.21165105

401

← TITLE
ENTRY

LONDON

Contents

Written by Lesley Reader
Magazine by Fiona Dunlop
Where to sections by Elizabeth Carter
Captions and additional writing by Tim Jepson

Copy edited by Lodestone Publishing
Page layout by Amanda Chauhan, Tony Truscott
Verified by Colin Follett
Indexed by Marie Lorimer

Edited, designed and produced by AA Publishing
© The Automobile Association 2000
Maps © The Automobile Association 2000

Published in the United States by AAA Publishing,
1000 AAA Drive, Heathrow, Florida 32746
Published in the United Kingdom by AA Publishing

ISBN 1-56251-329-X

Color separation by Leo Reprographics
Printed and bound in China by Leo Paper Products

10 9 8 7 6 5 4 3 2 1

London

the magazine

DOUBLE DESTRUCTION

London's double whammy of the Great Fire and the Blitz, although three centuries apart, left smoldering ruins. Yet, phoenix-like, out of the ashes arose new approaches to urban living that were to transform the face of the capital.

London's burning!

The flames crackled and cinders whirled into the night sky: It was September 2, 1666, the king's bakery on Pudding Lane was on fire and 80 percent of the city of London was about to go up in smoke. It was not the first time this medieval town of wood had seen a fire, but this one was to be by far the most destructive. As the flames raged, the Lord Mayor dithered, unwilling to rouse himself, and announced dismissively that "a woman might piss it out." That woman unfortunately did not materialize, and the fire soon spread to riverside warehouses filled with combustible materials. The blaze took hold.

Even the efforts of King Charles II, his brother the Duke of York and armies of fire-fighters were to no avail and four nights later, when the wind

The Great Fire of London, 1666

abated and the fire finally died down, over 13,000 houses had bitten the dust, along with 76 churches, 44 livery company halls, the Guildhall, the Royal Exchange and St. Paul's Cathedral. Remarkably, there were only 9 deaths but 100,000 people became homeless.

It didn't take long for the king to issue new building regulations: All new construction was to be in brick or stone and all streets were to be wide enough for carriages to pass along them. This Rebuilding Act was the forerunner of legislation that was to regulate the standard of housing for the next two centuries. Although Sir Christopher Wren's plan for a model urban layout was rejected because speed was the number one priority, some improvements were made, notably a continuous quay between the Tower of London and London Bridge. Rebuilding took about 10 years – not counting St. Paul's and 50 or so churches, all designed by Wren – but the most important spinoff was the accelerated drift to the suburbs, either across the river to Southwark or west to Westminster. The old city of London thus lost its hold, its population plummeted, and the embryo of suburban London took shape.

Survivors

Not every City church succumbed to the flames of the Great Fire. Among the ecclesiastical survivors in the Bishopsgate area were St. Botolph-without-Bishopsgate, the tiny St. Ethelburga and, above all, the remarkable St. Helen's, once part of a 12th-century Benedictine nunnery. However, all three were to suffer extensive damage in 1993 when an IRA bomb blasted out Bishopsgate, leaving over $1 billion worth of damage. To the west, the beautiful medieval parish church of St. Bartholomew-the-Great, much restored in the 19th century, also escaped the fire, together with London's oldest hospital, commonly known as St. Bart's.

Sir Christopher Wren, architect of St. Paul's Cathedral and some 50 London churches

Although thousands of steel bomb shelters were issued to Londoners who had back yards, many East Enders used the public shelters. The largest was an underground goods yard in Stepney, where 16,000 people would spend the night in overcrowded conditions. Far better in terms of facilities was a network of caverns at Chislehurst, Kent, where electric light, bunk beds, toilets and an old piano all added to the rousing atmosphere of solidarity. But top of the popularity stakes were the subway stations. Tickets were issued for regulars, bunk beds set up and impromptu sing-alongs took place as rats scuttled by. By the end of the war 53 million entries to these underground dormitories had been clocked up.

London Blitz

Blackouts and wailing sirens were the prelude to London's World War II drama: the Blitz. The aerial assault of the city began on September 7, 1940, when some 320 Luftwaffe bombers flew up the Thames to unleash their devastation on the East End. The bombing continued mercilessly for 57 consecutive nights, then intermittently for a further 6 months with over 27,000 bombs and countless incendiaries dropped on the city, and by November more than 11,000 people had been killed and 250,000 were homeless. Initially the East End, Docklands and the City were the targets but attacks on central London soon followed. The last raid came on May 10, 1941, when 550 bombers hammered the capital, destroying the Chamber of the House of Commons (among other buildings) and killing over 1,400 people.

After the war, priority was given to planning new satellite towns and filling the craters that pockmarked the urban landscape. Thus the late 1950s and 1960s witnessed a building bonanza of offices and public housing with tower blocks often over-shadowing a Wren church or Regency row houses. Slum clearance, too, gave way to high-rises, but it took two decades and the inner city riots during Margaret Thatcher's years as prime minister in the 1980s before these concrete jungles were recognized as nonviable. Like them or not, they're part of London's history and have created a social patchwork across the capital.

The most ingenious torture on the Blitz agenda came in 1944, when terrifying doodlebugs (flying bombs) were launched from northern France, soon followed by the even faster and more devastating V2 rockets which razed entire rows of houses. Well over 1 million houses crumbled in this last-ditch Nazi assault.

St. Paul's Cathedral, a miraculous survivor of the London Blitz

It took over 50 years to set up, but in 1999 a memorial to the 30,000 Londoners who died in the Blitz was unveiled by the Queen Mother in the courtyard of St. Paul's Cathedral. The choice of this royal dedicator was particularly appropriate because, at the height of bombing, the then wife of King George VI tirelessly toured the bomb sites. When Buckingham Palace received a direct hit, she remarked "I'm glad we've been bombed. It makes me feel I can look the East End in the face."

THE FACTS OF LONDON LIFE

London, Europe's largest city, covers more than 610 square miles (1,579 sq km).

London recieves 29 million visitors annually, and despite 95,000 hotel rooms, around 20,000 more beds are needed to keep up with demand.

Daytime traffic crawls at an average speed of 10 m.p.h. (16k.p.h.) through the city. No wonder every day around 5 million people opt to use the subway.

Westminster, the most visited part of the capital, has around 90 tons of garbage collected from its streets each day.

London's population today, hovering around the 7 million mark, is the same as it was in 1900 when it was the world's most populated city.

The city's financial institutions process about $300 billion in foreign exchange daily and manage half the world's ship brokering, company mergers and acquisitions.

The Millennium Dome, the largest structure of its kind in the world, could accommodate Nelson's Column standing upright and the Eiffel Tower placed horizontally.

One-third of Londoners live alone.

The city has 1,700 parks in an area of 70 square miles (181sq km) and it's possible to walk from Westminster to Notting Hill, a distance of 2 miles (3.2km), through parkland alone.

The Millennium Bridge connecting Tate Modern with St. Paul's Cathedral is the first pedestrian bridge to be built across the Thames since 1900.

At the height of the recession in 1992, the freshly completed but unoccupied Canary Wharf was losing $61 million per day.

There are 40,000 tulips planted each year in front of Buckingham Palace and 250,000 more at Hampton Court.

The 1,020-foot (314-m) length of Canary Wharf station is enough to accommodate the adjacent Canary Wharf Tower, Britain's tallest building, placed horizontally.

Battersea Dogs Home is the world's oldest home for lost or unwanted dogs.

Canary Wharf Tower, at the heart of the Docklands redevelopment

Tracking down the glitterati

Literary, Arty, Musical, Political or Thinking London... the metropolis bristles with blue plaques posted on the former residences of its illustrious inhabitants. Today, with well-defined areas still attracting high-profile personalities, you may just bump into a living legend. London is constantly evolving, so you are unlikely still to see cutting-edge artists in upscale Hampstead or Chelsea. Increasing real estate values have sent them running to Hackney, whose lofts house the greatest concentration of artists in Europe, if not the world. Hang out in the "cool" new bars of Shoreditch and spot tomorrow's meteor, then move on to that haven of affluent bohemia, Notting Hill, to shadow entrepreneur Richard Branson, comedian Ruby Wax, writer Martin Amis or singer Annie Lennox.

Above: Richard Branson chooses to live in Holland Park, near Notting Hill

Creative Londoners

London has inspired the pens of thousands of writers over the centuries. Top areas for the more successful are the northern districts of Hampstead, Camden Town and Islington (chosen by pre-fatwa author Salman Rushdie, composer Michael Nyman and actress Cate Blanchett), reflecting a remarkable continuity with the past. Some houses have even been home to more than one famous inhabitant, as at 23 Fitzroy Road, Primrose Hill, once occupied by the Irish poet W. B. Yeats and later by the American poet Sylvia Plath. Plath was drawn to Yeats's blue plaque when on her way to visit her doctor and instantly decided that it was "the street and the house" for her. Within minutes of persuading builders to let her in, she was at the realtor's office, negotiating the lease for the top-floor apartment.

George Orwell (1903–50), in keeping with his sociopolitical concerns, lived closer to the pulse of less-erudite streets, gravitating between Camden Town and rent-free rooms above a bookshop in South End Green where he worked. He later moved to 27 Canonbury Square in Islington – at the time a far from gentrified address. Another socially concerned writer, H. G. Wells (1866–1946), meanwhile lived in style overlooking Regent's Park from 13 Hanover Terrace. When negotiating the lease he said, "I'm looking for a house to die in." This he did 10 years later, having survived the world war that he had so grimly predicted.

Not to be outdone, Chelsea has seen a stream of luminaries ever since Sir Thomas More (the 16th-century author of *Utopia*, later beheaded for denouncing Henry VIII's wife-changing habits) built his stately house in Cheyne Walk – now long gone. Exoticism and scandal always went hand in hand here, but its notoriety really took off in Victorian times when custom-built artists' studios became the rage. At this time, Oscar Wilde (1854–1900) penned plays at 34 Tite Street, home to his wife and children. Wilde was partying madly with his boyfriend "Bosie," so indulging in the angst of a double life perfectly reflected in *The Picture of Dorian Gray*.

Before the American John Singer Sargent (1856–1925) became London's most fashionable portraitist from his Tite Street home, his compatriot James Whistler

(1834–1903) was painting Chelsea's riverscapes from 96 Cheyne Walk. He was not the first, however, as the great J. M. W. Turner (1775–1851) had already been inspired into abstraction from windows at No. 119.

In the 20th century Chelsea continued to attract creative souls and it was in Cheyne Row that Ian Fleming pounded out

his first James Bond novel, *Casino Royale*, on a gold-plated typewriter while T. S. Eliot lived below. The latter's checkered marital life was exposed at 24 Russell Square in Bloomsbury, where for 40 years he worked for the publishers Faber & Faber. Literary hopefuls who mounted the steps often spotted Eliot's first wife, Vivienne, who would arrive wearing placards saying "I am the wife he abandoned."

Money is now everything in Chelsea; gone are the bearded bohemians, royal mistresses and struggling actors, today replaced by the likes of former prime minister Margaret Thatcher (Chester Square), actress Joan Collins (Eaton Square), architect Sir Richard Rogers (Turks Row) and everyone's favorite foppish Englishman, actor Hugh Grant, together with the woman who wore "that dress," Liz Hurley.

T. S. ELIOT, O.M.
1888–1965
Poet
lived and died here

Both T. S. Eliot (above) and Ian Fleming (left), the creator of James Bond, were residents of exclusive Cheyne Row in Chelsea

Actress Joan Collins has a home in Eaton Square

Blue plaques of Hampstead

John Keats (1795–1821), Wentworth Place, Keats Grove
Katherine Mansfield (1888–1923), 17 East Heath Road
D. H. Lawrence (1885–1930), 1 Byron Villas
John Constable (1776–1837), 40 Well Walk
George Romney (1734–1802), Holly Bush Hill
Anna Pavlova (1885–1931), Ivy House, North End Road
Sigmund Freud (1856-1939), 20 Maresfield Gardens

London's creative coterie *par excellence* was the Bloomsbury Group that took its name from its location. Members included writers Clive Bell and E. M. Forster, painters Roger Fry and Lytton Strachey, the painter Vanessa Bell and her writer sister, Virgina Woolf (1882–1941). Virginia and her husband, Leonard Woolf, marked the group's heyday in 1924 when they moved the Hogarth Press from Richmond to Tavistock Square, in the shadow of London's august university. It was scandal all the way, including Woolf's lesbian love affair with Vita Sackville-West, to whom she dedicated her historical fantasy, *Orlando*.

Virginia Woolf, novelist and leading light of the Bloomsbury Group

Political exiles

With democracy stamped on the nation's soul and tolerance on its psyche, it is hardly surprising that numerous politicos on the run made London their base, although it was never such a hotbed of revolutionaries as Paris. Yet even Napoleon III (1808–73), Bonaparte's nephew, found himself exiled in London twice over and in 1848 lived at 1 King Street, in the gentlemanly heart of St. James's. He became so inspired by the parks of the English capital that on his subsequent coronation as emperor he ordered his city architect to set about copying them in Paris. A century later, another Gallic exile, General Charles De Gaulle (1890–1970), was notoriously less of an anglophile, despite an equally salubrious address at 4 Carlton Gardens. This was his base for organizing the Free French Forces while broadcasting to resistance fighters before a triumphal return at liberation.

At the other end of the spectrum was Karl Marx (1818–83) who, after expulsion from Germany, settled in London to pursue a rocky, often impecunious existence. From 1851 to 1856 he lived in what was then a seedy Soho, at 28 Dean Street, later writing much of *Das Kapital* in the British Museum's Reading Room. He was buried in Highgate Cemetery beneath a gigantic bearded bust bearing those pithy words "Workers of the World Unite."

Marx's wealthier compatriot, supporter and fellow thinker, Friedrich Engels (1820–95), was also buried in Highgate Cemetery after spending much of his life in London. From 1870 to 1892 he lived at 121 Regent's Park Road, a plush address overlooking the park. Communist theoreticians continued to be inspired by no less a figure than Vladimir Ilyich Lenin (1870–1924), who in 1905 lived at 16 Percy Circus, near King's Cross (now the Royal Scot Hotel), within walking distance of the London Patriotic Society in Clerkenwell where he worked. This neoclassical 1737 building now houses the Marx Memorial Library (37a Clerkenwell Green).

This stern image of Karl Marx tops his burial place in Highgate Cemetery

London's rural retreats

Visit London in winter and it looks colorless. Visit in summer and you'll be greeted by huge splashes of green, from perfectly manicured lawns to towering plane or lime trees lining streets and avenues. The great British love for all things rural is undeniable and the fact that the capital, despite rising pollution and traffic, manages to preserve this aspect must stem from some psychic feat of collective willpower. The squares of central London are bucolic havens carved out of the general mayhem. With a break in the clouds, Londoners are out there, on deck chairs, bikini-clad on the grass or striding across the parks.

Holland Park

One of London's prettiest and most secluded parks is a favorite getaway for residents of Kensington and Notting Hill. In 54 acres of grounds wilderness and order are juxtaposed, although only the east wing of the Jacobean mansion survived a bomb in 1941. The park's intrinsic leafiness attracted a colony of wealthy artists to its fringes in Victorian days; they

Urban Green

included Frederic Leighton (made a Lord on his deathbed), who built an extraordinary arabesque extravaganza of a house, now a museum. Today's well-heeled and well-behaved *habitués* of the park take in art exhibitions at the Ice House, lunch at the Orangery, or indulge in summer evening concerts in a tent on the lawn. Meanwhile, well-spoken families gather at the teahouse; squirrels, peacocks and rabbits roam in the woods of the northern half; and nannies and au pairs watch over their juvenile charges in the playground of the formal gardens. The Kyoto Japanese Garden offers a meditative retreat to the northwest of Holland House.

Kids rule

"Adults must be accompanied by children." This is the rule at Coram's Fields, in Bloomsbury, a large green space with playgrounds and grazing sheep, set up in the 1740s beside a Foundling Hospital.

A statue of Lord Holland presides over the park to which he gave his name

The Kyoto Japanese Garden in Holland Park

desirable, white stuccoed residences within which lies the Inner Circle of botanical glories with their fantastically diverse and fragrant rose gardens (including a Japanese-style waterfall, a favorite for Chinese wedding photos) and an open-air theater that optimistically stages Shakespeare productions on summer evenings. The open, northern section is where soccer players vie with the zoo's mountain goats for attention. On the western perimeter looms the copper dome of the London Central Mosque, and cosmospolitan strollers include Gulf Arabs, members of the orthodox Jewish community, and Chinese or Americans (the residence of the U.S. ambassador stands in the park).

Islington squares

The liberal intelligentsia of Islington's gentrified squares has been dubbed the "chattering classes," although they are now joined by bankers eager to live within spitting distance of the City. Unlike Kensington and Chelsea, the essentially Georgian and Regency squares of Islington are mainly public and surpris-ingly well maintained, despite the regular onslaught of office workers' picnics, local children and, at times, the homeless. Southern Islington offers the

Regent's Park

The most northerly of the royal parks is the work of John Nash, "a thick squat dwarf with round head, snub nose and little eyes" (his own self-appraisal). Appearances aside, this visionary architect came up with the prototype for England's garden suburbs and cities, combining urban and rural in one fell swoop in order to lure the nobility to what was then considered far north of the fashionable West End. The 494-acre circular park is edged by the Outer Circle of highly

Parklife

In summer, the northern side of Hyde Park's Serpentine (► 130–131) sees Londoners out in force to picnic on the grass, often with portable televi-sions. Far more energetic is the nearby roller-blading fraternity.

intimacy of Wilmington Square
and its crumbling 1920s
garden kiosk, the harmonious
Palladian-style Lloyd Square
(unusually private, because it is
part of an estate) and vast,
church-dominated Myddelton
Square. Barnsbury, to the
north, is home to elegant
Gibson Square with its curious
brick folly – in reality a ventila-
tion shaft for the London
Underground's Victoria line –
and Milner Square, unique for
its neoclassical architecture. In
contrast are Lonsdale Square's
unexpected gray-brick neo-
Gothic houses.

Battersea Park

On 200 acres of land where the
Duke of Wellington and the
Marquis of Winchelsea once
fought an absurd pistol duel
(they both missed), Battersea
Park was created in 1858. It
catered for "tens of thousands

of mechanics, little tradesmen,
apprentices, and their wives
and sweethearts." Today, its
location directly across the
river from Chelsea (earning
Battersea the sobriquet "south
Chelsea") makes it an obvious
escape for the people who live
and work there, among others,
interior decorators or antiques
dealers from the King's Road
musing on potential deals.

On the park's eastern edge
loom the stacks of Battersea
Power Station, closed since
1983 and now being redeveloped as a leisure complex.
Bungy jumpers leap from a
crane here and every Friday
motorcyclists congregate to rev
up and compare horse-power.
The park's big surprise,
however, is the Peace Pagoda, a
two-tier building erected in
1985 by Japanese Buddhists.

Left: the
Buddhist Peace
Pagoda stands
right by the
Thames in
Battersea Park

COOL

BRITANNIA

S uddenly, in 1997, it became cool to be British. Coinciding with a youthful, newly elected Labour government, a fresh face of the nation was propelled to fame from the galleries, studios, restaurants, clubs and stores of the capital. And it looks set to continue well into the new millennium. No other

Check out budding designers' clothes at markets such as Portobello (in stalls under the overpass) and Camden Lock, keeping a close eye on other shoppers to gauge the latest trends. Then cruise down Monmouth Street for emerging talent, and Bond Street and Brompton Cross for the big labels.

Fashion from Vivienne Westwood (below)

European capital can claim the same buzz, flair and above all hype that London generates as it rides high on a wave of prosperity and self-confidence. Fashion, art, architecture, design, music and film are the ingredients stirred into this heady mix that makes it one of the world's most vibrant cities. It is not the first time that London has been swinging. The hippy-dippy 1960s also saw a tidal wave of inventiveness, spearheaded by rock groups who did not necessarily originate in the capital but who just had to be there; The Beatles came from Liverpool, but their Abbey Road recording studios were the focus of the nation's music. London was the uncontested pulse of the nation with Carnaby Street, Kensington Market and the King's Road setting the tone for fashion victims, while Mary Quant, Biba, Ossie Clark or Mr. Freedom cut the patterns to match. Today, Carnaby Street may be a tacky

Millennium Dome

It's London's most ambitious architectural project ever. At a cost of over $1 billion, the gigantic Millennium Dome crowns Docklands, Greenwich and, of course, Cool Britannia. Reviled and mythologized, its 163-foot high teflon-coated glass fiber shell is stretched tautly over a 2,600-foot circumference and held in place by yellow antennas. Lift-off to the future?

tourist haunt with its own website and the King's Road is drifting into mainstream, but homegrown designers have matured into realism. Some, such as Alexander McQueen, John Galliano and Stella McCartney, even steer the fortunes of top couture houses in France, while London's grande dame, Vivienne Westwood, continues to stun. Above all, street fashion is still big. Even Parisian couturiers such as Jean-Paul Gaultier and Christian Lacroix admit to pillaging ideas from London's trend-setting young clubbers.

Facelifting

Less ephemeral in nature are London's innovative architects who are chiseling the capital's facelifted image. Architectural conservatism was the rule until the late 1980s, and included many misguided abominations, but great stylish swathes of glass and steel are now slotting into the city fabric. Many of these new buildings were designed by Sir Norman Foster and Sir Richard Rogers, originally partners in the 1960s before working separately on major projects in Europe and the Far East. Rogers' earliest landmark is the towering high-tech Lloyd's Building in the financial heart of London, which opened its doors in 1986, just before the yuppie bubble burst and recession set in. His latest contribution, and the capital's most controversial construction ever, is the Millennium Dome in Greenwich. In his turn, Foster, who in Hong Kong designed the headquarters

Richard Rogers' Lloyd's Building

of the Hong Kong & Shanghai Bank and the new airport, and in Berlin majestically rejuvenated the Reichstag, has created the Millennium Bridge (currently under construction), a much-delayed result of decades of handwringing about the

Thames. Not least, it is the first pedestrian bridge to be built over the Thames since 1900. This purist "blade of light" connecting the new Bankside Tate Modern with St. Paul's marks the general shift eastward of the capital's cultural foci. In 1999 Foster was awarded the prestigious Pritzker architectural prize, so endowing him with true godfather status.

Another Millennium project, the much-delayed and overbudget subway Jubilee line extension, is a showcase for architectural audacity with each station the work of a different designer, from Foster at Canary Wharf, to Will Alsop at North

Best contemporary art galleries

The best public galleries to see exhibitions of cutting-edge contemporary art are the **Serpentine, Camden Arts Centre** and the **Hayward**. Private galleries vary from established dealers on and off Cork Street to the up and coming scattered all over Shoreditch and Whitechapel. Out on a geographical limb, but consistently showing significant British work, is the **Lisson Gallery** (67 Lisson Street and 52–54 Bell Street, NW1).

Greenwich, Ian Ritchie at Bermondsey and the award-winning Chris Wilkinson at Stratford.

Art for art's sake

Provocative, sometimes scandalous, the Britpack (a convenient label for Britain's youngest generation of artists) is firmly anchored in the galleries and studios of the capital. Love it or hate it, their work has become increasingly well known, particularly as star artist Damien Hirst

launches himself into restaurants and bars. Much of the impetus for London's most controversial artists came in the 1980s from advertising mogul Charles Saatchi who, in his vast gallery space in St. John's Wood, continues to promote many of the artists whose work he collects. These include Hirst, the Chapman brothers and Gary Hume – all graduates of the University of London's Goldsmiths College, an institution that has consequently attained near-legendary status. Maturer London-based artists include Rachel Whiteread,

Far left: spotted in all the right places – Damien Hirst, *enfant terrible* of the British art scene

Anish Kapoor, Cornelia Parker, Richard Deacon and those unforgettable doyens of East End living, the double act of Gilbert and George, whose house in Fournier Street is a work of art in itself.

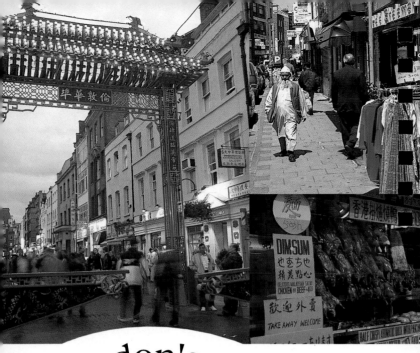

London's global
villages

The Tower of Babel?
London's tapestry of
cultures has had far-
reaching influences on its
character, its music, its
literature, its streetlife and, not
least, its eating habits. Ever
since London's founders
arrived in AD 43, namely the
Roman army of Emperor
Claudius, its citizens have
descended from a variety of
cultures, whether Angles,
Saxons or Normans, all adding
to an unbeatable cosmopolitan
flavor. Religious persecution
later brought French
Huguenots and members of
the European Jewish

community, while economic
necessity brought Italians, Irish
and Chinese. However, large-
scale immigration really kicked
off after World War II when
there was a huge influx of
people from newly independent Commonwealth countries
that became a much-exploited
low-paid workforce.

Today, inner-city areas
encapsulate a kaleidoscope of
37 different cultures, making
up 20 percent of the population. Tension between com-
munities has in the past
exploded in riots (Notting Hill
in 1958, Whitechapel in the
1970s and Brixton in 1981).

A taste of Italy

The Italian festival takes place every year on the Sunday closest to July 16. A procession leaves St. Peter's on Clerkenwell Road, and food stalls are set up around the corner on Warner Street.

The East End Jewish community has a lengthy list of rags-to-riches tales, such as hairdresser Vidal Sassoon and playwrights Harold Pinter and Steven Berkoff.

Whitechapel

Walking down Brick Lane, you'll hear the wail from the mosque or the beat of *bhangra* music, see traditionally dressed Bangladeshi men and women, and smell the pungent aromas of a string of inexpensive curry restaurants. The heart of this East End garment district, where street-name signs are written in Bengali, beats in the shadow of the Jamme Masjid, once a Huguenot church, in 1897 a synagogue and, since 1976, the Great Mosque, each reincarnation pointing to the dominant culture of the time. In 1700, London absorbed around 25,000 Huguenots escaping persecution in France, and many set up silk-weaving businesses here, some with

But as integration develops, it is increasingly difficult to separate the immigrants of yesteryear from those who were born and raised in London.

Young Asians have a high profile in the music world, joining more traditional roles in business, finance, law and restaurants. A first-generation success story is that of millionaire Muquim Amed (born in 1963 in Bangladesh) who, starting from nothing in Brick Lane, now owns a chain of restaurants and is on first-name terms with Prime Minister Tony Blair. Writers Salman Rushdie and Hanif Kureishi have also both imposed their global mark.

The black community has produced one of England's most popular news presenters, Trevor McDonald, as well as endless sportspeople, actors, musicians and politicians such as M.P. Oona King and Trevor Phillips, also a TV presenter and candidate for London mayor.

London's streets reflect its ethnic diversity

Don't miss the 24-hour bagel shop, Beigel Bake, at the top of Brick Lane (No 159), an East End institution popular with taxi-drivers. The place is bustling at all times and on Sunday mornings, when Brick Lane's junk market is in full swing lines stretch down the street

A family affair – dressing up for the Notting Hill Carnival

outlets in Petticoat Lane market. By the 1880s came another wave, this time from the Eastern European Jewish community, who worked in the shoe and clothing industries. As they prospered and moved out, Bengalis replaced them to set up, in their turn, leather-clothes workshops.

Clerkenwell

Hip Clerkenwell, inner London's epicenter of loft lifestyles, is shaking off its history of crafts-people and immigrants. Huguenots, again, were the first, joined in the 19th century by Italians who peaked at around 10,000 between the world wars, living parallel to the Hasidic Jewish community which still runs London's diamond trade from Hatton Garden. Although prosperity has scattered the Italian community, Little Italy preserves some trusty relics: grocery stores (Gazzano at 171 Farringdon Road for authentic customers and conversation), cafés (Carlo's at 8 Exmouth Market) and churches (St. Peter's is the official Italian Church, but the Holy Redeemer in Exmouth Market truly echoes

Opposite: dancers at the Notting Hill Carnival

Chinese New Year

Chinese New Year is celebrated in true snake-dance style with fireworks, papier-mâché headgear, paper money (lots of it) and teeming, vociferous crowds. It takes place in late January or early February and centers on Gerrard Street.

Italianate style) are steeped in Italian character and chatter.

Soho

It's official and you can't miss it: Soho's Gerrard Street is London's Chinatown, lavishly announced by pagoda-style gateways and phonebooths, at night joined by flashing neon ideograms. London's Chinese community dates back to the late 18th century when East India Company ships bringing goods from the Far East disgorged sailors into the docklands. Some settled there to open stores, restaurants or opium dens, but it was after World War II that Chinese (mainly Cantonese) fleeing the Communist regime focused on the labyrinth of streets south of Shaftesbury Avenue. Few of London's 60,000 Chinese now live here, but this area is the best window on Chinese culture. You can pick up that much-prized giant fruit, the stinking durian; a wok; a newspaper fresh off the presses of Beijing; an embroidered *cheong san* dress or devour a Peking duck in one of the cheek-by-jowl restaurants.

Notting Hill

The first group of 500 West Indian immigrants shivered in the cold of Tilbury docks in 1948 but since then have made their exuberant presence felt. The Notting Hill Carnival (held on the last weekend in August) is the zenith of Caribbean culture in Britain, with technicolor floats and elaborate costumes, throbbing reggae music, steel bands, impromptu food stands and cavorting crowds making it the world's second largest carnival after Rio de Janeiro. Ongoing gentrification is changing this part of the city, however, and the unofficial clubs and relaxed cafés of the Afro-Caribbean community are slowly disappearing.

Two types of watering hole exemplify the often eccentric social traditions of London. By their very essence, gentlemen's clubs are reserved for the happy, privileged few who pay annual dues to relax in the hushed atmosphere while traditionally perusing *The Times* over a Scotch. Pubs, meanwhile, are open to all comers, male and female alike, rich or poor, their often warm, smoky, jostling atmospheres a welcoming retreat for downing pints of beer while chatting to friends or strangers. On warmer days, customers at popular pubs will overflow onto the street.

Pubs & Clubs

Gentlemen's Clubs

There is no doubt about it, St. James's Street and Pall Mall are the epicenter of London's most distinguished and discreetly aging gentlemen's clubs. You won't be allowed in but their stately façades betray just a hint of what goes on inside. These are the bastions of upper-class England where new members are admitted only on personal recommendation. Business deals, "old boy" networking, introductions and society gossip are the bottom line, while in the background a Reuters telex spews out the latest on City stocks and shares.

When first established as gambling dens, these clubs saw a string of scandals in the fine upper-class tradition of waywardness and eccentricity. Money was rarely a problem and vast amounts were lost or gained on the most trivial of bets – although in extreme cases this inspired bankruptcy and even suicide. At the oldest club, White's (1693), the diarist Horace Walpole recorded a typical incident: "A man dropped down dead at the door, was carried in and the

club immediately made bets on whether he was dead or not." Brooks' and Boodle's were established soon after White's, setting a similar standard of excellence, and even today these three clubs remain top of the list for those in the upper echelons of British society.

Opposite: a taste for tradition – the Wig and Pen Club and Restaurant in Fleet Street

The Reform Club, founded by reformist Liberals in 1841, was a haunt of author Henry James and a hole was bored in the door of his favorite room so that the valet knew whether or not to disturb him. It was from the club's drawing room that Phileas Fogg, Jules Verne's

The RAC Club in Pall Mall

Since the 1970s, some clubs have relaxed the ban on women members although the Carlton Club, a bastion of the Conservative Party, had to make a special case to admit Margaret Thatcher. In others, women will be admitted as guests only or, as at the Athenaeum, only to a basement restaurant, keeping the main dining room a male-only preserve.

fictional hero, bet that he could travel around the world in just 80 days.

At the nearby Athenaeum, easily recognizable for its neo-Grecian frieze and dazzling gilt statue of Pallas, writers William Thackeray and Anthony Trollope both labored away in the library, while Charles Dickens was another pen-pushing member.

Members-only clubs continue to proliferate, above all in Soho, but the new generation is a far cry from its predecessors in St. James's. Women are accepted on an equal footing with men and it's the thirty-somethings who dominate. But the bottom line is the same: you are allowed entry only if signed in by a member. Today's most high-profile club is Groucho's, on Dean Street, home to the media and movie *cognoscenti* who graduate from bar to restaurant.

Victoriana rules

Many pubs still preserve the etched glass screens (known as snob screens), mirrors, tiles, wood paneling and lofty boarded ceilings of Victorian times. Track down these classics:

Red Lion
2 Duke of York Street, SW1 (St. James's)
Dog & Duck
18 Bateman Street, W1 (Soho)
The Lamb
94 Lamb's Conduit Street, WC1 (Bloomsbury)
Salisbury Tavern
90 St. Martin's Lane, WC2 (Covent Garden)
Paxton's Head
153 Knightsbridge, SW1 (Knightsbridge)
Prince Alfred
9 Formosa Street, W9 (Maida Vale)
Camden Head
2 Camden Walk, N1 (Islington)

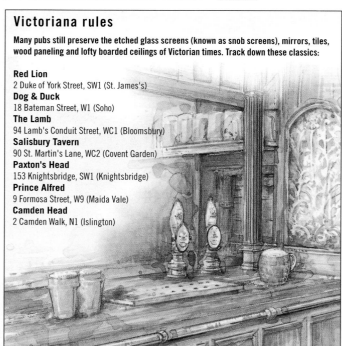

Pub etiquette

Pubs operate a system of first come, first served, so be prepared to elbow your way to the bar to order and pay for your drinks before sitting down – if you can. And remember closing is at 11 p.m. (10:30 p.m. on Sundays) – sometimes it's announced by "Time ladies and gentlemen please" and sometimes by the ringing of a bell. Beware of theme pubs and brewery chains: The true sense of a "free house" is that the pub sells beers from different breweries and the decor should reflect the landlord's and landlady's often idiosyncratic personal taste.

Pubs

Pubs are moving with the times, too. Some now produce cuisine that easily compares with top restaurants (see panel "Upgraded pubs") making for hazy distinctions between the two. Others have opted for satellite television on a big screen to boost pub crowds, with rousing atmospheres during major sporting events. But whatever the changes, pubs are still the mainstay for neighborhood or after-work socializing. They may have gone a long way from their origins, but the aim is the same – drinking and conversation.

It was the Victorian era that saw pubs multiply, but in the more egalitarian late 20th century the classic division between unadorned "public bar" (where the serious drinking was done) and carpeted "saloon bar" (for couples and the middle social classes) has virtually vanished. Changes in licensing hours, too, have encouraged long afternoons that are spent Continental-style at outdoor tables, and the cloistered atmosphere of Victorian times is fast disappearing.

Standards of comfort and decor vary wildly, as does pub food, but if you find the right one you may have the bonus of an upstairs fringe theater, art gallery or live music.

Traditional London pubs like the Dog and Duck are under threat from bland "theme" pubs

The Fitzroy Tavern

No longer what it was in its 1920s heyday, this pub on the corner of Charlotte and Windmill streets has a heady history of disreputable local characters. Its queen, a fast-living character called Nina Hamnett, was immortalized by artists such as Modigliani and Gaudier-Breszka, befriended by Picasso and, as the saying goes, bedded by almost everyone else. Other permanent fixtures were Augustus John, resplendent in gypsy earrings and hat, and the poet Dylan Thomas, who fed his self-destructive alcoholic trajectory here.

Upgraded pubs

The Engineer, 65 Gloucester Avenue, NW1 (Primrose Hill) is a lively bar serving light meals as well as offering a full-blown restaurant. A patio garden and mirrored upstairs rooms add to its charms.

Market Bar, 240a Portobello Road, W11 (Notting Hill) draws the antiques-market crowds mixed with local bohemia to its neo-Gothic bar and restaurant.

The Peasant, 240 St. John Street, EC1 (Clerkenwell), plum in the middle of loft London, has a wonderful ornate bar with a tiled mural of St. George and a cool designer restaurant upstairs.

LONDON'S

BEST . . .

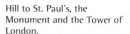

BEST FREE MUSIC
• In **Covent Garden's piazza** on a sunny day you'll hear anything from Vietnamese xylophones to Peruvian flutes or a homegrown electric guitar – or all at once.
• **The Barbican Centre** on Sunday lunchtime holds free jazz concerts in the bar.

BEST BUS ROUTES
• **No. 7** – be spirited past the throngs of shoppers at Oxford Street department stores to reach Marble Arch, the Middle Eastern enclave of Edgware Road, Paddington station, hip Westbourne Grove and, through the backstreets of Notting Hill, end at Portobello Road.
• **No. 15** – cruise past the views from the shopping hub of Oxford Circus to Piccadilly Circus, Trafalgar Square, the Strand and Aldwych. Continue along Fleet Street, once the newspaper mecca, and up Ludgate

Hill to St. Paul's, the Monument and the Tower of London.
• **No. 38** – enjoy a ride from Victoria through Belgravia, passing Buckingham Palace gardens, then along Piccadilly to Soho, the bookstores of Charing Cross Road and finally Bloomsbury – a few steps from the British Museum. Stay on longer for Clerkenwell and Islington.

BEST ANTIQUE AND JUNK MARKETS
• **Bermondsey Market** (Bermondsey Square, SE1) glitters with silverware, paintings, odd furniture and obsolete objects. Go at dawn on Friday to jostle with sharp-eyed professional antiques dealers for bargains.
• **Camden Market** (Camden Lock, Chalk Farm Road, NW1) is for anyone hankering after London street fashion, crafts, jewelry, ethnic knickknacks, design objects or furniture. Fight your way through teeming youth for fortification at countless drink and snack stalls. Saturday and Sunday.
• **Portobello** (► 131) for anything and everything, from fruits and vegetables to specialty bric-a-brac, young designer fantasies or antiques – fake or sublimely real. Friday and Saturday.

BEST BRIDGE VIEWS
• **Albert Bridge** (1873). Not just another of Queen Victoria's odes to her defunct husband,

Top: the Oxo
Tower Restaurant

Left: one of
London's famous
red buses

but a magically illuminated suspension bridge between Battersea Park and Chelsea. Take in views of the exclusive Chelsea Harbour development and Cheyne Walk to the north and monumental Battersea Power Station to the east.

• **Blackfriar's Bridge** (1869). The widest bridge on the Thames offers views of the expanding skyline of Southwark to the south, including the new Bankside Tate, St. Paul's Cathedral, the spires, and high-rises in the City to the north, the Southbank Centre, Waterloo Bridge and Westminster to the west.

• **Tower Bridge** (1894). From this virtual pastiche and symbol of London you can see burgeoning waterside lofts replacing wharves as well as HMS *Belfast* on the south bank, and the dwarfed turrets and walls of the Tower of London alongside St. Katharine's Dock to the north. Its jaws open for river traffic about 500 times a year.

Above: street performers in Covent Garden

Right: all that glitters... a stall in Portobello Road market

If you go to only one...

...stand–up comedy show, head for the Comedy Store (1a Oxendon Street, SW1) with impromptu amateur acts or sets by polished professional comedians. Beware of hard-hitting audience participation.

...Continental coffee shop, indulge at Soho's Pâtisserie Valérie or for loftier surroundings its offshoot on the second floor of art-deco RIBA, 66 Portland Place, W1.

...bar with a view, hit the terrace of the Oxo Tower restaurant around sunset (▶ 109).

For and against

London is the only place in which the child grows completely up into the man.
William Hazlitt (1778-1830)

London is a modern Babylon.
Benjamin Disraeli (1804-81)

Town life nourishes and perfects all the civilized elements in man. Shakespeare wrote nothing but doggerel verse before he came to London and never penned a line after he left.
Oscar Wilde (1854-1900)

London, that great cesspool into which all the loungers and idlers of the Empire are irresistibly drained.
Sir Arthur Conan Doyle (1859-1930)

Of course I got lost: for London is laid out as haphazardly as a warren. It is a myriad of Streets High and Low, of Courts and Cloisters and Crescents and full Circles, Paths and Parks and Parkways, and Yards, and Mews, and Quays, Palace and Castles and Mansions and Halls and mere Houses... there are Ways to go and Ends to be arrived at... London is, in other words, a maze, but I was simply amazed, surprised that it had taken me so long to realize I was lost.
Dale Peck, "Granta 65: London," 1999

I've learned to accept London as my muse. Initially, there I was, sitting on the tube, when she came in: filthy, raddled, smelly, old and drunk. But now we're inseparable, going round and round the Circle Line, arm in arm, perhaps for eternity.
Will Self, "Granta 65: London," 1999

I hate this daily ten-minute walk, along the outlines of the cold squares, past dark shopfronts where cats claw at the window panes, then into the tingling strip of Queensway, through shuddering traffic and the sweet smell of yesterday's trash.
Martin Amis "Success" 1978

London hates to let you go... If you drive out of London towards Brighton, there are seventy-five sets of traffic lights before you reach the motorway, and a dozen false dawns.
Ian Parker, "Granta 65: London," 1999

It is not a pleasant place; it is not agreeable or cheerful or easy or exempt from reproach. It is only magnificent.
Henry James (1843-1916)

The vast town is always in movement night and day, wide as an ocean, with the grind and howl of machinery..., commercial adventure..., the Thames befouled, the atmosphere packed with coal dust; the superb parks and squares... the city with its vast moneybags.
Dostoevsky (1821-81)

A wet Sunday in London: shops closed, streets almost empty; the aspect of a vast and well-kept graveyard. The few people in this desert of squares and streets, hurrying beneath their umbrellas, look like unquiet ghosts; it is horrible.
Hippolyte Taine (1828-93)

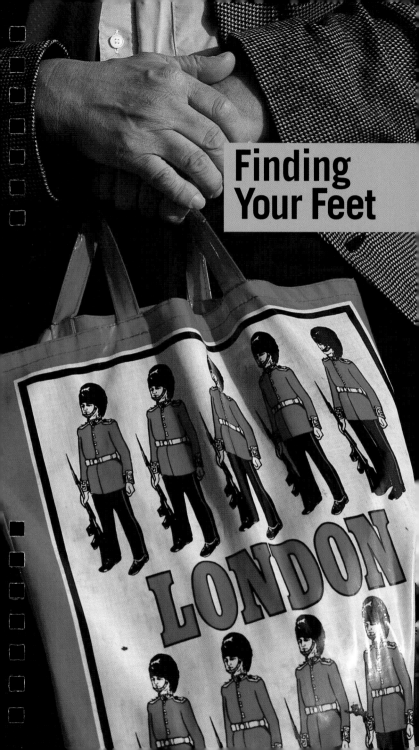

Finding Your Feet

First Two Hours

Heathrow and Gatwick are the principal airports serving London. However, Stansted and London City Airport are increasingly busy with traffic from continental Europe.

From Heathrow

Heathrow (code LHR) lies 15 miles west of central London and is served by good road and rail connections. All the services below go from all four terminals and are well signposted.

- **The London Underground** (tel: 020 7222 1234), Piccadilly line, serves Heathrow from 4:58 a.m. to 11:54 p.m. (Mon.–Sat.) and 5:57 a.m. to 11:16 p.m. (Sun). The journey to central London takes about an hour. It can get crowded in the rush hour but is the most convenient, best-value option.
- **The Heathrow Express** (tel: 0845 600 1515) is a high-speed rail link to Paddington station. It runs from 5:10 a.m. to 11:40 p.m. every 15 minutes and the journey takes 15 to 20 minutes – it's fast but expensive.
- There are two **Airbus Heathrow Shuttle** routes (tel: 020 7222 1234), each operating daily, usually every 30 minutes from 5:40 a.m. to 9:53 p.m. Buses make more than 20 stops along the way and trips typically take about an hour to Victoria (longer to King's Cross). Heavy traffic can add considerably to this. No reservation is required. Airbuses are accessible for wheelchairs.
- Pick up a black metered **taxi** outside any terminal. Expect around an hour's journey time and $50 or more on the meter by the time you get to central London. Don't forget to allow for a 10 percent tip for the driver.

From Gatwick

Public transportation from Gatwick (code LGW), which lies 27 miles south of the city center, includes a 24-hour rail service.

- **Gatwick Express** (tel: 0990 301 530) rail service runs to Victoria Station in central London. It is a 24-hour service, every 15 minutes most of the day and hourly most of the night; journey time is 30 minutes. There are also slightly slower, cheaper 24-hour rail services (tel: 0845 484 950) into the center.
- **Flightline buses** (tel: 0990 747777) operate every 1 to 2 hours from 5 a.m. to 8:10 p.m. to Victoria Coach Station and take up to 1 hour 30 minutes.
- **Taxis** operate from outside the terminal – journey time to central London is usually more than 1 hour 30 minutes and prices are around $80.

From Stansted

Stansted (code STN), open less than a decade, lies 35 miles northeast of the city center.

- **Stansted Skytrain** (tel: 0845 48 49 50) to Liverpool Street station runs daily from 6 a.m. until 11:59 p.m. and journeys take about 40 minutes.
- **Flightline buses** (tel: 0990 747777) operate daily to Victoria Coach Station hourly from 8 a.m. to 6 p.m., then at 8 p.m. and 10:15 p.m. to Victoria and take up to 1 hour 45 minutes.
- There's a **taxi** reservation desk inside the terminal and a taxi costs at least $80 into central London.

From London City Airport

London City Airport (code LCY) is the most central of the capital's airports, lying just 9 miles east of the city center.

- The best option is the **Airport Shuttle Bus** (tel: 020 7646 0088). Buses run to Liverpool Street station every 10 minutes Mon. to Fri. 6:50 a.m.–9:10 p.m., Sat. 6:50 a.m.–1:10 p.m. and Sun. 11 a.m.–9:10 p.m. The journey takes 25 minutes and costs around $8 one way.
- Black metered **taxis** wait outside the terminal – journey time is about 30 minutes into Liverpool Street and the cost will be around $22. Expect to pay $32 upwards to central London, depending on traffic.

Rail Arrivals

International rail services (Eurostar tel: 0990 186 186) from France (Lille and Paris) and Belgium (Brussels) arrive at Waterloo International Terminal where you connect with the subway system.

Getting Around

Buses and the Underground (London's subway system) operate from roughly 5:30 a.m. until just after midnight, after which there is a network of night buses until early morning. The system is divided into zones – six for the Underground and four for the bus system. These are marked on bus and Underground maps and displayed at stations. On both buses and the Underground you must have a ticket valid for the zone you are in or you are liable for an on-the-spot fine.

Travelcards and Bus Passes

If you are going to do a lot of traveling over a day or a week, buy a pass that gives you unlimited travel in that period. Make sure it covers all the zones you need – most of the places in the main part of this guide are in Zones 1 and 2.

- **Travelcards** are valid on buses, the Underground, the Docklands Light Railway and National Railways' services in the London area after 9:30 a.m. during the week and any time at weekends or on public holidays. **Weekend Travelcards** and **Family Travelcards** are also good value.
- If you need to travel before 9:30 a.m., then a **One Day LT Card** is available. All Travelcards can be purchased at Underground stations, London Travel Information Centres and National Railways' stations in the London area, or newsagents' (news-sellers) stores displaying a London Transport logo.
- For a weekly or monthly pass, you'll need a passport-size photograph.
- Reduced-price passes are available for children.

The Underground

The Underground is easy to use and good for longer journeys in London. The system operates on 12 lines, which are consistently color-coded on maps and signs. Once you know which line you need and the direction you'll be taking (north, south, east or west), follow signs to the relevant platform.

- **Tickets** are available from machines or ticket offices in Underground stations.
- If you are going to do three or more Underground trips in one day, or a mix

of bus and Underground trips, then consider **buying a Travelcard** (see above).
• A **Carnet of 10** Zone 1 Underground tickets is a cheaper option if you will be making a number of trips in central London spread over several days. They are available from Zone 1 Underground stations or designated newsagents.

Buses

An extensive bus network operates in London. Buses are better than the Underground for shorter journeys (and have the advantage that you can see where you're going), but they tend to be slower on longer journeys.

• Some buses have a back entrance with no doors and a conductor to take fares; find a seat and show your pass or pay when the conductor comes along.
• On buses with two sets of doors, you enter via the door at the front to pay the driver or show your pass and get off through the doors farther back.
• You need to know your destination and have change to pay for the fare.

Docklands Light Railway (DLR)

This is an above-ground rail system operating from Bank Underground station to Lewisham. Most visitors to London use it to get to Greenwich. Through tickets are available between D.L.R. and Underground stations, and Travelcards are valid on the DLR.

Taxis

Black cabs (now often painted in gaudy colors) are available from taxi ranks outside stations and hotels but you can also hail them from the roadside.

• Cabs available for hire will have the yellow "For Hire" sign lit.
• All taxis are metered and the fare will depend on journey time; there are surcharges in the evenings. Drivers expect a 10 percent to 15 percent tip.
• To ring for a taxi, **Radio Taxis** (tel: 020 7272 0272) and **Dial-a-Cab** (tel: 020 7253 5000) are both 24-hour services.
• **Black Taxi Tours of London** (tel: 020 7289 4371) offer a 2-hour tailor-made sightseeing tour.

Sightseeing Buses

Several companies operate private bus routes that cover the main tourist sights. The tour is usually in open-topped buses with a commentary in several languages. It's a hop-on, hop-off service, with stops throughout central London. For more information contact:
    Big Bus Company (tel: 020 8944 7810)
    London Pride Sightseeing (tel: 01708 631122)
    Original London Sightseeing Tour (tel: 020 8877 1722)

Car Rental

A car can be a liability in London; traffic is congested and parking expensive and elusive. Parking illegally can result in a parking ticket or having your car immobilized by a wheel clamp: It is a major expense and hassle to get a clamped car released. It's only really worth renting a car for an excursion from the city. All the main international car rental companies have branches in central London. Prices start at around $40 daily; longer rentals are more economical.

Alamo tel: 0990 993 000	**Europcar** tel: 0870 6075000
Avis tel: 0990 900 500	**Hertz** tel: 0990 996 699

Driving

To drive in the United Kingdom, you need a full driver's license or an International Driver's Permit (available from national motoring organizations in your own country).

- Traffic in the United Kingdom drives on the left.
- It is obligatory to wear seat belts.
- The speed limit in built-up areas is 30 m.p.h.; 60 m.p.h. on highways; and 70 m.p.h. on divided highways and freeways.
- There are stringent laws against drinking and driving.
- Private cars are banned from bus lanes – watch out for signs informing you when they are in operation.
- Double yellow lines painted on the road mean no parking at any time.

City Center Tourist Offices

British Tourist Authority
- ✉ 1 Regent Street
- ☎ 020 8846 9000 for information
- ◉ Tue.–Fri. 9–6:30 (Mon. 9:30–6:30), Sat. 9–5, Sun. 10–4

London Tourist Board
- ✉ Victoria Station
- ☎ 020 7971 0026 for recorded information and details of local tourist offices

Admission Charges

The cost of admission for museums and places of interest mentioned in the text is indicated by price categories

inexpensive – up to $8   **moderate** – $8–$16   **expensive** – over $16

Accommodations

London is an expensive city and its hotels reflect this. The capital is simply too popular, and with not enough beds to go around, market forces push prices for accommodations ever higher.

Hotels

The hotels listed below are the pick of the bunch: Some are magnificent buildings with restaurants to match, others have been converted from large 19th-century town houses, or are more modern and custom built. What they offer in terms of service, character, charm and standard of facilities is second to none, and most can now be contacted by e-mail.

Bed-and-Breakfasts

Bed-and-breakfasts (B&Bs), a great British institution, can be a budget alternative to hotels. At their simplest, B&Bs offer a bedroom in a private house with a shared bathroom, but further up the scale are rooms with private bathrooms in beautiful old houses, with all the personal touches that are missing in a grand hotel. The annual *AAA Bed and Breakfast Guide to Britain* contains a useful London listing covering a range of prices.

Seasonal Discounts

July, August and September are the capital's busiest months, though Easter and pre-Christmas are also popular periods, when room prices and availability are at a premium. In the winter months, especially November, January and February, rooms may be discounted. Indeed, one of the best times to visit London is the period between Christmas and New Year when, apart from the busy sales crowds thronging the major shopping areas, the city and its hotels are relatively quiet (many hotels offer special rates after Boxing Day and before New Year's Eve – but you have to ask for them).

Prices Prices are per night for a double room
$ under $240 $$ $240–400 $$$ over $400

The Academy $$
This cozy, light, Bloomsbury hotel – not far from the British Museum – has been carved out of four Georgian town houses. Bedrooms in particular have been thoroughly updated and are now fully air-conditioned; studio rooms are the most spacious and the best equipped. Food is good, too: the breakfast buffet is a cornucopia of fresh fruits, compotes, warm rolls and croissants, while the various lunch and dinner menus offer food with a Mediterranean slant.

➕ 201 E3 ✉ 17–21 Gower Street, WC1 ☎ 020 7631 4115; fax: 020 7636 3442; e-mail: academyh@aol.com
Ⓖ Goodge Street

Athenaeum Hotel $$$
Overlooking Green Park and just a few steps from Hyde Park Corner, the Athenaeum exudes an air of peace and tranquility despite the bustle outside. Bedrooms have a quiet charm and are comfortably appointed. The Windsor Lounge, decorated in English country-house style, is perfect for afternoon tea or an evening drink. Amenities include a health and fitness suite for the exclusive use of guests.

➕ 200 C5 ✉ 116 Piccadilly, W1 ☎ 020 7499 3464; fax: 020 7493 1860; e-mail: www.athenaeumhotel.com
Ⓖ Hyde Park Corner

Basil Street Hotel $$
This hotel, whose location just behind Harrods could not be bettered, is one of the more characterful and old-fashioned London hotels. It wears a genteel faded air, boosted by the charm of the antique elevator, grand staircase and well-proportioned public rooms. Bedrooms vary in size and not all of them are *en suite*, but they are excellent value for money.

➕ 202 A4 ✉ Basil Street, SW3 ☎ 020 7581 3311; fax: 020 7581 3693; e-mail: thebasil@aol.com
Ⓖ Knightsbridge

Bryanston Court $–$$
Look for the attractive blue awning that marks out this well-run hotel in the Georgian row not far from Marble Arch. The bar looks and feels like a gentlemen's club with its leather chairs and old portraits; breakfast is served in the pretty basement restaurant where evening snacks are available during the week. Bedrooms vary in size but are thoroughly up-to-date.

➕ 200 A2 ✉ 60 Great Cumberland Place, W1 ☎ 020 7262 3141; fax: 020 7262 7248l

Claridge's $$$
Claridge's has, for over a century, enjoyed the patronage of visiting royalty, heads of state and dignitaries. A major refurbishment has brought the hotel's facilities right up-to-date, though outwardly little appears to have changed. Bedrooms now have the latest service systems and telecommunications, as well as a privacy button alongside those for maid, valet and floor waiter. Suites and deluxe rooms are particularly outstanding.

➕ 200 C2 ✉ Brook Street, W1 ☎ 020 7629 8860; fax 020 7499 2210; e-mail: info@claridges.co.uk
Ⓖ Bond Street

The Dorchester $$$

Since a lavish refurbishment program, when top designers were commissioned on a no-expense-spared budget to give every room an individual feel, the Dorchester has successfully combined the ultimate in old-fashioned luxury with modern comfort. The glorious original decor in the public rooms gives way to a more traditionally English, but still sumptuous, style in the bedrooms. Antique furniture and rich fabrics give the rooms an air of opulence, while managing to avoid chintzy excesses.

🞖 202 B5 ✉ Park Lane, W1
☎ 020 7629 8888; fax: 020 7409 0114;
e-mail: info@dorchesterhotel.com
🚇 Hyde Park Corner

Five Sumner Place $$

Entering this upbeat Victorian town house feels like walking into someone's very classy home. The personal service is second to none and there are just a dozen bedrooms, all of which have a traditional feel and good facilities. Breakfast is served in the huge airy conservatory, which doubles as a lounge. The South Kensington location is surprisingly quiet.

🞖 Off map ✉ 5 Sumner Place, SW7
☎ 020 7584 7586; fax: 020 7823 9962;
e-mail: no.5@dial.pipex.com 🚇 South Kensington

Goring Hotel $$$

One of the few top hotels in the capital to be independently run, the Goring was built in 1910 by the great-grandfather of the present owner, George Goring, and is a wonderful example of a good old-fashioned British hotel – as such, it is very popular. Guests are drawn to this establishment by the blue-blooded appeal of the classic decor, the exemplary staff (many of whom have been there for years) and the absolutely up-to-date facilities which run to fully air-conditioned bedrooms and power showers.

🞖 202 C3 ✉ Beeston Place, Grosvenor Gardens, SW1 ☎ 020 7396 9000; fax: 020 7834 4393; e-mail: reception@goringhotel.co.uk
🚇 Victoria

Halcyon Hotel $$$

The Halcyon is an elegant town house on a grand scale, offering a peaceful environment on chic Holland Park Avenue. The original Victorian character has been updated in a fashionable period style that mixes fine antiques and paintings with a light, modern color scheme. Bedrooms are spacious and well equipped with every conceivable extra including lavish marble bathrooms. The restaurant is highly regarded, delivering some top-quality modern British cooking.

🞖 Off map ✉ 81 Holland Park, W11
☎ 020 7727 7288; fax: 020 7229 8516;
e-mail: halcyon_hotel@compuserve.com
🚇 Holland Park

Hotel 167 $

This well-kept small hotel, not far from Harrods and the South Kensington museums, has 19 bedrooms, all with *en suite* bathrooms, mini-fridges and in-house video. Breakfast is served at a few tables in the charming lobby. The hotel's modest prices and good location make it essential to reserve well in advance.

🞖 Off map ✉ 167 Old Brompton Road, SW5 ☎ 020 7373 3221; fax: 020 7373 3360 🚇 South Kensington

London County Hall Travel Inn Capital $

This is one of several hotels in the Thames-side building that once housed the now defunct Greater London Council. It may not have the river views of the grander London Marriott County Hall (➤ 38), but it scores points for its exemplary pricing policy (all rooms are a standard price). With neatly designed bedrooms and *en suite* bathrooms, it is one of the best deals for such a central location.

🞖 204 B2 ✉ County Hall, SE1
☎ 020 7902 1600; fax: 020 7902 1619
🚇 Westminster

London Hilton on Park Lane $$$

With everything from a barber's shop and newsstand to a florist and fitness center, the Hilton makes life so comfortable that guests need never leave the building. It has been designed primarily to cater for the needs of business travelers, which it does superbly. Standard rooms are comfortable with good facilities, but the executive floor offers access to a clubroom and a host of complimentary extras.

➕ 202 C5 ✉ 22 Park Lane, WI
☎ 020 7493 8000; fax: 020 7493 4957
Ⓜ Hyde Park Corner

London Marriott County Hall $$–$$$

The hotel, with spectacular views of the Houses of Parliament, Westminster Bridge and a broad sweep of the Thames, provides an excellent range of leisure facilities to accompany the well-laid-out bedrooms. It shares the vast site on the South Bank (formerly home to the Greater London Council) with the London Aquarium (➤ 105).

➕ 204 B2 ✉ County Hall, SE1
☎ 020 7928 5200; fax: 020 7928 5300
Ⓜ Westminster

The Ritz $$$

César Ritz opened the hotel in 1906 following the success of the Hotel Ritz, Paris. It remains one of London's most fashionable hotels, distinguished by an exterior that is pure Parisian elegance and an interior that has been restored in *belle époque* style. French period furniture, colorful chintzes and gilt detailing to the molded-plaster walls, together with modern facilities like video recorders, provide exceptional levels of comfort in the bedrooms.

➕ 203 D5 ✉ 150 Piccadilly, WI
☎ 020 7493 8181; fax: 020 7493 2687;
e-mail: enquire @theritzhotel.co.uk
Ⓜ Green Park

Royal Garden Hotel $$$

This 10-story building next door to Kensington Palace has been transformed by a $30 million refurbishment into an ultramodern hotel. Bedrooms are models of comfort. The nicest have seating areas with park views, but all have up-to-the-minute facilities including fax/modem lines, voice mail and room safes, together with sumptuous bathrooms. There's also a health club, a choice of bars and cafés, as well as a highly rated restaurant on the eleventh floor.

➕ 198 B2 ✉ 2–24 Kensington High Street, W8 ☎ 020 7937 8000; fax: 020 7361 1991; e-mail: guest@royalgdn.co.uk Ⓜ High Street Kensington

The Stafford $$$

Tucked away in St. James's, this discreet hotel puts the emphasis on personal service, and public areas create a look of cultured charm. A collection of American club and university ties decorates the American Bar. The individually designed bedrooms are luxurious, with marble-clad bathrooms.

➕ 203 D5 ✉ 16–18 St. James's Place, SW1 ☎ 020 7493 0111; fax: 020 7493 7121; e-mail: info@thestaffordhotel.co.uk
Ⓜ Green Park

The Westbury $$$

Opened in 1955, this sister hotel to the Westbury in New York is in the perfect location for shopaholics – just off exclusive Bond Street. The original owners had a passion for polo – both hotels are named after the Long Island polo ground – and the Polo Lounge and Polo Bar remain popular features. A major makeover has thoroughly updated the hotel, so that once again it offers every modern facility to the highest standard.

➕ 201 D1 ✉ Bond Street, W1 ☎ 020 7629 7755; fax: 020 7495 1163
Ⓜ Oxford Circus, Piccadilly Circus, Bond Street

The White House $$–$$$

Since its transformation from a 1930s apartment block into a hotel, The White House has come to be regarded by aficionados as one of London's best-kept secrets. It exudes charm, and the promised emphasis on hospitality and comfort is met with dedication. Rooms are modern and comfortable; reserve floor bedrooms are the most spacious. The peaceful location is a short walk from the West End.

➕ 200 C4 ✉ Albany Street, NW1
☎ 020 7387 1200; fax: 020 7388 0091
Ⓜ Great Portland Street

Food and Drink

At one time, British food meant fish and chips, steak and kidney pie or bangers (sausages) and mash. Now London is regarded as one of the restaurant capitals of the world, boasting food styles and chefs from all corners of the globe, and finding a restaurant table in London on a Saturday night is no easy task.

New Trends

The explosion of new restaurants, even pubs, simply serving excellent food means that there is a wider choice of places to eat than ever before. Exciting new trends have completely revolutionized Londoners' eating habits. Fusion cooking, incorporating ideas from all over the world, plus an entirely new school of modern Italian cooking, and the reworking of traditional British dishes into lighter modern cuisine have all made their mark. And to crown it all, some of the finest French cuisine to be found in the capital is being created by British chefs. For the food lover there has never been a better time to visit London.

Movers and Shakers

In the 1990s two men from widely different backgrounds influenced the London dining scene more than anyone else. When, in 1989, the designer-cum-businessman Sir Terence Conran opened the Design Museum and adjoining Blue Print Café in a disused riverside warehouse, few realized the impact this would have on the capital. It was a relatively modest opening for the trail-blazing Conran, who was already noted for the stylish **Bibendum** in Brompton Cross (► 132). From the amazing **South Bank Gastrodome**, which also includes **Le Pont de la Tour**, **Cantina del Ponte** (► 108) and **Butlers Wharf Chop House**, he has transformed dining habits in fashionable districts, first with megarestaurants **Quaglino's** (► 64), **Mezzo** (► 157) and **Bluebird** at the King's Road Gastrodome (► 132), and then with more controlled spaces such as **The Orrery** in Marylebone (► 157).

Marco Pierre White has always been considered the *enfant terrible* of the London restaurant scene. Arguably the best native-born chef in England, he occupies pole position among London's star chefs and attracts success and controversy like a giant magnet. Although he has mellowed with time, he has grown into an astute businessman, scooping up prime sites, mainly in the West End, and relaunching them stamped with his own exemplary style of modern British cooking. Two stand out: his premier restaurant, **The Oak Room**, in the Meridien Piccadilly (► 63), and the **Mirabelle** (► 63).

Up and Coming

With big bucks dominating the West End, the burgeoning restaurant scene has pushed out the boundaries of fashionable London. To check up on the latest openings, look in the *Evening Standard* newspaper every Tuesday when formidable restaurant critic Fay Maschler digests the pick of the crop. Saturday and Sunday editions of *The Times* and *The Independent* newspapers also carry good reviews of restaurants which are generally London based.

But be prepared to travel out of the center in search of the latest hit restaurant – the area around Smithfield meat market, for example, or Clerkenwell and Farringdon. At the end of the 1980s these areas were grim and deserted after dark; now property values are booming, with young professionals, stylish bars, stores and galleries jostling for the available space. Such is the power of food.

The Drinking Scene

Both Sir Terence Conran and Marco Pierre White can claim to have put the style back into drinking. Until the start of the 1990s, the usual meeting place for

Londoners was the pub, where smoky, crowded conditions were often made worse by indifferent service. The new breed of megarestaurants changed all that.

One of the sharpest features of Conran's **Quaglino's** and **Mezzo**, and Marco Pierre White's **Quo Vadis** (► 158) are the chic American-style bars that act as a magnet for London's coolest when looking for a little recreation. Popularity bred success, so much so that both **Bank** (► 156) and Oliver Peyton's acclaimed **Atlantic Bar & Grill** (► 62) made a real feature of their bars. Indeed, so popular have they become that they use vaguely intimidating door policies to retain an exclusive feel; the dress code is not strict and door policies do not apply if you have a reservation for dinner.

You can drink just about anything in these bars. Champagne, of course, is always a good choice, but all boast excellent wine lists, with many wines available by the glass and prices to suit all pockets. Bottled beers are classy European brands, and English real ales are often on tap – microbreweries such as Mash produce their own beers; and hard liquor runs to quality brands not usually seen in pubs – Bombay Sapphire gin and East European vodkas, for example. The bartenders have their own following; some even run bartending columns in national newspapers.

London's Coolest Bars
These are the places to go if you want to hang out with the some of the hippest folk in town.

Atlantic Bar & Grill	Bank	Fifth Floor Restaurant at Harvey Nichols	Mash Quaglino's	Mezzo Quo Vadis

Welcome to the Gastrodome
Conran's mega-eaterie on the South Bank, close to Tower Bridge, is home to several top-quality restaurants.

Blue Print Café Cantina del Ponte	Butlers Wharf Chop House Le Pont de la Tour

Afternoon Tea
It may be a fixture on a tourist itinerary, but many Londoners also regard afternoon tea in a grand hotel as the ultimate treat. It's an excuse to dress up (nearly all the hotels listed here adhere to a jacket-and-tie code), is cheaper than lunch but often just as satisfying, and is an agreeable way to spend the afternoon. Don't worry about which tea to order and whether to drink it with milk or lemon; if you are unsure just ask for the house blend, which can be drunk with either, or order a herbal tea.

The Savoy $$
The Savoy is the most accessible of the capital's grand hotels, with tea served in the stately Thames Foyer. To the sound of a tinkling piano an exquisite array of doll's house food is served, including miniature sandwiches, scones with jam and cream, and a selection of delicious cakes and pastries.

🕀 204 B3 ⊠ The Strand, WC2 ☎ 020 7836 4343 🕔 Daily 3–5:30 🚇 Charing Cross, Embankment

The Ritz $$
The Palm Court, with its opulent Louis XVI decor, is the quintessential location for tea at the Ritz. This very touristy afternoon tea is expensive, but it remains an unforgettable experience. A reservation for either of the two sittings is required one month in advance (three months if you want to go at a weekend).

🕀 203 D5 ⊠ Piccadilly, W1 ☎ 020 7493 8181 🕔 Daily 2–6, reserved sittings at 3:30 and 5 🚇 Green Park

The Dorchester $$

The Promenade, where tea is served, is soothing and luxurious, with deeply comfortable armchairs and thick carpets. A piano plays in the background and tea brings mouthwatering pâtisserie. Booking is advisable.

🔲 202 B5 ⊠ 54 Park Lane, W1
☎ 020 7629 8888 🕒 Daily 3–6
🚇 Hyde Park Corner

Brown's Hotel $–$$

Tea in the Drawing Room of Brown's is a cozy experience; it's like being in an English country house. There is a splendid Victoria sponge cake, as well as delicate sandwiches and fresh scones, jam and cream. Indulge yourself in the whole tea but be prepared to forgo dinner. Reservations are advisable, especially in summer.

🔲 201 D1 ⊠ 33–4 Albemarle Street, W1 ☎ 020 7518 4108 🕒 Daily 3–6
🚇 Green Park

Meridien Waldorf $–$$

The Meridien Waldorf has a larger Palm Court than at the Ritz, and probably the best setting for tea of all the hotels. It's like stepping back in time to the 1930s, especially if you go to the tea dance and celebrate with the set champagne tea. There's no formal dress code, but it is worth making the effort.

🔲 204 B4 ⊠ Aldwych, WC2 ☎ 020 7836 2400 🕒 Mon.–Fri. 3-5:30; tea dance: Sat. 2:30– 5:30, Sun. 4–6:30
🚇 Covent Garden

Fish and Chips

Fish and chips (French fries) is the one dish tourists to London want to try most. Forget fusion, modern British cooking and the rest of the food revolution, here are five expert "chippies." If you're having a takeout, you may be asked if you want salt and vinegar (malt) sprinkled over, or condiments may be available at the counter for you to serve yourself.

Fish Central $

Regarded by many as the capital's best fish-and-chip shop, there is also a restaurant where all manner of piscine delights are listed, from sea bass to sole. Reserve in advance.

🔲 Off map ⊠ King Square, 151 Central Street, EC1 ☎ 020 7253 4970
🕒 Mon.–Sat. 11–2:30, 4:45–10:30
🚇 Angel, Old Street

North Sea Fish Restaurant $

This is where the cabbies (taxi drivers) come. They usually occupy the back room, while the rest of the clientele sit in the front, among the pink velvet upholstery and stuffed fish. Portions are gigantic, and the fish is very fresh. Reservations are recommended for dinner, and there is a takeout service.

🔲 201 F5 ⊠ 7–8 Leigh Street, WC1 ☎ 020 7387 5892 🕒 Mon.–Sat. noon–2:30, 5:30–10:30. Closed Sun. dinner 🚇 Russell Square

Rock and Sole Plaice $

This claims to be the oldest surviving chippie in London, opened in 1871. The Covent Garden location draws a pretheater crowd to the restaurant and reservations are recommended for dinner. There is also a takeout service.

🔲 204 A4 ⊠ 47 Endell Street, WC2 ☎ 020 7836 3785 🕒 Mon.–Sat. 11:30– 10, Sun. 11:30–9 🚇 Covent Garden

Sea Shell $

Probably the most famous of London's chippies, the Sea Shell is certainly the most popular with tourists – lines are common as reservations are not taken for parties of fewer than six.

🔲 Off map ⊠ 49–51 Lisson Grove, NW1 ☎ 020 7723 8703 🕒 Mon.–Fri. noon–2, 5:15– 10:30, Sat. noon–10:30, Sun. noon–2:30. Closed Sun. dinner 🚇 Marylebone

Geales $

Tucked away down a tiny back street in a fashionable residential area of Kensington, this long-standing chippie offers both takeout and a very popular restaurant. Reservations are taken for large parties only – go early.

🔲 198 A3 ⊠ 2 Farmer Street, W8 ☎ 020 7727 7969 🕒 Noon–3, 6–11. Closed Sun. dinner 🚇 Notting Hill Gate

Shopping

A vital wave of change has swept through the city's stores, and you will find an enthusiastic mood and glimpse a new modernism in London's shopping streets. Traditional institutions and long-established stores, however, continue to provide top-quality goods and deserve time on any visit.

Fashion

The capital's stores cater to a wide variety of tastes and pockets, whether you are looking for designer labels, a top-quality made-to-measure suit, or moderately priced current fashion.

- Chain stores sell good-quality clothes at moderate prices. **Oxford Street** (► 66), **Covent Garden** (► 159) and **Chelsea and Kensington** (► 134) have the best choice.
- Boutiques and classy department stores are the best bet for **designer names,** and lovers of international designer labels will have fun finding their favorite names on either **Bond Street** (► 65) or **Sloane Street** (► 134). Both streets underwent a transformation in the late 1990s and are vibrant and exciting.
- For those who favor a classical approach, **Burberry** has two outlets, one on Haymarket, the other on Regent Street. **Savile Row** (► 65), a shrine to pinstriped cloth and made-to-measure gentlemen's wear, also contains discreetly subversive tailors such as Ozwald Boateng.
- To find everything under one roof try the fashion-oriented department stores: **Harrods** (► 116), **Harvey Nichols** (► 134), **Liberty's** (► 65) and **Selfridges** (► 66).

Art and Antiques

A thriving commercial art scene has both antiques and art from a time before Samuel Johnson's London, as well as pictures so fresh the paint is still drying. London caters for every visual taste.

- The **galleries of Mayfair**, primarily Cork Street and Bond Street, show established names and certain investments, with plenty of late 20th-century work.
- Many young artists have warehouse studios in the East End and a number of galleries here show exciting work at attractive prices. Listings magazines contain weekly updates of exhibitions and studio shows.
- If antiques are your passion the auction houses of **Sotheby's** on New Bond Street, **Christie's** in South Kensington and, to a lesser extent, **Bonham's** in Chelsea, provide the best hunting ground.
- The **New King's Road** (► 135) in Chelsea and **Kensington Church Street** (► 134) are two long stretches of road lined by shops stuffed with furniture, ceramics, memorabilia and jewelry – eye-catching displays make for great window-shopping.

Contemporary Furniture

Habitat, **Heal's** and **Conran** are still popular for furniture but are definitely resting on their design laurels; these days they are generally considered to be middle-of-the-road, disguised as modernist. Two stores selling furniture designs that are right up-to-date are **Purves & Purves** (80–81 and 83 Tottenham Court Road, W1, tel: 020 7580 8223) and **Viaduct** (1–10 Summers Street, EC1, tel: 020 7278 8456).

Specialty Food Stores

- **The Conran Shop** at Brompton Cross and Conran's **Bluebird** on the King's Road (➤ 132) are terrific for stylish food purchases.
- Historic **Fortnum & Mason** (➤ 65) stocks a fabulous range of teas and a choice of 50 types of marmalade among other foods.
- **Harrods** food hall, with its lush displays and own-brand comestibles, is irresistible to Londoners and tourists alike.

Markets

- Antiques hunters have to be at **Portobello Road market** (➤ 131) at the crack of dawn, but if you're hunting for clothes or are just plain curious you can afford to visit at a more leisurely hour.
- **Portobello** and **Camden markets** (➤ 152) are probably the two best markets for secondhand and unusual designer clothes, and just fun browsing.

Gift Ideas
Patum Peperium Gentlemen's Relish from Fortnum & Mason (➤ 65)
Luggage tags from Smythson's (➤ 134)
A classic silk tie with spots from Turnbull & Asser (➤ 65)
A silk scarf from Liberty's (➤ 65)
Hologram cufflinks from Paul Smith (➤ 159)

Entertainment

The choice of entertainment in London is vast and listings magazines are invaluable for detailing what's on, whether it's theater, movies, art exhibitions or gigs. *Time Out*, published every Tuesday, covers the whole spectrum of entertainment and is the best buy. Thursday editions of the *Evening Standard* (London's evening newspaper) and Saturday editions of national newspapers such as *The Times* and *The Independent* also have listings magazines for London.

Music
Diversity sums up the London music scene, and supports a serious claim to the title of music capital of Europe. Classical music is celebrated by five symphony orchestras as well as various smaller outfits, several first-rate concert halls and high standards of performance. The ever-changing pop music culture that is the driving force behind London fashion and stylish restaurants and bars can feature more than a hundred gigs on a Saturday night alone, from pub bands to big rock venues.

- If you enjoy classical music, the **Proms**, an annual festival at the Royal Albert Hall, is held from mid-July to mid-September (➤ 136).
- In summer, informal **open air concerts** are held at Kenwood House (tel: 020 7973 3427) and in Holland Park.
- The **Royal Opera** at Covent Garden (Floral Street, WC2, tel: 020 7240 1066), stages elaborate productions with performances by the major stars. Alternatively, try the **English National Opera** (London Coliseum, St. Martin's Lane, WC2, tel: 020 7836 3161), where works are sung in English.

Dance

Dance can mean anything from classical to flamenco and jazz tap, with London playing host to top international performers throughout the year.

• The **Royal Festival Hall** at the South Bank Centre has an eclectic mix of dance programs, as does **Sadler's Wells** (tel: 020 7863 8000), Islington, although it is better known for ballet. The **Royal Ballet** is based at the Royal Opera House, Covent Garden.
• **Dance Umbrella**, an international festival of contemporary dance, is held at various venues around London during October and November (tel: 020 8741 5881 for information).

Theater

Some **West End musicals** might look a bit tired now – *Cats*, *Starlight Express*, *Les Misérables* and *Miss Saigon* have all been running for over a decade – but the genre maintains its excitement, with current productions such as *Chicago* winning praise for a fresh approach. Theater is strong, too. Agatha Christie's thriller *The Mousetrap* has been running for more than half a century and is a firm fixture on the tourist itinerary, but new plays also open regularly.

• The **Royal National Theatre** at the South Bank Centre (tel: 020 7928 3002) has three theaters producing all manner of drama, and the Royal Shakespeare Company (focusing mainly on Shakespeare) occupies two theaters at the **Barbican Centre** (➤ 88). Also worth visiting is **Shakespeare's Globe** at Bankside (➤ 106). The Royal Court and the Old Vic are the most dynamic theaters promoting the works of young unknowns as well as major new plays by avant-garde writers.
• "Off-West End" and fringe theater has a healthy reputation. The **Almeida** and **Donmar Warehouse** are the major players, but theaters such as the **Gate** and **King's Head** are worth checking out.

Buying Tickets

The best way to buy a ticket for any London theater production is to contact the venue directly (so avoiding agency commissions). However, tickets for hit plays and musicals are hard to come by, particularly at short notice, and often are *only* obtainable through ticket agencies. **First Call** (tel: 0870 906 3700) is the most reliable ticket agency, though there are many others throughout the West End.

• Buy your tickets directly from the concert or theater venue or from ticket agencies. **Never buy from ticket touts**; the practice is illegal and you may well end up with forgeries.
• If you are flexible about which production you want to see, try the **Half-Price Ticket Booth** at Leicester Square (➤ 160). Expect to wait in line and remember that tickets are limited to two pairs per person.
• The most inexpensive seats are always at the top of the theater, known as the "gods," but you will probably need binoculars.
• **Matinées** are less expensive than evening performances and tickets are far easier to come by.
• Some theaters offer **restricted-view seats** in the stalls at a reduced rate.

Movie Theaters

For movie-goers, The Odeon, Leicester Square, is recommended for the most modern and up-to-date movie experience the capital can offer.

St. James's, Mayfair and Piccadilly

Getting Your Bearings

The area between Buckingham Palace and Trafalgar Square is one of London's quintessential quarters, and if you have time for only a day in the city, you should consider spending it here.

A district of considerable wealth and architectural grandeur, this area contains the leafy squares and prestigious residential buildings of Mayfair, the exclusive gentlemen's clubs of St. James's, and the long-established stores and hotels of Piccadilly, one of London's great thoroughfares.

Here, too, is Buckingham Palace, the monarch's official residence, and reputedly the world's most photographed building.

The area owes its original development to St. James's Palace, built by Henry VIII in the 1530s and subsequently the home of several later sovereigns, including Elizabeth I and Charles I (in our own time, the Prince of Wales moved here after his separation from Diana, Princess of Wales in 1992). The royal palace loaned the area considerable social cachet, particularly after the 17th century, when King Charles II opened two of London's loveliest London parks, St. James's Park and Green Park, to the public for the first time. By the 18th century, members of the aristocracy who wished to be close to court had built fine mansions such as Spencer House and Burlington House. In time, splendid arcades and exclusive Piccadilly stores sprang up to serve the area's high-spending visitors and residents. The character of the area changed little in the 19th century when Queen Victoria moved the court to Buckingham Palace, which was nearby, nor in the 20th century, which saw the building of the present grand ceremonial route along The Mall between Buckingham Palace and Trafalgar Square.

Today, the area's elegance and refinement make it unique in the capital, with a sense of gentility and grandeur missing in other areas. You can enjoy the parks and grand walkways, the fine old houses, the stores and galleries (notably the Royal Academy, scene of major art exhibitions), and the principal sights at either end of The Mall: Buckingham Palace, with its famous ceremonial Changing of the Guard, and Trafalgar Square with the National Gallery, the country's premier art gallery.

Previous page and above: pomp and circumstance: the Horse Guards on parade

HYDE PARK CORNER

GROSVENOR PLACE

⭐ Don't Miss

At Your Leisure

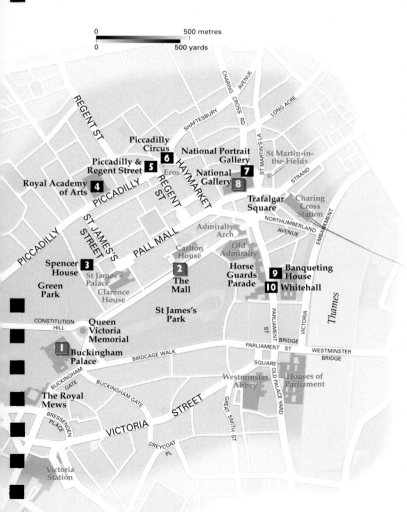

Enjoy a couple of royal palaces, some of the best-known sights of London, countless artistic masterpieces and – the real bonus – peaceful swathes of green in the heart of the city.

St. James's, Mayfair and Piccadilly in a Day

One of the recommended highlights is the State Rooms in Buckingham Palace (➤ 50–51), but they're open only two months every year (early August to early October) – and if you do visit them then it's unlikely you'll be able to find a

good vantage point afterward to watch the Changing of the Guard (or have the time to walk to Horse Guards Parade to see it there ➤ 53). Come back another day if you have your heart set on seeing the ceremony. You can still follow the plan below after visiting the palace, however – you'll just be doing everything a couple of hours later.

9:00 a.m.

Start at **Buckingham Palace** (left, ➤ 50–51) – either ogle the grand façade through the railings or, if you are in London at the right time of year, visit the magnificent State Rooms. To avoid queuing on the day see Top tips (➤ 51).

9:30 a.m.

Stroll through **St. James's Park**, a tranquil oasis, and then walk along the broad, majestic, tree-lined **Mall** (➤ 52–53) to Horse Guards Parade to see the Changing of the Guard, one of London's most impressive ceremonies. Be in place by 10 a.m. to find a good vantage point.

11:45 a.m.

The Changing of the Guard over, walk through to **Trafalgar Square** (above right ➤ 53) for a close encounter with lions (statues) and pigeons (real). It's busy, noisy and surrounded by traffic, but it remains a natural meeting place, a national symbol of past glories, and an essential stop on any London visit.

12:30 p.m.

Time for lunch. St. Martin-in-the-Fields (above), adjacent to the National Gallery at the top of Trafalgar Square, has an inexpensive café in its crypt, and the gallery itself has a coffee bar and brasserie.

1:30 p.m.

Spend the afternoon seeing the gems of the superlative art collection at the **National Gallery** (➤ 54-57) – spend as long as you wish. If you're here on a Wednesday, the gallery doesn't close until 9 p.m.

4:00 p.m.

Stop off at the **National Portrait Gallery** (➤ 60–61) for a look at its appealing collection of portraits of famous and infamous Brits.

5:00 p.m.

Make your way to **Piccadilly Circus** (➤ 60). From here you can take in some of Mayfair's squares and back lanes or the **exclusive stores** of Piccadilly (right ➤ 58–59). You're also just around the corner from Leicester Square, the heart of Theaterland, with sleazy, flamboyant Soho and exotic Chinatown nearby.

Buckingham Palace

The British sovereign's grandiose London home was built between 1701 and 1705 by the 1st Duke of Buckingham, but was redeveloped as a palace by King George IV in the 1820s, and became the official royal residence in the reign of Queen Victoria in 1837. Although it's a must-see on all London itineraries, at first glance it doesn't look terribly impressive – its stolid lines appear plain, solid and dependable rather than an exuberant celebration of majesty in stone.

While the palace isn't anything special from the outside, its interior is a different story altogether. The **State Rooms** were first opened to the public in 1993, a move prompted by changing attitudes within the Royal Family, and a desire to contribute funds toward the restoration of Windsor Castle (➤ 164). They shouldn't be missed if you're in London at the right time.

Above: the white marble Queen Victoria Memorial in front of the palace

☎ Enquiries 020 7839 1377; Recorded information 020 7799 2331; Credit card reservations 020 7321 2233 🕐 Green Park ticket office, near the palace: Daily 9–4, Aug.–Oct. State Rooms: Daily 9:30–4:30 (last entry), early Aug.–Oct. Royal Mews: Mon.–Thu. noon–4, Oct.–Jul.; Mon.–Thu. 10:30–4:30, Aug.–Sep. 🚇 Green Park, St. James's Park, Victoria 🚌 Piccadilly 3, 8, 9, 14, 19, 22; Victoria Street 11, 24, 211; Grosvenor Place 2, 8, 16, 36, 38, 52, 73, 82 💷 Palace expensive; mews inexpensive

Right: Buckingham Palace, The Mall, Queen Victoria Memorial and St. James's Park

The State Rooms are where the real work of royalty goes on, providing a stage for state entertaining, investitures, receptions and official banquets. Their sheer richness and decorative theatricality are mesmerizing, from the grand marble staircase and the brightly furnished drawing rooms to the Throne Room and the elaborate red-and-gilt State Dining Room. Your feet sink softly into plush red carpets, wall coverings are almost works of art in themselves, and balustrades, doors, chandeliers and windows all display spellbinding and unforgettable detail. Equally compelling are the paintings that hang in the Picture Gallery, including works by Van Dyck, Rembrandt and Rubens, the Classical sculptures and exquisite furniture. Look in particular for the thrones and the fabulously ornamental ceilings, which are some of the most elaborate imaginable. Don't expect to meet any of the Royal Family – they move elsewhere when the general public come to call.

BUCKINGHAM PALACE: INSIDE INFO

Top tips To avoid waiting in line, **reserve tickets in advance** by credit card and collect them on the day from the Green Park ticket office. Arrangements can be made to have tickets sent out by mail. Allow 10 days for United Kingdom and three weeks for overseas addresses. No concessions are available on tickets reserved this way.
- Buy an **Official Guide** on the way in – it's invaluable, as nothing in the State Rooms is labeled.
- Look at the flags: if the gold, blue and red Royal Standard flies from the roof, the Queen is in residence.
- The **Changing of the Guard** ceremony with bands and standard bearers takes place at 11:30 a.m. in the palace forecourt and lasts 40 minutes. Get there by 10 a.m. to get a good position – by the front railings between the gates is best.

In more detail Visit the **Royal Mews** to see the state carriages and coaches together with their horses. The collection's gem is the Gold State Coach, a beautifully elaborate carriage straight out of a fairy tale.

The Mall to Trafalgar Square

The Mall is the grand, tree-lined processional avenue between Buckingham Palace and Trafalgar Square, a thoroughfare that comes into its own on ceremonial occasions such as the State Opening of Parliament and Trooping the Colour. Near the Mall are two royal parks: Green Park, which is particularly lovely in spring when the daffodils are in flower, and St. James's Park, which is a delight at any time of year.

To start your exploration, turn your back on Buckingham Palace and cross the road to the **Queen Victoria Memorial**. This white marble statue, the Mall and Admiralty Arch were laid out in the early 20th century as a memorial to Queen Victoria, who died in 1901. The statue depicts a rather dour-looking Victoria surrounded by figures representing the glories of the British Empire.

These days the Mall is a busy, traffic-filled thoroughfare, although one whose grandeur and dignity remain majestically intact. Until the 17th century, however, it was a small country lane, its confines used by King James I to play a French game known as *palle-maille* (anglicized to pell mell). A hybrid of golf and croquet, the game has long gone out of fashion, but it is remembered in the names of the Mall and Pall Mall, one of Piccadilly's main streets. Later, King Charles II improved the area, most notably by opening St. James's Park and Green Park to the public, a move that made this *the* fashionable spot in the capital to take a daily constitutional.

Above: Changing the Guard at Buckingham Palace

Right: the sweeping façade of Admiralty Arch

Top right: Nelson's Column dominates Trafalgar Square

Looking down the Mall on the left you can see 19th-century Clarence House, named after its first resident, the Duke of Clarence, who became King William IV in 1830. In 1953, when Queen Elizabeth II acceded to the throne, it became the London home of the Queen Mother. Behind Clarence House rise the red-brick Tudor turrets of St. James's Palace, built by Henry VIII (who died here). Since 1992, it has been home to the Prince of Wales, heir to the throne.

From the Queen Victoria Memorial you may want to enter **St. James's Park**, following shady paths toward the lake; at the bridge you have a choice: One route takes you back to the Mall and a right turn past Carlton House Terrace, distinguished by its early 19th-century white stucco façade, leads you along the Mall to Admiralty Arch. Another allows you to continue along the lake to the far end of the park.

Either way, you should take in **Horse Guards**, the huge parade ground at the park's eastern end that provides the stage for the daily **Changing of the Guard** (➤ Inside Info, below). Then walk through Admiralty Arch to **Trafalgar Square**, laid out in 1820 as a memorial to British naval hero Admiral Horatio Nelson, who stands three times life-size on the 170-foot column at the square's heart. Reliefs at the column's base depict four of his greatest naval victories, of which Trafalgar against the French in 1805 – where Nelson died – was the most famous. The square's celebrated lions were added in the late 1860s.

The square's northern flank is dominated by the National Gallery (➤ 54–57), and – to its right – the fine spire of St.-Martin-in-the-Fields, burial place of Nell Gwynne, the most beautiful of King Charles II's many mistresses.

TAKING A BREAK

Try **Chor Bizarre** (➤ 62) for an exciting range of Indian regional cooking, including a wide choice of vegetarian dishes and tandoori favorites.

THE MALL TO TRAFALGAR SQUARE: INSIDE INFO

Top tips The celebrated **Changing of the Guard**, where the mounted guards change over their duties, takes place in Horse Guards Parade, off Whitehall (Mon.–Sat. 11 a.m., Sun. 10 a.m.). The same ceremony for foot soldiers proceeds in the fore-court of Buckingham Palace (➤ 50–51). If the weather is bad, the ceremony may be canceled at short notice. (Daily 11:30, Apr.–Jul.; alternate days 11:30, Aug.–Mar., tel: 020 7930 4466).

• If you have the chance, try to attend one of the **candlelight classical music concerts** held regularly in St.-Martin-in-the-Fields. For information and credit card reservations tel: 020 7839 8362 – the reservation line is open Mon. to Fri. 10 a.m. to 4 p.m. Tickets are also available Mon. to Sat. 10 a.m. to 6 p.m. from the box office in the crypt.

National Gallery

The National Gallery has one of the world's greatest collections of paintings. Covering the years 1260 to about 1900, it presents the cream of the nation's art collection, including some 2,200 works of European art hung in a succession of light, well-proportioned rooms. Think of almost any famous painter from almost any era, and the chances are they'll be represented here – Botticelli, Canaletto, Cézanne, Constable, Leonardo da Vinci, Monet, Rembrandt, Renoir, Raphael, Titian, Turner, Van Gogh.

Suggested Route

The gallery is divided into **four wings**, each covering a chronological period: it makes sense to visit the wings in this order:

- **Sainsbury Wing** 1260 to 1510 Rooms 51–66
- **West Wing** 1510 to 1600 Rooms 2–13
- **North Wing** 1600 to 1700 Rooms 14–32
- **East Wing** 1700 to 1900 Rooms 33–34

The National Gallery was designed as the architectural focus of Trafalgar Square

✉ Trafalgar Square, WC2
☎ 020 7747 2885; e-mail: www.nationalgallery.org.uk
🕐 Daily 10–6 (Wed. 10–9); The Micro Gallery: daily 10–5:30 (Wed. 10–8:30). Closed

Jan. 1, Good Friday and Dec. 24–26
🚇 Charing Cross, Leicester Square
🚌 3, 6, 9, 11, 12, 13, 15, 23, 24, 29, 53, 77A, 88, 91, 109, 159, 176
🎫 Admission free

Sainsbury Wing

The wonderfully airy Sainsbury Wing (named after the supermarket dynasty that sponsored it) was designed by architect Robert Venturi and opened in 1991. Although it is the newest part of the gallery, it displays the oldest paintings, in particular the masterpieces of the various Italian schools after about 1300. Two of its loveliest works are by Leonardo da Vinci (Room 51). The unfinished *The Virgin of the Rock* (1508) depicts Mary, John the Baptist and Christ with an angel in a rocky landscape. Some of the work may be by pupils, but the sublime expression on the angel's face suggests pure Leonardo. In a specially darkened room nearby, da Vinci's cartoon of

An allegory of motherhood – the celebrated Leonardo da Vinci cartoon in the National Gallery depicts the Madonna and Child with a young John the Baptist and St. Anne, the mother of the Virgin Mary

The Virgin and Child with St. Anne and St. John the Baptist (1508) is an exquisitely beautiful depiction of a meeting never mentioned in the Bible – Christ and his maternal grandmother.

Be certain to see *The Wilton Diptych* (Room 53), a late 14th-century altarpiece commissioned by Richard II for his private prayers: It shows the king kneeling on the left and being presented to the Madonna and Child. Both the artist and his nationality remain a mystery. Less tantalizing but no less beautiful are two portraits, Van Eyck's *Arnolfini Portrait* (Room 56) and Giovanni Bellini's matchless *Doge Leonardo Loredan* (Room 61).

West Wing

Turn around as you cross from the Sainsbury to the West Wing for the gallery's most remarkable view – a series of receding archways designed to frame a Renaissance altarpiece on a distant wall. Once in the West Wing, you're treated to mostly French, Italian and Dutch works from the High Renaissance, of which perhaps the most memorable is Hans Holbein the Younger's *The Ambassadors* (1533) – almost life-size portraits of Jean de Dinteville and Georges de Selve (Room 4). The picture is crammed with symbol and allusion, most aimed at underlining the fleeting nature of earthly life and the dark span of death and eternity. In the middle foreground of the picture, for example, is a white disk; move to the right side of the painting and it's revealed as a human skull, a *memento mori*.

North Wing

Painters who challenged the primacy of the Italians during the 16th and 17th centuries are the stars of the North Wing – Rubens, Rembrandt, Van Dyck, Velázquez, Vermeer and Claude, to name but a handful. Velázquez's *The Toilet of Venus* (also known as *The Rokeby Venus* after Rokeby Hall where it once hung) is one of the best-known paintings (Room 29). It is an unusual work, first because it shows a back view of the goddess (with an extraordinary face captured in a mirror), and second because it is a nude, a genre frowned upon by the Inquisition in Spain when the work was completed in 1651.

East Wing

The East Wing is often extremely busy, mainly because it contains some of the best-known of all British paintings. Chief among these is John Constable's *The Hay Wain* (Room 34), first exhibited in 1821 when the fashion was for blended brushwork and smooth painted texture: Contemporary critics disapproved of what they saw as its rough and unfinished nature. Today it represents an archetype of an all-but-vanished English rural landscape. More works by the same artist are displayed in the Victoria and Albert Museum (➤ 117–120) and the Tate Britain (➤ 94–96).

Another great English painter, J. M. W. Turner, was a contemporary of Constable but developed a radically different style. In his day he was considered madly eccentric, particularly in his later works, yet it is these mature paintings that have the most profound modern-day resonance. Two of the greatest, *The Fighting Téméraire* (1838) and *Rain, Steam and Speed* (1844), display the powerful and almost hallucinatory effects of light on air and water characteristic of the painter (Room 34). More of the same can be seen in the Tate Gallery's Turner Bequest (➤ 95).

Equally as popular as the Turners and Constables are the National's numerous Impressionist masterpieces (Rooms 44 and 45), including a wealth of instantly recognizable paintings such as Van Gogh's *Sunflowers* (1889) and Seurat's *The Bathers at Asnières* (1884), the latter's shimmering clarity a fitting memory to take with you back into Trafalgar Square.

TAKING A BREAK

You can get light refreshments at the **National Gallery coffee bar** and **brasserie**.

The splendid interior of the National Gallery provides a suitably grand setting for one of the greatest collections of paintings in Europe

The Bathers at Asnières by Georges Seurat is among the best known of the National Gallery's many Impressionist masterpieces

NATIONAL GALLERY: INSIDE INFO

Top tips The gallery displays many British artists, but many more – especially modern British painters – are better represented in the Tate Gallery's collection (➤ 94).
• **Soundtrack** is an excellent portable CD guide. It covers the entire collection – simply dial up the number beside the picture to hear a commentary. Although this is in English, there is a highlights tour of 30 major works which is available in six languages. It's free, but a donation is requested.

In more detail The **Micro Gallery** in the Sainsbury Wing contains a computerized information system with information on every painting and artist in the collection.

Hidden gems Most of the pictures owned by the National Gallery are on display – those not in the main galleries are in the **lower-floor galleries** in the main building. Telephone before visiting to make sure that these lower galleries are open; when staffing levels are low they are closed.

At Your Leisure

3 Spencer House

Spencer House is London's finest surviving 18th-century town house and one of the capital's best-kept secrets. Excellent hour-long guided tours provide background information on the house, its painstaking 10-year restoration and its original incumbents, the Spencer family, the most famous member of which was Lady Diana Spencer, later Diana, Princess of Wales (1961–97).

The house was built for the first Earl Spencer and his wife, Georgiana, who desired a London home to complement their country seat at Althorp in Northamptonshire. Virtually all of the decoration celebrates the pair's love for one another – a rare thing when aristocratic marriages were effectively arranged – and is distinguished by a surfeit of cherubs, roses, palms and turtle doves.

The Dining Room and Great Room are impressive for their size and grandeur, while book lovers will long for a few private hours in the Library with its towering wooden bookcases and leather-bound books. Most people will love the ground floor's Palm Room, where each column is covered with elaborately carved and gilded palm fronds (the furniture has a matching motif). The painted ceilings, walls, friezes and gilded ornamentation are breathtaking throughout.

✉ 27 St. James's Place, SW1
☎ 020 7499 8620
🕐 Sun. 10:30– 5:30, Feb.–Jul. and Sep.–Dec. Last tour 4:45. Children aged under 10 not admitted
🍴 Cafés and restaurants along Piccadilly
🚇 Green Park
🚌 8, 9, 14, 19, 22, 38
💷 Moderate

4 Royal Academy of Arts

Burlington House is one of the few remaining 18th-century Piccadilly mansions. Today it houses one of London's most illustrious art galleries, the Royal Academy, which stages a variety of high-profile exhibitions. June to August sees its annual Summer Exhibition, when every aspiring artist in the country hopes to have a piece selected – the result is a *mélange* of modern British art.

✉ Burlington House, Piccadilly, W1
☎ 020 7439 7438 🕐 Daily 10–6 (Fri. 6–8:30) 🍴 Café and restaurant
🚇 Piccadilly Circus 🚌 9, 14, 19, 22, 38 💷 Admission charge depends on the exhibition

5 Piccadilly and Regent Street shopping

If you need a change from sightseeing, take time off to visit some of London's most exclusive stores: Piccadilly, St. James's and Regent Street (▶ 65–66) are home to some of London's finest stores.

The best of the Piccadilly stores are the old-fashioned bookstore,

REGENT ST

Piccadilly
Circus

Piccadilly &
Regent Street **5** Eros

Royal Academy **4**
of Arts PICCADILLY

HAYMARKET

REGENT ST

PICCADILLY

ST JAMES'S
STREET

Spencer **3**
House

St James's
Palace

Green
Park

Clarence
House

PALL MALL

CONSTITUTION
HILL

Hatchards, the high-class grocery turned department store, **Fortnum & Mason** (➤ 65), and the covered arcades of prestigious stores that lead off to left and right. **Burlington Arcade**, where top-hatted beadles ensure shoppers act with due decorum (there are regulations against singing and hurrying), is the best-known. Piccadilly itself was named in honor of a 17th-century tailor who made his fortune from collars known as "picadils." The mansion he built became known as Piccadilly Hall, in time lending its name to the entire street. These days much of the tailoring has moved north of Piccadilly to

Savile Row and south to **Jermyn Street** (➤ 65).

Liberty's in Regent Street is a department store of class and character, with plush carpets, wood paneling and a balconied hall hung with glorious fabrics (➤ 65).

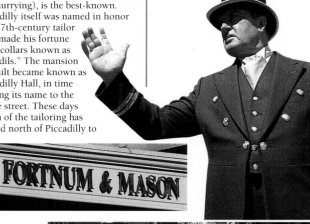

Piccadilly and Regent Street are home to exclusive stores such as Fortnum & Mason (above), famed for its sumptuous food, and Liberty's, whose interior (right) is an Aladdin's Cave of luxury goods. At elegant Burlington Arcade, beadles (top right) enforce regulations against singing and hurrying

Regent Street is one of the capital's premier shopping streets

the mentally ill. The neon advertisements were introduced in the 20th century, and are probably the main reason to visit the area – come after dark for the most dramatic effects.

For all its faults, the Circus is useful as a jumping-off point to other sights; along Shaftesbury Avenue toward Chinatown or Soho, along Coventry Street to Leicester Square, or to Regent Street and Piccadilly.

7 National Portrait Gallery

The gallery houses a fascinating and strangely beguiling collection of paintings, sculptures and photographs of eminent Britons past and present. The material dates from the early 16th century to the modern era, and includes some of history's most recognizable portraits. Whatever your fields of interest, you will almost certainly find something here to interest you.

The monarchs represented include Richard III, Henry VII, Henry VIII, Elizabeth I (depicted several times) and many members of the present Royal Family. However, it is the portraits of commoners that are most memorable. There is a supposed portrait of Shakespeare, a drawing of Jane Austen by her sister, the Brontë sisters by their brother Patrick and fabulous photographs of Oscar Wilde, Virginia Woolf and Alfred, Lord Tennyson.

6 Piccadilly Circus

While Piccadilly Circus features large in the minds of visitors to the city (a photograph in front of the statue at its heart is almost obligatory), most Londoners dismiss it as a slightly down-at-heel mêlée of tourists, traffic and noise.

The Eros statue, which actually represents the Angel of Christian Charity, not the Greek god of love, was erected in 1893 to commemorate Antony Cooper, 7th Earl of Shaftesbury (1801–85), a tireless campaigner for workers, the poor and

Eros and the bright lights of Piccadilly Circus are best seen at night

Among recent literary stars are Salman Rushdie and Dame Iris Murdoch.

Politicians and figures from the arts, sciences, sports and media are also well represented. Some of the most interesting portraits are those of previous British prime ministers Margaret Thatcher and Harold Wilson, scientist Stephen Hawking, film director Alfred Hitchcock and soccer player Bobby Charlton.

St. Martin's Place, WC2 020 7306 0055 Mon.–Sat. 10–6, Sun. noon–6; closed Jan. 1, Good Friday, May Day public holiday and Dec. 24–26 Charing Cross, Leicester Square Café in the basement 3, 6, 9, 11, 12, 13, 15, 23, 24, 29, 53, 77A, 88, 91, 109, 159, 176 Admission free (charge for some exhibitions)

9 Banqueting House

The Banqueting House is the only remaining part of the old Palace of Whitehall, formerly the monarch's official home, which was destroyed by fire in 1698. It was built by the great architect Inigo Jones in the early 17th century, and included a painted ceiling by Flemish artist Peter Paul Rubens as its decorative centerpiece. The ceiling was commissioned in 1635 by the king, Charles I, who paid the artist $1,890, an astronomical sum at that time. This, and other paintings – still the building's highlights – were all conceived as paeans to Charles's father, James I.

It was from a window of the Banqueting House that, on January 30, 1649, Charles I, tried and convicted for high treason following the defeat of Royalist forces in the English Civil War, stepped onto the scaffold and faced his executioner. As he went to his death, branded an enemy of state, he remarked, "I have a good cause and a gracious God on my side."

Whitehall 020 7930 4179 Mon.–Sat. 10–5; closed public holidays, and for special functions Westminster, Charing Cross 3, 11, 12, 24, 53, 77A, 88, 109, 159 Inexpensive; an audio guide included

10 Whitehall

This busy but undistinguished street, lined by the bland façades of government offices, takes you south from Trafalgar Square through the heart of British Government. Downing Street, a side turning blocked off by a large gate, is where the British prime minister has his (or her) official residence. Traditionally this is at No. 10, while No. 11 plays host to the Chancellor of the Exchequer, though the present prime minister Tony Blair and his family reside at the larger No. 11. The only real patch of color is provided by the mounted soldiers at Horse Guards.

At the center of Whitehall is the Cenotaph, a memorial to the war dead and the solemn focus of the annual Remembrance Day Ceremony in November.

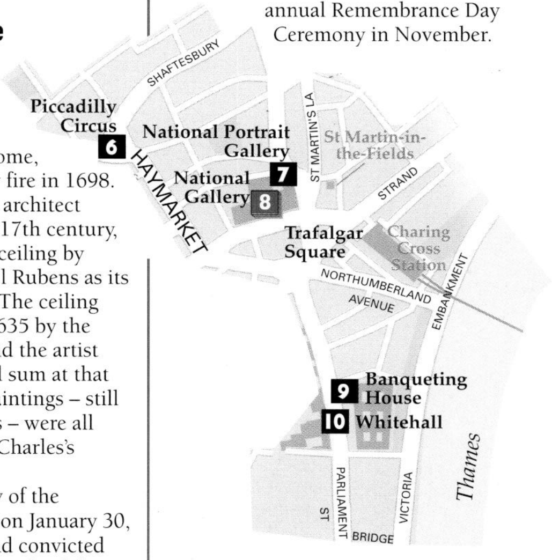

For Kids

- The colorful Changing of the Guard ceremony at Buckingham Palace and/or Horse Guards
- Feeding the pigeons in Trafalgar Square
- A visit to Hamleys toy store and the Disney Store, both in Regent Street
- Feeding the ducks in St. James's Park (take bread)

Where to...
Eat and Drink

Prices
Expect to pay per person for a meal excluding drinks and service
$ under $40 $$ under $80 $$$ over $80

Atlantic Bar & Grill $$

Sweep down the grand staircase into a noisy, dramatically lit cavernous space, filled with a cosmopolitan crowd. Some are here just for a drink at the clamorous bar, but the food is worth investigation. There's a slight Mediterranean-cum-oriental twist to the whole menu, but the classics are equally pleasing. Dinner reservations are essential. Good standard of dress is required.

✚ 201 E1 ⊠ 20 Glasshouse Street, W1 ☎ 020 7734 4888; fax: 020 7734 3609 ⊚ Lunch Mon.–Fri. noon–3; dinner daily 6–midnight
Ⓔ Piccadilly Circus

Le Caprice $$–$$$

This famous restaurant, tucked neatly behind the Ritz hotel, attracts a chic celebrity crowd. Despite the stark white walls and black-and-chrome furniture, the atmosphere is far from intimidating, and the fast-paced service remains friendly at all times. The menu is a great mix of classic brasserie dishes balanced by some more lively up-to-date ideas.

✚ 203 D5 ⊠ Arlington Street, SW1 ☎ 020 7629 2239; fax: 020 7493 4008 ⊚ Lunch Mon.–Sat.; dinner Mon.–Sat. noon–3:30; dinner Mon.–Sat. 5:30–midnight, Sun. 6–midnight
Ⓔ Green Park

Chez Nico at Ninety Park Lane $$$

The restaurant adjoining Grosvenor House Hotel has the feel of an exclusive St. James's gentlemen's club: A spacious, comfortable interior, muted colors, lots of wood paneling, and formally clad staff. In this wonderful, discreet environment you can enjoy some of the best haute cuisine in London. The menus are described in a sparse, understated way, emphasizing the fact that chef Nico Ladenis's food is based as much on the very best ingredients as on a high level of accomplishment.

✚ 200 B1 ⊠ 90 Park Lane, W1 ☎ 020 7409 1290; fax: 020 7355 4877 ⊚ Lunch Mon.–Fri. noon–2; dinner Mon.–Sat. 7–11. Closed 10 days Christmas Ⓔ Marble Arch

Chor Bizarre $$

This overseas branch of the New Delhi restaurant embraces its name (which means "thieves' market") with gusto, displaying a crowded, exotic collection of Indian antiques and artifacts. The menu explores the regions of India with some imagination, and provides a good choice of vegetarian dishes and tandoori favorites. The wine list has been carefully compiled to complement the food.

✚ 201 D1 ⊠ 16 Albemarle Street, W1 ☎ 020 7629 9802/629 8542; fax: 020 7493 7756 ⊚ Daily noon–2:45, 6–11:30 Ⓔ Green Park

Le Gavroche $$$

This, London's longest-running and greatest French restaurant, is comfortable rather than opulent, with tables that are generous in size and service that's warmly, soothingly efficient. For many years Albert Roux's classic French cooking was the solid rock on which the restaurant's seasonally changing menus were built, but now that son Michel has taken over, ideas, although firmly rooted in that same classic tradition, have moved with the times. The cooking is still confident and skilled, but with a lighter touch. The wine list is aristocratic, with prices to match.

➕ 200 B1 ☒ 43 Upper Brook Street, W1 ☎ 020 7408 0881/7499 1826; fax: 020 7409 0939/7491 4387
🕐 Mon.–Fri. noon–2, 7–11
Ⓜ Marble Arch

Mirabelle $$–$$$

Rescued from oblivion by chef Marco Pierre White, the Mirabelle has reemerged as one of the most fashionable places to eat in London, serving MPW's trademark first-class classic French-style cooking. The restaurant's revamped decor matches an easier, less formal style, though tables are perhaps a little too close together. Lunch is especially good value, with the keenly priced menu ensuring that the place is packed. Get a reservation for a patio table in fine weather.

➕ 202 C5 ☒ 56 Curzon Street, W1 ☎ 020 7499 4636; fax: 020 7499 5449
🕐 Daily noon–2.30, 6–midnight
Ⓜ Green Park

Mitsukoshi $$

This classy, comfortable restaurant is situated on the lower ground floor of a Japanese department store. The a la carte selection includes classic Japanese dishes, but choosing one of the many set meals will give an excellent introduction to the cuisine. These range from a simple *hana*, which includes an appetizer, tempura, grilled fish, rice, miso soup and pickles, to the ten-course *kaiseki* feasts which must be ordered in advance. The separate sushi menu is recommended.

➕ 201 E1 ☒ Dorland House, 14–20 Lower Regent Street, SW1 ☎ 020 7930 0317; fax: 020 7839 1167
🕐 Mon.–Sat. noon–2, 6–9.30
Ⓜ Piccadilly Circus

Nicole's $$

This is a fashionable place in every respect, from the chic setting in the basement of Nicole Farhi's Bond Street store to the ladies-that-lunch who come to toy with the light, ultramodish food. The restaurant's

less figure-conscious clientele will be equally satisfied – an earthier approach can be discerned with such rustic fare as duck confit appearing on the menu. Breakfast is served from 10 to 11.

➕ 200 C2 ☒ 158 New Bond Street, W1 ☎ 020 7499 8408; fax: 020 7409 0381 🕐 Lunch Mon.–Fri. noon–3.30, Sat. noon–4; dinner Mon.–Fri. 6:30–10.45 Ⓜ Green Park, Bond Street

Nobu $$$

Nobuyuki Matsuhisa brings the full force of his pan-American experience (which ranges from restaurants in the United States to travels in South America) to bear on the second floor of the seriously chic Metropolitan Hotel. This is the ultimate place to see-and-be-seen, with "A-list" personalities in abundance. The combination of the ultramodern, Philippe Starck-like interior and the trendy clientele add up to an irresistible package, especially when New York-style service

and spiced-up Japanese cooking are thrown into the equation. Reservations are essential.

➕ 202 C5 ☒ Metropolitan Hotel, 19 Old Park Lane, W1 ☎ 020 7447 4747; fax: 020 7447 4749 🕐 Lunch Mon.–Fri. noon–2.15; dinner 6–10:15 Ⓜ Hyde Park Corner, Green Park

The Oak Room $$$

This is the principal restaurant of London's best-known chef, Marco Pierre White. The intensity for which his cooking is famed is there in large measure. The menu is full of *joie gras*, truffles, morels, caviar and oysters, and the room is opulent with lots of gold, chandeliers and generous space, all devoted to the service of food in much comfort. Prices reflect this, but it is the ultimate in luxury and perfection. Highly recommended.

➕ 201 E1 ☒ Le Meridien Piccadilly, 21 Piccadilly, W1 ☎ 020 7437 0202
🕐 Lunch Mon.–Fri. noon–2.30; dinner Mon.–Sat. 7–11:15; closed 2 weeks Aug. and 2 weeks Christmas Ⓜ Piccadilly

Quaglino's $$

Make an entrance down the sweeping staircase, feel the buzz and experience a bit of Hollywood glitz. The most glamorous of London's megarestaurants is owned by the Conran group and it's a slick operation. Just go for a drink in the bar or try out a menu that has a strong French bistro feel. If you prefer, traditional English classics such as fish and chips with tartare sauce make a welcome appearance. The crustacean bar is a major feature.

🛱 203 D5 ⊠ 16 Bury Street, St. James's, SW1 ☎ 020 7930 6767; fax: 020 7839 2866 ⓦ Daily noon–3, 5.30–midnight (also Fri.–Sat. midnight–1 a.m., Sun. 5.30–11) ⓠ Green Park

Rasa W1 $–$$

Das Sreedharan opened this lavish, spacious restaurant after the huge success of his first restaurant in East London. His exquisite vegetarian food from the Kerala region is considered some of the best Indian cooking in town. The menu offers a wide range of poppadums, stuffed pastries, curries, dosas, lentil patties, and some excellent breads.

🛱 200 C2 ⊠ 6 Dering Street, W1 ☎ 020 7629 1346 ⓦ Lunch Mon.–Sat. noon–3; dinner daily 6–11 (also Fri.–Sat. 11–midnight) ⓠ Oxford Circus

Richoux Coffee Company $

The Richoux chain is something of a London institution. A facelift has given this spacious Piccadilly branch a new lease of life, but service is reassuringly motherly. Drop in for an early breakfast, morning coffee and cake, or for a light lunch of salads, sandwiches and quiches.

🛱 201 D1 ⊠ 171 Piccadilly, W1 ☎ 020 7629 4991 ⓦ Mon.–Fri. 7 a.m.–7 p.m., Sat.–Sun. 9–7 ⓠ Green Park

Sotheby's, The Café $

One of Bond Street's best-kept secrets is tucked away in the lobby of Sotheby's auction house. It's open for stylish breakfasts, light lunches and afternoon tea. The cosmopolitan clientele add more than a touch of interest, and reservations are essential for lunch.

🛱 200 C2 ⊠ 34 Bond Street, W1 ☎ 020 7293 5077 ⓦ Sun.–Fri. 9:30–5 ⓠ Bond Street

The Square $$$

Nigel Platts-Martin's exceptional restaurant combines the allure of chic, spacious premises with a prestigious setting near Berkeley Square. His highly regarded chef and partner, Philip Howard, offers imaginative, yet classically based, modern French cooking. Dishes are prepared with an immense precision and such great attention to detail that it takes in the championing of free-range/organic produce.

🛱 200 C1 ⊠ 6 Bruton Street, W1 ☎ 020 7495 7100; fax 020 7495 7150 ⓦ Lunch Mon.–Fri. noon–3; dinner Mon.–Sat. 6:30–10:45, Sun. 6:30–10 ⓠ Bond Street

Tamarind $$

This fashionable Indian restaurant serves an imaginative interpretation of Indian regional cooking in its comfortable, discreetly designed basement dining room. Whenever possible, dishes are prepared with specially imported herbs and spices to create some memorable flavors.

🛱 202 C5 ⊠ 20 Queen Street, W1 ☎ 020 7629 3561; fax: 020 7499 5034 ⓦ Lunch Mon.–Fri. noon–3, Sun. noon–2:30; dinner Mon.–Sat. 6–11:30, Sun. 6–10:30 ⓠ Green Park

Titanic $–$$

This blockbuster restaurant has proved a big hit, especially in the evening when it draws a fashionable young crowd. There's a large open lobby, a centerpiece bar and a sprawling, noisy dining room. Breakfast is served from midnight until 3 a.m. – great for clubbers.

🛱 201 E1 ⊠ 81 Brewer Street, W1 ☎ 020 7437 1912 ⓦ Lunch noon–2:30; dinner 5:30–midnight (also 3 a.m. for breakfast) ⓠ Green Park

Where to...
Shop

Savile Row and Jermyn Street

Traditions linger here, in what was the heart of 18th-century London. Several tailors on Savile Row have been in business since the 19th century, and continue to provide top-quality bespoke men's clothes: **Henry Poole** (15 Savile Row, W1, tel: 020 7734 5985), established in 1806, and **Kilgour, French & Stanbury** (8 Savile Row, W1, tel: 020 7734 6905), dating from 1882.

Jermyn Street has the monopoly on men's shirtmakers. Try **Turnbull & Asser** (71–72 Jermyn Street, W1, tel: 020 79300502), **Harvie & Hudson** (77 Jermyn Street, W1, tel: 020 7930 3949), and **Hilditch & Key** (73 Jermyn Street, W1, tel: 020 7930 5336), which does excellent ready-to-wear for women.

Regent Street

The broad sweep of Regent Street is home to stores on a grand scale. **Aquascutum** (100 Regent Street, W1, tel: 020 7734 6090) is *the* place to buy the classic English raincoat and tailored, tweedy jackets for both men and women, **Burberrys** (165 Regent Street, W1, tel: 020 7734 4060) is the home of the distinctive English trenchcoat, and **Austin Reed** (103–13 Regent Street, W1, tel: 020 7734 6789) is good for Savile Row-style clothes at rather lower prices.

At the Oxford Circus end of the Regent Street is **Liberty's** (210–20 Regent Street, W1, tel: 020 7734 1234), the famed department store. Even the façade, a black-and-white mock-Tudor extravaganza, exudes great character. Within, the store is a treasure trove of antiques, oriental carpets, furnishings, dress fabrics, needlework and leather goods, as well as cutting-edge fashion for men and women, upscale cosmetics and wonderful accessories.

Regent Street is also home to **Hamleys** (188–96 Regent Street, W1, tel: 020 7734 3161), one of the world's largest toy stores, suitable for kids of all ages. Prices here are higher than elsewhere and at weekends it's packed, but there are magic tricks and toy demonstrations galore.

Piccadilly

Occupying a central position on Piccadilly is **Fortnum & Mason** (tel: 020 7734 8040), internationally renowned for its food emporium selling everything from own-brand marmalades, teas and condiments to hams, pâtés, cheeses, bread and fresh fruit. It is also a delightfully unusual department store including a sharply up-to-date women's designer fashion floor and a splendid stationery and gift section.

Another favorite shopping stop in Piccadilly is **Waterstones** (203–206 Piccadilly, tel: 020 7851 2400), the place to go if you are looking for a good book to read on vacation.

Bond Street and New Bond Street

Bond Street, though pandering to the image of exclusivity, is a showcase for designers who cannot afford to be seen looking backward. Fast-paced, upscale fashion is represented on this street by every major international designer, exhibited in their own innovative stores, including **Donna Karen** (19 New Bond Street, W1, tel: 020 7495 3100), **Gucci** (32–33 Old Bond Street, W1, tel: 020 7629 2716) and **Versace** (34–36 Old Bond Street, W1, tel: 020 7499 1862).

Also setting out their wares are jewelers such as **Tiffany & Co.** (25 Old Bond Street, W1, tel: 020 7409 2790), **Asprey & Garrard** (167 New Bond Street, W1, tel: 020 7734 7020) and **Cartier** (175 New Bond Street, W1, tel: 020 7493 6962); two great auction houses, **Sotheby's** (34–35 New Bond Street, W1, tel: 020 7493 8080) and **Phillips** (101 New Bond Street, W1, tel: 020 7629 6602), and major representatives of the art and antiques dealing world, notably the **Fine Art Society** (148 New Bond Street, W1, tel: 020 7629 5116). Here, too, is **Fenwick** (63 New Bond Street, W1, tel: 020 7629 9161), a charming, fashion-oriented department store stocking Ben de Lisi, Jasper Conran, Alberta Ferretti and Nicole Farhi, among many others. The first floor is given over to one of the best accessory collections in town, the basement to a dazzling selection of gifts at less-than-Bond Street prices.

South Molton Street
On South Molton Street there are smaller, quirkier boutiques, among them **Browns** (23–27 South Molton Street, W1, tel: 020 7491 7833) – a series of interconnected little stores at the knife-edge of fashion.

Gray's Antique Market (58 Davies Street, W1, tel: 020 7629 7034) hosts an impressive collection of stalls run by knowledgeable people. It's noted for antique jewelry

(check out Brian and Lyn Holmes's stall) and oriental artifacts, but there is much more.

Oxford Street
Oxford Street is big, brash and noisy, with buses and taxis bumper to bumper and unceasing crowds. Department stores are punctuated by chains like Gap, Kookai and Wallis. **John Lewis** (278–306 Oxford Street, W1, tel: 020 7629 7711) sells everything from dress fabrics to computers, **Marks & Spencer**, at both Marble Arch (458 Oxford Street, W1, tel: 020 7935 7954) and north of Oxford Circus (173 Oxford Street, W1, tel: 020 7437 7722) is good for basic wardrobe staples and sells good-value knitwear, and **Selfridges** (400 Oxford Street, W1, tel: 020 7629 1234) has Europe's largest perfume department, as well as a massive cosmetics section, two vast floors of current women's fashions, and a good food hall with various cafés (even a sushi bar).

Where to...
Be Entertained

Cut away from the traffic and bright lights of Piccadilly into Pall Mall, St. James's and the area around Curzon Street and you'll enter a world of wealth and privilege. This area is home to many of London's gentlemen's clubs. Major movie theaters and some splendid theaters occupy Haymarket and Piccadilly Circus (▶ 59–60 for information on how to obtain tickets).

Movie Theaters
The **Curzon Mayfair** (38 Curzon Street, W1, tel: 020 7369 1720) shows art-house, foreign and main-stream movies. **The Institute of Contemporary Arts (ICA)** (Nash House, The Mall, W1, tel: 020 7930 3647) has a small movie theater and hosts intelligent groupings of

movies linked by director, style or theme, usually far removed from the blockbuster genre.

Clubs
100 Club (100 Oxford Street, W1, tel: 020 7636 0933), where The Rolling Stones, The Kinks, The Sex Pistols and The Clash have all played, follows an eclectic booking policy that also takes in traditional jazz, blues, jive and swing.

Music
The little-known **British Music Information Centre** (10 Stratford Place, W1, tel: 020 7499 8565) hosts twice-weekly recitals of modern British music. There is also a library of books, scores and audio and visual recordings.

The City

Getting Your Bearings

The City of London, the commercial heart of the capital, is one of the busiest financial centers in the world, with banks, corporate headquarters and insurance companies occupying dramatic showcases of modern architecture. Yet alongside the glass-and-steel office buildings, you find beautiful 17th-century churches, cobbled alleyways, historic markets and even fragments of the original Roman city wall.

The modern City stands on the site of the Roman settlement of Londinium, and has long been a center of finance and government. Historically, it had an identity separate to that of the rest of the capital. When Edward the Confessor moved his palace from the City of London to Westminster in 1042, the area retained some of its ancient privileges, and later in the 14th century secured charters granting it the

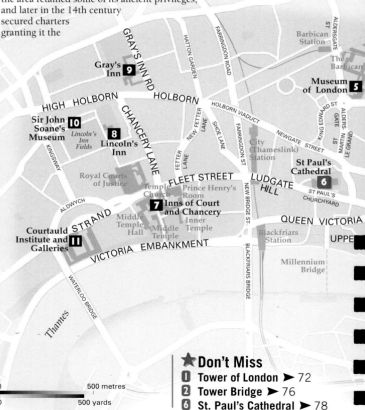

right to elect its own mayor and council. Even the sovereign could not enter the City without formal permission. Today, the legacy of these privileges still survives. The Corporation of London, the successor to the original council, which is overseen by the Lord Mayor, administers the City through council meetings held in the Guildhall.

Much of the medieval City was destroyed by the Great Fire of 1666, although the Tower of London survived. In the construction boom that followed, architect Sir Christopher Wren was commissioned to build over 50 churches, the most prominent and well-known of which is St. Paul's Cathedral. Many of the lesser-known Wren churches survived the severe bombing of World War II, and remain tucked away in quiet streets.

The City is also home to the modern Barbican complex, with its theater, movie house and concert hall, as well as several fine museums. Among them are the Museum of London, where the story of the capital is brought to life; the Bank of England Museum on Bartholomew Lane, which gives a fascinating insight into the City's financial history; Sir John Soane's Museum, an unaltered time capsule of 19th-century life; and a stunning collection of Impressionist and post-Impressionist paintings at the Courtauld Gallery. Just outside the City is the heart of legal London, the historic Inns of Court.

At Your Leisure

Previous page: the distinctive dome of St. Paul's Cathedral

Barbican Centre

Moorgate Station

MOORGATE

Liverpool Street Station

LONDON WALL

Guildhall

International Financial Centre

BISHOPSGATE

HOUNDSDITCH

BEVIS MARKS

Stock Exchange

Bank of England Museum **4**

THREADNEEDLE ST

POULTRY

CORNHILL

GRACECHURCH ST

LEADENHALL ST

ALDGATE

MINORIES

3 **Leadenhall Market**

STREET

KING WILLIAM ST

FENCHURCH ST

Fenchurch Street Station

CANNON ST

EASTCHEAP

GREAT TOWER ST

...MES ST

MONUMENT ST

LOWER THAMES STREET

BY WARD ST

TOWER HILL

Cannon Street Station

LONDON BRIDGE

Thames

I **Tower of London**

St Katharine Dock

DUKE ST HILL

HMS *Belfast*

Hays Galleria

London Bridge Station

TOOLEY STREET

2 **Tower Bridge**

ST THOMAS'S STREET

Upper Pool

Three of London's most evocative sights – cathedral, ancient fortress and bridge – are the day's highlights, offering magnificent views over the city.

The City in a Day

9:00 a.m.

Try to be at the **Tower of London** (➤ 72–75) by 9 a.m. to beat the worst of the crowds, even if this means you may get caught up in the morning rush hour. The rewards are jewels, ravens, Beefeaters (left), and an insight into the long and often bloody history of London from the perspective of its famous fortress.

11:30 a.m.

Walk up onto nearby **Tower Bridge** (below, ➤ 76–77) and visit the Tower Bridge Experience for an excellent history of the structure. Stunning views of the River Thames make the climb to the top worthwhile.

1:00 p.m.

Take a break for lunch. For top-quality fare head across to the south bank of the river to **Cantina del Ponte** (➤ 108). Reservations are recommended.

2:15 p.m.

Walk back across the bridge and catch the number 15 bus from Tower Hill, the main road to the north of the Tower, which will deliver you outside St. Paul's Cathedral.

3:00 p.m.

More breathtaking views are revealed from the dome of **St. Paul's Cathedral** (below, ➤ 78–81). There's a café in the Crypt if you need a break after climbing the dome. Then soak up the magnificence of the architecture and artifacts around you.

5:00 p.m.

You may want to stay on in St. Paul's for evensong – the times of services are posted inside and outside the cathedral.

To move on from St. Paul's catch the number 15 bus back to Trafalgar Square or use St. Paul's Underground station, which is just beside the cathedral.

Tower of London

The Tower of London has always fascinated visitors – even 300 years ago it was a popular attraction – and today it is one of the city's top two or three tourist sights. Begun by William the Conqueror shortly after 1066, it has survived for over 900 years as a palace, prison, place of execution, arsenal, royal mint and jewel house. Throughout this time it has remained woven into the fabric of London and its history, while maintaining its essential character as a fortress and self-contained world within the defensive walls.

St. Edward's Crown, one of the many priceless treasures making up the Crown Jewels

The Crown Jewels

Archive footage of the coronation of Queen Elizabeth II puts you in the mood while you wait to see the Crown Jewels, providing a prelude to and preview of one of the world's richest collections of jewelry (many of the jewels in the footage are on display in the Jewel House's inner sanctum). The collection's most dazzling piece is the **Imperial State Crown**, used by the monarch at the State Opening of Parliament in October or November, and crusted with 2,868 diamonds, 17 sapphires, 11 emeralds, 5 rubies and 273 pearls. Also look for the **Sovereign's Sceptre** (which contains the world's largest cut diamond, Cullinan I) and the crown of Queen Elizabeth the Queen Mother, the collection's only platinum crown. It contains the fabulous Koh-i-Noor diamond, which is used only in a woman's crown as it is believed to bring bad luck to men.

For some fascinating background on the Crown Jewels, visit the "Crowns and Diamonds" display in the Martin Tower, accessed via the Salt Tower, whose walls still bear graffiti carved by early prisoners.

✉ Tower Hill, EC3 ☎ 020 7709 0765
🕐 Mon.–Sat. 9–5, Sun. 10–5, Mar.–Oct.; Tue.–Sat. 9–4, Sun.–Mon. 10–4, Nov.–Feb. Closed Jan.1 and Dec. 24–26
🍴 Coffee stall inside, café and restaurant just outside
🚇 Tower Hill 🚌 15, 25, 42, 78, 100, D1 💷 Expensive

Tower Green

This benign-looking spot was the place of execution of seven high-ranking prisoners, the most notable of whom were Anne Boleyn and Catherine Howard, Henry VIII's second and fifth wives (both beheaded following charges of adultery). Execution here was an option reserved for the illustrious – less socially elevated prisoners met a much slower, more painful end on nearby Tower Hill. The executioner's axe and block are on display in the Martin Tower.

The White Tower

The Tower's oldest and most striking feature is the White Tower, begun around 1078, its basic form having remained unchanged for more than 900 years. Today its highlight is a superlative collection of armor, a display that manages to be awe-inspiring and strangely beautiful at the same time. Henry VIII's personal armor forms its main attraction, but smaller

The Tower of London was begun in 1066, its position affording clear views of any enemy forces that might approach up the Thames

pieces, such as the suits crafted for young boys, are equally interesting. Be sure to see the evocative St. John's Chapel on the second floor, one of England's earliest remaining church interiors, and also take a peep into some of the tower's "garderobes" – 11th-century toilets.

The Tower Ravens

Ravens have been associated with the Tower throughout its history. Legend tells how King Charles II wanted to get rid of the birds, but was told that if they ever left the White Tower the kingdom would fall and disaster would strike. No chances are taken these days – the feathers of one wing of each raven are clipped so the birds can't fly away.

The White Tower (1078) is one of the oldest parts of the Tower of London. It took its name after Henry III had its exterior whitewashed in 1241

The Bloody Tower

Not all prisoners in the Tower lived – and died – in terrible conditions. Some passed their time in more humane lodgings. One such prisoner was Sir Walter Ralegh, explorer, philosopher and scientist, who was imprisoned in the Bloody Tower from 1603 to 1616, accused of plotting against James I. The Tower's most notorious incumbents, partly the reason for its name, were the "Princes in the Tower." Following the death of King Edward IV, the princes – the king's sons Edward (the heir to the throne) and his younger brother Richard – were put in the Tower under the "protection" of their uncle, Richard, Duke of

The forbidding walls of the Tower, built to keep attackers out, were later used to confine those perceived to be enemies of the Crown

Beefeaters

The Tower's colorfully costumed guards, or Yeoman Warders, are commonly known as Beefeaters, though how they came by the name is not known for certain. About 40 in number, they all have a military background, and perform ceremonial duties both inside and outside the Tower – they'll also answer your questions and give you directions.

Gloucester. However, the boys mysteriously vanished and, in their absence, their uncle was crowned King Richard III. The bodies of two boys, presumed to be those of the princes, were found hidden in the White Tower 200 years later. Richard's involvement, or otherwise, in the boys' death has been much debated since, but never proved one way or the other.

Traitors' Gate was the Tower of London's entrance from the river

The Medieval Palace

The entrance to the Medieval Palace lies just beside the infamous Traitors' Gate, the river entrance to the Tower through which many prisoners arrived for their execution. The palace is laid out as it would have been in Edward I's reign (1272–1307), and staffed by costumed guides who describe the lives that might have been led by people of the time.

From the palace you should stroll along the Wall Walk on the Tower's south side, a route that offers fine views of Tower Bridge (➤ 76–77). This route also takes you through the Wakefield Tower, in whose upper chamber Edward I's throne room has been dramatically reconstructed.

TAKING A BREAK

The **Apprentice Restaurant** (➤ 108), across the river from the Tower, serves inexpensive food in an informal environment.

TOWER OF LONDON: INSIDE INFO

Top tips Come **early** in the morning to avoid the crowds.
• Buy admission tickets at London Underground stations to **avoid the long lines** at the main ticket office.
• On arrival, head straight for the Waterloo Barracks and visit the **Crown Jewels** – this is the Tower's most popular attraction and soon becomes crowded.
• Be **flexible** in your approach to what you visit and when: If one part of the Tower is busy, give it a miss and return later.
• If you have time, the Yeoman Warders (Beefeaters) lead free, hour-long **guided tours** throughout the day. Most of the guides are great characters and bring the history of the Tower wonderfully alive.

Tower Bridge

Tower Bridge is one of London's most familiar landmarks and the views from its upper walkway are some of the city's best, yet it has occupied its prominent place on the capital's skyline for only a little over a hundred years.

By the late 1800s, crossing the River Thames had become a major problem. London Bridge was then the city's most easterly crossing, but more than a third of the population lived even farther east. Building a new bridge, however, posed a dilemma for architects and planners. Any construction had to allow tall-masted ships to reach the Upper Pool, one of the busiest stretches of river in the world, handling ships and goods from all corners of the British Empire. It also needed to be strong and adaptable enough to allow for the passage of motor and horse-drawn vehicles. Though designs had been submitted to Parliament since the 1850s (over 50 were rejected), it wasn't until 1886 that one was finally approved. The plan for a remarkable lifting roadway (known as a "bascule" bridge after

Above: shipping by Tower Bridge in 1908

Top: the bridge is a prominent feature of the capital's night-time skyline

📞 020 7378 1928; bridge opening 020 7378 7700
🕐 Daily 10–6:30, Apr.–Oct.; 9:30–6, Nov.–Mar. Closed Jan. 1 and Dec. 24-26. Last entry 75 minutes before closing time
🚇 Tower Hill, London Bridge
🚌 15, 42, 47, 78, 100, D1, P11
♿ Moderate

VITAL STATISTICS

❏ The bridge took eight years to build.

❏ Its structure is steel, but it is clad in Portland stone and granite to complement the nearby Tower of London.

❏ Though the Tower of London suffered significant bomb damage during World War II, Tower Bridge escaped relatively unscathed.

❏ Each moving bascule weighs 1,320 tons.

❏ The height from the road to the upper walkways is 108 feet.

---

the French word for seesaw), was the brainchild of architect Horace Jones and engineer John Wolfe Barry.

Access to the bridge's towers and walkways is via the **Tower Bridge Experience**, an extensive exhibition that uses life-size moving models, film, artifacts and photographs to explain the history, construction and operation of the bridge. The Experience's highlight, however, is the view from the upper walkway, where there are also some fascinating archive photographs taken during construction, as well as interactive computers offering more detail on Tower Bridge and the surrounding area.

TAKING A BREAK

If you fancy a treat, head across to the south bank of the river for lunch at **Cantina del Ponte** (➤ 108). The food is great, as are views of the bridge.

TOWER BRIDGE: INSIDE INFO

Top tips Try to see the **bridge lifting**; telephone for times.
• Make a return visit to see the bridge at **nighttime** – it looks fabulous when spotlit.
• A portable **audio-translation** of the exhibition is available in several languages.

St. Paul's Cathedral

The towering dome of St. Paul's Cathedral has stood sentinel over London for almost 300 years, a lasting testament to the revolutionary genius of its architect, Sir Christopher Wren. Innovative and controversial, the cathedral rose from the ashes of the Great Fire of London in the 17th century, making it a positive youngster when compared with the medieval cathedrals of most European countries. Centuries later it became a symbol of London's unbeatable spirit, standing proud throughout the wartime Blitz of 1940–41, while more recently it has been the scene of national events such as the wedding of Prince Charles to Diana, Princess of Wales (then Lady Diana Spencer) in 1981.

Wren's design for St. Paul's was submitted just six days after the Great Fire of London

The entrance to the cathedral is in the **West Front** between the towers, where you pay an admission charge even though this is a church. Be prepared for noise and crowds, and remember the cathedral is enormous.

On first entering St. Paul's, take a few moments to just stand and soak up something

☎ 020 7246 8348
✉ Ludgate Hill, EC4
🕐 Mon.–Sat. 10–4:15
🍴 Café in the crypt.
Ⓢ St. Paul's
🚌 4, 11, 15, 17, 23, 26, 76, 172
💷 Inexpensive; galleries extra

VITAL STATISTICS

❑ The cathedral's largest bell, Great Paul, which weighs almost 19 tons, is rung at 1 p.m. every day for 5 minutes.

❑ The distance from ground level to the very top of the cross on the cathedral's roof measures just short of 370 feet.

❑ The clock, Big Tom, on the right-hand tower on the cathedral's West Front, is almost the same size as the clock at Big Ben. The clock face is 16 feet in diameter and the minute hand 10 feet long.

Monochrome frescoes depicting the life of St. Paul decorate the interior of the dome

of the building's grandeur. Soaring arches lead the eye toward the huge open space below the main dome, and on to a series of smaller, brilliantly decorated domes that rise above the choir and distant high altar.

Then move to the center of the nave, marked by an intricate black-and-white compass pattern and a memorial to Wren that includes the line "Reader, if you seek his monument, look around you." Looking up into the **dome** from here you can

admire the Whispering Gallery, the monochrome frescoes by 18th-century architectural painter Sir James Thornhill (1716–19) of the life of St. Paul, and the windows in the upper lantern. Wren was 75 years old by the time the upper lantern was underway, but still insisted on being hauled up to the galleries in a basket several times a week to check on progress. What he wouldn't have seen are the ceiling's shimmering mosaics, completed in the 1890s and made from an estimated 30 million or more pieces of glass. They depict biblical scenes and figures such as evangelists, prophets, the Creation, the Garden of Eden and the Crucifixion.

Then take in the area around the **altar**, a part of the cathedral filled with exquisite works of art. Master woodcarver Grinling Gibbons, noted for his high-relief carvings, designed the limewood choir stalls – the cherubs are especially fine – and Jean Tijou, a Huguenot refugee, created the intricate ironwork gates (both were completed in 1720). The canopy is based on a similar bronze canopy in St. Peter's, Rome, designed by the 16th-century baroque architect Bernini. In St. Paul's, however, the canopy is made of English oak and, although it dates from as recently as 1958, is based on a design by Wren.

The Galleries

The dome has three galleries, all of them open to the public and all unmissable if you've the time, energy and a head for heights. The views of the cathedral's interior and of London are breathtaking – but there are over 500 steps to climb to the top before you can enjoy them. The best interior views come from the **Whispering Gallery** (259 steps), where the building's patterned floor and sheer scale can be enjoyed to the full. The gallery's name describes the strange acoustic effect that allows something said on one side of the gallery to be heard on the other. For panoramas of London you'll need to climb to the top two galleries, the **Stone Gallery** (378 steps from the bottom) and the **Golden Gallery** (a further 172 steps).

At the other extreme, downstairs, is the crypt, a peaceful and atmospheric space supported by massive piers and redoubtable vaulting. This is the largest such crypt in Europe, and contains around 200 graves and memorials, the grandest of which belong to national heroes such as Admiral Lord Nelson and the Duke of Wellington, who defeated Napoleon at the battle of Waterloo in 1815.

The Whispering Gallery, where secrets whispered on one side of the gallery can be heard on the other

TAKING A BREAK

Enjoy some great wines at **Balls Brothers** (6–8 Cheapside, EC2, tel: 020 7248 2708). Food is served – sausages, fish cakes and chicken wings – but it is secondary to the wines.

ST. PAUL'S CATHEDRAL: INSIDE INFO

Top tips No photography is allowed inside the building.
• **Guided tours** (90 min.–120 min.; additional charge) run at 11, 11:30, 1:30 and 2.

Hidden gem Attend a **"sung" service**, in which the choir takes part. Evensong on weekdays is usually at 5 p.m., but check on the lists posted at the cathedral for more information or call for details.

At Your Leisure

3 Leadenhall Market

This iron-and-glass Victorian food hall, built on the site of a medieval market, now caters to the needs of City workers, with plenty of eating places, tailors, shoestores, bookstores, druggists and grocers. The huge glass roof and finely renovated and painted ironwork, plus the bustle of the crowds, make this one of the best places in the City to shop, grab a snack or linger over lunch.

✉ Whittington Avenue, EC3
🕐 Mon.–Fri. 7–4 Ⓜ Monument
🚌 25, 40

5 Museum of London

This fascinating museum details the story of London from prehistoric times to the present day, its magnificent array of information and exhibits laid out chronologically to present a cogent and colorful account of the city's evolution.

The Roman Gallery is particularly well illustrated, and includes excellent reconstructions of Roman-era rooms. Look also for the paneled Stuart interior of a prosperous merchant's home, complete with appropriate music, and the streets of Victorian stores, with the requisite fittings and goods.

4 Bank of England Museum

You won't see mountains of gold, but the material that is on display is surprisingly interesting – and is helped along by an excellent audio-guide. There are a couple of gold ingots on show which always draw a big crowd, but more fascinating are the displays explaining how bank notes are printed and the complex security devices employed to beat counterfeiters. If you fancy yourself as a financial whizz kid, there are interactive computer programs that allow you to simulate trading on the foreign exchange markets – after a few minutes trying to get to grips with the processes you begin to see how real City superstars justify their big annual bonuses.

✉ Bartholomew Lane, EC2 ☎ 020 7601 5545 🕐 Mon.–Fri. 10–5 Ⓜ Bank
🚌 8, 21, 23, 25, 43, 76, 133, 242
🎟 Admission free

On a smaller scale the working model of the Great Fire of London, accompanied by the words of Samuel Pepys, is an excellent illustration of the drama of this cataclysmic event (▶ 6–7). Perhaps the most gorgeous exhibit, however, is the Lord Mayor's Coach, commissioned in 1757. A confection of color and ornament, it is covered in magnificent carvings and sculptures, while its side panels are by the Florentine artist Cipriani. The coach is still used during the annual Lord Mayor's Parade in November and the coronation of a new sovereign.

✉ London Wall ☎ 020 7600 3699;
www.museumoflondon.org.uk
🕐 Mon.–Sat. 10–5:50, Sun. noon–5:50;

Elaborately carved and gilded: the Lord Mayor's Coach

last admission 5:30. Closed Jan. 1 and Dec. 24–26 ⛔ Café 🚇 St. Paul's, Barbican 🚌 8, 11, 15, 23, 25 💷 Moderate – tickets valid for a year. Free admission after 4:30

🅦–🅩 The Inns of Court

Entered through narrow, easy-to-miss gateways, the four Inns of Court are a world away from the busy city outside. Their historic buildings, well-kept gardens and hushed atmosphere create an aura of quiet industry. Home to London's legal profession, the Inns began life in the 14th century as hostels where lawyers stayed. Until the 19th century, the only way to obtain legal qualifications was to serve an apprenticeship at the Inns, and even today barristers must be members of an Inn.

While most of the buildings are private, some are open to the public; even if you don't see inside any of the august institutions, it is enough simply to wander the small lanes and cobbled alleyways, stumbling upon unexpected courtyards and gardens and breathing the rarefied legal air.

The way to see the Inns is to start at the Temple and then walk to Lincoln's Inn and Gray's Inn.

For Kids
- Tower of London
- Tower Bridge Experience
- St. Paul's Cathedral galleries
- Museum of London

Inner and Middle Temple

Consecrated in 1185, Temple Church originally had links with the Knights Templar, a confraternity of soldier monks whose role was to protect pilgrims traveling to the Holy Land. This may account for the building's unusual circular plan, which mirrors that of the Church of the Holy Sepulchre in Jerusalem. The floor of the church has ancient effigies of the Knights' patrons, though few date after the 13th century as the Knights fell out of favor and were abolished in 1312. The church is a tranquil oasis in a busy part of the city.

The imposing **Middle Temple Hall** retains its 16th-century oak-paneled interior, where it is said Queen Elizabeth I attended the first performance of Shakespeare's *Twelfth Night*.

✉ Access from Fleet Street, just opposite end of Chancery Lane, EC4 🕐 Temple Church: Wed.–Fri. 10–4; Middle Temple Hall: irregular – check with the porter at the entrance

Prince Henry's Room

This remarkable little building – just outside the Temple proper – was built in 1610 as part of a Fleet Street tavern. The room, decorated to commemorate the investiture of Henry, eldest son of James I, as Prince of Wales, retains the plaster ceiling inscribed with the Prince of Wales' feathers and part of its original oak paneling. It now houses memorabilia associated with the diarist Samuel Pepys (1633–1703), who lived locally but who was probably not directly associated with the building.

✉ 17 Fleet Street, EC4 🕐 Mon.–Sat. 11–2

Lincoln's Inn

Lincoln's Inn is large, well maintained and spacious, and its red-brick buildings are constructed on a grand scale, particularly the four-storied mansions, New Hall and library of New Square (begun in 1680). Many illustrious British politicians studied here, among them Pitt the Younger, Walpole, Disraeli, Gladstone and Asquith. Other former students include William Penn, founder of Pennsylvania, and 17th-century poet John Donne. Make a special point of seeing the Inn's chapel (Mon.–Fri. noon–2:30), built above a beautiful undercroft with massive pillars and dramatic vaulting.

> ✉ **Entrances off Chancery Lane and Lincoln's Inn Fields, WC2** 🕐 **Mon.–Fri. 7 a.m.–7 p.m.**

Gray's Inn

Entrances off High Holborn, Gray's Inn Road, Theobald's Road, WC1. This Inn dates from the 14th century, but was much restored after damage during World War II. Famous names to have passed through its portals include the writer Charles Dickens, who was a clerk here between 1827 and 1828. Its highlights are the extensive gardens or "Walks" as they are commonly known (Mon.–Fri. noon–2:30), once the setting for some infamous duels and where diarist Samuel Pepys used to admire the ladies promenading. The chapel is also open to the public (Mon.–Fri. 10–6), but lacks the charm of its Lincoln's Inn equivalent (see above).

🔟 Sir John Soane's Museum

This remarkable museum is the 19th-century house of an affluent gentleman, architect and art collector, providing a charming artistic and social showcase that has remained unchanged for over 150 years. Nor will it change in the future, for Sir John left the property and its contents to the nation on his death in 1837 on condition that nothing was altered – the conditions were even enshrined in a special Act of Parliament.

Soane was the architect of the Bank of England, among other buildings, and wealthy enough to indulge his passion for collecting, a passion that seems to have been more or less unchecked or unguided – he simply bought whatever caught his eye. As a result the house's various rooms are packed with a miscellany of beautiful but eclectic objects, with ceramics, paintings, books, statues, even a skeleton, all jostling for space. At the same time, there is no doubt Soane adored his treasures – when the ancient Egyptian sarcophagus of Pharaoh Seti I arrived, for example, he greeted it with a three-day reception party. The tomb is one of the collection's many highlights, carved from a single block of limestone and engraved with scenes from the afterlife to guide the soul of the deceased.

For many years this eccentric jewel was known to only the well-informed few. Now

A beautiful miscellany – just some of the treasures in Sir John Soane's eclectic collection

that the secret is out, you can expect more people; come early or late on weekdays to avoid the worst crowds.

📧 13 Lincoln's Inn Fields, WC2 ☎ 020 7405 2107 ⏱ Tue.–Sat. 10–5 (also first Tue. of month 6–9 p.m. with some candlelit rooms). Groups of six or more must make advance reservation 🚇 Holborn 🚌 1, 8, 25, 68, 91, 168, 171, 188, 242 💷 Admission free

⓫ Courtauld Gallery

The Courtauld has a stunning but manageable collection of art displayed in superb surroundings, making it a wonderful antidote if you are overwhelmed by the size of the large London galleries. Many of the Courtauld's works were a gift of the textile baron Samuel Courtauld (1876–1947), who donated his collection of 19th-century paintings to the University of London in 1932.

The gallery's reputation rests largely on the Impressionist and post-Impressionist paintings – works by Cézanne, Seurat, Gauguin, Renoir, Monet, Toulouse-Lautrec, Van Gogh and Modigliani and, in particular, *Bar at the Folies-Bergère* by Manet, perhaps this painter's best-known work.

Another celebrated painting here is Van Gogh's *Self-Portrait with a Bandaged Ear*, painted in 1889 soon after the painter left hospital following his self-mutilation, the result of an argument with fellow artist Paul Gauguin.

Rooms on lower floors contain earlier paintings, many of them early religious works that formed parts of church altars or movable altars intended for private prayer. Particularly outstanding is a *Triptych* by the Master of Flemalle in Room 1, which depicts the entombment of Christ, and the Resurrection. It is one of the masterpieces of 15th-century Dutch painting – notice the wonderful facial expressions and the angel in the middle panel, wiping away a tear as Christ is laid in the tomb. Also striking is an *Adam and Eve* by Lucas Cranach the Elder (1526), distinguished by Adam's genuinely bewildered expression as an apparently knowing Eve hands him the apple.

📧 Somerset House, Strand, WC2 ☎020 7873 2526 ⏱ Mon.–Sat. 10–6, Sun. noon–6 🍴 The Coffee Gallery offers drinks, snacks and lunches (Mon.–Sat. 10–5:30, Sun. noon–5:30) 🚇 Covent Garden, Temple, Embankment 🚌 1, 4, 6, 9, 11, 13, 15, 23, 26, 76, 77A, 91, 168, 171, 171A, 176, 188 💷 Inexpensive; free Mon. 10–2

Where to...
Eat and Drink

Prices
Expect to pay per person for a meal excluding drinks and service
$ under $40 $$ under $80 $$$ over $80

Alba $-$$
This classy, modern Italian restaurant, just a short walk from the Barbican Centre, is deservedly popular. It provides excellent value for money and is always busy: the place is filled with businesspeople at lunchtime and theater-goers in the evening.

The modern Italian menu is sensibly short, encouraging some serious cooking. Fish or meat dishes, such as Trentino lamb stew, and classics such as chicken cacciatore are prepared with first-rate ingredients. The helpfully annotated wine list gives an impressive selection of wines from the best Italian vineyards.

🚹 Off map 🗺 107 Whitecross Street, EC1 ☎ 020 7588 1798; fax: 020 7638 5793 🕐 Mon.–Fri. noon–3, 6–11; closed 10 days Christmas, public holidays 🚇 Barbican

City Rhodes $$$
At City Rhodes, television celebrity chef Gary Rhodes has created an upscale setting in which to sample his reworking of classic English dishes. The well-spaced, sparsely decorated room comes with a pricey menu, but the cooking is first class with sound standards and technique. Stunning presentation stirs up the appetite and old-fashioned ingredients are frequently given an interesting new spin. Dessert should not be missed; bread-and-butter pudding is a signature dish. The service is young, well-paced, enthusiastic and efficient. Highly recommended.

🚹 205 D4 🗺 1 New Street Square, EC4 ☎ 020 7583 1313; fax: 020 7353 1662 🕐 Mon.–Fri. noon–2.30, 6–8.45 🚇 Blackfriars

Club Gascon $$-$$$
Pascal Aussignac, from Toulouse in Southwest France, has rapidly established a name for himself in this gastronomically evolving part of London. He offers top-class Gascon cooking with the emphasis on *foie gras* and duck, ingredients which are supplied direct by French farmers and producers in Gascony. Although traditionally prepared dishes are Aussignac's specialties, he is not afraid to experiment. Tables may be cramped but the atmosphere at Club Gascon is vibrant. Highly recommended. Reservations are essential.

🚹 205 E5 🗺 57 West Smithfield, EC1 ☎ 020 7796 0600 🕐 Lunch Mon.–Fri. noon–2.30; dinner Mon.–Sat. 7–10.15 🚇 Farringdon

The Eagle $-$$
The Eagle was one of the pioneers of converted pubs specializing in very good food and still leads the field. Choose from a short but mouth-watering selection of mainly Spanish- and Portuguese-influenced dishes; all are great value for money. Reservations are not taken and as this establishment is lively and often crowded, you need to arrive early to secure a table and have the best choice from the blackboard menu. You order and pay for your food and drink at the bar.

🚹 Off map 🗺 159 Farringdon Road, EC1 ☎ 020 7837 1353 🕐 Lunch Mon.–Fri. noon–2.30 (also Sat. 2.30–3.30, Sun. 2.30–4); dinner Mon.–Sat. 6–10.30 🚇 Farringdon

Maison Novelli $$-$$$

The imaginative cooking pioneered by Jean-Christophe Novelli matches the sheer panache of the chic, dining room, which is filled with fresh flowers, big mirrors and bold blue-purple colors. Novelli classics such as stuffed braised pig's trotter and hot-and-cold chocolate pudding are never off the menu, but there are plenty of daring combinations using Asian, oriental and European influences. Next door, Novelli EC1 offers a less-expensive alternative.

✛ Off map ⊠ 29 Clerkenwell Green, EC1 ☎ 020 7251 6606; fax: 020 7490 1083 ⓒ Lunch Mon.–Fri. noon–3; dinner Mon.–Sat. 6:30–11:15
ⓖ Farringdon

Moro $$

The opening of this restaurant caused a great frisson of excitement among the capital's food critics. The minimalist decor with a long zinc bar down one wall, an open-plan kitchen along another, and plain, close-packed wooden tables creates an informal setting. The food is magical, largely Spanish and Arabic in origin, with good raw materials simply cooked in a wood-burning oven or char-grilled. Reservations need to be made well in advance.

✛ Off map ⊠ 34–6 Exmouth Market, EC1 ☎ 020 7833 8336; fax: 020 7833 9338 ⓒ Mon.–Fri. 12:30–2:30, 7–10:30 ⓖ Farringdon

Quality Chop House $$

Much of the original character of this informal former Victorian chop house has been preserved, including high-backed mahogany booths. The food is a fashionable mix of updated traditional English dishes and French brasserie classics, with eggs, bacon and chips, fish soup with *rouille*, confit of duck, and Toulouse sausage with mash and onion gravy never off the menu. No credit cards are taken.

✛ Off map ⊠ 94 Farringdon Road, EC1 ☎ 020 7837 5093 ⓒ Lunch Sun.–Fri. 12:30–2:55; dinner daily 7–11:25 ⓖ Farringdon, King's Cross

St. John $$

Back-to-basics eating is the principle behind this remarkable Clerkenwell hot spot close to Smithfield. The decor of the former smokehouse is starkly white and minimalist, and an open-plan kitchen adds to the general informality. Traditional old-English recipes are reworked – offal is greatly favored – and sit happily alongside modern Mediterranean dishes on the short menu. The kitchen adopts a simple approach, using fresh prime produce.

✛ Off map ⊠ 26 St. John Street, EC1 ☎ 020 7251 0848, 020 7251 4998; fax: 020 7251 4090 ⓒ Lunch Mon.–Fri. noon–3; dinner Mon.–Sat. 6–11:30 ⓖ Farringdon

Stephen Bull Smithfield $$

The Smithfield branch is the least formal, least expensive of the Stephen Bull chain of restaurants, and the most spacious. Its short menus offer simple, light food, very much in the modern idiom although influences tend to look no further than the Mediterranean. Wines are thoughtfully chosen with plenty available by the glass.

✛ Off map ⊠ 71 St. John Street, EC1 ☎ 020 7490 1750; fax: 020 7490 3128 ⓒ Lunch Mon.–Fri. noon–2:30; dinner Mon.–Sat. 6–10:30 ⓖ Farringdon

BAR

Cicada $

Minimalist bar/restaurant that's open all day, but where drinkers frequently outnumber those eating in the evening. Cicada attracts a young and stylish crowd who create an atmosphere that is lively, noisy and fun. The food, should you wish to eat here, is oriental in style, backed up by some excellent, inexpensive wines from a list that includes chilled sake by the flask.

✛ Off map ⊠ 132–6 St. John Street, EC1 ☎ 020 7608 1550 ⓒ Mon.–Fri. noon–11 ⓖ Farringdon

Where to...
Shop

The City of London is not a significant shopping area, particularly when compared with other parts of the capital.

Stores in the City are geared to the needs of office workers, and sandwich bars, wine bars and pubs dominate, with a few tourist gift shops near the City sights. However, the few **markets** that remain in this part of London have strong historic and social roots and make a pleasant, easy outing. Most are held at weekends when traffic congestion is at its lightest.

Columbia Road Flower Market
(Columbia Road, E2, open: Sun. 8–2) is where many Londoners come to stock up with plants for their decks and window boxes. Even if you don't want to buy a massive yucca or tray of begonias, it's worth a visit.

Petticoat Lane market
(Middlesex Street and beyond, E1, open: Sun. 9–2) is an East London institution. It's *the* place to buy inexpensive clothes and shoes. However, coachloads of tourists add to the crush and make browsing difficult. The end of the market by Aldgate East Underground station is devoted to leather jackets; it is possible to get a bargain if you are prepared to haggle. Take cash not credit cards to get the best deal.

The giant Victorian covered marketplace at **Spitalfields Market** (Commercial Street between Lamb Street and Brushfield Street, E1, open: Mon.–Fri. 11–3, Sun. 9:30–5) is filled with craft stalls and an array of fast-food outlets selling a range of foods from crêpes to sushi and tandoori. The market has a very good organic food section every Friday and Sunday.

Where to...
Be Entertained

Much of the City remains quiet in the evenings. The Barbican Centre and Broadgate Centre are the area's focal points.

When the **Barbican Centre** (Silk Street, EC2. Box Office tel: 020 7638 8891; general information tel: 020 7638 4141) first opened, journalists wrote critical reviews about how difficult it was for concert-goers to find their way around this behemoth in a featureless part of the City. Music and theater-lovers crowd in, however, lured by the center's proximity to Clerkenwell, London's latest culinary hot spot, as well as by the cultural program.

The Barbican is the home of the London Symphony Orchestra, who offer 85 concerts a year with performances by some of the world's top musicians. It is also the London base of the Royal Shakespeare Company and has two movie screens showing the latest releases.

It's well worth stopping by the Barbican's lobby, especially on weekends when a variety of free entertainment is on offer. There are also various cafés on the different levels.

The Barbican is best reached by Underground. Barbican and Moorgate stations are the closest, and have the bonus of clearly marked directions that take you straight to the complex.

At the **Broadgate Centre** (Broadgate Circus, Eldon Street, EC2) tiers of stores and restaurants line an impressive outdoor ice rink.

Westminster and Bankside

Getting Your Bearings

Stand on one of the bridges or embankments
and as you gaze at the slowly flowing
River Thames you can't help but
notice the contrast between
the water's stately progress
and the noise and
drama of the
surrounding city.

Inns of Court
& Chancery

Somerset
House

VICTORIA
EMBANKMENT

Cleopatra's
Needle

**Waterloo
Bridge**

**Oxo
Tower** 8

Charing Cross
Station

NORTHUMBERLAND
AVE

**Embankment
Pier**

Royal
National
Theatre

STAMFORD STREET

Royal
Festival Hall

7 **South
Bank
complex**

EMBANKMENT

WHITEHALL

Jubilee
Gardens

YORK ROAD

Waterloo
Station

WATERLOO ROAD

**London
Aquarium**
5

County
Hall

VICTORIA

4

PARLIAMENT

**Westminster
Bridge**

WESTMINSTER

BRIDGE

Central
Hall

SQUARE

**Big
Ben** 3

BAYLIS ROAD

2

**Westminster
Abbey**

**Houses of
Parliament**

ROAD

PALACE

ROAD

KENNINGTON

ROAD

MARSHAM

MILLBANK

Thames

LAMBETH

Archbishop's
Park

**Imperial
War
Museum**
6

Lambeth
Palace

LAMBETH

ROAD

HORSEFERRY ROAD

LAMBETH
BRIDGE

STREET

STREET

Millbank
Tower

MILLBANK

JOHN

I **Tate Britain**

VAUXHALL BRIDGE

ISLIP

The river's banks
present two contrast-
ing images. The north
bank is lined, in general,
with stately buildings connected with money, power and
government, such as the Houses
of Parliament, Westminster Abbey,
the Savoy hotel and Somerset
House, providing the focus for
administrative offices and large
commercial enterprises. The status
quo is occasionally disturbed by new

buildings – Charing Cross train station is a notable example –
but generally the river's north side is stable and established,
retaining the political, historical and religious significance it
has enjoyed for centuries.

The south bank has a very different history. In the early 20th
century it was a mixture of wasteland and heavy industry. The Bankside Power Station, transformed into a major art
gallery, is an

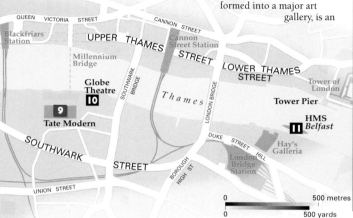

eloquent memorial to the area's industrial past. After World
War II, the South Bank cultural complex, and the Royal
Festival Hall in particular, marked the start of a makeover for
the south bank, although a localized one – travel even a few
hundred feet beyond the waterfront's often innovative developments and you encounter grimy arterial roads and shabby
housing.

In a day the best of both banks can be sampled: on the north,
Westminster Abbey and the Houses of Parliament, respectively
the country's foremost religious building and its seat of government, and Tate Britain, and on the south bank the eponymous
cultural complex. You can also relax and enjoy the Thames
itself from one of the boats that ply their way up- and down-
stream, or take a stroll along the riverside.

★ Don't Miss

At Your Leisure

Art, religion, the world's most famous clock and a river walk form the heart of this day in London. Avoid this itinerary at weekends: Westminster Abbey closes early on Saturday and is closed all day Sunday for services.

Westminster and Bankside in a Day

10:00 a.m.

Take your pick of the two Tate galleries, **Tate Britain** in Millbank and the new **Tate Modern** in Bankside (➤ 94–96). Put aside a couple of hours to browse among the magnificent works of art in either one of these significant collections.

12:00 noon

If you are coming from Millbank, it's about 30 minutes' gentle walk along the river to Westminster Abbey and the Houses of Parliament. The number 77A bus provides an alternative means of transportation. From Bankside, cross to the north side of the river and pick up the number 11 bus from Ludgate Hill to take you back to Westminster.

12:30 p.m.

Stop for a snack lunch in the **Pimlico Wine Vaults** (19–22 Upper Tachbrook Street, SW1, tel: 020 7834 7429), close to Westminster Abbey.

1:30 p.m.

Allow 2 hours to enjoy the grandeur of **Westminster Abbey** (above,
➤ 98–101). Look for the numerous memorials to royalty and literary figures
among the stunning chapels and aisles.

3:30 p.m.

Admire the **Houses of Parliament**
(right) and **Big Ben** (➤ 102) and
from there begin the **river walk**
across **Westminster Bridge**, along
the south bank (plenty of refreshment and cultural opportunities
here) and then back across
Waterloo Bridge, with a spectacular view of the Thames.
Alternatively, walk to Westminster
Pier near the Houses of
Parliament and buy tickets for
boat trips up or down the river
(➤ 104).

Tate Galleries

The Tate Gallery has traditionally held two outstanding major collections: British art since 1500 and international modern and contemporary art. The gallery was opened in 1897 and soon outgrew its Millbank home, which has room to hang only around 20 percent of the total collection. One of London's most thrilling developments has been the transformation of the huge Bankside Power Station (across the river from St. Paul's Cathedral) into Tate Modern. From May 2000, this will accommodate the modern and contemporary collection, with the Millbank gallery (to be relaunched in 2000 as Tate Britain) retaining all British works from 1500 to the present day.

Tate Britain on Millbank is named after the sugar magnate Henry Tate, who donated 67 paintings and almost $130,000 to the nation in 1889

Tate Britain

The Tate's British collection illustrates the broad development of portrait, landscape and other painting across some five centuries. Its oldest work, *A Man in a Black Cap*, was painted by John Bettes in 1545, one of many portraits that dominate the 16th- and 17th-century galleries. Among the most distinctive of these portraits is *The Cholmondeley Sisters* (c1600–10), painted in typically formal Tudor style by an unknown painter – the

✉ Millbank SW1 ☎ 020 7887 8000; www.tate.org.uk
🕐 Daily 10–5:50; closed Dec. 24–26
🍴 Café, espresso bar and restaurant
Ⓜ Pimlico 🚌 88, 77A, C10
💷 Admission free; charge for major loan exhibitions

sisters were twins who were married and gave birth to children on the same day. Equally appealing is *The Saltonstall Family* (*c*1636–37) by David Des Granges, a deceptively simple picture of a father showing off a new baby, which actually amounts to an entire family history.

Norham Castle, Sunrise by J. M. W. Turner, part of the Tate Gallery's extensive collection of work by the 19th-century painter

The 18th century is dominated by the lively works of Hogarth, the first great British painter, and the portraits by Joshua Reynolds and Thomas Gainsborough. Both Reynolds and Gainsborough depicted many of their subjects as mythological or historical characters. The 1773 *Three Ladies Adorning a Term of Hymen (The Montgomery Sisters)* by Reynolds is a typical work, with the sisters shown in Classical costume paying homage to the god of marriage.

The stars of the early 19th century are two contrasting landscape painters, John Constable and J. M. W. Turner. They are now rightly regarded as among Britain's greatest painters, but neither achieved full recognition in his lifetime. Constable's style was considered overly rough and unfinished, while the distinctive depictions of light and atmosphere in Turner's later works were described by one critic as "so much soapsuds and whitewash." Today Turner has his own wing, the Clore Gallery, adapted to accommodate the Turner Bequest, a collection of hundreds of oil paintings and thousands of watercolors and drawings left to the nation by the artist. More of Turner's work can be seen in the National Gallery (➤ 54–57), while the National Gallery and the Victoria & Albert Museum (➤ 117–120) have more paintings by Constable.

Arguably the most striking paintings of the late 19th century were those of the Pre-Raphaelite Brotherhood, whose members created serious, symbolic works – often with profound spiritual and social themes – painted in a highly realistic style. Its leading lights, all well represented at the Tate, were John Everett Millais, William Holman Hunt, Dante Gabriel Rossetti, Edward

Burne-Jones and Frederic, Lord Leighton. Two of the Tate's most popular paintings are by the Pre-Raphaelites – Millais' *Ophelia* (c1851) and Rossetti's *Beata Beatrix* (c1864–70); the model in both cases was Rossetti's wife-to-be, Elizabeth Siddal.

The gallery's more recent works include sculptures by Barbara Hepworth, Henry Moore, Jacob Epstein and Eduardo Luigi Paolozzi, and paintings by Stanley Spencer, Francis Bacon, Lucien Freud, Frank Auerbach, David Hockney, Patrick Caulfield and Howard Hodgkin.

Detail of *Ophelia* by John Everett Millais. The highly realistic style is characteristic of the Pre-Raphaelite movement

Tate Modern
Open May 2000

This gallery embraces virtually all modern art movements, beginning in earnest with 19th-century Impressionism and early 20th-century post-Impressionism, chronicling the years when artists such as Cézanne, Seurat, Gauguin and Van Gogh dominated the artistic firmament. Next come the early works of Picasso and Matisse, exemplified by paintings from the former's "Blue" and "Pink" periods; the Tate's *Girl in a Chemise* (c1905) is one of the best known "Pink" period works. Picasso was later one of the leading exponents of cubism, in which form was reduced to geometric outline. His *Seated Nude* (1909–10) here is one of the style's seminal works, as, too, is *Clarinet and Bottle of Rum on a Mantelpiece* (1911) by Georges Braque.

Abstract art is also extensively reviewed, abstraction being the process by which an artist abstracts an element from the object being painted to simplify its representation. Paintings by Kandinsky and Mondrian exemplify the style's early development, while the Abstract Expressionism of the 1940s – which aimed to portray human psychology through abstract art – is represented by Willem de Kooning, Jackson Pollock and Mark Rothko. The Minimal Art of the 1960s that evolved from Expressionism is represented, among other works, by Carl Andre's now infamous 1966 work *Equivalent VIII* (a pile of bricks), which caused a furor in the British press when it was first exhibited.

Surrealism is represented by the *Metamorphosis of Narcissus* (1937) by Salvador Dali, a favorite among many visitors, as are the 1960s works of Pop Art and New Realism, which incorporate images of popular culture: Andy Warhol's *Marilyn Diptych* and Roy Lichtenstein's *Whaam!* are two of the genre's most familar images.

TAKING A BREAK

For a real treat, go to the **Tate Gallery Restaurant** (Millbank, SW1, tel: 020 7887 8877). In a superb setting, surrounded by murals by Whistler, you can enjoy old-English recipes as well as more modern fare. Open for lunch only.

A Bigger Splash by David Hockney. The simplicity of the image and economy of technique is typical of Hockney's work.

The former Bankside Power Station has been converted into a new home for much of the Tate Gallery's permanent collection (computer-generated image)

TATE BRITAIN: INSIDE INFO

Top tips Avoid Sunday afternoons. The gallery is very popular and sometimes gets so crowded that it is forced to close.
• Call ahead to find which gallery contains a work of art you may particularly want to see. Some modern British paintings may move between the galleries.
• Check for details of any current major temporary exhibitions.
• **TateInform** is an excellent audio guide to the works on show.

Westminster Abbey

Britain's greatest religious building is a church, a national shrine, the setting for coronations and a burial place for some of the most celebrated figures from almost a thousand years of British history. Most of the country's sovereigns from William the Conqueror to Queen Elizabeth II have been crowned and buried at Westminster, while in 1997 it was the setting for the funeral of Diana, Princess of Wales. The building has ancient roots, but construction of the present structure, a masterpiece of medieval architecture, began in the 13th century. Since then the building has grown and evolved, a process that continues to the present day as ever more modern memorials are erected.

Westminster Abbey is one of London's top tourist destinations, drawing huge crowds. It's impossible to appreciate all the abbey's abundance of riches in one visit, so concentrate on the selected highlights below.

Visitors follow a set route around the abbey. From the entrance through the North Door you head first along the ambulatory, the passageway leading to the far end of the abbey. At the top of the steps, the chapel on the left contains the **tomb of Elizabeth I** (1533–1603) and her older half-sister, Mary Tudor (1516–58), daughters of the much-married Henry VIII. Although they lie close in death, there was little love lost beween them in life – Mary was a Catholic, Elizabeth a Protestant at a time when religious beliefs

---

Left: the nave and vaulting of Westminster Abbey

Above: the West Towers

✉ Broad Sanctuary, SW1 ☎ 020 7222 5152; www.westminster-abbey.org
🕐 Mon.–Fri. 9:30–3:45 (also Wed. 6–7:45), Sat. 9:30–1:45. Last admission 1 hour before closing. Sun. open for worship only. College Garden: Tue. and Thu. 10–6, Apr.–Sep.; Tue. and Thu. 10–4, Oct.–Mar.
🍴 Coffee counter in cloisters and Broad Sanctuary
🚇 Westminster, St. James's Park 🚌 3, 11, 12, 24, 53, 77A, 88, 109, 159, 211
💷 Inexpensive; half price Wed. evening

divided the country and persecution was rife.

Next comes the sublime **Henry VII Chapel** built by King Henry VII in 1512, possibly to ease a conscience troubled by his violent route to the throne. The abbey's most gorgeous chapel, it was described by one commentator as *orbis miraculum*, or a wonder of the world. The brilliantly detailed and gilded fan vaulting of the roof is particularly fine, as are the vivid banners of the Knights of the Order of the Bath (an order of chivalry bestowed by the monarch) above the oak choir stalls. Behind the altar are the magnificent tombs and

Breathtakingly delicate fan vaulting in the Henry VII Chapel

gilded effigies of Henry VII and his wife, Elizabeth, created to a personal design by Henry himself.

As you leave this area, a side chapel holds the tomb of Mary, Queen of Scots (1542–87), imprisoned by Elizabeth I as a rival claimant to the throne for 19 years before her execution in 1587. Mary's son, James VI of Scotland, became James I of England when the unmarried, childless Elizabeth died. He had his mother's body exhumed and brought to the abbey 25 years after her death and erected the monuments to both Elizabeth I and Mary – but his mother's is much the grander.

WILLIAM SHAKESPEARE 1564 - 1616
BURIED AT STRATFORD-ON-AVON

NOËL COWARD
Playwright · Actor · Composer
16 December 1899
26 March 1973
Buried in Jamaica
'A TALENT TO AMUSE'

Poets' Corner Notables

Alfred, Lord Tennyson
Dylan Thomas
Henry James
T. S. Eliot
George Eliot
William Wordsworth
Jane Austen
The Brontë sisters

As you go back down the stairs don't miss the unassuming chair facing you. This is the **Coronation Chair**, dating from 1296, and has been used at the coronation of most British monarchs. For several centuries anyone could sit on it: many who did left their mark amid its historic graffiti.

Next comes **Poets' Corner**, packed with the graves and memorials of literary superstars. You'll spot Geoffrey Chaucer, author of *The Canterbury Tales*; Shakespeare, commemorated by a memorial as he is

The Battle of Britain window contains the badges of the 65 fighter squadrons who took part in that World War II battle

buried in Stratford-upon-Avon; and Charles Dickens, who was buried here against his wishes on the orders of Queen Victoria. Thomas Hardy's ashes are here but his heart was buried in Dorset, setting for many of his novels.

From Poets' Corner, walk toward the center of the abbey and the highly decorated altar and choir stalls. One of the loveliest views in the abbey opens up from the steps leading to the altar, looking along the length of the nave to the window above the West Door. For a restful interlude you should then head into the 13th-century **cloisters**, a stone-paved, covered passageway around a small garden once used for reflection by the abbey's monks. Contemplation is also the effect created by virtually the last thing you see in the abbey – the **Tomb of the Unknown Soldier**, an eloquent memorial to the dead of war.

WESTMINSTER ABBEY: INSIDE INFO

Top tips Attend a **choral service** to see the abbey at its best. Evensong is at 5 p.m. on weekdays. Times of other services are displayed, otherwise call for details.
• Entry is **half price** on Wednesday evening. This is the only time when you can take photographs inside the abbey.
• **Guided tours** led by abbey vergers leave several times daily (90 min., additional charge). Make a reservation at the information desk. There is also an **audio guide**, available in several languages, which provides good additional background (charge).

In more detail Explore the **side chapels** off the ambulatory near Henry VII Chapel, which are packed with highly decorated tombs.

Hidden gems The **College Garden**, open on Tuesdays and Thursdays, is a haven of tranquility. Access is from the cloisters, via the delightful Little Cloister.
• Look for the new **statues above the West Door**. These celebrate modern Christian martyrs from around the world.

The Thames

This short but fascinating walk takes in Westminster and Waterloo bridges and some of the best sights of the river's south and north banks. It offers an opportunity to appreciate a selection of London's finest views and a chance to enjoy a different outlook on examples of the capital's historical and more modern architecture.

Start on the north bank in front of the **Houses of Parliament** (a complex officially known as the Palace of Westminster), which is the country's seat of government. Much of the structure was rebuilt in the 19th century following a fire, but Westminster Hall, part of the original palace, dates from 1097. The Victoria Tower (335 feet tall) stands at one end and the tower holding Big Ben (326 feet tall) at the other. Strictly speaking **Big Ben** is the name of the tower's 14-ton bell, not the tower itself. How the name was coined is uncertain – the bell may have been named after the heavyweight boxing champion, Benjamin Caunt, or the works commissioner Sir Benjamin Hall, who supervised installation.

Walk across **Westminster Bridge** to the south bank of the river for the best views of the Houses of Parliament. Today this bridge (built in 1862) is one of over 30 across the Thames, but in 1750 the original bridge on this site was only the second crossing, built after London Bridge. As you walk across look at the water which, despite its murky appearance, supports over a hundred species of fish, including salmon – there have even been sightings of seals in the river.

On the bridge's south side turn left along the footpath beside the river. The huge building to your right is County Hall, once the seat of London's metropolitan council. The building's fate after the Greater London Council was abolished in 1986 was

uncertain, but it now houses the **London Aquarium** (➤ 105), hotels and a Chinese restaurant. Look across the river from here for dramatic views of modern Charing Cross station.

Farther along the riverside you come to the rather drab looking concrete buildings of the **South Bank complex**, one of the city's main cultural and arts venues (➤ 106 and 110).

Climb the steps up onto **Waterloo Bridge** for one of the finest views of London. Looking east, the dominant landmarks are St. Paul's Cathedral (➤ 78– 81), St. Bride's Church spire, the International Finance Centre (NatWest Tower), Lloyd's Building (➤ 173) and – in the far distance – Canary Wharf, London's tallest building. In the near distance, on the right, stands the Oxo Tower (➤ 106).

As you walk to the north side of the bridge, the grand building just to the right is Somerset House, the only remaining example of the 18th-century mansions that once lined the Strand. It now houses the Courtauld Gallery (➤ 85).

Walk down the steps on to Victoria Embankment on the river's north bank. The road is busy and noisy, but you can look back to the south bank from here and there are plenty of seats to rest weary feet en route to Westminster. You also pass Cleopatra's Needle, a 60-foot-high Egyptian obelisk from 1475 BC, given to Britain in 1819 by the Viceroy of Egypt, Mohammed Ali.

Near Westminster Bridge stop at Westminster Pier to check

on the times, prices and destinations of the river trips (➤ 104–105) available.

TAKING A BREAK

There are plenty of refreshment opportunities in the **South Bank complex**. Try the Royal Festival Hall's bar, buffet lunch area and coffee shop, or stop for a pre-theater meal at the **People's Palace** (➤ 109).

At Your Leisure

4 River Trips

A trip along the Thames is a tremendous way to see the city, away from the Underground or traffic-clogged streets. Piers in central London from which you can take trips are Westminster, Charing Cross/Embankment, Temple and the Tower of London. Services east to Greenwich (with connections out to the Thames Barrier) pass through a largely urban and industrial landscape, but offer excellent views of Greenwich (► 176–179). Services upstream to Hampton Court via Kew (► 162–163), Putney, Richmond and on to Kingston are more rural, the river meandering through parks and alongside some of London's more village-like residential enclaves. An evening cruise is also a lovely way to see the city, the river banks enlivened by the twinkling and gleaming of a million lights. Note that timetables vary from month to month, so be sure to go to the piers or telephone for latest details.

For Kids
- London Aquarium
- Boat trip on the river
- HMS *Belfast*

direction between Westminster Pier and Greenwich Pier, and the Docklands Light Railway (DLR) in the other between Tower Gateway DLR station and Island Gardens DLR station. Island Gardens is linked to Greenwich via a pedestrian tunnel under the river. Tickets are available at Greenwich and Westminster piers, the DLR information center at Island Gardens and some DLR ticket machines.

Embankment Pier

Royal Festival Hall

Jubilee Gardens

EMBANKMENT

VICTORIA

London Aquarium 5

County Hall

YORK ROAD

Waterloo Station

WATERLOO ROAD

4

Big Ben 3 **Westminster Bridge**

Houses of Parliament

MILLBANK

Thames

PALACE ROAD

LAMBETH

Archbishop's Park

Lambeth Palace

WESTMINSTER BRIDGE ROAD

BAYLIS ROAD

KENNINGTON ROAD

Imperial War Museum 6

LAMBETH ROAD

From Westminster Pier
Upriver to Putney (45 min.), Kew (1½ hours), Richmond (3 hours) and Hampton Court (4½ hours) tel: 020 7930 2062 or 020 7930 4721.
Downriver to Tower Pier (30 min.) tel: 020 7237 5134 and Greenwich (1 hour) tel: 020 7930 4097.
Buy a "Sail and Rail" ticket, which allows you to take the boat in one

Evening cruises From May until September evening cruises (1 hour 45 min.) run three evenings weekly from Westminster to the Millennium Dome just beyond Greenwich (tel: 020 7930 2062).

From Embankment Pier
Downriver to Greenwich (1 hour) and Circular Cruise (50 min.) nonstop to Houses of Parliament/Tower Bridge tel: 020 7987 1185.

From Tower Pier
Upriver to Westminster (30 min.) tel: 020 7515 1415 and Embankment (25 min.) tel: 020 7987 1185.
Downriver to Greenwich (30–40 min.) tel: 020 7987 1185.
Evening cruises On an evening dinner cruise (3 hours) you can sightsee while wining and dining. Woods River Cruises operate three times weekly tel: 020 7480 7770 and Bateaux London daily tel: 020 7925 2215.

5 London Aquarium

Even if you hate the idea of living things being kept in cages, you are likely to be entranced by this modern aquarium. Its centerpiece is a huge glass tank, several stories high, in which all manner of sea life swims serenely as visitors spiral down wide walkways and gaze in from all levels. There is something mesmeric about the apparently gentle glide of the sharks, the sheer ugliness of the gigantic eels and the bottom-hugging immobility of the giant rays. Smaller surrounding tanks are devoted to different watery environments, and there's an open tank full of rays for visitors to stroke (the rays appear to relish the attention).

📧 County Hall, Westminster Bridge Road, SE1 ☎ 020 7967 8000 Daily 10–6 🍴 Fast-food outlets
🚇 Westminster, Waterloo 🚌 12, 53, 76, 109, 171A, 211, P11 💷 Moderate

Aquatic marvels at the London Aquarium

Fighter planes and rockets in the Imperial War Museum's main hall

6 Imperial War Museum

This fascinating but sobering museum is much more than a display of military might or a glorification of war – despite the name, the monstrous guns in the forecourt and the militaristic slant of the vehicles on show in the main hall. The museum's real emphasis and strengths are the way in which it focuses on the effects of war in the 20th century on the lives of soldiers and civilians alike. This is achieved through a comprehensive collection of artifacts, documents, photographs, works of art, and sound and film archive footage. Some of the most moving testimonies come from oral descriptions recorded by ordinary people whose lives were deeply affected by their wartime experiences. If you've ever wondered what war is like, this is the place to deepen your understanding.

📧 Lambeth Road, SE1
☎ 020 7416 5320; www.iwm.org.uk
🕐 Daily 10–6; closed Dec. 24–26
🍴 Café 🚇 Lambeth North, Elephant and Castle, Waterloo 🚌 1, 12, 45, 53, 63, 68, 168, 171, 172, 176, 188, 344
💷 Moderate; free admission after 4:30 daily

7 The South Bank Complex

The vibrant, all-encompassing South Bank arts complex is crammed with theaters, concert halls, movie theaters, bars and restaurants – not to mention a gallery and poetry library. Architecturally austere, it is not a particularly pretty place but on a warm summer's day it can still be a pleasant spot in which to relax. There is a genuine buzz to the complex, thanks to the crowds of people drawn to its bars and cafés, and the (often free) concerts and exhibitions held in the lobbies of the major arts venues. Start in either the main lobby of the Royal Festival Hall or Royal National Theatre and explore from there.

🚇 Waterloo 🚌 Waterloo Bridge 1, 4, 26, 68, 76, 168, 171, 171A, 176, 188; York Road 76, 77, 171A, 211, P11

8 Oxo Tower

A landmark building, the Oxo Tower houses a dynamic mixture of private and public housing, restaurants and bars (► 109), exhibition spaces and designer workshops. The tower's windows are carefully placed to spell out the word "OXO" (a brand of stock cube), a clever ploy by the architect to evade regulations against riverside advertising. It's worth a visit for the superb views from the observation area alone.

✉ Bargehouse Street, SE1 ☎ 020 7401 3610 🕐 Observation area, Level 8: daily 9:30 a.m.–10:30 p.m. (earlier if weather bad); studios and shops 11–6 🚇 Blackfriars, Waterloo 🚌 45, 63, 149, 172, P11 💷 Admission free

10 Shakespeare's Globe

How about a visit to Shakespeare's theater? Well, almost: This Globe is a reconstruction of the Globe Theatre (whose original site lay less than a quarter mile away) in which Shakespeare was an actor and shareholder, and in which many of his greatest plays were first performed.

The project was the brainchild of Sam Wanamaker, the American movie actor and director, who died before its completion. His legacy is an extraordinary achievement, not least because

the theater itself is a wonderfully intimate and atmospheric space. It is built of unseasoned oak held together with 9,500 oak pegs, topped by the first thatched roof completed in the city since the Great Fire of London in 1666. It is also partly open to the elements, as was Shakespeare's original Globe, with standing room in front of the stage where theater-goers can heckle the actors in true Elizabethan fashion. A small indoor theater is currently under construction to allow performances to be held outside the summer months. It is scheduled to open at the end of 2000.

A visit to the exhibition and a tour of the theater is highly worthwhile and will leave you almost certainly scrabbling for tickets for a performance. The tours cover the history of the project, future plans and costumes from past productions.

Inns of Court & Chancery

VICTORIA EMBANKMENT

Waterloo Bridge

Oxo Tower **8**

Embankment Pier

Royal National Theatre

EMBANKMENT

Royal Festival Hall

7 *South Bank complex*

STAMFORD STREET

✉ New Globe Walk, Bankside, SE1 ☎ 020 7902 1500; box office 020 7401 9919 🕐 Exhibition and tours: daily 9–noon, May–Sep.; 10–5, Oct.–Apr. During theater season (May–Sep.) times and access may vary 🍴 Coffee bar, café and restaurant 🚇 Mansion House, London Bridge, Cannon Street 🚌 Blackfriars Bridge 45, 63, 172; Southwark Street 149, 344, P11 💷 Moderate

11 HMS *Belfast*

This World War II vessel, the biggest cruiser ever built by the Royal Navy, took part in the Normandy landings, and remained in service until 1965. Preserved in the state it enjoyed

The Globe is a faithful re-creation of Shakespeare's original Elizabethan theater

(Map showing area with labels: QUEEN VICTORIA STREET, Blackfriars Station, Millennium Bridge, UPPER THAMES STREET, CANNON STREET, Cannon Street Station, LOWER THAMES STREET, Tower of London, SOUTHWARK BRIDGE, Globe Theatre 10, Thames, LONDON BRIDGE, Tower Pier, 9 Tate Modern, HMS Belfast 11, DUKE STREET HILL, Hay's Galleria, SOUTHWARK STREET, London Bridge Station)

during active service, the ship is now moored between Tower Bridge and London Bridge on the south side of the Thames. It houses displays connected with recent Royal Navy history, but the ship itself remains the true attraction. You can explore all the way from the bridge to engine and boiler rooms nine decks below, taking in the cramped quarters of the officers and crew, the galleys, punishment cells and sick bays, as well as the gun

HMS *Belfast*, high seas warrior until 1965

turrets, magazines and shell rooms.
✉ Off Morgans Lane, SE1 ☎ 020 7940 6300; www. hms belfast.org.uk
🕐 Daily 10–6, Mar–Oct.; 10–5, Nov.–Feb. (last admission 45 min. before closing). Closed Dec. 24–26 🍴 Many nearby in Hay's Galleria (➤ 110) 🚇 London Bridge, Tower Hill, Monument 🚌 42, 47, 78, P11
💷 Inexpensive; free for children 15 or under

Where to...
Eat and Drink

Prices
Expect to pay per person for a meal excluding drinks and service
$ under $40 $$ under $80 $$$ over $80

Apprentice Restaurant $

This restaurant, set in an old spice warehouse, is a chef's training school and gives out a modest feel with plain bentwood chairs and simple blue tables offset against red brick walls. The style of cooking is modern British, prices are inexpensive, and the service is informal. The food and service come with lots of enthusiasm, making this an appealing place to come for a meal.

➕ 206 F2 ✉ 31 Shad Thames, SE1 ☎ 020 7234 0254; fax: 020 7403 2638 🍴 Mon.–Fri. noon–1:30, 6:30–8:45 Ⓔ London Bridge, Tower Hill

Bengal Clipper $$

A building that was once a cardamom warehouse, next to the Conran gastrodome at Butlers Wharf, makes a particularly fitting setting for this respected Indian restaurant. The spacious dining room is dominated by a central grand piano, the surroundings have a strong sense of style and comfort, and the service is elegant. The short menu specializes in mainly Bengal and Goan dishes.

➕ 206 F2 ✉ Butlers Wharf, SE1 ☎ 020 7357 9001; fax: 020 7357 9002 🍴 Daily noon–3, 7–11:30 Ⓔ London Bridge, Tower Hill

Cantina del Ponte $-$$

This busy, informal Conran eaterie designed in simple Italian style is set on the quayside by Tower Bridge and has fabulous views back over the City. This is the least expensive of the Conran Gastrodome restaurants and the mainly Italian-inspired menu brings a simple choice of grilled or roasted meats and fish. In summer, ask for a table on the terrace backing onto the River Walk.

➕ 206 F2 ✉ Butlers Wharf Building, 36c Shad Thames, SE1 ☎ 020 7403 5403; fax: 020 7403 0267 🍴 Daily noon–3, 6–11 Ⓔ London Bridge, Tower Hill

The Circle Bar Restaurant $-$$

The Circle is one of a collection of fashionable eateries to be found at Butlers Wharf on the south bank of the Thames by Tower Bridge. The unusual layout features a restaurant set on a balconied mezzanine, which in turn overlooks the popular bar (where informal snacks are available). There's a definite buzz to the atmosphere and the kitchen copes well with the mix of styles on the globally influenced menu.

➕ 206 F2 ✉ The Circle, Queen Elizabeth Street, SE1 ☎ 020 7407 1122; fax: 020 7407 0123 🍴 Lunch Mon.–Fri. 11:30–2:30; dinner Mon.–Sat. 6–10:15 Ⓔ London Bridge, Tower Hill

Fina Estampa $

The capital's only Peruvian restaurant is set not far from London Bridge and just a short walk from the London Dungeon. The cooking is authentic and good value, the surroundings extremely kitsch, but as peaceful as you can get with non-stop traffic rushing by. Shellfish is excellent, as is the seviche, and it should all be washed down with a pisco sour. Otherwise the rest of the cooking is bulked out with beans and potatoes. Interesting.

➕ 206 D2 ✉ 150–152 Tooley Street, SE1 ☎ 020 7403 1342 🍴 Lunch noon–3 p.m.; dinner 6–10 Ⓔ London Bridge

Globe Café $

There are stunning river views from the Georgian building that forms part of the Shakespeare's Globe theater complex on the south bank. This light, bright café is an absolute treasure, serving light lunch and supper dishes such as pasta and salads, as well as cakes and sandwiches. The grill/restaurant on the second floor has the same river views, and offers an a la carte menu as well as good-value pre- and post-theater menus.

➕ 205 F3 ☒ New Globe Walk, Bankside, SE1 ☎ 020 7902 1576 ⏰ Daily 10 a.m.–11 p.m., May–Sep.; 10–6, Oct.–Apr. 🚇 Cannon Street, London Bridge, Mansion House

Konditor & Cook $

Bright colors, plate-glass windows with light streaming through them, and aluminum furniture characterize this ultramodern café close to Waterloo train station. Open from breakfast through to dinner, the café serves a varied menu, with classics such as scrambled eggs and smoked salmon as well as Californian-Italian pasta dishes. The delicious cakes, made by their own bakery, are hard to resist, and the superb bread is baked here, too. Coffee is excellent.

➕ 205 D2 ☒ Young Vic, 66 The Cut, SE1 ☎ 020 7620 2700 ⏰ Mon.–Fri. 8:30 a.m.–11 p.m., Sat. 10:30 a.m.–11 p.m. 🚇 Waterloo

Livebait $$

The menu at this informal and slightly cramped seafood restaurant incorporates traditional dishes such as rock and native oysters, cock crabs from Poole, and langoustines with mayonnaise. Added to this are a selection of very interesting contemporary dishes that reflect Asian, oriental and Mediterranean influences (often on the same plate). Close to the Old Vic and South Bank complex.

➕ 205 D2 ☒ 43 The Cut, SE1 ☎ 020 7928 7211; fax: 020 7928 2279 ⏰ Mon.–Sat. noon–2:45, 5:30–11:30 🚇 Waterloo

Oxo Tower $$–$$$

Be warned: the Oxo Tower may be a Thames-side landmark but it can be hard to find. However, the elevator that expresses you to the 8th floor brings ample reward in stunning river vistas taking in St. Paul's and the Houses of Parliament. Window tables are not essential, as the view dominates the entire ultrachic space. Dishes are drawn from a global melting pot of influences, but in the evening there are more classic interpretations of European cooking.

➕ 205 D3 ☒ 8th Floor, OXO Tower Wharf, Barge House Street, SE1 ☎ 020 7803 3888; fax: 020 7803 3812 ⏰ Lunch Sun.–Fri. noon–3; dinner daily 6–11:15 🚇 Blackfriars

People's Palace $$

This restaurant runs along the entire frontage of the Royal Festival Hall and is very convenient for the South Bank theaters and concert halls. The best seats are those by the windows overlooking the Thames, so reserve early. The cooking is fashionable with strong Mediterranean and Asian accents. Pretheater dinners are excellent value with ultra-efficient service.

➕ 204 B2 ☒ Level 3, Royal Festival Hall, Belvedere Road, SE1 ☎ 020 7928 9999; fax: 020 7928 2355 ⏰ Daily noon–3, 5:30–11 🚇 Waterloo

RSJ $$

The name RSJ refers to the steel joist that crosses the ceiling of this long-established family-owned restaurant. Among its numerous charms are a comfortably warm but contemporary interior; good, modern Anglo-French cooking strong on seasonal ingredients, great vegetarian dishes, and a much-applauded wine list. The set-price lunch is excellent value should you be heading for a matinée at the Royal National Theatre. Recommended.

➕ 204 C2 ☒ 13a Coin Street, SE1 ☎ 020 7633 0881; fax: 020 7401 2455 ⏰ Lunch Mon.–Fri. noon–3; dinner Mon.–Sat. 6–11 🚇 Waterloo

Where to...
Shop

Borough Market (open: Mon.–Sat. 5:30–noon), at the junction of Borough High Street and Southwark Street, sells fruit and vegetables. Though there has been a market on this site since the 13th century, current threats of development mean that it is facing extinction. It's worth a visit if only to glimpse one of the few truly Dickensian areas left in London.

Hay's Galleria, opening onto the River Walk by the Thames, was one of the first warehouse developments. An impressive Victorian-style iron-and-glass roof covers a huge atrium that is surrounded by a mixture of offices, stores and cafés. The Galleria is noted for some quirky stores, but during the week the stores and eateries tend to cater to the needs of office workers. Though not worth a detour in itself, Hay's Galleria provides a pleasant watering hole if you are looking for a respite from some of the nearby attractions.

Gabriel's Wharf (Upper Ground, SE1), by Waterloo Bridge, close to the South Bank arts center, is a great place to buy unusual gifts. The lively complex of design and craft workshops includes silversmiths selling their own jewelry, and ceramists, as well as cafés. In summer a number of open-air events create a lively atmosphere.

The **Riverside Walk Market**, which sells secondhand books, is set up on the wide, paved space by the Thames under Waterloo Bridge every weekend between 10 a.m. and 5 p.m., and irregularly during the week. The stalls stock mostly old paperbacks, but there are a few gems, including children's books, plays, poetry, science fiction and old map prints, to be found if you persevere.

Where to...
Be Entertained

South Bank complex

Within the South Bank Centre proper (tel: 020 7928 3002; recorded information: 020 7633 0932) are three venues, all of which stage music and dance events: **Royal Festival Hall (RFH1)**, the **RFH2**, (formerly the Queen Elizabeth Hall) and **RFH3** (formerly the Purcell Room). The complex is also home to **The Royal National Theatre** (Lyttelton, Olivier and Cottesloe theaters) and **National Film Theatre** (tel: 020 7928 3232), one of London's major movie theaters, showing subtitled foreign movies as well as mainstream releases. A major restoration project to improve the complex is underway

The retrospectives and exhibitions of contemporary art, painting, sculpture and photography at the

Hayward Gallery (Belvedere Road, SE1, tel: 020 7960 4242) are a must for art lovers.

Movie Theaters

Visit the newly opened **British Film Institute London Imax Cinema** (1 Charlie Chaplin Walk, SE1, tel: 020 7902 1234) and see 3D films on the largest screen in Europe.

Clubs

Try the cutting-edge **Ministry of Sound** (103 Gaunt Street, SE1, tel: 020 7378 6528). As with many London clubs, MoS plays different music on different nights (with dress codes in operation), so check listings magazines in advance for details. This is one of London's best-known clubs and an evening here won't be low budget.

Knightsbridge, Kensington and Chelsea

ERECTED
WAS

Getting Your Bearings

Portobello Road Market **9**

PORTOBELLO ROAD
KENSINGTON PARK ROAD
PEMBRIDGE ROAD

QUEENSWAY
INVERNESS TERR
LEINSTER TERR

NOTTING HILL GATE

BAYSWATER ROAD

KENSINGTON

PALACE GDNS TERRACE

THE BROAD WALK

Kensington Gardens **8**

Round Pond

Kensington Palace **7**

CHURCH STREET

KENSINGTON HIGH ST

KENSINGTON ROAD

PALACE GATE

GLOUCESTER RD

These premier residential districts were once leafy villages, favored for their healthy distance from the dirt and pollution of early London. Today they still retain an ambience of exclusivity and wealth: Their houses are grand, the streets still leafy, and the area has attracted many consulates and embassies to its genteel environs.

Kensington first gained its fashionable reputation in the late 17th century when royalty moved to Kensington Palace on the edge of what is now Kensington Gardens. The palace remains a royal home – though parts are open to the public – and the gardens are among London's prettiest. Separated from Kensington Gardens by the Serpentine, an artificial lake, the larger Hyde Park extends all the way to Marble Arch, affording a magnificent swath of green at the very heart of the city.

Much of Kensington is scattered with monuments to Queen Victoria's husband, Prince Albert, who died at the age of 41. The Albert Memorial on the edge of Kensington Gardens is the principal monument, but more subtle reminders of the royal consort survive elsewhere. It was the Prince's idea that profits from the Great Exhibition (held in Hyde Park in 1851) should be used to establish an education center in the area. The many colleges and institutions of South Kensington were the result, among them three of the capital's foremost museums: the Victoria & Albert Museum, the Science Museum and the Natural History Museum.

Knightsbridge is Kensington's neighbor to the east and, if anything, is even more exclusive as a residential address. It also has an upscale commercial aspect, including the department store Harrods. More affluent residents use it as a local store, but most Londoners and tourists are content with a voyeuristic look at the richness and variety of its stock, lavish interiors and tempting food halls.

Previous page: the decorative frieze on the Royal Albert Hall depicts the Triumph of Arts and Letters

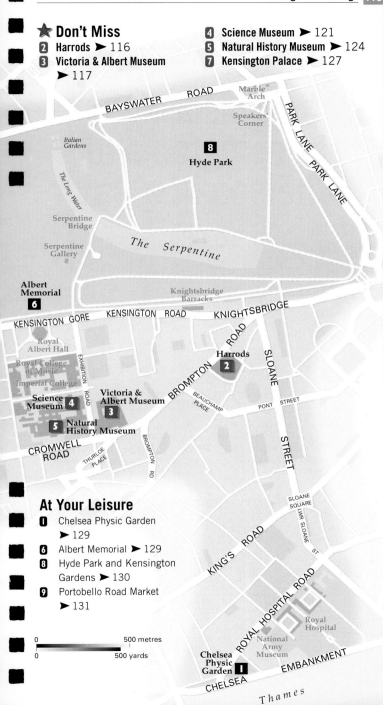

★ **Don't Miss**
2 Harrods ➤ 116
3 Victoria & Albert Museum
➤ 117

4 Science Museum ➤ 121
5 Natural History Museum ➤ 124
7 Kensington Palace ➤ 127

BAYSWATER ROAD
Marble Arch
Speakers' Corner
PARK LANE
PARK LANE

Italian Gardens

8 Hyde Park

The Long Water

Serpentine Bridge

The Serpentine

Serpentine Gallery

Albert Memorial
6

Knightsbridge Barracks

KENSINGTON GORE   KENSINGTON ROAD   KNIGHTSBRIDGE

Royal Albert Hall

Royal College of Music

Imperial College

EXHIBITION ROAD

ROAD

Harrods
2

SLOANE

Science Museum 4

Victoria & Albert Museum 3

BROMPTON

BEAUCHAMP PLACE

PONT STREET

5 Natural History Museum

CROMWELL ROAD

THURLOE PLACE

BROMPTON RD

STREET

SLOANE SQUARE

LWR SLOANE ST

At Your Leisure
1 Chelsea Physic Garden
➤ 129
6 Albert Memorial ➤ 129
8 Hyde Park and Kensington
Gardens ➤ 130
9 Portobello Road Market
➤ 131

KING'S ROAD

ROYAL HOSPITAL ROAD

Royal Hospital

National Army Museum

0 ——— 500 metres
0 ——— 500 yards

Chelsea Physic Garden 1

EMBANKMENT

CHELSEA

Thames

Ensure a relaxed start to your day by browsing or luxury shopping in Harrods before heading to South Kensington's three principal museums and a royal palace set in beautiful gardens.

Knightsbridge, Kensington and Chelsea in a Day

10:00 a.m.

Harrods (➤ 116) is essential viewing even if you don't want to spend any money. Don't miss the food halls, the pet department and the exotic Egyptian Hall. Try to catch the bagpipers and have a coffee in one of the many in-store cafés.

11:30 a.m.

Stroll along **Brompton Road**, lined with exclusive stores, to the Victoria & Albert Museum. Alternatively, if you don't fancy the half-mile walk, catch a number 14, 74 or C1 bus, any of which will take you near the museum. The other museums are nearby.

The **Victoria & Albert Museum** (➤ 117–120), the national museum of art and design, is filled with all manner of beautiful objects; the **Natural History Museum** (entrance hall, below, ➤ 124–126) covers the earth's flora, fauna and geology; and the **Science Museum** (➤ 121–123) investigates every imaginable aspect of science. The best approach is to choose one museum and give it a couple of hours – don't try to tackle too much in one visit.

1:30 p.m.

Have a leisurely lunch in the area at one of the museum cafés or a patisserie or pub on nearby Brompton Road.

2:45 p.m.

Walk north up Exhibition Road, turn left onto Kensington Gore to the Royal Albert Hall and admire the exuberant **Albert Memorial** opposite (➤ 129). If the weather is fine head into Kensington Gardens and across to the Round Pond and Kensington Palace. Otherwise, buses number 9, 10 or 52 run toward Kensington High Street along Kensington Gore; get off at the Broad Walk (it's just a couple of stops along) and walk straight into the gardens near the palace. Check Kensington Palace closing times, especially in winter.

3:30 p.m.

Look around **Kensington Palace** (➤ 127–128), less grand than Buckingham Palace, but the sort of place where you can imagine people actually living. The palace's royal dress collection is especially good.

5:00 p.m.

Have a break in the **Orangery** (➤ 133) and then enjoy an evening walk through **Kensington Gardens** and into **Hyde Park** (above, ➤ 130–131): you could even take a row boat out on the Serpentine as a peaceful finale to the afternoon.

Harrods

Harrods is a London institution. It began life when Henry Charles Harrod, a grocer and tea merchant, opened a small store in 1849. Today it contains over 300 departments spread across seven floors, still striving to fulfill its motto "Omnia Omnibus Ubique" – all things, for all people, everywhere.

Harrods works hard to maintain its reputation as London's premier department store. Liveried commissionaires (known as Green Men) patrol the doors and if you are deemed to be dressed inappropriately you'll be refused entry. Backpacks, leggings, shorts or revealing clothing are to be avoided.

The store's most popular departments are the cavernous first-floor **food halls**, resplendent with decorative tiles and vaulted ceilings, where cornucopian displays of fish, fruit and myriad other foodstuffs tempt shoppers. Handsomely packaged teas, coffees, cookies and jars, all bearing the distinctive Harrods logo, are available: an inexpensive way to acquire the trade-mark carrier bag!

Also worth a special look are the **Egyptian Hall**, complete with sphinxes (also on the first floor) and the **Egyptian Escalator** that carries you to the store's upper floors. One perennial favorite is the **pet department** (on the third floor), whose most publicized sale was a baby elephant in 1967; the store keeps smaller livestock these days.

During your visit, keep an ear open for the distinctive sound of bagpipes. The Harrods' bagpipers perform daily, usually in the late morning on the first floor, but telephone for details.

Harrods' food halls are the most famous of the store's 300 or more departments

The Harrods experience isn't complete unless you come back after dark when the vast exterior is brilliantly illuminated with thousands of lights.

TAKING A BREAK
Stop in the first-floor food halls at the **Harrods Famous Deli** for delicious salt beef bagels or smoked salmon on rye.

✉ 87–135 Brompton Road, SW1   ☎ 020 7730 1234
🕐 Mon.–Tue. and Sat. 10–6; Wed., Thu., Fri. 10–7
🍴 19 bars and restaurants including a deli, pizzeria, sushi bar and a pub (serving Harrods' own beer)   Ⓡ Knightsbridge   🚌 C1, 14, 74

Victoria & Albert Museum

The Victoria & Albert Museum (also known as the V&A), the national museum of art and design, was founded in 1852 with the aim of making art accessible, educating working people, and inspiring designers and manufacturers. One of Europe's great museums, its 6 miles of galleries are crammed with exquisite exhibits from across the world and across the centuries.

This is the sort of place where you want to take just about everything home: some Meissen, perhaps, a few Persian carpets, an Indian throne, or the Heneage Jewel once owned by Queen Elizabeth I. The range of objects is staggering – sculpture, ceramics, glass, furniture, metalwork, textiles, paintings, photography, prints, drawings, jewelry, costume and musical instruments. In addition to the wealth of beautiful works of art, the V&A also has the most peaceful atmosphere and most interesting shop of all the major London museums.

Casts and copies from the Italian Renaissance – just a fraction of the many beautiful works in the Victoria & Albert Museum

✉ Cromwell Road, SW7 ☎ 020 7938 8500; www.vam.ac.uk
🕐 Tue.–Sun. 10–5:45; Mon. noon–5:45 (also late opening Wed. 6:30–9:30, Jan.–Jul.); Henry Cole Wing 10–5:30; closed Dec. 24–26 🚇 South Kensington
🚌 C1, 14, 74. 💷 Moderate; free for under-18s and students and after 4:30

One of many highlights in the **Medieval Treasury** is the Limoges enamel Becket Casket, dating from 1180. It is covered with images depicting the death of St. Thomas à Becket at the hands of four knights loyal to King Henry II, who Becket had angered by refusing to let Church authority be compromised by the Crown. The casket reputedly contained a bloodstained scrap of fabric from the clothes St. Thomas was wearing at his death. Look also for the early church vestments, especially the Butler-Bowden Cope, embellished with fine embroidery.

The **Nehru Gallery of Indian Art** features a fine display of textiles and paintings, together with a variety of other interesting artifacts such as a white jade wine cup and thumb ring belonging to Shah Jehan (a 17th-century Mogul emperor of

Suggested Route
- Medieval Treasury
- Nehru Gallery of Indian Art
- Raphael Cartoons
- Dress Collection
- Morris, Gamble and Poynter Rooms
- Canon Photography Gallery
- Cast Rooms
- Silver Gallery
- Glass Gallery

India and the builder of the Taj Mahal). One of the museum's most idiosyncratic items is also here – Tipu's Tiger (c1790), a life-size wooden automaton from Mysore which shows a tiger eating a man. A musical box inside the tiger's body can reproduce the growls of the tiger and screams of the victim.

Tipu's Tiger, one of the museum's most popular exhibits, shows a tiger mauling a British soldier – complete with sound effects

The V&A's **Raphael Cartoons** were commissioned by Pope Leo X in 1515 as designs for tapestries to hang in the Sistine Chapel in the Vatican. The word *cartoon* properly refers to a full-size preparatory drawing for works in other media. Important works of art, they depict scenes from the lives of St. Peter and St. Paul.

The **Dress Collection** traces the development of men's, women's and children's clothing through the ages. One of the museum's most popular sections, it gives you a chance to smirk at the fashions of your forebears, admire the often sumptuous dresses of centuries past, or marvel at historical oddities such as the 5-foot-wide mantua, a formal dress worn by 18th-century women for ceremonial occasions. Clothes from names such as Dior, Issey Miyake, Versace and Chanel represent modern fashion.

A thousand years of fashion – the V&A's collection of historic dress is a highlight of any visit

The **Morris, Gamble and Poynter Rooms** are named after and decorated in the styles of three leading 19th-century artists and designers; the hugely influential William Morris (1834–96), who designed furniture and textiles, among much else; James Gamble (1835–1919), who worked as part of the museum's design team and produced stained glass and ceramics for his room, and artist Edward Poynter (1836–1919). They retain their original function as public refreshment rooms, the V&A having been the first museum in the world to provide its patrons with such facilities. Their painted tiles, friezes, columns, quotations and glass windows provide plenty to admire as you sip your coffee. Look in particular for some of the quotations that form part of the decorative scheme.

Left: the Italian Rooms display remarkable examples of Renaissance art and craftsmanship

A selection of the museum's 300,000 photographic works is displayed in the **Canon Photography Gallery**, alongside two changing displays. This is one of the few spaces devoted to

photography in a major London museum.

The **Cast Rooms** contain some of the museum's largest exhibits – yet nothing is original. Everything here is a reproduction, often a cast of a European sculpture made in the 19th century when students were less able to travel to study masterpieces at first hand. The rooms are packed with statues, windows, pulpits and altars: Size was clearly of no concern – parts of Trajan's Column in Rome and the enormous Portico de la Gloria from Santiago de Compostela in Spain are both reproduced.

The Victoria and Albert Museum moved to its present home in 1857. Until 1899 it was known as the South Kensington Museum

The **Silver Gallery** traces the history of silver from the 14th century, with examples of every size, shape and provenance. Exhibits range from the dramatic 18th-century Macclesfield Wine Service, testimony to an era of grand living and extravagant entertaining, to the silver snuff box that King Charles II gave to Nell Gwynn, the most beautiful of his many mistresses. In "How Do We Know" you learn how to identify a forgery, and in the discovery area visitors handle some of the exhibits.

The sparkling **Glass Gallery** tells the story of glass from 2500 BC to the present day. Make a special point of seeing The Luck of Edenhall, a 13th-century Syrian vessel probably brought home by a Crusader, but said by legend to have been created by fairies. A fabulous example of modern glass design is provided by the balustrade up to the mezzanine floor, the work of the American glass artist Danny Lane.

TAKING A BREAK

Stop at **Emporio Armani Express** (191 Brompton Road, SW3, tel: 020 7823 8854), an elegant second-floor café on Brompton Road where Armani-clad waiters serve delicious modern Italian food.

VICTORIA & ALBERT MUSEUM: INSIDE INFO

Top tips Late view takes place on Wednesday evenings (6:30–9:30 p.m.) with selected galleries open, live music, lectures and food.
• Sunday **Jazz brunches** with live music take place weekly in the New Restaurant (from 11–3). Make advance reservations.

Hidden gems Take time to see the office of Pittsburgh department store proprietor Edgar J. Kaufmann, designed by American architect Frank Lloyd Wright (1869–1959). It is the only example of Wright's work in Europe.
• The **John Constable Collection** is the world's largest collection of works by this leading 19th-century British landscape artist.

Science Museum

Technophobes needn't be afraid of this museum: The science here is presented in a simple and user-friendly way, with plenty of child-pleasing hands-on displays and clever devices to make sense of complex and everyday items alike. The museum embraces all branches of pure and applied science from their beginnings to modern times, covering the ground with enormous visual panache and a real desire to communicate the excitement and vibrancy of science.

Great working engines from the Industrial Revolution are popular exhibits at the Science Museum

With 7 floors and 40 individual galleries – not to mention the big new Wellcome Wing – it's best to explore a few galleries carefully by following the suggested route.

Power (first floor – East Hall). This dramatic gallery features an array of early engines, the best (right next to the café) being a mill engine dating from 1903 that was used until 1970 in northwest England to drive 1,700 looms (it is still run daily for

visitors). The gallery also holds one of the world's oldest steam engines, built in 1788 by Boulton and Watt, a fine example of the early engines that powered – quite literally – Britain's Industrial Revolution.

The **Exploration of Space** (first floor). This gallery runs the gamut of space exploration – everything from how to drink a can of cola in a weightless environment to the big debate about what the universe might contain. Perhaps the most wonderful exhibit is the Apollo 10 Command Module that orbited the moon in May 1969; it is still charred and scorched from its reentry through the earth's atmosphere. Next to the tiny capsule is a full-size replica of the Lunar Excursion Module

---

✉ Exhibition Road, SW7
☎ 020 7938 8080 or 8008; www.nmsi.ac.uk
🕐 Daily 10–6; closed Dec. 24–26   🍴 Kiosk and café
Ⓜ South Kensington 🚌 Nearby 9, 10, 14, 49, 52, 74, 345, C1
✋ Moderate; free after 4:30

Above: the Exploration of Space Gallery contains a replica of the Apollo lunar module

Below: historic planes on show in the Flight Gallery

from the Apollo 11 mission that took the first men to the moon in 1969.

Foucault's pendulum (first floor). In 1851 the French physicist Jean Bernard Léon Foucault (1819–68) realized that once a pendulum was set in motion it continued to swing in the same direction while the earth rotated around it. The museum's huge pendulum repeats and confirms Foucault's experiment. Notice where it is swinging in relation to the marks on the floor early in your visit and then see how much the earth has moved by the time you leave.

The **Flight** gallery (fourth floor) traces the history of human flight, from early balloons and gliders through to the powered planes, of which the museum has many. The Wright Flyer on show is a reconstruction of the plane in which Wilbur and Orville Wright achieved the first controlled human flight in 1903. Other original planes include a Spitfire and a Hurricane, two World War II British fighter planes; Amy Johnson's Gipsy Moth, *Jason*, in which she completed the first solo Britain-to-Australia flight in 1930; and the machine in which Alcock and Brown first crossed the Atlantic nonstop in 1919. The Flight Lab next door demonstrates the mechanics of flight, looking at helicopters, balloons and airplanes.

The Challenge of Materials (second floor). A glass-and-steel bridge suspended across the museum floor forms part of this wide-ranging gallery, which looks at the materials we

encounter in everyday life, their properties, how they are suited for their task and how we dispose of them at the end of their useful life.

TAKING A BREAK

La Brasserie (272 Brompton Road, SW3, tel: 020 7584 1668) serves unpretentious French cooking, including salads, omelettes, moules and pasta.

Detailed models and innumerable hands-on displays around the museum help to bring science to life

For Kids

The museum is committed to involving children and the four specialist galleries for them are all staffed by informative "Explainers."

- The Garden (basement): aimed at 3-to-6-year-olds.
- Things (basement): aimed at 7-to-11-year-olds.
- Flight Lab (fourth floor): explains the mysteries of flight.
- Launch Pad (second floor): a range of scientific principles explained in a fun, hands-on environment. It gets crowded during school vacations and it is sometimes necessary to make a reservation at the information desk in the Power gallery on the first floor.

SCIENCE MUSEUM: INSIDE INFO

Top tips If you only want a quick look around the museum, remember that after 4:30 p.m. **admission is free**.

In more detail The **Science and Art of Medicine** (sixth floor) provides a fascinating and detailed history of medicine. It also looks at how different cultures interpret and treat illnesses. The range of items on display is remarkable, and includes old medical instruments, skulls, costumes, anatomical models and even shrunken heads.

- The **Secret Life of the Home** (in the basement) houses a fun collection illustrating how the everyday household items we take for granted have evolved and operate. There's also a set of household objects that never caught on – visitors are invited to guess their function.

Natural History Museum

The Natural History Museum's staggering 68 million specimens, many of which (but not all) are on display, cover life forms and the earth's building blocks from the most distant past to the modern day. Everything in, under or on the earth is here, the flora and fauna – from dinosaurs, whales and butterflies to trees, monkeys, snakes, hummingbirds and human beings – in the Life

Galleries, and the geological material in the Earth Galleries. Throughout both sets of galleries the displays are visual and interactive – if there's a fault, it's that there's almost too much to see.

Before you go in, look at the museum building, designed in the late 19th century in the style of a cathedral. Measuring over 650 feet from end to end, it was the first building in Britain to be entirely faced in terra cotta.

The suggested route below will take about two hours. Alternatively, the free museum plan has a useful breakdown of the museum's highlights.

The Natural History Museum is home to more than 68 million exhibits

Life Galleries

The Wonders of the Natural History Museum (Gallery 10). This remarkable three-story gallery is the entrance hall to the Life Galleries and contains a variety of breathtaking exhibits. The 85-foot-long cast of the fossilized skeleton of a Diplodocus dinosaur holds center stage, but the alcoves around the hall display remarkable items such as the fossilized egg of the Madagascan elephant bird (which is as big as a rugby ball). Follow the stairs to the fourth floor to see the section of a giant sequoia tree from San Francisco (giant sequoias are the largest

✉ Cromwell Road, SW7 ☎ 020 7938 9123; www.nhm.ac.uk
🕐 Mon.–Sat. 10–5:50, Sun. 11–5:50 (last admission 5:30); closed Dec. 23–26
🍴 Coffee bar, café, restaurant, snack bar and fast-food restaurant
🚇 South Kensington 🚌 Nearby 14, 49, 70, 74, 345, C1 💷 Moderate; free after 4:30 Mon.–Fri. and after 5 Sat., Sun. and public holidays

Dinosaur skeletons are among the largest and most popular of the museum's exhibits. Of the 350,000 items that come to the museum every year, 250,000 are insect specimens

living things on the planet) and notice how the dates of major historical events are marked in their appropriate place on the tree's "rings."

Dinosaurs (Gallery 21). The dramatic and popular displays here examine many aspects of most species of dinosaur, including some of the many theories as to why they became extinct. A raised walkway enables visitors to get close to the exhibits, and the exhibition includes a robotics display of dinosaurs in action.

Special raised walkways bring you face to face with the likes of Tyranosaurus Rex in the Dinosaur Gallery

Mammals (Galleries 23–24). Some of the material in these galleries consists of stuffed animals behind glass, and has been part of the museum for years. This said, the straightforward displays are almost a relief after the overwhelming variety of exhibits in other galleries: The model of the blue whale (92 feet long) in particular is a perennial favorite.

Ecology (Gallery 32). This is one of the most visually impressive areas in the museum, with a striking mirrored video display of the Water Cycle, and a walk-in leaf to illustrate just how vital plants are to the life of the planet. It does a good job of explaining often complex ecological issues and the need for responsibility with regard to the environment.

The dramatic entrance to the Earth Galleries

Creepy Crawlies (Gallery 33). You'll never look at your house in the same way again after discovering all the bugs and beasties it can harbor. You learn more than you ever wanted to know about insects, spiders, crustaceans and centipedes; not for the squeamish.

Earth Galleries

Visions of Earth (Gallery 60). An escalator carries visitors away from the Earth Galleries' impressive entrance hall through a huge revolving earth sculpture into the upper galleries. It's a stunning introduction to this part of the museum, but before you go up examine the displays behind the tiny portholes in the walls: Many of the specimens on show here are beautifully shaped and have almost impossibly brilliant colors. Look, in particular, for the piece of moon rock and the ancient fossils once believed to have been the devil's toenail and the weapons of Zeus.

The Power Within (Gallery 61). This highly visual gallery seeks to explain volcanoes and earthquakes; its memorable centerpiece is a mockup of a supermarket that simulates the 1995 Kobe earthquake in Japan, which killed 6,000 people.

The Earth's Treasury (Gallery 64). Such is the beauty and variety of the items on show, it takes awhile to realize that what is on display is simply specimens of gems, rocks and minerals. Exhibits range from priceless diamonds, emeralds and sapphires to grains of sand: You'll never look at a humble rock in quite the same way again.

A fossil exhibit

TAKING A BREAK

Stop for lunch at either **Emporio Armani Express** (▶ 120) or **La Brasserie** (▶ 123), both on the Brompton Road.

NATURAL HISTORY MUSEUM: INSIDE INFO

Top tips The main museum entrance on Cromwell Road leads into the Life Galleries; the entrance on Exhibition Road takes you to the Earth Galleries. The two are joined by Gallery 50.

• The museum is **quietest** early or late on weekdays, but all periods during school vacations are busy.

• The **Discovery Centre** (Gallery B2) includes lots of child-friendly exhibits.

Kensington Palace

Kensington Palace has been the home of various members of royalty for many centuries, but came most prominently to public notice only when the late Diana, Princess of Wales moved here. This is an attractive and historic palace, well worth a visit for its setting, art treasures, State Rooms, fine furnishing and Royal Ceremonial Dress Collection.

Detail of the intricately designed, gilded gates of Kensington Palace

The mansion began life as a country house in 1605, but was converted into a palace by Sir Christopher Wren for King William III and Queen Mary II following their accession to the throne in 1689. Later resident monarchs included Queen Anne, George I and George II, while Queen Victoria was born, baptized and grew up in the palace. It was also here that she was woken one morning in June 1837 to be told that her uncle (William IV) had died and that she was Queen. Today, Princess Margaret, the Duke and Duchess of Gloucester and Prince and Princess Michael of Kent all have private apartments in the palace.

The south front of Kensington Palace was designed in 1695 by Nicholas Hawksmoor

Visits to the palace begin downstairs with the **Royal Ceremonial Dress Collection** and then move upstairs to the **State Apartments**. The former features the sumptuous clothes that would have been worn by those being presented at court at

✉ The Broad Walk, Kensington Gardens, W8

☎ 020 7937 9561

🕐 Daily 10–5 (last entry) Apr.–Oct.; daily 10–4 (last entry) Nov.–Mar. Times may change, telephone for details

🍴 Restaurant in the Orangery (▶ 133) serving light meals and snacks

🚇 High Street Kensington, Queensway

🚌 9, 10, 49, 52, 70

♿ Moderate

the turn of the 19th century. Less dramatic but equally interesting is a selection of dresses, hats and purses belonging to the present queen, Elizabeth II.

Upstairs, the apartments of King William III and (less grand) rooms of his wife, Queen Mary II, have been restored to their 18th-century appearance. Their most impressive corner is the Cupola Room, decorated in the style of ancient Rome with an excess of gilded statues and classical painting: It was here that Queen Victoria's baptism took place in 1819. The room's centerpiece is an 18th-century clock called *The Temple of the Four Grand Monarchies of the World*, whose intricate decoration far outshines the tiny clockface itself.

Top: the King's Gallery displays the palace's finest paintings

Above: the King's Staircase, with portraits of royal courtiers

The palace has seen its share of tragedy. Mary II succumbed to smallpox here at the age of 32 in 1694, and when Queen Anne's beloved husband, Prince George, died in 1708, she did not return to the palace for many months. Like Mary, she also died here six years later, at 49 years of age, a sad figure who, despite 18 pregnancies, saw none of her children live beyond the age of 11. King George II ended his days here, too – while on the toilet.

TAKING A BREAK

Enjoy a classic English afternoon tea in pleasant surroundings in the **Orangery** (► 133).

KENSINGTON PALACE: INSIDE INFO

Top tips Access to the palace is from the back of the building, from the Broad Walk in Kensington Gardens.
- Note there is no official monument here to Diana, Princess of Wales, though people continue to bring flowers to the palace.
- Be sure to visit the **Orangery** (► 133), built for Queen Anne and now a restaurant, and don't miss the pretty Sunken Garden.

At Your Leisure

❶ Chelsea Physic Garden

This small garden is a quiet corner of pretty, rural tranquility in the heart of the city, with over 5,000 species of plants growing in attractive profusion. Established in 1673, it was founded by the Royal Society of Apothecaries to study medicinal plants, making it the oldest botanical garden in England after Oxford's. It also retains the country's oldest rockery (1773) and the first cedars in England were planted here in 1683. After green-seeded cotton from the West Indies was nurtured in the garden, seed was sent to Georgia in the American colonies in 1732 and contributed to what would become the huge cotton plantations of the South.

> ✉ Swan Walk, 66 Royal Hospital Road, SW3 ☎ 020 7352 5646 🕐 Wed. noon–5, Sun. 2–5, Apr.–Oct. Ⓔ Sloane Square 🚌 239 💷 Inexpensive

❻ Albert Memorial

It's worth detouring from any Kensington itinerary to see this memorial, perhaps the most florid and exuberant of all London statues, now gleaming after restoration. The monument was com-pleted in 1872 by Sir George Gilbert Scott, win-ner of a competition to design a national memorial to Prince Albert of Saxe-Coburg-Gotha (1819–61), Queen Victoria's husband, though it was not unveiled until four years later. Victoria and Albert married in 1840, but Albert died of typhoid aged just 41 years, a blow from which Victoria never quite recovered.

For Kids
- Science Museum
- Natural History Museum
- Boating on the Serpentine in Hyde Park
- Feeding the ducks in Kensington Gardens and Hyde Park
- Toy department of Harrods

What Albert – who didn't want a memorial – would have made of the neo-Gothic pile is hard to imagine: His spectacularly gilded statue is some three times life size, and the edifice as a whole rises 180 feet, its apex crowned with the figures of Faith, Hope and Charity. The figures around the edges portray artistic and scientific subjects such as astronomy, poetry and sculpture, plus enterprises close to Albert's heart such as agriculture, manufacturing and commerce. The 169 sculptures around the statue's base portray figures from history – there's not one woman among them – while those set slightly apart are allegories of the four continents: Europe, Africa, America and Asia.

> ✉ South Carriage Drive, Kensington Gardens, SW7 ☎ 020 7495 0916 for guided tours Ⓔ High Street Kensington, Knightsbridge 🚌 9, 10, 52

The Albert Memorial, restored to its original gilded glory

Above: boating on the Serpentine in the rural haven of Hyde Park. Below: sculpture by Henry Moore in Hyde Park

BAYSWATER ROAD

Marble Arch

Speakers' Corner

BAYSWATER ROAD

Italian Gardens

The Long Water

8
Hyde Park

8
Kensington Gardens

Round Pond

Serpentine Bridge

Serpentine Gallery

The Serpentine

Albert Memorial
6

Knightsbridge Barracks

KENSINGTON GORE   KENSINGTON ROAD

8 Hyde Park and Kensington Gardens

Look at the map of London and you'll see a large swath of green at its heart southwest of Marble Arch. Most of this is Hyde Park, but Kensington Gardens, formerly the grounds of Kensington Palace, occupies an area to the west of the Serpentine (see below).

Originally a tract of land set aside for Henry VIII to go hunting, **Hyde Park** was opened to the public in the early 17th century by James I, and today provides a magnificent and peaceful area in which to escape the city. **Speakers' Corner**, at its north-eastern edge near Marble Arch, is the place to air your views – anyone is entitled to stand up here and speak his or her mind: Sunday afternoons draw the most orators. Farther west stretches the **Serpentine**, an artificial lake created in 1730 by Caroline, queen to George II, for boating and bathing. It's now a good a place to

Above: Hyde Park's Speakers' Corner

while away an hour on the water – row boats and pedaloes are available for rent on the northern bank. You can also swim at certain times in a designated area off the south shore near one of the lake's two cafés.

The **Serpentine Gallery** at the heart of **Kensington Gardens** shows a changing program of modern and often controversial art throughout the year. Other art in the park includes a variety of statues, most famously Peter Pan (1912), the boy who never grew up, paid for by the story's author, J. M. Barrie, who lived nearby. It's just off a walkway on the Serpentine's west bank, near the lake's northern limit.

Hyde Park
🕐 Daily 5 a.m.–midnight 🚇 Hyde Park Corner, Knightsbridge, Lancaster Gate, Marble Arch

Kensington Gardens
🕐 Daily 5 a.m.–midnight 🚇 High Street Kensington, Bayswater, Queensway, Lancaster Gate

Serpentine Gallery
☎ 020 7402 6075 🕐 Daily 10–6
🆓 Admission free

🟦 Portobello Road Market

Portobello is London's largest market, the long street and its environs hosting a wide variety of food, modern clothing, crafts and junk markets, as well as the specialty small shops and antiques stores (and stalls) that first made it famous. On Saturdays it is the scene of what is reputedly the world's largest antiques market, with over 1,500 traders, the majority of whom are at the street's southern end after the junction with Westbourne Grove (itself lined with galleries and stores). Fruit stalls dominate beyond Elgin Crescent, while junk, secondhand clothes and offbeat shops and stalls take over beyond the "Westway" freeway overpass.

The range and quality of antiques and other goods is enormous. At the top end prices are as high as any in London, but bargains and one-offs can still be found; it's great fun to browse and people-watch even if you don't want to spend anything.

Note that on fine summer days the market is often extremely crowded (beware of pickpockets).

🕐 Antiques: Sat. 4–6. Clothes/bric-a-brac: Fri. 7–4, Sat. 8–5, Sun. 9–4. General: Mon.–Wed. 8–6, Thu. 9–1, Fri.–Sat. 7–7 🚇 Notting Hill Gate, Ladbroke Grove 🚌 7, 23, 27, 28, 31, 52, 70, 302

A colorful corner of Portobello Road

Where to...
Eat and Drink

Prices
Expect to pay per person for a meal excluding drinks and service
$ under $40 $$ under $80 $$$ over $80

Bibendum $$–$$$

Sir Terence Conran opened this, his premier restaurant, in the acclaimed Michelin building in 1987. It is both relaxed and highly professional, and the magnificent dining room provides a great setting for some serious cooking. The wide range of classic European dishes on the menu are given a modern twist. The extraordinary depth of the wine list is a real talking point.

🚫 Off map 🏠 Michelin House, 81 Fulham Road, SW3 ☎ 020 7581 5817; fax: 020 7823 7925 ⓦ Daily noon–2:30, 7–11:30 🚇 South Kensington

Bluebird $$

A flower shop, café, high-profile bar, kitchen store, and classy super-market are all part of the experience of this fashionable high-volume eaterie. There's a great buzz from the chic restaurant. The menu is simply conceived, with dishes from the crustacean bar, rotisserie, and the large wood-fired brick oven where a wide variety of meats, fish, poultry and vegetables are cooked over different types of wood.

🚫 Off map 🏠 350 Kings Road, SW3 ☎ 020 7559 1000; fax: 020 7559 1111 ⓦ Mon.–Sat. noon–3:30, 6–11:30; Sun. noon–4:30, 6–11 🚇 Sloane Square

Fifth Floor at Harvey Nichols $$

The Fifth Floor restaurant, on the top floor of the designer-label Harvey Nichols department store (▶ 134), forms part of a food lover's paradise that takes in a food hall, café and bar, even *kaiten zushi* (a conveyor-belt sushi bar). The dining room is cool and chic, while the food incorporates imaginative Italian, Middle Eastern and oriental influences. Both the restaurant and bar can become crowded at peak times. Reservations are essential.

🚫 202 A4 🏠 Harvey Nichols, Knightsbridge, SW1 ☎ 020 7235 5250; fax: 020 7823 2207 ⓦ Lunch daily noon–3; dinner Mon.–Sat. 6–11:30 🚇 Knightsbridge

Gordon Ramsay Restaurant $$$

The former Glasgow Rangers soccer player took the fast track to the top of the catering profession, gaining experience along the way with some of London's premier chefs as well as in France, in the kitchens of Guy Savoy and Joël Robuchon. Now installed at the former La Tante Claire (discreetly restyled), Gordon Ramsay continues to enthrall customers with a rich, yet light style of haute cuisine. The best value – and the best way to sample the Ramsay style – is the set three-course lunch. Reservations well in advance are essential.

🚫 202 A1 🏠 68 Royal Hospital Road, SW3 ☎ 020 7352 4441 ⓦ Mon.–Fri. noon–2, 6:45–11 🚇 Sloane Square

Hilaire $$

Chef/proprietor Bryan Webb has ensured that this is one of the great small restaurants of London. Whether you're in one of the curved windows of the first-floor dining room or in a cozy basement alcove, a meal here is always a civilized experience. Uncompromising standards in choice of ingredients and exact technique produce consistently memorable results from a kitchen that eschews fashion, but nevertheless provides some of the best modern British cooking in this part of London.

✚ Off map ⊠ 68 Old Brompton Road, SW7 ☎ 020 7584 8993; fax: 020 7581 2949 ⓦ Lunch Mon.–Fri. 12:15–2:30; dinner Mon.–Sat. 6:30–11:30 🚇 South Kensington

The Orangery $

The elegant, white, light Orangery provides a pleasant, informal setting for English afternoon tea. Three set teas are offered, the grandest including champagne, or you could just opt for a selection of delicious cakes and a pot of tea. Light lunches are available between noon and 2:30.

✚ 198 B3 ⊠ Kensington Palace, Kensington Gardens, W8 ☎ 020 7376 0239 ⓦ Daily 10–4, Oct.–Easter; 10–6 Easter–Sep. 🚇 High Street Kensington

Stefano Cavallini Restaurant at The Halkin Hotel $$$

The discreet hotel entrance, the sparsely decorated restaurant

(renamed after the chef who has inspired a new school of modern Italian cooking), the professional, charming Armani-clad staff, are the epitome of Italian chic. Menus are absorbing, packed with innovative and unusual combinations, dishes an exploration of modern ideas, textures and flavors. Balance is everything, with dishes served tepid to emphasize flavors.

✚ 202 B4 ⊠ Halkin Hotel, Halkin Street, SW1 ☎ 020 7333 1000; fax: 020 7333 1100 ⓦ Lunch Mon.–Fri. 12:30–2:30; dinner daily 7:30–11 p.m. 🚇 Hyde Park Corner

La Tante Claire $$$

Pierre Koffmann has followed in the steps of top London chefs Nico Ladenis and Marco Pierre White in moving his restaurant into a grand London hotel. In Koffmann's case the move has come after 21 years, and relocating from his former Chelsea base to the quiet and elegant Berkeley Hotel in the heart of Knightsbridge has proved an

immediate success. The menu has changed little, continuing to offer simple preparations of classic French cooking, much of it based on the traditions of Koffmann's native Gascony.

✚ 202 B4 ⊠ The Berkeley Hotel, Wilton Place, SW1 ☎ 020 7823 2003; fax: 020 7823 2001 ⓦ Lunch Mon.–Fri. 12:30–2; dinner Mon.–Sat. 7–11 p.m. 🚇 Knightsbridge, Hyde Park Corner

Zafferano $$

In an understated room, the plain walls, terra cotta floor, comfortable chairs and closely set tables all contribute to an air of upscale informality. Chef/proprietor Giorgio Locatelli's cooking comes as a breath of fresh air, presenting Italian food with an understanding and flair that many more pretentious establishments have difficulty matching. Uncluttered and simply conceived dishes based on first-class ingredients, exact technique and clear flavors are the driving force

behind lunch and dinner menus. In this expensive part of London, a meal at Zafferano's is a positive bargain.

✚ 202 B3 ⊠ 15 Lowndes Street, SW1 ☎ 020 7235 5800; fax: 020 7235 1971 ⓦ Mon.–Sat. noon–2:30, 7–11 🚇 Knightsbridge

BAR

Boisdale $$

An astonishing range of single malt whiskies is available at London's premier malt whisky bar. Furnishings offer the odd spot of tartan to emphasize the Scottish theme. Despite the presence of a cigar bar, this is not in any way a male preserve. Indeed, it's a pleasant place, with an attractive courtyard, a cozy, dark, atmospheric bar, and an adjoining restaurant that specializes in Scottish dishes.

✚ 202 C3 ⊠ 15 Eccleston Street, SW1 ☎ 020 7730 6922 ⓦ Mon.–Fri. noon–11 🚇 Victoria

Where to... Shop

The streets of Knightsbridge, Kensington and Chelsea provide some of London's most blue-blooded shopping, with the sophisticated coexisting alongside the traditional. Many stores don't open until 10 a.m., generally closing at 6 p.m. On a Sunday this becomes noon to 5 p.m. in most instances. Late-night shopping in this neighborhood is Wednesday (Kensington High Street, Thursday) with stores generally adding an extra hour onto their usual closing times.

Famous Knightsbridge Stores

Harvey Nichols (109–125 Knightsbridge, SW1, tel: 020 7235 5000). Fashion addicts can indulge themselves on three floors of designer womenswear, two floors of menswear and a first floor given over to up-to-the-minute accessories such as Wolford hosiery, Dolce e Gabbana sunglasses and all manner of scarves, perfumes and cosmetics. Minimalist surroundings house an industrial steel-and-glass sixth-floor food emporium with an opulent food hall, sushi bar, café, bar and restaurant.

Harrods (87–135 Brompton Road, SW1, tel: 020 7730 1234), probably London's best-known department store, is a must on most tourist itineraries (▶ 116). The store is renowned for food as well as high fashion.

Sloane Street

Sloane Street is a serious showcase for international designers. Italy is represented by the romantic designs of **Alberta Ferretti** (205–206 Sloane Street, SW1, tel: 020 7235 2349) – gauzes and shimmering silks in a chandeliered setting; by that master of understated neutrality, **Armani** (37 Sloane Street, SW1, tel: 020 7235 6232); and by the funky uniformity of **Prada** (44–45 Sloane Street, SW1, tel: 020 7235 0008). French designers include the colorful **Christian Lacroix** (8a Sloane Street, SW1, tel: 020 7235 2400) and **Christian Dior** (22 Sloane Street, SW1, tel: 020 7235 1357), while **Katherine Hamnett** (20 Sloane Street, SW1, tel: 020 7823 1002) and **Tomasz Starzewski** (177–178 Sloane Street, SW1, tel: 020 7235 4526) present two very different faces of contemporary British design.

There are fantastic shoes at **Gina** (189 Sloane Street, SW1, tel: 020 7235 2932) and just around the corner, **Agent Provocateur** (16 Pont Street, SW1, tel: 020 7235 0229) sells top-quality lingerie.

If all the choice of high fashion sends you into a wardrobe crisis, slip into the old-established stationery sanctuary of **Smythson's** (135 Sloane Street, SW1, tel: 020 7730 5520) to scoop up leather-bound calendars and notebooks (available at significantly less expensive prices than in comparable stores), along with perfect engraved paper and envelopes.

Kensington High Street and Kensington Church Street

Kensington High Street might be less slick, but it is very long and has lots of useful stores clustered around the High Street Kensington Underground station, including a major branch of Marks & Spencer and the department store Barkers.

Running north, opposite Barkers, is Kensington Church Street, an antiques lover's dream, with a fabulous concentration of dealers. Important 19th- and early 20th-century designers such as William Morris and Pugin are for sale at **Haslam & Whiteway** (105 Kensington Church Street, W8, tel: 020 7229 1145). Early English ceramics, including Staffordshire figures and early Wedgwood pieces, are available at **Jonathan Horne** (66c Kensington Church Street, W8, tel: 020 7221 5658), and Cornishware, Midwinter and Poole potteries are the specialty at **Richard Dennis** (144 Kensington Church Street, W8, tel: 020 7727 2061). Both dealers can organize shipping, as can **John Jesse** (160 Kensington Church Street, W8, tel: 020 7229 0312), who stocks 20th-century design, including art nouveau prints. Wherever you buy, don't forget to thoroughly inspect the goods, haggle (it is expected) and request a receipt with an accurate description of the item.

South Kensington

Individual shops at the **Natural History Museum** (▶ 124–126), the **Science Museum** (▶ 121–123) and the **Victoria & Albert Museum** (▶ 117–120) stock all the educational lines that you might expect: pocket-money toys, dinosaurs and pretty minerals at the Natural History Museum; rockets and robots at the Science Museum. The museum shops, however, are also a good hunting ground for top-quality gifts for discerning grown-ups. The **Victoria & Albert Museum shop** is a real Aladdin's cave. A Crafts Council section sells contemporary works by British artists – one-off presents and future collectibles – while the main, attractively laid-out section is filled with clever reproductions of 18th-century ceramics, antique dolls and teddy bears, a vast selection of William Morris memorabilia and lavish coffee-table art books. At the Science Museum, adults can browse an unusual range of gadgetry and scientific instruments.

King's Road

The young and young at heart flock to this Chelsea thoroughfare for its boutiques and other interesting stores. A promenade can start at Sloane Square and take in the entire length of the long road, or just a fraction; either way there is a crop of coffee bars, from the chains such as Costa Coffee, Coffee Republic and Starbucks to independent cafés, with which to fuel your progress.

Peter Jones department store (Sloane Square, SW1, tel: 020 7730 3434) is on Sloane Square itself. Whistles, Kookai, Warehouse, Oasis and Next begin a roll call of mid-price fashion names as you begin to stroll down the King's Road. Farther along, the vintage clothes shop **Steinberg & Tolkein** (193 King's Road, SW3, tel: 020 7376 3660) has a dazzling array of garments from past decades, including original Pucci shirts, 1970s kaftans and cases of old jewelry and wacky accessories.

Angelic (194 King's Road, SW3, tel: 020 7351 1557) is a divine shop full of atmospheric candles to go with any decor; floating, votive, or aromatherapy. Downwind of the outlet **Lush** (123 King's Road, SW3, tel: 020 7376 8348), you can smell in advance the intensely fragrant natural cosmetics before you see them: soaps sliced from huge blocks to order, fizzing bath bombs and gooey hand-mixed face packs, plus fun packaging and labeling.

A branch of **Heal's** (224 King's Road, SW3, tel: 020 7349 8411) has nice things for the home, from furniture to photo frames, as does the fashionable **Designers' Guild** (267–271 & 275–277 King's Road, SW3, tel: 020 7351 5775) toward the World's End of the King's Road. Food fans might enjoy trekking this far along to discover the **Bluebird** gastrodome (▶ 132) with its café, bar, restaurant and food and flower market. Check out the bakery's lovely fresh breads such as rosemary or spinach, the delicatessen counters and curious dry goods.

Opposite, the sweet-toothed can indulge at **Rococo** chocolates (321 King's Road, SW3, tel: 020 7352 5857) with its artisan bars of dark and milk chocolate flavored with ingredients like Earl Grey tea, chili pepper, nutmeg, cardamom and wild mint leaves.

Where to...
Be Entertained

This is a cosmopolitan, well-heeled part of the city, with plenty of entertainment choices. Although it's an expensive area, there is no dearth of great-value venues.

Movie Theaters

Commercial choice is divided between the **two multi-screen Virgin movie theaters**, showing all the recently released blockbusters (279 King's Road, SW3, tel: 0870 907 0710 and 142 Fulham Road, SW10, tel: 0870 907 0711).

For art-house and subtitled movies try the **Curzon Cinema** (45 Knightsbridge, SW1, tel: 020 7369 1723). It's ideally positioned if you're looking for a respite from Knightsbridge shopping, and the small adjoining café serves good

salads, Italian snacks and espresso. The **Chelsea Cinema** (206 King's Road, SW3, tel: 020 7351 3742) shows similar movies, with the bonus of the most comfortable theater seats in town. It also has a small bar. At the **Gate Cinema** (Notting Hill Gate, W11, tel: 020 7727 4043) both trendy art-house movies and mainstream block-busters are screened.

Classical Music

The **Proms**, as the Henry Wood Promenade Concerts are more popularly known, are advertised by the BBC as the world's greatest music festival. Concerts are held nightly at the **Royal Albert Hall** (Kensington Gore, tel: 020 7930 2377) for a seven-week period every summer. Visiting international

orchestras, soloists and conductors join the BBC Symphony Orchestra to perform a wide-ranging selection of music. If you are prepared to line up, you can buy tickets to "prom" or stand that cost around $5. For those with less stamina there are seats ranging in price from $8–$100.

Clubs

Nightclubs are not found in abundance in this part of the city. Try **Cuba** (11 Kensington High Street, W8, tel: 020 7938 4137), a chic place with a fashionable clientele. It offers a broad spectrum of Latin music, with occasional live bands.

Jazz

If you like jazz, try the **606 Club** (90 Lots Road, SW10, tel: 020 7352 5953), where groups such as the bluesy modern jazz Julian Siegel Quartet play. It is open to non-members. At the sophisticated **Pizza on the Park** (11–13 Knightsbridge, SW1, tel: 020 7235 5273), you can listen to live music. Jazz greats such

as veteran singer George Melly have performed in the basement room.

Theater

Whether shocking, disturbing or just plain brilliant, the **Royal Court** (Sloane Square, SW1, tel: 020 7565 5000), home of the English Stage Company, has nurtured some of the best modern playwrights in Britain, and it is the place to see modern theater at its very best. A multi-million dollar refurbishment has uplifted the experience for theater-goers, replacing cramped conditions in the two theaters with state-of-the-art facilities. The **Holland Park Theatre** (Holland Park W8, tel: 020 7602 7856) is a popular open-air theater that operates only in the summer months. With the ruins of the 17th-century Holland House as a backdrop, and occasional accompaniment from the peacocks roaming freely through the park, the theater plays host to the Royal Ballet as well as offering a well-regarded opera season.

Covent Garden, Bloomsbury and Soho

Getting Your Bearings

Exploration of these districts underlines London's amazing variety: Within the space of a few streets an area's character can change from upscale to run down, from retail to residential, and from busy and exciting to genteel and refined.

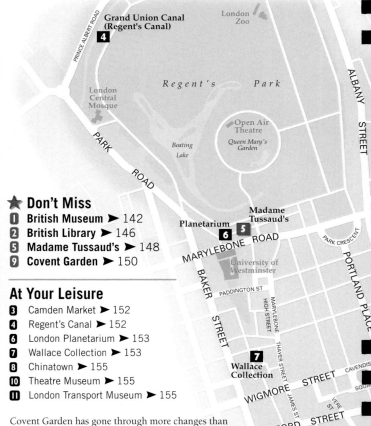

★ Don't Miss

1 British Museum ➤ 142
2 British Library ➤ 146
5 Madame Tussaud's ➤ 148
9 Covent Garden ➤ 150

At Your Leisure

3 Camden Market ➤ 152
4 Regent's Canal ➤ 152
6 London Planetarium ➤ 153
7 Wallace Collection ➤ 153
8 Chinatown ➤ 155
10 Theatre Museum ➤ 155
11 London Transport Museum ➤ 155

Covent Garden has gone through more changes than most London districts. Up until the 1970s it was the site of London's wholesale fruit and vegetable market, but when this moved south of the Thames, the market building was transformed into a small shopping center and crafts market. Gentrification has since spread, and the market and whole surrounding area have become a vibrant shopping and entertainment district full of stores, market stalls, fun museums, bars, cafés and restaurants.

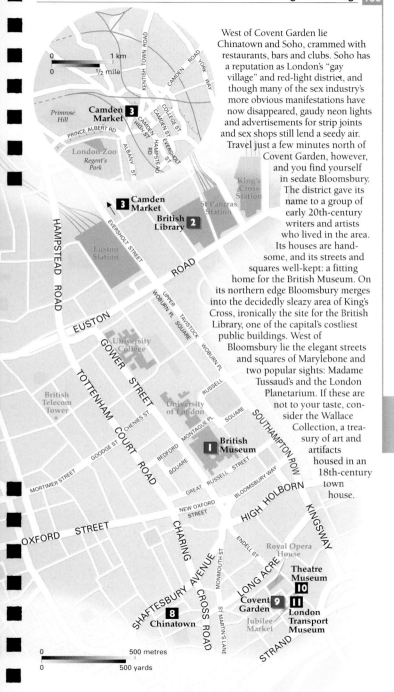

West of Covent Garden lie Chinatown and Soho, crammed with restaurants, bars and clubs. Soho has a reputation as London's "gay village" and red-light district, and though many of the sex industry's more obvious manifestations have now disappeared, gaudy neon lights and advertisements for strip joints and sex shops still lend a seedy air. Travel just a few minutes north of Covent Garden, however, and you find yourself in sedate Bloomsbury. The district gave its name to a group of early 20th-century writers and artists who lived in the area. Its houses are handsome, and its streets and squares well-kept: a fitting home for the British Museum. On its northern edge Bloomsbury merges into the decidedly sleazy area of King's Cross, ironically the site for the British Library, one of the capital's costliest public buildings. West of Bloomsbury lie the elegant streets and squares of Marylebone and two popular sights: Madame Tussaud's and the London Planetarium. If these are not to your taste, consider the Wallace Collection, a treasury of art and artifacts housed in an 18th-century town house.

A variety of tempting cultural experiences awaits in a day that takes in the ancient treasures of the British Museum, the priceless books and manuscripts of the British Library, and the waxwork models of the rich, famous and notorious in Madame Tussaud's.

Covent Garden, Bloomsbury and Soho in a Day

10:00 a.m.

Opening time at the **British Museum** (Elgin Marbles, left, ➤ 142–145): enjoy the classical façade and then explore galleries full of beautiful artifacts from bygone civilizations.

12:00 noon

Have lunch in one of the many cafés and pubs near the museum or bring along a picnic to eat in leafy Russell Square.

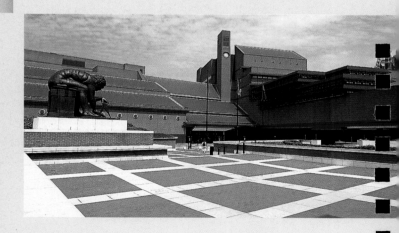

1:00 p.m.

From Russell Square catch a number 91 bus or take a 30-minute walk through Bloomsbury to the **British Library** (➤ 146–147). Look at the outside of the building from the spacious piazza (below left) then admire some of the world's loveliest old books and manuscripts. Have a café break to set you up for the next few hours.

2:30 p.m.

The number 30 bus takes you along Euston Road to Marylebone Road and **Madame Tussaud's** (➤ 148–149). The waxworks are enjoyable and rightly popular – but note our advice on how to avoid the lines.

4:00 p.m.

Take the Underground from Baker Street to **Covent Garden** (above, ➤ 150–151) for the market, stores, street entertainers and the area's great choice of restaurants, pubs and bars. It's a short walk from here to many West End theaters (➤ 160) if you're catching a show in the evening.

British Museum

The British Museum is one of the world's foremost museums, containing a wealth of antiquities illuminating the history of civilizations and cultures from across the globe. Founded in 1753 around the private collection of Sir Hans Sloane, it now possesses over 6 million artifacts arranged in a magnificent building with several miles of galleries. The exhibits on display include ancient carvings and sculpture, sublime paintings, exquisite jewelry and a host of other treasures.

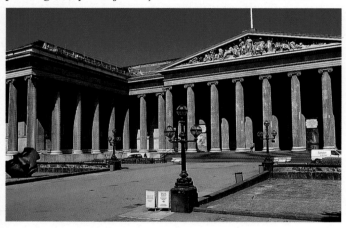

The colonnaded main building of the British Museum was built in 1844 to replace the earlier Montagu House, which had become too small to house the museum's growing collection

The British Museum is vast, with more than enough beautiful exhibits to sustain several lengthy visits, so for those with only a short amount of time to explore, the key to surviving and enjoying the museum is not to try to see it all in one visit. Be ruthlessly selective, know what you'd like to see before you go, and try not to get too distracted en route.

The **Eygptian galleries,** which house one of the best collections of Egyptian antiquities outside Egypt, are among the museum's highlights. Many of the exhibits in these galleries came into the museum's possession after the Napoleonic Wars, the British taking from the French what they in turn had taken from the Egyptians. Other finds came directly from Egypt,

✉ Great Russell Street, WC1
☎ 020 7636 1555; www.british-museum.ac.uk ⏰ Mon.–Sat. 10–5, Sun. noon–6; closed Jan. 1, Good Fri., Dec. 24-26
🍴 Café and restaurant 🚇 Holborn, Tottenham Court Road, Russell Square
🚌 Tottenham Court Road, northbound, and Gower Street, southbound 10, 24, 29, 73, 134; Southampton Row 68, 91, 199; New Oxford Street 8, 19, 22b, 25, 38, 55, 98; Great Russell Street 7 ♿ Admission free

The Egyptian Sculpture Gallery is home to statues, sarcophagi and the Rosetta Stone, one of the most important artifacts in the British Museum

acquired by British envoys and ambassadors or discovered in the explorations of Egypt Exploration Fund. Funerary art and artifacts dominate, with exquisitely decorated coffins, mummies, sarcophagi, jewelry, models and scrolls. The gilded inner coffin of Henutmehyt (*c*1290 BC) is particularly impressive. Look for the case containing "Ginger," the 5,000-year-old mummified body of an Egyptian man, whose leathery remains always draw a crowd. He still has a few tufts of red hair, but is missing his left index finger (it was "collected" by an early visitor to the museum).

The most important exhibit in these galleries, and perhaps the entire museum, is the **Rosetta Stone** (196 BC). Its significance lies in the three languages of its inscriptions: Greek at the bottom, Egyptian hieroglyphs at the top, a cursive form of the Egyptian between the two. Discovered accidentally in 1799, the stone enabled Egyptian hieroglyphs to be deciphered for the first time, allowing much of Egyptian civilization to be understood. Less important, but more visually arresting, is the huge granite **head of Rameses II**, which towers over the gallery: It was carved for the ruler's memorial temple in Thebes in the 13th century BC.

Suggested Route

Follow this route to cover the museum's highlights with minimum backtracking.

First floor:
Room 25 Egyptian Sculpture Gallery
Room 8 The Sculptures of the Parthenon
Rooms 16 and 17 Assyrian Galleries

Second floor:
Room 41 Early Medieval (Sutton Hoo)
Rooms 49 and 50 Weston Gallery of Roman Britain (Mildenhall)
Rooms 61–66 Egyptian Galleries

The museum's most controversial sculptures are the **Elgin Marbles**, named after Lord Elgin, a British diplomat who brought them to England in 1816. Most are taken from a 5th-century BC frieze removed from the Parthenon, the most important temple in ancient Athens, and probably depict a festival in honor of Athena, the city's patron goddess. Modern Greece believes the Marbles should be returned, claiming it is wrong that a foreign museum should possess such important national cultural relics.

The Assyrians, who lived in what is now northern Iraq, are represented in the museum by, among other things, the entrance of **Khorsabad, Palace of Sargon** (721–705 BC), a glorious example of the massive carvings of winged bulls with human heads that guarded their palaces. Equally beguiling are the reliefs of King Ashurbanipal, the last great Assyrian king; they depict a lion hunt, and once adorned his palace in Ninevah.

British artifacts are also celebrated. The 7th-century Anglo-Saxon **Sutton Hoo Ship Burial exhibits** – weapons and helmets in particular – provide a valuable insight into the Dark Ages, a period of British and European history about which relatively little is known. The treasures were found in 1939

An imposing reconstruction of the Nereid monument from Xanthos in the southwest of present-day Turkey

Beautiful Greek sculpture from the Nereid monument

during excavations of ancient burial mounds close to the River Deben near the town of Woodbridge in Suffolk, a site which before the construction of sea walls lay just 600 feet from the high-water level. The **Mildenhall Treasure**, an important collection of 4th-century Roman silverware, was found at Mildenhall, in Suffolk, just a few years later. Some mystery still surrounds the discovery of the treasure, which was not immediately declared to the authorities. Its centerpiece is the 18-lb. Great Dish, decorated with images of Neptune, the sea god, with a beard of seaweed and dolphins leaping from his hair.

TAKING A BREAK

The **Coffee Gallery** (23 Museum Street, WC1, tel: 020 7405 3211), serving salads, filled bagels, chili chicken and mixed *meze*, is a great place to stop for a light lunch.

BRITISH MUSEUM: INSIDE INFO

Top tips The museum has two entrances: the main one on Great Russell Street and a quieter one on **Montague Place**.
• Video and still photography, including flash, is allowed.
• **Guided tours** of the museum's highlights (60 and 90 mins.; charge) or individual galleries (50 mins.; free) are available. Reserve at entrance information points.

In more detail The **Mexican Gallery (Room 33)** contains several impressive displays, the loveliest of which are the turquoise mosaic statues from the Mixtec–Aztec era (1400–1521).
• If you have time, admire the craftsmanship of the gold and silver **Oxus Treasure (Room 52)**, a collection of Persian artifacts dating from the 5th or 4th century BC.

One to miss The **Portland Vase**, a piece of Roman blown glass, is one of the museum's best-known treasures. It is actually rather small and unimpressive, however, and repairs carried out after it was smashed into a couple of hundred pieces by a drunken visitor in 1845 are all too clearly visible.

British Library

The British Library ranks alongside the National Library of Congress in Washington and the Bibliothèque Nationale in Paris as one of the three greatest libraries in the world. The facts and figures about the library are startling enough, but the modern, airy building itself amounts to an attractive, user-friendly set of galleries and facilities, while its contents include some of the world's most incredible printed treasures. Exhibits span almost three millennia, from the Buddhist

Diamond Sutra of 868 BC, the world's oldest printed book, up to modern manuscripts by Paul McCartney and John Lennon. Along the way they take in Shakespeare, the Gutenberg Bible, the Magna Carta and the notebooks of Leonardo da Vinci.

The **John Ritblat Gallery** contains some of the library's principal treasures, including maps, sacred religious texts, historical documents, letters and literary and musical manuscripts. The gallery is remarkable for the fame, age,

The binding of the Lindisfarne Gospels (*CAD* 698)

breadth and quality of its collection. The light is kept low to protect the material and the atmosphere is almost hallowed – as indeed it should be in the presence of the Lindisfarne Gospels and Bedford Hours, two of the loveliest early English illuminated manuscripts. Among the other treasures on display are original manuscripts by Jane Austen and Charlotte Brontë, scores by Mozart and Handel, including that of the *Messiah*, letters from Gandhi, and Lord Nelson's last (unfinished) love letter to Lady Hamilton.

For an interactive experience head for **Turning the Pages**, a unique computer-based system (just off the John Ritblat Gallery) that allows visitors to "browse" through some of the treasures a page at a time.

✉ 96 Euston Road, NW1 C020 7412 7332
🕐 Mon.–Fri. 9:30–6 (also Tue. 6–8), Sat. 9:30–5, Sun. and public holidays 11–5
🍴 Restaurant, coffee shop and café 🚇 King's Cross
🚌 10, 30, 46, 73, 91, 214 ♿ Admission free

The library's two other galleries offer a more practical look at books. The **Pearson Gallery of Living Words** considers the development of writing, children's books and scientific records (with some fine examples) and provides a small reading area to sit and enjoy a selection of books. The **Workshop of Words, Sounds and Images** investigates the technology of book production, printing and sound recording. It offers an interactive, computer-based chance to design a book page – there are often also printing demonstrations.

TAKING A BREAK

Visit the library's café (➤ Inside Info, below). Alternatively, try **Patisserie Deux Amis** (63 Judd Street, WC1, tel: 020 7383 7029), a simple café serving filled baguettes and delicious cakes.

The new British Library came in three times over budget and eight years over schedule. Prince Charles described it as "a dim collection of sheds groping for some symbolic significance"

VITAL STATISTICS

❑ The library basement is equivalent to eight stories and holds 150 miles of shelving.

❑ Some 12 million books are stored in the basement, but the library's total collection numbers over 150 million.

❑ The library receives a free copy of every book, comic, newspaper, map and magazine published in the United Kingdom. This means it receives an average of 10,000 new items weekly.

❑ The library building was discussed in the 1950s, but opened only in 1998, by which time it had cost three times its original budget.

BRITISH LIBRARY: INSIDE INFO

Top tips Visit the **café or restaurant** beside the multistory glass tower that houses the 65,000 leather-bound volumes of King George III's library.

• The **piazza** in front of the library is a fine public space: Notice Paolozzi's statue of *Newton* (1995) and the views of the Gothic pinnacles of St. Pancras Station.

• **Guided tours** provide an excellent introduction to the history and workings of the Library (1 hour, additional charge, Mon., Wed. and Fri. 3 p.m., Sat. 10:30 a.m. and 3 p.m. Only three tours also include a visit to one of the reading rooms (Tue. 6:30 p.m. and Sun. 11:30 a.m. and 3 p.m.).

Madame Tussaud's

One of London's most deservedly popular tourist attractions offers you the chance to meet James Bond, see how tall actor Arnold Schwarzenegger really is and have your photograph taken with boxing legend Mohammad Ali – or at least waxwork models of these and over 400 other characters. A visit provides a fun-packed couple of hours' entertainment for adults and children alike.

A splitting image – actress and singer Kylie Minogue, with her waxwork twin

The displays proper start with **The Garden Party**, where many of the collection's contemporary figures – including film stars and sporting greats – are portrayed as if relaxing at a social gathering. You move on to displays detailing the story of Madame Tussaud, who learned her art in 18th-century France, came to Britain with a traveling show, and 33 years later, in 1835, founded the museum. A sequence of exhibits shows how the models are made. Each model takes about six months and costs almost $50,000 to create. Look for the shelves of old body parts, including heads, of ex-celebrities who have faded from the

✉ Marylebone Road, NW1
☎ 020 7935 6861
🕐 Mon.–Fri. 10–5:30 (last entry), Sat.–Sun. 9:30–5:30; closed Dec. 25
🍴 Café Tussaud's for meals and snacks, but a better choice in Baker Street nearby
🚇 Baker Street
🚌 13, 18, 27, 30, 74, 82, 113, 159, 274
💷 Moderate

FACTS AND FIGURES

❏ Early techniques involved casts being made of the model's head. Napoleon had to have straws stuck up his nostrils so that he could breathe as his cast was made, and was so distressed he held Josephine's hand throughout.

❏ All the hair used on the models is real and is regularly washed and styled.

❏ The wax used is similar to candle wax and the exhibition has no windows so that models don't melt in the sunlight.

limelight and lost their place in the show.

Upstairs in the **Grand Hall** there are models of religious leaders, members of the Royal Family, politicians and world leaders as well as figures from the arts such as Picasso, Beethoven and The Beatles.

From here you plunge into the **Chamber of Horrors**, perhaps the exhibition's best-known – and certainly most ghoulish – section. Torture, execution and murder are dealt with, together with lots of gruesome sound effects. It's a part of the show those with young children may wish to avoid.

The climax of the exhibition is the **Spirit of London** section, in which visitors take a ride in a model taxi through a fabulously colorful tableau of 400 years of London's history.

As if it were yesterday – John, Paul, George and Ringo, as they appeared at the start of their career

TAKING A BREAK

Try the dim sum at the hugely popular **Royal China** (40 Baker Street, W1, tel: 020 7487 4688).

MADAME TUSSAUD'S: INSIDE INFO

Top tips The exhibition quickly becomes very crowded, and there are long lines for admittance. To avoid the queues **reserve tickets by credit card**, which allows you to enter by the ticket holders' entrance.

• The exhibition space opens earlier during **school vacations**, but avoid visiting at this time, if possible. The exhibition is quieter later in the afternoon: If you arrive by 4:30 you'll still have time to see everything.

• A saving can be made on admission charges by purchasing a **combined ticket** for Madame Tussaud's and the adjoining London Planetarium (➤ 153).

Covent Garden

When London's wholesale fruit and vegetable market moved out of Covent Garden in the 1970s, the scene was set for its transformation into one of the city's most lively, entertaining and popular districts. Weekends are best for exploring the superb shopping, market and entertainment area, with plenty of excellent bars, cafés and restaurants. There are also a couple of fun museums, theaters and the newly reopened opera house.

The district's heart is the piazza, the area surrounding the restored 19th-century market building that now houses small stores and the handmade crafts stalls of the Apple Market. Close by is the dignified Royal Opera House and the indoor Jubilee Market (clothes, crafts and leather goods), while the Theatre Museum (► 155) and the London Transport Museum (► 155) will provide a good couple of hours' diversion.

One of the piazza's highlights is the variety of street entertainers who congregate here, embracing everything from Chinese orchestras and South American pan pipe musicians to acrobats, mime artists and didgeridoo players. They generate much of the "buzz" and atmosphere of the place. The many small streets, especially Floral Street and the area north of the Covent Garden Underground station, are also well worth exploring for their individual and unusual stores (► 159) and tucked-away cafés, bars and restaurants.

Street performers entertain Covent Garden visitors

Far right: fruit and vegetable stalls in Covent Garden have given way to a wide variety of cafés, bars and craft stalls

🚇 Covent Garden 🚌 Along Strand 6, 9, 11, 13, 15, 23, 77A, 91, 176

COVENT GARDEN: INSIDE INFO

Top tips Don't leave Covent Garden without spending some time strolling down **Neal Street**. There are some interesting stores here, including **Neal Street East** (5 Neal Street, WC2, tel: 020 7240 0135), which specializes in Asian goods, and **The Tea House** (15 Neal Street, WC2, tel: 020 7240 7539), selling a huge range of teas and teapots of all shapes and sizes.

• Don't miss **Neal's Yard Remedies** (15 Neal's Yard, WC2, tel: 020 7379 7222), where you can buy herbal remedies, top-quality oils and toiletries (all sold in distinctive blue bottles) from knowledgeable staff. The store also has a good selection of books on herbal and alternative medicine.

• For delicious English cheeses, try **Neal's Yard Dairy** (17 Shorts Gardens, WC2, tel: 020 7379 7646).

Hidden gem For a break from shopping and the chance to enjoy one of the best cups of coffee in London, stop at **Monmouth Coffee Company** (► 157).

At Your Leisure

🔞 Camden Market

Camden Market is actually a con-
glomeration of several markets in
Camden Town, spreading out from
Camden Lock along Chalk Farm
Road and Camden High Street. A visit
here is a good way to spend a Sunday,
when all the markets are open (some
are also open on other days: see
below), but you should bear in mind
that the whole area is usually
extremely crowded, especially in the
summer. The market is particularly
good for modern clothing, jewelry
and crafts.

Camden Lock

Renovated warehouses beside the
canal are packed solid with stalls selling arts, crafts, old and new clothing,
tapes and CDs, plus food and drink.
🔵 Sat.–Sun. 10–6

Camden Canal Market

This market is located to the north of
the canal between Chalk Farm Road
and Castle Haven Road. The entrance

is small, but the place is packed with
stalls selling collectible items such as
books and clothes – even bicycles.
🔵 Sat.–Sun. 10–6; indoor stalls:
Tue.–Sat. 10–6

Stables Market

This is the most northerly of the markets (off Chalk Farm Road). It sells
pretty much the same range of items
as Camden Lock but with some furniture and antiques as well.
🔵 Sat.–Sun. 9–5

Electric Market

Selling secondhand clothes, plus
some new items, this market has an
emphasis on the weird and way-out.
✉ Camden High Street, just north of
Camden Town Underground 🔵 Sun.
9–5:30

Camden Market

Look here for old and new clothing,
music, jewelry and tapes.
✉ Camden High Street 🔵 Thu.–Sun.
9–5:30

🔞 Regent's Canal

The 19th-century Regent's Canal, an
extension of the Grand Union Canal,
provides an unusual view of London,
the city's traffic replaced by stately
canal barges and its buildings by trees
and flowers. A gentle stroll along the
canal banks is a delightful antidote to
sightseeing.
     Built in 1820, the canal runs for
8 miles between Little Venice in west
London to Limehouse in the east,
where it eventually joins the Thames.
Little Venice is an attractive enclave,
the canal at its heart dotted with decorated houseboats that are awash with
potted plants and flowers in the summer.
     Several boat companies offer canal
trips between Little Venice and

Regent's Canal, a peaceful backwater

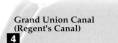

**Grand Union Canal
(Regent's Canal)**
4

London Zoo

Regent's Park

London Central Mosque

Open Air Theatre

Boating Lake

Queen Mary's Garden

PARK ROAD

Camden Lock (around 50 min. each way): Contact the companies below for more details. Alternatively, you could walk on the towpath from Camden Lock, close to Camden Market (► 152), toward the northern perimeter of Regent's Park. Although built up in its early stretches, this is one of the most peaceful parts of the canal; you can keep walking until you get tired and then take one of the paths up to rejoin the city at any point, or you may want to relax in Regent's Park.

Planetarium
6

Madame Tussaud's
5

MARYLEBONE ROAD

University of Westminster

PADDINGTON ST

BAKER STREET

MARYLEBONE HIGH STREET

Wallace Collection
7

For Kids
- Madame Tussaud's
- Covent Garden street entertainers
- Canal boat trip
- British Museum
- Theatre Museum

6 London Planetarium

The centerpiece of the London Planetarium is a 30-minute star show (available in several languages) projected onto the building's domed ceiling by the world's most advanced star projector. The show takes viewers on a colorful and dramatic journey through the universe, but as most people come here immediately after visiting nearby Madame Tussaud's (► 148–149) lines can be long, and you may have to wait for up to 40 minutes for the next show – not a good thing if your energy levels are low after the Tussaud's waxworks.

✉ Marylebone Road, NW1 ☎ 020 7935 6861 🕒 Mon.–Fri. first show at 12:20 then every 40 min. until last show at 5; Sat.–Sun. and school vacations first show at 10:20; closed Dec. 25 🍴 Good choice in Baker Street nearby 🚇 Baker Street 🚌 18, 27, 30 💷 Inexpensive. Combined tickets available with Madame Tussaud's (► 148)

7 Wallace Collection

This remarkable collection of objets d'art is made all the more alluring by its setting, Manchester House, a beautiful 18th-century mansion acquired in 1797 by the 2nd Marquess of Hertford. Its collection of artifacts was bequeathed to the nation on condition it should never be sold, loaned or removed from central London.

Every room is filled with treasures, though most people's favorite is Room 22, where a wonderful collection of Old Masters by Titian, Rubens, Murillo, Van Dyck and others is on display. The collection's most well-

London Waterbus Company
☎ 020 7482 2660 🕒 Sat.–Sun. 10–5 all year; Mon.–Fri. 10–5 end Mar.–Oct. Hourly departures.
Jason's Trip
☎ 020 7286 3428 🕒 Three times daily late Mar.–Oct.
Jenny Wren
Sightseeing trips from Camden Town to Little Venice and return (90 min.)
☎ 020 7485 4433 🕒 Daily Mar.–Oct. (3 trips per day, 4 trips at weekends and during school vacations); Sat.–Sun. only, Nov.–Feb.

known work is also here, Frans Hals' *The Laughing Cavalier* – the portrait of an unknown young man painted in 1624. While obviously a figure of substance, the man in question is neither laughing nor a cavalier: The title was coined in 1888 when the picture was lent to the Royal Academy Old Masters Exhibition. Nearby is another portrait of an unknown sitter, Velázquez's *Lady With A Fan*.

On a more general level, one of the collection's main charms is its

Manchester House provides an elegant setting in which to display the Wallace Collection's *objets d'art*

sheer variety, and the chance it provides to admire things you might normally overlook. Many people might expect to be distinctly underwhelmed by the displays of armor, for example, but the late 15th-century German *Complete War-Harness for Man and Horse* is one of several surprisingly attractive pieces in the collection.

✉ Hertford House, Manchester Square, W1 ☎ 020 7935 0687 🕐 Mon.–Sat. 10–5, Sun. 2–5 🍴 Café under construction in the courtyard developments 🚇 Bond Street 🚌 2, 13, 30, 74, 82, 113, 139, 159, 189, 274 💳 Admission free

Gerrard Street, the heart of London's Chinatown, is enriched with the aromas of eastern cuisine

8 Chinatown

The few blocks around Gerrard Street provide a magnet for London's 60,000-strong Chinese community. Many live elsewhere, but flock here on Sundays when the area is most lively. The streets are full of Chinese signs, restaurants (► 156), grocers and bookstores. Even the telephone booths resemble pagodas.

✉ Around Gerrard Street, W1
Ⓔ Leicester Square 🚌 14, 19, 24, 29, 38, 176

10 Theatre Museum

The museum has a wide range of artifacts from some 400 years of British theater history and is unmissable for anyone who enjoys the performing arts. Younger visitors should enjoy the museum's program of activities, especially the costume workshops and stage makeup demonstrations. Most of the museum guides are "resting" actors, and use their professional skills to entertain their audience.

The museum's displays embrace every aspect of theater: Gilbert and Sullivan and the Music Hall, for example, have their own sections, and many theatrical characters are featured, including Sir Henry Irving, Ellen Terry and Nöel Coward. Other sections look at the technical aspects of the theater, notably "The Wind in the Willows – From Page to Stage," which details the process of creating a production from finance to casting, design, marketing, the stage manager's role and the voice coaching given to actors.

Memorable images at the Theatre Museum

Some of what you learn here is startling.

✉ Russell Street, Covent Garden, WC2
☎ 020 7836 7891 🕐 Tue.–Sun. 10–6 (last admission 5:30) Ⓔ Covent Garden
🚌 Along Strand 6, 9, 11, 13, 15, 23, 77A, 91, 176 💷 Inexpensive

11 London Transport Museum

This museum offers an intriguing view of the history of London over the last 200 years through its buses, trams and trains. It looks at the way that transportation has affected and continues to affect the lives of people in the city, and provides a glimpse into what it takes to shift millions of travelers around the capital daily. Visitors can see just how the London Underground and bus systems were built and operate today and ponder the demise of the tram. The museum looks forward as well as back, with displays illustrating the impact of increasing car ownership on the capital's transportation network.

✉ Covent Garden, WC2
☎ 020 7836 8557
🕐 Sat.–Thu. 10 a.m.–6 p.m., Fri. 11 a.m.–6 p.m. Last admission 5:15 p.m.
🍴 Coffee shop Ⓔ Covent Garden 🚌 Along Strand 6, 9, 11, 13, 15, 23, 77A, 91, 176 💷 Inexpensive

Where to...
Eat and Drink

Prices
Expect to pay per person for a meal excluding drinks and service
$ under $40 $$ under $80 $$$ over $80

Alastair Little Soho $$

Everything about Alastair Little's eponymous restaurant is understated – from the bare aquamarine walls and stripped floorboards, to the casual but informed service and the fresh, deceptively simple food. An Italian influence sits well with the refreshingly seasonal ingredients, the quality of which shines through in every dish. The fixed-price menus (there is no à la carte) are very good value for money.

➕ 201 E2 ▢ 49 Frith Street, W1
☎ 020 7734 5183 🕐 Lunch
Mon.–Fri. noon–3; dinner Mon.–Sat.
6–11 Ⓔ Leicester Square

Bank $$

An enormous contemporary brasserie, this is undoubtedly the most colorful of London's large-scale restaurants, where there's something for everyone at any time of the day. The menu combines French favorites with new metropolitan ideas. All dishes are highly enjoyable and of a consistently good standard. The waiting staff provide fast, super-efficient and polished service.

➕ 204 B4 ▢ 1 Kingsway, WC2
☎ 020 7379 9011; fax: 020 7379 9014
🕐 Daily noon–3, 5.30–11.30
Ⓔ Holborn

Christopher's $–$$

Set on two floors in a grand Victorian building, Christopher's serves some of the best classic American food in London. The steaks, specially imported from the United States, Maine lobsters, tasty grills and Maryland crab cakes are unmissable; portions are ample. The restaurant is lively and popular and advance reservations are recommended. The clamorous café-bar has greater informality and a separate menu of salads and sandwiches as well as some of the Grill's dishes.

➕ 204 B3 ▢ 18 Wellington Street,
WC2 ☎ 020 7240 4222; fax: 020
7836 3506 🕐 Lunch daily noon–2:45;
dinner Mon.–Sat. 6–11:30
Ⓔ Covent Garden

Fung Shing $$

Chinatown may be wall-to-wall with Chinese restaurants, and Lisle Street in particular a crowded run-down part of it, but the long-standing Fung Shing remains one of the best places to eat. It serves authentic Cantonese food, the high quality of which further distinguishes the restaurant from its neighbors. The staff are very adept and patient at explaining the menu.

➕ 201 F1 ▢ 15 Lisle Street, WC2
☎ 020 7437 1539; fax: 020 7734 0284
🕐 Daily noon–11:15 Ⓔ Leicester
Square

The Ivy $$

The Ivy ranks as one of London's most fashionable eating places, close to achieving cult status; regulars return again and again for their favorite dishes. What they enjoy is best described as classic brasserie food. Traditional British ideas are tempered by modern European and oriental additions. Over a dozen wines are available by the glass. Making a reservation well in advance is an absolute essential.

➕ 201 F2 ▢ 1 West Street, Covent
Garden, WC2 ☎ 020 7836 4751; fax:
020 7240 9333 🕐 Daily noon–3,
5:30–midnight Ⓔ Leicester Square,
Covent Garden

J. Sheekey $$

A major facelift has injected new life into this restaurant, one of the oldest and best known seafood restaurants in the capital. Now run by the team that is responsible for such gastronomic temples as The Ivy and Le Caprice, J. Sheekey's is the place to go for traditional British fish dishes. Adding an extra dimension to the menu are a selection of more modern creations.

➕ 201 F1 ☒ 28–32 St. Martin's Court, WC2 ☎ 020 7240 2565
🕐 Daily noon–3 (also Sun. 3–3:30), 5:30–midnight ◉ Leicester Square

Lindsay House $$

There are strong reminders here of the private Georgian house this once was – you even have to ring the front-door bell in order to be admitted – but otherwise Lindsay House has been discreetly and sympathetically decorated, with a restful cream color scheme enhanced by some stylish modern touches. Irish chef Richard Corrigan has won great accolades for his cooking. His Celtic roots are still very evident in his gutsy, almost robust style, but his creations also incorporate a delicate touch. Offal is something of a passion for Corrigan, and his treatment of fish dishes is particularly imaginative.

➕ 201 E2 ☒ 21 Romilly Street, W1
☎ 020 7439 0450; fax: 020 7437 7349
🕐 Lunch Mon.–Fri. noon–2:15; dinner Mon.–Sat. 6–10.45. Closed last 2 weeks Aug. ◉ Leicester Square

Mash $–$$

The policy at this modernistic bar, deli and restaurant is to show customers exactly what they are getting. The bar is backed by a visible state-of-the-art microbrewery, and the second-floor restaurant is adjacent to a partially open-to-view kitchen. The dining area is in a light, expansive room, filled with generously spaced tables. Breakfast, which merges into a good brunch at weekends, forms part of a varied menu that also offers imaginative pizzas from a traditional wood-fired oven, char-grilled meat and fish dishes, and sumptuous calorie-laden desserts.

➕ 201 D2 ☒ 19–20 Great Portland Street, W1 ☎ 020 7637 5555; fax: 020 7637 7333 🕐 Daily 8–11 ◉ Oxford Circus

Mezzo $$

This is one of the largest eateries in Europe and high standards are consistent at Sir Terence Conran's Soho branch. The lively Mezzonine (on the first floor), specializes in Pacific Rim food in comfortable canteen-style surroundings. The flagship basement restaurant, Mezzo, continues that theme, but includes some modern European ideas. Shellfish from the excellent crustacean bar is recommended.

➕ 201 E2 ☒ 100 Wardour Street, W1 ☎ 020 7314 4000 🕐 Mezzo: lunch Sun.–Fri. noon–3; dinner Mon.–Sat. 6–midnight (also Sat. midnight–1 a.m.), Sun. 6–11. Mezzonine: open Sat. lunch ◉ Piccadilly Circus

Monmouth Coffee Company $

One of Soho's best-kept secrets – from the front it is nothing more than a store selling bags of coffee beans from all the world's coffee growing regions. But, at the back are eight tables, newspapers to read and a delectable selection of pastries. It's the perfect place to stop, relax and sample some great coffees from the wide-ranging stock.

➕ 201 F2 ☒ 27 Monmouth Street, WC2 ☎ 020 7836 5272
🕐 Mon.–Sat. 9–6:30, Sun. 11–5
◉ Covent Garden

The Orrery $$

This is one of the smallest restaurants in the famous Conran group, with just 80 seats, plus a shop and food store. However, the family design traits are all there: arched windows, lots of natural lighting, blond wood; a classy, stylish look. The short menu explores French classics, giving them a modern twist. The food bears many of Conran's trademark Mediterranean characteristics; raw ingredients especially have a true freshness and are of the best quality.

➕ 200 B3 ☒ 55–7 Marylebone High Street, W1 ☎ 020 7616 8000; fax: 020 7616 8080 ⓖ Daily noon–2:30, 7–11 Ⓜ Baker Street, Regent's Park

Le Palais du Jardin $$

This vast, popular brasserie at the heart of Covent Garden has a strong Parisian feel, especially with the all-day seafood counter, and the hustle and bustle of traditionally clad waiters. Those in the know come here for the seafood – lobster in particular, but there is also a good selection of dishes for meat-eaters. This is a great place for a pretheater meal.

➕ 204 A4 ☒ 136 Long Acre, WC2 ☎ 020 7379 5353; fax: 020 7379 1846 ⓖ Daily noon–3:30, 6–11:45 Ⓜ Covent Garden, Leicester Square

Patisserie Valerie $

The cramped but cozy old-fashioned tearoom is very much a Soho institution with shared tables and motherly waitresses; you won't want to leave. The patisserie is superb (check out the window display), but there are also good salads, Croque Monsieur and savory quiches to go with tea, coffee or hot chocolate.

➕ 201 E2 ☒ 44 Old Compton Street, W1 ☎ 020 7437 3466 ⓖ Mon.–Fri. 8–8, Sat. 8–7, Sun. 9.30–6 Ⓜ Leicester Square

La Porte des Indes $$

A fabulous Indian restaurant filled with lush, tropical greenery and decked out in rich colors. The kitchen explores the relationship between France and its Indian colonies through such dishes as *beignets d'aubergines* – slices of eggplant filled with cheese and herb pâté. Lunch consists of a spectacular buffet, which offers one of the best-value deals in the area.

➕ 200 A2 ☒ 32 Bryanston Street, W1 ☎ 020 7224 0055; fax: 020 7224 1144 ⓖ Lunch Sun.–Fri. noon–2:30; dinner Mon.–Sat. 7–midnight, Sun. 6–10:30 Ⓜ Marble Arch

Quo Vadis $$–$$$

The restaurant is the epitome of Cool Britannia, where the megatalents of chef Marco Pierre White and artist Damien Hirst merge. The contemporary restaurant is filled with Hirst's startling art (the flayed bovine heads preserved in formaldehyde are in the upstairs bar). The cooking is classic with a French twist. *Larousse Gastronomique* dictionary definitions pepper the menu: sauce diable, sauce Bercy, matched with more than a streak of modernism.

➕ 201 E2 ☒ 26–29 Dean Street, W1 ☎ 020 7437 9585; fax: 020 7434 9972 ⓖ Lunch Mon.–Fri. noon–3; dinner Mon.–Sat. 6–11.30, Sun. 6–10:30 Ⓜ Leicester Square

Stephen Bull Restaurant $$

This is a small, intimate room, with tables necessarily close and the only decoration a controlled use of color. The focus is firmly on the food. Short menus, a simple, light, touch and a straightforward approach show Stephen Bull maintaining the innovative streak that has kept him at the forefront of the London culinary scene for a generation. It is essential to make a reservation here.

➕ 200 B3 ☒ 5–7 Blandford Street, W1 ☎ 020 7486 9696; fax: 020 7490 3128 ⓖ Lunch Mon.–Fri. 12:15–2:30; dinner Mon.–Sat. 6:30–10:30 Ⓜ Bond Street

Sugar Club $$

The ultrafashionable Sugar Club is the place to come for some of the sharpest cutting-edge fusion food in town. Despite moving to new premises, antipodean Peter Gordon's philosophy remains unaltered, with strong Pacific Rim influences to the fore, at least when it comes to hot, powerful spicing – this is where flavors and temperatures collide.

➕ 201 D1 ☒ 21 Warwick Street, W1 ☎ 020 7437 7776 ⓖ Daily noon–2:30, 6–10:30 Ⓜ Oxford Circus

Where to... Shop

This central part of London acts as a visitor magnet and shopping here takes in both extremes of tourist clichés and sophisticated specialty goods.

Covent Garden

Covent Garden's pedestrianized piazza, where you can stroll, eat ice cream and browse, is a popular visitor's choice. Traders here are keen to capitalize on the crowds and many stores stay open till 7 or 8 p.m.

The Market itself is a good starting point. Stand and watch performing clowns and jugglers or meander the arcades for curiosities. The Candle Shop (30 The Market, WC2, tel: 020 7836 9815) sells all styles, perfumes and colors of candle. Culpeper Herbalists (8 The Market, WC2, tel: 020 7379 6698) stocks English herbs, oils, bath salts, potpourri and toiletries that make great presents. Benjamin Pollock's Toy Shop (44 The Market, WC2, tel: 020 7379 7866) is an amazing emporium of handmade puppets, theaters and other toys.

If you are looking for clothes, Paul Smith (40–44 Floral Street, WC2, tel: 020 7379 7133), British designer, sells superb casual wear, sharp suits, and unusual socks, ties and cufflinks. Robot (37 Floral Street, WC2, tel: 020 7836 6156) is stocked with trendy sunglasses, hats and cool clothing for men.

Bloomsbury

Bloomsbury is home to University College London and the British Museum (▶ 142–145), and an intellectual feel permeates the streets.

The British Museum's shop (Great Russell Street, WC1, tel: 020 7323 8613) sells reproduction jewelry, Egyptian artifacts and Michelangelo mementos.

Bloomsbury is also the traditional home of London's publishing houses, so there are bookstores galore. Charing Cross Road is the place for bookworms: Foyles, Books etc, Blackwell's and Waterstone's are the big four. Any Amount of Books (62 Charing Cross Road, WC2, tel: 020 7240 8140) sells secondhand books and has a bargain basement. Ulysses (40 Museum Street, WC1, tel: 020 7831 1600) specializes in first editions.

Soho

Chinatown lies at the heart of Soho, and Gerrard Street is at the heart of Chinatown. It is the cultural and financial center of Britain's Chinese community, with an amazing choice of restaurants, supermarkets, electrical stores and Chinese herbalists.

Soho itself is better known for its range of restaurants than for conventional shopping. Food, however, is a serious draw. Berwick Street Market (52 Old Compton Street, W1, tel: 020 7437 2480), a Monday to Saturday "fruit and veg" extravaganza, is worth a visit. On Old Compton Street there are I Camisa & Co (35 Old Compton Street, W1, tel: 020 7734 3477), which sells Italian deli foods; the Algerian Coffee Store (61 Old Compton Street, W1, tel: 020 7437 7610) for a range of fresh coffees, and the wonderful Pâtisserie Valerie (44 Old Compton Street, W1, tel: 020 7437 3466) for delicious French cakes; all crammed in between the sex shops that reflect a seedier but declining side to the area.

There's also American Retro (35 Old Compton Street, W1, tel: 020 7734 3477), a great source of unusual gifts from its stock of funky accessories. In Brewer Street check out the Vintage Magazine Shop (39–43 Brewer Street, W1, tel: 020 7439 8525), a good place to search out an old movie poster or rare movie and music magazines.

London's clubbers help to keep places open later in Soho than in other parts of the capital.

Where to...
Be Entertained

This is the heart of London entertainment, and on a Saturday night it can seem as if the whole of the metropolis has squeezed itself into taxis or Underground carriages to surface at Leicester Square and Covent Garden stations. Late on a Friday or Saturday night the sidewalks are still thronged with people who spill onto the streets, and the atmosphere is highly charged. There is much to take in when considering the choice of theaters, movies and clubs.

Theater

The choice ranges from the long-running blockbusters of Shaftesbury Avenue to Off-West End at the

Donmar Warehouse (tel: 020 7369 1732). Although you can go directly to the individual theater's box office, you might be able to pick up a half-price ticket at the **Half-Price Ticket Booth** (Mon.–Sat. noon–6:30, Sun. noon–3) in the clocktower building on the south side of Leicester Square piazza – there is no telephone number. There is a service charge of up to $3, strictly cash only and tickets are restricted to two pairs of tickets per person and are for a performance on that day. For a popular show, it is often your only chance of getting a ticket. Be prepared to get there before noon to be as close to the front of the line as possible. Do make a careful note that there are other more-expensive ticket booths in the square, so be

careful to join the right line. Also, never buy from touts who may approach you while you are waiting. They are working illegally and the tickets could well be fakes.

Another option is the charity ticket hotline **West End Cares** (tel: 020 7833 3939). Tickets for popular West End shows, for example *Miss Saigon*, *Les Misérables*, *The Phantom of the Opera*, are available and the price includes a donation to AIDS charities.

Ticketmaster (tel: 020 7413 1142) can otherwise help you find seats. There will be a service charge for credit card sales.

Clubs

London is king of the hill as far as the music scene is concerned and in its clubs a wide spectrum of tastes are catered to, from mainstream rock acts, country and jazz, to techno, indie and hip hop sounds. The listings magazine *Time Out* (published every Tuesday) is the most authoritative and comprehen-

sive of all the London magazines. As music and themes vary from night to night, it is essential to check for up-to-date information. For example, **Heaven** (Under The Arches, Villiers Street, WC2, tel: 020 7930 2020), a huge gay club with a laid back and friendly atmosphere, is also popular with straight men and women.

Other popular club venues worth checking out:

The Astoria (157 Charing Cross Road, WC2, tel: 020 7434 0403), a brilliant venue for up-to-the-minute sounds as well as rock and reggae.

Café de Paris (3 Coventry Street, W1, tel: 020 7734 7700), a glam dance hall, overlooked by a galleried restaurant.

The Gardening Club (4 The Piazza, WC2, tel: 020 7497 3153/4), cave-like; varied but mostly house beats.

The Rock Garden (6–7 The Piazza, Covent Garden, WC2, tel: 020 7240 3961), a burger joint noted for showcasing new talent in a variety of musical areas.

Excursions

Kew

Kew is an excellent day out. Not only is it convenient – just a short boat or train ride from central London – but its highlight, the Royal Botanic Gardens, is the world's foremost botanical garden and one of the loveliest spots in the capital.

The Royal Botanic Gardens' 300 acres contain around 30,000 species of plants, including 13 species extinct in the wild. Keen botanists and gardeners will revel in the floral diversity, but nonexperts can also easily savor the gardens' overall beauty. Visits outside the summer months can be especially rewarding – September to November produces wonderful fall colours, camellias bloom in January, and February to May sees the first blooms of spring.

It would be easy to wander here for days, but to see the highlights visit the glasshouses in the order suggested below. Look for the glasshouses' display boards, which offer entertaining information about some of the plants.

The **Princess of Wales Conservatory** features 10 computer-regulated climate zones. Wander from orchids in the humid tropical zone to cacti in the dry tropical zone to

The 10-story Kew Pagoda. During World War II, the RAF drilled holes in its floors to test model bombs

Top tips
• Kew, 9 miles from the city center, is accessible by public transportation.
• The seasonal highlights are listed on a free map available at the entrance.

Previous page: the moat at Windsor Castle has been transformed into lovely gardens

Kew Gardens
☎ 020 8940 1171 (24-hour recorded information) ⏰ Daily 9:30–dusk (telephone for exact closing times). The glasshouses and galleries close earlier. Closed Jan. 1, Dec. 25
🍽 Several cafés and restaurants in the gardens and other options nearby
🚇 Kew Gardens
🚌 Kew Bridge 63, 391; also R68 (Sun. only) For information on river trips to Kew from central London
► 104 🎫 Moderate

appreciate the huge influence of climate on floral types. The most bizarre plants are the lithops of Namibia, also called "living stones," which are indistinguishable from stones until they produce brilliantly colored flowers.

The **Palm House** is a masterpiece of Victorian engineering, constructed between 1844 and 1848 with some 16,000 sheets of glass. Climb one of the wrought-iron spiral staircases to the raised walkways to view its lush rain-forest interior containing tropical species from across the globe, such as coconut, banana and rubber, and don't miss the basement with its marine plants and habitats, in particular the coral reef. Kew is one of the few places in Britain with living coral, something that is notoriously difficult to cultivate in captivity.

The **Temperate House** is the largest of the glasshouses (590 by 140 feet). An elegant structure, it was begun in 1860, but work was stopped after the central block was finished and the building was not finally completed until almost 40 years later. Today its highlights are a Chilean wine palm, planted in the mid-19th century and now one of the world's largest indoor palms, and subtropical plants such as citrus trees, tea trees and Himalayan rhododendrons.

Just behind the Temperate House is the **Evolution House**, which traces the development of the most ancient plants. A bubbling primordial sludge has been re-created, duplicating – it is thought – the earliest "soil." From here, plant evolution is traced from the first bacteria through algae, mosses and ferns to conifers and flowering plants.

The 10-story **Pagoda** is perhaps the gardens' most celebrated landmark. It was completed in 1762 for Princess Augusta, the mother of George III, and at the time was the most accurate reproduction of a Chinese building in Europe.

Top: the Palm House at Kew incorporates 16,000 panes of glass and took four years to build

Above: luxuriant tropical plants thrive in its controlled climate

Windsor

Windsor Castle is the obvious centerpiece for this excursion, but the town is attractive in its own right. There is also the chance to visit historic Eton College, a school for the sons of the rich and famous, and – a treat for the children – the modern theme park of Legoland.

Top tips

- The Changing of the Guard takes place at 11 a.m. daily (except Sundays) from April to June and on alternate days for the rest of the year.

- Buy a guidebook on the way in, as very little is labeled.

Visitor Information Centre

✉ 24 High Street, Windsor
☎ 01753 743900
🕙 Daily including most public holidays; times vary throughout the year

Windsor Castle

☎ 01753 831118 (24 hour) or 01753 868286
🕙 Daily 10–5:30 (last admission 4), Mar.–Oct.; 10–4 (last admission 3) Nov.–Feb. Closed Good Fri., Easter Sun. morning, Dec. 25–26, Service for the Order of the Garter in Jun. St. George's Chapel closed to visitors Sun. Subject to full or partial closure at other times 💷 Expensive (reduced price on days of partial closure)

Eton College

☎ 01753 671177; visits@etoncollege .org.co.uk
🕙 Opening times vary between school terms and holidays
💷 Inexpensive; tours moderate

Legoland Windsor

✉ Winkfield Road
☎ 0990 040404
🕙 10–6 (or dusk if earlier) mid-Mar.–end Oct.; (also daily 6–8 mid-Jul.–early Sep.)
💷 Expensive (2-day tickets available)

Windsor Castle

Windsor Castle looks the part of a castle to perfection – towers, turrets and battlements rise skyward guarded by uniformed soldiers – and possesses a grandeur that far outshines that of Buckingham Palace (➤ 50–51). Britain's largest inhabited castle, Windsor was founded by William the Conqueror in about 1080, when it formed part of the defenses around London. In time it became a royal residence, partly because of the opportunities for hunting afforded by the surrounding countryside. Henry I had quarters in the castle in 1110, and almost 900 years later the sovereign is still resident. Queen Elizabeth II spends most weekends here, as well as much of April and June.

The most notorious episode in the castle's recent history occurred on the night of November 20, 1992, when a fire (probably started by the heat of a spotlight too close to a curtain) destroyed 115 rooms, among them several State Rooms which included St. George's Hall, the Grand Reception Room, the State Dining Room and the Crimson Drawing Room. It burned for 15 hours and needed 2 million gallons of water to extinguish. Restoration took five years and cost over $60 million, most of which was met by the Royal Family with money earned from the annual opening of Buckingham Palace and visitor admissions to the precincts of Windsor Castle.

Left: Windsor Castle is an imposing sight, especially from the Thames

Above: Henry VIII's gate

Areas of the castle open to the public include the State Rooms (all year), Semi-State Rooms (October to March only) and St. George's Chapel (daily, all year except Sundays). All are grand and all are worth seeing, their vast array of treasures embracing fabulous Gobelin tapestries, ornate antique furniture and paintings by artists such as Van Dyck, Rubens, Gainsborough, Dürer, Rembrandt, Reynolds and Canaletto.

Visitors follow a set route, the key highlights of which are as follows:

Queen Mary's Dolls' House is an entire house built on a scale of 1:12. Look especially for the tiny leather-bound books in the library, and the vacuum cleaner, faucets, crockery, kitchen equipment, the miniature works of art on the walls, and a sewing machine that actually works.

The **Grand Staircase** and **Grand Vestibule** provide a magnificent introduction to the State Apartments. Both are lined with statues, firearms, armor and huge cases filled with miscellaneous treasures – among them, in the Grand Vestibule, the bullet that killed Admiral Lord Horatio Nelson at the Battle of Trafalgar in 1805 (currently on display at the National Maritime Museum in Greenwich, ➤ 179).

The opulent **Grand Reception Room** was designed for King George IV, a monarch with a passion for ornate French design, which is why everything from walls and ceiling to furniture and chandeliers is intricately gilded and adorned.

St. George's Hall – superbly restored since the 1992 fire – is the grandest of the castle's rooms. At over 140 feet long, it is impressive for its size alone, but is also remarkable for its decoration – crests, busts and suits of armor – and the wonderful oak hammerbeam roof. Notice the King's Champion mounted on horseback on the balcony at the far end – as fine and dignified a display of armor as you'll see anywhere.

Ten monarchs are buried in **St. George's Chapel**, a beautifully decorated space distinguished, among other things, by its choir stalls, altar and gilded vaulting. It also contains Prince Albert's Memorial Chapel, built in memory of Victoria's beloved husband who died at Windsor in 1861. It's a startling piece of work, laden with statues, Venetian mosaics, inlaid marble panels: Albert himself is depicted in medieval armor, with his favorite dog, Eos, at his feet.

St. George's Chapel, the burial place of 10 British monarchs, including the executed Charles I

Windsor

If you've more time to spend in the area, **Eton College** lies a 15-minute walk across the river from Windsor. One of Britain's oldest private schools, Eton was founded in 1440, and pupils still wear formal dress. Today it is highly prestigious; most pupils come from rich and influential families and go on to assume positions of considerable importance. More than 18 of Britain's prime ministers were educated here. The school yard, oldest classroom, museum and chapel are open to the public, and afternoon guided tours are available.

Legoland Windsor, a theme park just 2 miles from Windsor, is ideally suited to children aged 2–12. It mixes rides and displays with constructions made from the popular Lego bricks, together with live-action shows. A half-hourly shuttle bus operates to Legoland from stops close to Windsor and Eton Central and Riverside train stations (tickets including admission, shuttle bus and rail travel are available from most major train stations in Britain).

Getting there

Windsor is 21 miles (34km) west of London.

Train (☎ 0845 484950) Direct trains to Windsor and Eton Riverside from Waterloo Station, every 30 min. Journey time approximately 55 min.
From Paddington Station to Windsor and Eton Central, changing trains at Slough, every 30 min. Journey time approximately 40 min.
Coach (☎ 020 8668 7261) From Victoria Coach Station, journey time 60–75 min., coaches hourly on Sundays and more frequently during the week. Telephone for times.

Walks & Tours

MAYFAIR SQUARES

Walk

DISTANCE 3 miles **TIME** 2 hours. Allow extra time for window-shopping, refreshment stops and visiting churches
START POINT Piccadilly Circus Underground station **END POINT** Oxford Circus Underground station

Elegant Burlington Arcade, off Piccadilly

Amid the noise and bustle of the surrounding streets, Mayfair (▶ 46–66) is an enclave of luxury and elegance. Originally laid out in the early 18th century by wealthy families such as the Grosvenors and Berkeleys, the area is the most expensive in London and retains evidence of past glories including fine houses, both grand and humble, leafy squares, elegant shopping arcades and the old-fashioned alleyways and cobbles of Shepherd Market.

As you walk, look for commemorative blue plaques that indicate a famous person is associated with the building, and for storefronts carrying royal crests; the companies awarded crests supply a member of the Royal Family – read the small print to find out which one.

1–2

Leave Piccadilly Circus Underground station by the Piccadilly (South Side) exit and walk straight along Piccadilly past St. James's Church, designed by Wren; Princes Arcade, lined with upscale stores, and Hatchards, booksellers since 1797. You'll soon reach the high-class grocery and department store of Fortnum & Mason, which was founded by a footman to Queen Anne in 1707. The store is very plush and exclusive – some of the salesmen even wear tailcoats.

2–3

Cross Piccadilly to Burlington House, an 18th-century mansion, now home to the Royal Academy of Arts (▶ 58). Its neighbor, Burlington Arcade, built in 1819, is the best known of the exclusive shopping

OXFORD STREET

HANOVER SQ

REGENT STREET

PRINCES STREET

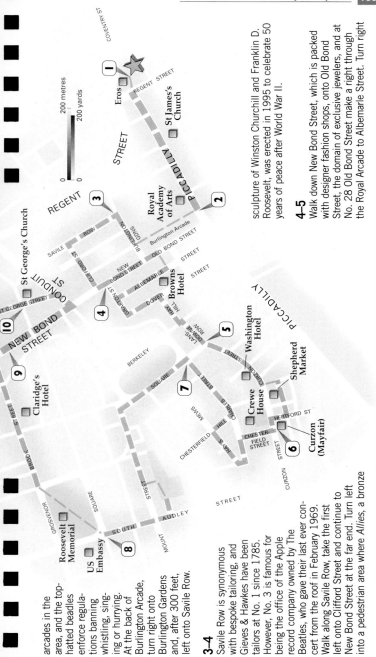

sculpture of Winston Churchill and Franklin D. Roosevelt, was erected in 1995 to celebrate 50 years of peace after World War II.

4–5

Walk down New Bond Street, which is packed with designer fashion shops, onto Old Bond Street, the domain of exclusive jewelers, and at No. 28 Old Bond Street make a right through the Royal Arcade to Albemarle Street. Turn right

arcades in the area, and the top-hatted beadles enforce regulations banning whistling, singing or hurrying. At the back of Burlington Arcade, turn right onto Burlington Gardens and, after 300 feet, left onto Savile Row.

3–4

Savile Row is synonymous with bespoke tailoring, and Gieves & Hawkes have been tailors at No. 1 since 1785. However, No. 3 is famous for being the office of the Apple record company owned by The Beatles, who gave their last ever concert from the roof in February 1969. Walk along Savile Row, take the first left onto Clifford Street and continue to New Bond Street at the far end. Turn left into a pedestrian area where *Allies*, a bronze and you'll see Brown's Hotel on the left: in 1876, Alexander Graham Bell made his first successful telephone call from here. At the top of Albemarle Street turn left onto Grafton Street, follow the road as it turns two corners and then turn right onto Hay Hill. Cross the road at the bottom onto pedestrianized Lansdowne Row and walk through here to Curzon Street.

5–6

Walk straight along Curzon Street and after about 600 feet, opposite the store of G. F. Trumper, Court Hairdresser and Perfumer, make a left through the covered entrance into Shepherd Market. The architect Edward Shepherd built Shepherd Market in 1735 and it

became an infamous red-light district. Today its lanes are filled with outdoor cafés, small shops and restaurants; everything here is on a smaller, older scale than the area around – whether it is still a red-light district is open to dispute.

At Ye Grapes pub, at the far end of the passageway, turn immediately right through a pedestrian area. Cross cobbled Trebeck Street and walk along the right side of Tiddy Dols Restaurant (named after a gingerbread seller in the original market). Turn right up Hertford Street past the Curzon Mayfair Cinema to Curzon Street. Across Curzon Street stands Crewe House (now the Saudi Arabian Embassy), which Shepherd built in 1730 as his own home.

6–7

Turn left onto Curzon Street and then right onto elegant Chesterfield Street, left at the top onto Charles Street, right at the Red Lion pub and right again into Hay's Mews, originally the stables for

Shepherd Market, with narrow streets, stores and pubs

the coach horses of the wealthy, now converted into highly desirable homes. Take the next right onto Chesterfield Hill and at the end turn left, back onto Charles Street. Follow this road to its end at Berkeley Square.

7–8

Berkeley Square, made a household name through the song "A Nightingale Sang in Berkeley Square," was originally laid out in the mid-18th century and retains its attractive, leafy feel. The nightingales are more likely to cough these days, as the traffic roaring along the surrounding streets detracts from the prettiness and pollutes the air. Walk up the left (west) side of the square, which retains the most character.

At the top left (northwest) corner make a left onto Mount Street; after about 600 feet turn left onto peaceful Mount Street Gardens, where there is an entrance to the solemn Church of the Immaculate Conception, well worth a look. Continue to the other side of the gardens and then turn right onto South Audley Street. This leads to Grosvenor Square, one of London's largest squares, with the modern U.S. Embassy to the left – it's certainly assertive, although hardly in keeping with the square's period style. There are statues here to U.S. presidents Roosevelt and Eisenhower.

8–9

Walk diagonally right across the square and
leave from the far (northeast) corner along
Brook Street. Continue straight ahead past
Claridge's (▶ 36), one of London's finest
hotels, which is often patronized by visiting royalty. Famous residents of Brook Street were
composer George Friderich Handel, who lived
and died at No. 25 (plans for a museum on the
site are currently on hold), and guitarist Jimi
Hendrix, who lived next door at No. 23 from
1968 to 1969.

9–10

At the next junction make a right onto New
Bond Street. Along on the left is Sotheby's, the
prestigious auction house – anyone can view the
often fabulous articles waiting to be sold. Take
the next left onto Conduit Street and turn
immediately left onto St. George Street, where
the imposing bulk of St. George's Church is
ahead on the right. Built in the 1720s, it was
the first church in London to have a portico.

10–11

Carry on to the end of St. George Street where
the statue of William Pitt, who became prime
minister at the age of only 24, marks the
entrance to Hanover Square. Take Princes Street

Berkeley Square is a green oasis in an exclusive area

from the top right corner of the square out to
Regent Street. Turn left and it is a short distance to Oxford Circus Underground station.

Taking a Break

Stop at one of the coffee shops or snack
bars on Lansdowne Row or try one of the
outdoor cafés or pubs in Shepherd
Market.

When?

Sunday is a bad time to do this walk
as the stores are closed. Saturday is not a
good day to visit the churches as wed-
dings are often scheduled.

Places to Visit

St. James's Piccadilly
☎ 020 7734 4511 Ⓖ Open to visitors
Mon.–Fri. 10–12:15, 2–5. Telephone for times
and dates of classical concerts

Church of the Immaculate Conception
⊠ Entrances from Farm Street and Mount
Street Gardens ☎ 020 7493 7811 Ⓖ Mon.–Fri.
9–11:30, 1:30–5:30; Sat. 9–10:30pm

St. George's
⊠ Hanover Square ☎ 020 7629 0874
Ⓖ Mon.–Fri. 8:15–3:30

2 THE CITY
Walk

DISTANCE 2 miles **TIME** 2 hours. Allow more time for visits
START POINT Monument Underground station **END POINT** Bank Underground station

The City of London (▲ 67–88), also known as the Square Mile, is a major world financial center bursting with banks, corporations, financial institutions and trading centers. The wheeling and dealing takes place behind closed doors, and security concerns mean that most buildings are closed to the public. However, the streets have a real buzz during the week (they're dead at weekends) and this walk takes in famous buildings, lovely city churches, excellent views and even an art gallery.

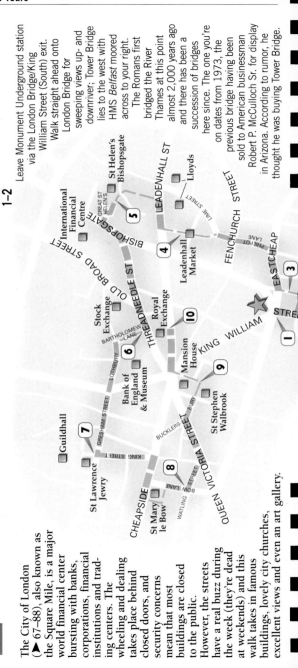

1–2

Leave Monument Underground station via the London Bridge/King William Street (South) exit. Walk straight ahead onto London Bridge for sweeping views up- and downriver; Tower Bridge lies to the west with HMS *Belfast* moored across to your right. The Romans first bridged the River Thames at this point almost 2,000 years ago and there has been a succession of bridges here since. The one you're on dates from 1973, the previous bridge having been sold to American businessman Robert P. McCulloch Sr. for display in Arizona. According to rumor, he thought he was buying Tower Bridge.

3–4

Walk up Fish Hill Street to Eastcheap at the top and turn right; the next road on the right is Pudding Lane, now lined with modern office buildings.

Cross Eastcheap onto Philpot Lane and look ahead for a view of the dramatically modern and highly controversial Lloyd's Building. Designed by Sir Richard Rogers, it houses the Lloyd's insurance market, the world center of insurance for over 200 years since it was founded in the coffee houses of the City. You'll either love or hate the steel-and-glass giant with the entrails of pipes and shafts exposed on the outside – it looks especially dramatic at night. Wits tell how Lloyd's started life in a coffee house and ended up in a percolator.

The Monument recalls the Great Fire

At the end of Philpot Lane, cross Fenchurch Street onto Lime Street and take the first street left, the cobbled Lime Street Passage, which leads into Leadenhall Market (▶ 82).

4–5

Leave the market through Whittington Avenue onto Leadenhall Street and turn right to the foot of the Lloyd's Building. Cross the road and head north across an open square to St. Helen Bishopsgate, one of the few churches to survive the Great Fire. There are 38 churches in the Square Mile; with almost no resident parishioners and not enough weekday worshippers to justify this number of buildings, the threat of closure hangs over many.

5–6

Turn left at the church and along St. Helen's Square to Bishopsgate. Look directly ahead to the International Finance Centre (NatWest Tower). Fifty-two stories high, it is one of the City's most distinctive landmarks.

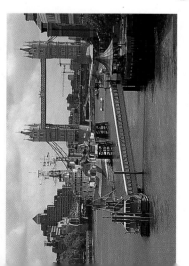

HMS Belfast

Tower Bridge and HMS Belfast

2–3

Walk back toward the Underground station and take the first road to the right, Monument Street, to the Monument. It was built by Sir Christopher Wren, architect of St. Paul's Cathedral, in the 1670s as a memorial to the Great Fire of 1666. It is 203 feet tall – the distance on the ground from its base to the place where the fire started in Pudding Lane – and there are 311 steps up to the viewing platform.

LONDON BRIDGE (2)

Thames

0 200 metres
0 200 yards

Turn left in Bishopsgate and cross at the traffic lights onto Threadneedle Street. At the junction with Old Broad Street a small sign proclaims the London Stock Exchange; electronic dealing has replaced its old trading floor where deals used to be done in person.

Continue along Threadneedle Street and turn right down Bartholomew Lane along one wall of the Bank of England. A visit to the Bank of England Museum (▶ 82) is the only way to get inside the bank.

6–7

Carry on to the end of Bartholomew Lane, where the Lothbury Gallery, a renovated banking hall, faces you. The gallery features changing displays of the NatWest Bank's art collection, mostly contemporary. There are plenty of easy chairs here so it's a great spot to relax.

On leaving the gallery turn right along Lothbury and onto Gresham Street. To your right, behind St. Lawrence Jewry Church, is Guildhall, the symbolic heart of the City. The original 15th-century building has undergone many reconstructions but the main hall remains the highlight,

bedecked with shields and banners and displaying figures of the legendary giants Gog and Magog.

7–8

With your back to Guildhall, cross Gresham Street onto King Street and continue down to Cheapside, where you turn right toward the huge steeple of St. Mary-le-Bow. The church's original Norman crypt still exists, while the spacious elegance of Wren's work is obvious both in the fine lines of the spire and in the elegant arches and vaulted roof of the interior. Traditionally, only those born within the sound of Bow bells can call themselves true Londoners.

Walk through Bow Churchyard next to the church, where there is a statue of Sir John Smith (1580–1631) who was a parishioner here before he became one of the first American colonists. Walk around the back of the church and turn right onto Bow Lane, where you will see Williamson's Tavern on the right. Turn left onto Watling Street; Ye Olde Watling pub, at the bottom, dates from 1666 and Sir Christopher Wren used it as an office while building St. Paul's Cathedral.

8–9

Walk along Watling Street to a large junction and cross onto Queen Victoria Street. Turn right onto Bucklersbury to St. Stephen Walbrook Church, built by Wren between 1672 and 1679; the dome is thought to have been a trial run for that of St. Paul's. The

Guildhall, the symbolic heart of the City, is where Lord Mayors of London are installed

the Royal Exchange, first granted a charter to trade in all kinds of commerce by Queen Elizabeth I in the 16th century, although this particular building dates from 1844. It is now the center of futures trading. The gardens in front are a good place for a rest, and if you stand with your back to the giant statue of the Duke of Wellington you will see a plaque that details the nearby buildings: The Mansion House, official residence of the Lord Mayor of London, is across to the left, and the solid bulk of the Bank of England, surrounded by its windowless walls, is on the right.

The walk ends here – Bank Underground station is nearby.

The Royal Exchange, founded in 1571

telephones on display in the church commemorate the founding in the rector's study, on November 2, 1953, of the first telephone helpline for the despairing, which eventually became the Samaritans organization.

9–10

From the church turn along Walbrook and then right at the end toward the huge, temple-like building at the far side of the junction. This is

Taking a Break

Plenty of coffee shops and snack bars; The Place Below in the Crypt of St. Mary-le-Bow, Williamson's Tavern, Ye Olde Watling pub.

When?

Monday to Friday.

Places to Visit

Monument
✉ Monument Street, EC3 ☎ 020 7626 2717
🕐 Mon.–Fri. 10–5:40; Sat.–Sun. 2–5:40
💷 Inexpensive

St. Helen Bishopsgate
✉ Great St. Helen's, EC3 ☎ 020 7283 2231
🕐 Mon.–Fri. 9–5 via Church Office
💷 Admission free

Bank of England Museum
✉ Bartholomew Lane, EC3 ☎ 020 7601 5545
🕐 Mon.–Fri. 10–5 💷 Admission free

Lothbury Gallery
✉ 41 Lothbury, EC2 ☎ 020 7726 1642/3
🕐 Mon.–Fri. 10–4 (last admission 3:30)
💷 Admission free

St. Mary-le-Bow
✉ Cheapside, EC3 ☎ 020 7248 5139
🕐 Mon.–Thu. 6:30–6, Fri. 6:30–4
💷 Admission free

St. Stephen Walbrook
✉ 39 Walbrook, EC4 ☎ 020 7283 4444
🕐 Mon.–Thu. 9–4, Fri. 9–3
💷 Admission free

3 GREENWICH
Walk

Greenwich, 8 miles down the River Thames from central London, overflows with royal, maritime and astronomical associations – and is known across the globe for Greenwich Mean Time and the Greenwich Meridian where East meets West. Add to that the rolling parkland, superb views and lively crafts market (Fri.–Sun.), and Greenwich begins to look unmissable.

DISTANCE 2 miles **TIME** 2 hours. Allow additional time for visits – you could easily spend a day here **START POINT** Greenwich Pier. Allow an hour from Westminster Pier to Greenwich by boat **END POINT** Greenwich Pier or Island Gardens

The Old Royal Naval College and National Maritime Museum

Launched in 1869, it was the fastest tea clipper of its time, on occasion covering over 360 miles in one day ferrying tea from China and wool from Australia. The exhibitions aboard the ship show what conditions were like for the crew (grim) and officers (not much better), and illustrate the history of the ship.

1–2
From Greenwich Pier walk straight ahead to the stately, tall-masted ship *Cutty Sark*.

public and there is an exhibition of replica Crown Jewels of the world in the undercroft. From the central gates there is a lovely view through the college to Queen's House, the elegant white building behind, and the Old Royal Observatory up on the hill.

There are also excellent views down the river to the Millennium Dome, focus of Britain's year 2000 celebrations, and across the river to the stainless steel and glass bulk of Canary Wharf – at over 800 feet and 50 stories, it is London's, and indeed the U.K.'s tallest building. Continue along the river path to Park Row and the Trafalgar Tavern.

Prince Charles learned seamanship at Greenwich

From *Gipsy Moth IV* walk back past the entrance to Greenwich Pier and east along the footpath beside the river. The Old Royal Naval College (now part of Greenwich University) is on the right, built on the site of the old Greenwich Palace where Henry VIII and his daughter Queen Elizabeth I were born. The college was built by architect Sir Christopher Wren, assisted by Nicholas Hawksmoor and Sir John Vanbrugh, starting in 1696. Generations of sailors, including Prince Charles, learned their trade here until its closure in 1995. The hall and chapel are open to the

The *Cutty Sark* takes its name from the robe worn by a witch in Robert Burns' poem "Tam O'Shanter"

There is also an enthralling display of ships' figureheads.

Nearby, on the riverside, the circular red-brick building with the glass, domed roof is the entrance to the Greenwich Foot Tunnel (▲ 179). The comparatively tiny yacht just beyond is the *Gipsy Moth IV*, in which Sir Francis Chichester completed the first solo voyage around the world in 1966 to 1967, a journey that lasted 226 days.

Map labels:
- Fan Museum
- CROOM'S HILL
- Old Royal Observatory
- Greenwich Park
- General Wolfe's Statue **5**
- BLACKHEATH AVENUE
- Park Café
- Reservoir
- Ranger's House
- **6**

2–3

The Trafalgar Tavern was built in 1837 and frequented by writer Charles Dickens: Sample its fare or turn away from the river and walk along Park Row and cross the main road (Romney Road). There is an entrance to the National Maritime Museum and Queen's House on the right.

The National Maritime Museum is a treasure trove of naval instruments, charts, models,

paintings, memorabilia and a royal barge. The history of seafaring is comprehensively and well illustrated in state-of-the-art exhibits and inter-active displays, including the exploratory as well as the military. One whole gallery is devoted to Admiral Lord Horatio Nelson. Exit back into Park Row and enter Greenwich Park.

3–4

Follow the first path in front of the Queen's House until you can turn right, then take the second path to the left which climbs steeply up One Tree Hill. Queen Elizabeth I often came here to enjoy the fine view, a custom commem-orated in verse on the benches.

4–5

From One Tree Hill either follow the paths or cut across the grass toward the Old Royal Observatory, the regal red-brick-and-white build-ing with the green dome on the next hill. You'll arrive at the statue of General James Wolfe; he was a local man who, in 1759, commanded the British army during the capture of Quebec, in which he was killed. There's another good view of London from here: Look for St. Paul's Cathedral, with the distinctive black bulk of the International Finance Centre (NatWest Tower) close to it.

The Old Royal Observatory was built by Sir Christopher Wren under orders from King Charles II. Astronomers now study the skies away from the blazing lights of London, but the exhibits illustrate the history of astronomy and the problems of measuring position and time. You can straddle the Prime Meridian, which links the North and South poles, and is where the eastern and western hemispheres meet, at 0° longitude.

5–6

With your back to General Wolfe, walk along Blackheath Road (usually lined with parked cars), with the Park Café on the left. At the small traffic circle turn right onto a path that follows a line of trees to a gate in the park wall. Turn left along the gravel drive to Crooms Hill.

If you want to visit the 17th-century Ranger's House, it is a 650-foot detour to the left. It has a large gallery and houses a collection of Jacobean portraits.

6–7

As you walk down the hill, admire the 17th- and 18th-century houses. Toward the bottom of Crooms Hill, you will find the Fan Museum, the only one of its kind in the world, located in two 18th-century houses. Founded in 1989 by

The Old Royal Observatory at Greenwich was founded by Charles II in 1675

Helen Alexander, whose personal collection of more than 2,000 fans is the basis of the exhibition, the museum displays stunning examples of the fanmaker's craft.

7–8

From the Fan Museum continue straight to the bottom of Croom's Hill, then walk ahead onto Stockwell Street; the Village Market is on the right, and make a right onto Greenwich Church Street with the Fountain Food Court on the bend. Continue along Greenwich Church Street and cross Nelson Road. The entrance to the main craft market, offering a varied selection of goods, is through a small alleyway to the right.

Return to Greenwich Church Street, turn right, cross College Approach, and after 300 feet you'll be back at the *Cutty Sark*.

8–9

Instead of returning to central London by boat, an alternative is to take the Docklands Light Railway (DLR) (▶ 34). Walk under the River Thames by the Greenwich Foot Tunnel, opened in 1902, to Island Gardens, where there's a good view of Greenwich, and catch the DLR from there; much of the rail journey back to the center takes you through the futuristic landscape of Docklands.

Taking a Break

Trafalgar Tavern, fast food in the Fountain Food Court, the Orangery of the Fan Museum and restaurants in Greenwich Church Street.

When?

Saturday or Sunday when the markets are open.

Places to Visit

Cutty Sark

🖂 King William Walk, SE10 ☎ 020 8858 3445
🕐 Daily 10–5. Closed Dec. 24–26
💷 Inexpensive

Old Royal Naval College

🖂 Entrance from King William Walk, SE10
☎ 020 8858 2154; information line: 020 8312 6565
🕐 Painted hall and chapel daily 10–5
💷 Admission free

National Maritime Museum and Old Royal Observatory

🖂 Greenwich Park, SE10
☎ 020 8858 4422
🕐 Daily 10–5 (last admission 4:30); closed Dec. 24–26
💷 Combined admission moderate

Ranger's House

🖂 Chesterfield Walk, Greenwich Park, SE10
☎ 020 8853 0035
🕐 Daily 10–6, Apr.–Oct.; Wed.–Sun. 10–1, 2–4, Nov.–Mar.; closed Dec. 24–26
💷 Inexpensive

Fan Museum

🖂 12 Crooms Hill, SE10
☎ 020 8305 1441
🕐 Tue.–Sat. 11–5, Sun. noon–5
💷 Inexpensive

4 HAMPSTEAD
Walk

DISTANCE 3.5 miles
TIME 3 hours. Allow more for refreshment stops and visiting the houses
START POINT Golders Green Underground station **END POINT** Hampstead Underground station

This walk through the charming village of Hampstead and across Hampstead Heath, 4 miles to the north of central London, offers some of the most rural scenery in the capital, a spectacular view from Parliament Hill, historic houses and delightful lanes. Hampstead has been a popular residential area, particularly with writers and artists, since the 18th century when visitors flocked to drink the restorative spa waters; famous inhabitants have included artist John Constable, poet John Keats, writers Ian Fleming and Agatha Christie, and actors Peter O'Toole, Elizabeth Taylor and Emma Thompson.

1–2

Catch the number 210 bus from outside Golders Green Underground station to Kenwood House – ask the driver to tell you where to alight. On the way look for two historic pubs: Jack Straw's Castle was built in 1962, but there has been an inn on the site for over 500 years, and Spaniard's Inn, associated with the highwayman Dick Turpin and literary figures Dickens, Keats, Shelley and Byron.

There are two entrances to Kenwood House a few hundred feet after Spaniard's Inn on the right – West Lodge and East Lodge; both lead to the house.

2–3

Kenwood House dates from the 18th century and is famed for the work of the Scottish architect Robert Adam. The highlight of the interior is the fabulously ornate library and the Iveagh Bequest art collection, which includes a Rembrandt self-portrait, the *Guitar Player* by Vermeer and works by J. M. W. Turner, Joshua Reynolds and

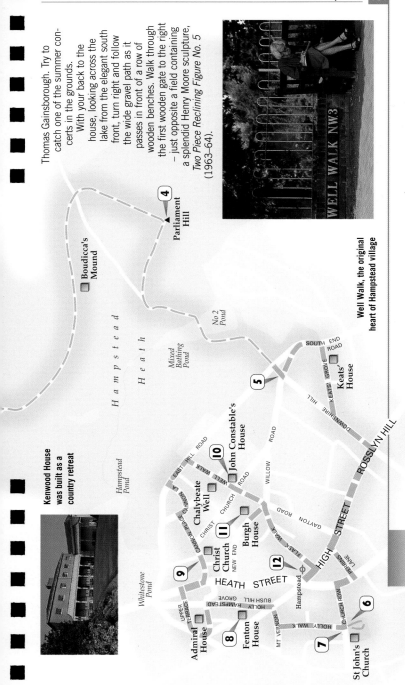

Thomas Gainsborough. Try to catch one of the summer concerts in the grounds.

With your back to the house, looking across the lake from the elegant south front, turn right and follow the wide gravel path as it passes in front of a row of wooden benches. Walk through the first wooden gate to the right – just opposite a field containing a splendid Henry Moore sculpture, *Two Piece Reclining Figure No. 5* (1963–64).

Kenwood House was built as a country retreat

Well Walk, the original heart of Hampstead village

Boudicca's Mound

H a m p s t e a d   H e a t h

▲ **4 Parliament Hill**

No 2 Pond

Mixed Bathing Pond

Hampstead Pond

Whitestone Pond

5

Keats' House

SOUTH END ROAD

KEATS GROVE

DOWNSHIRE HILL

EAST HILL ROAD

WELL WALK

10 John Constable's House

CHURCH ROAD

WILLOW ROAD

ROSSLYN HILL

Chalybeate Well

CANNON PLACE

CHRIST

11 Christ Church

NEW END

Burgh House

GAYTON ROAD

FLASK WALK

Hampstead ◆

12

HEATH STREET

HIGH STREET

PERRINS LANE

9 Admiral House

UPPER TERRACE

8 Fenton House

HAMPSTEAD GROVE

BUSH HILL

HOLLY HILL

HOLLY WALK

MT VERNON

CHURCH ROW

7

6 St John's Church

poet John Keats (1795–1821) lived for two years, wrote some of his best-known work and fell in love with the girl next door. The house contains many of his possessions and manuscripts.

Continue along Keats' Grove and turn left onto Downshire Hill and then right onto Rosslyn Hill. Turn left just after the King William IV pub onto Perrins Lane, right at the end onto Heath Street and then take the first turning left onto elegant Church Row.

6–7

At the far end of Church Row enter the left gate of St. John's Church and turn immediately left along the rough path. At the bottom of the churchyard on the left, behind a small iron fence, is the grave of the landscape artist John Constable (1776–1837), a noted Hampstead resident, his wife and their eldest son.

Walk up to the church, which has a pleasantly proportioned interior, fine stained glass and, at the front to the right of the choir, a memorial to John Keats.

7–8

Leave the church and, with your back to the church door, turn left and cross the churchyard. Now cross the road onto Holly Walk to start the stretch of the walk through the back lanes of

From Parliament Hill, there are superb, panoramic views of the capital

Follow the path straight through the next intersection of paths, then take the next path to your right and you'll spot Parliament Hill directly ahead, bare of trees and with benches on the skyline.

4–5

On Parliament Hill look for the plaque identifying the London landmarks laid out below. Facing the plaque, turn right and walk straight along the path that leads you between two of the many ponds on the Heath; the Mixed Bathing Pond is on the right and Hampstead Number Two pond on the left. Follow the path left along the side of Hampstead Number Two pond and out to the main road, East Heath Road.

5–6

Cross East Heath Road at the pedestrian crossing and walk left down East Heath Road. Take the third turning right onto Keats' Grove, with Keats' House along on the left. This is where the

3–4

Take the gravel path to the left and stay on it as another path joins from the right. After less than a quarter mile you'll pass through an iron gate. Fork left and descend through the trees to a large gravel area where you continue straight across. At the next intersection, marked by a wooden post, go straight across and after160 feet, at the next intersection, again marked by a wooden post, make a left. You'll descend gradually and to the right will see Boudicca's Mound, planted with trees and enclosed by a fence. Boudicca, Queen of the Iceni tribe, led her people against the Romans in the 1st century AD, slaughtering 70,000 of the enemy before her defeat. Legend claims this as her burial place.

Hampstead village. On the right, the row of quaint cottages in Benhams Place dates from 1813. At the end of Holly Walk turn right onto Mount Vernon, follow the path to the left of the last house and take the lower path to the left as it swings around to the left onto Holly Bush Hill. At the top of Holly Bush Hill, the black-and-gold gates across the grass belong to Fenton House, one of the oldest and grandest Hampstead houses, with a large collection of early musical instruments.

8–9

Walk along the right side of Fenton House onto Hampstead Grove and turn left onto Admiral's Walk. Along on the right, the startling Admiral's House was turned into a facsimile of a ship by a former owner – who also used to fire cannons to commemorate naval victories. Continue along Admiral's Walk to Lower Terrace, turn right and then right again onto Upper Terrace, and head straight across a small crossroads to the main road (Heath Street). Turn right and take the first left, a small lane, onto Hampstead Square.

9–10

Walk straight across the top of the square, with Christ Church Hampstead on the right, continuing straight into Cannon Place. At the end of

the road turn right down the hill, left onto Cannon's Lane and you'll reach East Heath Road. Turn right and take the second road on the right, Well Walk.

10–11

To your right is the now-defunct Chalybeate Well, where the spring water, rich in iron salts, was discovered in the 18th century. Just opposite the well is 40 Well Walk, one of the Hampstead homes of John Constable. Cross

Christchurch Hill and at the end turn right into New End Square, where you will see historic Burgh House on the right. Built in 1703, it now houses the local history museum and art gallery.

11–12

From Burgh House head back down New End Square and take the first turning right onto Flask Walk. This leads up to Hampstead High Street, where a right turn leads the short way to Hampstead Underground station.

Taking a Break

The Brew House at Kenwood House, numerous coffee shops on Rosslyn Hill, the Buttery in Burgh House.

When?

Weekends are the best time to see kite-flying on Parliament Hill, but the stores are shut on Sunday.

Places to Visit

Kenwood House

🏠 Hampstead Lane, NW3 ☎ 020 8348 1286
🕐 Daily 10–6, Apr.–Sep.; 10–5 Oct.; 10–4 Nov.–Mar.; closed Dec. 24–25 💷 Admission free

Keats' House

🏠 Keats' Grove, NW3 ☎ 020 7435 2062
🕐 Mon.–Fri. 10–1, 2–6, Sat. 10–1, 2–5, Sun. 2–5, Apr.–Oct.; Mon.–Fri. 1–5, Sat. 10–1, 2–5, Sun. 2–5 Nov.–Mar. 💷 Admission free

Fenton House

🏠 20 Hampstead Grove, NW3 ☎ 020 7435 3471
🕐 Wed.–Fri. 2–5:30, Sat.–Sun. and public holidays 11–5:30, Apr.–Oct.; Sat.–Sun. 2–5, Mar. 💷 Inexpensive

Burgh House

🏠 New End Square, NW3 ☎ 020 7431 0144
🕐 Wed.–Sun. noon–5 (closed some Sats.), public holidays 2–5 💷 Admission free

5 No. 15 Bus Trip

From Marble Arch to the Tower of London

This bus trip takes in many of the major London sights including Marble Arch, Piccadilly Circus, Trafalgar Square and St. Paul's Cathedral, plus well-known thoroughfares – Oxford Street, Regent Street, Haymarket and the Strand. Sit upstairs on the bus and as close to the front as possible for the best views.

TIME 1 hour depending on traffic
START POINT Marble Arch Underground station
END POINT Tower Hill Underground station

BUS STOP		
Towards Oxford Circus		
Marble Arch		
6	12	15
23	94	159
N3	N6	N12
N15		N16 N23	N16 N98

1–2

Leave Marble Arch Underground station by Subway 1, Marble Arch and Oxford Street North.

Look across to the right to the huge marble edifice on the vast traffic island in the middle of the one-way system – this is the Marble Arch that gives the area its name. Built for the forecourt of Buckingham Palace, it was moved to its current site in 1851 because it was too narrow for the state coach to pass through.

Turn left out of the subway and catch the No. 15 bus at the second stop you come to, stop L. Ask for the Tower of London.

Hop on the bus at Marble Arch

The bus goes along Oxford Street, one of London's most-visited shopping streets, lined with department stores. Much of Oxford Street is now shabby, but look for the grand frontage of Selfridges on the left. The store was built by an American, Gordon Selfridge, early in the 20th century and certainly rivals Harrods for contents, if not fame and exclusivity.

2–3

At Oxford Circus the bus turns right onto Regent Street, and a different world architecturally. Grand and unified, it is one remnant of the Nash Sweep, a processional route running from St. James's Park, through Trafalgar Square to Regent's Park,

MARBLE ARCH ① ⊖ Marble Arch

Marble Arch ★

OXFORD STREET

NEW BOND ST

REGENT STREET

② OXFORD CIRCUS / REGENT ST

GREAT MARLBOROUGH STREET

4–5

As the bus continues along Duncannon Street, look toward the Charing Cross train station forecourt with its highly ornate reproduction of an Eleanor Cross. In 1290, King Edward I built 12 crosses along the funeral route of his wife, Eleanor of Castile, from Nottinghamshire to Westminster Abbey, each cross marking the spot where her body rested on the 12-day journey.

The bus passes along the Strand, which was once famed for its music halls and theaters, and arches around Aldwych, rejoining the Strand at St. Clement Danes church in the center of the road with the Royal Courts of Justice on the left. In the center of the road, the griffin statue marks the boundary of the City of London – the sovereign stops here on ceremonial occasions to ask the permission of the Lord Mayor of London to enter the City.

Left: Regent Street; Below: the Law Courts

with the fountain and Eros to the right (▶ 60).

3–4

The bus turns right down Haymarket, named for the market which sold hay for the royal horses stabled in the area until 1830, and then left across the north side of Trafalgar Square. The National Gallery is on the left, Nelson on his column on the right and the fine spire of St. Martin-in-the-Fields rises ahead (▶ 53).

PICCADILLY CIRCUS
Trocadero Centre
REGENT ST
PALL MALL
HAYMARKET
Eros ③
LEICESTER SQUARE
National Gallery ④
ST MARTIN'S LANE
TRAFALGAR SQUARE
DUN CANNON ST
Charing Cross Station
Victoria Embankment Gardens
STRAND
STRAND
ALDWYCH
KINGSWAY
St Clement Danes
Royal Courts of Justice ⑤
FLEET STREET
Inns of Court and Chancery
St Bride's Church ⑥
LUDGATE CIRCUS

Thames

0 ——— 200 metres
0 ——— 200 yards

designed by architect John Nash (1752–1835). Most distinctive of the stores is Liberty's department store – look along Great Marlborough Street for the black-and-white mock Tudor entrance of this lovely emporium (▶ 65).

At the end of Regent Street neon advertisements announce arrival at Piccadilly Circus,

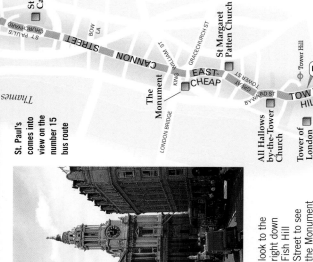

5–6

The road now becomes Fleet Street, which was once the publishing center for the British national press, although the newspapers have now moved to modern premises in Docklands. On the left is Ye Olde Cheshire Cheese pub, dating from the mid-17th century. Dr. Samuel Johnson, compiler of the first English dictionary, was a regular customer here, and it became popular with later authors, including Dickens, Thackeray and Mark Twain. Look out on the right for the white spire of St. Bride's Church, one of Sir Christopher Wren's most distinctive creations – it is said that soon after it was built a baker copied the design for a tiered wedding cake and a tradition was born.

6–7

The bus crosses Ludgate Circus onto Ludgate Hill, heading straight toward the dramatic West Front of St. Paul's Cathedral, then it passes to the right of the cathedral, onto Cannon Street. Look to the left for the International Finance Centre (NatWest Tower) and a few hundred feet later, just after Monument Underground station, look to the right down Fish Hill Street to see the Monument (▶ 173). The bus then heads along Eastcheap,

past All Hallows church, with its distinctive green roof, and along Great Tower Street to the solid fortress of the Tower of London on the right. The bus stops just outside the Tower Hill Memorial, which was built to honor the 24,000 men in the merchant navy and fishing fleets who lost their lives in World War I with "no grave but the sea."

Either cross the road and return to the start at Marble Arch on the number 15 bus or follow the signs to Tower Hill Underground station, a few feet away.

St. Paul's comes into view on the number 15 bus route

St Paul's Cathedral

The Monument

St Margaret Patten Church

EASTCHEAP

All Hallows by-the-Tower Church

Tower of London

TOWER HILL

 Tower Hill (7)

0   200 metres
0   200 yards

When?

Any time, but avoid rush hours (8–9:30 a.m., 4:30–6 p.m. weekdays).

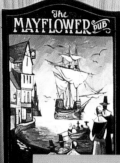

Practicalities

GETTING ADVANCE INFORMATION

Websites
- British Tourist Authority
  www.visitbritain.com/
  england
- U.K. Travel Guide
  www.uktravel.com
- London Tourist Board
  www.LondonTown.com
- London Travel Service
  www.bridge-travel.co.uk

In the U.K.
London Tourist Board
Glen House
Stag Place
London SW1E 5LT
☎ (020) 7932 2000

BEFORE YOU GO

WHAT YOU NEED

- Required
- ○ Suggested
- ▲ Not required

	U.K.	Germany	U.S.A.	Canada	Australia	Ireland	Netherlands	Spain
Passport/National Identity Card	▲	●	●	●	●	▲	●	●
Visa	▲	▲	▲	▲	▲	▲	▲	▲
Onward or Return Ticket	▲	○	○	○	○	○	○	○
Health Inoculations (tetanus and polio)	▲	▲	▲	▲	▲	▲	▲	▲
Health Documentation (➤ 192, Health)	▲	●	●	●	●	●	●	●
Travel Insurance	○	○	○	○	○	○	○	○
Driver's License (national)	●	●	●	●	●	●	●	●
Car Insurance Certificate	▲	●	n/a	n/a	n/a	●	●	●
Car Registration Document	▲	●	n/a	n/a	n/a	●	●	●

WHEN TO GO

[ ] High season   [ ] Low season

JAN	FEB	MAR	APR	MAY	JUN	JUL	AUG	SEP	OCT	NOV	DEC
43°F	43°F	46°F	50°F	55°F	61°F	66°F	66°F	61°F	55°F	48°F	45°F

☀ Sun   ☀ Sun/Showers   ☁ Wet   ☁ Very wet

The chart above shows **average daily** temperatures for each month.
London experiences defined seasons. **Spring** (March to May) has a mixture of
sunshine and showers, although winter often encroaches on it. **Summer** (June to
August) can be unpredictable; clear skies and searing heat one day followed by
sultry grayness and thunderstorms the next. **Fall** begins in September, but clear
skies can give a summery feel. Real fall starts in October and the colder weather
sets in during November. **Winter** (December to February) is generally mild and
snow is rare, but expect the occasional "cold snap."
Be prepared for the **unpredictability** of the British climate – dress in layers and
carry rainwear or an umbrella.

In the U.S.A.	In Australia	In Canada
British Tourist Authority	British Tourist Authority	British Tourist Authority
7th Floor	Level 16	5915 Airport Road
551 Fifth Avenue	Gateway 1	Suite 120
New York	Macquarie Place	Mississauga
NY 10176-0799	Sydney NSW 2000	Ontario L4V 1T1
☎ 212/986 2200	☎ (02) 9377 4400	☎ (905) 405 1840

GETTING THERE

By Air London has two main **airports**, Heathrow and Gatwick. Heathrow handles all major airline scheduled flights, while Gatwick handles worldwide scheduled and charter flights. In addition, there are smaller airports at Luton, Stansted and London City (Docklands), handling mainly European charter and business flights.

There are **direct flights** to London from most European, U.S and Canadian cities. Flights from Australia and New Zealand stop en route in either Asia or the U.S.

Approximate **flying times** to London: Dublin (1¼ hours), New York (7½ hours), Los Angeles (11 hours), Vancouver (10 hours), Montréal (7 hours), Toronto (7 hours), east coast of Australia (22 hours), New Zealand (24 hours).

Ticket prices are lower from November to April, excluding Easter and Christmas. Check with the airlines, travel agents, flight brokers, travel sections in newspapers, and the Internet for current special offers. Make reservations well in advance for discounted APEX fares or wait on standby for last-minute cut-price deals.

All **airport taxes** are usually included in the price of a ticket.

By Train An alternative option for travelers from Europe is the train. The Channel Tunnel offers a direct link between London and Paris or Brussels for foot passengers aboard "Eurostar" trains (tel: (0990) 186186), while the car-carrying train "Le Shuttle" (tel: (0990) 353535) operates between Calais (France) and Folkestone (England).

By Ferry Passenger and car ferries operate from Ireland, France, Belgium, Netherlands, Germany, Scandinavia and Spain.

TIME

London is on Greenwich Mean Time (GMT) in winter, but from late March until late October British Summer Time (BST, i.e. GMT+1) operates.

CURRENCY AND FOREIGN EXCHANGE

Currency Britain's currency is the pound (£) sterling. There are 100 pennies or pence (p) to each pound. **Notes** are issued in denominations of £5, £10, £20 and £50. **Coins** come in denominations of 1p, 2p, 5p, 10p, 20p, 50p, £1 and £2. An unlimited amount of British currency can be imported or exported.

Sterling **travelers' checks** are the most convenient way to carry money. They may be accepted as payment by some hotels, restaurants and large department stores.

Credit cards (MasterCard, Visa and American Express) are widely accepted.

Exchange You can exchange foreign currency and travelers' checks at banks and bureaux de change. There are exchange facilities at larger travel agents, in large department stores and hotels, at most main post offices or at bureaux de change on the street. Be sure to check the rate of exchange and the commission charged before any transaction as they do vary. It is possible to obtain local currency through automated cash machines (ATMs) using a debit or credit card. ATMs are found inside or outside most banks. Your bank will provide details of where your cards will be accepted in London.

TIME DIFFERENCES

GMT	London	U.S.A. (NY)	U.S.A. (West Coast)	Sydney	Germany
12 noon	12 noon	← 7 A.M.	← 4 A.M.	→ 10 P.M.	→ 1 P.M.

WHEN YOU ARE THERE

CLOTHING SIZES

Australia/U.K.	Rest of Europe	U.S.A.	
36	46	36	
38	48	38	
40	50	40	
42	52	42	Suits
44	54	44	
46	56	46	
7	41	8	
7.5	42	8.5	
8.5	43	9.5	
9.5	44	10.5	Shoes
10.5	45	11.5	
11	46	12	
14.5	37	14.5	
15	38	15	
15.5	39/40	15.5	
16	41	16	Shirts
16.5	42	16.5	
17	43	17	
8	34	6	
10	36	8	
12	38	10	
14	40	12	Dresses
16	42	14	
18	44	16	
4.5	38	6	
5	38	6.5	
5.5	39	7	
6	39	7.5	Shoes
6.5	40	8	
7	41	8.5	

NATIONAL HOLIDAYS

Jan. 1	New Year's Day
Mar./Apr.	Good Friday
Mar./Apr.	Easter Monday
First Mon. May	May Day Holiday
Last Mon. May	Spring Bank Holiday
Last Mon. Aug.	Late Summer Bank Holiday
Dec. 25	Christmas Day
Dec. 26	Boxing Day

Almost all attractions close on Christmas Day. On other holidays some attractions open, often with reduced hours. There are no general rules regarding the opening times of restaurants and stores, so check before making a special journey. Bear in mind that public transportation services are likely to be less frequent on public holidays.

OPENING HOURS

○ Stores   ● Post Offices
● Offices   ● Museums/Monuments
● Banks   ● Pharmacies

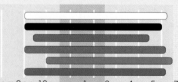

8 a.m. 9 a.m. 10 a.m. noon 1 p.m. 2 p.m. 4 p.m. 5 p.m. 7 p.m.

☐ Day   ▨ Midday   ☐ Evening

Stores Many stores in central London open for longer hours and also on Sunday.
Banks Many banks are also open Saturday morning and bureaux de change are open daily until late.
Museums Smaller museums may close one day or more a week.
Pharmacies When pharmacies are closed a sign in the window gives details of the nearest one that operates extended hours or is on 24-hour duty.

POLICE 999

FIRE 999

AMBULANCE 999

PERSONAL SAFETY

London is generally a safe city and police officers are often seen on the beat (walking the streets) in the central areas. They are usually friendly and approachable. To help prevent crime:

● Do not carry more cash than you need.

● Do not leave a bag unattended in public places.

● Beware of pickpockets in markets, on the Underground, in tourist sites or crowded places.

● Avoid walking alone in parks or dark alleys at night.

Police assistance:
 999 from any phone

ELECTRICITY

The power supply in Britain is 230/240 volts.
Sockets accept only three- (square)-pin plugs, so an adaptor is needed for continental European and U.S appliances. A transformer is also needed for appliances operating on 110–120 volts.

TELEPHONES

£1 coins (10p is the minimum charge), but card-operated phones are often more convenient. British Telecom phonecards are available from post offices and many stores. Hotel phones are expensive. To call the operator dial 100.

The traditional red phone booths are now rare; instead kiosks come in a wide variety of different designs and colors. Coin-operated phones take 10p, 20p, 50p and

International Dialing Codes
Dial 00 followed by

Ireland:	353
U.S.A.:	1
Canada:	1
Australia:	61
New Zealand:	64
Germany:	49
Netherlands:	31
Spain:	34

MAIL

Post offices are open Mon.–Fri. 9–5:30, Sat. 9–1. The only exception is Trafalgar Square Post Office, 24–28 William IV Street, open Mon.–Fri. 8–8, Sat. 9–8. Poste restante mail may also be collected here.

TIPS/GRATUITIES

Yes ✓   No ✗

Restaurants (if service not included)	✓	10%
Bar service	✗	
Tour guides	✓	$2–$3
Hairdressers	✓	10%
Taxis	✓	10%
Chambermaids	✓	$1–$1.50 per day
Porters	✓	$1–$1.50 depending on number of bags
Usherettes	✗	

EMBASSIES AND CONSULATES

U.S.A
020 7499 9000

Ireland
020 7235 2171

Australia
020 7379 4334

Canada
020 7258 6600

New Zealand
020 7930 8422

HEALTH

Insurance
Nationals of E.U. countries, Australia and New Zealand can get free or reduced-cost medical treatment in Britain with Form E111 (EU nationals) or a passport. Medical insurance is still advised, and is essential for all other visitors.

Dental Services
Visitors qualifying for free or reduced-cost medical treatment (see Insurance above) are entitled to concessionary dental treatment, providing the treatment is by a National Health dentist. Private medical insurance is still recommended, and is essential for all other visitors.

Weather
The sun can shine a lot in July and August. Some sights involve being outdoors for prolonged periods when you should "cover up," apply sunscreen and drink plenty of water.

Drugs
Prescription and nonprescription drugs are available from druggists (chemists). Pharmacists can advise on medication for common ailments. Drug stores operate a rota so there will always be one open; notices in all drug store windows give details.

Safe Water
Tap water is safe to drink. Mineral water is widely available but is often expensive.

CONCESSIONS

Students Holders of an International Student Identity Card may obtain concessions on travel, entrance fees and some goods and services. Check the National Union of Students' website (www.nus.org.uk).
Senior Citizens Senior citizens (usually over 60) will find discounts on travel, entrance fees and some events and shows. Proof of age may be required.
GoSee, The White Card This is a pass to 15 of the capital's top museums and galleries, including the V&A, the Science Museum and the Natural History Museum. It is valid for three or seven days and can be bought in some stores and tourist information centers.

TRAVELING WITH A DISABILITY

Provision is generally good for visitors with disabilities. Many of the capital's sights have access for wheelchair users but transportation can be a problem; not all Underground stations have elevators and ramps. Most public houses are not adapted for wheelchairs. The London Tourist Board's *London For All* details facilities and access for people with special needs.

CHILDREN

London offers a great deal of child-centered entertainment. Details of activities are given in *Kids Out* magazine.
Baby-changing facilities are available in most family-oriented attractions.
Under 16s pay half fare on public transportation, while under 5s travel free.

RESTROOMS

The cleanest restrooms are usually found in department stores, hotels and restaurants.

LOST PROPERTY

Airports
Heathrow ☎ 020 8745 7727
Gatwick ☎ (01293) 503162
Trains ☎ 020 7928 5151
Underground/buses ☎ 020 7486 2496
Taxis ☎ 020 7833 0996

Picture Credits

Acknowledgments

Streetplan

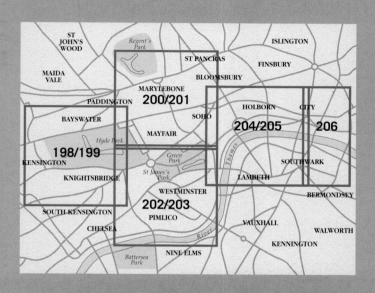

ST JOHN'S WOOD
Regent's Park
ISLINGTON
ST PANCRAS
FINSBURY
MAIDA VALE
BLOOMSBURY
MARYLEBONE
200/201
PADDINGTON
HOLBORN
CITY
BAYSWATER
SOHO
204/205
206
MAYFAIR
Hyde Park
198/199
Green Park
KENSINGTON
SOUTHWARK
St James's Park
KNIGHTSBRIDGE
LAMBETH
Thames
WESTMINSTER
BERMONDSEY
SOUTH KENSINGTON
202/203
PIMLICO
CHELSEA
VAUXHALL
WALWORTH
River
KENNINGTON
Battersea Park
NINE ELMS

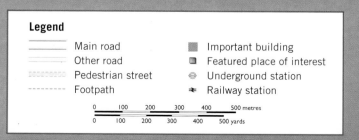

Legend

——— Main road
——— Other road
▒▒▒▒ Pedestrian street
- - - - Footpath

▨ Important building
▢ Featured place of interest
⊜ Underground station
⇌ Railway station

0   100   200   300   400   500 metres
0   100   200   300   400   500 yards

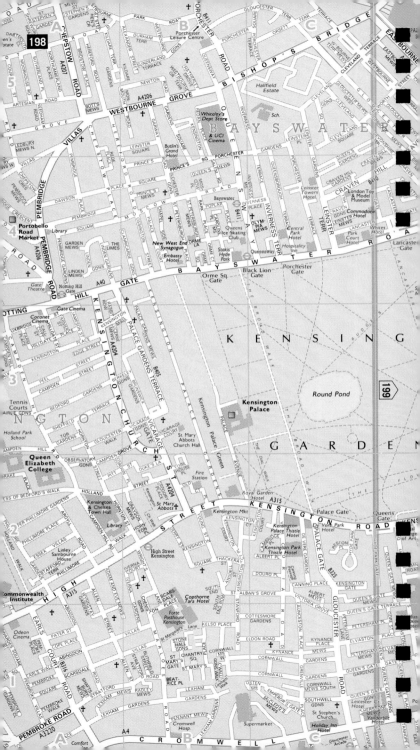

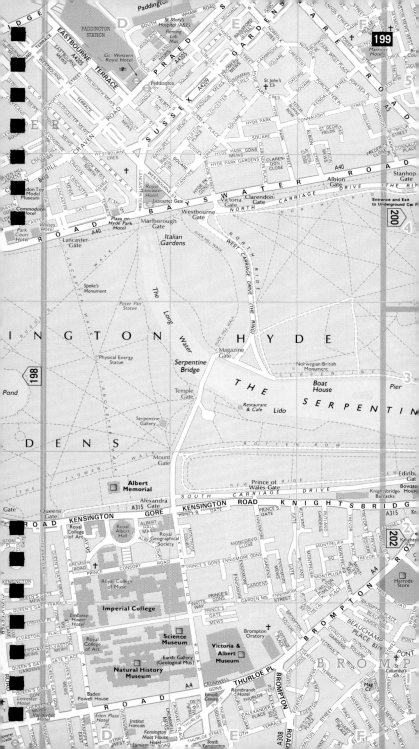

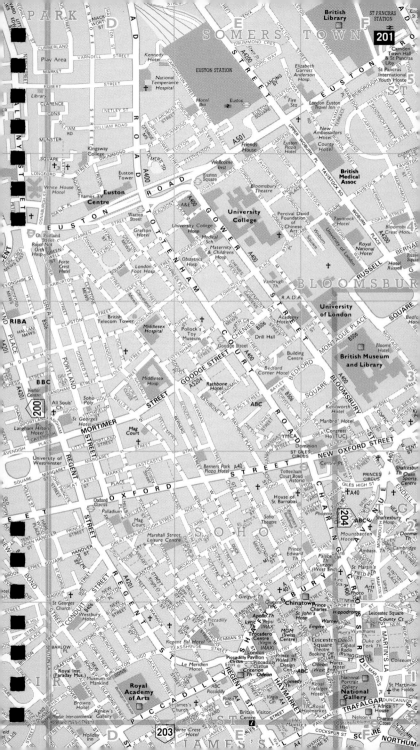

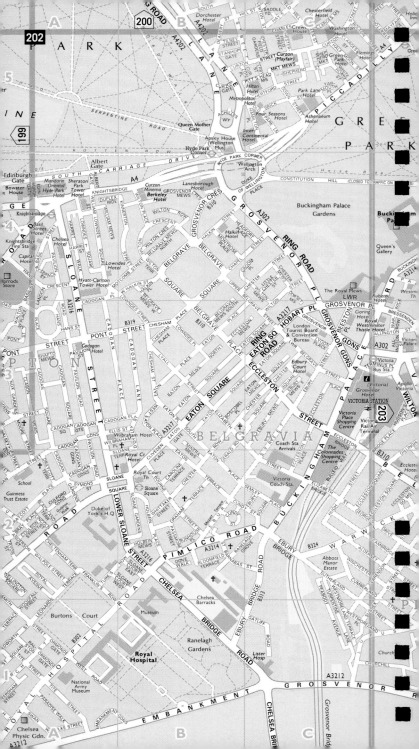

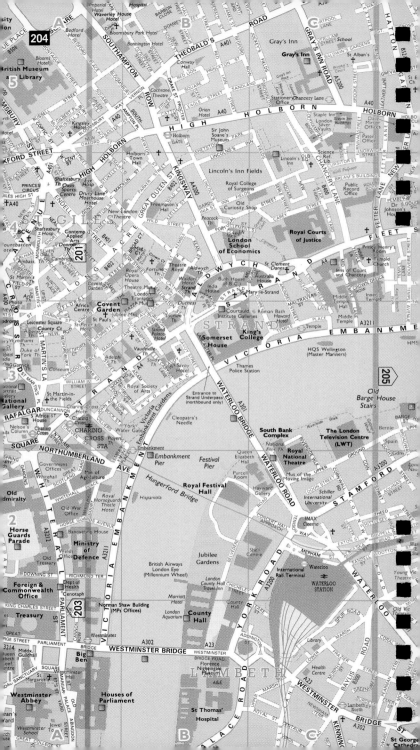

SPIRAL GUIDES

Questionnaire

Dear Traveler

Your comments, opinions and recommendations are very important to us. So please help us to improve our travel guides by taking a few minutes to complete this simple questionnaire.

Send to: Spiral Guides, MailStop 66, 1000 AAA Drive, Heathrow, FL 32746–5063

Your recommendations...

We always encourage readers' recommendations for restaurants, nightlife or shopping – if your recommendation is added to the next edition of the guide, we will send you a FREE AAA Spiral Guide of your choice. Please state below the establishment name, location and your reasons for recommending it.

_____

_____

_____

_____

_____

Please send me AAA Spiral_____

(see list of titles inside the back cover)

About this guide...

Which title did you buy?

_____ **AAA Spiral**

Where did you buy it? _____

When? mm/ y y

Why did you choose a AAA Spiral Guide? _____

_____

_____

_____

Did this guide meet your expectations?

Exceeded ☐ Met all ☐ Met most ☐ Fell below ☐

Please give your reasons _____

_____

_____

_____

continued on next page...

Were there any aspects of this guide that you particularly liked?

Is there anything we could have done better?

About you...

Name (Mr/Mrs/Ms) ______

Address ______

______ Zip ______

Daytime tel nos. ______

Which age group are you in?

Under 25 ☐ 25–34 ☐ 35–44 ☐ 45–54 ☐ 55–64 ☐ 65+ ☐

How many trips do you make a year?

Less than one ☐ One ☐ Two ☐ Three or more ☐

Are you a AAA member? Yes ☐ No ☐

Name of AAA club ______

About your trip...

When did you book? m m / y y When did you travel? m m / y y

How long did you stay? ______

Was it for business or leisure? ______

Did you buy any other travel guides for your trip? ☐ Yes ☐ No

If yes, which ones? ______

Thank you for taking the time to complete this questionnaire.

All information is for AAA internal use only and will NOT be distributed outside the organization to any third parties.

HOUGHTON MIFFLIN HARCOURT

Literacy and Language Guide

Consultants
Irene C. Fountas
Shane Templeton

Grade K

Printed in the U.S.A.

ISBN   978-0-547-86645-1

6 7 8 9 10   0914   21 20 19 18 17 16 15 14 13

4500401503   A B C D E F G

HOUGHTON MIFFLIN HARCOURT
School Publishers

Literacy and Language Guide
Table of Contents

- Introduction
- Spelling/Phonics Lessons
- Oral Vocabulary Development Lessons

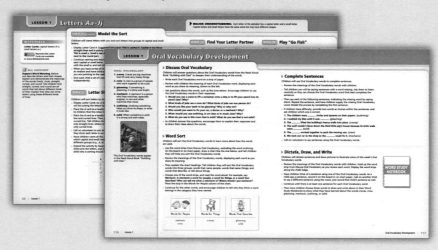

- Whole-Group Lessons
- Teaching Genre

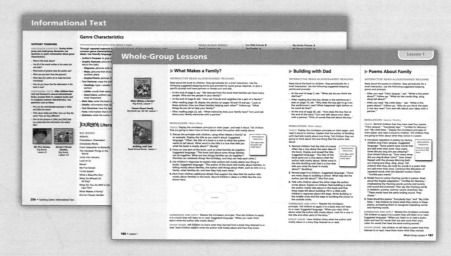

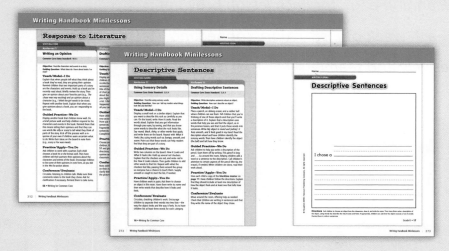

- **Linguistic Transfer Support**
- **Qualitative Spelling Inventory**
- **Comprehensive Word List**
- **Leveled Readers Database**
- **Literature Discussion**
- **Bibliography**

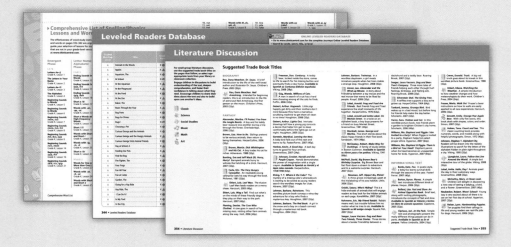

Literacy and Language Guide
Overview

In this Guide, you will find weekly lesson plans for Word Study, Reading, and Writing. A Planning page for each lesson provides a clear pathway through each week of instruction, connecting the parts of the plan cohesively and seamlessly.

INSTRUCTIONAL FOCUS
Each week's instructional focus at a glance—literature selections, comprehension skills, word work, and writing

READING SELECTIONS
Reading selections for the week from the *Journeys* Big Book and Read Aloud Book

WORD STUDY
Spelling/Phonics and Oral Vocabulary Development lessons for the week

WRITING
Writing minilessons connect to *Journeys* instruction and provide children with additional handbook resources for writing practice during the week

GUIDED READING
Options for small-group teaching also appear in the complete Leveled Readers Database in the Resources section of this Guide

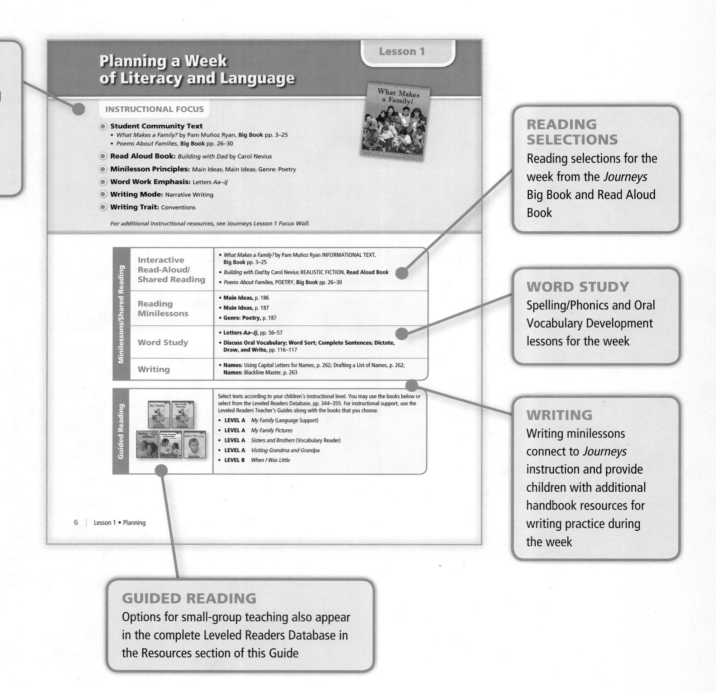

Lesson 1

Planning a Week of Literacy and Language

INSTRUCTIONAL FOCUS

- **Student Community Text**
  - *What Makes a Family?* by Pam Muñoz Ryan, **Big Book** pp. 3–25
  - *Poems About Families*, **Big Book** pp. 26–30
- **Read Aloud Book:** *Building with Dad* by Carol Nevius
- **Minilesson Principles:** Main Ideas; Main Ideas; Genre: Poetry
- **Word Work Emphasis:** Letters *Aa–Jj*
- **Writing Mode:** Narrative Writing
- **Writing Trait:** Conventions

For additional instructional resources, see Journeys Lesson 1 Focus Wall.

Minilessons/Shared Reading		
Interactive Read-Aloud/ Shared Reading	• *What Makes a Family?* by Pam Muñoz Ryan INFORMATIONAL TEXT, **Big Book** pp. 3–25 • *Building with Dad* by Carol Nevius REALISTIC FICTION, **Read Aloud Book** • *Poems About Families*, POETRY, **Big Book** pp. 26–30	
Reading Minilessons	• **Main Ideas**, p. 186 • **Main Ideas**, p. 187 • **Genre: Poetry**, p. 187	
Word Study	• **Letters *Aa–Jj***, pp. 56–57 • **Discuss Oral Vocabulary; Word Sort; Complete Sentences; Dictate, Draw, and Write**, pp. 116–117	
Writing	• **Names:** Using Capital Letters for Names, p. 262; Drafting a List of Names, p. 262; **Names:** Blackline Master, p. 263	

Guided Reading

Select texts according to your children's instructional level. You may use the books below or select from the Leveled Readers Database, pp. 344–355. For instructional support, use the Leveled Readers Teacher's Guides along with the books that you choose.

- **LEVEL A**   *My Family* (Language Support)
- **LEVEL A**   *My Family Pictures*
- **LEVEL A**   *Sisters and Brothers* (Vocabulary Reader)
- **LEVEL A**   *Visiting Grandma and Grandpa*
- **LEVEL B**   *When I Was Little*

6 | Lesson 1 • Planning

Table of Contents

Instructional Focus and Planning

Planning a Week of Literacy and Language

INSTRUCTIONAL FOCUS

- **Student Community Text**
  - *What Makes a Family?* by Pam Muñoz Ryan, **Big Book** pp. 3–25
  - *Poems About Families*, **Big Book** pp. 26–30
- **Read Aloud Book:** *Building with Dad* by Carol Nevius
- **Minilesson Principles:** Main Ideas; Main Ideas; Genre: Poetry
- **Word Work Emphasis:** Letters *Aa–Jj*
- **Writing Mode:** Narrative Writing
- **Writing Trait:** Conventions

For additional instructional resources, see Journeys *Lesson 1 Focus Wall.*

Minilessons/Shared Reading

Interactive Read-Aloud/ Shared Reading	• *What Makes a Family?* by Pam Muñoz Ryan INFORMATIONAL TEXT, **Big Book** pp. 3–25 • *Building with Dad* by Carol Nevius REALISTIC FICTION, **Read Aloud Book** • *Poems About Families*, POETRY, **Big Book** pp. 26–30
Reading Minilessons	• **Main Ideas,** p. 186 • **Main Ideas,** p. 187 • **Genre: Poetry,** p. 187
Word Study	• **Letters *Aa–Jj*,** pp. 56–57 • **Discuss Oral Vocabulary; Word Sort; Complete Sentences; Dictate, Draw, and Write,** pp. 116–117
Writing	• **Names:** Using Capital Letters for Names, p. 262; Drafting a List of Names, p. 262; **Names:** Blackline Master, p. 263

Guided Reading

Select texts according to your children's instructional level. You may use the books below or select from the Leveled Readers Database, pp. 344–355. For instructional support, use the Leveled Readers Teacher's Guides along with the books that you choose.

- **LEVEL A** *My Family* (Language Support)
- **LEVEL A** *My Family Pictures*
- **LEVEL A** *Sisters and Brothers* (Vocabulary Reader)
- **LEVEL A** *Visiting Grandma and Grandpa*
- **LEVEL B** *When I Was Little*

Planning a Week of Literacy and Language

INSTRUCTIONAL FOCUS

◉ **Student Community Text**
- *How Do Dinosaurs Go to School?* by Jane Yolen, **Big Book** pp. 2–30
- "My School Bus" by Stephen Schaffer, **Big Book** pp. 31–38

◉ **Read Aloud Book:** *Friends at School* by Rochelle Bunnett

◉ **Minilesson Principles:** Understanding Characters; Main Ideas; Genre: Informational Text

◉ **Word Work Emphasis:** The Letters in Your Name

◉ **Writing Mode:** Narrative Writing

◉ **Writing Trait:** Word Choice

For additional instructional resources, see Journeys Lesson 2 Focus Wall.

Minilessons/Shared Reading		
Interactive Read-Aloud/ Shared Reading	• *How Do Dinosaurs Go to School?* by Jane Yolen FANTASY, **Big Book** pp. 2–30 • *Friends at School* by Rochelle Bunnett INFORMATIONAL TEXT, **Read Aloud Book** • "My School Bus" by Stephen Schaffer INFORMATIONAL TEXT, **Big Book** pp. 31–38	
Reading Minilessons	• **Understanding Characters,** p. 188 • **Main Ideas,** p. 189 • **Genre: Informational Text,** p. 189	
Word Study	• **The Letters in Your Name,** pp. 58–59 • **Discuss Oral Vocabulary; Paired Yes/No Questions; Guess the Word; Dictate, Draw, and Write,** pp. 118–119	
Writing	• **Labels:** Describing a Picture, p. 264; Drafting Labels, p. 264; **Labels:** Blackline Master, p. 265	

Guided Reading

Select texts according to your children's instructional level. You may use the books below or select from the Leveled Readers Database, pp. 344–355. For instructional support, use the Leveled Readers Teacher's Guides along with the books that you choose.

- **LEVEL A** *At School* (Vocabulary Reader)
- **LEVEL A** *My Backpack*
- **LEVEL A** *Show and Tell*
- **LEVEL A** *Tell All About It* (Language Support)
- **LEVEL D** *Helping Mr. Horse*

Planning a Week of Literacy and Language

INSTRUCTIONAL FOCUS

- **Student Community Text**
  - *Please, Puppy, Please* by Spike Lee and Tonya Lewis Lee, **Big Book** pp. 2–30
  - "Different Kinds of Dogs" by Linda Ruggieri, **Big Book** pp. 31–38

- **Read Aloud Book:** *I Have a Pet!* by Shari Halpern

- **Minilesson Principles:** Story Structure; Story Structure; Main Ideas

- **Word Work Emphasis:** Letters *Aa–Tt*

- **Writing Mode:** Narrative Writing

- **Writing Trait:** Ideas

For additional instructional resources, see Journeys Lesson 3 Focus Wall.

Minilessons/Shared Reading		
Interactive Read-Aloud/ Shared Reading	• *Please, Puppy, Please* by Spike Lee and Tonya Lewis Lee REALISTIC FICTION, **Big Book** pp. 2–30 • *I Have a Pet!* by Shari Halpern REALISTIC FICTION, **Read Aloud Book** • "Different Kinds of Dogs" by Linda Ruggieri INFORMATIONAL TEXT, **Big Book** pp. 31–38	
Reading Minilessons	• **Story Structure,** p. 190 • **Story Structure,** p. 191 • **Main Ideas,** p. 191	
Word Study	• **Letters *Aa–Tt*,** pp. 60–61 • **Discuss Oral Vocabulary; This or That; "Because" Sentences; Dictate, Draw, and Write,** pp. 120–121	
Writing	• **Captions:** Telling About a Picture, p. 266; Drafting Captions, p. 266; **Captions:** Blackline Master, p. 267	

Guided Reading

Select texts according to your children's instructional level. You may use the books below or select from the Leveled Readers Database, pp. 344–355. For instructional support, use the Leveled Readers Teacher's Guides along with the books that you choose.

- **LEVEL A** *My Cat*
- **LEVEL A** *My Dog*
- **LEVEL A** *My Pet Cat* (Language Support)
- **LEVEL A** *The Puppy* (Vocabulary Reader)
- **LEVEL D** *Lola, the Muddy Dog*

Planning a Week of Literacy and Language

INSTRUCTIONAL FOCUS

- **Student Community Text**
  - *Everybody Works* by Shelley Rotner and Ken Kreisler, **Big Book** pp. 2–30
  - *Traditional Tales,* **Big Book** pp. 31–38

- **Read Aloud Book:** *Pizza at Sally's* by Monica Wellington

- **Minilesson Principles:** Genre: Informational Text; Text and Graphic Features; Genre: Traditional Tales

- **Word Work Emphasis:** The Alphabet

- **Writing Mode:** Narrative Writing

- **Writing Trait:** Ideas

For additional instructional resources, see Journeys Lesson 4 Focus Wall.

Minilessons/Shared Reading		
	Interactive Read-Aloud/ Shared Reading	• *Everybody Works* by Shelley Rotner and Ken Kreisler INFORMATIONAL TEXT, **Big Book** pp. 2–30 • *Pizza at Sally's* by Monica Wellington REALISTIC FICTION, **Read Aloud Book** • *Traditional Tales,* **Big Book** pp. 31–38
	Reading Minilessons	• **Genre: Informational Text,** p. 192 • **Text and Graphic Features,** p. 193 • **Genre: Traditional Tales,** p. 193
	Word Study	• **The Alphabet,** pp. 62–63 • **Discuss Oral Vocabulary; Riddles; Word Sort; Dictate, Draw, and Write,** pp. 122–123
	Writing	• **Story Sentences:** Choosing Events to Describe, p. 268; Drafting Story Sentences, p. 268; **Story Sentences:** Blackline Master, p. 269

Guided Reading	
	Select texts according to your children's instructional level. You may use the books below or select from the Leveled Readers Database, pp. 344–355. For instructional support, use the Leveled Readers Teacher's Guides along with the books that you choose. • **LEVEL A** *The Fire Fighter* • **LEVEL A** *Let's Sell Things!* (Language Support) • **LEVEL A** *Our Jobs* (Vocabulary Reader) • **LEVEL A** *Selling Things* • **LEVEL D** *Jobs on the Farm*

Planning a Week of Literacy and Language

INSTRUCTIONAL FOCUS

◉ **Student Community Text**
- *The Handiest Things in the World* by Andrew Clements, **Big Book** pp. 2–39
- "Stone Soup," **Big Book** pp. 40–44

◉ **Read Aloud Book:** *The Little Red Hen* Retold by Heather Forest

◉ **Minilesson Principles:** Details; Details; Genre: Folktales

◉ **Word Work Emphasis:** Beginning Sounds in Words

◉ **Writing Mode:** Narrative Writing

◉ **Writing Trait:** Ideas

For additional instructional resources, see Journeys Lesson 5 Focus Wall.

Minilessons/Shared Reading		
Interactive Read-Aloud/ Shared Reading	• *The Handiest Things in the World* by Andrew Clements INFORMATIONAL TEXT, **Big Book** pp. 2–39 • *The Little Red Hen* Retold by Heather Forest FOLKTALE AND FABLE, **Read Aloud Book** • "Stone Soup" TRADITIONAL TALE/FOLKTALE, **Big Book** pp. 40–44	
Reading Minilessons	• **Details,** p. 194 • **Details,** p. 195 • **Genre: Folktales,** p. 195	
Word Study	• **Beginning Sounds in Words,** pp. 64–65 • **Discuss Oral Vocabulary; True or Not True; Secret Word Game; Dictate, Draw, and Write,** pp. 124–125	
Writing	• **Class Story:** Telling a Story in Words and Pictures, p. 270; Drafting a Class Story, p. 270; **Class Story:** Blackline Master, p. 271	

Guided Reading

Select texts according to your children's instructional level. You may use the books below or select from the Leveled Readers Database, pp. 344–355. For instructional support, use the Leveled Readers Teacher's Guides along with the books that you choose.

- **LEVEL A** *At the Playground*
- **LEVEL A** *I Can Do It!*
- **LEVEL A** *Make a Kite* (Vocabulary Reader)
- **LEVEL A** *The Playground* (Language Support)
- **LEVEL B** *Fun with Friends*

Planning a Week of Literacy and Language

INSTRUCTIONAL FOCUS

- **Student Community Text**
  - *My Five Senses* by Aliki, **Big Book** pp. 2–31
  - *Poems About Senses,* **Big Book** pp. 32–38

- **Read Aloud Book:** *Listen, Listen* by Phillis Gershator

- **Minilesson Principles:** Text and Graphic Features; Compare and Contrast; Genre: Poetry

- **Word Work Emphasis:** Beginning Sounds in Words

- **Writing Mode:** Informative Writing

- **Writing Trait:** Word Choice

For additional instructional resources, see Journeys Lesson 6 Focus Wall.

Minilessons/Shared Reading		
Interactive Read-Aloud/ Shared Reading	• *My Five Senses* by Aliki INFORMATIONAL TEXT, **Big Book** pp. 2–31 • *Listen, Listen* by Phillis Gershator INFORMATIONAL TEXT, **Read Aloud Book** • *Poems About Senses,* POETRY, **Big Book** pp. 32–38	
Reading Minilessons	• **Text and Graphic Features,** p. 196 • **Compare and Contrast,** p. 197 • **Genre: Poetry,** p. 197	
Word Study	• **Beginning Sounds in Words,** pp. 66–67 • **Discuss Oral Vocabulary; Word Associations; Describe It; Dictate, Draw, and Write,** pp. 126–127	
Writing	• **Descriptive Sentences:** Using Sensory Details, p. 272; Drafting Descriptive Sentences, p. 272; **Descriptive Sentences:** Blackline Master, p. 273	

Guided Reading

Select texts according to your children's instructional level. You may use the books below or select from the Leveled Readers Database, pp. 344–355. For instructional support, use the Leveled Readers Teacher's Guides along with the books that you choose.

- **LEVEL A** *Choosing a Pet* (Language Support)
- **LEVEL A** *Look at Me!* (Vocabulary Reader)
- **LEVEL A** *The Market*
- **LEVEL A** *My Pet*
- **LEVEL B** *My House*

Planning a Week of Literacy and Language

For additional instructional resources, see Journeys Lesson 7 Focus Wall.

INSTRUCTIONAL FOCUS

○ **Student Community Text**
- *Mice Squeak, We Speak* by Tomie dePaola, **Big Book** pp. 2–31
- "The Fort Worth Zoo," **Big Book** pp. 32–38

○ **Read Aloud Book:** *Amelia's Show-and-Tell Fiesta* by Mimi Chapra

○ **Minilesson Principles:** Compare and Contrast; Understanding Characters; Genre: Informational Text

○ **Word Work Emphasis:** Beginning Sounds /m/m, /s/s

○ **Writing Mode:** Informative Writing

○ **Writing Trait:** Word Choice

Minilessons/Shared Reading	**Interactive Read-Aloud/ Shared Reading**	• *Mice Squeak, We Speak* by Tomie dePaola REALISTIC FICTION, **Big Book** pp. 2–31 • *Amelia's Show-and-Tell Fiesta* by Mimi Chapra REALISTIC FICTION, **Read Aloud Book** • "The Fort Worth Zoo," INFORMATIONAL TEXT, **Big Book** pp. 32–38
	Reading Minilessons	• **Compare and Contrast,** p. 198 • **Understanding Characters,** p. 199 • **Genre: Informational Text,** p. 199
	Word Study	• **Beginning Sounds /m/m, /s/s,** pp. 68–69 • **Discuss Oral Vocabulary; Paired Yes/No Questions; Complete Sentences; Dictate, Draw, and Write,** pp. 128–129
	Writing	• **Descriptive Sentences:** Showing Information in a Drawing, p. 274; Drafting Descriptive Sentences, p. 274; **Descriptive Sentences:** Blackline Master, p. 275

Guided Reading

Select texts according to your children's instructional level. You may use the books below or select from the Leveled Readers Database, pp. 344–355. For instructional support, use the Leveled Readers Teacher's Guides along with the books that you choose.

- **LEVEL A** *At the Zoo*
- **LEVEL A** *On the Farm* (Vocabulary Reader)
- **LEVEL A** *Visiting the Zoo* (Language Support)
- **LEVEL A** *A Walk in the Woods*
- **LEVEL C** *Winter Sleep*

Planning a Week of Literacy and Language

INSTRUCTIONAL FOCUS

◉ **Student Community Text**
- *Move!* by Steve Jenkins and Robin Page, **Big Book** pp. 2–31
- "The Hare and the Tortoise" retold by Rob Greco, **Big Book** pp. 32–38

◉ **Read Aloud Book:** *Jonathan and His Mommy* by Irene Smalls

◉ **Minilesson Principles:** Details; Details; Understanding Characters

◉ **Word Work Emphasis:** Beginning Sounds /m/*m*, /s/*s*, /t/*t*

◉ **Writing Mode:** Informative Writing

◉ **Writing Trait:** Word Choice

For additional instructional resources, see Journeys *Lesson 8 Focus Wall.*

Minilessons/Shared Reading	**Interactive Read-Aloud/ Shared Reading**	• *Move!* by Steve Jenkins and Robin Page INFORMATIONAL TEXT, **Big Book** pp. 2–31 • *Jonathan and His Mommy* by Irene Smalls REALISTIC FICTION, **Read Aloud Book** • "The Hare and the Tortoise" retold by Rob Greco FOLK TALE AND FABLE, **Big Book** pp. 32–38
	Reading Minilessons	• **Details,** p. 200 • **Details,** p. 201 • **Understanding Characters,** p. 201
	Word Study	• **Beginning Sounds /m/*m*, /s/*s*, /t/*t*,** pp. 70–71 • **Discuss Oral Vocabulary; This or That; Describe It or Act It Out; Dictate, Draw, and Write,** pp. 130–131
	Writing	• **Captions:** Using Words for Colors and Shapes, p. 276; Drafting Caption Sentences, p. 276; **Captions:** Blackline Master, p. 277

Guided Reading		Select texts according to your children's instructional level. You may use the books below or select from the Leveled Readers Database, pp. 344–355. For instructional support, use the Leveled Readers Teacher's Guides along with the books that you choose. • **LEVEL A** *The Aquarium* (Language Support) • **LEVEL A** *At the Aquarium* • **LEVEL A** *Let's Climb!* • **LEVEL B** *In the Rainforest* • **LEVEL B** *Visiting a Park* (Vocabulary Reader)

Planning a Week of Literacy and Language

INSTRUCTIONAL FOCUS

◉ **Student Community Text**
 • *What Do Wheels Do All Day?* by April Jones Prince, **Big Book** *pp.* 3–32
 • "Wheels Long Ago and Today," **Big Book** pp. 33–38

◉ **Read Aloud Book:** *Good Morning, Digger* by Anne Rockwell

◉ **Minilesson Principles:** Text and Graphic Features; Text and Graphic Features; Compare and Contrast

◉ **Word Work Emphasis:** Beginning Sounds /t/t, /k/c, /p/p

◉ **Writing Mode:** Informative Writing

◉ **Writing Trait:** Word Choice

For additional instructional resources, see **Journeys** *Lesson 9 Focus Wall.*

Minilessons/Shared Reading		
Interactive Read-Aloud/ Shared Reading	• *What Do Wheels Do All Day?* by April Jones Prince INFORMATIONAL TEXT, **Big Book** pp. 3–32 • *Good Morning, Digger* by Anne Rockwell, REALISTIC FICTION, **Read Aloud Book** • "Wheels Long Ago and Today," INFORMATIONAL TEXT, **Big Book,** pp. 33–38
Reading Minilessons	• **Text and Graphic Features,** p. 202 • **Text and Graphic Features,** p. 203 • **Compare and Contrast,** p. 203
Word Study	• **Beginning Sounds /t/t, /k/c, /p/p,** pp. 72–73 • **Discuss Oral Vocabulary; Guess the Word; Word Sort; Dictate, Draw, and Write,** pp. 132–133
Writing	• **Description:** Choosing Descriptive Words, p. 278; Revising a Description with Number Words, p. 278; **Description:** Blackline Master, p. 279

Guided Reading	
	Select texts according to your children's instructional level. You may use the books below or select from the Leveled Readers Database, pp. 344–355. For instructional support, use the Leveled Readers Teacher's Guides along with the books that you choose. • **LEVEL A** *Going for a Hay Ride* (Language Support) • **LEVEL A** *The Hay Ride* • **LEVEL A** *In the City* • **LEVEL A** *My Bike* (Vocabulary Reader) • **LEVEL D** *Going Fast*

Planning a Week of Literacy and Language

Mouse Shapes

Ellen Stoll Walsh

INSTRUCTIONAL FOCUS

◉ **Student Community Text**
  • *Mouse Shapes* by Ellen Stoll Walsh, **Big Book** pp. 2–30
  • "Signs and Shapes," **Big Book** pp. 31–38

◉ **Read Aloud Book:** *David's Drawings* by Cathryn Falwell

◉ **Minilesson Principles:** Story Structure; Story Structure; Text and Graphic Features

◉ **Word Work Emphasis:** Ending Sounds in Words

◉ **Writing Mode:** Informative Writing

◉ **Writing Trait:** Word Choice

For additional instructional resources, see Journeys *Lesson 10 Focus Wall.*

Minilessons/Shared Reading		
	Interactive Read-Aloud/ Shared Reading	• *Mouse Shapes* by Ellen Stoll Walsh, FICTION, **Big Book** pp. 2–30 • *David's Drawings* by Cathryn Falwell REALISTIC FICTION, **Read Aloud Book** • "Signs and Shapes," INFORMATIONAL TEXT, **Big Book** pp. 31–38
	Reading Minilessons	• **Story Structure,** p. 204 • **Story Structure,** p. 205 • **Text and Graphic Features,** p. 205
	Word Study	• **Ending Sounds in Words,** pp. 74–75 • **Discuss Oral Vocabulary; True or Not True; "Because" Sentences; Dictate, Draw, and Write,** pp. 134–135
	Writing	• **Description:** Using Peer Feedback to Revise, p. 280; Revising a Description with Size and Shape Words, p. 280; **Description:** Blackline Master, p. 281

Guided Reading

Select texts according to your children's instructional level. You may use the books below or select from the Leveled Readers Database, pp. 344–355. For instructional support, use the Leveled Readers Teacher's Guides along with the books that you choose.

• **LEVEL A** *It's a Party!*
• **LEVEL A** *Making a Tree House* (Language Support)
• **LEVEL A** *The Tree House*
• **LEVEL B** *Our Classroom* (Vocabulary Reader)
• **LEVEL C** *A Hat for Cat*

Planning a Week of Literacy and Language

INSTRUCTIONAL FOCUS

○ **Student Community Text**
 • *Jump Into January* by Stella Blackstone **Big Book** pp. 2–25
 • "Holidays All Year Long" by Roy Grindall **Big Book** pp. 26–30

○ **Read Aloud Book:** *Every Season* by Shelley Rotner and Anne Love Woodhull

○ **Minilesson Principles:** Compare and Contrast; Compare and Contrast; Genre: Informational Text

○ **Word Work Emphasis:** Ending Sounds /s/s, /p/p, /t/t

○ **Writing Mode:** Narrative Writing

○ **Writing Trait:** Word Choice

For additional instructional resources, see Journeys Lesson 11 Focus Wall.

Minilessons/Shared Reading		
Interactive Read-Aloud/ Shared Reading	• *Jump Into January* by Stella Blackstone INFORMATIONAL TEXT, **Big Book,** pp. 2–25 • *Every Season* by Shelley Rotner and Anne Love Woodhull INFORMATIONAL TEXT, **Read Aloud Book** • "Holidays All Year Long" by Roy Grindall INFORMATIONAL TEXT, **Big Book,** pp. 26–30	
Reading Minilessons	• **Compare and Contrast,** p. 206 • **Compare and Contrast,** p. 207 • **Genre: Informational Text,** p. 207	
Word Study	• **Ending Sounds /s/s, /p/p, /t/t,** pp. 76–77 • **Discuss Oral Vocabulary; Describe It; This or That; Dictate, Draw, and Write,** pp. 136–137	
Writing	• **Story Sentences:** Writing a Great Beginning, p. 282; Drafting Story Sentences, p. 282; **Story Sentences:** Blackline Master, p. 283	

Guided Reading

Select texts according to your children's instructional level. You may use the books below or select from the Leveled Readers Database, pp. 344–355. For instructional support, use the Leveled Readers Teacher's Guides along with the books that you choose.

 • **LEVEL A** *Fun All Year*
 • **LEVEL A** *October Days*
 • **LEVEL A** *A Year of Fun* (Language Support)
 • **LEVEL B** *Fun in July* (Vocabulary Reader)
 • **LEVEL C** *June Vacation*

Planning a Week of Literacy and Language

INSTRUCTIONAL FOCUS

- ⦿ **Student Community Text**
  - *Snow* by Manya Stojic, **Big Book** pp. 2–30
  - "How Water Changes," **Big Book** pp. 31–38

- ⦿ **Read Aloud Book:** *Storm Is Coming!* by Heather Tekavec

- ⦿ **Minilesson Principles:** Conclusions; Conclusions; Genre: Informational Text

- ⦿ **Word Work Emphasis:** Short *a* /ă/

- ⦿ **Writing Mode:** Narrative Writing

- ⦿ **Writing Trait:** Word Choice

For additional instructional resources, see Journeys Lesson 12 Focus Wall.

Minilessons/Shared Reading		
Interactive Read-Aloud/ Shared Reading	• *Snow* by Manya Stojic FANTASY, **Big Book** pp. 2–30 • *Storm Is Coming!* by Heather Tekavec FANTASY, **Read Aloud Book** • "How Water Changes" INFORMATIONAL TEXT, **Big Book** pp. 31–38	
Reading Minilessons	• **Conclusions,** p. 208 • **Conclusions,** p. 209 • **Genre: Informational Text,** p. 209	
Word Study	• **Short *a* /ă/,** pp. 78–79 • **Discuss Oral Vocabulary; Guess the Word; Describe It or Act It Out; Dictate, Draw, and Write,** pp. 138–139	
Writing	• **Story Sentences:** Reacting to Events, p. 284; Drafting Story Sentences, p. 284; **Story Sentences:** Blackline Master, p. 285	

Guided Reading

Select texts according to your children's instructional level. You may use the books below or select from the Leveled Readers Database, pp. 344–355. For instructional support, use the Leveled Readers Teacher's Guides along with the books that you choose.

- **LEVEL A** *Bears Through the Year*
- **LEVEL A** *Look at the Bears* (Language Support)
- **LEVEL A** *Winter Vacation*
- **LEVEL B** *Animals in the Snow* (Vocabulary Reader)
- **LEVEL D** *No Snow!*

Planning a Week of Literacy and Language

INSTRUCTIONAL FOCUS

● **Student Community Text**
- *What Do You Do With a Tail Like This?* by Steve Jenkins and Robin Page, **Big Book** pp. 2–31
- *Poems About Animals* **Big Book** pp. 32–37

● **Read Aloud Book:** *A Zebra's World* by Caroline Arnold

● **Minilesson Principles:** Author's Purpose; Author's Purpose; Genre: Poetry

● **Word Work Emphasis:** Words with *-an, -ap, -at*

● **Writing Mode:** Narrative Writing

● **Writing Trait:** Ideas

For additional instructional resources, see Journeys **Lesson 13 Focus Wall.**

Minilessons/Shared Reading		
Interactive Read-Aloud/ Shared Reading	• *What Do You Do With a Tail Like This?* by Steve Jenkins and Robin Page INFORMATIONAL TEXT, **Big Book** pp. 2–31 • *A Zebra's World* by Caroline Arnold INFORMATIONAL TEXT, **Read Aloud Book** • *Poems About Animals* POETRY, **Big Book** pp. 32–37	
Reading Minilessons	• **Author's Purpose**, p. 210 • **Author's Purpose**, p. 211 • **Genre: Poetry**, p. 211	
Word Study	• **Words with *-an, -ap, -at*,** pp. 80–81 • **Discuss Oral Vocabulary; Secret Word Game; Complete Sentences; Dictate, Draw, and Write,** pp. 140–141	
Writing	• **Story Sentences:** Writing a Strong Ending, p. 286; Drafting Story Sentences, p. 286; **Story Sentences:** Blackline Master, p. 287	

Guided Reading	
	Select texts according to your children's instructional level. You may use the books below or select from the Leveled Readers Database, pp. 344–355. For instructional support, use the Leveled Readers Teacher's Guides along with the books that you choose. • **LEVEL A** *Lots of Flowers* (Language Support) • **LEVEL A** *My Flower Garden* • **LEVEL A** *The Pet Show* • **LEVEL B** *Lots of Birds* (Vocabulary Reader) • **LEVEL D** *In the Desert*

Planning a Week of Literacy and Language

INSTRUCTIONAL FOCUS

- **Student Community Text**
  - *Turtle Splash!* by Cathryn Falwell **Big Book** pp. 2–29
  - "Where Animals Live" by Anne Rogers **Big Book** pp. 30–38

- **Read Aloud Book:** *Home for a Tiger, Home for a Bear* by Brenda Williams and Rosamund Fowler

- **Minilesson Principles:** Cause and Effect; Details; Main Ideas

- **Word Work Emphasis:** Beginning Sounds /n/n, /m/m

- **Writing Mode:** Narrative Writing

- **Writing Trait:** Organization

For additional instructional resources, see Journeys *Lesson 14 Focus Wall.*

Minilessons/Shared Reading	**Interactive Read-Aloud/ Shared Reading**	• *Turtle Splash!* by Cathryn Falwell INFORMATIONAL TEXT, **Big Book** pp. 2–29 • *Home for a Tiger, Home for a Bear* by Brenda Williams and Rosamund Fowler INFORMATIONAL TEXT, **Read Aloud Book** • "Where Animals Live" by Anne Rogers INFORMATIONAL TEXT, **Big Book** pp. 30–38
	Reading Minilessons	• **Cause and Effect,** p. 212 • **Details,** p. 213 • **Main Ideas,** p. 213
	Word Study	• **Beginning Sounds /n/n, /m/m,** pp. 82–83 • **Discuss Oral Vocabulary; This or That; "Because" Sentences; Dictate, Draw, and Write,** pp. 142–143
	Writing	• **Story:** Organizing a Story, p. 288; Drafting a Story, p. 288; **Story:** Blackline Master, p. 289

Guided Reading		Select texts according to your children's instructional level. You may use the books below or select from the Leveled Readers Database, pp. 344–355. For instructional support, use the Leveled Readers Teacher's Guides along with the books that you choose. • **LEVEL A** *At the Pond* • **LEVEL A** *Four Frogs* (Language Support) • **LEVEL A** *Splash!* • **LEVEL B** *How Many Ducks?* (Vocabulary Reader) • **LEVEL C** *Look in the Woods*

Planning a Week of Literacy and Language

INSTRUCTIONAL FOCUS

◉ **Student Community Text**
- *What a Beautiful Sky!* by Yanitzia Canetti **Big Book** pp. 2–25
- "What Will the Weather Be Like?" **Big Book** pp. 26–30

◉ **Read Aloud Book:** *How Many Stars in the Sky?* by Lenny Hort

◉ **Minilesson Principles:** Details; Sequence of Events; Genre: Informational Text

◉ **Word Work Emphasis:** Short *a* Words and High-Frequency Words

◉ **Writing Mode:** Narrative Writing

◉ **Writing Trait:** Organization

For additional instructional resources, see Journeys *Lesson 15 Focus Wall.*

<table>
<tr><td rowspan="4">Minilessons/Shared Reading</td><td>Interactive Read-Aloud/ Shared Reading</td><td>• What a Beautiful Sky! by Yanitzia Canetti INFORMATIONAL TEXT, Big Book pp. 2–25
• How Many Stars in the Sky? by Lenny Hort REALISTIC FICTION, Read Aloud Book
• "What Will the Weather Be Like?" INFORMATIONAL TEXT, Big Book pp. 26–30</td></tr>
<tr><td>Reading Minilessons</td><td>• Details, p. 214
• Sequence of Events, p. 215
• Genre: Informational Text, p. 215</td></tr>
<tr><td>Word Study</td><td>• Short a Words and High-Frequency Words, pp. 84–85
• Discuss Oral Vocabulary; Riddles; True or Not True; Dictate, Draw, and Write, pp. 144–145</td></tr>
<tr><td>Writing</td><td>• Story: Revising a Story, p. 290; Editing a Story, p. 290; Story: Blackline Master, p. 291</td></tr>
</table>

<table>
<tr><td rowspan="2">Guided Reading</td><td rowspan="2"></td><td>Select texts according to your children's instructional level. You may use the books below or select from the Leveled Readers Database, pp. 344–355. For instructional support, use the Leveled Readers Teacher's Guides along with the books that you choose.</td></tr>
<tr><td>• LEVEL A Look Up!
• LEVEL A Rain Today (Language Support)
• LEVEL A Rainy Day
• LEVEL C In the Sky (Vocabulary Reader)
• LEVEL D The Storm</td></tr>
</table>

Planning a Week of Literacy and Language

INSTRUCTIONAL FOCUS

- **Student Community Text**
  - *What Is Science?* by Rebecca Kai Dotlich, **Big Book** pp. 2–31
  - "Benjamin Franklin, Inventor," by Linda Ruggieri, **Big Book** pp. 32–38

- **Read Aloud Book:** *Dear Mr. Blueberry* by Simon James

- **Minilesson Principles:** Details; Genre: Fantasy; Details

- **Word Work Emphasis:** Beginning Sounds /p/p, /f/f

- **Writing Mode:** Opinion Writing

- **Writing Trait:** Organization

For additional instructional resources, see Journeys *Lesson 16 Focus Wall.*

Minilessons/Shared Reading	**Interactive Read-Aloud/ Shared Reading**	• *What Is Science?* by Rebecca Kai Dotlich POETRY, **Big Book** pp. 2–31 • *Dear Mr. Blueberry* by Simon James FANTASY, **Read Aloud Book** • "Benjamin Franklin, Inventor" by Linda Ruggieri INFORMATIONAL TEXT, **Big Book** pp. 32–38
	Reading Minilessons	• **Details,** p. 216 • **Genre: Fantasy,** p. 217 • **Details,** p. 217
	Word Study	• **Beginning Sounds /p/p, /f/f,** pp. 86–87 • **Discuss Oral Vocabulary; Guess the Word; Complete Sentences; Dictate, Draw, and Write,** pp. 146–147
	Writing	• **Message:** Writing Facts and Opinions, p. 292; Drafting a Message, p. 292; **Message:** Blackline Master, p. 293

Guided Reading 	Select texts according to your children's instructional level. You may use the books below or select from the Leveled Readers Database, pp. 344–355. For instructional support, use the Leveled Readers Teacher's Guides along with the books that you choose. • **LEVEL A** *Animals in the Woods* • **LEVEL A** *In My Yard* (Language Support) • **LEVEL A** *My Yard* • **LEVEL B** *Camping Under the Stars* (Vocabulary Reader) • **LEVEL C** *In the Tree*

Planning a Week of Literacy and Language

INSTRUCTIONAL FOCUS

⦿ **Student Community Text**
- *From Caterpillar to Butterfly* by Deborah Heiligman, **Big Book** pp. 2–29
- "Anansi and Grasshopper" Retold by Olivia Dean **Big Book** pp. 30–35

⦿ **Read Aloud Book:** *It Is the Wind* by Ferida Wolff

⦿ **Minilesson Principles:** Sequence of Events; Conclusions; Genre: Traditional Tale

⦿ **Word Work Emphasis:** Short *i* /ĭ/

⦿ **Writing Mode:** Opinion Writing

⦿ **Writing Trait:** Voice

For additional instructional resources, see Journeys Lesson 17 Focus Wall.

Minilessons/Shared Reading	**Interactive Read-Aloud/ Shared Reading**	• *From Caterpillar to Butterfly* by Deborah Heiligman INFORMATIONAL TEXT, **Big Book** pp. 2–29 • *It Is the Wind* by Ferida Wolff REALISTIC FICTION, **Read Aloud Book** • "Anansi and Grasshopper" Retold by Olivia Dean, TRADITIONAL TALE, **Big Book** pp. 30–35
	Reading Minilessons	• **Sequence of Events,** p. 218 • **Conclusions,** p. 219 • **Genre: Traditional Tale,** p. 219
	Word Study	• **Short *i* /ĭ/,** pp. 88–89 • **Discuss Oral Vocabulary; Sentence Clue Game; Synonyms; Dictate, Draw, and Write,** pp. 148–149
	Writing	• **Thank-You Note:** Expressing Thanks, p. 294; Drafting a Thank-You Note, p. 294; **Thank-You Note:** Blackline Master, p. 295

Guided Reading 	Select texts according to your children's instructional level. You may use the books below or select from the Leveled Readers Database, pp. 344–355. For instructional support, use the Leveled Readers Teacher's Guides along with the books that you choose. • **LEVEL A** *Bugs!* (Vocabulary Reader) • **LEVEL A** *Bug Parts* • **LEVEL A** *Find the Bug* • **LEVEL A** *Look for Bugs* (Language Support) • **LEVEL D** *Rosie and the Bug Jar*

Planning a Week of Literacy and Language

Atlantic
G. Brian Karas

INSTRUCTIONAL FOCUS

- **Student Community Text**
  - *Atlantic* by G. Brian Karas, **Big Book** pp. 2–31
  - *Poems About the Sea,* **Big Book** pp. 32–38

- **Read Aloud Book:** *One-Dog Canoe* by Mary Casanova

- **Minilesson Principles:** Author's Purpose; Author's Purpose; Genre: Poetry

- **Word Work Emphasis:** Ending Sounds /g/g, /b/b

- **Writing Mode:** Opinion Writing

- **Writing Trait:** Conventions

For additional instructional resources, see Journeys *Lesson 18 Focus Wall.*

Minilessons/Shared Reading	**Interactive Read-Aloud/ Shared Reading**	• *Atlantic* by G. Brian Karas INFORMATIONAL TEXT, **Big Book** pp. 2–31 • *One-Dog Canoe* by Mary Casanova FICTION, **Read Aloud Book** • *Poems About the Sea* POETRY, **Big Book** pp. 32–38
	Reading Minilessons	• **Author's Purpose,** p. 220 • **Author's Purpose,** p. 221 • **Genre: Poetry,** p. 221
	Word Study	• **Ending Sounds /g/g, /b/b,** pp. 90–91 • **Discuss Oral Vocabulary; Paired Yes/No Questions; Word Sort; Dictate, Draw, and Write,** pp. 150–151
	Writing	• **Letter:** Using Parts of a Letter, p. 296; Drafting a Letter, p. 296; **Letter:** Blackline Master, p. 297

Guided Reading 	Select texts according to your children's instructional level. You may use the books below or select from the Leveled Readers Database, pp. 344–355. For instructional support, use the Leveled Readers Teacher's Guides along with the books that you choose. • **LEVEL A** *Let's Swim* • **LEVEL A** *The Sea* • **LEVEL A** *Swimming* (Language Support) • **LEVEL B** *At the Beach* (Vocabulary Reader) • **LEVEL B** *By the Sea*

Planning a Week of Literacy and Language

Sheep Take a Hike
Nancy Shaw
Illustrated by Margot Apple

INSTRUCTIONAL FOCUS

◉ **Student Community Text**
  - *Sheep Take a Hike* by Nancy Shaw, **Big Book** pp. 3–28
  - *Fairy Tales/Traditional Tales,* **Big Book** pp. 29–38

◉ **Read Aloud Book:** *Nicky and the Rainy Day* by Valeri Gorbachev

◉ **Minilesson Principles:** Cause and Effect; Cause and Effect; Understanding Characters

◉ **Word Work Emphasis:** Words with Short *a* and Short *i*

◉ **Writing Mode:** Opinion Writing

◉ **Writing Trait:** Word Choice

For additional instructional resources, see Journeys Lesson 19 Focus Wall.

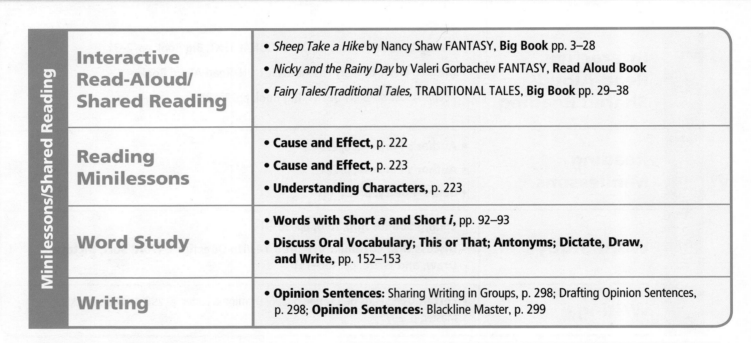

Minilessons/Shared Reading		
	Interactive Read-Aloud/ Shared Reading	• *Sheep Take a Hike* by Nancy Shaw FANTASY, **Big Book** pp. 3–28 • *Nicky and the Rainy Day* by Valeri Gorbachev FANTASY, **Read Aloud Book** • *Fairy Tales/Traditional Tales,* TRADITIONAL TALES, **Big Book** pp. 29–38
	Reading Minilessons	• **Cause and Effect,** p. 222 • **Cause and Effect,** p. 223 • **Understanding Characters,** p. 223
	Word Study	• **Words with Short *a* and Short *i*,** pp. 92–93 • **Discuss Oral Vocabulary; This or That; Antonyms; Dictate, Draw, and Write,** pp. 152–153
	Writing	• **Opinion Sentences:** Sharing Writing in Groups, p. 298; Drafting Opinion Sentences, p. 298; **Opinion Sentences:** Blackline Master, p. 299

Guided Reading

Select texts according to your children's instructional level. You may use the books below or select from the Leveled Readers Database, pp. 344–355. For instructional support, use the Leveled Readers Teacher's Guides along with the books that you choose.

- **LEVEL A** *Fun at Camp* (Language Support)
- **LEVEL A** *Summer Camp*
- **LEVEL A** *Taking Pictures*
- **LEVEL B** *Going for a Hike* (Vocabulary Reader)
- **LEVEL D** *Come for a Swim!*

Planning a Week of Literacy and Language

INSTRUCTIONAL FOCUS

- ◉ **Student Community Text**
  - *Margret and H. A. Rey's Curious George's Dinosaur Discovery,* by Catherine Hapka, **Big Book** pp. 2–24
  - "Exploring Land and Water," **Big Book** pp. 25–30
- ◉ **Read Aloud Book:** *Duck & Goose* by Tad Hills
- ◉ **Minilesson Principles:** Sequence of Events; Sequence of Events; Genre: Informational Text
- ◉ **Word Work Emphasis:** Words with *-ig, -in, -it*
- ◉ **Writing Mode:** Opinion Writing
- ◉ **Writing Trait:** Word Choice

For additional instructional resources, see Journeys *Lesson 20 Focus Wall.*

<table>
<tr><td rowspan="4" style="writing-mode:vertical-lr">Minilessons/Shared Reading</td><td>Interactive Read-Aloud/ Shared Reading</td><td>• Margret and H. A. Rey's Curious George's Dinosaur Discovery by Catherine Hapka, FANTASY, Big Book pp. 2–24
• Duck & Goose by Tad Hills FANTASY, Read Aloud Book
• "Exploring Land and Water" INFORMATIONAL TEXT, Big Book pp. 25–30</td></tr>
<tr><td>Reading Minilessons</td><td>• Sequence of Events, p. 224
• Sequence of Events, p. 225
• Genre: Informational Text, p. 225</td></tr>
<tr><td>Word Study</td><td>• Words with -ig, -in, -it, pp. 94–95
• Discuss Oral Vocabulary; True or Not True; "Because" Sentences; Dictate, Draw, and Write, pp. 154–155</td></tr>
<tr><td>Writing</td><td>• Opinion Sentences: Changing Words, p. 300; Revising Opinion Sentences, p. 300; Opinion Sentences: Blackline Master, p. 301</td></tr>
</table>

Guided Reading

Select texts according to your children's instructional level. You may use the books below or select from the Leveled Readers Database, pp. 344–355. For instructional support, use the Leveled Readers Teacher's Guides along with the books that you choose.

- **LEVEL A** *Curious George and the Animals* (Language Support)
- **LEVEL A** *Curious George and the Hungry Animals*
- **LEVEL A** *Curious George Visits Animal Friends*
- **LEVEL C** *Curious About the Animal Park* (Vocabulary Reader)
- **LEVEL E** *Curious George Visits the Woods*

Planning a Week of Literacy and Language

INSTRUCTIONAL FOCUS

- ⦿ **Student Community Text**
  - *Zin! Zin! Zin! a Violin* by Lloyd Moss, **Big Book** pp. 2–29
  - *Poems About Music*, **Big Book** pp. 30–35

- ⦿ **Read Aloud Book:** *Simon and Molly plus Hester* by Lisa Jahn-Clough

- ⦿ **Minilesson Principles:** Details; Understanding Characters; Genre: Poetry

- ⦿ **Word Work Emphasis:** Beginning Sounds /d/d, /r/r, /g/g

- ⦿ **Writing Mode:** Informative Writing

- ⦿ **Writing Trait:** Organization

For additional instructional resources, see Journeys *Lesson 21 Focus Wall.*

Minilessons/Shared Reading		
Interactive Read-Aloud/ Shared Reading	• *Zin! Zin! Zin! a Violin* by Lloyd Moss POETRY, **Big Book** pp. 2–29 • *Simon and Molly plus Hester* by Lisa Jahn-Clough REALISTIC FICTION, **Read Aloud Book** • *Poems About Music* POETRY, **Big Book** pp. 30–35	
Reading Minilessons	• **Details,** p. 226 • **Understanding Characters,** p. 227 • **Genre: Poetry,** p. 227	
Word Study	• **Beginning Sounds /d/d, /r/r, /g/g,** pp. 96–97 • **Discuss Oral Vocabulary; Paired Yes/No Questions; Guess the Word; Dictate, Draw, and Write,** pp. 156–157	
Writing	• **List:** Making Lists for Different Purposes, p. 302; Drafting a List, p. 302; **List:** Blackline Master, p. 303	

Guided Reading	
	Select texts according to your children's instructional level. You may use the books below or select from the Leveled Readers Database, pp. 344–355. For instructional support, use the Leveled Readers Teacher's Guides along with the books that you choose. • **LEVEL A** *Mouse and Bear* • **LEVEL A** *Mouse and Bear are Friends* (Language Support) • **LEVEL A** *The Show* • **LEVEL B** *Friends* (Vocabulary Reader) • **LEVEL E** *Kevin and Lucy*

Planning a Week of Literacy and Language

INSTRUCTIONAL FOCUS

◉ **Student Community Text**
- *Leo the Late Bloomer* by Robert Kraus **Big Book** pp. 2–30
- "What Can a Baby Animal Do?" by Andrew Kasparyan **Big Book** pp. 31–38

◉ **Read Aloud Book:** *A Tiger Grows Up* by Anastasia Suen

◉ **Minilesson Principles:** Story Structure; Sequence of Events; Conclusions

◉ **Word Work Emphasis:** Short o /ŏ/

◉ **Writing Mode:** Informative Writing

◉ **Writing Trait:** Organization

For additional instructional resources, see Journeys *Lesson 22 Focus Wall.*

Minilessons/Shared Reading	**Interactive Read-Aloud/ Shared Reading**	• *Leo the Late Bloomer* by Robert Kraus FANTASY, **Big Book** pp. 2–30 • *A Tiger Grows Up* by Anastasia Suen INFORMATIONAL TEXT, **Read Aloud Book** • "What Can a Baby Animal Do?" by Andrew Kasparyan, **Big Book** pp. 31–38
	Reading Minilessons	• **Story Structure,** p. 228 • **Sequence of Events,** p. 229 • **Conclusions,** p. 229
	Word Study	• **Short o /ŏ/,** pp. 98–99 • **Discuss Oral Vocabulary; Describe It or Act It Out; Word Sort; Dictate, Draw, and Write,** pp. 158–159
	Writing	• **Lists:** Writing Lists with Numbers, p. 304; Drafting a Numbered List, p. 304; **Lists:** Blackline Master, p. 305

Guided Reading		Select texts according to your children's instructional level. You may use the books below or select from the Leveled Readers Database, pp. 344–355. For instructional support, use the Leveled Readers Teacher's Guides along with the books that you choose. • **LEVEL A**　*A Day at School* • **LEVEL A**　*Our Family Vacation* • **LEVEL A**　*Our School* (Language Support) • **LEVEL B**　*Family Fun* (Vocabulary Reader) • **LEVEL D**　*Good Job, Sam!*

Planning a Week of Literacy and Language

INSTRUCTIONAL FOCUS

⬤ **Student Community Text**
- *Zinnia's Flower Garden* by Monica Wellington, **Big Book** pp. 2–31
- "Growing Sunflowers," **Big Book** pp. 32–37

⬤ **Read Aloud Book:** *Oscar and the Frog* by Geoff Waring

⬤ **Minilesson Principles:** Sequence of Events; Text and Graphic Features; Sequence of Events

⬤ **Word Work Emphasis:** Words for One and More than One (*-s*)

⬤ **Writing Mode:** Informative Writing

⬤ **Writing Trait:** Organization

For additional instructional resources, see Journeys Lesson 23 Focus Wall.

Minilessons/Shared Reading	**Interactive Read-Aloud/ Shared Reading**	• *Zinnia's Flower Garden* by Monica Wellington INFORMATIONAL TEXT, **Big Book** pp. 2–31 • *Oscar and the Frog* by Geoff Waring INFORMATIONAL TEXT, **Read Aloud Book** • "Growing Sunflowers" INFORMATIONAL TEXT, **Big Book** pp. 32–37
	Reading Minilessons	• **Sequence of Events,** p. 230 • **Text and Graphic Features,** p. 231 • **Sequence of Events,** p. 231
	Word Study	• **Words for One and More than One (*-s*),** pp. 100–101 • **Discuss Oral Vocabulary; Word Associations; "Because" Sentences; Dictate, Draw, and Write,** pp. 160–161
	Writing	• **Invitation:** Choosing Important Information, p. 306; Drafting an Invitation, p. 306; **Invitation:** Blackline Master, p. 307

Guided Reading	Select texts according to your children's instructional level. You may use the books below or select from the Leveled Readers Database, pp. 344–355. For instructional support, use the Leveled Readers Teacher's Guides along with the books that you choose. • **LEVEL A** *The Garden* (Language Support) • **LEVEL A** *In the Garden* • **LEVEL A** *The Vegetable Garden* • **LEVEL B** *The Flower* (Vocabulary Reader) • **LEVEL C** *A City Garden*

Planning a Week of Literacy and Language

INSTRUCTIONAL FOCUS

◉ **Student Community Text**
- *Chameleon, Chameleon* by Joy Cowley, **Big Book** pp. 2–31
- "Amazing Animal Bodies" by Margaret Bishop, **Big Book** pp. 32–38

◉ **Read Aloud Book:** *Red Eyes or Blue Feathers* by Patricia M. Stockland

◉ **Minilesson Principles:** Conclusions; Compare and Contrast; Conclusions

◉ **Word Work Emphasis:** Words with *-at, -it, -ot*

◉ **Writing Mode:** Informative Writing

◉ **Writing Trait:** Ideas

For additional instructional resources, see Journeys *Lesson 24 Focus Wall.*

Minilessons/Shared Reading	**Interactive Read-Aloud/ Shared Reading**	• *Chameleon, Chameleon* by Joy Cowley INFORMATIONAL TEXT, **Big Book** pp. 2–31 • *Red Eyes or Blue Feathers* by Patricia M. Stockland INFORMATIONAL TEXT, **Read Aloud Book** • "Amazing Animal Bodies" by Margaret Bishop INFORMATIONAL TEXT, **Big Book** pp. 32–38
	Reading Minilessons	• **Conclusions**, p. 232 • **Compare and Contrast**, p. 233 • **Conclusions**, p. 233
	Word Study	• **Words with *-at, -it, -ot*,** pp. 102–103 • **Discuss Oral Vocabulary; True or Not True; Word Sort; Dictate, Draw, and Write,** pp. 162–163
	Writing	• **Report:** Researching Facts, p. 308; Drafting a Report, p. 308; **Report:** Blackline Master, p. 309

Guided Reading

Select texts according to your children's instructional level. You may use the books below or select from the Leveled Readers Database, pp. 344–355. For instructional support, use the Leveled Readers Teacher's Guides along with the books that you choose.

- **LEVEL A**   *Bugs for Dinner*
- **LEVEL A**   *Feeding Our Pets*
- **LEVEL A**   *Pets at School* (Language Support)
- **LEVEL B**   *The Lion* (Vocabulary Reader)
- **LEVEL D**   *What Animals Eat*

Planning a Week of Literacy and Language

INSTRUCTIONAL FOCUS

⦿ **Student Community Text**
  • *Pie in the Sky* by Lois Ehlert, **Big Book** pp. 2–36
  • "From Apple Tree to Store," **Big Book** pp. 37–45

⦿ **Read Aloud Book:** *Bread Comes to Life* by George Levenson

⦿ **Minilesson Principles:** Text and Graphic Features; Text and Graphic Features; Sequence of Events

⦿ **Word Work Emphasis:** Words with Short *o* and Short *e*

⦿ **Writing Mode:** Informative Writing

⦿ **Writing Trait:** Ideas

For additional instructional resources, see Journeys *Lesson 25 Focus Wall.*

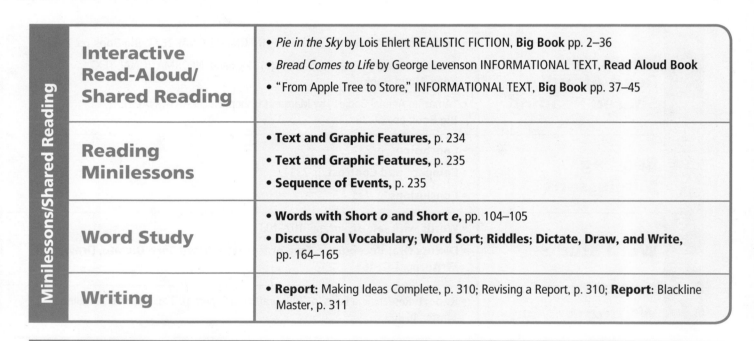

Minilessons/Shared Reading		
Interactive Read-Aloud/ Shared Reading	• *Pie in the Sky* by Lois Ehlert REALISTIC FICTION, **Big Book** pp. 2–36 • *Bread Comes to Life* by George Levenson INFORMATIONAL TEXT, **Read Aloud Book** • "From Apple Tree to Store," INFORMATIONAL TEXT, **Big Book** pp. 37–45	
Reading Minilessons	• **Text and Graphic Features,** p. 234 • **Text and Graphic Features,** p. 235 • **Sequence of Events,** p. 235	
Word Study	• **Words with Short *o* and Short *e*,** pp. 104–105 • **Discuss Oral Vocabulary; Word Sort; Riddles; Dictate, Draw, and Write,** pp. 164–165	
Writing	• **Report:** Making Ideas Complete, p. 310; Revising a Report, p. 310; **Report:** Blackline Master, p. 311	

Guided Reading

Select texts according to your children's instructional level. You may use the books below or select from the Leveled Readers Database, pp. 344–355. For instructional support, use the Leveled Readers Teacher's Guides along with the books that you choose.

• **LEVEL A** *Apples*
• **LEVEL A** *The Baker*
• **LEVEL A** *We Like Apples* (Language Support)
• **LEVEL C** *Making a Mud Pie*
• **LEVEL C** *Snack Time* (Vocabulary Reader)

Planning a Week
of Literacy and Language

INSTRUCTIONAL FOCUS

◉ **Student Community Text**
  - *Kitten's First Full Moon* by Kevin Henkes, **Big Book** pp. 2–31
  - *Poems About Trying and the Moon,* **Big Book** pp. 32–38

◉ **Read Aloud Book:** *Curious George Makes Pancakes* by Margret and H.A. Rey

◉ **Minilesson Principles:** Conclusions; Cause and Effect; Genre: Poetry

◉ **Word Work Emphasis:** Words with *-et* and *-en*

◉ **Writing Mode:** Opinion Writing

◉ **Writing Trait:** Voice

For additional instructional resources, see Journeys Lesson 26 Focus Wall.

Minilessons/Shared Reading		
	Interactive Read-Aloud/ Shared Reading	• *Kitten's First Full Moon* by Kevin Henkes FICTION, **Big Book** pp. 2–31 • *Curious George Makes Pancakes* by Margret and H.A. Rey FANTASY, **Read Aloud Book** • *Poems About Trying and the Moon* POETRY, **Big Book** pp. 32–38
	Reading Minilessons	• **Conclusions,** p. 236 • **Cause and Effect,** p. 237 • **Genre: Poetry,** p. 237
	Word Study	• **Words with *-et* and *-en*,** pp. 106–107 • **Discuss Oral Vocabulary; Synonyms; Word Sort; Dictate, Draw, and Write,** pp. 166–167
	Writing	• **Response to Literature:** Writing an Opinion, p. 312; Drafting a Response to Fiction, p. 312; **Response to Literature:** Blackline Master, p. 313

Guided Reading	
	Select texts according to your children's instructional level. You may use the books below or select from the Leveled Readers Database, pp. 344–355. For instructional support, use the Leveled Readers Teacher's Guides along with the books that you choose. • **LEVEL A** *Time for Breakfast!* • **LEVEL B** *I Can!* (Vocabulary Reader) • **LEVEL B** *Things I Can Do* • **LEVEL B** *Things I Like to Do* (Language Support) • **LEVEL C** *Team Work*

Planning a Week of Literacy and Language

INSTRUCTIONAL FOCUS

◉ **Student Community Text**
  • *One of Three* by Angela Johnson, **Big Book** pp. 2–30
  • "Cross-Country Trip," **Big Book** pp. 31–38

◉ **Read Aloud Book:** *Someone Bigger* by Jonathan Emmett

◉ **Minilesson Principles:** Compare and Contrast; Story Structure; Genre: Informational Text

◉ **Word Work Emphasis:** Short *u* /ŭ/

◉ **Writing Mode:** Opinion Writing

◉ **Writing Trait:** Ideas

For additional instructional resources, see Journeys Lesson 27 Focus Wall.

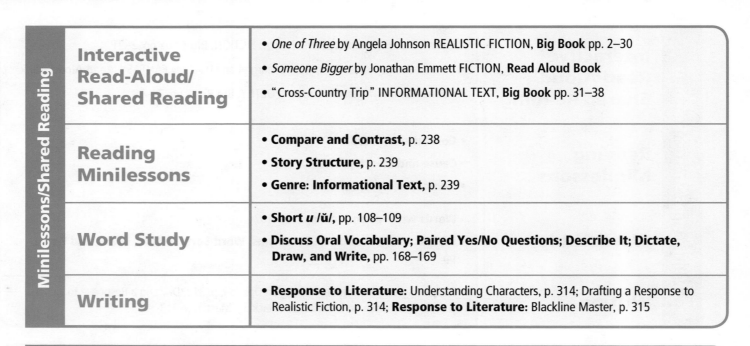

Minilessons/Shared Reading		
Interactive Read-Aloud/ Shared Reading	• *One of Three* by Angela Johnson REALISTIC FICTION, **Big Book** pp. 2–30 • *Someone Bigger* by Jonathan Emmett FICTION, **Read Aloud Book** • "Cross-Country Trip" INFORMATIONAL TEXT, **Big Book** pp. 31–38	
Reading Minilessons	• **Compare and Contrast,** p. 238 • **Story Structure,** p. 239 • **Genre: Informational Text,** p. 239	
Word Study	• **Short *u* /ŭ/,** pp. 108–109 • **Discuss Oral Vocabulary; Paired Yes/No Questions; Describe It; Dictate, Draw, and Write,** pp. 168–169	
Writing	• **Response to Literature:** Understanding Characters, p. 314; Drafting a Response to Realistic Fiction, p. 314; **Response to Literature:** Blackline Master, p. 315	

Guided Reading

Select texts according to your children's instructional level. You may use the books below or select from the Leveled Readers Database, pp. 344–355. For instructional support, use the Leveled Readers Teacher's Guides along with the books that you choose.

• **LEVEL A** *Our Room*
• **LEVEL B** *Let's Have Fun!* (Vocabulary Reader)
• **LEVEL B** *My Big Brother Ned*
• **LEVEL B** *My Brother* (Language Support)
• **LEVEL C** *Dan and His Brothers*

Planning a Week of Literacy and Language

INSTRUCTIONAL FOCUS

- ◉ **Student Community Text**
  - *Margret and H.A. Rey's You Can Do It, Curious George!* by Catherine Hapka, **Big Book** pp. 2–25
  - *Poems About Things You Can Do,* **Big Book** pp. 26–30
- ◉ **Read Aloud Book:** *The Little Engine That Could* retold by Watty Piper
- ◉ **Minilesson Principles:** Story Structure; Genre: Fantasy; Genre: Poetry
- ◉ **Word Work Emphasis:** Words with Short *e* and Short *u*
- ◉ **Writing Mode:** Opinion Writing
- ◉ **Writing Trait:** Ideas

For additional instructional resources, see Journeys *Lesson 28 Focus Wall.*

Minilessons/Shared Reading	**Interactive Read-Aloud/ Shared Reading**	• *Margret and H.A. Rey's You Can Do It, Curious George!* by Catherine Hapka FANTASY, **Big Book** pp. 2–25 • *The Little Engine That Could* retold by Watty Piper FANTASY, **Read Aloud Book** • *Poems About Things You Can Do* POETRY, **Big Book** pp. 26–30
	Reading Minilessons	• **Story Structure,** p. 240 • **Genre: Fantasy,** p. 241 • **Genre: Poetry,** p. 241
	Word Study	• **Words with Short *e* and Short *u*,** pp. 110–111 • **Discuss Oral Vocabulary; Word Sort; Riddles; Dictate, Draw, and Write,** pp. 170–171
	Writing	• **Response to Literature:** Understanding Different Kinds of Writing, p. 316; Drafting a Response to Literature, p. 316; **Response to Literature:** Blackline Master, p. 317

Guided Reading	Select texts according to your children's instructional level. You may use the books below or select from the Leveled Readers Database, pp. 344–355. For instructional support, use the Leveled Readers Teacher's Guides along with the books that you choose. • **LEVEL A** *Up and Away, Curious George* • **LEVEL B** *Curious About Playing Ball* (Vocabulary Reader) • **LEVEL B** *Curious George Goes for a Ride* • **LEVEL B** *Curious George Likes to Ride* (Language Support) • **LEVEL F** *Curious George and the Newspapers*

Planning a Week of Literacy and Language

INSTRUCTIONAL FOCUS

- **Student Community Text**
  - *Look at Us* by Isabel Campoy, **Big Book** pp. 2–25
  - "The Three Little Pigs" retold by Ana Waters, **Big Book** pp. 26–30

- **Read Aloud Book:** *Baby Brains* by Simon James

- **Minilesson Principles:** Main Ideas; Story Structure; Story Structure

- **Word Work Emphasis:** Words with *-ap*, *-up*, *-op*

- **Writing Mode:** Opinion Writing

- **Writing Trait:** Voice

For additional instructional resources, see Journeys Lesson 29 Focus Wall.

Minilessons/Shared Reading		
Interactive Read-Aloud/ Shared Reading	• *Look at Us* by Isabel Campoy INFORMATIONAL TEXT, **Big Book** pp. 2–25 • *Baby Brains* by Simon James FICTION, **Read Aloud Book** • "The Three Little Pigs" retold by Ana Waters TRADITIONAL TALE, **Big Book** pp. 26–30	
Reading Minilessons	• **Main Ideas,** p. 242 • **Story Structure,** p. 243 • **Story Structure,** p. 243	
Word Study	• **Words with *-ap*, *-up*, *-op*,** pp. 112–113 • **Discuss Oral Vocabulary; Antonyms; Complete Sentences; Dictate, Draw, and Write,** pp. 172–173	
Writing	• **Journal:** Responding in a Journal, p. 318; Drafting a Journal Entry, p. 318; **Journal:** Blackline Master, p. 319	

Guided Reading	
	Select texts according to your children's instructional level. You may use the books below or select from the Leveled Readers Database, pp. 344–355. For instructional support, use the Leveled Readers Teacher's Guides along with the books that you choose. • **LEVEL A** *Zoom!* • **LEVEL B** *Going to School* (Language Support) • **LEVEL B** *Riding to School* • **LEVEL C** *Lots of Helpers* • **LEVEL C** *My School* (Vocabulary Reader)

Planning a Week of Literacy and Language

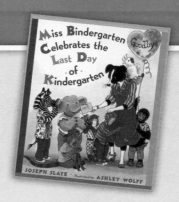

INSTRUCTIONAL FOCUS

- ◉ **Student Community Text**
  - *Miss Bindergarten Celebrates the Last Day of Kindergarten* by Joseph Slate, **Big Book** pp. 2–40
  - "Schools Then and Now," **Big Book** pp. 41–46

- ◉ **Read Aloud Book:** *Pet Show!* by Ezra Jack Keats

- ◉ **Minilesson Principles:** Understanding Characters; Understanding Characters; Compare and Contrast

- ◉ **Word Work Emphasis:** Words with Short Vowels

- ◉ **Writing Mode:** Opinion Writing

- ◉ **Writing Trait:** Voice

For additional instructional resources, see Journeys *Lesson 30 Focus Wall.*

Minilessons/Shared Reading		
Interactive Read-Aloud/ Shared Reading	• *Miss Bindergarten Celebrates the Last Day of Kindergarten* by Joseph Slate FANTASY, **Big Book** pp. 2–40 • *Pet Show!* by Ezra Jack Keats REALISTIC FICTION, **Read Aloud Book** • "Schools Then and Now" INFORMATIONAL TEXT, **Big Book** pp. 41–46	
Reading Minilessons	• **Understanding Characters,** p. 244 • **Understanding Characters,** p. 245 • **Compare and Contrast,** p. 245	
Word Study	• **Words with Short Vowels,** pp. 114–115 • **Discuss Oral Vocabulary; Sentence Clue Game; Word Associations; Dictate, Draw, and Write,** pp. 174–175	
Writing	• **Journal:** Using Your Own Voice, p. 320; Sharing Your Work Online, p. 320; **Journal:** Blackline Master, p. 321	

Guided Reading

Select texts according to your children's instructional level. You may use the books below or select from the Leveled Readers Database, pp. 344–355. For instructional support, use the Leveled Readers Teacher's Guides along with the books that you choose.

- **LEVEL A** *Our Class Band*
- **LEVEL B** *The Costume Box*
- **LEVEL B** *Dressing Up* (Language Support)
- **LEVEL C** *Trip to the Fire Station* (Vocabulary Reader)
- **LEVEL D** *A Very Nice Lunch*

Teacher's Notes

Word Study

Table of Contents

(continued)

Word Study

Table of Contents

Oral Vocabulary Development

Why Is Word Study Important?

Word study is a developmentally based approach to phonics, spelling, and vocabulary instruction. Because of the critical role that word knowledge plays in reading and in writing, it is essential that our instruction be matched to students' developmental levels. The word study approach is grounded in research that has identified how learners develop an understanding of the structure of written words and how this structure reflects the alphabetic, pattern, and meaning layers of the language (Templeton, 2011).

Effective word study develops students' underlying *orthographic knowledge*—the understanding of how letters and letter patterns represent sound and meaning in language. As the diagram shown below illustrates, over time students move from an understanding of (1) alphabetic/sound relationships to (2) pattern/sound relationships to (3) *morphology*, or meaning, relationships. Orthographic knowledge forms the foundation of students' development in fluency, reading comprehension, and writing.

By understanding how we can best assess what our students know about word structure, we can then target our instruction most effectively at those aspects of word study that each of our students needs and is ready to learn (Bear, Invernizzi, Templeton, & Johnston, 2012).

ALPHABET	PATTERN	MEANING	
Letter Name	Within Word ↓ Vowel Patterns	Between Syllables ↓ Syllable Patterns ↓ Basic Word-Formation Processes: Bases + Affixes	More Advanced Word-Formation Processes: Bases + Affixes, Greek/Latin Roots + Affixes

▸ Engaging and Effective Word Study

For word study to be effective, we need to make sure that our students are experiencing, examining, and talking about words from a variety of perspectives—taking them apart and putting them together (Ehri, 2005; Templeton & Bear, 2011). Through this type of analysis and synthesis, students will best internalize the features of words and apply this understanding efficiently in their reading and writing.

The most effective framework in which students may productively explore words and their patterns is through the process of comparing, contrasting, and analyzing in interactive word sort activities. Word sorts actively engage and motivate students, and the discussions allow students to share insights and discover generalizations about words. Word sorting combines student-exploratory and teacher-directed learning.

In *Journeys* and in this Guide, you are provided with words that will support students' discoveries and generalizations about the spelling of words at the alphabet, pattern, and meaning layers. First, you will guide students' explorations with appropriate modeling and questioning. As students follow up in their seatwork, they internalize these questions and develop ways to think critically about words.

Because word sorts are hands-on, they are motivating to students. Students work with *known* words because they cannot search for and discover patterns if they cannot identify some or most of the words they are examining. This involvement is in sharp contrast to many phonics and spelling approaches in which the "rule" is stated at the beginning of the lesson. Sorting words leads students towards generating the rule themselves. This framework supports the kind of processing that is the foundation of efficient, fluent reading and spelling.

Types of Word Sorts

The two primary types of word sorts are *closed* and *open*.

- In **closed sorts**, you provide the categories into which students will sort the words: words with long *a* and words with short *a*, for example. After sorting, students discuss what spelling features they think distinguish long *a* spellings from short *a* spellings.

- In **open sorts**, students sort the words provided by you any way that they wish—all options are open. They may sort by spelling features they notice or by meaning.

Variations of closed and open sorts are described on the next page and used throughout the lessons in this Guide.

Word Sort Variations

Repeated Sorting It is important that students have multiple opportunities to sort and write the words for the week. Repeated sorting may be done after the initial group sort on Day 1. You may also send words home to be sorted with family members.

Blind Sorts A blind sort focuses on strengthening the bond between sound and spelling. In blind sorts, students do not see the words to be sorted; they sort them based on the targeted sound/feature that the words represent. Words are shuffled and read aloud by you or a buddy without showing them to the writer. A key word is used to represent each of the sort categories. Students write the word that is called out under the appropriate key word.

Word Hunts This activity helps students establish the connection between spelling words and reading words. After exploring the targeted features/patterns through sorting, students look back through familiar reading selections, hunting for words that are examples of these features/patterns. They record their discoveries in their Word Study Notebooks (see below).

Picture Sorts Children in the early phases of spelling development sort both words and pictures. Pictures are particularly effective when children are focusing on sound because they must attend to particular sound patterns or phonemes within the pronounced word. Then they are able to focus more precisely on the sounds as they are represented either alphabetically or by spelling pattern.

Draw and Label, Cut-and-Paste As children are learning the names and sounds of particular letters, they will draw pictures of things that begin with or contain these sounds. They label the pictures with the appropriate letter or try to spell as much of the label as they are able. Later, when words are sorted, they may be pasted into categories.

Guess My Category This activity involves students in trying to guess categories after words have been sorted by you or by other students. The categories may be based on spelling patterns or on concepts. Students grow more creative in their categorization and guessing as they are exposed to more words and their features.

Speed Sorts As students sort the words later in the week, they enjoy timing their sorts to see how rapidly they are able to complete the sort while maintaining accuracy. Many students keep track of their progress in their Word Study Notebooks.

Meaning/Concept Sorts Pictures and words may be sorted according to meaning categories. When known words are grouped in different ways, new conceptual relationships are established. For example, younger children may sort a group of pictures according to things that may be found *indoors* and those that may be found *outdoors*; older students may sort a group of words according to concepts such as *mammal*, *amphibian*, or *bird*.

Word Study Notebooks

The Word Study Notebook is the home for word sorts, writing sorts, word hunts, interesting new words encountered in reading, and important new vocabulary. For younger children, the notebook may be a few pages of construction paper stapled or tied together. For older students, a loose-leaf binder works especially well because as more words and patterns are explored it is easy to add pages. Students may record and work with new spelling and vocabulary words—doing concept sorts, creating graphic organizers, or drafting sentences for the vocabulary.

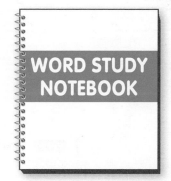

▶ Spelling/Phonics

The spelling/phonics lessons in this Guide may be used apart from or to complement the lessons in *Journeys*, providing additional exposure to and exploration of targeted word features. The five-day format of each lesson begins with an introduction and walk-through of the features and patterns in the spelling words. On subsequent days, the spelling words are compared and contrasted through the variety of sorts and activities described on page 41.

Throughout each lesson, there are several opportunities for students to share and discuss what they are observing and thinking with partners and with the group. The fifth day of each lesson is an assessment. Dictation sentences that include the spelling words are provided in Grades 1–6.

It is important that students interact with the spelling words every day. At all levels, you will introduce important phonics and spelling features at the beginning of the lesson. Depending on the students' developmental level, you may meet with some students on subsequent days. Every day, however, activities are provided that may be completed by the students at their seats, either in small groups or independently.

Components of a Typical Kindergarten Spelling/Phonics Lesson

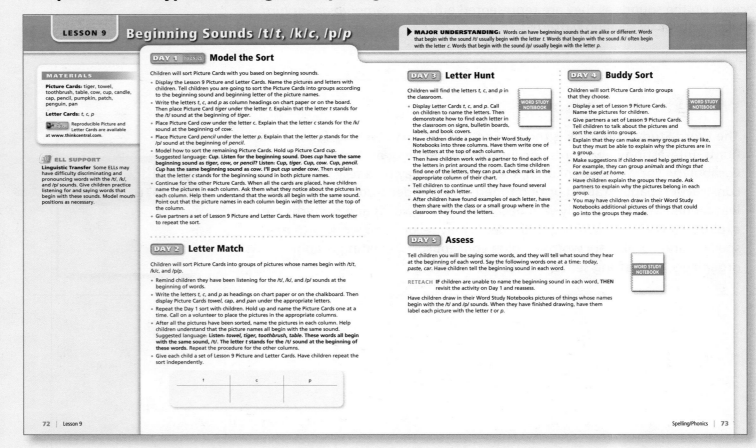

Characteristics of Most Kindergarten Spellers

- At the beginning of the kindergarten year, most children are emergent spellers. As they learn the names of the alphabet letters and begin to explore beginning and ending consonant sounds, you will see them including these in their writing.

- When children are consistently representing beginning and ending sounds in their writing, they are very close to having a concept of word in print and will be ready to explore medial vowel sounds and the letters that represent them.

- It is important to encourage young children to "have a go" at spelling as they write, applying what they know about letters and sounds. Research in emergent and beginning literacy underscores the importance of this, particularly for children who have not had the benefit of lots of literacy experiences at home during the preschool years.

- Short *a* is the first short vowel that children in the alphabetic-letter name phase usually spell conventionally. Following are the most commonly used "letter name" spellings for the other short vowels: *a* for short *e, e* for short *i, i* for short *o.*

- Children at this phase will use a single vowel letter to stand for a long vowel sound: LAT for *late,* RAN for *rain.*

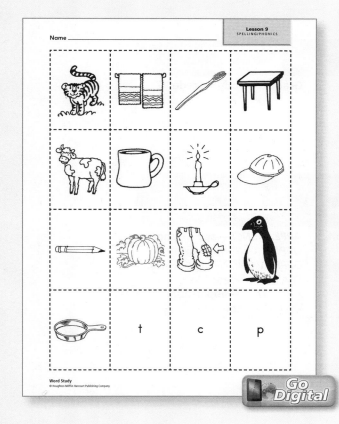

Word Study Spelling/Phonics Lessons

- **Day 1:** Beginning consonant sounds and the letters that represent them are compared and contrasted. The teacher models sorting pictures that begin with targeted sounds and then children repeat the sort with a partner.

- **Day 2:** Children deepen understanding by independently sorting pictures according to targeted beginning sounds.

- **Day 3:** Children extend their developing understanding of beginning sounds and the letters that represent them by doing a letter hunt around the classroom.

- **Day 4:** Children deepen understanding by thinking about different ways in which pictures and the sounds/concepts they represent may be categorized.

- **Day 5:** Assesses children's understanding.

Reproducible Picture and Letter Cards

- Available at **www.thinkcentral.com**
- The lesson's Picture and Letter Cards are used in a variety of ways throughout the week.

▸ Spelling/Phonics Development

What the Research Says

Word study instruction must match the needs of each student. A student's **instructional level** is a powerful determinant of what may be learned. Simply put, we must teach within each child's zone of understanding. The word features that are examined at each grade in *Journeys* should match the developmental level of most students. Students for whom the word study curriculum is not the appropriate developmental "fit," however, will have appropriate patterns and words provided.

The lower chart below presents the developmental nature of orthographic knowledge as students learn the relationships between letters in the printed word and the types of information the letters represent. The spellings reflect the types of orthographic information to which developing learners pay attention, from alphabetic through a deeper understanding of the structure of single-syllable words, two-syllable and multisyllabic words, and morphological relationships.

A developmental perspective on phonics and spelling instruction reveals that knowledge does not occur simply through repetition and memorization. For most students throughout the primary, intermediate, and middle grades, memory for words and patterns is supported by an awareness of underlying interrelationships among sound, spelling, meaning, and morphology.

Levels of Literacy Development

Emergent Literacy	Beginning Literacy	Transitional Literacy	Intermediate Literacy	Skilled/Advanced Literacy
Pre-K to middle of Grade 1	Kindergarten to middle of Grade 2	Grade 1 to middle of Grade 4	Grade 3 through Grade 8	Grade 5 through Grade 12

Levels of Spelling Development

Emergent Phase	Letter Name-Alphabetic Phase	Within Word Pattern Phase	Syllables and Affixes Phase	Derivational Relations Phase
B—bed *CUS*—see you soon	*DT*—dot *BAD*—bed *SEP*—ship *LUP*—lump *JRIV*—drive	*TRANE*—train *FLOWT*—float *CATOL*—cattle *THOUT*—throat	*HABBIT*—habit *CAPCHURE*—capture *MIDDEL*—middle	*APPEARENCE*—appearance *OPPISITION*—opposition *DEPRAVATION*—deprivation *FEASABLE*—feasible *APARITION*—apparition *CLORINE*—chlorine

Phases of Spelling Development

Emergent Most preschoolers and kindergartners, as well as some first graders at the beginning of the school year, are emergent spellers. Emergent spelling may range from random marks to recognizable letters that correspond in some way to sound. Notably, children at the emergent phase are not yet phonemically aware—that is, they are not able consciously to attend to consonant and vowel sounds within syllables.

Letter Name-Alphabetic Becoming letter name-alphabetic spellers depends upon learning the *alphabetic principle*—the understanding that letters represent sounds in a systematic way and that words can be segmented into phonemes from left to right. Early on, children use the names of the letters to represent sounds. Beginning and ending sounds in syllables are represented, and medial vowels come in a bit later: BD spells *bed*; *we* may be spelled YE because the name of letter *y* contains the /w/ sound.

Typically, short vowel sounds may be spelled with the letter whose name is *closest* to the sound the child wants to spell: *bed* is spelled BAD because the name of the letter *a* is pronounced with a mouth position that is very similar to the mouth position that is used to pronounce the short *e* sound—more similar than any other vowel sound. As children learn about the conventional spellings for short vowel sounds, they learn about consonant digraphs and also blends, or how to separate the sound that each letter represents.

Within Word Pattern Within word pattern spellers are able to spell correctly most single-syllable short-vowel words, consonant blends, consonant digraphs, and the sounds that *m* and *n* represent when they occur before consonants, as in *bump* and *stand*. They are able to think in more than one dimension about word structure—how letters may be grouped into patterns that correspond predictably to sound—and they examine words by sound and pattern simultaneously. Because of this, within word pattern spellers come to understand that how sounds are spelled often depends on the following: where the sounds occur within words (long *a* at the end of words is spelled *ay*; in the middle, usually *a*-consonant-*e* or *ai*); other sounds that are around them (if a long vowel comes before a /j/ sound, /j/ is spelled *ge*; otherwise, /j/ is spelled *dge*); letters provide clues about the pronunciation of other letters within the word (the final *e* in *slide*).

During the within word pattern phase, students will first explore the common long vowel patterns (long *o* can be spelled *o*-consonant-*e* as in *broke*, *oa* as in *boat*, and *ow* as in *grow*), then less common patterns (VCC pattern in *told* and *host*), and later more challenging patterns (*au* in *taught*, *ough* in *through* and *though*).

Students begin to explore the role of *meaning* in the spelling system when they examine *homophones* such as *sail/sale* and *pail/pale*. The different spellings for the same sound are often explained by the fact that they occur in homophones, and we support children as they keep the word's meaning in mind while examining its spelling.

Syllables and Affixes Students' understanding about spelling patterns in single-syllable words is the foundation that supports their growth into the syllables and affixes phase. This understanding helps them to explore two-syllable words and the syllable patterns that determine what goes on at the juncture of syllables and morphemes. The juncture conventions all depend on an awareness of the relationship between sound and spelling. Morphological analysis—the exploration of word-formation processes involved in combining prefixes, suffixes, base words, and roots—may be facilitated by exploring how these units are represented in spelling.

The syllables and affixes phase is typically achieved in the intermediate grades. The first major convention to be explored at this phase is the addition of inflectional endings to base words. The vowel pattern in the base word determines what happens at the juncture of the base word and the ending: *make* + *ing* = *making* (drop *e*); *hit* + *ing* = *hitting* (double the final consonant to keep the short vowel sound in the base word); *wait* + *ing* = *waiting* (vowel pair in the base word, so no change when adding the ending).

Students' understanding of the relationship between short and long vowel sounds/patterns in base words and how they determine spelling when inflectional endings are added provides a solid foundation for their exploration of syllable patterns—what happens *within* words at the juncture of syllables. The vowel-consonant-consonant-vowel (VC/CV) pattern in *hitting* occurs in *hammer*. In both cases, the doubled consonant keeps the vowel in the first syllable short. The vowel-consonant-vowel (V/CV) pattern in *making* occurs in *diner*. In both cases, the single consonant signals a long vowel in the first syllable.

Derivational Relations Some students may move into the derivational relations phase in Grade 4 or 5, but most students in this phase are in middle school and above. It is important to note that students will be *reading* many of the words to be studied at this phase when they are still syllables and affixes spellers.

In this phase, students explore the full range in which words are *derived* from a common base or Greek/Latin root to form spelling-meaning families. Word study at this level has the potential to expand students' vocabularies exponentially because most words students will encounter in specific domains of study will be understood and learned by examining their morphological structure. Students' spelling errors at this level are fairly sophisticated: schwas in unaccented syllables within multisyllabic words (DEPRAVATION/*deprivation*, DOMINENT/*dominant*) and consonant doubling in assimilated or "absorbed" prefixes (APARITION/*apparition*). Assimilated prefixes reflect the convention of changing the last consonant in a prefix to the first consonant of the base word or root (*in* + *mediate* = *immediate*; *ad* + *point* = *appoint*).

Where Do the Spelling/Phonics Words Come From?

The resources we have drawn upon to guide the selection of words in *Journeys* and in this Guide include extensive word frequency counts of English (Zeno et al., 1996). This informs us about the most frequently occurring words at each grade level in oral language as well as in print. To determine which words are likely to be known by students at different grade levels, we have used Biemiller's (2005) adaptation of Dale et al.'s (1981) extensive study. We have also drawn upon the developmental research that, as described above, has determined the scope and sequence of word features (Henderson & Templeton, 1986; Templeton & Bear, 1992).

Consolidating this information allows us to select words representing the features that need to be addressed at each developmental level.

At the beginning of each grade, several lessons address important patterns that were also addressed in the previous grade. The words that represent the patterns, however, are appropriate for the new grade level. This is done in order to revisit and consolidate knowledge that may not have been exercised over the preceding break. If you teach in a year-round or multi-track system, you may decide whether or which students need to work through these lessons.

▶ Vocabulary

The vocabulary lessons in this Guide build on and extend the lessons and activities in *Journeys*. Each lesson addresses the research-based criteria for effective instruction using a grade-appropriate approach:

- Develop **word consciousness**—the appreciation of and interest in words, their meanings, and how they are used.

- Through discussion, **activate background knowledge** to determine what students already know about the words and the concepts they represent. Usually there is a range of understandings among students, so getting them involved in discussion is very important.

- Use a **variety of activities** that involve students in using words and thinking about their meanings. These include **sorting/categorizing** words, thinking of **words that are related** morphologically and semantically, **discussing** the words with examples and non-examples, and using **graphic organizers**.

- Reinforce how the structure or **morphology** of the words—affixes, base words, and roots—provides clues to their meanings.

- Teach and model the development of independent word-learning strategies that integrate the use of **contextual and morphological clues**.

- When necessary, **explain the meaning and give examples** of how the words are used. Make a point of using the words often.

Components of a Typical Kindergarten Oral Vocabulary Development Lesson

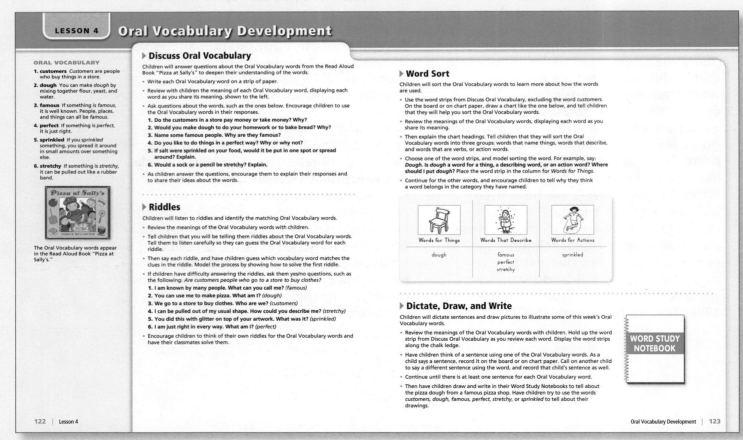

Word Study Vocabulary Lessons

- Oral Vocabulary words that appear in a *Journeys* Read Aloud Book are introduced using student-friendly definitions. Oral questioning focuses on applying the words to various contexts to support an understanding of their meanings.

- Meaning is reinforced through wordplay and game-like activities in which children apply their knowledge of the Oral Vocabulary words.

- A word sort activity with teacher prompting has children categorize Oral Vocabulary words by how they are used.

- Children apply their understanding by dictating sentences and drawing pictures about a given topic that is based on the Oral Vocabulary words. Children then write about their drawings using the lesson's Oral Vocabulary words.

▶ Vocabulary Development

What the Research Says

We know that vocabulary knowledge is the single most powerful predictor of reading comprehension and academic learning. In Kindergarten and Grade 1, developing *oral* vocabulary is critical and absolutely necessary as a foundation for later vocabulary growth and learning.

For younger children who are not yet reading widely, there is a substantial, convincing body of research that supports the role of teacher read-alouds in developing language and vocabulary (Santoro, Chard, Howard, & Baker, 2008; Pilkulski & Templeton, 2010). However, significant vocabulary growth will occur only when you spend time with *explicit* attention to vocabulary in the contexts of both narrative and informational texts.

In Grades 2–6, we need to address the two major areas of vocabulary development: general academic vocabulary and content-area, or domain-specific, vocabulary (*Common Core State Standards*, 2010).

- **General academic vocabulary** includes those words that do not often occur in everyday spoken language—for example *transmit*, *paradox*, and *product*—but which students may encounter frequently in their reading across all content areas. These words also occur in more formal spoken language, such as a lecture format. Students may often have the underlying concept that such a word represents, but they lack the label that stands for that concept.

- **Content-area or domain-specific vocabulary** refers to words that occur primarily in specific content or subject matter areas such as science, history and social science, mathematics, and the arts. In contrast to general academic vocabulary, much content-specific academic vocabulary—for example *equilateral*, *condensation*, and *feudalism*—represents new concepts, and can therefore be more challenging to learn.

Journeys and this Guide offer a research-based, rich, and robust approach to vocabulary instruction using the important words that students need to learn. The lessons also teach them *about* words—for example, how prefixes, suffixes, base words, and roots combine to result in the meaning of words. When learners understand how this process works, they possess one of the most powerful understandings for vocabulary growth.

Where Does the Target Vocabulary Come From?

As with the selection of words for the spelling/phonics lessons, at Grades 2–6 we used Biemiller's (2005) adaptation of Dale et al.'s (1981) study to guide the selection of words for a particular grade level. We then used Zeno et al.'s frequency corpus (1996) as well as Hiebert's corpus (2005) to identify morphologically related words and cross-checked with Harris-Jacobsen (1982), Dale-Chall, and the Academic Word List.

This process ensured that words would be sufficiently challenging to be academic rather than conversational vocabulary, yet not so challenging that students will find them too difficult to learn and remember, even with good instruction and careful repetition. In Kindergarten and Grade 1, we used Zeno as well as cross-checking with traditional word frequency lists that still correlate highly with recent analyses.

▶ Addressing the Common Core State Standards

The approach to word study in this Guide will help students develop and reach reading foundational skills and language standards targeted in the *Common Core State Standards for English Language Arts (CCSS)*. The depth and breadth of word knowledge developed through this approach to word study will also support the emphasis in the *CCSS* on students' reading of more complex literary and informational texts. Because this approach is embedded in the reading and writing in which students are engaged, it strongly supports the *CCSS*'s emphasis on "an integrated model of literacy" (p. 4).

Word knowledge is a central aspect of the Grades K–5 Reading Foundational Skills that relate to the decoding and identification of words during reading. Word knowledge is also a central aspect of the Grades K–6 Language Standards that relate to the spelling of words in writing. While "spelling" is classified in the CCSS as a convention of written language, the standards are explicit about spelling knowledge being "inseparable" from reading and writing. The research in developmental word knowledge confirms this interconnectedness. Students' spelling knowledge provides the foundation for word knowledge that they use to *read* words as well as to *write* words (Templeton, 2011).

In the *CCSS*, the standards in word recognition, phonics, and spelling that are presented across the grades follow in large part the sequence identified in the developmental research. Because the word study in *Journeys* and in this Guide is developmentally based, we can be assured that students will learn and effectively apply knowledge of spelling patterns. All students, including those students whose instructional levels are below their grade-level placement, will be making productive progress toward the anchor standards.

The sequence of standards in the *CCSS* follows the developmental course of the relationship between learning to read words and learning to spell words identified in research. For beginning readers in Kindergarten and Grade 1, this relationship is quite close. As children learn about consonant and vowel sounds within single-syllable words, they are able to spell and read words that follow the basic consonant-vowel-consonant pattern.

As children progress, however, their ability to accurately read words runs ahead of their ability to accurately spell those same words. The sequence of instruction in the *CCSS* reflects this fact. For example, the spelling standards for Grades 1 and 2 address single-syllable words while the phonics and word recognition skills address two-syllable words. There are no expectations that children will correctly spell two-syllable words. Continued experience with such words through reading, together with your decoding instruction, will build the foundation of word knowledge that moves children toward understanding, learning, and correctly spelling words they have already learned to read.

The *CCSS* also address *morphology* in reading, spelling, and vocabulary development. At the syllables and affixes and the derivational relations phases, students explore word formation processes. This develops generative vocabulary knowledge as well as spelling knowledge. It is not sufficient to know what the meanings of particular affixes are; students must understand how they affect the meanings of base words and roots. *Journeys* and this Guide systematically build morphological knowledge, supporting students' learning of the meanings of affixes and also the ways in which they combine (Templeton, 2012).

Developmental word study accommodates the needs of a range of learners at each grade level. The *CCSS* are clear about not every student being able to attain grade-level standards: "No set of grade-specific standards can fully reflect the great variety in abilities, needs, learning rates, and achievement levels of students in any given classroom" (*CCSS*, p. 6). The standards emphasize, therefore, that "Instruction should be differentiated . . . The point is to teach students what they need to learn . . . to discern when particular children or activities warrant more or less attention" (*CCSS*, p. 15). Each grade-level of this Guide and the online resources provided accommodate a wide span of developmental levels, ensuring that all students' needs are met.

▸ Differentiated Instruction

Teachers differentiate for appropriate reading levels in their classrooms. It is important that children and older students be placed at their appropriate levels for word study as well. This will ensure that they have the experience with words and patterns that they are ready to explore.

Specific guidelines for determining your students' appropriate developmental levels for word study are provided in the Resources section of this Guide on the next page and on pages 329–342. The Qualitative Spelling Inventory will help you determine your students' developmental spelling levels at the beginning of the school year. It may be administered again at the middle of the school year, and then toward the end of the year.

The relationship between word knowledge and reading level is very close. You will likely find that your below-level, on-level, and above-level students in word study are almost always your below-, on-, and above-level readers. This allows you to differentiate your instruction more effectively. For example, when meeting with your below-level reading group at the beginning of the week, you may introduce and sort the leveled spelling words after students have read an appropriately leveled selection.

For most students, the grade-level words and features that are presented in *Journeys* and in this Guide will be appropriate. For your students who are not on grade level, the Struggling and Advanced words and features offered in each lesson will address the needs of most. For those students who are significantly below- or above-level, use the word lists on pages 332–342 and access the appropriate lessons in another grade level of this Guide on **www.thinkcentral.com**.

Occasionally, it may be necessary to adjust the level for particular students, just as you adjust reading levels. The weekly assessments on Day 5 of each spelling/phonics lesson provide effective progress monitoring so that you will be able to know how students are progressing. This insight is also very helpful as you evaluate students' writing since that is where the depth of your students' learning is observed.

ELL ELL SUPPORT

In addition to the point-of-use notes located in the spelling/phonics lessons in this Guide, the information on the next page and on pages 324–328 of the Resources section will help you address the unique transfer support needs of your students who are English language learners (ELLs).

▶ Assessment to Inform Instruction

Assessing a student's spelling developmental phase is a powerful and precise method for planning instruction. By following the steps below and using the tools on the pages that follow, you can determine the phase of spelling development for each of your students and use the results to select appropriate lessons for students at varying phases.

① ASSESS

Administer the Qualitative Spelling Inventory (QSI) on page 329 in the Resources section of this Guide. Also collect a selection of each student's first-draft writing for comparison. The QSI results combined with examples from daily writing will offer a strong sampling for analysis. Emphasize to students that the assessment is not a test for a grade and it is okay if they don't know all the answers. Explain that their work will help you understand what they already know and what you need to help them learn.

② ANALYZE

Determine a spelling developmental phase for each student. Use the Qualitative Spelling Inventory Checklist (pages 330–331) to guide your decisions.

③ PLAN AND MONITOR

Organize small groups based on your diverse classroom needs. Monitor students' progress, and reorganize groups as needed throughout the year. For on-level students, use the lessons in your grade-level of this Guide. Select lessons for Struggling and Advanced students:

- Suggested lessons for Differentiated Instruction are provided in each lesson in Grades 1–6.
- If your students' needs do not align with the suggested lessons, select an appropriate lesson using the word lists organized by spelling phase on pages 332–342.

Letters *Aa–Jj*

Model the Sort

Children will name letters with you and sort letters into groups of capital and small letters.

- Display Letter Card *A*. Suggested language: **This is capital *A*. Capital *A* has three straight lines and is pointy at the top.** Display Letter Card *a*. Suggested language: **This is small *a*. Small *a* has a curved line that is round like a circle and a straight line next to the round part.**

- Continue naming and describing the other capital and small letters. As you identify each capital or small letter, ask children if you should put it with the capital *A* or with the small *a*, and tell why.

- When you have sorted all the letters as capital and small letters, point to Letter Cards at random and have children name the letter each time. Have them say whether you are pointing to the capital or small letter.

- Give each child a set of Lesson 1 Letter Cards, and have them repeat the sort independently.

MATERIALS

Letter Cards: capital letters *A–J*; small letters *a–j*

 Reproducible Letter Cards are available at **www.thinkcentral.com**.

ELL SUPPORT

Support Word Meaning Before you describe letters and their shapes, explain and demonstrate the meanings of the words *line(s)*, *circle*, *straight*, *curved*, and *round*. Tell children that *straight*, *curved*, and *round* are all words that tell about different kinds of lines. Explain that they can write letters using these different kinds of lines.

Letter Shape Sort

Children will sort letters by the types of lines in the letters.

- Display Letter Cards *Aa–Jj* at the top of a pocket chart. Tell children that today you will be sorting the letters by the kinds of lines they have.

- Place the *A* card as a heading below the other letters in the pocket chart. Point out to children that this letter has only straight lines.

- Place the *B* card as a heading for another column. Point out that it has a straight line and curved lines. Then place the *C* card, and tell children that it has only a curved line. Tell children that they will be sorting letters into groups: letters with only straight lines, letters with straight and curved or round lines, and letters with only curved lines.

- Call on volunteers to sort the letters. Encourage classmates to comment on whether they think each letter is correctly sorted.

- Have children name all the capital and small letters in each group and identify which capital and small letters are in the same group (e.g., *B, b*), and which are in different groups (e.g., *A, a*).

- Extend the activity by having partners take turns sorting some of the letters. One child sorts the letters, and his or her partner tells how the letters are sorted. The child who is sorting should be able to explain to the partner how he or she sorted.

A	B	C
E	D	c
F	G	g
H	J	j
I	a	
i	b	
	d	
	e	
	f	
	h	

DAY 3 Find Your Letter Partner

Children will match capital letters to small letters.

- Display and name Letter Cards *Aa–Jj*. Then make two piles of Letter Cards, one for capital letters and one for small letters.
- Tell children that they are going to play a game. You will give each child a Letter Card. Children have to find the classmate who has the capital or small letter that matches the letter on their card. That child is their "letter partner."
- Give each child a Letter Card. Have children find their letter partners.
- When children have found their partners, have each child in a pair say the name of his or her letter.
- Extend the activity by asking the pairs of children to stand in ABC order. Help children as needed. Then have them say the name of their letter in turn so they repeat the alphabet in order from *Aa* to *Jj*.

DAY 4 Play "Go Fish"

Children will play a game to match capital and small letters.

- Remind children that there are two forms for each letter, a capital letter and a small letter. Tell children that they are going to play a game called "Go Fish" with capital and small letters.
- Tell children how to play the game. Explain that partners each take five Letter Cards. The rest of the cards are placed face down in a pile.
- Explain that the first child then chooses one of his or her cards and asks the second child if he or she has a match. For example, if the child chooses a capital letter, he or she asks the second child for the matching small letter.
- If the second child does not have the matching letter, he or she says, "Go fish." Then the first child picks a card from the pile. The game is over when all the capital and small Letter Cards are matched.
- Organize children into pairs. Then give partners a set of Lesson 1 Letter Cards to play the game.
- After all the Letter Cards have been matched, have partners name the capital and small letters.

DAY 5 Assess

Tell children that you will be naming letters and asking children to hold up the Letter Card that shows the letter. One at a time, name capital and small letters, and have children hold up the corresponding Letter Card.

RETEACH **IF** children are unable to name three or more letters, **THEN** revisit the activity on Day 1 and reassess.

Have children use the Letter Cards as a model to write in their Word Study Notebooks some of the letters *Aa–Jj*. When they have finished writing the letters, have them say the names of the letters they wrote.

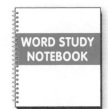

WORD STUDY NOTEBOOK

The Letters in Your Name

MATERIALS

Blank name cards

 Reproducible blank name cards are available at **www.thinkcentral.com**.

 **ELL SUPPORT**

Support Word Meaning Before you discuss the length of children's names, use classroom objects, such as blocks or string, to demonstrate the meanings of the words *short* and *long*. Explain that these words can be used to describe names, too.

DAY 1 PHONICS **Model the Sort**

Children will identify their names and sort name cards with you into groups of short and long names.

- Write each child's name on a blank name card.
- Display a name card for a child with a short name. Suggested language: **This is the name of someone in our class. It is (Lin's) name. Lin's name begins with a capital *L*. It is a short name. It only has three letters in it. All of the letters have straight lines in them. One of the letters has a curved line, too.**
- Point out the letters with straight and curved lines in the child's name. Then tell children you will start a category for names that are short. Remind children that short names only have a few letters.
- Display a name card for a child with a long name. Suggested language: **This is (Christopher's) name. Christopher's name begins with a capital *C*. It is a long name. It has many letters in it.**
- Use the child's name to start a category for names that are long. Remind children that long names have many letters.
- Continue with the name cards for the other children in the group. As you display each name, ask children if you should put it with the short name or the long name and tell why. Encourage discussion between children about whether a name is long or short.
- When you have sorted all the names, read aloud the name cards at random. Have children take their cards when they hear their names.
- Call on children in alphabetical order. Have them independently place their name cards in the group with short or long names.

DAY 2 **Find Your Name**

Children will discuss the letters in their names and find their own name cards.

- Remind children that they have been learning about the letters in their names. Then recall the story "Building with Dad" with children. Display a card with the name *Dad* in a pocket chart.
- Describe the name for children. Suggested language: **This is the name of a person in the story "Building with Dad." This is a name card that says *Dad*. *Dad* begins with a capital letter. All the letters have straight and curved lines in them.**
- Choose a child's name card and place it in the pocket chart. Call on children to tell what they notice about the name. Repeat with other children's name cards.
- Tell children you are going to hold up name cards one at a time. They should raise their hands when they see their names.
- For variation, you may give clues about name cards you are holding. Suggested language: **I have a card for a long name. It starts with a capital *S* and ends with a letter that has a straight line and a round line. Whose name is it?** *(Samantha)*
- If there are two or more children with the same name and spelling, you may either color code the cards or use their last initial.

| Deepak | Antonio | Samantha | Lia | Carlos |

DAY 3 Letter Hunt

Children will find letters from their names in the classroom.

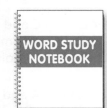

WORD STUDY NOTEBOOK

- Display the *Dad* name card from Day 2. Say each letter in the name. Then demonstrate how to find the letters on classroom signs, on bulletin boards, and in books.
- Tell children that they are going to play a game. First they will say the letters in their names. Then they will try to find some or all of the letters somewhere in the classroom.
- Give children their name cards. Tell them to take turns searching the classroom for letters in their names. Have children point to and say each letter that they find.
- Ask children to use their Word Study Notebooks to write the letters as they find them. Then have them write their names in their Word Study Notebooks.
- Extend the activity by having children compare the letters in their names with those in a partner's.

DAY 4 Share Your Name

Children will say the letters in their names.

- Display the *Dad* name card from Day 2. Say each letter in the name for children. Suggested language: **This is Dad's name. There are three letters in the name *Dad*. *Dad* begins with a capital *D*. The next letter is a small *a*. The last letter is a small *d*.**
- Tell children that they will now say the letters in their names. Give children their name cards. Then have them take turns saying each letter in their names.
- Extend the activity by saying the alphabet in order. Have children raise their hands each time you say a letter that is in their names.

DAY 5 Assess

Tell children they will be writing their own names. Give children their name cards. Have them trace the names on the cards. Then have them write their names in their Word Study Notebooks.

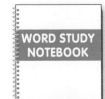

WORD STUDY NOTEBOOK

RETEACH **IF** children are unable to write their names, **THEN** have children practice tracing their names and practice writing each letter.

Have children use their name cards as a model to write their names in their Word Study Notebooks. When they have finished writing their names, have them say the letters in their names.

DAY 1 PHONICS **Model the Sort**

MATERIALS

Letter Cards: capital letters *A–T*; small letters *a–t*

 Reproducible Letter Cards are available at www.thinkcentral.com.

 **ELL SUPPORT**

Support Word Meaning Before you discuss letter pairs that look the same or different, use classroom objects to demonstrate the meanings of the words *same* and *different*. For example, show two blocks that are the same and two blocks that are different. Then have children point out and name other objects in the classroom that are the same and different.

Children will sort letters with you into groups of letters whose capital and small letters look the same or almost the same and whose capital and small letters look different. Then children will name the letters.

- Display the Letter Cards for capital *C* and small *c*. Suggested language: **This letter is capital C. This is small c. Capital C and small c look the same. They both have one curved line.** Tell children that you are going to start a category for letter pairs that look the same.

- Display the Letter Cards for capital *A* and small *a*. Suggested language: **This is capital A. This is small a. Capital A and small a look different. Capital A has straight lines. Small a has one curved line and one straight line.** Tell children that you are now going to start a category for letter pairs that look different.

- Continue naming other pairs of capital and small letters. As you display and name each letter pair, ask children if you should put it in the *same* group or in the *different* group.

- When you have sorted all the letters, point to each pair of Letter Cards at random and have children name the capital and small letters.

- Give partners a set of Lesson 3 Letter Cards, and have them repeat the sort.

DAY 2 **Letter Pair Sort**

Children will sort pairs of capital and small letters into groups whose capital and small letters look the same and whose capital and small letters look different.

- Remind children that they have been learning that some capital and small letters look the same or almost the same and some capital and small letters look different.

- Place the Letter Cards *A* and *a* as a heading in a pocket chart. Remind children that these letters look different.

- Place the Letter Cards *C* and *c* as a heading in a pocket chart. Remind children that these letters look the same.

- Call on volunteers to sort the remaining pairs of capital and small letters. Have classmates tell whether they think each letter pair has been sorted correctly.

- After children have sorted all the cards, have them name the letters in each group.

Aa	Cc
Bb	Pp
Ee	Mm
Gg	Ss

DAY 3 | Letter Hunt

Children will find capital and small letters in the classroom.

- Display Letter Cards *Aa–Tt*. Then make two piles of cards, one for capital letters and one for small letters.
- Tell children they are going to hunt for letters in the classroom. You will give each child a capital Letter Card and a small Letter Card. Children will try to find examples of the letters somewhere in the classroom.
- Give each child a pair of Letter Cards. Have children say the names of the letters on their cards. Then have them take turns searching the classroom for the letters.
- Have children come together to display their Letter Cards and tell where they found each letter in the classroom.
- Extend the activity by saying the letter names in alphabetical order. When children hear the name of a letter on one of their cards, they should place it in order in a pocket chart or on the chalk ledge.

DAY 4 | Letter Match

Children will match capital and small letters.

- Remind children that there are two forms for each letter, a capital letter and a small letter. Then tell them they are going to play a matching game with a partner.
- Give partners a set of Lesson 3 Letter Cards. Have children sort the cards into two piles, one for capital letters and one for small letters.
- Tell children that they will take turns choosing and naming a capital Letter Card. Then their partners will find the matching small Letter Card. Children will continue taking turns until all of the capital and small Letter Cards are matched.
- Extend the activity by having children sort the pairs of Letter Cards into different groups, one group for letters whose capital and small letters look the same or almost the same and one group for letters whose capital and small letters look different.

DAY 5 | Assess

Tell children that they will be identifying letter pairs. Have children identify two pairs of letters whose capital and small letters look the same or almost the same. Then have them identify two pairs of letters whose capital and small letters look different.

RETEACH **IF** children are unable to identify four pairs of letters, **THEN** revisit the activity on Day 1 and reassess.

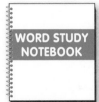

Have children paste in their Word Study Notebooks the pairs of Letter Cards that they identified as the same and different. When they have finished pasting their letter pairs, have them say the names of the letters.

The Alphabet

MATERIALS

Letter Cards: capital letters *A–Z*; small letters *a–z*

 Reproducible Letter Cards are available at **www.thinkcentral.com**.

 **ELL SUPPORT**

Linguistic Transfer Children from some language backgrounds may be unfamiliar with the concept of the alphabet. Help these children to understand that the words we read and write are made up of letters.

DAY 1 PHONICS **Model the Sort**

Children will name the letters of the alphabet with you as you place them in order.

- Tell children that you are going to sing a song about the alphabet. Point to an alphabet chart or a set of capital and small Letter Cards placed in alphabetical order. Suggested language: **This is the alphabet. The alphabet is made up of all the letters we use to write words. Listen as I name all of the letters in this song.**

- Sing "The Alphabet Song" for children, pointing to each letter as it is named in the song. Then sing the song again. Encourage children to join in with you. Tell children that when we say or sing the alphabet, we always say or sing the letters in this order.

- Hold up Letter Card *A*, and have children repeat its name as you place the card in a pocket chart or along the chalk ledge. Continue with the rest of the alphabet, one letter at a time. Repeat and reinforce that the letters in the alphabet are always in this order.

- Repeat the procedure with the small Letter Cards, having children repeat each letter name as you place the Letter Cards in a pocket chart or along the chalk ledge. Remind children that the letters in the alphabet are always in this order.

- Give partners a set of Lesson 4 Letter Cards. Have them work together to place the capital and small letters in alphabetical order. Tell children to use the alphabet chart or the alphabet you made with Letter Cards to guide them.

DAY 2 **Letter Name**

Children will name letters and place them in alphabetical order.

- Remind children that they have been learning about the letters in the alphabet. Sing "The Alphabet Song" with children. Display Letter Card *A*. Call on a volunteer to say the name of the letter and then place it in a pocket chart or on the chalk ledge.

- Continue with the remaining capital Letter Cards, having volunteers place each letter in order. Then have children point to the cards as they say the names of the letters in order.

- Display Letter Card *a*. Call on a volunteer to name the letter and then place it in a pocket chart or on the chalk ledge.

- Continue with the remaining small Letter Cards, having volunteers place them in alphabetical order. Then have children point to the cards as they say the names of the letters in order.

- Extend the activity by having small groups work together to place a set of Lesson 4 Letter Cards in alphabetical order.

A	B	C	D	E	F

DAY 3 Alphabet Sort

Children will arrange letters in alphabetical order.

WORD STUDY NOTEBOOK

- Give partners a set of capital and small Letter Cards. Tell children that they will work together to place all of the letters in alphabetical order.

- Have children put each set of Letter Cards in alphabetical order, starting with the capital letters. Then have them say the names of the letters to recite the alphabet.

- You may have children place the small Letter Cards beneath the capital Letter Cards to reinforce their understanding of capital and small letters.

- Extend the activity by having children write the letters of the alphabet in their Word Study Notebooks. Have them use an alphabet chart or the Letter Cards as a guide.

DAY 4 Letter Match

Children will match capital and small letters and place them in order.

- Remind children that each letter has a capital and a small form. Tell children that they are going to match capital and small letters.

- Pass out a set of capital and small Letter Cards to partners.

- Have children work together to place each capital letter with its matching small letter.

- Then have them work together to place the letter pairs in alphabetical order. Children can use an alphabet chart in the classroom as a guide.

DAY 5 Assess

Tell children they will be putting Letter Cards in alphabetical order. Have children place the capital letters in alphabetical order. Then have them place the small letters in alphabetical order.

WORD STUDY NOTEBOOK

RETEACH **IF** children are unable to place the letters in alphabetical order, **THEN** revisit the activity on Day 1 and reassess.

Have children use the Letter Cards as a model to write the letters of the alphabet in their Word Study Notebooks. When they have finished writing the letters, have them say the names of the letters in order.

Beginning Sounds in Words

DAY 1 PHONICS Model the Sort

Children will sort Picture Cards with you based on beginning sounds.

- Display the Lesson 5 Picture Cards, and name each picture with children. Tell children that together you will sort the Picture Cards into groups of pictures whose names have the same beginning sound. Set aside the Picture Cards with beginning sounds /l/, /f/, and /d/.

- Place Picture Cards *mouse* and *sun* as headings in a pocket chart. Point to the *mouse* card and name the picture. Suggested language: **Mouse. I hear the /m/ sound at the beginning of *mouse*. /m/ is the first sound I hear. Listen again: *mouse*.**

- Point to the *sun* card and name the picture. Suggested language: **Sun. I hear the /s/ sound at the beginning of *sun*. /s/ is the first sound I hear. Listen again: *sun*.** Explain that the words *mouse* and *sun* have different beginning sounds.

- Model how to sort the Picture Cards. Display Picture Card *moon*. Suggested language: **Listen: *Mouse, moon. Sun, moon*. Does *moon* begin like *mouse* or does *moon* begin like *sun*? *Moon* and *mouse* have the same sound at the beginning. Listen: *mouse, moon*. I'll put *moon* under *mouse* because they have the same beginning sound.**

- Repeat for the remaining /m/ and /s/ Picture Cards. When all the cards are placed, have children listen as you name each picture to make sure all the words begin with the same sound.

- Repeat the process with the Picture Cards that begin with the /l/, /f/, and /d/ sounds.

- Give partners a set of Lesson 5 Picture Cards. Have them work together to repeat the sort.

DAY 2 Picture Sort

Children will sort Picture Cards into groups of pictures whose names have the same beginning sounds.

- Remind children that they have been learning about the sounds at the beginning of words. Then repeat the sort from Day 1 with the /m/ words and /s/ words.

- Display Picture Cards *mop, dog, saw, lion,* and *feather* as headings in a pocket chart. Name the pictures, enunciating the beginning sounds so children can hear them clearly.

- Then draw attention to the beginning sound in each word. Suggested language: **This is a *mop*. *Mop*. I hear the /m/ sound at the beginning of *mop*. Listen again: *mop*.** Repeat for each card you will use as a heading.

- Display the remaining Lesson 5 Picture Cards one at a time. Name each picture for children, emphasizing the beginning sound. Then call on a volunteer to place it in the appropriate column.

- After all the pictures have been sorted, name the pictures in each column and help children understand that the words all begin with the same sound. Suggested language: **Listen: *mop, mouse, moon*. These words all begin with the same /m/ sound.**

- Give each child a set of Lesson 5 Picture Cards. Have them repeat the sort independently.

DAY 3 Buddy Sort

Children will sort Picture Cards into groups of their own making.

- Display the Lesson 5 Picture Cards. Name the pictures for children.
- Tell children that you are going to sort the pictures in a new way. Model thinking about the Picture Cards. Say: **I am going to sort the pictures into two groups. One group will have pictures of animals. The other group will have pictures of other things.**
- Use the Picture Cards to create the groups. Then discuss with children the groups you made.
- Give partners a set of Lesson 5 Picture Cards. Tell them to sort the pictures into groups that they talk about and choose together.
- Tell children that they will have to be able to explain why they sorted the pictures into the groups that they did. You may suggest various groups for children, such as things you see in the sky, animals, or things you can find in a house.
- Have partners share how they sorted the Picture Cards.

DAY 4 Brainstorming

Children will think of words that have the same beginning sounds as the Picture Card names.

- Remind children that some words begin with the same sound. Suggested language: **Listen to these words:** *mouse, moon, mop*. **They all begin with the /m/ sound.**
- Tell children that you can name some other words that begin with the /m/ sound. Say the words *mat* and *mother*. Point out that they have the same beginning sound as *mouse*, *moon*, and *mop*.
- Give partners a set of Lesson 5 Picture Cards. Have children name the pictures.
- Then have one child hold up a picture while the other child says a different word that begins with the same sound. Have children take turns until all the cards have been used.
- You may extend the activity by having children draw in their Word Study Notebooks pictures of things that begin with each of the sounds.

DAY 5 Assess

Tell children you will hold up and name a Picture Card and they will say its beginning sound. One at a time, display and name Picture Cards *moon*, *socks*, *lamp*, *duck,* and *fan*. Have children say the beginning sound of each word.

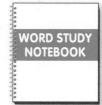

RETEACH **IF** children are unable to identify the beginning sounds for three of the cards, **THEN** revisit the activity on Day 1 and reassess.

Have children draw in their Word Study Notebooks pictures of one thing that begins with the /s/ sound and one thing that begins with the /m/ sound. When they have finished drawing their pictures, have them name the pictures, enunciating the sound at the beginning of each word.

Beginning Sounds in Words

MATERIALS

Picture Cards: nail, nest, nut, pan, pencil, pool, comb, camel, carrot, two, tire, tomato

 Reproducible Picture Cards are available at **www.thinkcentral.com**.

 **ELL SUPPORT**

Linguistic Transfer The /n/ sound should be familiar to most ELLs. Some children may be unfamiliar with the /p/, /t/, and /k/ sounds. Give them additional practice pronouncing words that begin with these sounds and discriminating the sounds.

DAY 1 PHONICS **Model the Sort**

Children will sort Picture Cards with you based on beginning sounds.

- Remind children that they have been working with the sounds at the beginning of words. Display the Lesson 6 Picture Cards, and name each picture with children. Tell children that together you will sort the Picture Cards into groups of pictures whose names begin with the same sound. Set aside the Picture Cards with beginning sounds /k/ and /t/.

- Place Picture Cards *nail* and *pan* as headings in a pocket chart. Then point to the *nail* card and name the picture, emphasizing the beginning sound. Suggested language: *Nail.* **I hear the /n/ sound at the beginning of *nail*. It is the first sound that I hear in the word. Listen:** *nail.*

- Point to the *pan* card and name the picture. Suggested language: *Pan.* **I hear the /p/ sound at the beginning of *pan*. It is the first sound I hear in the word. Listen:** *pan.* Explain that these two picture names have different sounds at the beginning. Suggested language: **Listen:** *nail, pan.* **These words have different sounds at the beginning.**

- Model how to sort cards by their beginning sounds. Display the following cards one at a time: *nest, pencil, nut, pool.* As you display each card, name the picture of the card you are showing and the picture of each heading card. Have children compare the sounds at the beginning of each picture name. Then place each Picture Card in the correct column.

- When all the cards are placed, name the pictures in each column. Have children listen to make sure all the words in each column begin with the same sound.

- Repeat the process with the Picture Cards whose names begin with the /k/ and /t/ sounds.

- Give partners a set of Lesson 6 Picture Cards. Have them work together to repeat the sort.

DAY 2 **Picture Sort**

Children will sort Picture Cards into groups of pictures whose names have the same beginning sounds.

- Remind children that they have been listening for the sounds at the beginning of words.

- Display Picture Cards *nest, pencil, camel,* and *tire* as headings in a pocket chart. Name the pictures, enunciating the beginning sounds so that children can hear them clearly. Then point out the beginning sound in each picture name. Suggested language: **This is a picture of a *nest*. *Nest*. I hear the /n/ sound at the beginning of *nest*. Listen again:** *nest.*

- Display the Lesson 6 Picture Cards one at a time. Name each picture for children, emphasizing the beginning sound. Then call on a volunteer to place it in the column with the picture whose name has the same beginning sound.

- After all the pictures have been sorted, name the pictures in each column, having children listen to make sure all the picture names begin with the same sound. Suggested language: **Listen:** *nest, nail, nut.* **Do they all begin with the same /n/ sound? Yes.**

- Give each child a set of Lesson 6 Picture Cards. Have them repeat the sort independently.

DAY 3 Brainstorming

Children will think of words that have the same beginning sounds as the Picture Card names.

WORD STUDY NOTEBOOK

- Remind children that they can listen to the beginning sounds in words and decide whether the words have the same beginning sounds. Suggested language: **Listen to these words:** *nail, nest, nut*. **They all begin with the /n/ sound.**

- Tell children you can name some other words that begin with the /n/ sound. Say the words *notebook* and *noise*. Point out that they have the same beginning sound as *nail*, *nest*, and *nut*.

- Give partners a set of Lesson 6 Picture Cards. Have children name the pictures. Then have one child hold up a picture while the other child thinks of a different word that begins with the same sound as the picture name.

- Have children take turns until all the Picture Cards have been used.

- You may want to extend the activity by having children draw in their Word Study Notebooks pictures of things whose names begin with each of the sounds in today's lesson.

DAY 4 Buddy Sort

Children will sort Picture Cards into groups of their own making.

- Display a set of Lesson 6 Picture Cards. Name the pictures for children.

- Tell children that you are going to sort the pictures in a new way. Suggested language: **I am going to sort the pictures into two groups. One group will have things I can eat. The other group will have things I cannot eat.**

- Use the Picture Cards to create the groups. Then discuss with children the groups you made.

- Give partners a set of Lesson 6 Picture Cards. Tell children to talk about the pictures and then sort them in their own ways. Explain that they can make as many groups as they want. Suggest examples for children to help them get started, such as *things they can use* or *foods*.

- Have partners share the groups they made with other pairs of children. Have them explain why they put each picture into its group.

DAY 5 Assess

Tell children that you will hold up a Picture Card, and they will say the beginning sound for each picture name. One at a time, display Picture Cards *nut*, *pool*, *carrot*, and *tomato*. Have children name each picture and then say the beginning sound in each picture name.

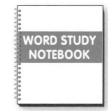

WORD STUDY NOTEBOOK

RETEACH **IF** children are unable to identify the beginning sounds for three of the cards, **THEN** revisit the activity on Day 1 and reassess.

Have children draw in their Word Study Notebooks pictures of two things whose names begin with the same sound. When they have finished drawing their pictures, have them name the pictures, enunciating the sound at the beginning of each picture name.

Beginning Sounds /m/*m*, /s/*s*

MATERIALS

Picture Cards: milk, mouse, monkey, man, mat, map, moon, salad, sink, saw, sandwich, seal, sun, soap

Letter Cards: *m, s*

 Reproducible Picture and Letter Cards are available at **www.thinkcentral.com**.

 ELL SUPPORT

Linguistic Transfer The /m/ and /s/ sounds should be familiar to most ELLs. If children have difficulty discriminating words that begin with /m/*m* and /s/*s*, give them additional practice listening to and saying words that begin with these sounds.

DAY 1 PHONICS **Model the Sort**

Children will sort Picture Cards with you into groups of pictures whose names begin with /m/*m* and /s/*s*.

- Display the Lesson 7 Picture and Letter Cards. Name the pictures and letters with children. Tell children that you are going to sort the Picture Cards into groups according to the beginning sound and beginning letter of the picture names.

- Display Letter Card *m* at the top of a pocket chart. Then place Picture Card *milk* under it. Explain that the letter *m* stands for the /m/ sound at the beginning of *milk*. Suggested language: **Listen to this word: *milk*, /m/. *Milk* begins with the /m/ sound. The letter *m* stands for the /m/ sound at the beginning of *milk*.**

- Display Letter Card *s* at the top of a pocket chart. Then place Picture Card *sun* under it. Repeat the process to explain that the letter *s* stands for the /s/ sound at the beginning of *sun*.

- Begin the sort by displaying Picture Card *mouse*. Ask children to name the picture and to say whether they hear /s/ or /m/ at the beginning of the word. Suggested language: ***Mouse*. Listen to the beginning sound. Does *mouse* begin with /m/ or /s/?** Place the Picture Card below the *milk* card. Suggested language: ***M, milk. M, mouse*.** Continue in a similar way until all the Picture Cards have been placed.

- When all the cards are placed, have children name the pictures in each column and listen to make sure all the words begin with the same sound. After repeating the words in a column, tell children that all the words begin with the letter *m* (or *s*).

- Give partners a set of Lesson 7 Picture and Letter Cards. Have them work together to repeat the sort.

DAY 2 **Picture Sort**

Children will sort Picture Cards into groups of pictures whose names begin with /m/*m* and /s/*s*.

- Remind children that they have been listening for the sounds at the beginning of words and learning about the letters that stand for those sounds.

- Display Letter Card *m* and Picture Card *mouse* as a heading in a pocket chart. Name the picture and beginning sound, /m/. Remind children that the letter *m* stands for the /m/ sound at the beginning of *mouse*.

- Repeat, using Letter Card *s* and Picture Card *soap* as another heading.

- Display the remaining Lesson 7 Picture Cards one at a time. Name each picture for children. Then call on volunteers to place the pictures in the /m/*m* or /s/*s* column.

- After all the pictures have been sorted, name the pictures in each column. Reinforce that the words all begin with the same letter. Suggested language: ***M, mouse. M, milk. M, monkey. M, man. M, mat. M, map. M, moon*. These words all begin with the /m/ sound. The letter *m* stands for the /m/ sound at the beginning of all these words.**

- Give each child a set of Lesson 7 Picture and Letter Cards. Have children repeat the sort independently.

DAY 3 Blind Sort

Children will sort words that you say aloud.

- Remind children they have been learning about words that begin with the /m/ sound and the letter *m*. Suggested language: **We have been learning about words that begin with *m*, such as *mouse*. The letter *m* stands for the /m/ sound at the beginning of *mouse*.**

- Remind children they have also been learning about words that begin with the /s/ sound and the letter *s*. Suggested language: **We have been learning about words that begin with *s*, such as *seal*. The letter *s* stands for the /s/ sound at the beginning of *seal*.**

- Give each child a copy of Letter Cards *m* and *s*.

- Tell children that you are going to say some words. If they hear the /m/ sound at the beginning of the word, they should hold up the letter *m*. If they hear the /s/ sound at the beginning of the word, they should hold up the letter *s*.

- Say the following words one at a time: *suit, mountain, make, sailboat, mattress, money, sit, minnow, mat, sip, mix, mud, sap, sing, mule, sister, mink, save, soft.*

- Check to make sure children are holding up the correct Letter Card for each word you say.

DAY 4 Draw and Label

Children will draw and label pictures of things whose names begin with the /m/ and /s/ sounds.

- Remind children they have been learning that the letter *m* stands for the /m/ sound at the beginning of the word *mouth*.

- Then remind children that they have also learned that the letter *s* stands for the /s/ sound at the beginning of the word *sun*.

- Tell children they will be drawing in their Word Study Notebooks pictures of things that begin with the /m/ and /s/ sounds.

- Have children draw pictures in their Word Study Notebooks. Then have them label each picture with the letter *m* if the beginning sound is /m/ and with the letter *s* if the beginning sound is /s/.

- Children can share their pictures with a partner. Have partners check each other's pictures to make sure they are labeled correctly.

DAY 5 Assess

Tell children you will be saying some words that begin with the /m/ or /s/ sounds, and they will hold up the Letter Card that stands for the sound they hear at the beginning of the word. Say the following words one at a time: *march, saddle, sail, merry, mirror, sand.* Have children hold up Letter Card *m* or *s* to match the beginning sound in each word.

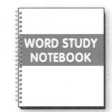

RETEACH IF children are unable to associate beginning sounds with letters, **THEN** revisit the activity on Day 1 and reassess.

Have children draw in their Word Study Notebooks a picture of one thing whose name begins with the /m/ sound and one thing whose name begins with the /s/ sound. When they have finished drawing, have children label each picture *m* or *s*.

Beginning Sounds /m/*m*, /s/*s*, /t/*t*

MATERIALS

Picture Cards: mat, monkey, map, moose, six, seal, soap, sack, top, turtle, taxi, tub, two

Letter Cards: *m, s, t*

  Reproducible Picture and Letter Cards are available at **www.thinkcentral.com**.

ELL SUPPORT

Linguistic Transfer Some speakers of Hmong may be unfamiliar with the /t/ sound. Give children additional practice listening for and pronouncing words that begin with *t*.

DAY 1 PHONICS Model the Sort

Children will sort Picture Cards with you based on beginning sounds.

- Display the Lesson 8 Picture and Letter Cards. Name the pictures and letters with children. Tell them you are going to sort the Picture Cards into groups of pictures with the same beginning sound.

- Write the letter *t* on chart paper or on the chalkboard. Then display Picture Card *top* under it. Explain that the letter *t* stands for the /t/ sound at the beginning of *top*. Suggested language: **Listen to this word: *top*, /t/. *Top* begins with the /t/ sound. The letter *t* stands for the /t/ sound at the beginning of *top*.**

- Repeat for the letters *m* and *s*, using Picture Cards *mat* and *six*.

- Model how to sort the remaining Picture Cards. Display Picture Card *turtle*. Suggested language: ***Turtle*. I will listen to see if it has the same beginning sound as *top*, *mat*, or *six*. Listen: *turtle*, /t/. *Turtle*, *top*. *Turtle*, *mat*. *Turtle*, *six*. *Turtle* has the same beginning sound as *top*. I'll put *turtle* under *top*.** Then explain that the letter *t* stands for the beginning sound in both picture names.

- Continue for the other Picture Cards. When all the cards are placed, have children name the pictures in each column and listen to make sure the words all have the same beginning sound. Suggested language: **Listen to these beginning sounds: *mat, monkey, map, moose*. These words all begin with the /m/ sound. The letter *m* stands for the sound we hear at the beginning of the words.**

- Give partners a set of Lesson 8 Picture and Letter Cards. Have them work together to repeat the sort.

DAY 2 Letter Match

Children will sort Picture Cards into groups of pictures whose names begin with /m/*m*, /s/*s*, and /t/*t*.

- Remind children they have been listening for the /m/, /s/, and /t/ sounds at the beginning of words.

- Write the letters *m, s,* and *t* as headings on chart paper or on the board. Then display Picture Cards *monkey, seal,* and *turtle* under the appropriate letters.

- Display the remaining Picture Cards one at a time. Name each picture for children. Then call on a volunteer to place the picture in the appropriate column.

- After all the pictures have been sorted, name the pictures in each column. Help children understand that they all have the same beginning sound. Suggested language: **Listen: *monkey, map, moose, mat*. These words all begin with the same /m/ sound. The letter *m* stands for the /m/ sound we hear at the beginning of these words.** Repeat the procedure with the other columns.

- Give each child a set of Lesson 8 Picture and Letter Cards. Have children repeat the sort independently.

m	s	t

DAY 3 Brainstorming

Children will think of words that have the same beginning sound as picture names of Picture Cards.

- Remind children they have been listening for words that begin with the /m/, /s/, and /t/ sounds. Suggested language: **We have been learning about words that begin with the /m/ sound in** *monkey*, **the /s/ sound in** *seal*, **and the /t/ sound in** *turtle*.

- Give partners a set of Lesson 8 Picture Cards. Have children place the pictures face down in a pile. Then have one child turn over and name a card. The other child will think of a different word that begins with the same sound.

- Have children continue until all the cards have been turned over.

- You may also have partners turn over and name a card. Then they can work together to name as many words as they are able that have the same beginning sound.

DAY 4 Buddy Sort

Children will sort Picture Cards into groups that they choose.

- Display a set of Lesson 8 Picture Cards. Name the pictures for children.

- Then model how to sort the cards into two groups: one for things that are alive and one for things that are not alive. Review the groups of cards you made. Explain to children why you put each card into its group.

- Give partners a set of Lesson 8 Picture Cards. Tell children to talk about the cards and sort them in a way that they choose. Explain to children that they can make as many different groups as they like. You may suggest different groups to help children get started, such as *animals* and *not animals*.

- Have partners discuss their groupings with another pair of children. Ask partners to explain why the pictures belong where they were placed.

- You may have children draw in their Word Study Notebooks additional pictures of things that would go into the groups they made.

DAY 5 Assess

Tell children you will be naming Picture Cards, and they will hold up the Letter Card that stands for the sound they hear at the beginning of each picture name. Display each Picture Card one at a time. Have children hold up Letter Card *m*, *s*, or *t* to match the beginning sound in each picture name.

RETEACH **IF** children are unable to associate beginning sounds with letters, **THEN** revisit the activity on Day 1 and reassess.

Have children draw in their Word Study Notebooks pictures of things whose names begin with the /m/, /s/, or /t/ sounds. When they have finished drawing their pictures, have them label each picture with the letter *m, s,* or *t*.

Beginning Sounds /t/t, /k/c, /p/p

MATERIALS

Picture Cards: tiger, towel, toothbrush, table, cow, cup, candle, cap, pencil, pumpkin, patch, penguin, pan

Letter Cards: t, c, p

 Reproducible Picture and Letter Cards are available at **www.thinkcentral.com**.

 **ELL SUPPORT**

Linguistic Transfer Some ELLs may have difficulty discriminating and pronouncing words with the /t/, /k/, and /p/ sounds. Give children practice listening for and saying words that begin with these sounds. Model mouth positions as necessary.

DAY 1 PHONICS **Model the Sort**

Children will sort Picture Cards with you based on beginning sounds.

- Display the Lesson 9 Picture and Letter Cards. Name the pictures and letters with children. Tell children you are going to sort the Picture Cards into groups according to the beginning sound and beginning letter of the picture names.
- Write the letters *t, c,* and *p* as column headings on chart paper or on the board. Then place Picture Card *tiger* under the letter *t*. Explain that the letter *t* stands for the /t/ sound at the beginning of *tiger*.
- Place Picture Card *cow* under the letter *c*. Explain that the letter *c* stands for the /k/ sound at the beginning of *cow*.
- Place Picture Card *pencil* under the letter *p*. Explain that the letter *p* stands for the /p/ sound at the beginning of *pencil*.
- Model how to sort the remaining Picture Cards. Hold up Picture Card *cup*. Suggested language: **Cup. Listen for the beginning sound. Does *cup* have the same beginning sound as *tiger, cow,* or *pencil*? Listen: *Cup, tiger. Cup, cow. Cup, pencil. Cup* has the same beginning sound as *cow*. I'll put *cup* under *cow*.** Then explain that the letter *c* stands for the beginning sound in both picture names.
- Continue for the other Picture Cards. When all the cards are placed, have children name the pictures in each column. Ask them what they notice about the pictures in each column. Help them understand that the words all begin with the same sound. Point out that the picture names in each column begin with the letter at the top of the column.
- Give partners a set of Lesson 9 Picture and Letter Cards. Have them work together to repeat the sort.

DAY 2 **Letter Match**

Children will sort Picture Cards into groups of pictures whose names begin with /t/t, /k/c, and /p/p.

- Remind children they have been listening for the /t/, /k/, and /p/ sounds at the beginning of words.
- Write the letters *t, c,* and *p* as headings on chart paper or on the chalkboard. Then display Picture Cards *towel, cap,* and *pan* under the appropriate letters.
- Repeat the Day 1 sort with children. Hold up and name the Picture Cards one at a time. Call on a volunteer to place the pictures in the appropriate columns.
- After all the pictures have been sorted, name the pictures in each column. Help children understand that the picture names all begin with the same sound. Suggested language: **Listen: *towel, tiger, toothbrush, table*. These words all begin with the same sound, /t/. The letter *t* stands for the /t/ sound at the beginning of these words.** Repeat the procedure for the other columns.
- Give each child a set of Lesson 9 Picture and Letter Cards. Have children repeat the sort independently.

t	c	p

DAY 3 | Letter Hunt

Children will find the letters *t, c,* and *p* in the classroom.

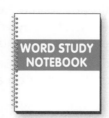

- Display Letter Cards *t, c,* and *p*. Call on children to name the letters. Then demonstrate how to find each letter in the classroom on signs, bulletin boards, labels, and book covers.

- Have children divide a page in their Word Study Notebooks into three columns. Have them write one of the letters at the top of each column.

- Then have children work with a partner to find each of the letters in print around the room. Each time children find one of the letters, they can put a check mark in the appropriate column of their chart.

- Tell children to continue until they have found several examples of each letter.

- After children have found examples of each letter, have them share with the class or a small group where in the classroom they found the letters.

DAY 4 | Buddy Sort

Children will sort Picture Cards into groups that they choose.

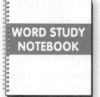

- Display a set of Lesson 9 Picture Cards. Name the pictures for children.

- Give partners a set of Lesson 9 Picture Cards. Tell children to talk about the pictures and sort the cards into groups.

- Explain that they can make as many groups as they like, but they must be able to explain why the pictures are in a group.

- Make suggestions if children need help getting started. For example, they can group *animals* and *things that can be used at home*.

- Have children explain the groups they made. Ask partners to explain why the pictures belong in each group.

- You may have children draw in their Word Study Notebooks additional pictures of things that could go into the groups they made.

DAY 5 | Assess

Tell children you will be saying some words, and they will tell what sound they hear at the beginning of each word. Say the following words one at a time: *today, paste, car*. Have children tell the beginning sound in each word.

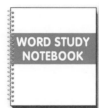

RETEACH **IF** children are unable to name the beginning sound in each word, **THEN** revisit the activity on Day 1 and reassess.

Have children draw in their Word Study Notebooks pictures of things whose names begin with the /t/ and /p/ sounds. When they have finished drawing, have them label each picture with the letter *t* or *p*.

Ending Sounds in Words

MATERIALS

Picture Cards: net, bat, kit, sun, van, pen, rug, wig, dog, cap, mop, cup, sock, beak, block, tack

 Reproducible Picture Cards are available at **www.thinkcentral.com**.

 **ELL SUPPORT**

Support Word Meaning Before discussing ending sounds with children, have them stand in a line. Develop meaning for the words *beginning* and *ending* by pointing to the first child and last child in line. Have children switch positions several times and tell who is at the beginning and end of the line.

DAY 1 PHONICS Model the Sort

Children will sort Picture Cards with you based on ending sounds.

- Display the Lesson 10 Picture Cards and name each picture with children. Tell children that they have already sorted Picture Cards whose names have the same beginning sound. Tell them that today you will sort Picture Cards into groups of pictures whose names have the same ending sound.
- Set aside the Picture Cards with ending sounds /g/, /p/, and /k/. Place Picture Card *net* as a heading in a pocket chart or on a tabletop. Then place Picture Card *sun* as another heading.
- Point to *net* and name the picture, emphasizing the final /t/. Suggested language: ***Net*. I hear the /t/ sound at the end of *net*. Listen again: *net*.**
- Point to *sun* and name the picture, emphasizing the final /n/. Suggested language: ***Sun*. I hear the /n/ sound at the end of *sun*. Listen again: *sun*.**
- Explain that the words *net* and *sun* have different sounds at the end. Suggested language: **Listen: *net, sun*. These words sound different at the end. *Net* ends with /t/. *Sun* ends with /n/.**
- Model how to sort cards by their sound. Display Picture Cards one at a time. As you display each card, name the picture that you are showing and the picture of each heading card. Suggested language: **Listen: *Bat, net. Bat, sun*. Which words have the same sound at the end? I hear /t/ at the end of *bat* and *net*. I'll put *bat* under *net* because they have the same ending sound.**
- When all the cards are placed, name the pictures in each column. Have children listen to make sure that the picture names in each column have the same ending sound.
- Repeat the process with the Picture Cards that end with the /g/, /p/, and /k/ sounds.
- Give partners a set of Lesson 10 Picture Cards. Have them work together to repeat the sort.

DAY 2 Picture Sort

Children will sort Picture Cards into groups of pictures whose names have the same ending sound.

- Remind children that they have been listening for the sounds at the ends of words.
- Display Picture Cards *bat, van, wig, mop,* and *beak* as headings in a pocket chart. Name the pictures, emphasizing their ending sounds. Suggested language: **This is a picture of a *bat*. *Bat*. I hear the /t/ sound at the end of *bat*. Listen again: *bat*.** Discuss each heading picture in a similar way.
- Display the remaining Lesson 10 Picture Cards one at a time. Name each picture, emphasizing the ending sound. Then call on a volunteer to place it below the picture whose name has the same ending sound.
- After all the pictures have been sorted, have children name the pictures in each column. Help them understand that all of the words end with the same sound. You may want to repeat each column, placing extra emphasis on the final sound in each word.
- Give each child a set of Lesson 10 Picture Cards. Have them repeat the sort independently.

DAY 3 Buddy Sort

Children will sort Picture Cards into groups of their own making.

- Display a set of Lesson 10 Picture Cards. Name the pictures for children.

- Tell children that you are going to sort the pictures in a new way. Suggested language: **I am going to sort the pictures into two groups. One group will be things you can hold in your hand. The other group will be things you cannot hold in your hand.**

- Use the Picture Cards to create the groups. Then discuss with children the groups you made.

- Give partners a set of Lesson 10 Picture Cards. Tell children to discuss the possible groups they can make and work together to sort the pictures into groups. Remind them that they should be able to explain why each picture belongs in a group.

- Have partners share with classmates how they sorted the pictures. Have them explain why each card is placed in its group.

DAY 4 Brainstorming

Children will think of words that have the same ending sounds as Picture Card names.

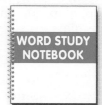

- Remind children that some words end with the same sound. Suggested language: **Listen to these words: *net, bat, kit.* I hear /t/ at the end of *net, bat,* and *kit.* The words all end with the same sound, /t/.**

- Tell children that you can name other words that end with the /t/ sound. Say the words *fit* and *kite.* Point out that these words also end with the /t/ sound.

- Give partners a set of Lesson 10 Picture Cards. Tell them that one child will name a Picture Card. Then the other child will think of a different word that ends with the same sound as the picture name. Children take turns until all the Picture Cards have been used.

- You may extend the activity by having children draw in their Word Study Notebooks a picture of something whose name has the same ending sound as one of the Picture Card names.

DAY 5 Assess

Tell children that you will be naming Picture Cards, and they will show you another Picture Card whose name has the same ending sound. Display the following Picture Cards one at a time: *net, van, wig.* Have children find one Picture Card whose name ends with the same sound.

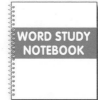

RETEACH **IF** children are unable to match Picture Cards whose names end with the same sound, **THEN** revisit the activity on Day 1 and reassess.

Have children draw in their Word Study Notebooks pictures of two things whose names have the same ending sound. When they have finished drawing their pictures, have them name the pictures, emphasizing the sound at the end of each one.

Ending Sounds /s/s, /p/p, /t/t

MATERIALS

Picture Cards: bus, gas, dress, grass, top, map, cup, mop, hat, pot, bat, jet, glass

Letter Cards: s, p, t

 Reproducible Picture and Letter Cards are available at **www.thinkcentral.com.**

 ELL SUPPORT

Use Minimal Pairs Some ELLs may have difficulty hearing and saying words with the /p/ and /t/ ending sounds. Give children practice discriminating these sounds by saying word pairs such as the following: *hop/hog, rat/rap, sat/Sam.* Have children raise their hands when they hear the /p/ or /t/ sound at the end of a word. Then have them practice saying the words.

DAY 1 PHONICS Model the Sort

Children will sort Picture Cards with you based on ending sounds.

- Display the Lesson 11 Picture and Letter Cards. Name the pictures and letters with children. Tell them you are going to sort the Picture Cards into groups of pictures whose names have the same ending sound.

- Write __s, __p, and __t as column headings on chart paper or on the board. Then place Picture Card *bus* under __s. Name the picture, emphasizing the final /s/ sound. Explain that the letter *s* stands for the /s/ sound at the end of *bus.* Suggested language: **Listen to the word: *Bus, /s/. Bus* ends with the /s/ sound. The letter *s* stands for the ending sound in *bus.***

- Repeat for __p and __t, using Picture Cards *top* and *hat.*

- Model sorting the remaining Picture Cards by naming each picture and saying its ending sound. Hold up Picture Card *gas.* Suggested language: ***Gas.* I will listen to see if it has the same ending sound as *bus, top,* or *hat.* Listen: *Gas, bus. Gas, top. Gas, hat. Gas* has the same ending sound as *bus.* I'll put *gas* under *bus.***

- Then explain that the letter *s* stands for the ending sound in both *gas* and *bus.*

- Continue with the other Picture Cards. When all the cards are placed, have children name the pictures in each column.

- Ask children what they notice about the pictures. Help them understand that the picture names in each column have the same ending sound. Point out that the letter at the top of each column stands for the ending sound of the picture names below it.

- Give partners a set of Lesson 11 Picture and Letter Cards. Have them work together to repeat the sort.

DAY 2 Guess My Category

Children will guess the category names for Picture Cards sorted by ending sound.

- Remind children they have been listening for the ending sounds of words.

- Display Picture Cards *gas, map,* and *pot* as headings in a pocket chart. Name the pictures, emphasizing each ending sound so children can hear it clearly.

- Display Picture Card *dress,* and place it under *gas.* Then place Picture Card *cup* under *map* and Picture Card *jet* under *pot.*

- Display the remaining Lesson 11 Picture Cards one at a time. Ask children where you should put each card.

- After all the pictures have been sorted, have children name the pictures. Have them tell how the pictures in each column are the same. Help them understand that the pictures in each column have names that end with the same sound.

- Give partners a set of Lesson 11 Picture and Letter Cards. Have children repeat the sort by grouping together Picture Cards whose names have the same ending sound.

DAY 3 Letter Hunt

Children will hunt for words that end with the letters *s, p,* and *t*.

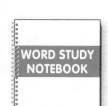

- Tell children they will be looking for words that end with the letters *s, p,* and *t* in a story and around the classroom.
- Have children divide a page in their Word Study Notebooks into three columns and write one of the following letters at the top of each column: *s, p, t.*

- Have partners work together to read aloud the Student Book selection "Come and See Me." Ask children to take turns naming any words that end with *t*.
- When children find a word, have them make tally marks in the appropriate column in their Word Study Notebooks. *(Possible responses: Pat, cat, sat)*
- Then ask children to make tally marks in their Word Study Notebooks for words around the classroom ending with *s, p,* and *t*. They may look at bulletin boards, on book covers, or in other places that you designate.
- Have children share their findings.

DAY 4 Brainstorming

Children will think of words that have the same ending sound as picture names on Picture Cards.

- Remind children that they have been learning about words that end with the /p/, /s/, and /t/ sounds. Suggested language: **We have been learning about words that end with the /p/ sound in *cup*, the /s/ sound in *glass*, and the /t/ sound in *jet*.**
- Tell children that you can name other words that end with the /p/ sound, such as *nap* and *lip*. Explain that children will be thinking of other words with the ending sounds /p/, /s/, and /t/.
- Give partners a set of Lesson 11 Picture Cards. Tell them one child will choose a Picture Card and name the picture. Then the other child will think of a different word that ends with the same sound.
- Have children take turns until all the Picture Cards have been used.
- You may also have children write in their Word Study Notebooks one word that ends with each of the sounds.

DAY 5 Assess

Tell children that you will be naming Picture Cards, and they will hold up the Letter Card that stands for the sound they hear at the end of each picture name. Display the Picture Cards one at a time. Have children hold up the *s, p,* or *t* Letter Card to match the ending sound in each picture name.

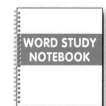

RETEACH **IF** children are unable to associate ending sounds with letters, **THEN** revisit the activity on Day 1 and reassess.

Have children draw in their Word Study Notebooks pictures of things whose names end with the /s/, /p/, or /t/ sound. When they have finished drawing their pictures, have children label their pictures with the letter *s, p,* or *t.*

Short *a* /ă/

DAY 1 PHONICS Model the Sort

Children will sort Picture Cards with you into groups of pictures whose names have the short *a* sound in the beginning or in the middle.

- Display the Lesson 12 Picture and Letter Cards. Name the pictures and letter with children. Tell children that all of the picture names have the short *a* sound. Explain that some picture names have the short *a* sound at the beginning. Other picture names have the short *a* sound in the middle.

- Display Letter Card *a* as a heading in a pocket chart. Then place Picture Card *apple* below it to one side. Explain that the letter *a* stands for the /ă/ sound at the beginning of *apple*. Suggested language: **Apple. Apple begins with the /ă/ sound. The letter *a* stands for the /ă/ sound at the beginning of *apple*.**

- Place Picture Card *cat* below *a* and to the side of the *apple* card. Explain that the letter *a* stands for the /ă/ sound in the middle of *cat*. Suggested language: **Cat. Cat has the /ă/ sound in the middle. The letter *a* stands for the /ă/ sound in the middle of *cat*.**

- Model sorting the Picture Cards according to the position of the short *a* sound. Hold up and read Picture Card *ax*. Suggested language: **Listen: *Ax*. Is the /ă/ sound at the beginning or in the middle of the word? *Ax*. The short *a* sound, /ă/, is at the beginning of the word. I'll put *ax* under *apple*.** Continue until all the Picture Cards are placed.

- When all the cards have been sorted, name the pictures in each column. Have children listen to make sure all the words are in the correct column.

- Give partners a set of Lesson 12 Picture and Letter Cards. Have them work together to repeat the sort.

DAY 2 Picture Sort

Children will sort Picture Cards into groups of pictures whose names have the short *a* sound in the beginning or in the middle.

- Remind children they have been listening for the short *a* sound and learning about the letter that stands for that sound.

- Display Letter Card *a* as a heading in a pocket chart. Place Picture Card *ax* below it to one side. Say the letter and name the picture, extending the short *a* sound at the beginning of *ax*. Remind children the letter *a* stands for the /ă/ sound at the beginning of *ax*.

- Display Picture Card *bat* below *a* and to the side of Picture Card *ax* in the pocket chart. Name the picture, extending the short *a* sound in the middle of *bat* so that children can hear it clearly. Remind children that the letter *a* stands for the /ă/ sound in the middle of *bat*.

- Display the remaining Lesson 12 Picture Cards one at a time. Name each picture for children. Then call on a volunteer to place the picture in the correct column.

- After all the pictures have been sorted, have children name the pictures in each column. Point out that all of the picture names in the first column have the short *a* sound at the beginning. Explain that all of the picture names in the second column have the short *a* sound in the middle.

- Give each child a set of Lesson 12 Picture and Letter Cards. Have children repeat the sort independently.

DAY 3 Letter Location

Children will place Letter Cards to show where they hear the short *a* sound.

- Remind children that they have been learning about words with the short *a* sound. Suggested language: **We have been learning about words that have the short *a* sound. The letter *a* stands for the /ă/ sound. Sometimes the /ă/ sound is at the beginning of a word. Sometimes the /ă/ sound is in the middle of a word.**

- Give each child an Elkonin box (or use Write-on/ Wipe-off Boards) and a copy of Letter Card *a*. Tell children you will say one word at a time. If they hear the /ă/ sound at the beginning of a word, they should place Letter Card *a* in the first box. If they hear the /ă/ sound in the middle of a word, they should place Letter Card *a* in the middle box.

- Model how to place Letter Card *a* in the first box as you say the word *add*. Then say the following words one at a time: *lap, ax, mat, at, sat, bad, Al, mad, after, ask, band, lab, acting.* Have children place Letter Card *a* in the correct box for each word.

a		

DAY 4 Letter Hunt

Children will hunt for the letter *a* in a familiar story.

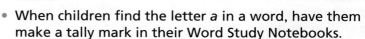

- Remind children that they have been learning about the short *a* sound at the beginning and in the middle of words. Remind them that the letter *a* often stands for the /ă/ sound.

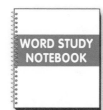

- Display Letter Card *a*. Tell children they will be looking for the letter *a* in words in the Student Book story "I Can Nap."

- Have partners work together to read aloud the story. Then have children take turns finding the letter *a* in words with the short *a* sound.

- When children find the letter *a* in a word, have them make a tally mark in their Word Study Notebooks.

- When children have completed their letter hunt, call on them to tell the class how many times they found the letter *a* in words with short *a*.

DAY 5 Assess

Tell children that you will be naming Picture Cards, and they will tell whether they hear the short *a* sound at the beginning or in the middle of the word. Display and name each Picture Card one at a time. Have children tell where they hear the short *a* sound.

RETEACH IF children are unable to tell where they hear the short *a* sound, **THEN** revisit the activity on Day 2 and reassess.

Have children draw in their Word Study Notebooks a picture of a thing whose name begins with the /ă/ sound and a picture of a thing whose name has the /ă/ sound in the middle. When they have finished drawing their pictures, have children label them with the letter *a*.

Words with -an, -ap, -at

MATERIALS

Picture Cards: man, pan, cat, map, cap, nap, mat, pat, fan, can, tap, fat

Word Cards: *man, pan, cat, map, cap, nap, mat, pat, fan, can, tap, fat*

 Reproducible Picture and Word Cards are available at **www.thinkcentral.com**.

ELL SUPPORT

Linguistic Transfer Speakers of Spanish, Vietnamese, Chinese, and Korean may have difficulty pronouncing the short *a* sound, /ă/. Provide additional opportunities for children to work with the words for the week by showing the Picture Cards, naming the pictures, and having children repeat the picture name each time.

DAY 1 [PHONICS] Model the Sort

Children will sort Picture Cards with you into groups of pictures with rhyming names.

- Display the Lesson 13 Picture Cards, and name each picture with children. Tell children that together you will sort the pictures according to rhyming names.
- Display Picture Card *man*, say *man*, and place the card as a heading in a pocket chart. Then display Picture Card *nap* as another heading. Point to the cards and name the pictures. Suggested language: ***Man*. I hear /ăn/ at the end of *man*. *Nap*. I hear /ăp/ at the end of *nap*. /m/ /ăn/, /n/ /ăp/. These words have different ending sounds. *Man* and *nap* do not rhyme.**
- Then place Picture Card *cat* as an additional heading. Repeat the process for *cat*.
- Then as you display each card, name the Picture Card and the heading card. Suggested language: **Listen: *Can*. *Can, man*. *Can, nap*. *Can, cat*. Where should I put *can*?** Have children listen carefully to each word and help you place each card correctly.
- When all the cards are placed, repeat the picture names in each column. Have children listen to make sure all the words in each column rhyme.
- Give partners a set of Lesson 13 Picture Cards. Have children work together to repeat the sort.

- -

DAY 2 Open Sort

Children will sort Picture Cards into categories of their own choosing.

- Tell children they will sort the pictures into groups that they create. Display the Picture Cards one at a time, and name each picture.
- Model how to think about the picture names, choose categories, and sort the Picture Cards. Point out that some of the pictures show living things and some do not.
- Start one group as *living things* with Picture Card *man*. Start another group as *not living things* with Picture Card *map*. Then sort the remaining Picture Cards into the correct categories.
- Have children take a moment to look at the Picture Cards and decide how they will sort them. Children may decide to sort the pictures into groups of pictures with rhyming words, as they did on Day 1. Other possible ways to sort include by beginning sounds, shapes of objects shown, or the uses of objects shown.
- As children sort the Picture Cards, encourage them to explain how they are sorting the cards.
- When children have sorted their cards, have them take turns telling a partner how they sorted the pictures.
- Then have children tell the group how they sorted the Picture Cards. On the board, record each way children sorted the cards. You may add tally marks to show how many children sorted the pictures each way.

DAY 3 Picture-Word Match

Children will match Picture Cards to the Word Cards that name each picture.

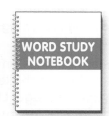

- Display the Lesson 13 Picture Cards, and remind children that they have been working with these picture names this week. Then display the Word Cards for the week.

- Tell children they will be reading the words on the cards and matching each one to a Picture Card.

- Display the Word Cards, and ask a volunteer to choose one. Have children blend the letter-sounds to read the word on the card. Then ask a child to find the Picture Card that matches the word on the Word Card.

- Continue until all the Picture Cards are matched with the Word Cards.

- Then have children work in pairs to match Picture and Word Cards.

- When children have finished matching the cards, have them write three of the words in their Word Study Notebooks. Then have them draw a picture to illustrate one of the words they wrote.

DAY 4 Pattern Sort

Children will sort words into groups by word endings *(-ap, -an, -at).*

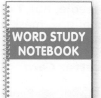

- Tell children they will be sorting words into groups of words that rhyme. Then display the Word Cards, and read each one with children.

- Read the Word Card *pan* and compare it to the Word Card *cap.* Suggested language: ***Cap. Blend with me: /c/ /ă/ /p/, cap. Pan. Let's blend: /p/ /ă/ /n/, pan. Cap, pan. Cap* and *pan* do not rhyme.**

- Repeat for *fat.* **What do you notice about the endings of *cap, pan,* and *fat?*** *(Possible response: They end with different letters.)*

- Create categories with the Word Cards *cap, pan,* and *fat.* Then sort the remaining Word Cards one at a time. Suggested language: **Listen: *Man. Man, cap. Man, pan. Man, fat.* Where should I put *man?***

- Read each group of rhyming words. Ask: **What is the same about the words in each group?** *(Possible response: They rhyme; they have the same letters and sounds at the end.)*

- Distribute the Lesson 13 Word Cards, and have children repeat the sort. Have them write one set of rhyming words in their Word Study Notebooks.

DAY 5 Assess

Tell children that you will be showing them Word Cards. They should look at their own Word Cards, find a rhyming word, and hold it up. Display the Word Card *fan,* and have children hold up a rhyming word. *(pan, man, can)* Repeat this procedure with Word Cards *cat* and *map.*

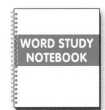

RETEACH **IF** children are unable to correctly match the rhyming letter patterns on the Word Cards, **THEN** revisit the activity on Day 4 and reassess.

Have children sort the Word Cards into groups of words that rhyme. Have them either glue the sets of rhyming Word Cards into their Word Study Notebooks or write the sets of rhyming words.

Beginning Sounds /n/*n*, /m/*m*

MATERIALS

Picture Cards: net, nurse, nail, needle, nut, nest, newspaper, mitten, mailbox, mask, milk, moon, marbles, monkey

Letter Cards: *n, m*

 Reproducible Picture and Letter Cards are available at **www.thinkcentral.com**.

ELL ELL SUPPORT

Linguistic Transfer The /n/ and /m/ sounds are similar, but they should be familiar to most ELLs. If children have difficulty discriminating words that begin with /n/*n* and /m/*m*, give them additional practice naming and sorting Picture Cards by beginning sounds.

DAY 1 PHONICS Model the Sort

Children will sort Picture Cards with you into groups of pictures whose names begin with /n/*n* and /m/*m*.

- Display the Lesson 14 Picture and Letter Cards. Name the pictures and letters with children. Tell children that you are going to sort the pictures into groups whose names have the same beginning sound.

- Write the letters *n* and *m* as headings on chart paper. Then place Picture Card *net* under the letter *n*. Explain that the letter *n* stands for the /n/ sound at the beginning of *net*. Suggested language: **Listen: *Net, /n/. Net* begins with the /n/ sound. The letter *n* stands for the /n/ sound at the beginning of *net*.**

- Repeat for the letter *m*, using Picture Card *mask*.

- Model how to sort the Picture Cards by their beginning sounds. Name each Picture Card and the picture in each heading. Ask children which picture names have the same beginning sound. Suggested language: **Listen: *Nurse, net. Nurse, mask. Nurse* and *net* both begin with the /n/ sound.**

- Then point to Letter Card *n,* and tell children that the letter *n* stands for the /n/ sound at the beginning of both words.

- When all the cards are placed, name the pictures in each column. Have children listen to make sure all the words in each column begin with the same sound. Point out that the sounds /n/ and /m/ are almost the same, so children should listen carefully as you say each picture name.

- Give partners a set of Lesson 14 Picture and Letter Cards. Have them work together to repeat the sort.

DAY 2 Blind Sort

Children will sort words that you say aloud.

- Remind children that they have been learning about words that begin with the /n/ and /m/ sounds and the letters that stand for these sounds. Suggested language: **We have been learning about words that begin with the /n/ sound, such as *nut*. We also learned about words that begin with the /m/ sound, such as *milk*.**

- Explain to children that the letter *n* stands for the /n/ sound at the beginning of *nut*. The letter *m* stands for the /m/ sound at the beginning of *milk*.

- Give each child a copy of Letter Cards *n* and *m*.

- Tell children you are going to say some words. If they hear the /n/ sound at the beginning of a word, they should hold up the letter *n*. If they hear the /m/ sound at the beginning of a word, they should hold up the letter *m*.

- Say the following words one at a time: *now, noon, meow, meadow, night, minute, morning, next, make, notebook, no, merry, mud, napkin, Nate, medal, meet.*

- Check to make sure that children hold up the correct Letter Card for each word.

DAY 3 Brainstorming

Children will think of words that have the same beginning sound as Picture Card names.

WORD STUDY NOTEBOOK

- Remind children that they have been learning about words that begin with the /n/ sound, such as *nail* and the /m/ sound, such as *moon*.

- Tell children that you can name other words that begin with the /n/ sound. Say the words *next* and *new*. Point out that these words also begin with the /n/ sound. Model naming other words that begin with the /m/ sound, such as *much* and *mountain*.

- Give partners a set of Lesson 14 Picture Cards. Tell children that they are going to take turns holding up a card and naming it. Then the other child will think of a different word that begins with the same sound as the picture name.

- Have children continue taking turns until all the cards have been used.

- You may extend the activity by having children work together to write in their Word Study Notebooks one word that begins with the /n/ sound and one word that begins with the /m/ sound.

DAY 4 Letter-Picture Match

Children will match Picture Cards with Letter Cards that show the beginning sounds of the picture names.

- Remind children that they have been learning that the letter *n* stands for the /n/ sound at the beginning of words, such as *nest*.

- Then remind children that they have also learned that the letter *m* stands for the /m/ sound at the beginning of words, such as *mitten*.

- Display Letter Cards *n* and *m* as headings in a pocket chart.

- Then display the Picture Cards one at a time. Name each picture for children. Call on volunteers to place the picture in the column with the letter that stands for the beginning sound of the picture name.

- Give each child a set of Lesson 14 Picture and Letter Cards. Have children repeat the sort independently.

DAY 5 Assess

Tell children you will be saying some words that begin with the /n/ or /m/ sound, and they will hold up the Letter Card that stands for the sound they hear at the beginning of each word. Say the following words one at a time: *monkey, nuts, mountain, neck, neighbor, most*. Have children hold up Letter Card *n* or *m* to match the beginning sound in each word.

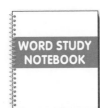

WORD STUDY NOTEBOOK

RETEACH **IF** children are unable to associate beginning sounds with letters, **THEN** revisit the activity on Day 2 and reassess.

Have children draw in their Word Study Notebooks a picture of one thing whose name begins with the /n/ sound and a picture of one thing whose name begins with the /m/ sound. When children have finished drawing their pictures, have them label each picture with the letter *n* or *m*.

Short *a* Words and High-Frequency Words

MATERIALS

Word Cards: *bat, cap, man, nap, pan, sat, tap, tan, I, like, the, a, and, see, we, to*

 Reproducible Word Cards are available at **www.thinkcentral.com**.

ELL SUPPORT

Linguistic Transfer The short vowel sound /ă/ will be unfamiliar to many ELLs. Have children listen for the short *a* sound. Point out mouth positions as you say the vowel sound. Then have children repeat the vowel sound several times. Correct their pronunciation as necessary.

DAY 1 PHONICS Model the Sort

Children will sort short *a* words and high-frequency words with you.

- Display the Lesson 15 Word Cards, and read each word aloud. Point out to children that these are words they know how to read, either by blending letter-sounds to read or by learning the word.
- Tell children that some of the words you just read have the short *a* sound in them, and others do not.
- Model sorting the Word Cards by whether they have the short *a* sound. Hold up and read the Word Card *bat*. Suggested language: *Bat*. **I'll listen for the short *a* sound. *Bat*. I hear the short *a* sound, /ă/, in the middle of *bat*. I'll start a group for words with the short *a* sound.**
- Hold up Word Card *I,* and read it aloud. Suggested language: *I*. **I do not hear the short *a* sound in *I*. I'm going to start a new group for words that do not have the short *a* sound.**
- Continue with the remaining Word Cards, helping children sort them into the appropriate groups. After all the words have been sorted, read each column aloud. Guide children to notice the short *a* sound in the words in the first column.
- Point out to children that the words in the second column are words they have already learned and that they will see many times when they read.
- Give partners a set of Lesson 15 Word Cards. Have them work together to repeat the sort.

· ·

DAY 2 Word Sort

Children will sort words into groups that have the short *a* sound or do not have the short *a* sound.

- Remind children that they have been learning how to read many words.
- Repeat the sort from Day 1, working with children to sort the Word Cards based on whether they have the short *a* sound. Model sorting several words for children. Then have volunteers place the remaining cards in the correct column.
- After all the words have been sorted, have children read the words in each column.
- Point out that all the words in the first column have the short *a* sound and that children have learned to blend letter-sounds to read them. Explain that the words in the second column do not have the short *a* sound, but children have been taught to read the words.
- Give each child a set of Lesson 15 Word Cards. Have children repeat the sort independently.

Short *a* Words	Other Words
bat	I
cap	like
man	the

DAY 3 Buddy Sort

Children will sort Word Cards into groups of their own choosing.

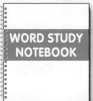

WORD STUDY NOTEBOOK

- Display the Lesson 15 Word Cards. Read the words aloud.
- Then tell children that you are going to sort the words in a new way. Suggested language: **I'm going to sort the words into two groups. One group will be for words that are things you can do. One group will be for other words.**
- Use the Word Cards to create the groups. Then discuss the groups you made with children.
- Give partners a set of Lesson 15 Word Cards. Tell them to sort the words into groups that they will choose together.
- Remind children that they will have to be able to explain why they sorted the words as they did. You may suggest various groups for children, such as words with certain letters (*p* or *t*). Children could also sort by the number of letters in the words.
- Have partners share how they sorted the Word Cards.
- Children may copy their sorts into their Word Study Notebooks.

DAY 4 Word Hunt

Children will find short *a* words and other words in a familiar story.

WORD STUDY NOTEBOOK

- Remind children that they have been learning to read many words, either by blending letter-sounds or by learning the whole word.
- Tell children that they will go on a word hunt to find short *a* words and other words they know in stories they have read.
- Have partners work together to read aloud the Student Book story "Pam Cat."

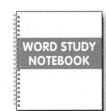

- Then have children take turns looking at a page and reading a word on the page. Partners should identify whether the word is a word with short *a* or a word they have learned to read.
- When children find a short *a* word, have them write it in their Word Study Notebooks.
- When children have completed their word hunt, they may compare their word lists with those of other children.

  (Possible responses: Mac, sat, Pam, cat, can, pat, fan)

DAY 5 Assess

Tell children that you will be showing them Word Cards they have been using this week. Have children hold up their copies of the Word Card that matches the word you show. Have children read each word and say whether it has the short *a* sound.

WORD STUDY NOTEBOOK

RETEACH **IF** children are unable to distinguish words with short *a* from other words, **THEN** revisit the activity on Day 1 and reassess.

Have children copy several short *a* words and high-frequency words into their Word Study Notebooks. Have them underline the letter *a* in each short *a* word.

Beginning Sounds /p/*p*, /f/*f*

ELL SUPPORT

Use Minimal Pairs Speakers of Korean may replace the /p/ sound with the /f/ sound. Give children practice listening to and saying word pairs such as the following: *pat/ fat, pan/fan, pail/fail*. Have children repeat. Model correct mouth positions as necessary. Use pictures if available to help children distinguish the meanings of the words.

DAY 1 PHONICS Model the Sort

Children will sort Picture Cards with you based on beginning sounds.

- Display the Lesson 16 Picture and Letter Cards. Name the pictures and letters with children. Tell them you are going to sort the Picture Cards into groups of pictures with the same beginning sound.

- Write the letters *p* and *f* as headings on chart paper or on the board. Then place Picture Card *pail* under the letter *p*. Explain that the letter *p* stands for the /p/ sound at the beginning of *pail*. Suggested language: **Listen: *Pail. Pail* begins with the /p/ sound. The letter *p* stands for the /p/ sound at the beginning of *pail*.**

- Repeat for the letter *f*, using Picture Card *fox*.

- Model how to sort the Picture Cards by naming each picture and the picture cards being used as headings. Suggested language: **Listen: *Feather, fox. Feather, pail. Feather* and *fox* have the same beginning sound. They both begin with the /f/ sound. I'll put *feather* under *fox*.**

- Point out that the letter *f* stands for the /f/ sound at the beginning of the words *feather* and *fox*. Repeat for the remaining Picture Cards.

- When all the cards are placed, name the pictures in each column. Have children listen to make sure all the words in each column begin with the same sound.

- Give partners a set of Lesson 16 Picture and Letter Cards. Have them work together to repeat the sort.

DAY 2 Picture Sort

Children will sort Picture Cards into groups of pictures whose names begin with /p/*p* or /f/*f*.

- Remind children they have been learning about the sounds at the beginning of words and the letters that stand for those sounds.

- Display Letter Card *p* and Picture Card *paintbrush* as a heading in a pocket chart. Say the letter and picture name, emphasizing the beginning sound of the picture name. Remind children that the letter *p* stands for the /p/ sound at the beginning of *paintbrush*.

- Display Letter Card *f* and Picture Card *fence* as another heading in the pocket chart. Say the letter and picture name, emphasizing the beginning sound. Remind children the letter *f* stands for the /f/ sound at the beginning of *fence*.

- Display the remaining Lesson 16 Picture Cards one at a time. Name each picture for children. Then call on volunteers to place the pictures in the /p/*p* or /f/*f* column.

- After all the pictures have been sorted, name the pictures in each column and help children understand that they all begin with the same sound and the same letter. Suggested language: **Listen: *fence, fox, feather, fish, feet, farm, five.* These words all begin with the same /f/ sound. The letter *f* stands for the /f/ sound at the beginning of these words.**

- Give each child a set of Lesson 16 Picture and Letter Cards. Have children repeat the sort independently.

DAY 3 Brainstorming

Children will think of words that have the same beginning sound as the names of Picture Cards.

WORD STUDY NOTEBOOK

- Remind children they have been learning about words that begin with /p/ and /f/. Suggested language: **We have been learning about words that begin with the /p/ sound in** *pan* **and the /f/ sound in** *feet*.

- Tell children that you can name other words that begin with the /p/ sound, such as *pal* and *purple*. You can also name other words that begin with /f/, such as *fantastic* and *fun*. Explain that children will think of other words that have the beginning sounds /p/ and /f/.

- Give partners a set of Lesson 16 Picture Cards. Tell them that one child will choose a Picture Card and name the picture. Then the other child will think of a different word that begins with the same sound.

- Have children continue until all the cards have been used.

- You may extend the activity by having children write in their Word Study Notebooks one word that begins with the /p/ sound and one word that begins with the /f/ sound.

DAY 4 Buddy Sort

Children will sort Picture Cards into groups of their own choosing.

- Display a set of Lesson 16 Picture Cards. Name the pictures for children.

- Tell children that you are going to sort the pictures in a new way. Suggested language: **I am going to sort the pictures into two groups. One group is for living things, and one group is for things that are not living.**

- Review the groups of cards you made. Discuss with children why you put each card into its group.

- Give partners a set of Lesson 16 Picture Cards. Tell children to discuss possible groups and then work together to sort the pictures into groups that they choose. Remind them that they should be able to explain why each picture belongs in a group.

- Have partners discuss the groups they made with other pairs of children. Ask pairs to take turns explaining why the pictures belong in the groups they made.

- As an alternative activity, children may try to guess the categories that other pairs made.

DAY 5 Assess

Tell children that you will be naming Picture Cards, and they will place each card into one of two groups: one for picture names that begin with /p/*p* and one for picture names that begin with /f/*f*. Have children place their Picture Cards in the correct group.

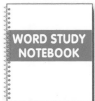

WORD STUDY NOTEBOOK

RETEACH **IF** children are unable to distinguish between words that begin with /p/*p* and /f/*f*, **THEN** revisit the activity on Day 2 and reassess.

Have children draw a line in the middle of a page in their Word Study Notebooks. Have them paste the letters *p* and *f* at the top of the columns. Then have them paste their Picture Cards under the Letter Card *p* or *f* to show whether the picture name begins with /p/*p* or /f/*f*.

Short *i* /ĭ/

MATERIALS

Picture Cards: pit, sit, pin, sip, man, cap, mat, pan

Word Cards: pit, sit, pin, sip, man, cap, mat, pan

 Reproducible Picture and Word Cards are available at **www.thinkcentral.com**.

 ELL SUPPORT

Linguistic Transfer Speakers of Spanish, Vietnamese, Tagalog, and Korean may have difficulty with the short *i* sound. Give children additional practice listening for and pronouncing words with short *i*.

DAY 1 PHONICS Model the Sort

Children will sort Picture and Word Cards with you based on medial vowel sound.

- Display the Lesson 17 Picture Cards and name them for children.
- Place Picture Card *pit* in a pocket chart. Then place Word Card *pit* next to it. Blend the letter-sounds to read the word aloud. Explain to children that the word *pit* matches the Picture Card *pit*.
- Tell children you are going to match the rest of the Picture Cards with the corresponding Word Cards. Display and name the remaining Picture Cards. Each time, have children blend letter-sounds to read and find the matching Word Cards.
- Model sorting the Picture and Word Cards by vowel sound. Tell children that some of these words have the short *i* sound. Place the Picture and Word Card *pit* as a heading in the pocket chart. Suggested language: **Listen: Pit. Pit has the /ĭ/ sound. The letter *i* stands for the short *i* sound, /ĭ/, in the middle of *pit*.**
- Place the Picture and Word Card *man* as another heading in the pocket chart. Suggested language: **Man. Man does not have the /ĭ/ sound in the middle. Pit, man. The middle sounds are not the same. I hear the short *a* sound, /ă/, in the middle of *man*.**
- Continue with the other pairs of Picture and Word Cards. When all the cards are placed, read the words in each column. Have children check that all the words are in the correct column.
- Give partners a set of Lesson 17 Picture and Word Cards. Have them work together to repeat the sort.

DAY 2 Picture-Word Match

Children will match Picture and Word Cards and then sort them based on medial vowel sound.

- Remind children they have been learning about words with the short *i* and short *a* sounds. They have been reading and sorting words by the vowel sound in the middle, /ĭ/*i* or /ă/*a*.
- Display the Picture Cards one at a time. Have volunteers find the matching Word Cards and place them with the Picture Cards.
- Display Picture and Word Card *pin* as a heading in a pocket chart. Name the picture and blend the letter-sounds to read the word. Remind children that the letter *i* stands for the /ĭ/ sound in the middle of *pin*.
- Repeat with Picture and Word Card *mat* as another heading. Point out that *mat* has the short *a* sound, /ă/, in the middle.
- Display the remaining pairs of Picture and Word Cards. Name each picture, and have children blend the letter-sounds to read the corresponding word. Then call on a volunteer to place the cards in the correct column.
- After all the cards have been sorted, have children blend the letter-sounds to read the words in each column. Have children identify the sound in the middle of the words in each column.
- Give each child a set of Lesson 17 Picture and Word Cards. Have children repeat the sort independently.

DAY 3 Open Sort

Children will sort Picture Cards into categories of their own choosing.

- Display a set of Lesson 17 Picture Cards. Name the pictures for children.
- Tell children you are going to sort the pictures in a new way. Suggested language: **I'm going to put all the pictures whose names begin with the /p/ sound into one group. Then I'll make other groups for picture names that begin with the /s/, /m/, and /k/ sounds.**
- Use the Picture Cards to create the groups. Then discuss with children the groups you made.
- Have children take a moment to look at the Picture Cards and decide how they will sort them. Remind them that they should be able to explain why each picture belongs in a group.
- You may make suggestions to help children get started. Children may group the cards by vowel sound, as they did on Day 2. They can also group the cards by beginning sound or ending sound.
- When children have sorted their cards, have them take turns telling a partner how they sorted the pictures.

DAY 4 Word Hunt

Children will find short *i* words in familiar stories.

- Remind children they have been learning about words with short *i*. Tell them that they will go on a word hunt to find short *i* words in stories they have read.

- Have partners work together to read aloud the Student Book story "What Is It?" Then have children take turns finding short *i* words in the story.
- When children find a short *i* word, have them write it in their Word Study Notebooks.

  (Possible responses: pin, it, is, bit, nip, fit, Tim)
- Then have partners repeat the procedure for the Student Book story "Fit in My Cab."

  (Possible responses: it, is, fit, in, bit, sit)
- When children have completed their word hunt, call on them to read aloud the short *i* words they wrote. Children can compare their word lists to those of other children.

DAY 5 Assess

Tell children you will be naming Picture Cards, and they will find the matching Word Card and read it. Display the Picture Cards one at a time. Have children match each Picture Card with the corresponding Word Card and then blend the letter-sounds to read the word.

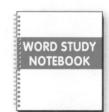

RETEACH **IF** children are unable to blend the letter-sounds to read words, **THEN** revisit the activity on Day 1 and reassess.

Have children copy the words with short *i* into their Word Study Notebooks. When they have finished writing the words, have them read each one aloud.

Ending Sounds /g/g, /b/b

Model the Sort

Children will sort Picture Cards with you based on ending sounds.

- Display the Lesson 18 Picture and Letter Cards. Name the pictures and letters with children. Tell them you are going to sort the Picture Cards into groups of pictures whose names have the same ending sound.
- Write __g and __b as headings on chart paper or on the board. Then place Picture Card *flag* under __g. Explain that the letter *g* stands for the /g/ sound at the end of *flag*.
- Place Picture Card *tub* under __b. Explain that the letter *b* stands for the /b/ sound at the end of *tub*.
- Model how to sort the remaining Picture Cards by naming each picture and the Picture Cards used as headings. Hold up Picture Card *web*. Suggested language: **Web. Does *web* have the same ending sound as *flag* or *tub*? Listen: *Web, flag. Web, tub. Web* has the same ending sound as *tub*. I'll put *web* under *tub*.**
- Explain that the letter *b* stands for the ending sound in both *web* and *tub*.
- Continue with the remaining Picture Cards. When all the cards are placed, name the pictures in each column. Ask children what they notice about the picture names in each column. *(They all have the same ending sound.)*
- Point out to children that the letter at the top of each column stands for the ending sound of the picture names below.
- Give partners a set of Lesson 18 Picture and Letter Cards. Have them work together to repeat the sort.

Picture Sort

Children will sort Picture Cards into groups of pictures whose names end with /g/g or /b/b.

- Remind children they have been learning about the sounds at the end of words and the letters that stand for those sounds.
- Display Letter Card __g and Picture Card *rug* as a heading in a pocket chart. Say the letter and picture name, emphasizing the ending sound in the picture name. Remind children that the letter *g* stands for the /g/ sound at the end of *rug*.
- Display Letter Card __b and Picture Card *crib* as another heading in the pocket chart. Say the letter and picture name, emphasizing the ending sound in the picture name. Remind children that the letter *b* stands for the /b/ sound at the end of *crib*.
- Display the remaining Lesson 18 Picture Cards one at a time. Name each picture for children. Then call on volunteers to place the pictures in the __g column if the picture names end with the /g/ sound and in the __b column if the picture names end with the /b/ sound.
- After all the pictures have been sorted, name the pictures in each column. Help children understand that in each column the picture names all end with the same sound. Suggested language: **Listen: *rug, frog, dog, flag, egg, wig, leg*. These words all end with the same sound, /g/. The letter *g* stands for the /g/ sound at the end of all these words.**
- Give each child a set of Lesson 18 Picture and Letter Cards. Have children repeat the sort independently.

MATERIALS

Picture Cards: frog, flag, rug, leg, dog, egg, wig, tub, cub, web, cab, crib, knob, sub

Letter Cards: *g, b*

 Reproducible Picture and Letter Cards are available at **www.thinkcentral.com**.

 ELL SUPPORT

Use Minimal Pairs Speakers of Spanish and Korean may have difficulty hearing and saying words with the /b/ sound. This sound is sometimes replaced by the /v/ sound. Give children practice discriminating these sounds from each other by saying word pairs, such as the following: *bet/vet; ban/van, bat/vat*. Have children repeat the words. When available, supply pictures of the words used to help children understand the words' meanings.

DAY 3 Brainstorming

Children will think of words that have the same ending sound as the picture names of Picture Cards.

- Remind children that they have been learning about words that end with the /g/ and /b/ sounds. Suggested language: **We have been learning about words that end with the /g/ sound in *dog* and the /b/ sound in *cab*.**

- Tell children you can name other words that end with the /g/ sound, such as *sag* and *big*. You can also name other words that end with the /b/ sound, such as *job* and *globe*. Explain to children that they will be thinking of other words that end with the sounds /g/ and /b/.

- Give partners a set of Lesson 18 Picture Cards. Tell them that one child will choose a Picture Card and say the picture name. Then the other child will think of a different word that ends with the same sound.

- Have children take turns until all the cards have been turned over.

- You may have children work together to write in their Word Study Notebooks one word that ends with each of the sounds.

DAY 4 Buddy Sort

Children will sort Picture Cards into groups of their own choosing.

- Display a set of Lesson 18 Picture Cards. Name the pictures for children.

- Then model how to sort the cards into two groups: one for animals and one for things that are not animals. Review the groups of cards you made. Then discuss with children why you put each card into its group.

- Give partners a set of Lesson 18 Picture Cards. Tell children to talk about the pictures and then sort the cards into groups that they choose. Remind them that they should be able to explain why each picture belongs in a group.

- Explain that they can sort the pictures by ending sounds as they did earlier in the week or they can sort in other ways.

- Have partners discuss with another pair of children how they sorted the pictures. Children can try to guess each other's categories. Have them explain why each picture was placed into its group.

DAY 5 Assess

Tell children you will be naming Picture Cards, and they will place each card into one of two groups: one for picture names that end with the /g/ sound and one for picture names that end with the /b/ sound. Have children place their Picture Cards in the correct group.

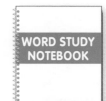

RETEACH **IF** children are unable to associate ending sounds with letters, **THEN** revisit the activity on Day 1 and reassess.

Have children draw a line in the middle of a page in their Word Study Notebooks. Have them color and paste the __*g* and __*b* cards at the top of the columns. Then have them paste their pictures under the Letter Card __*g* or __*b* to show if the picture names end with /g/*g* or /b/*b*.

Words with Short *a* and Short *i*

MATERIALS

Picture Cards: bat, fan, bag, hat, map, tag, van, six, hill, lid, fish, ship, wig, crib

Letters Cards: *a*, *i*

 Reproducible Picture and Letter Cards are available at **www.thinkcentral.com**.

 ELL SUPPORT

Linguistic Transfer Many ELLs may have difficulty discriminating and pronouncing the short *a* and short *i* sounds. Give children additional practice listening for and pronouncing words that have these sounds. Children can take turns naming the Picture Cards with a partner who is a proficient English speaker.

DAY 1 PHONICS Model the Sort

Children will sort Picture Cards with you based on the medial vowel sound in the picture names.

- Display the Lesson 19 Picture Cards and name them for children.
- Write the letters *a* and *i* as headings on chart paper. Then place Picture Card *bat* under the letter *a*. Suggested language: **Listen: *Bat.* *Bat* has the /ă/ sound in the middle. The letter *a* stands for the short *a* sound, /ă/, in the middle of *bat*.**
- Display Picture Card *six* under the letter *i*. Suggested language: **Listen: *Six.* *Six* has the /ĭ/ sound in the middle. The letter *i* stands for the short *i* sound, /ĭ/, in the middle of *six*.**
- Tell children you are going to sort the remaining Picture Cards by the short *a* sound or short *i* sound in the middle of their names.
- Model sorting the Picture Cards according to the vowel sound in their names. Hold up and name Picture Card *hill*. Suggested language: **Listen: *Hill.* Do you hear /ă/ or /ĭ/ in the middle of *hill*? *Hill.* I hear /ĭ/, the short *i* sound, in the middle of *hill*. I'll put Picture Card *hill* under *six*.** Continue with the remaining Picture Cards.
- When all the cards are placed, name the pictures in each column. Have children listen to make sure all the words are in the correct column.
- Give partners a set of Lesson 19 Picture Cards. Have them work together to repeat the sort.

DAY 2 Picture Sort

Children will sort Picture Cards into groups of pictures whose names have the short *a* or short *i* sound.

- Remind children they have been learning about words with the short *a* and short *i* sounds and the letters that stand for those sounds.
- Display Letter Card *a* and Picture Card *fan* as a heading in a pocket chart. Name the picture. Point out that the letter *a* stands for the /ă/ sound in the middle of *fan*.
- Display Letter Card *i* and Picture Card *ship* as another column. Name the picture. Remind children that the letter *i* stands for the /ĭ/ sound in the middle of *ship*.
- Display the remaining Picture Cards one at a time. Name each picture and call on a volunteer to place it in the short *a* or short *i* column.
- After all the pictures have been sorted, have children name the pictures in each column. Point out that all of the words in the first column have the short *a* sound. Guide children to recognize that all of the words in the second column have the short *i* sound.
- Give each child a set of Lesson 19 Picture Cards. Have children repeat the sort independently.

DAY 3 Buddy Sort

Children will sort Picture Cards into categories of their own choosing.

- Tell children they will sort pictures into groups they create. Then display and name the Lesson 19 Picture Cards.

- Give partners a set of Picture Cards. Tell children to talk about the pictures and then work together to sort the cards as they decide.

- Children may want to group the cards by vowel sound, as they did on Day 2, or by beginning or ending sound. They may also sort the cards in other ways, based on what the pictures show.

- Remind children that they should be able to explain why each Picture Card is in a particular group.

- After partners have sorted their cards, have them compare the groups they made with those of other pairs. Children can discuss why they put each card into the groups they made.

- Challenge children to come up with other groupings for sorting the cards.

DAY 4 Word Hunt

Children will find words with short *a* and short *i* in a familiar story.

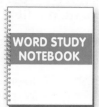

- Remind children they have been learning about words with short *a* and short *i*. Tell them that they will go on a word hunt to find short *a* and short *i* words in a story they have read.

- Have partners work together to read aloud the Student Book story "D Is for Dad" Then have children take turns finding short *a* and short *i* words in the story.

- Children can make two columns in their Word Study Notebooks: one for short *a* words and one for short *i* words. When children find a short *a* or a short *i* word, have them write it in the appropriate column.

- When children have completed their word hunt, call on them to read aloud the words they wrote. Children can compare their word lists with those of other children.

(Possible responses: at, bat, can, Dad, is, big, dig, dip, in, it, rig, sit)

DAY 5 Assess

Tell children you will be naming Picture Cards, and they will hold up the Letter Card that stands for the vowel sound in the middle of the picture name. Display the Picture Cards one at a time. Have children hold up the letter *a* or *i* to match the vowel sound in each picture name.

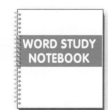

RETEACH **IF** children are unable to associate vowel sounds with letters, **THEN** revisit the activity on Day 1 and reassess.

Have children draw in their Word Study Notebooks pictures of things whose names have the short *a* or the short *i* sound. When they have finished drawing their pictures, have children label each picture with the letter *a* or *i* to show the letter that stands for the short vowel sound in the picture name.

Words with *-ig, -in, -it*

MATERIALS

Picture Cards: dig, rig, pig, pin, bin, fin, sit, pit, fit

Word Cards: *dig, rig, pig, pin, bin, fin, sit, pit, fit*

Reproducible Picture and Word Cards are available at **www.thinkcentral.com**.

ELL SUPPORT

Linguistic Transfer Speakers of Spanish, Vietnamese, Tagalog, and Korean may have difficulty pronouncing the short *i* sound. Provide additional opportunities for children to work with the Picture Cards. Name the pictures, and have children repeat the picture names.

DAY 1 PHONICS Model the Sort

Children will sort Picture Cards with you into groups of pictures with rhyming names.

- Display the Lesson 20 Picture Cards, and name each picture with children. Tell children that together you will sort the pictures into groups of picture names that rhyme.

- Display Picture Card *dig,* say *dig,* and place the card as a heading in a pocket chart. Then display Picture Card *fin* as another heading. Point to the cards, and name the pictures. Suggested language: ***Dig*. I hear /ĭg/ at the end of *dig*. *Fin*. I hear /ĭn/ at the end of *fin*. /d/ /ĭg/, /f/ /ĭn/. These words have different ending sounds. *Dig* and *fin* do not rhyme.**

- Place Picture Card *sit* as an additional heading. Repeat the process for *sit*.

- Then as you display each card, name the picture and the heading card. Suggested language: **Listen: *Rig. Rig, dig. Rig, fin. Rig, sit*. Where should I put *rig*? I will put it under *dig* because *rig* and *dig* rhyme.** Have children listen carefully to each word and help you place each card correctly.

- When all the cards are placed, repeat the picture names in each column. Have children listen to make sure all the words in each column rhyme.

- Give partners a set of Lesson 20 Picture Cards. Have children work together to repeat the sort.

DAY 2 Picture Sort

Children will sort Picture Cards into groups of rhyming picture names.

- Tell children they will sort pictures into groups of picture names that rhyme.

- Display the Picture Cards, and name them for children. Then create categories with the Picture Cards *rig, pin,* and *pit*. Sort the remaining Picture Cards one at a time. Begin with *fit*. Suggested language: **Listen: *Fit, rig. Fit, pin. Fit, pit*. Where should I put *fit*? I will put it with *pit* because *pit* and *fit* have the same sounds at the end.**

- After all the Picture Cards have been sorted, ask children what is the same about all the pictures in each group. *(Their names rhyme; their names have the same ending sounds.)*

- Give each child a set of Lesson 20 Picture Cards. Then have children repeat the sort independently.

DAY 3 Picture-Word Match

Children will match Picture Cards to Word Cards for each picture name.

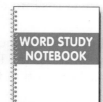

- Display the Lesson 20 Picture Cards, and remind children that they have been working with these Picture Cards this week. Then display the Word Cards for the week.

- Tell children they will be reading the words on the cards and matching the cards to the pictures on the Picture Cards.

- Display the Word Cards, and ask a volunteer to choose one. Have children blend the letter-sounds to read the word on the card.

- Then ask a child to find the Picture Card that matches the word on the Word Card. Continue until all the Picture Cards are matched with the Word Cards.

- Then have children work in pairs to match Picture and Word Cards.

- When children have finished matching the cards, have them write three of the rhyming words in their Word Study Notebooks.

DAY 4 Pattern Sort

Children will sort words into groups by word endings (-ig, -in, -it).

- Tell children they will be sorting words into groups of words that rhyme. Then display the Word Cards, and read each one with children.

- Read the Word Card *pig*, and compare it to the Word Card *bin*. Suggested language: **Pig. Blend with me: /p/ /ĭ/ /g/, pig. Bin. Let's blend: /b/ /ĭ/ /n/, bin. Pig, bin. Pig and bin do not rhyme.**

- Repeat for *fit*. Then ask: **What do you notice about the endings of the words pig, bin, and fit?** (Possible response: They end with different letters).

- Create categories with the Word Cards *pig, bin,* and *fit*. Then sort the remaining Word Cards one at a time, beginning with *pit*. Suggested language: **Listen: Pit. Pit, pig. Pit, bin. Pit, fit. Where should I put pit?**

- Read each group of rhyming words. Ask: **What is the same about the words in each group?** (Possible response: They rhyme; they have the same letters and sounds at the end.)

- Distribute the Lesson 20 Word Cards, and have children repeat the sort. Have them write one set of rhyming words in their Word Study Notebooks.

DAY 5 Assess

Tell children you will be showing them Word Cards. They should look at the Word Cards in front of them, find a rhyming word, and hold it up. Display the Word Card *rig*, and have children hold up another Word Card with a rhyming word. (*dig, pig*) Repeat this procedure with the Word Cards *fin* and *pit*.

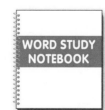

RETEACH IF children are unable to correctly match the rhyming letter-patterns on the Word Cards, THEN revisit the activity on Day 4 and reassess.

Have children sort the Word Cards into groups of words that rhyme. Have them glue the sets of rhyming Word Cards into their Word Study Notebooks.

Beginning Sounds /d/d, /r/r, /g/g

MATERIALS

Picture Cards: door, dog, duck, desk, ring, rocket, rabbit, rope, goat, gate, guitar, gas, garden

Letter Cards: d, r, g

 Reproducible Picture and Letter Cards are available at **www.thinkcentral.com**.

 ELL SUPPORT

Linguistic Transfer Speakers of Cantonese, Mandarin, and Korean may have difficulty discriminating and pronouncing words with the /d/ and /r/ sounds. Give children practice listening for and saying words that begin with these sounds. Model mouth positions as necessary. Use pictures if available to help reinforce word meanings.

DAY 1 — PHONICS — Model the Sort

Children will sort Picture Cards with you based on beginning sounds.

- Display the Lesson 21 Picture Cards. Name the pictures with children. Tell them you are going to sort the Picture Cards into groups of pictures with the same beginning sounds.

- Write the letters *d*, *r*, and *g* as column headings on chart paper or on the board. Then place Picture Card *door* under the letter *d*. Name the picture, emphasizing the /d/ sound at the beginning. Explain that the letter *d* stands for the /d/ sound at the beginning of *door*.

- Repeat for the letter *r*, using Picture Card *ring*, and for the letter *g*, using Picture Card *goat*.

- Model sorting the remaining cards by the beginning sounds in their names. Hold up Picture Card *rabbit*. Suggested language: **Listen:** *Rabbit*. **Does** *rabbit* **have the same beginning sound as** *door, ring*, **or** *goat*? *Rabbit, door. Rabbit, ring. Rabbit, goat.* *Rabbit* **has the same beginning sound as** *ring*. **I'll put** *rabbit* **under** *ring*. Explain that the letter *r* stands for the /r/ sound at the beginning of *rabbit* and *ring*.

- Continue with the other Picture Cards. When all the cards are placed, name the pictures in each column. Have children listen to make sure all the words in each column begin with the same sound.

- Give partners a set of Lesson 21 Picture and Letter Cards. Have them work together to repeat the sort.

DAY 2 — Picture Sort

Children will sort Picture Cards into groups of pictures whose names begin with /d/d, /r/r, and /g/g.

- Remind children they have been listening for the sounds at the beginning of words and learning about the letters that stand for those sounds.

- Display Letter Card *d* and Picture Card *duck* as a heading in a pocket chart. Name the letter and picture, emphasizing the beginning sound of the picture name. Remind children that the letter *d* stands for the /d/ sound at the beginning of *duck*.

- Repeat for the letter *r*, using Letter Card *r* and Picture Card *rabbit*, and for the letter *g*, using Letter Card *g* and Picture Card *guitar*.

- Display the remaining Picture Cards one at a time. Name each picture for children. Then call on volunteers to place the pictures in the /d/d, /r/r, or /g/g column.

- After all the pictures have been sorted, name the pictures in each column and help children understand that they all begin with the same sound.

- Give each child a set of Lesson 21 Picture and Letter Cards. Have children repeat the sort independently.

d	r	g

DAY 3 Brainstorming

Children will think of words that have the same beginning sound as Picture Card picture names.

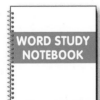
WORD STUDY NOTEBOOK

- Remind children they have been learning about words that begin with the sounds /g/, /r/, and /d/. Suggested language: **We have been learning about words that begin with /g/, such as** *gate,* **words that begin with /r/, such as** *rocket,* **and words that begin with /d/, such as** *desk.*

- Tell children you can name other words that begin with /g/. Say the words *get* and *go.* Point out that they have the same beginning sound as *gate.* Repeat for /d/, using the words *dig* and *duke,* and for /r/, using *rock* and *rip.*

- Give partners a set of Lesson 21 Picture Cards. Tell them that one child will choose a Picture Card and name the picture. Then the other child will think of a different word that begins with the same sound.

- Have children continue until all the cards have been used once.

- You may extend the activity by having children write in their Word Study Notebooks words that begin with the /d/, /r/, and /g/ sounds.

DAY 4 Guess My Category

Children will guess the category names for Picture Cards sorted by beginning sounds.

- Remind children they have been listening for the /d/, /r/, and /g/ sounds at the beginning of words.

- Display Picture Cards *dog, rope,* and *gas* as headings in a pocket chart. Name the pictures, emphasizing each beginning sound so children can hear it clearly.

- Display Picture Card *duck* and place it under *dog.* Then place Picture Card *rocket* under *rope,* and Picture Card *gate* under *gas.*

- Display the remaining Lesson 21 Picture Cards one at a time. Ask children where you should put each card.

- After all the pictures have been sorted, have children name the pictures in each column. Ask them to tell how the pictures in each column are the same. Help them understand that the picture names in each column all begin with the same sound.

DAY 5 Assess

Tell children that you will be naming Picture Cards, and they will place each card into one of three groups: one for picture names that begin with the /d/ sound, one for picture names that begin with the /r/ sound, and one for picture names that begin with the /g/ sound. Have children place Picture Cards into the correct group.

WORD STUDY NOTEBOOK

RETEACH **IF** children are unable to distinguish between words that begin with /d/, /r/, and /g/, **THEN** revisit the activity on Day 2 and reassess.

Have children divide a page in their Word Study Notebooks into three columns. Have them paste the letters *d, r,* and *g* at the top of the columns. Then have them color and paste the Picture Cards under the corresponding Letter Card to show whether the picture name begins with /d/d, /r/r, or /g/g.

MATERIALS

Picture Cards: fox, log, pot, hop, top, lock, doll, box, bat, cap, fish, wig, sun, bed, pen

Letter Card: o

 Reproducible Picture and Letter Cards are available at **www.thinkcentral.com.**

 **ELL SUPPORT**

Use Minimal Pairs Speakers of Spanish, Tagalog, and Korean may pronounce the short o sound like the long o. Give children practice saying pairs of words, such as the following: *hop/hope, cop/cope, cot/coat, not/note.* Display visuals or use gestures when appropriate to help children understand each word's meaning.

DAY 1 PHONICS **Model the Sort**

Children will sort Picture Cards with you based on medial sound, focusing on the short o sound.

- Display the Lesson 22 Picture Cards, and name them for children. Tell children that some of the picture names have the short o sound and others do not.

- Model sorting the Picture Cards by whether they have the short o sound or another sound in the middle. Hold up Picture Card *fox*. Suggested language: **Listen:** *Fox. Fox* **has the /ŏ/ sound in the middle. The letter o stands for the short o sound, /ŏ/, in the middle of** *fox*.

- Display Picture Card *fish*. Suggested language: **Listen:** *Fish. Fish* **does not have the /ŏ/ sound in the middle. It has the short** *i* **sound, /ĭ/, in the middle. I'm going to start a new group for words that do not have the short o sound.**

- Continue with the remaining Word Cards, helping children sort them into the appropriate groups. After all the words have been sorted, read each column aloud. Guide children to notice the short o sound in the words in the first column.

- When all the cards are placed, name the pictures in each column. Have children listen to make sure all the words are in the correct column.

- Give partners a set of Lesson 22 Picture Cards. Have them work together to repeat the sort.

· ·

DAY 2 **Picture Sort**

Children will sort Picture Cards based on medial sound.

- Remind children they have been listening for words with the short o sound and learning about the letter that stands for that sound.

- Display Letter Card o as a heading in a pocket chart. Remind children that the letter o stands for the /ŏ/ sound. Display Picture Card *doll*. Name the picture, elongating the short o sound in the middle. Tell children you will place Picture Card *doll* under Letter Card o because *doll* has the short o sound in the middle.

- Display Picture Card *sun* as another heading. Name the picture, elongating the vowel sound in the middle. Point out that this word does not have the short o sound in the middle.

- Display the remaining Picture Cards one at a time. Name each picture. Then call on a volunteer to place each card under Letter Card o if the picture name has the short o sound in the middle or under Picture Card *sun* if the picture name has another sound in the middle.

- After all the pictures have been sorted, have children name the pictures in each column. Point out that all of the picture names in the first column have the short o sound in the middle. Explain that all of the picture names in the second column have another sound in the middle.

- Give each child a set of Lesson 22 Picture Cards. Have children repeat the sort independently.

DAY 3 Brainstorming

Children will think of words that have the short *o* sound.

WORD STUDY NOTEBOOK

- Remind children they have been learning about words with the short *o* sound. Suggested language: **Listen to these words:** *fox, hop, pot*. **They all have the /ŏ/ sound in the middle.**

- Tell children that you can name other words with the /ŏ/ sound in the middle. Say the words *fog* and *not*. Point out that they have the same sound in the middle as *fox*, *hop*, and *pot*.

- Give partners a set of the following Picture Cards: *fox, log, pot, hop, top, lock, doll, box*. Tell them that one child will choose a Picture Card and name it. Then the other child will think of a different word that has the same sound in the middle.

- Have children continue until all the cards have been used once.

- You may extend the activity by having children work together to write words that have the short *o* sound in their Word Study Notebooks.

DAY 4 Buddy Sort

Children will sort Picture Cards into categories of their own choice.

- Tell children that they will sort pictures into groups they create.

- Give partners a set of Lesson 22 Picture Cards. Tell children to talk about the pictures and then sort the cards into groups that they choose. Remind them that they should be able to explain why each picture belongs in a group.

- Children may want to group the cards by vowel sound as they did on Day 2. They can also choose to sort the cards in other ways, based upon the characteristics of the pictures. For example, they could make groups for *animals* or *things found in a house*.

- After partners have sorted their cards, have them compare the groups they made with those of another pair of children. Children can discuss why they put each card into a group.

- After children discuss their groups with others, challenge them to think of other ways they can group the pictures.

DAY 5 Assess

Tell children that you will be naming Picture Cards, and they will hold up the Letter Card *o* if they hear the short *o* sound. Display the Picture Cards one at a time. Have children hold up the letter *o* when they hear the short *o* sound in a picture name.

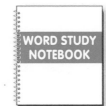

WORD STUDY NOTEBOOK

RETEACH IF children are unable to discriminate the short *o* sound, **THEN** revisit the activity on Day 1 and reassess.

Have children draw in their Word Study Notebooks pictures of things whose names have the short *o* sound. When they have finished drawing their pictures, have children label the pictures with the letter *o*.

MATERIALS

Picture Cards: *pan, cap, top, pit, pans, caps, tops, pits*

Word Cards: *pan, cap, top, pit, pans, caps, tops, pits*

 Reproducible Picture and Word Cards are available at **www.thinkcentral.com**.

ELL SUPPORT

Linguistic Transfer In many languages, there are no plural forms for nouns. Some ELLs may need additional support with this concept. Have them name groups of objects in the classroom and complete sentence frames, such as the following: *This is one _____. These are two _____.*

DAY 1 PHONICS Model the Sort

Children will sort Picture and Word Cards with you based on whether they represent one or more than one.

- Display the Lesson 23 Picture Cards, and name them for children.
- Place Picture Cards *pan* and *pans* as headings in a pocket chart. Name each picture. Point out that Picture Card *pan* shows only one pan, and Picture Card *pans* shows more than one pan.
- Then display the Word Card *pan*. Read the word. Explain that the word *pan* matches the Picture Card *pan* because it means only one pan. Place the Word Card *pan* under Picture Card *pan*.
- Use a similar procedure to match the Word Card *pans* to Picture Card *pans*.
- Point to the *s* at the end of the word *pans*. Remind children that they can add an *s* to the end of a word to make it mean more than one.
- Then model sorting the Picture Cards by whether they show one or more than one. Hold up and name Picture Card *cap*. Suggested language: **Cap. This picture shows only one cap. I'll put the Picture Card *cap* under *pan*. Then I'll find the Word Card that matches the picture name. /k/ /ă/ /p/. This is the card. The Word Card *cap* matches the Picture Card *cap* because it means one cap.**
- Repeat the procedure with the Picture and Word Cards for *caps*, placing them under *pans*.
- Continue with the other Picture and Word Cards. When all the cards are placed, name the pictures and read the words in each column. Have children listen to make sure all the Picture and Word Cards are in the correct column.
- Give partners a set of Lesson 23 Picture and Word Cards. Have them repeat the sort.

DAY 2 Picture/Word Sort

Children will sort Picture and Word Cards based on whether they represent one or more than one.

- Remind children they have been learning about words that name one thing or that name more than one thing.
- Display Picture Card *pit* as a heading in a pocket chart. Name the picture. Remind children that this is a picture of one pit. Then display Picture Card *pits* as another heading. Name the picture. Point out that this is a picture of more than one pit.
- Remind children that they can add an *s* to the end of many naming words to make them mean "more than one."
- Display the remaining Picture Cards one at a time. Name each picture. Then call on a volunteer to place the picture in the correct column.
- Hold up the Word Card *pit* and place it beside Picture Card *pit*. Explain that this word means "one pit." Then hold up the Word Card *pits*. Point to the *s* at the end of the word, and explain that this word means "more than one pit." Then place it beside Picture Card *pits*.
- After all the Picture and Word Cards have been sorted, have children name the pictures and read the words in each column. Ask children what they see at the end of all the words that mean "more than one." *(-s)*
- Give each child a set of Lesson 23 Picture and Word Cards. Have children repeat the sort independently.

DAY 3 Word Sort

Children will sort words into groups based on whether they mean "one" or "more than one."

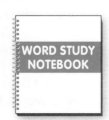
WORD STUDY NOTEBOOK

- Display a set of Lesson 23 Word Cards. Model how to blend the letter-sounds to read several words. Then have volunteers blend the remaining words.
- Tell children they are going to sort the words to show which ones mean one thing and which ones mean more than one thing.
- Give partners a set of Lesson 23 Word Cards. Tell them they are going to make two groups: one for words that mean "one" and another for words that mean "more than one."
- Have children take turns reading a Word Card and placing it in the correct group.
- When children have sorted their cards, have them read the words in each column. Then have them copy their sorts into their Word Study Notebooks.

DAY 4 Play "Go Fish"

Children will play a game to match words that mean "one" or "more than one."

WORD STUDY NOTEBOOK

- Remind children that you can add an *s* to the end of many words to make them mean "more than one." Then tell them they are going to play a game called "Go Fish" with the Word Cards.
- Remind children how to play the game. Explain that partners will each take two Word Cards. The rest of the cards are placed face down in a pile.
- Explain that the first child then chooses one of his or her cards and asks the second child if he or she has a match. For example, if the first child chooses Word Card *pan*, he or she asks the second child for Word Card *pans*.
- If the second child does not have the matching Word Card, he or she says, "Go fish." Then the first child picks a card from the pile. The game is over when all the Word Cards are matched.
- Divide children into pairs. Then give partners a set of Lesson 23 Word Cards, and have them play the game.
- After all the Word Cards have been matched, have partners read the words aloud. Then have them copy one set of words into their Word Study Notebooks.

DAY 5 Assess

Tell children that you will be holding up two Word Cards, and they will point to the word that means more than one thing. Display the Word Cards *top* and *tops*. Have children point to the word that means "more than one top." Then have them tell why they chose that particular word. *(It has an* s *at the end.)* Repeat for the other word pairs.

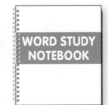
WORD STUDY NOTEBOOK

RETEACH **IF** children are unable to recognize which words mean "more than one," **THEN** revisit the activity on Day 1 and reassess.

Have children copy the words into their Word Study Notebooks. When they have finished writing the words, have them underline the *s* at the end of each word that means "more than one."

Words with *-at, -it, -ot*

 **ELL SUPPORT**

Linguistic Transfer Many ELLs may have difficulty pronouncing short vowel sounds. Provide additional opportunities for children to work with the words for the week by showing the Picture Cards, naming the pictures, and having children repeat the picture name each time.

DAY 1 PHONICS Model the Sort

Children will sort Picture Cards with you into groups of pictures with rhyming names.

- Display the Lesson 24 Picture Cards, and name each picture with children. Tell children that together you will sort the pictures according to rhyming picture names.

- Display Picture Card *bat*, say *bat*, and place the card as a heading in a pocket chart. Then display Picture Card *kit* as another heading. Point to the cards, and name the pictures. Suggested language: **Bat. I hear /ăt/ at the end of *bat*. Kit. I hear /ĭt/ at the end of *kit*. /b/ /ăt/, /k/ /ĭt/. These words have different ending sounds. *Bat* and *kit* do not rhyme.**

- Then place Picture Card *cot* as an additional heading. Repeat the process for *cot*.

- Then, as you display each card, name the Picture Card and the heading card. Suggested language: **Listen: *Cat. Cat, bat. Cat, kit. Cat, cot*. Where should I put *cat*? *Cat* and *bat* have the same ending sounds, so I'll put *cat* under *bat*.** Have children listen and help you place each card correctly.

- When all the cards are placed, repeat the picture names in each column. Have children listen to make sure all the words in each column rhyme.

- Give partners a set of Lesson 24 Picture Cards. Have children work together to repeat the sort.

DAY 2 Open Sort

Children will sort Picture Cards into categories of their own choice.

- Tell children that today they will sort pictures into groups they create. Display the Picture Cards one at a time, and name each picture.

- Have children take a moment to look at the Picture Cards and decide how they will sort them. Children may decide to sort the pictures into groups of rhyming words, as they did on Day 1. Children may also choose to sort words by beginning sound or to create groups for *animals* and *non-animals*. Remind children that they should be able to explain why each Picture Card belongs in a group.

- As children sort the Picture Cards, circulate to have them tell how they are sorting the cards.

- When children have sorted their cards, have them take turns sharing with a partner how they sorted the pictures.

- Then have children tell the group how they sorted the Picture Cards. On the board, record each way children sorted the cards. You may add tally marks to show how many children sorted the pictures each way.

DAY 3 Picture-Word Match

Children will match each Picture Card to the Word Card that names it.

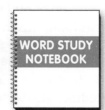

- Display the Lesson 24 Picture Cards, and remind children that they have been working with these picture names this week. Then display the Word Cards for the week.
- Tell children they will be reading the words on the cards and matching the Word Cards to the Picture Cards.
- Have a volunteer choose a Word Card. Have children blend the letter-sounds to read the word. Then ask a child to find the Picture Card that matches the word on the Word Card.
- Continue until all the Picture Cards are matched with the Word Cards.
- Give partners a set of Picture and Word Cards. Then have them work together to match Picture Cards to Word Cards.
- When children have finished matching the cards, have them write three of the words in their Word Study Notebooks.

DAY 4 Pattern Sort

Children will sort words into groups by word endings *(-at, -it, -ot)*.

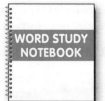

- Tell children they will be sorting words into groups of words that rhyme. Display the Word Cards and read each one with children.
- Create categories with the Word Cards *cat, hit*, and *dot*.
- Then model how to sort the Word Cards into rhyming groups. Suggested language: **Listen to this word:** *Pit.* ***Pit, cat. Pit, hit. Pit, dot.*** **The words** *pit* **and** *hit* **rhyme. They have the same ending sounds. I will put** *pit* **under** *hit.* Then point out that the words *pit* and *hit* both end with the letters *-it.*
- Give partners a set of Lesson 24 Word Cards. Have them sort the words into groups of words that rhyme.
- After children have sorted the words, have them read aloud the words in each column. Ask: **What is the same about the words in each group?** *(They rhyme; they have the same letters and sounds at the end.)*
- Have children write one set of rhyming words in their Word Study Notebooks.

DAY 5 Assess

Tell children that you will be showing them Word Cards. They should look at the Word Cards in front of them, find a rhyming word, and hold it up. Display the Word Card *hat*, and have children hold up another Word Card with a rhyming word. *(cat, hat, mat)* Repeat this procedure for the Word Cards *pit* and *pot*.

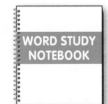

RETEACH **IF** children are unable to correctly match the rhyming letter-patterns on the Word Cards, **THEN** revisit the activity on Day 4 and reassess.

Have children sort the Word Cards into groups of words that rhyme. Have them either glue the sets of rhyming Word Cards into their Word Study Notebooks or write the sets of rhyming words.

Words with Short *o* and Short *e*

 **ELL SUPPORT**

Linguistic Transfer Many ELLs may have difficulty discriminating and pronouncing the short *o* and short *e* sounds. Pair ELLs with more-proficient English speakers when doing partner activities. For example, when doing the Word Hunt on Day 4, have the more-proficient speaker say words for their partners to help them discriminate the vowel sounds in the words.

DAY 1 PHONICS Model the Sort

Children will sort Picture Cards with you based on whether the picture names have the short *o* or short *e* sound.

- Display the Lesson 25 Picture Cards, and name them for children.
- Place Letter Cards *o* and *e* as headings in a pocket chart. Then place Picture Card *lock* under Letter Card *o*. Suggested language: **Listen:** *Lock. Lock* **has the /ŏ/ sound in the middle. The letter** *o* **stands for the short** *o* **sound, /ŏ/, in the middle of** *lock.*
- Display Picture Card *bed* under Letter Card *e*. Suggested language: **Listen:** *Bed. Bed* **has the /ĕ/ sound in the middle. The letter** *e* **stands for the short** *e* **sound, /ĕ/, in the middle of** *bed.*
- Model sorting the Picture Cards according to the vowel sounds in their names. Hold up and name Picture Card *top*. Suggested language: *Top.* **I'll listen to see if I hear /ŏ/ or /ĕ/ in the middle.** *Top.* **I hear the short** *o* **sound, /ŏ/, in the middle of** *top.* **I'll put the Picture Card** *top* **under** *lock.* Repeat with Picture Card *ten* and the sound for short *e*.
- Continue with the remaining Picture Cards. When all the cards are placed, name the pictures in each column. Have children listen to make sure all the words are in the correct column.
- Give partners a set of Lesson 25 Picture Cards. Have them work together to repeat the sort.

DAY 2 Guess My Category

Children will guess the category names for Picture Cards sorted by medial short *o* and short *e* sounds.

- Remind children that they have been listening for the short *o* and short *e* sounds in the middle of words.
- Display Picture Cards *top* and *hen* as headings in a pocket chart. Name the pictures, emphasizing each vowel sound so children can hear it clearly.
- Display Picture Card *sock,* and place it under *top*. Then place Picture Card *net* under *hen*.
- Display the remaining Lesson 25 Picture Cards one at a time. Ask children where you should put each card.
- After all the pictures have been sorted, have children name the pictures in each column. Ask them to tell how the pictures in each column are the same. Help them understand that the pictures in the first column have names with the short *o* sound, and the pictures in the second column have names with the short *e* sound.
- Give partners a set of Lesson 25 Picture and Letter Cards. Have children repeat the sort by grouping together Picture Cards whose names have the same medial sound.

DAY 3 **Brainstorming**

Children will think of words that have the short *o* or short *e* sound.

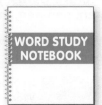

- Remind children they have been learning about words with the short *o* and short *e* sounds. Suggested language: **We have been learning about words with the short *o* sound in the middle, such as *mop*, and about words with the short *e* sound in the middle, such as *leg*.**

- Tell children that you can name other words with the short *o* sound. Say the words *got* and *lot*. Point out that they have the same vowel sound as *mop*. Then say the words *men* and *deck*. Point out that they have the same vowel sound as *leg*.

- Give partners a set of Lesson 25 Picture Cards. Tell them that one child will choose a Picture Card and name the picture. The other child will think of a different word that has the same sound in the middle.

- Have children continue until all the cards have been used once.

- You may extend the activity by having children write in their Word Study Notebooks one word that has the short *o* sound and one word that has the short *e* sound.

DAY 4 **Word Hunt**

Children will find short *o* and short *e* words in a familiar story.

- Remind children they have been learning about words with short *o* and short *e*. Tell them they will go on a word hunt to find short *o* and short *e* words in a story they have read.

- Have partners work together to read aloud the Student Book story "Six Pigs Hop." Then have children take turns naming short *o* and short *e* words in the story.

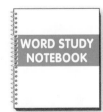

- Tell children to make two columns in their Word Study Notebooks, one for short *o* words and one for short *e* words. When children find a short *o* or short *e* word, have them write it in the appropriate column.

- When children have completed their word hunt, call on them to read aloud their words to the group. Children can compare their word lists with those of other children.

(Possible responses: Jen, pen, hop, top)

DAY 5 **Assess**

Tell children that you will be naming Picture Cards, and they will hold up the Letter Card that stands for the vowel sound they hear in the middle of each picture name. Display the Picture Cards one at a time. Have children hold up the letter *o* or *e* to match the vowel sound in each picture name.

RETEACH **IF** children are unable to associate vowel sounds with letters, **THEN** revisit the activity on Day 1 and reassess.

Have children divide a page in their Word Study Notebooks into two columns. Have them paste the letters *o* and *e* at the top of the columns. Next, have them color and then paste their Picture Cards under the corresponding Letter Card to show the letter that stands for the vowel sound in each picture name.

Words with -*et* and -*en*

 **ELL SUPPORT**

Linguistic Transfer Speakers of Spanish, Vietnamese, Cantonese, Mandarin, Tagalog, and Korean may have difficulty pronouncing short *e* words. Model mouth positions as you say words with the short *e* sound. Then have children repeat each word several times. During the course of the week, give children opportunities to practice saying the short *e* picture names for the week.

DAY 1 PHONICS **Model the Sort**

Children will sort Picture Cards with you into groups of pictures with rhyming names.

- Display the Lesson 26 Picture Cards, and name each picture with children. Tell children that together you will sort the pictures according to rhyming picture names.

- Display Picture Card *jet,* say *jet,* and place the card as a heading in a pocket chart. Then display Picture Card *hen* as another heading. Point to the cards, and name the pictures. Suggested language: ***Jet.* I hear /ĕt/ at the end of *jet. Hen.* I hear /ĕn/ at the end of *hen.* /j/ /ĕt/, /h/ /ĕn/. These words have different ending sounds. *Jet* and *hen* do not rhyme.**

- Then, as you display each Picture Card, name the picture and the heading card. Suggested language: **Listen to this word: *Pen. Pen, jet. Pen, hen.* Which two words have the same sounds at the end?** *Pen* and *hen* sound the same at the end. **I'll put *pen* under *hen.*** Have children listen and help you name the rhyming words. Then place each card into the correct group.

- When all the cards are placed, name the pictures in each column. Have children listen to make sure all the words in each column rhyme.

- Give partners a set of Lesson 26 Picture Cards. Have children work together to repeat the sort.

DAY 2 **Open Sort**

Children will sort Picture Cards into categories of their own choice.

- Tell children that today they will sort the pictures into groups they create. Display the Picture Cards one at a time, and name each picture.

- Have children look at the Picture Cards and think about different ways they can sort them. You may make some suggestions to help children get started. Children may decide to sort the pictures into groups of rhyming words, as they did on Day 1. They might also make groups for *animals*, *things people use*, and so on.

- As children sort the Picture Cards, remind them that they should be able to explain why each picture belongs in a group. Circulate to ask children about how they are sorting the cards.

- When children have sorted their cards, have them take turns telling a partner how they sorted the pictures. Challenge partners to work together to figure out other ways to sort the pictures.

DAY 3 Picture-Word Match

Children will match Picture Cards to the Word Cards that name each picture.

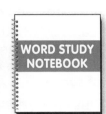

- Display the Lesson 26 Picture Cards, and remind children they have been working with these picture names this week. Then display the Word Cards for the week.

- Tell children they will be reading the words on the cards and matching the words to the pictures on the Picture Cards.

- Display the Word Cards, and ask a volunteer to choose one. Have children blend the letter-sounds to read the word on the card. Then ask a child to find the Picture Card whose name matches the word on the Word Card.

- Continue until all the Picture Cards are matched with the Word Cards.

- Then have children work in pairs to match the Picture Cards to the Word Cards.

- When children have finished matching the cards, have them write three of the words in their Word Study Notebooks.

DAY 4 Pattern Sort

Children will sort words into groups by word endings (-et, -en).

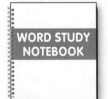

- Tell children they will be sorting words into groups of words that rhyme. Then display the Word Cards, and read each one with children.

- Create categories with the Word Cards *pet* and *ten*.

- Then model how to sort the Word Cards into groups that rhyme. Suggested language: **Listen: *Men. Men, pet. Men, ten.* I will put the Word Card *men* under *ten*. The words *men* and *ten* rhyme. They have the same ending sounds.** Then point out that the words *men* and *ten* both end with the letters -en.

- Give partners a set of Lesson 26 Word Cards. Have them sort the words into groups of rhyming words.

- After children have sorted the words, have them read the words in each column aloud. Ask: **What is the same about the words in each group?** (Possible response: They rhyme; they have the same letters and sounds at the end.)

- In their Word Study Notebooks, have children write two sets of rhyming words: one set with words that end with -et and one set with words that end with -en.

DAY 5 Assess

Tell children that you will be showing them a Word Card. They should look at the word, find a rhyming Word Card, and hold it up. Display the Word Card *wet,* and have children hold up a Word Card with a rhyming word. (net, jet, pet) Repeat this procedure for the Word Card *pen.*

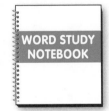

RETEACH **IF** children are unable to correctly match letter patterns on the Word Cards, **THEN** revisit the activity on Day 4 and reassess.

Have children sort the Word Cards into groups of words that rhyme. Then have them glue the sets of rhyming Word Cards into their Word Study Notebooks.

 **ELL SUPPORT**

Linguistic Transfer Speakers of Spanish, Cantonese, Mandarin, and Korean may have difficulty discriminating and pronouncing words that have the short *u* sound. Give children practice by displaying and naming pictures whose names have the short *u* sound. Have children repeat the picture names each time.

DAY 1 PHONICS | Model the Sort

Children will sort Picture Cards with you based on medial sound, focusing on the short *u* sound.

- Display the Lesson 27 Picture Cards, and name them for children.
- Model sorting the Picture Cards by whether they have the short *u* sound or another sound in the middle. Hold up Picture Card *sun*. Suggested language: **Listen to this word:** *Sun. Sun* **has the /ŭ/ sound in the middle. The letter** *u* **stands for the short** *u* **sound, /ŭ/, in the middle of** *sun*.
- Display Picture Card *fan*. Suggested language: **Listen:** *Fan. Fan* **does not have the /ŭ/ sound in the middle. It has a different sound, /ă/, in the middle. I'm going to start a new group for words that do not have the short** *u* **sound.**
- Continue with the remaining Picture Cards, helping children sort them into appropriate groups. After all the cards have been sorted, name each picture. Guide children to notice the short *u* sound in the words in the first column.
- Give partners a set of Lesson 27 Picture Cards. Have them work together to repeat the sort.

DAY 2 | Picture Sort

Children will sort Picture Cards based on medial sound.

- Remind children that they have been listening for the middle sound in words. They have been sorting words with the short *u* sound and learning about the letter that stands for that sound.
- Display Letter Card *u* as a heading in a pocket chart. Then hold up Picture Card *tub*. Name the picture, extending the short *u* sound, /ŭ/, in the middle. Remind children that the letter *u* stands for the /ŭ/ sound in the middle of *tub*.
- Display Picture Card *hill* as another heading. Name the picture, elongating the vowel sound. Point out that this word does not have the short *u* sound in the middle.
- Display the remaining Picture Cards one at a time. Name each picture. Then call on a volunteer to place each card under Letter Card *u* if the picture name has the short *u* sound in the middle or under Picture Card *hill* if the picture name has another sound in the middle.
- After all the pictures have been sorted, have children name the pictures in each column. Point out that all of the picture names in the first column have the short *u* sound in the middle. Reinforce that all of the picture names in the second column have a different sound in the middle.
- Give each child a set of Lesson 27 Picture Cards. Have children repeat the sort independently.

DAY 3 Brainstorming

Children will think of words that have the short *u* sound in them.

- Remind children that they have been learning about words with the short *u* sound and words with other vowel sounds. Suggested language: **We have been learning about words with short *u*, such as *sun* and *cup*. We have been comparing short *u* words to words with other vowel sounds.**

- Tell children that you can name other words with the /ŭ/ sound. Say the words *luck* and *run*. Point out that they have the same sound in the middle as *sun, tub,* and *cup*.

- Give partners a set of the following Picture Cards: *sun, tub, cup, duck, rug, sub, nut.* Tell children that one child will choose a Picture Card and name the picture. Then the other child will say a different word that has the same vowel sound, /ŭ/.

- Have children continue until all the cards have been used.

- You may extend the activity by having children write some of the words they named in their Word Study Notebooks.

DAY 4 Buddy Sort

Children will sort Picture Cards into categories of their choosing.

- Tell children that they will sort pictures into groups that they create.

- Give partners a set of Lesson 27 Picture Cards. Tell children to talk about the pictures and then sort the cards into groups that they choose. Remind them that they should be able to explain why each picture belongs in a group.

- Children may repeat the sort from Day 2 or make groups for all the different vowel sounds in the picture names. They may also choose to sort the cards in other ways, such as by beginning sounds, by ending sounds, or based upon what the pictures show.

- After partners have sorted their cards, have them compare the groups they made with those of another pair of children. Children can discuss why they put each card into a group.

- After children discuss their groups with others, challenge them to think of other ways they can group the pictures.

DAY 5 Assess

Tell children that you will be naming Picture Cards, and they will hold up the Letter Card *u* if they hear the short *u* sound. Display the Picture Cards one at a time. Have children hold up the letter *u* when they hear the short *u* sound in a picture name.

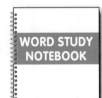

RETEACH **IF** children are unable to discriminate the short *u* sound in words, **THEN** revisit the activity on Day 1 and reassess.

Have children draw in their Word Study Notebooks pictures of things whose names have the short *u* sound. When they have finished drawing their pictures, have children label the pictures with the letter *u*.

Words with Short *e* and Short *u*

MATERIALS

Picture Cards: bell, nest, web, pen, net, bed, vet, truck, cup, plug, bug, cub, bus, drum

Letter Cards: *e, u*

 Reproducible Picture and Letter Cards are available at www.thinkcentral.com.

 **ELL SUPPORT**

Use Minimal Pairs Many ELLs may have difficulty discriminating and pronouncing the short *e* and short *u* sounds. Give children additional practice listening for and pronouncing word pairs, such as the following: *bed/bud, but/bet, pep/pup, duck/deck, rest/rust.* Use pictures if available to help reinforce word meanings.

DAY 1 PHONICS Model the Sort

Children will sort Picture Cards with you based on the medial vowel sounds in the picture names.

- Display the Lesson 28 Picture Cards, and name them for children.
- Place Letter Cards *e* and *u* in a pocket chart as headings. Display Picture Card *bell* under Letter Card *e*. Suggested language: **Listen as I say this word: *Bell. Bell* has the /ĕ/ sound in the middle. The letter *e* stands for the sound, /ĕ/, in the middle of *bell*.**
- Display Picture Card *truck* under Letter Card *u*. Suggested language: **Now listen to this word: *Truck. Truck* has the /ŭ/ sound in the middle. The letter *u* stands for the short *u* sound, /ŭ/, in the middle of *truck*.**
- Model sorting the Picture Cards according to the vowel sound in their names. Hold up and name Picture Card *nest*. Suggested language: ***Nest.* I'll listen to see if I hear the /ĕ/ sound or the /ŭ/ sound in the word. *Nest.* I hear the short *e* sound, /ĕ/, in the middle of *nest*. I'll put the Picture Card *nest* under *bell*.** Repeat with Picture Card *cup* and the sound for short *u*.
- Continue with the remaining Picture Cards. When all the cards are placed, name the pictures in each column. Have children listen to make sure all the words are in the correct column.
- Give partners a set of Lesson 28 Picture Cards. Have them work together to repeat the sort.

DAY 2 Picture Sort

Children will sort Picture Cards by medial vowel sound, short *e* or short *u*.

- Remind children they have been listening for the short *e* and short *u* sounds in words, and they have also been learning about the letters that stand for those sounds.
- Write the letters *e* and *u* as column headings on chart paper or on the board. Then place Picture Card *bed* under the letter *e*. Name the picture, elongating the vowel sound. Point out that the letter *e* stands for the /ĕ/ sound in the middle of *bed*.
- Place Picture Card *bug* under the letter *u*. Name the picture, elongating the vowel sound. Point out that the letter *u* stands for the /ŭ/ sound in the middle of *bug*.
- Display the remaining Picture Cards one at a time. Name each picture. Then call on a volunteer to place each card under the appropriate heading.
- After all the pictures have been sorted, have children name the pictures in each column. Help children understand that the picture names in the first column have the same middle sound, the short *e* sound, and that the picture names in the second column have the short *u* sound.
- Give each child a set of Lesson 28 Picture and Letter Cards. Have children repeat the sort independently.

DAY 3 Buddy Sort

Children will sort Picture Cards into categories of their choosing.

- Tell children that they will sort pictures into groups that they create. Then display and name the Lesson 28 Picture Cards.

- Give partners a set of Picture Cards. Tell them to talk about the pictures and then sort the cards into groups that they choose. Remind them that they should be able to explain why each picture belongs in a group.

- Children may want to group the cards by vowel sound as they did on Day 2. They can also choose to sort the cards by beginning sound, by ending sound, or in other ways, based on what the pictures show.

- If children have difficulty getting started, offer a few suggestions. For example, children can make groups, such as *vehicles*, *animals*, *things found in nature*, *musical instruments*, and so on.

- After partners have sorted their cards, have them compare the groups they made with those of other pairs of children. Children can discuss why they put each card into a group.

- After children discuss their groups with others, challenge them to think of other ways they can sort the pictures.

DAY 4 Brainstorming

Children will think of words that have the short *e* or short *u* sound.

WORD STUDY NOTEBOOK

- Remind children they have been learning about words with the short *e* and short *u* sounds. Suggested language: **We have been learning about words with the short *e* sound, such as** *nest.* **We also have been learning about words with the short *u* sound, such as** *drum.*

- Tell children that you can name other words with the short *e* sound. Say the words *mess* and *let*. Point out that they have the same vowel sound as *nest*. Then say the words *must* and *jump*. Point out that these words have the same vowel sound as *drum*.

- Give partners a set of Lesson 28 Picture Cards. Tell them that one child will choose a Picture Card and name the picture. Then the other child will think of a different word with the same vowel sound.

- Have children continue until all the cards have been used.

- You may extend the activity by having children write in their Word Study Notebooks one word that has the short *e* sound and one word that has the short *u* sound.

DAY 5 Assess

Tell children that you will be naming Picture Cards, and they will hold up the Letter Card that stands for the short vowel sound they hear in the middle of each picture name. Display the Picture Cards one at a time. Have children hold up the letter *e* or *u* to match the vowel sound in each picture name.

WORD STUDY NOTEBOOK

RETEACH **IF** children are unable to associate vowel sounds with letters, **THEN** revisit the activity on Day 1 and reassess.

In their Word Study Notebooks, have children draw pictures of things whose names have the short *e* or short *u* sound. When they have finished drawing, have children label each picture with the letter *e* or *u*.

LESSON 29 — Words with *-ap, -up, -op*

MATERIALS

Picture Cards: *cap, lap, map, nap, tap, pup, cup, up, mop, top, pop, hop*

Word Cards: *cap, lap, map, nap, tap, pup, cup, up, mop, top, pop, hop*

 Reproducible Picture and Word Cards are available at **www.thinkcentral.com**.

 **ELL SUPPORT**

Linguistic Transfer Many ELLs may have difficulty pronouncing short vowel sounds. Provide additional opportunities for children to work with the words for the week by showing the Picture Cards, naming the pictures, and having children repeat the picture name each time.

DAY 1 PHONICS — Model the Sort

Children will sort Picture Cards with you into groups of pictures with rhyming names.

- Display the Lesson 29 Picture Cards, and name each picture with children. Tell children that together you will sort the pictures according to picture names that rhyme.
- Display Picture Card *cap*, say *cap*, and place the card as a heading in a pocket chart. Then display Picture Card *pup* as another heading. Point to the cards, and name the pictures. Suggested language: ***Cap*. I hear /ăp/ at the end of *cap*. *Pup*. I hear /ŭp/ at the end of *pup*. *Cap, pup*. These words have different ending sounds. *Cap* and *pup* do not rhyme.**
- Then place Picture Card *mop* as an additional heading. Repeat the process for *mop*.
- Then as you display each Picture Card, name the picture and the heading card. Suggested language: **Listen: *Lap*. *Lap, cap*. *Lap, pup*. *Lap, mop*. Which word rhymes with *lap*? *Lap* rhymes with *cap*. They both have the same sounds at the end. I'll put Picture Card *lap* under *cap*.**
- Have children listen and help you place each Picture Card in the correct column.
- When all the cards are placed, repeat the picture names in each column. Have children listen to make sure all the words in each column rhyme.
- Give partners a set of Lesson 29 Picture Cards. Have children work together to repeat the sort.

DAY 2 — Open Sort

Children will sort Picture Cards into categories of their own choosing.

- Tell children that today they will sort the pictures into groups that they create. Display the Picture Cards one at a time, and name each picture.
- Give children a moment to look at the Picture Cards. Have them think about different ways to sort the cards. Remind them that they should be able to explain why each picture belongs in a group.
- Tell children to sort the cards as they choose. Children may decide to sort the pictures into groups of rhyming words, as they did on Day 1. They may also sort by beginning or ending sound or according to what the pictures show.
- If children need help getting started, suggest possible ways to sort the cards. For example, they can sort words into groups for *living things*, *things that move*, *things found in a home*, and so on.
- As children sort the Picture Cards, circulate and ask them about how they are sorting the cards.
- When children have sorted their cards, have them take turns telling a partner how they sorted the pictures. Have children compare the ways they sorted the cards.

DAY 3 Picture-Word Match

Children will match Picture Cards to the Word Cards that name each picture.

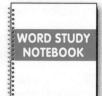

- Display the Lesson 29 Picture Cards, and remind children that they have been working with these picture names. Then display the Word Cards for the week.

- Tell children that today they will be reading the words on the cards and matching the cards to the pictures on the Picture Cards.

- Model how to match Picture and Word Cards. Display a Word Card, and blend the letter-sounds to read the word on the card. Find the Picture Card that matches the Word Card. Suggested language: **Listen as I blend the sounds: /m/ /ă/ /p/, *map*. The word is *map*. Here is the Picture Card that shows a map.**

- Give partners a set of Lesson 29 Picture and Word Cards. Have children work together to match Picture Cards to Word Cards.

- When children have finished matching, have them write three of the words in their Word Study Notebooks.

DAY 4 Pattern Sort

Children will sort words into groups by word endings *(-ap, -up, -op)*.

- Tell children that they will be sorting words into groups of words that rhyme. Display the Word Cards, and read each one with children.

- Create categories with the Word Cards *tap*, *up*, and *hop*. Model how to sort the Word Cards into groups that rhyme. Suggested language: **Listen: *Top. Top, tap. Top, up. Top, hop.* I will put the Word Card *top* under *hop*. *Top* and *hop* have the same ending sounds. These words rhyme.** Then point out that the words *top* and *hop* both end with the letters *-op*.

- Give partners a set of Lesson 29 Word Cards. Have them sort the words into groups of words that rhyme.

- After children have sorted the words, have them read aloud the words in each column. Ask: **What is the same about the words in each group?** *(They rhyme; they have the same letters and sounds at the end.)*

- Have children write three pairs of rhyming words in their Word Study Notebooks.

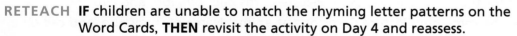

DAY 5 Assess

Tell children that you will be showing them Word Cards. They should look at their Word Cards, find a word that rhymes, and hold it up. Display the Word Card *nap*, and have children hold up a Word Card with a rhyming word. *(lap, map, cap, tap)* Repeat this procedure for the Word Cards *cup* and *top*.

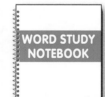

RETEACH **IF** children are unable to match the rhyming letter patterns on the Word Cards, **THEN** revisit the activity on Day 4 and reassess.

Have children sort the Word Cards into groups of words that rhyme. Then have them glue the sets of rhyming Word Cards into their Word Study Notebooks.

Words with Short Vowels

DAY 1 PHONICS

Model the Sort

MATERIALS

Picture Cards: hat, bag, pan, six, pin, lid, net, bed, mop, log, sun, cup

Word Cards: hat, bag, pan, six, pin, lid, net, bed, mop, log, sun, cup

 Reproducible Picture and Word Cards are available at **www.thinkcentral.com**.

ELL SUPPORT

Linguistic Transfer Many ELLs may have difficulty discriminating and pronouncing short vowel sounds. Provide opportunities for children to work with more-proficient English speakers when doing partner activities. The more-proficient speaker can say picture names and read words to help children complete activities.

Children will sort Picture Cards with you based on the short vowel sounds in the picture names.

- Display the Lesson 30 Picture Cards, and name them for children.
- Place Picture Card *hat* as a heading in a pocket chart. Suggested language: **Listen for the vowel sound in this word:** *Hat.* **Hat has the /ă/ sound in the middle. The letter *a* stands for the short *a* sound, /ă/, in the middle of *hat*.**
- Place Picture Card *six* as another heading. Suggested language: **Listen:** *Six. Six* **has the /ĭ/ sound in the middle. The letter *i* stands for the short *i* sound, /ĭ/, in the middle of *six*.**
- Repeat for Picture Cards *net, mop,* and *sun.* Tell children that you are going to sort the remaining Picture Cards into groups by their vowel sounds.
- Model sorting the Picture Cards according to the vowel sound in the picture names. Hold up and name Picture Card *pin.* Suggested language: *Pin.* **I'll listen to see which vowel sound I hear in the word.** *Pin.* **I hear the short *i* sound, /ĭ/, in the middle of *pin*. That's the same vowel sound I hear in *six*. I'll put Picture Card *pin* under *six*.**
- Continue with the remaining Picture Cards. When all the cards are placed, name the pictures in each column. Have children listen to make sure all the words are in the correct column.
- Give partners a set of Lesson 30 Picture Cards. Have them work together to repeat the sort.

DAY 2

Picture Sort

Children will sort Picture Cards into groups of pictures whose names have the same short vowel sound.

- Remind children they have been listening for short vowel sounds in words and learning about the letters that stand for those sounds.
- Write the letters *a, e, i, o,* and *u* as headings on chart paper or on the board. Place Picture Card *bag* below the letter *a.* Name the picture, elongating the vowel sound. Remind children that the letter *a* stands for the /ă/ sound in the middle of *bag.*
- Repeat for the other vowels, using Picture Cards *bed, pin, log,* and *cup.*
- Display the remaining Picture Cards one at a time. Name each picture, and call on a volunteer to place it in the appropriate column.
- After all the pictures have been sorted, have children name the pictures in each column. Point out that the picture names in each column have the same vowel sound.
- Give each child a set of Lesson 30 Picture Cards. Have children repeat the sort independently.

MAJOR UNDERSTANDING: Words with different vowel sounds are spelled with different vowels.

DAY 3 Picture-Word Match

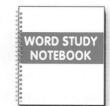

Children will match Picture Cards to the Word Cards that name each picture.

- Display the Lesson 30 Picture Cards, and remind children that they have been working with these picture names. Then display the Word Cards for the week.

- Tell children that today they will be reading the words on the cards and matching the cards to the pictures on the Picture Cards.

- Display the Word Cards, and ask a volunteer to choose one. Have children blend the letter-sounds to read the word on the card. Then ask a child to find the Picture Card whose name matches the word on the Word Card.

- Continue until all the Picture Cards are matched with Word Cards.

- After all the cards have been matched, have children write one word for each short vowel sound in their Word Study Notebooks.

DAY 4 Word Sort

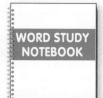

Children will sort words into groups based on short vowel sounds.

- Tell children that they will be sorting words into groups of words with the same vowel sound. Display the Lesson 30 Word Cards, and read each one with children.

- Create categories with Word Cards *pan, lid, net, mop,* and *sun.*

- Then model how to sort the Word Cards into groups according to their vowel sounds. Suggested language: **I will blend the sounds to read this word: /p/ /ĭ/ /n/,** *pin.* ***Pin, pan. Pin, lid. Pin, net. Pin, mop. Pin, sun. I will put the Word Card for*** *pin* **under** *lid.* **Both** *pin* **and** *lid* **have the short** *i* **sound, /ĭ/.**

- Give partners a set of Lesson 30 Word Cards. Have them sort the words into groups according to vowel sound.

- After children have sorted the words, have them read the words in each column aloud. Ask: **What is the same about the words in each group?** *(They have the same vowel sound. The same letter stands for the vowel sound in the words.)*

- Have children write one word for each vowel in their Word Study Notebooks.

DAY 5 Assess

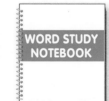

Tell children that you will be displaying Picture Cards, and they will place their own Picture Cards into groups based on vowel sounds. On a sheet of paper, have children write the letters *a, e, i, o,* and *u* as headings. Display the Picture Cards one at a time. Have children place each Picture Card under the letter that stands for the short vowel sound in the word.

RETEACH **IF** children are unable to match short vowel sounds to the vowels that stand for the sounds, **THEN** revisit the activity on Day 2 and reassess.

Have children divide two pages in their Word Study Notebooks into five columns. Have them write one vowel at the top of each column. Then have them paste each Word Card under the letter that stands for the vowel sound in the word.

Oral Vocabulary Development

ORAL VOCABULARY

1. **cranes** *Cranes* are big machines that lift and carry heavy things.

2. **crew** A *crew* is a group of people who work together to do a job.

3. **gleaming** If something is *gleaming,* it is shiny and bright.

4. **mechanic** A *mechanic* is a person who fixes machines, especially engines, in cars and other machines that move.

5. **outlining** *Outlining* something helps you show its shape, or what it looks like.

6. **solid** When something is *solid,* it is strong and well made.

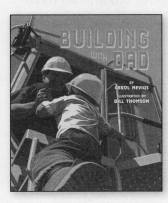

The Oral Vocabulary words appear in the Read Aloud Book "Building with Dad."

▶ Discuss Oral Vocabulary

Children will answer questions about the Oral Vocabulary words from the Read Aloud Book "Building with Dad" to deepen their understanding of the words.

- Write each Oral Vocabulary word on a strip of paper.

- Review with children the meaning of each Oral Vocabulary word, displaying each word as you share its meaning, shown to the left.

- Ask questions about the words, such as the ones below. Encourage children to use the Oral Vocabulary words in their responses.

   1. **Would you use a crane to lift a container onto a ship or to lift your pencil into its pencil case? Why?**
   2. **What kinds of jobs can a crew do? What kinds of jobs can one person do?**
   3. **Would you like your teeth to be gleaming? Why or why not?**
   4. **Who would you want to fix your car, a doctor or a mechanic? Why?**
   5. **When would you use outlining, in art class or in music class? Why?**
   6. **What do you see in this room that is solid? What do you see that is not solid?**

- As children answer the questions, encourage them to explain their responses and to share their ideas about the words.

▶ Word Sort

Children will sort the Oral Vocabulary words to learn more about how the words are used.

- Use the word strips from Discuss Oral Vocabulary, excluding the word *outlining*. On the board or on chart paper, draw a chart like the one below, and tell children they will help you sort the Oral Vocabulary words.

- Review the meanings of the Oral Vocabulary words, displaying each word as you share its meaning.

- Then explain the chart headings. Tell children they will sort the Oral Vocabulary words into three groups: words that name people; words that name things; and words that describe, or tell about things.

- Choose one of the word strips, and read the word aloud. For example, say: *Mechanic.* **Is *mechanic* a word for people, a word for things, or a word that describes? Who can tell me what a *mechanic* is? Where should I put *mechanic*?** Place the strip in the *Words for People* column of the chart.

- Continue for the other words, and encourage children to tell why they think a word belongs in the category they have named.

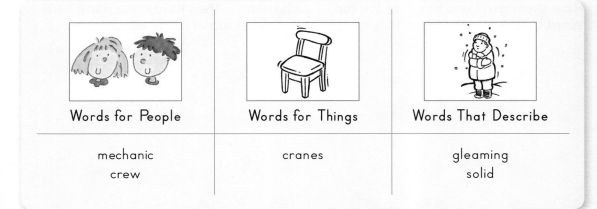

Words for People	Words for Things	Words That Describe
mechanic crew	cranes	gleaming solid

▶ Complete Sentences

Children will use Oral Vocabulary words to complete sentences.

- Review the meanings of the Oral Vocabulary words with children.

- Tell children you will be saying sentences with a word missing. Ask them to listen carefully so they can choose the Oral Vocabulary word that best completes the sentence.

- Then say each of the following sentences, indicating the missing word by saying *blank*. Repeat the sentence, and have children supply the missing Oral Vocabulary word. Model the process by completing the first sentence.

- If children have difficulty, provide two words as choices within the sentences, and ask children which one is correct.

  1. The children were _____ circles and squares on their papers. *(outlining)*

  2. I washed my bike until it was _____. *(gleaming)*

  3. The _____ lifted the building's heavy walls into place. *(cranes)*

  4. The wolf couldn't blow down the third little pig's house because its brick walls were _____. *(solid)*

  5. The _____ worked together to pack the moving van. *(crew)*

  6. We took our car to the shop so the _____ could fix it. *(mechanic)*

- Call on volunteers to say sentences using the Oral Vocabulary words.

▶ Dictate, Draw, and Write

Children will dictate sentences and draw pictures to illustrate some of this week's Oral Vocabulary words.

- Review the meanings of the Oral Vocabulary words with children. Hold up the word strip from Discuss Oral Vocabulary as you review each word. Display the word strips along the chalk ledge.

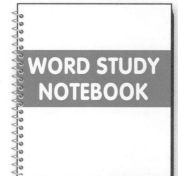

- Have children think of a sentence using one of the Oral Vocabulary words. As a child says a sentence, record it on the board or on chart paper. Call on another child to say a different sentence using the word, and record that child's sentence as well.

- Continue until there is at least one sentence for each Oral Vocabulary word.

- Then have children choose three words to draw and write about in their Word Study Notebooks to show what they have learned about the words *cranes, crew, gleaming, mechanic, outlining,* or *solid.*

ORAL VOCABULARY

1. **busy** If a place is *busy,* it is full of people and lots of things are happening there.

2. **company** You have *company* when people come to your house to visit.

3. **container** A *container* is something that holds things.

4. **job** A *job* is any work that you do.

5. **scoop** If you *scoop* something, you use a tool to dig it out of something else.

6. **tortoises** *Tortoises* are a kind of turtle.

The Oral Vocabulary words appear in the Read Aloud Book "Friends at School."

▶ Discuss Oral Vocabulary

Children will answer questions about the Oral Vocabulary words from the Read Aloud Book "Friends at School" to deepen their understanding of the words.

• Write each Oral Vocabulary word on a strip of paper.

• Review with children the meaning of each Oral Vocabulary word, displaying each word as you share its meaning, shown to the left.

• Ask questions about the words, such as the ones below. Encourage children to use the Oral Vocabulary words in their responses.

1. **Which place do you think would be busy, a football game or a quiet room? Why?**
2. **What do you like to do when you have company?**
3. **Look around the classroom. What kinds of things are kept in containers?**
4. **What are some jobs you do at home? What are some jobs you do at school?**
5. **What are some things that people can scoop?**
6. **What do tortoises look like?**

• As children answer the questions, encourage them to explain their responses and to share their ideas about the words.

▶ Paired Yes/No Questions

Children will answer paired questions about Oral Vocabulary words to show what they know about the words.

• Prepare yes/no cards for each child by drawing a smiling face on one card and a frowning face on another. You may also choose to have children make their own cards.

• Tell children that they will be answering questions about the Oral Vocabulary words with a smile card for *yes* and a frown card for *no.*

• Review the meanings of the Oral Vocabulary words, displaying each word as you share its meaning.

• Read a set of paired questions to children. Ask: **Would a crowded store be busy?** *(yes/smile)* **Would an empty store be busy?** *(no/frown)* Encourage children to explain their answers.

• Continue with the following questions, and encourage children to explain their answers.

1. **Would you have company when you brush your teeth?** *(no/frown)* **Would you have company when you have a party?** *(yes/smile)*
2. **Is a table a kind of container?** *(no/frown)* **Is a jar a kind of container?** *(yes/smile)*
3. **Are you doing a job when you swing on the swings?** *(no/frown)* **Are you doing a job when you clean your room?** *(yes/smile)*
4. **Could you scoop sand in a sandbox?** *(yes/smile)* **Could you scoop a tissue from a box?** *(no/frown)*
5. **Do tortoises have hard shells?** *(yes/smile)* **Do tortoises move fast?** *(no/frown)*

▶ Guess the Word

Children will listen to clues and identify Oral Vocabulary words.

- Review the meanings of the Oral Vocabulary words with children.

- Tell children you will be saying clues about the Oral Vocabulary words. Tell them to listen carefully so they can guess the Oral Vocabulary word for each clue.

- Then say each clue below, and have children guess the Oral Vocabulary word. Model the process with the first clue.

    1. Digging ice cream out of a tub and into a cone *(scoop)*

    2. Tells about a place that is full of people *(busy)*

    3. Kinds of turtles *(tortoises)*

    4. Cleaning out your backpack *(job)*

    5. People who come to visit *(company)*

    6. Something that holds your crayons *(container)*

- After children have guessed the correct word, ask volunteers to give other examples of when they might use the word.

. . . .

▶ Dictate, Draw, and Write

Children will dictate sentences and draw pictures to illustrate some of this week's Oral Vocabulary words.

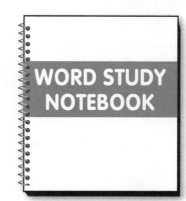

- Review the meanings of the Oral Vocabulary words with children. Hold up the word strip from Discuss Oral Vocabulary as you review each word. Display the word strips along the chalk ledge.

- Have children think of a sentence using one of the Oral Vocabulary words. As a child says a sentence, record it on the board or on chart paper. Call on another child to say a different sentence using the word, and record that child's sentence as well.

- Continue until there is at least one sentence for each Oral Vocabulary word.

- Then have children choose three words to draw and write about in their Word Study Notebooks to show what they have learned about the words *busy, company, container, job, scoop,* or *tortoises*.

ORAL VOCABULARY

1. **cooperate** You *cooperate* with others when you work together.

2. **curious** A *curious* person wants to find out about things.

3. **interesting** Something is *interesting* if it makes you want to know more about it.

4. **slimy** If something is *slimy,* it is wet and slippery.

5. **smooth** If something is *smooth,* it is even and not rough or bumpy.

6. **vet** A *vet* is an animal doctor.

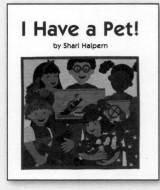

The Oral Vocabulary words appear in the Read Aloud Book "I Have a Pet!"

▶ Discuss Oral Vocabulary

Children will answer questions about the Oral Vocabulary words from the Read Aloud Book "I Have a Pet!" to deepen their understanding of the words.

- Write each Oral Vocabulary word on a strip of paper.

- Review with children the meaning of each Oral Vocabulary word, displaying each word as you share its meaning, shown to the left.

- Ask questions about the words, such as the ones below. Encourage children to use the Oral Vocabulary words in their responses.

  1. If you cooperate with others, does it make a job harder or easier to do? Why?
  2. What are some things that you are curious about?
  3. Name an interesting thing that you know about. Why is it interesting to you?
  4. Would a cotton ball feel slimy? Why or why not?
  5. If you had a smooth rock, how would it look?
  6. When would you visit a vet?

- As children answer the questions, encourage them to explain their responses and to share their ideas about the words.

▶ This or That

Children will sort the Oral Vocabulary words into groups of words that describe or don't describe something.

- Use the word strips from Discuss Oral Vocabulary. Draw a chart like the one below, and tell children they will help you sort the Oral Vocabulary words.

- Review the meanings of the Oral Vocabulary words, displaying each word as you share its meaning.

- Explain the chart headings. Tell children they will sort the Oral Vocabulary words into two groups: words that describe or tell about things and words that do not.

- Choose and read a word strip. For example, say: *Curious.* **Does** *curious* **describe something? Where should I put** *curious***?** Place the strip under *Describes Things*.

- Continue for the other words, having children tell why they think a word belongs in the category they have named.

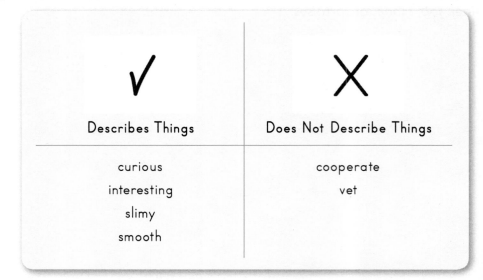

✓	✗
Describes Things	Does Not Describe Things
curious	cooperate
interesting	vet
slimy	
smooth	

▶ "Because" Sentences

Children will use the Oral Vocabulary words to complete sentences.

- Review the meanings of the Oral Vocabulary words with children.

- Tell children you will be saying part of a sentence that ends with the word *because*. Tell them they will finish the sentence by showing what they know about the meaning of the Oral Vocabulary word in the sentence.

- Then say each of the following sentences, allowing children to finish the sentences to show understanding of the Oral Vocabulary words. Model the process by completing the first sentence for them.

- Ask two or more children to complete each sentence to demonstrate a variety of possible responses.

  1. **Mom took our dog to the vet because...** *(Possible response: it was sick.)*
  2. **Ben slipped on the slimy rock because...** *(Possible response: it was slippery.)*
  3. **I am curious about whales because...** *(Possible response: I want to know more about them.)*
  4. **Maria thinks bugs are interesting because...** *(Possible response: there are many different kinds of them.)*
  5. **It is easier to ice skate on smooth ice because...** *(Possible response: it isn't bumpy.)*
  6. **We need to cooperate in class because...** *(Possible response: we can do more together.)*

▶ Dictate, Draw, and Write

Children will dictate sentences and draw pictures to illustrate some of this week's Oral Vocabulary words.

- Review the meanings of the Oral Vocabulary words with children. Hold up the word strip from Discuss Oral Vocabulary as you review each word. Display the word strips along the chalk ledge.

- Have children think of a sentence using one of the Oral Vocabulary words. As a child says a sentence, record it on the board or on chart paper. Call on another child to say a different sentence using the word, and record that child's sentence as well.

- Continue until there is at least one sentence for each Oral Vocabulary word.

- Then have children draw and write in their Word Study Notebooks to tell about something interesting that they are curious about. Have children try to use the words *cooperate, curious, interesting, slimy, smooth,* or *vet* to tell about their drawings.

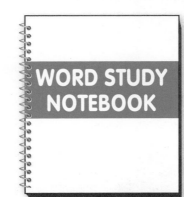

WORD STUDY NOTEBOOK

Oral Vocabulary Development

ORAL VOCABULARY

1. **customers** *Customers* are people who buy things in a store.

2. **dough** You can make *dough* by mixing together flour, yeast, and water.

3. **famous** If something is *famous,* it is well known. People, places, and things can all be *famous.*

4. **perfect** If something is *perfect,* it is just right.

5. **sprinkled** If you *sprinkled* something, you spread it around in small amounts over something else.

6. **stretchy** If something is *stretchy,* it can be pulled out like a rubber band.

The Oral Vocabulary words appear in the Read Aloud Book "Pizza at Sally's."

▶ Discuss Oral Vocabulary

Children will answer questions about the Oral Vocabulary words from the Read Aloud Book "Pizza at Sally's" to deepen their understanding of the words.

- Write each Oral Vocabulary word on a strip of paper.

- Review with children the meaning of each Oral Vocabulary word, displaying each word as you share its meaning, shown to the left.

- Ask questions about the words, such as the ones below. Encourage children to use the Oral Vocabulary words in their responses.

  1. **Do the customers in a store pay money or take money? Why?**
  2. **Would you make dough to do your homework or to bake bread? Why?**
  3. **Name some famous people. Why are they famous?**
  4. **Do you like to do things in a perfect way? Why or why not?**
  5. **If salt were sprinkled on your food, would it be put in one spot or spread around? Explain.**
  6. **Would a sock or a pencil be stretchy? Explain.**

- As children answer the questions, encourage them to explain their responses and to share their ideas about the words.

▶ Riddles

Children will listen to riddles and identify the matching Oral Vocabulary words.

- Review the meanings of the Oral Vocabulary words with children.

- Tell children that you will be telling them riddles about the Oral Vocabulary words. Tell them to listen carefully so they can guess the Oral Vocabulary word for each riddle.

- Then say each riddle, and have children guess which vocabulary word matches the clues in the riddle. Model the process by showing how to solve the first riddle.

- If children have difficulty answering the riddles, ask them yes/no questions, such as the following: *Are customers people who go to a store to buy clothes?*

  1. **I am known by many people. What can you call me?** *(famous)*
  2. **You can use me to make pizza. What am I?** *(dough)*
  3. **We go to a store to buy clothes. Who are we?** *(customers)*
  4. **I can be pulled out of my usual shape. How could you describe me?** *(stretchy)*
  5. **You did this with glitter on top of your artwork. What was it?** *(sprinkled)*
  6. **I am just right in every way. What am I?** *(perfect)*

- Encourage children to think of their own riddles for the Oral Vocabulary words and have their classmates solve them.

▶ Word Sort

Children will sort the Oral Vocabulary words to learn more about how the words are used.

- Use the word strips from Discuss Oral Vocabulary, excluding the word *customers*. On the board or on chart paper, draw a chart like the one below, and tell children that they will help you sort the Oral Vocabulary words.

- Review the meanings of the Oral Vocabulary words, displaying each word as you share its meaning.

- Then explain the chart headings. Tell children that they will sort the Oral Vocabulary words into three groups: words that name things, words that describe, and words that are verbs, or action words.

- Choose one of the word strips, and model sorting the word. For example, say: **Dough. Is *dough* a word for a thing, a describing word, or an action word? Where should I put *dough*?** Place the word strip in the column for *Words for Things*.

- Continue for the other words, and encourage children to tell why they think a word belongs in the category they have named.

Words for Things	Words That Describe	Words for Actions
dough	famous perfect stretchy	sprinkled

- -

▶ Dictate, Draw, and Write

Children will dictate sentences and draw pictures to illustrate some of this week's Oral Vocabulary words.

- Review the meanings of the Oral Vocabulary words with children. Hold up the word strip from Discuss Oral Vocabulary as you review each word. Display the word strips along the chalk ledge.

- Have children think of a sentence using one of the Oral Vocabulary words. As a child says a sentence, record it on the board or on chart paper. Call on another child to say a different sentence using the word, and record that child's sentence as well.

- Continue until there is at least one sentence for each Oral Vocabulary word.

- Then have children draw and write in their Word Study Notebooks to tell about the pizza dough from a famous pizza shop. Have children try to use the words *customers, dough, famous, perfect, stretchy,* or *sprinkled* to tell about their drawings.

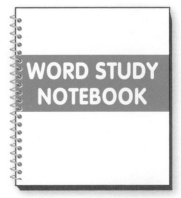

WORD STUDY
NOTEBOOK

Oral Vocabulary Development

ORAL VOCABULARY

1. admired If you *admired* something, you looked at it with pleasure.

2. delicious A *delicious* food tastes very good.

3. delight You feel *delight* when you are very happy.

4. doubt When you have *doubt* about something, you are not sure about it.

5. fable A *fable* is a story that teaches a lesson.

6. sigh When you *sigh,* you let out a long, deep breath to show that you are not happy.

The Oral Vocabulary words appear in the Read Aloud Book "The Little Red Hen."

▶ Discuss Oral Vocabulary

Children will answer questions about the Oral Vocabulary words from the Read Aloud Book "The Little Red Hen" to deepen their understanding of the words.

- Write each Oral Vocabulary word on a strip of paper.

- Review with children the meaning of each Oral Vocabulary word, displaying each word as you share its meaning, shown to the left.

- Ask questions about the words, such as the ones below. Encourage children to use the Oral Vocabulary words in their responses.

  1. If you admired a group's singing, would you like the way the group sang? Why or why not?

  2. What are some delicious foods you have eaten? Why do you think they are delicious?

  3. Would you feel delight if you got a new pet? Why or why not?

  4. Would you have doubt about doing something hard? Why or why not?

  5. If you are reading a fable, are you reading something that teaches a lesson or something that gives information?

  6. Would you sigh if you lost your favorite toy or if you found your favorite toy? Explain.

- As children answer the questions, encourage them to explain their responses and to share their ideas about the words.

▶ True or Not True

Children will listen to sentences about the Oral Vocabulary words and tell which ones are true and which ones are not true.

- Review the meanings of the Oral Vocabulary words with children.

- Tell children that you will be saying sentences about the Oral Vocabulary words. Tell them to listen carefully so they can decide if each sentence is true or not true.

- Then say each sentence, and have children decide whether it is true or not true. Model how to tell if the first sentence is true or not true.

  1. You might learn a lesson from a fable. *(true)*

  2. You are sure about something when you have doubt about it. *(not true)*

  3. You could be sad if you felt delight. *(not true)*

  4. You sigh when everything is great. *(not true)*

  5. I admired a painting that I didn't like. *(not true)*

  6. People like to eat delicious foods at parties. *(true)*

- Revisit the items that are not true. Encourage children to reword the sentences to make them true.

▶ Secret Word Game

Children will ask yes/no questions to guess a secret word.

- Review the meanings of the Oral Vocabulary words with children. Then tell them that they will play a game called the Secret Word Game.

- Explain that you will choose a secret word, which is one of the Oral Vocabulary words, and they can ask questions to guess the word. The questions must be able to be answered *yes* or *no*.

- For practice, assign an Oral Vocabulary word to children and tell them it's the secret word. Then ask yes/no questions for them to answer about the word.

- Ask questions such as these: **Does the word name an action? Does the word tell how food tastes? Does the word rhyme with** *buy*?

- Then choose your Oral Vocabulary word, and have children ask questions until they identify the secret word. Help them with clues as necessary.

▶ Dictate, Draw, and Write

Children will dictate sentences and draw pictures to illustrate some of this week's Oral Vocabulary words.

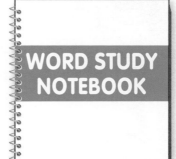

- Review the meanings of the Oral Vocabulary words with children. Hold up the word strip from Discuss Oral Vocabulary as you review each word. Display the word strips along the chalk ledge.

- Have children think of a sentence using one of the Oral Vocabulary words. As a child says a sentence, record it on the board or on chart paper. Call on another child to say a different sentence using the word, and record that child's sentence as well.

- Continue until there is at least one sentence for each Oral Vocabulary word.

- Then have children choose three words to draw and write about in their Word Study Notebooks to show what they have learned about the words *admired, delicious, delight, doubt, fable,* or *sigh*.

Oral Vocabulary Development

ORAL VOCABULARY

1. drift When you *drift,* you float along from one place to another.

2. ripen When fruits or vegetables *ripen,* they grow to their full size.

3. scurry When you *scurry,* you move quickly.

4. sizzle When things *sizzle,* they get very hot and make a hissing sound.

5. whisper You speak in a very quiet voice when you *whisper.*

6. whistle When things *whistle,* they make a very high sound.

The Oral Vocabulary words appear in the Read Aloud Book "Listen, Listen."

▶ Discuss Oral Vocabulary

Children will answer questions about the Oral Vocabulary words from the Read Aloud Book "Listen, Listen" to deepen their understanding of the words.

- Write each Oral Vocabulary word on a strip of paper.

- Review with children the meaning of each Oral Vocabulary word, displaying each word as you share its meaning, shown to the left.

- Ask questions about the words, such as the ones below. Encourage children to use the Oral Vocabulary words in their responses.

    1. If clouds drift in the sky, do they move or or stay in one place? Explain.

    2. Would you pick apples before they ripen? Why or why not?

    3. Which animal can scurry, an elephant or a mouse? Explain.

    4. Which would sizzle, meat cooking in a pan or bread toasting in a toaster?

    5. Would you whisper if you wanted one person or many people to hear you? Why?

    6. Do you know how to whistle? Show me.

- As children answer the questions, encourage them to explain their responses and to share their ideas about the words.

▶ Word Associations

Children will answer questions about the Oral Vocabulary words.

- Review the meanings of the Oral Vocabulary words with children.

- Tell children that you will be asking questions about the Oral Vocabulary words. Have them listen carefully to decide which Oral Vocabulary word answers each question.

- Read aloud the first question and model how to figure out which Oral Vocabulary word answers it.

- Then read aloud each of the remaining questions for children and have them name the Oral Vocabulary word that answers it. If they have difficulty answering, provide two answer choices for each question.

    1. Which word describes talking quietly? *(whisper)*

    2. Which word tells about something a small boat might do? *(drift)*

    3. Which word describes a bug that is moving very quickly? *(scurry)*

    4. Which word tells what the wind could do on a stormy night? *(whistle)*

    5. Which word is what you want a banana to do before you eat it? *(ripen)*

    6. Which word tells how something cooking in a hot pan might sound? *(sizzle)*

- Have children think of other ways they can use the Oral Vocabulary words in sentences.

▶ Describe It

Children will respond to prompts about Oral Vocabulary words to show understanding of the words.

- Review the meanings of the Oral Vocabulary words with children.

- Tell children you are going to ask them to say or do something to show that they understand the Oral Vocabulary words.

- Read the following prompts. Allow several children to provide descriptions for each prompt.

  1. Describe how a rabbit would scurry. *(Possible response: The rabbit would move fast.)*

  2. Tell about the sound eggs make when they sizzle in a frying pan. *(Possible response: They hiss and pop.)*

  3. Describe what apples look like when they ripen. *(Possible response: They get big and red.)*

  4. Tell or show how you would whistle. *(Possible response: I would blow air out of my mouth.)*

  5. Tell about how you would whisper to a friend. *(Possible response: I would speak softly into my friend's ear.)*

  6. Describe how a feather might drift in a pond. *(Possible response: It might float from one place to another.)*

▶ Dictate, Draw, and Write

Children will dictate sentences and draw pictures to illustrate some of this week's Oral Vocabulary words.

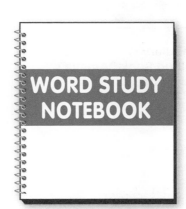

- Review the meanings of the Oral Vocabulary words with children. Hold up the word strip from Discuss Oral Vocabulary as you review each word. Display the word strips along the chalk ledge.

- Have children think of a sentence using one of the Oral Vocabulary words. As a child says a sentence, record it on the board or on chart paper. Call on another child to say a different sentence using the word, and record that child's sentence as well.

- Continue until there is at least one sentence for each Oral Vocabulary word.

- Then have children choose three words to draw and write about in their Word Study Notebooks to show what they have learned about the words *drift, ripen, scurry, sizzle, whisper,* or *whistle.*

Oral Vocabulary Development

1. **foolish** If someone is being *foolish,* the person is acting silly or not making sense.

2. **frowns** When someone *frowns,* the person makes an unhappy face.

3. **ruffled** When something is *ruffled,* it is gathered together.

4. **special** Something that is *special* is not ordinary, or not usual.

5. **treasures** If you collect *treasures,* you collect things that are valuable and important to you.

6. **tropical** Something *tropical* comes from a place where it is always warm.

The Oral Vocabulary words appear in the Read Aloud Book "Amelia's Show-and-Tell Fiesta."

▶ Discuss Oral Vocabulary

Children will answer questions about the Oral Vocabulary words from the Read Aloud Book "Amelia's Show-and-Tell Fiesta" to deepen their understanding of the words.

• Write each Oral Vocabulary word on a strip of paper.

• Review with children the meaning of each Oral Vocabulary word, displaying each word as you share its meaning, shown to the left.

• Ask questions about the words, such as the ones below. Encourage children to use the Oral Vocabulary words in their responses.

  1. **Would a clown or a police officer be more likely to be foolish? Explain.**

  2. **If someone frowns, is that person happy or unhappy? Why?**

  3. **If you had a ruffled shirt, would your shirt be fancy or plain? Tell why.**

  4. **Would you wear special clothes to a playground or to a party? Why?**

  5. **Why are some things treasures and some things not treasures? Explain.**

  6. **Could you go snow sledding in a tropical place? Why or why not?**

• As children answer the questions, encourage them to explain their responses and to share their ideas about the words.

▶ Paired Yes/No Questions

Children will answer paired questions about Oral Vocabulary words to show what they know about the words.

• Prepare yes/no cards for each child by drawing a smiling face on one card and a frowning face on another. You may also choose to have children make their own cards.

• Tell children that they will be answering questions about the Oral Vocabulary words using a smile card for *yes* and a frown card for *no.*

• Review the meanings of the Oral Vocabulary words, displaying each word as you share its meaning.

• Read a set of paired questions to children. Ask: **Would tropical food come from a place that is always warm?** *(yes/smile)* **Is a tropical breeze always cold?** *(no/frown)* Encourage children to explain their answers.

• Continue with the remaining questions, and encourage children to explain their answers.

  1. **Could you have a ruffled pen?** *(no/frown)* **Could you have a ruffled hat?** *(yes/smile)*

  2. **Would the same sandwich you eat every day be a special lunch?** *(no/frown)* **Would your birthday be a special day?** *(yes/smile)*

  3. **Would you frown if someone gave you something that you wanted?** *(no/frown)* **Would you frown if someone took away something that you wanted?** *(yes/smile)*

  4. **Would you feel foolish if you forgot to bring your lunch to the cafeteria?** *(yes/smile)* **Would you feel foolish if you made your best drawing ever?** *(no/frown)*

  5. **Would you keep your treasures in a special place?** *(yes/smile)* **Would you leave your treasures outside at night?** *(no/frown)*

▶ Complete Sentences

Children will use Oral Vocabulary words to complete sentences.

- Review with children the meanings of the Oral Vocabulary words.

- Tell children you will be saying sentences with a word missing. Ask them to listen carefully so they can choose the Oral Vocabulary word that best completes the sentence.

- Then say each of the following sentences, indicating the missing word by saying *blank*. Repeat the sentence, and have children supply the missing Oral Vocabulary word. Model the process by completing the first sentence.

- If children have difficulty, provide two words as choices within the sentences, and ask them which one is correct.

   1. **These _____ fruits can grow only where it is warm for many months in a row.** *(tropical)*
   2. **My little sister _____ when she can't play with me.** *(frowns)*
   3. **I have a _____ uniform that I only wear to soccer games.** *(special)*
   4. **The _____ dog always chases its tail.** *(foolish)*
   5. **Ana's skirt is _____ at the bottom.** *(ruffled)*
   6. **My grandmother keeps her _____ in a wooden box.** *(treasures)*

- Call on volunteers to say sentences using the Oral Vocabulary words.

▶ Dictate, Draw, and Write

Children will dictate sentences and draw pictures to illustrate some of this week's Oral Vocabulary words.

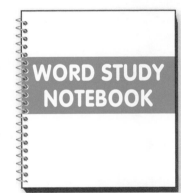

- Review the meanings of the Oral Vocabulary words with children. Hold up the word strip from Discuss Oral Vocabulary as you review each word. Display the word strips along the chalk ledge.

- Have children think of a sentence using one of the Oral Vocabulary words. As a child says a sentence, record it on the board or on chart paper. Call on another child to say a different sentence using the word, and record that child's sentence as well.

- Continue until there is at least one sentence for each Oral Vocabulary word.

- Then have children choose three words to draw and write about in their Word Study Notebooks to show what they have learned about the words *foolish, frowns, ruffled, special, treasures,* or *tropical*.

Oral Vocabulary Development

ORAL VOCABULARY

1. **backward** If you move *backward,* you move with your back first.

2. **beat** When you *beat* a drum, you pound on it.

3. **leap** When you *leap,* you jump.

4. **strange** If something is *strange,* it is odd or different.

5. **wiggle** When you *wiggle,* you move fast from side to side.

6. **zigzag** If you *zigzag,* you make quick turns one way and then another way.

The Oral Vocabulary words appear in the Read Aloud Book "Jonathan and His Mommy."

▶ Discuss Oral Vocabulary

Children will answer questions about the Oral Vocabulary words from the Read Aloud Book "Jonathan and His Mommy" to deepen their understanding of the words.

• Write each Oral Vocabulary word on a strip of paper.

• Review with children the meaning of each Oral Vocabulary word, displaying each word as you share its meaning, shown to the left.

• Ask questions about the words, such as the ones below. Encourage children to use the Oral Vocabulary words in their responses.

1. **Could you walk backward and see where you are going? Why or why not?**
2. **If you were beating a drum, would the sound be loud or quiet? Why?**
3. **Could you leap over a puddle or leap over a mountain? Why?**
4. **Would it be strange to see a zebra on your street? Why or why not?**
5. **Where would it be better to wiggle, in the lunchroom or in the gym? Explain.**
6. **Would you zigzag as you walked if you were in a hurry to go home? Explain.**

• As children answer the questions, encourage them to explain their responses and to share their ideas about the words.

▶ This or That

Children will sort the Oral Vocabulary words into groups of words that tell how things can move and words that don't tell how things can move.

• Use the word strips from Discuss Oral Vocabulary. On the board, draw a chart like the one below, and tell children they will help you sort the Oral Vocabulary words.

• Review the Oral Vocabulary words, displaying each word as you share its meaning.

• Tell children they will sort the Oral Vocabulary words into two groups: words that tell how things can move and words that don't tell how things can move.

• Choose a word strip, and model how to sort the word. For example, say: *Wiggle.* **Does *wiggle* tell how something can move? Where should I put *wiggle*?** Place the word strip in the column for *Ways Things Can Move.*

• Continue for the other words, encouraging children to tell why they think a word belongs in a category they have named.

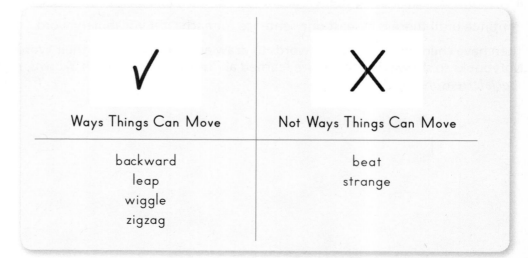

✓	✗
Ways Things Can Move	Not Ways Things Can Move
backward	beat
leap	strange
wiggle	
zigzag	

▶ Describe It or Act It Out

Children will describe or act out Oral Vocabulary words to demonstrate understanding.

- Review the meanings of the Oral Vocabulary words with children.

- Tell children that you are going to ask some questions about the Oral Vocabulary words. Explain that they will respond to the questions either by describing an Oral Vocabulary word or by acting it out.

- Ask each of the following questions. Have children respond by providing a description or by acting out the word's meaning.

  1. **How would you zigzag across the room?** *(Possible responses: I would make quick turns.* The child may also walk in a *zigzag.)*

  2. **How would you look if you saw something strange?** *(Possible responses: I might look surprised or scared.* The child may also pantomime seeing something *strange.)*

  3. **How does your heart beat?** *(Possible responses: It goes ba-bump, ba-bump.* The child may also pantomime a heart *beating.)*

  4. **How would you walk backward?** *(Possible responses: I would walk with my back first.* The child may also walk *backward.)*

  5. **How would you leap?** *(Possible responses: I would jump into the air.* The child may also demonstrate *leaping.)*

  6. **How would you wiggle?** *(Possible responses: I would move fast from side to side.* The child may also demonstrate *wiggling.)*

▶ Dictate, Draw, and Write

Children will dictate sentences and draw pictures to illustrate some of this week's Oral Vocabulary words.

- Review the meanings of the Oral Vocabulary words with children. Hold up the word strip from Discuss Oral Vocabulary as you review each word. Display the word strips along the chalk ledge.

- Have children think of a sentence using one of the Oral Vocabulary words. As a child says a sentence, record it on the board or on chart paper. Call on another child to say a different sentence using the word, and record that child's sentence as well.

- Continue until there is at least one sentence for each Oral Vocabulary word.

- Then have children draw and write in their Word Study Notebooks about different ways that they can move. Have children try to use the words *backward, beat, leap, strange, wiggle,* or *zigzag* to tell about their drawings.

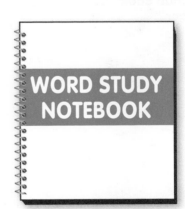

WORD STUDY NOTEBOOK

Oral Vocabulary Development

ORAL VOCABULARY

1. **cement** People use *cement* to make sidewalks and floors.

2. **community** Your *community* is the neighborhood where you live.

3. **early** If you do something *early,* you do it at the beginning of or before a period of time.

4. **vacant** A place that is *vacant* is empty.

5. **weeds** *Weeds* are wild plants that grow where you don't want them.

6. **welding** If you are *welding,* you are using heat to join pieces of metal together.

The Oral Vocabulary words appear in the Read Aloud Book "Good Morning, Digger."

▶ Discuss Oral Vocabulary

Children will answer questions about the Oral Vocabulary words from the Read Aloud Book "Good Morning, Digger" to deepen their understanding of the words.

- Write each Oral Vocabulary word on a strip of paper.

- Review with children the meaning of each Oral Vocabulary word, displaying each word as you share its meaning, shown to the left.

- Ask questions about the words, such as the ones below. Encourage children to use the Oral Vocabulary words in their responses.

   1. **Is cement hard or soft? How do you know?**
   2. **Do you have to go far to visit your community? Why or why not?**
   3. **If you finished a job early, did you finish before you thought you would finish or after you thought you would finish? Explain.**
   4. **Would you go shopping in a vacant building? Explain.**
   5. **Would you want weeds in your garden? Why or why not?**
   6. **Would you see someone welding parts of a car or parts of a book? Explain.**

- As children answer the questions, encourage them to explain their responses and to share their ideas about the words.

▶ Guess the Word

Children will listen to clues and identify Oral Vocabulary words.

- Review the meanings of the Oral Vocabulary words with children.

- Tell children you will be saying some clues about the Oral Vocabulary words. Tell them to listen carefully so they can guess the Oral Vocabulary word for each clue.

- Then say each clue below, and have children guess the Oral Vocabulary word. Model the process with the first clue.

   1. **An empty lot** *(vacant)*
   2. **People and places that are near your house** *(community)*
   3. **Joining together pieces of a metal door** *(welding)*
   4. **Finishing your work before it's time to stop** *(early)*
   5. **Wild plants that grow along the side of a road** *(weeds)*
   6. **Something used to make sidewalks** *(cement)*

- After children have guessed the correct word, ask volunteers to give other examples of when they might use the word.

▶ Word Sort

Children will sort the Oral Vocabulary words to learn more about how the words are used.

- Use the word strips from Discuss Oral Vocabulary. On the board or on chart paper, draw a chart like the one below, and tell children they will help you sort the Oral Vocabulary words.

- Review the meanings of the Oral Vocabulary words, displaying each word as you share its meaning.

- Then explain the chart headings. Tell children they will sort the Oral Vocabulary words into three groups: words that name things, words that describe, and verbs, or action words.

- Choose a word strip, and model sorting the word. For example, say: **Cement. Is cement a word that names a thing, a word that describes, or an action word? Who can tell me what cement is? Where should I put cement?** Place the strip in the *Words for Things* column of the chart.

- Continue for the other words, and encourage children to tell why they think a word belongs in the category they have named.

Words for Things	Words That Describe	Words for Actions
cement weeds community	early vacant	welding

....

▶ Dictate, Draw, and Write

Children will dictate sentences and draw pictures to illustrate some of this week's Oral Vocabulary words.

- Review the meanings of the Oral Vocabulary words with children. Hold up the word strip from Discuss Oral Vocabulary as you review each word. Display the word strips along the chalk ledge.

- Have children think of a sentence using one of the Oral Vocabulary words. As a child says a sentence, record it on the board or on chart paper. Call on another child to say a different sentence using the word, and record that child's sentence as well.

- Continue until there is at least one sentence for each Oral Vocabulary word.

- Then have children draw and write in their Word Study Notebooks about a vacant field in the middle of a community. Have children try to use the words *cement, community, early, vacant, weeds,* or *welding* to tell about their drawings.

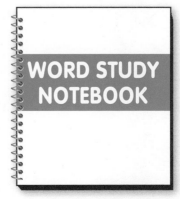

WORD STUDY NOTEBOOK

Oral Vocabulary Development

ORAL VOCABULARY

1. **add** When you *add* to something, you put in something new.

2. **fluffy** If something is *fluffy,* it is light, soft, and puffy.

3. **fresh** If something is *fresh,* it is new or hasn't been used yet.

4. **grinned** If a person *grinned,* the person smiled.

5. **moment** A *moment* is a very small amount of time.

6. **shyly** If you say something *shyly,* you say it in a bashful way.

The Oral Vocabulary words appear in the Read Aloud Book "David's Drawings."

▶ Discuss Oral Vocabulary

Children will answer questions about the Oral Vocabulary words from the Read Aloud Book "David's Drawings" to deepen their understanding of the words.

• Write each Oral Vocabulary word on a strip of paper.

• Review with children the meaning of each Oral Vocabulary word, displaying each word as you share its meaning, shown to the left.

• Ask questions about the words, such as the ones below. Encourage children to use the Oral Vocabulary words in their responses.

1. **If you add crayons to a box, do you put in crayons or take out crayons? Why?**
2. **Is an alligator fluffy? Why or why not?**
3. **If you just bought some fruit from a farmer, is it fresh or not fresh? Why?**
4. **If someone grinned at you, would you think he liked you or didn't like you? Explain.**
5. **What takes a moment, snapping your fingers or taking a bath? Why?**
6. **What would be an example of doing something shyly? Explain.**

• As children answer the questions, encourage them to explain their responses and to share their ideas about the words.

▶ True or Not True

Children will listen to sentences about the Oral Vocabulary words and tell which ones are true and which ones are not true.

• Review the meanings of the Oral Vocabulary words with children.

• Tell children that you will be saying some sentences about the Oral Vocabulary words. Tell them to listen carefully so they can decide if each sentence is true or not true.

• Then say each sentence, and have children decide whether it is true or not true. Model how to tell if the first sentence is true or not true.

1. **A rotten tomato is fresh.** *(not true)*
2. **You act shyly when you are with your best friends.** *(not true)*
3. **A moment is a long time.** *(not true)*
4. ***Grinned* and *frowned* mean the same thing.** *(not true)*
5. **A porcupine is fluffy.** *(not true)*
6. **You can add numbers together.** *(true)*

• Revisit the items that are not true. Encourage children to reword the sentences to make them true.

▶ "Because" Sentences

Children will use the Oral Vocabulary words to complete sentences.

- Review the meanings of the Oral Vocabulary words with children.

- Tell children you will be saying part of a sentence that ends with the word *because*. Tell them they will finish the sentence by showing what they know about the meaning of the Oral Vocabulary word in the sentence.

- Then say each of the following sentences, allowing children to finish the sentences to show understanding of the Oral Vocabulary words. Model the process by completing the first sentence for them.

- Allow two or more children to complete each sentence to demonstrate a variety of possible responses.
  1. **The vegetables were fresh because...** *(Possible response: they were just picked.)*
  2. **Lin grinned because...** *(Possible response: she saw her best friend.)*
  3. **I shyly asked the children if I could play because...** *(Possible response: I didn't know them.)*
  4. **Jamal will add water to the paint because...** *(Possible response: it is dried out.)*
  5. **Mom waited a moment to cross the street because...** *(Possible response: the light was red.)*
  6. **I like fluffy pillows because...** *(Possible response: they are comfortable.)*

▶ Dictate, Draw, and Write

Children will dictate sentences and draw pictures to illustrate some of this week's Oral Vocabulary words.

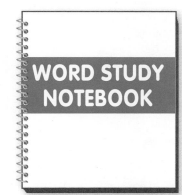

- Review the meanings of the Oral Vocabulary words with children. Hold up the word strip from Discuss Oral Vocabulary as you review each word. Display the word strips along the chalk ledge.

- Have children think of a sentence using one of the Oral Vocabulary words. As a child says a sentence, record it on the board or on chart paper. Call on another child to say a different sentence using the word, and record that child's sentence as well.

- Continue until there is at least one sentence for each Oral Vocabulary word.

- Then have children choose three words to draw and write about in their Word Study Notebooks to show what they have learned about the words *add, fluffy, fresh, grinned, moment,* or *shyly.*

ORAL VOCABULARY

1. **bloom** When they *bloom*, the buds of flowers open.

2. **peck** When birds *peck*, they hit something with their beaks.

3. **scatter** When things *scatter*, they go in many different directions.

4. **speckled** If something is *speckled*, it has spots.

5. **store** When you *store* something, you put it away to keep for later.

6. **tracks** Something that moves over the ground or snow can make *tracks*.

The Oral Vocabulary words appear in the Read Aloud Book "Every Season."

▶ Discuss Oral Vocabulary

Children will answer questions about the Oral Vocabulary words from the Read Aloud Book "Every Season" to deepen their understanding of the words.

- Write each Oral Vocabulary word on a strip of paper.

- Review with children the meaning of each Oral Vocabulary word, displaying each word as you share its meaning, shown to the left.

- Ask questions about the words, such as the ones below. Encourage children to use the Oral Vocabulary words in their responses.

  1. **Do most flowers bloom in the spring or in the winter? Why?**
  2. **Why would a bird peck the ground?**
  3. **What happens to leaves when they scatter in the wind?**
  4. **If something is speckled, is it one color or more than one color? Explain.**
  5. **What things do you store on shelves at school?**
  6. **What kinds of tracks might you be able to see in snow? Explain.**

- As children answer the questions, encourage them to explain their responses and to share their ideas about the words.

▶ Describe It

Children will respond to prompts about Oral Vocabulary words to show understanding of the words.

- Review the meanings of the Oral Vocabulary words with children.

- Tell children you are going to ask them to describe things to show that they understand the Oral Vocabulary words.

- Read the following prompts. Allow several children to provide descriptions for each prompt.

  1. **Describe what a speckled frog might look like.** *(Possible response: It has black and brown spots.)*
  2. **Tell what happens when children scatter at recess.** *(Possible response: They go in many directions.)*
  3. **Tell how chickens peck the ground.** *(Possible response: They bend so they can use their beaks to find food on the ground.)*
  4. **Tell how you could make tracks in a sandbox.** *(Possible response: I could walk through the sand or drive a toy car through it.)*
  5. **Tell where in your house you store your favorite things.** *(Possible response: I store them in a drawer in my room.)*
  6. **Describe what happens when flowers bloom.** *(Possible response: The flowers open up.)*

▶ This or That

Children will sort the Oral Vocabulary words into groups for action words and words that are not action words.

- Use the word strips from Discuss Oral Vocabulary. On the board or on chart paper, draw a chart like the one below, and tell children they will help you sort the Oral Vocabulary words.

- Review the meanings of the Oral Vocabulary words, displaying each word as you share its meaning.

- Then explain the chart headings. Tell children they will sort the Oral Vocabulary words into two groups: actions words and words that are not action words.

- Choose one of the word strips, and read the word aloud. For example, say: *Peck.* **Is** *peck* **an action word? Where should I put** *peck*? Place the word strip in the column for *Action Words*. Explain that the word *peck* tells about an action that birds can do.

- Continue with the other words, and encourage children to tell why they think a word belongs in the category they have named.

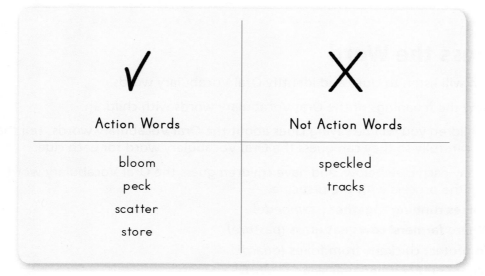

✓	✗
Action Words	Not Action Words
bloom	speckled
peck	tracks
scatter	
store	

▶ Dictate, Draw, and Write

Children will dictate sentences and draw pictures to illustrate some of this week's Oral Vocabulary words.

- Review the meanings of the Oral Vocabulary words with children. Hold up the word strip from Discuss Oral Vocabulary as you review each word. Display the word strips along the chalk ledge.

- Have children think of a sentence using one of the Oral Vocabulary words. As a child says a sentence, record it on the board or on chart paper. Call on another child to say a different sentence using the word, and record that child's sentence as well.

- Continue until there is at least one sentence for each Oral Vocabulary word.

- Then have children draw and write in their Word Study Notebooks about a speckled bird making tracks in a yard. Have children use the words *peck, speckled,* and *tracks* to tell about their drawings. Ask children to add to their drawings and use the words *bloom, scatter,* or *store* to tell about what they added.

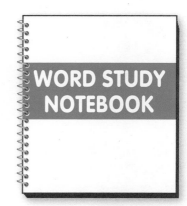

WORD STUDY NOTEBOOK

Oral Vocabulary Development

ORAL VOCABULARY

1. **guard** When you *guard* something, you protect it from danger.

2. **huddle** When you *huddle*, you gather close together with others.

3. **nodded** If you *nodded*, you moved your head up and down.

4. **pasture** A *pasture* is a field where animals eat grass.

5. **silent** When it is *silent*, there is no sound or noise.

6. **stampede** A *stampede* happens when a group of animals all run together.

The Oral Vocabulary words appear in the Read Aloud Book "Storm Is Coming!"

▶ Discuss Oral Vocabulary

Children will answer questions about the Oral Vocabulary words from the Read Aloud Book "Storm Is Coming!" to deepen their understanding of the words.

- Write each Oral Vocabulary word on a strip of paper.

- Review with children the meaning of each Oral Vocabulary word, displaying each word as you share its meaning, shown to the left.

- Ask questions about the words, such as the ones below. Encourage children to use the Oral Vocabulary words in their responses.

  1. **Would your dad guard your dog from a snake or from a kitten? Explain.**
  2. **When would you huddle with your friends—when you are talking with them or when you are in line to go to lunch? Why?**
  3. **If your friend nodded, did your friend agree or not agree with you? Explain.**
  4. **Would you see sheep or fish eating in a pasture? Why?**
  5. **Where would you be silent, at a ball game or in the library? Why?**
  6. **Do you think you could see a stampede in our cafeteria? Why or why not?**

- As children answer the questions, encourage them to explain their responses and to share their ideas about the words.

▶ Guess the Word

Children will listen to clues and identify Oral Vocabulary words.

- Review the meanings of the Oral Vocabulary words with children.

- Tell children you will be saying clues about the Oral Vocabulary words. Tell them to listen carefully so they can guess the Oral Vocabulary word for each clue.

- Then say each clue below, and have children guess the Oral Vocabulary word. Model the process with the first clue.

  1. **Horses running together** (*stampede*)
  2. **Where farmers' cows eat grass** (*pasture*)
  3. **To protect chickens from foxes** (*guard*)
  4. **What you are when you sleep** (*silent*)
  5. **What your mom did when she agreed with you** (*nodded*)
  6. **Football players on the same team do this** (*huddle*)

- After children have guessed the correct word, ask volunteers to give other examples of when they might use the word.

▶ Describe It or Act It Out

Children will describe or act out Oral Vocabulary words to demonstrate understanding.

- Review the meanings of the Oral Vocabulary words with children.

- Tell children that you are going to ask some questions about the Oral Vocabulary words. Explain that they will respond to the questions either by describing an Oral Vocabulary word or by acting it out.

- Ask each of the following questions. Have children respond by providing a description or by acting out the word's meaning.

  1. **How do you nod?** (*Possible responses: I move my head up and down.* The child might also *nod* his or her head.)

  2. **How would you describe a pasture?** (*Possible response: It is a grassy field where sheep or cows eat grass.*)

  3. **How would you be silent?** (*Possible responses: I would not say a word.* The child might also be *silent.*)

  4. **How would you guard a bird from a cat?** (*Possible responses: I would put it into a cage.* The child might also pantomime *guard* by pretending to put a bird into a cage.)

  5. **How do animals act in a stampede?** (*Possible responses: They run fast.* The child might also run in place.)

  6. **How would you huddle with some classmates?** (*Possible responses: I would get close to them.* The child might also *huddle* with some classmates.)

▶ Dictate, Draw, and Write

Children will dictate sentences and draw pictures to illustrate some of this week's Oral Vocabulary words.

- Review the meanings of the Oral Vocabulary words with children. Hold up the word strip from Discuss Oral Vocabulary as you review each word. Display the word strips along the chalk ledge.

- Have children think of a sentence using one of the Oral Vocabulary words. As a child says a sentence, record it on the board or on chart paper. Call on another child to say a different sentence using the word, and record that child's sentence as well.

- Continue until there is at least one sentence for each Oral Vocabulary word.

- Then have children choose three words to draw and write about in their Word Study Notebooks to show what they have learned about the words *guard, huddle, nodded, pasture, silent,* or *stampede.*

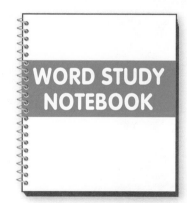

WORD STUDY NOTEBOOK

Oral Vocabulary Development

1. **daily** Something that happens *daily* happens every day.

2. **herd** A *herd* is a group of animals that live together.

3. **muscles** Your *muscles* are the parts of your body that make you move.

4. **pattern** A *pattern* is a design with parts that repeat.

5. **several** *Several* means more than two.

6. **usually** If something *usually* happens, it is what normally happens.

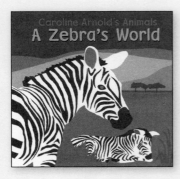

The Oral Vocabulary words appear in the Read Aloud Book "A Zebra's World."

▶ Discuss Oral Vocabulary

Children will answer questions about the Oral Vocabulary words from the Read Aloud Book "A Zebra's World" to deepen their understanding of the words.

- Write each Oral Vocabulary word on a strip of paper.

- Review with children the meaning of each Oral Vocabulary word, displaying each word as you share its meaning, shown to the left.

- Ask questions about the words, such as the ones below. Encourage children to use the Oral Vocabulary words in their responses.

   1. **What is something you do daily, eat breakfast or go on vacation? Explain.**
   2. **If you saw a cow in a barn, did you see a herd? Why or why not?**
   3. **What muscles do you use to run? What muscles do you use to write?**
   4. **Look around the classroom. Where do you see a pattern? Tell about it.**
   5. **If you had several pencils, could you share pencils with more than one friend? Explain.**
   6. **What are some things you usually do at school?**

- As children answer the questions, encourage them to explain their responses and to share their ideas about the words.

▶ Secret Word Game

Children will ask yes/no questions to guess a secret word.

- Review the meanings of the Oral Vocabulary words with children. Then tell them that they will play the Secret Word Game.

- Remind children how to play the game. Explain that you will choose a secret word that is one of the Oral Vocabulary Words, and children will ask questions to guess the word. The questions must be able to be answered *yes* or *no*.

- Model how to ask yes/no questions by assigning an Oral Vocabulary word to children. Tell them it is the secret word.

- Then ask questions such as these: **Does the word name something? Does the word tell about parts of your body? Does the word start with the letter *m*?**

- Then choose your Oral Vocabulary word, and have children ask yes/no questions to identify the secret word. Help them with additional clues as necessary.

▶ Complete Sentences

Children will use Oral Vocabulary words to complete sentences.

- Review the meanings of the Oral Vocabulary words with children.

- Tell children you will be saying sentences with a word missing. Ask them to listen carefully so they can choose the Oral Vocabulary word that best completes the sentence.

- Then say each of the following sentences, indicating the missing word by saying *blank*. Repeat the sentence, and have children supply the missing Oral Vocabulary word. Model the process by completing the first sentence.

- If children have difficulty, provide two words as choices within the sentences, and ask which one is correct.

  1. Dan saw a _____ of goats in a field. *(herd)*

  2. I _____ go to the park over the weekend. *(usually)*

  3. The teacher gave us _____ pieces of paper for an art project. *(several)*

  4. The soccer player worked hard to make his _____ strong. *(muscles)*

  5. I like the _____ of stripes on my shirt. *(pattern)*

  6. The dentist told me to brush my teeth twice _____. *(daily)*

- Call on volunteers to say sentences using the Oral Vocabulary words.

▶ Dictate, Draw, and Write

Children will dictate sentences and draw pictures to illustrate some of this week's Oral Vocabulary words.

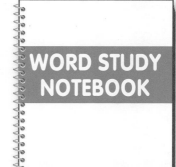

- Review the meanings of the Oral Vocabulary words with children. Hold up the word strip from Discuss Oral Vocabulary as you review each word. Display the word strips along the chalk ledge.

- Have children think of a sentence using one of the Oral Vocabulary words. As a child says a sentence, record it on the board or on chart paper. Call on another child to say a different sentence using the word, and record that child's sentence as well.

- Continue until there is at least one sentence for each Oral Vocabulary word.

- Then have children choose three words to draw and write about in their Word Study Notebooks to show what they have learned about the words *daily, herd, muscles, pattern, several,* or *usually.*

Oral Vocabulary Development

ORAL VOCABULARY

1. **burrow** A *burrow* is a hole an animal digs under the ground.

2. **desert** A *desert* is a very dry place.

3. **lodge** A *lodge* is a place where a group of animals lives.

4. **patient** If you are *patient,* you do not complain while you wait.

5. **shade** *Shade* is a dark spot made when light is blocked.

6. **soaring** If something is *soaring,* it is rising up in the air.

The Oral Vocabulary words appear in the Read Aloud Book "Home for a Tiger, Home for a Bear."

▶ Discuss Oral Vocabulary

Children will answer questions about the Oral Vocabulary words from the Read Aloud Book "Home for a Tiger, Home for a Bear" to deepen their understanding of the words.

- Write each Oral Vocabulary word on a strip of paper.

- Review with children the meaning of each Oral Vocabulary word, displaying each word as you share its meaning, shown to the left.

- Ask questions about the words, such as the ones below. Encourage children to use the Oral Vocabulary words in their responses.

  1. **Where would a rabbit make a burrow, in the ground or in a tree? Explain.**
  2. **Does it rain a lot in the desert? Why or why not?**
  3. **Why do beavers build a lodge? Explain.**
  4. **Is it easy to be patient while waiting for your birthday? Why or why not?**
  5. **Would you find shade under a tree or in the middle of a field? Explain.**
  6. **Would you be more likely to see a bird soaring or a bear soaring? Why?**

- As children answer the questions, encourage them to explain their responses and to share their ideas about the words.

▶ This or That

Children will sort the Oral Vocabulary words into groups for words that name places and words that don't name places.

- Use the word strips from Discuss Oral Vocabulary. On the board or on chart paper, draw a chart like the one below, and tell children they will help you sort the words.

- Review the meanings of the Oral Vocabulary words, displaying each word as you share its meaning.

- Then explain the chart headings. Tell children they will sort the words into two groups: words that name places and words that don't name places. Choose one of the word strips, and read the word aloud. For example, say: *Desert.* **Is** *desert* **a word for a place or not a word for a place? Where should I put** *desert*? Place the word strip in the column *Words for Places*.

- Continue with the other words, and encourage children to tell why they think a word belongs in the category they have named.

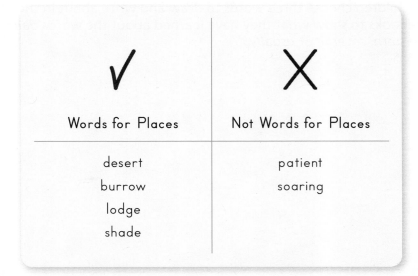

✓	✗
Words for Places	Not Words for Places
desert	patient
burrow	soaring
lodge	
shade	

▶ "Because" Sentences

Children will use the Oral Vocabulary words to complete sentences.

- Review the meanings of the Oral Vocabulary words with children.

- Tell children you will be saying part of a sentence that ends with the word *because*. Tell them they will finish the sentence by showing what they know about the meaning of the Oral Vocabulary word in the sentence.

- Then say each of the following sentences, allowing children to finish the sentences to show understanding of the Oral Vocabulary words. Model the process by completing the first sentence for them.

- Allow two or more children to complete each sentence to demonstrate a variety of possible responses.

   1. **We were thirsty when we hiked in the desert because...** *(Possible response: it was very dry.)*

   2. **I was patient while I waited in the lunch line because...** *(Possible response: it wasn't taking too long.)*

   3. **The soaring seagull looked very small because...** *(Possible response: it was so high in the sky.)*

   4. **Ann rested in the shade because...** *(Possible response: she wanted to get out of the sun.)*

   5. **At night the beavers go back to their lodge because...** *(Possible response: they live inside it.)*

   6. **The rabbit was safe in the burrow because...** *(Possible response: the fox could not get it there.)*

▶ Dictate, Draw, and Write

Children will dictate sentences and draw pictures to illustrate some of this week's Oral Vocabulary words.

- Review the meanings of the Oral Vocabulary words with children. Hold up the word strip from Discuss Oral Vocabulary as you review each word. Display the word strips along the chalk ledge.

- Have children think of a sentence using one of the Oral Vocabulary words. As a child says a sentence, record it on the board or on chart paper. Call on another child to say a different sentence using the word, and record that child's sentence as well.

- Continue until there is at least one sentence for each Oral Vocabulary word.

- Then have children draw and write in their Word Study Notebooks about different animal homes. Have children try to use the words *burrow, desert, lodge, patient, shade,* or *soaring* to tell about their drawings.

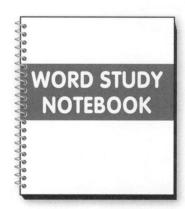

WORD STUDY NOTEBOOK

Oral Vocabulary Development

1. **dazzling** If something is *dazzling,* it is very bright.

2. **distance** *Distance* is the space that is very far away from you.

3. **gazing** If you are *gazing,* you are looking out at something.

4. **leaned** If something *leaned,* it bent out or away in a different direction.

5. **planet** A *planet* is a huge object out in space.

6. **tunnel** A *tunnel* is a long path for cars or trains that goes under the ground or under water.

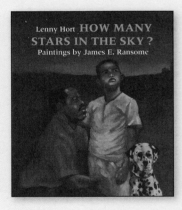

The Oral Vocabulary words appear in the Read Aloud Book "How Many Stars in the Sky?"

▶ Discuss Oral Vocabulary

Children will answer questions about the Oral Vocabulary words from the Read Aloud Book "How Many Stars in the Sky?" to deepen their understanding of the words.

- Write each Oral Vocabulary word on a strip of paper.

- Review with children the meaning of each Oral Vocabulary word, displaying each word as you share its meaning, shown to the left.

- Ask questions about the words, such as the ones below. Encourage children to use the Oral Vocabulary words in their responses.

  1. **If you saw a dazzling light, do you think it would hurt your eyes? Why or why not?**

  2. **If you see someone in the distance, would you be able to tell who it is? Explain.**

  3. **Are you gazing at something if your eyes are closed? Why or why not?**

  4. **If you leaned over the water fountain, would you be standing straight or bent over to get a drink? Why?**

  5. **Would you need a boat or a rocket to visit a planet? Explain.**

  6. **Would you drive through a tunnel to go under a mountain or to go over a river? Why?**

- As children answer the questions, encourage them to explain their responses and to share their ideas about the words.

▶ Riddles

Children will listen to riddles and identify the matching Oral Vocabulary words.

- Review the meanings of the Oral Vocabulary words with children.

- Tell children that you will be telling them riddles about the Oral Vocabulary words. Tell them to listen carefully so they can guess the Oral Vocabulary word that answers each riddle.

- Then say each riddle, and have children guess which Oral Vocabulary word answers the riddle. Model the process by showing how to solve the first riddle.

- If children have difficulty answering the riddles, ask them yes/no questions, such as the following: *Does a tunnel go under the ground?*

  1. **I am a long path under the ground. What am I?** *(tunnel)*

  2. **I am a big object in space that you can read about in a science book. What am I?** *(planet)*

  3. **I am a bright, sparkling light. What could you call me?** *(dazzling)*

  4. **You did this when you reached out to pick some flowers. What was it?** *(leaned)*

  5. **You see me when you look far away. What am I?** *(distance)*

  6. **You do this when you are looking at the moon. What is it?** *(gazing)*

▶ True or Not True

Children will listen to sentences about the Oral Vocabulary words and tell which ones are true and which ones are not true.

- Review the meanings of the Oral Vocabulary words with children.

- Tell children that you will be saying some sentences about the Oral Vocabulary words. Tell them to listen carefully so they can decide whether each sentence is true or not true.

- Then say each sentence, and have children decide whether it is true or not true. Model how to tell if the first sentence is true or not true.

  1. A planet is a huge object out in space. *(true)*

  2. A tree in the distance is very close to you. *(not true)*

  3. A dark room is dazzling. *(not true)*

  4. A tunnel goes up into the sky. *(not true)*

  5. You would have leaned over to reach a high shelf. *(not true)*

  6. You use your eyes when you are gazing. *(true)*

- Revisit the items that are not true. Encourage children to reword the sentences to make them true.

▶ Dictate, Draw, and Write

Children will dictate sentences and draw pictures to illustrate some of this week's Oral Vocabulary words.

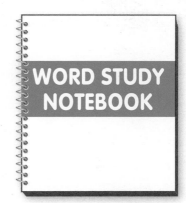

- Review the meanings of the Oral Vocabulary words with children. Hold up the word strip from Discuss Oral Vocabulary as you review each word. Display the word strips along the chalk ledge.

- Have children think of a sentence using one of the Oral Vocabulary words. As a child says a sentence, record it on the board or on chart paper. Call on another child to say a different sentence using the word, and record that child's sentence as well.

- Continue until there is at least one sentence for each Oral Vocabulary word.

- Then have children choose three words to draw and write about in their Word Study Notebooks to show what they have learned about the words *dazzling, distance, gazing, leaned, planet,* or *tunnel*. Encourage children to use the words to tell about their drawings.

ORAL VOCABULARY

1. **information** When you learn facts about something, you have *information* about it.

2. **perhaps** *Perhaps* is another way of saying "maybe."

3. **pleased** If something *pleased* you, it made you happy.

4. **pond** A *pond* is a small body of water.

5. **spurt** When things *spurt*, they pour out quickly.

6. **travel** When you *travel*, you go from one place to another.

The Oral Vocabulary words appear in the Read Aloud Book "Dear Mr. Blueberry."

▶ Discuss Oral Vocabulary

Children will answer questions about the Oral Vocabulary words from the Read Aloud Book "Dear Mr. Blueberry" to deepen their understanding of the words.

- Review with children the meaning of each Oral Vocabulary word, displaying each word as you share its meaning, shown to the left.

- Ask questions about the words, such as the ones below. Encourage children to use the Oral Vocabulary words in their responses.

   1. **What information would you like to have about dinosaurs?**
   2. **If you say that perhaps you will read a book, will you read it? Explain.**
   3. **If you are pleased by a birthday gift, do you like it? Why or why not?**
   4. **Which animal lives in a pond, a fish or a horse? Explain.**
   5. **Which of these things would be likely to spurt, a water hose or a jump rope? Why?**
   6. **Name some different ways that you can travel.**

- As children answer the questions, encourage them to explain their responses and to share their ideas about the words.

▶ Guess the Word

Children will listen to clues and identify Oral Vocabulary words.

- Review the meanings of the Oral Vocabulary words with children.

- Tell children you will be saying clues about the Oral Vocabulary words. Tell them to listen carefully so they can guess the Oral Vocabulary word for each clue.

- Then say each clue below, and have children guess the Oral Vocabulary word. Model the process with the first clue.

   1. **Water pouring out of an elephant's trunk** *(spurt)*
   2. **If you might go to the park, but might not go** *(perhaps)*
   3. **A place where fish and ducks live** *(pond)*
   4. **Facts about pets** *(information)*
   5. **Visiting another country** *(travel)*
   6. **To be happy about a painting you made** *(pleased)*

- After children have guessed the correct word, ask volunteers to give other examples of when they might use the word.

▶ Complete Sentences

Children will use Oral Vocabulary words to complete sentences.

- Review the meanings of the Oral Vocabulary words with children.

- Tell children you will be saying sentences with a word missing. Ask them to listen carefully so they can choose the Oral Vocabulary word that best completes the sentence.

- Then say each of the following sentences, indicating the missing word by saying *blank*. Repeat the sentence, and have children supply the missing Oral Vocabulary word. Model the process by completing the first sentence.

- If children have difficulty, provide two words as choices within the sentences, and ask them which one is correct.

    1. In the summer, my family will _____ to Canada. *(travel)*

    2. The librarian gave me a book full of _____ about bears. *(information)*

    3. Eduardo was _____ about the cap he chose to buy. *(pleased)*

    4. The juice started to _____ out of the bottle when I opened it. *(spurt)*

    5. Sarah tried to catch a frog, but it jumped into the _____. *(pond)*

    6. If the weather is hot, _____ we will go to the beach. *(perhaps)*

- Call on volunteers to say sentences using the Oral Vocabulary words.

▶ Dictate, Draw, and Write

Children will dictate sentences and draw pictures to illustrate some of this week's Oral Vocabulary words.

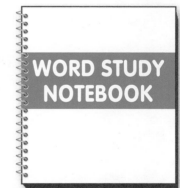

- Review the meanings of the Oral Vocabulary words with children. Hold up the word strip from Discuss Oral Vocabulary as you review each word. Display the word strips along the chalk ledge.

- Have children think of a sentence using one of the Oral Vocabulary words. As a child says a sentence, record it on the board or on chart paper. Call on another child to say a different sentence using the word, and record that child's sentence as well.

- Continue until there is at least one sentence for each Oral Vocabulary word.

- Then have children choose three words to draw and write about in their Word Study Notebooks to show what they have learned about the words *information*, *perhaps*, *pleased*, *pond*, *spurt*, or *travel*. Encourage children to use the words to tell about their drawings.

Oral Vocabulary Development

ORAL VOCABULARY

1. **creaks** When something *creaks*, it makes a squeaky sound.

2. **hare** A *hare* is a kind of rabbit.

3. **hinge** A *hinge* is a part of a door or gate that allows it to swing open and closed.

4. **howling** When something is *howling*, it is making a long crying or wailing sound.

5. **path** A *path* is a road or trail.

6. **sways** When something *sways*, it swings back and forth.

The Oral Vocabulary words appear in the Read Aloud Book "It Is the Wind."

▶ Discuss Oral Vocabulary

Children will answer questions about the Oral Vocabulary words from the Read Aloud Book "It Is the Wind" to deepen their understanding of the words.

• Write each Oral Vocabulary word on a strip of paper.

• Review with children the meaning of each Oral Vocabulary word, displaying each word as you share its meaning, shown to the left.

• Ask questions about the words, such as the ones below. Encourage children to use the Oral Vocabulary words in their responses.

  1. **Have you ever heard something that creaks? What was it? Why did it creak?**
  2. **What does a hare look like? Describe it.**
  3. **Where would you probably find a hinge, on a gate or on a floor? Explain.**
  4. **Would a dog more likely be howling if it was happy or if it was sad? Why?**
  5. **Which would you do on a path, swim or walk? Why?**
  6. **If a tree branch sways, is it moving or is it still? Explain.**

• As children answer the questions, encourage them to explain their responses and to share their ideas about the words.

▶ Sentence Clue Game

Children will use sentence clues to explain the meanings of Oral Vocabulary words.

• Review the meanings of the Oral Vocabulary words with children. Then tell them they will play a game called the Sentence Clue Game.

• Tell children that you will first ask what a word means. Then you will say sentences that give clues about the word's meaning. Children will explain the word's meaning, trying to explain the word after as few sentence clues as possible.

• In the first sentence clue, provide general information. Add details in subsequent sentences until children can explain the word.

• Begin with the word *hinge*. Ask: **What is a *hinge*?** Pause after each sentence clue to allow children to identify the word: **A *hinge* is part of a door. A *hinge* helps you open or close a door.** (Possible response: A hinge *is the part of a door or gate that allows it to swing open and closed.*)

• Continue with *creaks*. Ask: **What does the word *creaks* mean? If something *creaks*, it makes a sound. An old chair *creaks* when someone sits in it. If a gate *creaks*, it sounds squeaky.** (Possible response: Creaks *means to make a squeaky sound.*)

• Repeat the steps with the other Oral Vocabulary words as time allows.

▶ Synonyms

Children will name synonyms for Oral Vocabulary words.

- Tell children that synonyms are words that mean the same or almost the same thing. Provide a few examples of synonym pairs, such as *small* and *little*, *big* and *large*, and *leap* and *jump*.

- On the board or on chart paper, draw a chart like the one below. Tell children they will help you name synonyms for the Oral Vocabulary words.

- Review the meanings of the Oral Vocabulary words, displaying each word as you share its meaning.

- Write the word *hare* in the first column. Guide children to describe or name words that mean almost the same thing. List their ideas in the second column. If children need help with word meanings, help them use a picture dictionary.

- Continue for the remaining Oral Vocabulary words. Then read the words and synonyms with children.

Word	Synonyms
hare	rabbit, bunny
howling	wailing, crying, screaming, groaning
path	trail, road, track
creaks	squeaks, screeches
sways	swings, moves, wobbles

▶ Dictate, Draw, and Write

Children will dictate sentences and draw pictures to illustrate some of this week's Oral Vocabulary words.

- Review the meanings of the Oral Vocabulary words with children. Hold up the word strip from Discuss Oral Vocabulary as you review each word. Display the word strips along the chalk ledge.

- Have children think of a sentence using one of the Oral Vocabulary words. As a child says a sentence, record it on the board or on chart paper. Call on another child to say a different sentence using the word, and record that child's sentence as well.

- Continue until there is at least one sentence for each Oral Vocabulary word.

- Then have children draw and write in their Word Study Notebooks to show what they have learned about the words *creaks*, *hare*, *hinge*, *howling*, *path*, or *sways*. Encourage children to use the words to tell about their drawings.

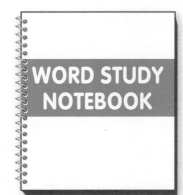

WORD STUDY NOTEBOOK

Oral Vocabulary Development

1. **canoe** A *canoe* is a kind of small boat.

2. **dew** *Dew* is drops of water that form outside at night on grass, trees, and other things.

3. **glided** If something *glided*, it moved very smoothly.

4. **paddle** A *paddle* is a tool that is used to row a boat.

5. **peered** If you *peered* at something, you looked at it closely.

6. **crew** A *crew* is a group of people who work together to do a job, such as handling a boat.

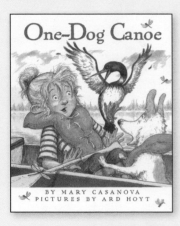

The Oral Vocabulary words appear in the Read Aloud Book "One-Dog Canoe."

▶ Discuss Oral Vocabulary

Children will answer questions about the Oral Vocabulary words from the Read Aloud Book "One-Dog Canoe" to deepen their understanding of the words.

• Write each Oral Vocabulary word on a strip of paper.

• Review with children the meaning of each Oral Vocabulary word, displaying each word as you share its meaning, shown to the left.

• Ask questions about the words, such as the ones below. Encourage children to use the Oral Vocabulary words in their responses.

1. **Would you use a canoe to travel on a lake or on a road? Why?**
2. **Where would you likely find dew, outside on the grass or inside on your floor? Explain.**
3. **If you were riding on something that glided, would the ride be bumpy or smooth? Why?**
4. **How would you use a paddle? Explain.**
5. **If you peered at something, what did you do?**
6. **What kinds of things might a crew do? Explain.**

• As children answer the questions, encourage them to explain their responses and to share their ideas about the words.

▶ Paired Yes/No Questions

Children will answer paired questions about Oral Vocabulary words to show what they know about the words.

• Prepare yes/no cards for each child by drawing a smiling face on one card and a frowning face on another. You may also choose to have children make their own cards.

• Tell children that they will be answering questions about the Oral Vocabulary words with a smile card for *yes* and a frown card for *no*.

• Review the meanings of the Oral Vocabulary words, displaying each word as you share its meaning.

• Read a set of paired questions to children. Ask: **Would you use a paddle to make a boat move?** (yes/smile) **Would you use a paddle to make a car move?** (no/frown) Encourage children to explain their answers.

• Continue with the other questions, and encourage children to explain their answers.

1. **If you peered out a window, would you be smelling something?** (no/frown) **If you peered out a window, would you be seeing something?** (yes/smile)
2. **Does a canoe travel in the air?** (no/frown) **Does a canoe travel in the water?** (yes/smile)
3. **Would a crew fix a boat?** (yes/smile) **Would a crew play on a boat?** (no/frown)
4. **If you glided on skates, would you fall a lot?** (no/frown) **If you glided on skates, would you skate well?** (yes/smile)
5. **Could you find dew on the ground when you wake up?** (yes/smile) **Could you find dew on the ground when you come home from school?** (no/frown)

▶ Word Sort

Children will sort the Oral Vocabulary words to learn more about how the words are used.

- Use the word strips from Discuss Oral Vocabulary, excluding the word *crew*. On the board or on chart paper, draw a chart like the one below, and tell children they will help you sort the Oral Vocabulary words.

- Review the meanings of the Oral Vocabulary words, displaying each word as you share its meaning.

- Then explain the chart headings. Tell children they will sort the Oral Vocabulary words into two groups: words that name things and words that are action words.

- Choose one of the word strips, and read the word aloud. For example, say: **Glided. Is *glided* a word that names a thing or is it an action word? Who can tell me what *glided* is? Where should I put *glided*?** Place the word strip in the *Words for Actions* column of the chart.

- Continue with the other words, and encourage children to tell why they think a word belongs in the category they have named.

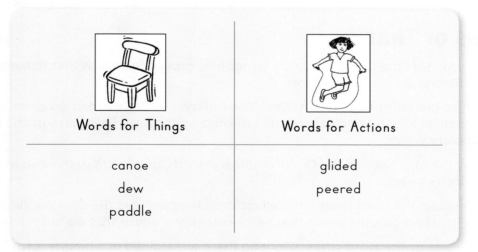

Words for Things	Words for Actions
canoe	glided
dew	peered
paddle	

▶ Dictate, Draw, and Write

Children will dictate sentences and draw pictures to illustrate some of this week's Oral Vocabulary words.

- Review the meanings of the Oral Vocabulary words with children. Hold up the word strip from Discuss Oral Vocabulary as you review each word. Display the word strips along the chalk ledge.

- Have children think of a sentence using one of the Oral Vocabulary words. As a child says a sentence, record it on the board or on chart paper. Call on another child to say a different sentence using the word, and record that child's sentence as well.

- Continue until there is at least one sentence for each Oral Vocabulary word.

- Then have children draw and write in their Word Study Notebooks about a canoe ride early in the morning. Have children try to use the words *canoe, dew, glided, paddle, peered,* or *crew* to tell about their drawings.

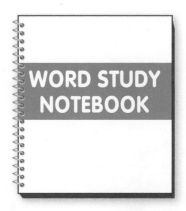

WORD STUDY NOTEBOOK

ORAL VOCABULARY

1. **blizzards** *Blizzards* are big snowstorms with a lot of wind.

2. **boring** If something is *boring*, it is not interesting.

3. **cliffs** *Cliffs* are high, steep walls of rock.

4. **impossible** If something is *impossible*, it cannot happen.

5. **jungle** A *jungle* is a hot place with many trees and plants.

6. **meadow** A *meadow* is flat land that is covered with tall grass.

The Oral Vocabulary words appear in the Read Aloud Book "Nicky and the Rainy Day."

▶ Discuss Oral Vocabulary

Children will answer questions about the Oral Vocabulary words from the Read Aloud Book "Nicky and the Rainy Day" to deepen their understanding of the words.

- Write each Oral Vocabulary word on a strip of paper.

- Review with children the meaning of each Oral Vocabulary word, displaying each word as you share its meaning, shown to the left.

- Ask questions about the words, such as the ones below. Encourage children to use the Oral Vocabulary words in their responses.

  1. **If you were visiting a place where there might be blizzards, would you bring a bathing suit or a warm coat? Why?**
  2. **If you like jumping rope, would you think it was boring? Why or why not?**
  3. **Do you think it would be easy to climb cliffs? Explain.**
  4. **Which is impossible to do, jump over a log or jump over a building? Why?**
  5. **What might you find in a jungle? Explain.**
  6. **Which animals might you see in a meadow, cows or whales? Why?**

- As children answer the questions, encourage them to explain their responses and to share their ideas about the words.

▶ This or That

Children will sort the Oral Vocabulary words into groups for words that name places and words that do not name places.

- Use the word strips from Discuss Oral Vocabulary. On the board or on chart paper, draw a chart like the one below, and tell children they will help you sort the Oral Vocabulary words.

- Review the meanings of the Oral Vocabulary words, displaying each word as you share its meaning.

- Then explain the chart headings. Tell children they will sort the Oral Vocabulary words into two groups: words that name places and words that do not name places.

- Choose one of the word strips, and read the word aloud. For example, say: *Meadow.* **Does** *meadow* **name a place? Could you go to a** *meadow*? **Where should I put** *meadow*? Place the word strip in the column for *Places.*

- Continue with the other words, and encourage children to tell why they think a word belongs in the category they have named.

✓ Places	✗ Not Places
meadow	blizzards
cliffs	boring
jungle	impossible

▶ Antonyms

Children will name antonyms for Oral Vocabulary words.

- Tell children that antonyms are words that mean the opposite of each other. Provide a few examples of antonym pairs, such as *big* and *little*, *tall* and *short*, and *happy* and *sad*.

- On the board or on chart paper, draw a chart like the one below. Tell children they will help you name antonyms for some of the Oral Vocabulary words.

- Review the meanings of the Oral Vocabulary words, displaying each word as you share its meaning.

- Write the word *boring* in the first column. Guide children to describe or name words that have the opposite meaning. List their ideas in the second column. If children need help with word meanings, help them use a picture dictionary.

- Repeat with the Oral Vocabulary words *impossible* and *cliffs*. Then read the words and antonyms with children.

Word	Antonyms
boring	interesting, exciting, fun
impossible	possible, likely, believable
cliffs	meadow, flat land

- -

▶ Dictate, Draw, and Write

Children will dictate sentences and draw pictures to illustrate some of this week's Oral Vocabulary words.

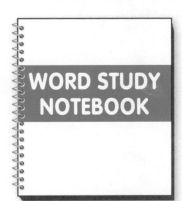

- Review the meanings of the Oral Vocabulary words with children. Hold up the word strip from Discuss Oral Vocabulary as you review each word. Display the word strips along the chalk ledge.

- Have children think of a sentence using one of the Oral Vocabulary words. As a child says a sentence, record it on the board or on chart paper. Call on another child to say a different sentence using the word, and record that child's sentence as well.

- Continue until there is at least one sentence for each Oral Vocabulary word.

- Then have children choose three words to draw and write about in their Word Study Notebooks to show what they have learned about the words *blizzards*, *boring*, *cliffs*, *impossible*, *jungle*, or *meadow*.

Oral Vocabulary Development

ORAL VOCABULARY

1. **apologized** If you *apologized*, you said you were sorry about something.

2. **attention** If something gets your *attention*, you are watching or looking at it.

3. **confusion** When things are all mixed up, there is a lot of *confusion*.

4. **notice** When you *notice* something, you see or hear it.

5. **snooze** If you take a *snooze*, you take a little nap.

6. **webbed** Something that is *webbed* is joined or connected by skin.

The Oral Vocabulary words appear in the Read Aloud Book "Duck & Goose."

▶ Discuss Oral Vocabulary

Children will answer questions about the Oral Vocabulary words from the Read Aloud Book "Duck & Goose" to deepen their understanding of the words.

- Write each Oral Vocabulary word on a strip of paper.

- Review with children the meaning of each Oral Vocabulary word, displaying each word as you share its meaning, shown to the left.

- Ask questions about the words, such as the ones below. Encourage children to use the Oral Vocabulary words in their responses.

  1. **Would you have apologized to a friend for giving him a present or for hurting his feelings? Explain.**
  2. **How might you get people's attention to warn them about a storm? Explain.**
  3. **What would cause more confusion, having five people or one person give you directions? Why?**
  4. **What are some things that you notice in the classroom?**
  5. **Why would you want to take a snooze, because you are sleepy or because you have something to do?**
  6. **Do a duck's webbed feet help it to swim or to fly? Explain.**

- As children answer the questions, encourage them to explain their responses and to share their ideas about the words.

▶ True or Not True

Children will listen to sentences about the Oral Vocabulary words and tell which ones are true and which ones are not true.

- Review the meanings of the Oral Vocabulary words with children.

- Tell children that you will be saying sentences about the Oral Vocabulary words. Tell them to listen carefully so they can decide if each sentence is true or not true.

- Then say each sentence, and have children decide whether it is true or not true. Model how to tell if the first sentence is true or not true.

  1. **A dog has webbed feet.** *(not true)*
  2. **If you apologized for something, you were proud to do it.** *(not true)*
  3. **You take a snooze when you feel tired.** *(true)*
  4. **If you notice something, you are not looking at it.** *(not true)*
  5. **A fire alarm will get your attention.** *(true)*
  6. **Confusion happens when things are very calm and quiet.** *(not true)*

- Revisit the items that are not true. Encourage children to reword the sentences to make them true.

▶ "Because" Sentences

Children will use the Oral Vocabulary words to complete sentences.

- Review the meanings of the Oral Vocabulary words with children.

- Tell children you will be saying part of a sentence that ends with the word *because*. Tell them they will finish the sentence by showing what they know about the meaning of the Oral Vocabulary word in the sentence.

- Then say each of the following sentences, allowing children to finish the sentences to show understanding of the Oral Vocabulary words. Model the process by completing the first sentence for them.

- Allow two or more children to complete each sentence to demonstrate a variety of possible responses.

    1. **There was confusion at the vet's office because…** *(Possible response: all the dogs started barking at once.)*

    2. **Berta apologized to her friend because…** *(Possible response: she forgot to invite the friend to her party.)*

    3. **Lara didn't notice that she dropped her pencil because…** *(Possible response: she was talking to her friend.)*

    4. **My father took a snooze because…** *(Possible response: he was tired.)*

    5. **Webbed feet are good for ducks because…** *(Possible response: they help the ducks swim better.)*

    6. **The noise got my attention because…** *(Possible response: it was so loud.)*

▶ Dictate, Draw, and Write

Children will dictate sentences and draw pictures to illustrate some of this week's Oral Vocabulary words.

- Review the meanings of the Oral Vocabulary words with children. Hold up the word strip from Discuss Oral Vocabulary as you review each word. Display the word strips along the chalk ledge.

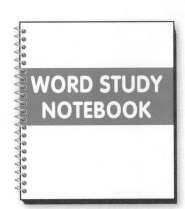

- Have children think of a sentence using one of the Oral Vocabulary words. As a child says a sentence, record it on the board or on chart paper. Call on another child to say a different sentence using the word, and record that child's sentence as well.

- Continue until there is at least one sentence for each Oral Vocabulary word.

- Then have children choose three words to draw and write about in their Word Study Notebooks to show what they have learned about the words *apologized*, *attention*, *confusion*, *notice*, *snooze*, or *webbed*.

Oral Vocabulary Development

ORAL VOCABULARY

1. **idea** An *idea* is something you think of.

2. **just** If you *just* have a sore throat, you have nothing more than a sore throat.

3. **plain** If you eat *plain* bread, you eat bread with nothing on it.

4. **teach** When you *teach* someone, you show that person how to do something.

5. **together** If you and a friend do something *together,* you do it with each other.

6. **until** If you stay at school *until* the bell rings, you stay at school up to the time when the bell rings.

Simon and Molly plus Hester

The Oral Vocabulary words appear in the Read Aloud Book "Simon and Molly plus Hester."

▶ Discuss Oral Vocabulary

Children will answer questions about the Oral Vocabulary words from the Read Aloud Book "Simon and Molly plus Hester" to deepen their understanding of the words.

- Write each Oral Vocabulary word on a strip of paper.
- Review with children the meaning of each Oral Vocabulary word, displaying each word as you share its meaning, shown to the left.
- Ask questions about the words, such as the ones below. Encourage children to use the Oral Vocabulary words in their responses.

   1. **If I have an idea about going swimming, am I swimming or thinking about swimming? Explain.**
   2. **If just you and a friend went to a movie, did anyone else go? Why?**
   3. **If you had plain spaghetti, did you have something on it or nothing on it? Why?**
   4. **What would you like someone to teach you? What could you teach someone?**
   5. **What are some things that you like to do together with your family? Why?**
   6. **If you play until your coach blows a whistle, are you playing after she blows the whistle? Why or why not?**

- As children answer the questions, encourage them to explain their responses and to share their ideas about the words.

▶ Paired Yes/No Questions

Children will answer paired questions about Oral Vocabulary words to show understanding of how to use the words correctly.

- Prepare yes/no cards for each child by drawing a smiling face on one card and a frowning face on another. You may also choose to have children make their own cards.
- Tell children that they will be answering questions about the Oral Vocabulary words with a smile card for *yes* and a frown card for *no.*
- Review the meanings of the Oral Vocabulary words, displaying each word as you share its meaning.
- Read a set of paired questions to children. Ask: **Would it be fun to play catch together with a friend?** *(yes/smile)* **Would it be safe to ride a bike together with a friend?** *(no/frown)* Encourage children to explain their answers.
- Continue with the other questions, and encourage children to explain their answers.

   1. **Would you need to have an idea to brush your teeth?** *(no/frown)* **Would you need to have an idea about what to make for an art project?** *(yes/smile)*
   2. **Did someone teach you how to write your name?** *(yes/smile)* **Did someone teach you how to breathe?** *(no/frown)*
   3. **If you had just enough time to get to school, would you have time to play before school?** *(no/frown)* **Would you want just enough popcorn to share with a friend?** *(yes/smile)*
   4. **If you ordered a plain dish of ice cream, would there be chocolate syrup on top?** *(no/frown)* **Would you order a plain dish of ice cream if you liked nothing on top?** *(yes/smile)*
   5. **If you read a book until lunchtime, would you read during lunchtime?** *(no/frown)* **Would you keep eating lunch until you ate all your food?** *(yes/smile)*

▶ Guess the Word

Children will listen to clues and identify Oral Vocabulary words.

- Review the meanings of the Oral Vocabulary words with children.

- Tell children you will be saying clues about the Oral Vocabulary words. Tell them to listen carefully so they can guess the Oral Vocabulary word for each clue.

- Then say each clue below and have children guess the Oral Vocabulary word. Model the process with the first clue.

   1. To show a friend how to do a cartwheel *(teach)*

   2. To have nothing more than a penny *(just)*

   3. To drink a glass of water with no ice *(plain)*

   4. Playing with a friend *(together)*

   5. Something that you think *(idea)*

   6. To sleep up to the time when your mom wakes you *(until)*

- After children have guessed the correct word, ask volunteers to give other examples of when they might use the word.

▶ Dictate, Draw, and Write

Children will dictate sentences and draw pictures to illustrate some of this week's Oral Vocabulary words.

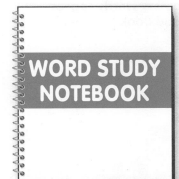

- Review the meanings of the Oral Vocabulary words with children. Hold up the word strip from Discuss Oral Vocabulary as you review each word. Display the word strips along the chalk ledge.

- Have children think of a sentence using one of the Oral Vocabulary words. As a child says a sentence, record it on the board or on chart paper. Call on another child to say a different sentence using the word, and record that child's sentence as well.

- Continue until there is at least one sentence for each Oral Vocabulary word.

- Then have children choose three words to draw and write about in their Word Study Notebooks to show what they have learned about the words *idea, just, plain, teach, together,* or *until.*

Oral Vocabulary Development

1. **blend** If you *blend* something, you mix it.

2. **cub** A *cub* is a baby animal, such as a tiger, lion, or bear.

3. **den** A *den* is a home for wild animals.

4. **pounces** When an animal *pounces*, it jumps on something and grabs it.

5. **prey** An animal that is hunted by another animal is called its *prey*.

6. **scraps** *Scraps* are pieces that are left over or thrown away.

The Oral Vocabulary words appear in the Read Aloud Book "A Tiger Grows Up."

▶ Discuss Oral Vocabulary

Children will answer questions about the Oral Vocabulary words from the Read Aloud Book "A Tiger Grows Up" to deepen their understanding of the words.

- Write each Oral Vocabulary word on a strip of paper.

- Review with children the meaning of each Oral Vocabulary word, displaying each word as you share its meaning, shown to the left.

- Ask questions about the words, such as the ones below. Encourage children to use the Oral Vocabulary words in their responses.

  1. **How can some animals blend in with their surroundings?**

  2. **If I saw a tiger cub at a zoo, would I have seen a young animal or an old animal? Explain.**

  3. **Which animal would live in a den—a bird or a lion? Why?**

  4. **If a cat pounces on a mouse, does it grab the mouse or let the mouse go? Explain.**

  5. **If a bird hunts for a worm, which one is the prey? How do you know?**

  6. **If you cut shapes from cloth, which are the scraps—the cloth shapes or the rest of the cloth? Explain.**

- As children answer the questions, encourage them to explain their responses and to share their ideas about the words.

▶ Describe It or Act It Out

Children will describe or act out Oral Vocabulary words to demonstrate understanding.

- Review the meanings of the Oral Vocabulary words with children.

- Tell children that you are going to ask some questions about the Oral Vocabulary words. Explain that they will respond to the questions either by describing an Oral Vocabulary word or by acting it out.

- Ask each of the following questions. Have children respond by providing a description or by acting out the word's meaning.

  1. **How do you think a cat pounces on a bug?** (*Possible responses: It jumps on it and grabs it. The child may also pantomime* pouncing.)

  2. **How would a bear find its prey?** (*Possible responses: It might hunt for it. The child may also pantomime a bear looking for* prey.)

  3. **How can a bird blend in with the trees?** (*Possible response: It would get mixed in with some leaves.*)

  4. **What do you think a fox's den looks like?** (*Possible response: It might have a soft place to sleep.*)

  5. **How could scraps be made from paper?** (*Possible response: The scraps of paper would be the pieces that are left over after I cut the pieces that I need.*)

  6. **What do you think a cub would do if it heard a strange noise?** (*Possible responses: It would stay close to its mother. The child may also pantomime a* cub *being frightened.*)

▶ Word Sort

Children will sort the Oral Vocabulary words to learn more about how the words are used.

- Use the word strips from Discuss Oral Vocabulary. On the board or on chart paper, draw a chart like the one below, and tell children they will help you sort the Oral Vocabulary words.

- Review the meanings of the Oral Vocabulary words, displaying each word as you share its meaning.

- Then explain the chart headings. Tell children they will sort the Oral Vocabulary words into two groups: words that name things and words that are action words.

- Choose a word strip, and read the word aloud. For example, say: **Cub. Is *cub* a word that names a thing or is it an action word? Who can tell me what *cub* is? Where should I put *cub*?** Place the strip in the *Words for Things* column of the chart.

- Continue with the other words, and encourage children to tell why they think a word belongs in the category they have named.

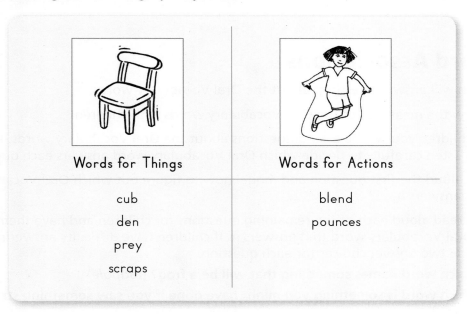

Words for Things	Words for Actions
cub	blend
den	pounces
prey	
scraps	

▶ Dictate, Draw, and Write

Children will dictate sentences and draw pictures to illustrate some of this week's Oral Vocabulary words.

- Review the meanings of the Oral Vocabulary words with children. Hold up the word strip from Discuss Oral Vocabulary as you review each word. Display the word strips along the chalk ledge.

- Have children think of a sentence using one of the Oral Vocabulary words. As a child says a sentence, record it on the board or on chart paper. Call on another child to say a different sentence using the word, and record that child's sentence as well.

- Continue until there is at least one sentence for each Oral Vocabulary word.

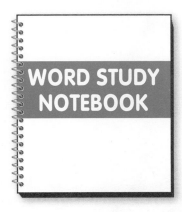

- Then have children draw and write in their Word Study Notebooks about a tiger cub. Have children try to use the words *blend, cub, den, pounces, prey,* or *scraps* to tell about their drawings.

Oral Vocabulary Development

1. **bank** The *bank* of a river is the ground on either side of the river.

2. **gills** *Gills* are the body part that help animals, such as fish, breathe under water.

3. **hatch** When baby birds *hatch*, they come out of eggs.

4. **shrink** When things *shrink*, they get smaller.

5. **stared** If you *stared* at something, you took a long look at it.

6. **tadpole** A *tadpole* is a baby frog.

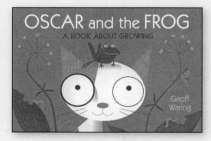

The Oral Vocabulary words appear in the Read Aloud Book "Oscar and the Frog."

▶ Discuss Oral Vocabulary

Children will answer questions about the Oral Vocabulary words from the Read Aloud Book "Oscar and the Frog" to deepen their understanding of the words.

- Write each Oral Vocabulary word on a strip of paper.

- Review with children the meaning of each Oral Vocabulary word, displaying each word as you share its meaning, shown to the left.

- Ask questions about the words, such as the ones below. Encourage children to use the Oral Vocabulary words in their responses.

   1. **If you stand on the bank of a river, are you in the water or out of the water? Why?**
   2. **Do gills help fish to breathe or to swim? Explain.**
   3. **Which would hatch, a chick or a puppy? Why?**
   4. **If your clothes shrink, will they still fit you? Why or why not?**
   5. **If you stared at a friend, did you look or listen? Why?**
   6. **What does a tadpole grow up to be? Explain.**

- As children answer the questions, encourage them to explain their responses and to share their ideas about the words.

▶ Word Associations

Children will answer questions about the Oral Vocabulary words.

- Review the meanings of the Oral Vocabulary words with children.

- Tell children you will be asking questions about the Oral Vocabulary words. Have them listen carefully to decide which Oral Vocabulary word answers each question.

- Read aloud the first question and model how to figure out which Oral Vocabulary word answers it.

- Then read aloud each of the remaining questions for children and have them name the Oral Vocabulary word that answers it. If children have difficulty answering, provide two answer choices for each question.

   1. **Which word names something that will be a frog?** *(tadpole)*
   2. **Which word is something you might have done if you saw something strange?** *(stared)*
   3. **Which word is something that helps animals breathe in water?** *(gills)*
   4. **Which word tells something baby birds might do in the spring?** *(hatch)*
   5. **Which word is something that could happen to clothes in a dryer?** *(shrink)*
   6. **Which word is something you can see on both sides of a river?** *(bank)*

- Have children think of other ways they can use the Oral Vocabulary words in sentences.

▶ "Because" Sentences

Children will use the Oral Vocabulary words to complete sentences.

- Review the meanings of the Oral Vocabulary words with children.

- Tell children you will be saying part of a sentence that ends with the word *because*. Tell them they will finish the sentence by showing what they know about the meaning of the Oral Vocabulary word in the sentence.

- Then say each of the following sentences, allowing children to finish the sentences to show understanding of the Oral Vocabulary words. Model the process by completing the first sentence for them.

- Ask two or more children to complete each sentence to demonstrate a variety of possible responses.

  1. **I stared at the cat because…** *(Possible response: I wanted to see what it would do.)*

  2. **We caught a tadpole because…** *(Possible response: we wanted to see it turn into a frog.)*

  3. **He walked carefully along the bank because…** *(Possible response: he didn't want to fall into the river.)*

  4. **My fish has gills because…** *(Possible response: it needs them to breathe under water.)*

  5. **The farmer waited for the eggs to hatch because…** *(Possible response: he wanted to see the chicks.)*

  6. **I did not want my pencils to shrink too much in the sharpener because…** *(Possible response: then they might be too small to write with.)*

▶ Dictate, Draw, and Write

Children will dictate sentences and draw pictures to illustrate some of this week's Oral Vocabulary words.

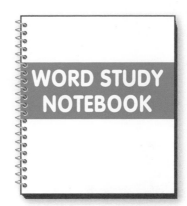

- Review the meanings of the Oral Vocabulary words with children. Hold up the word strip from Discuss Oral Vocabulary as you review each word. Display the word strips along the chalk ledge.

- Have children think of a sentence using one of the Oral Vocabulary words. As a child says a sentence, record it on the board or on chart paper. Call on another child to say a different sentence using the word, and record that child's sentence as well.

- Continue until there is at least one sentence for each Oral Vocabulary word.

- Then have children draw and write in their Word Study Notebooks to tell about a tadpole that grows into a frog. Have children try to use the words *bank, gills, hatch, shrink, stared,* or *tadpole* to tell about their drawings.

Oral Vocabulary Development

ORAL VOCABULARY

1. communicate When you *communicate* with others, you share your thoughts or feelings with them.

2. mood Your *mood* is the way you feel.

3. scent A *scent* is the special way something smells.

4. sly If an animal is *sly*, it is smart and sneaky.

5. survive When animals *survive*, they stay alive.

6. temperature The *temperature* of something is how hot or cold it is.

Red Eyes or Blue Feathers
A Book About Animal Colors
by Patricia M. Stockland
Illustrated by Todd Ouren

The Oral Vocabulary words appear in the Read Aloud Book "Red Eyes or Blue Feathers."

▶ Discuss Oral Vocabulary

Children will answer questions about the Oral Vocabulary words from the Read Aloud Book "Red Eyes or Blue Feathers" to deepen their understanding of the words.

- Write each Oral Vocabulary word on a strip of paper.

- Review with children the meaning of each Oral Vocabulary word, displaying each word as you share its meaning, shown to the left.

- Ask questions about the words, such as the ones below. Encourage children to use the Oral Vocabulary words in their responses.

  1. What are some ways you can communicate with a friend? Explain.

  2. If you were in a good mood, would you smile or frown? Why?

  3. Would a dog follow a scent if it wanted to find something? Why or why not?

  4. Would a sly fox be able to figure out how to get into a barn at night? Explain.

  5. What do you think helps baby animals survive? Explain.

  6. What do you like to do when the temperature is hot? What do you like to do when the temperature is cold?

- As children answer the questions, encourage them to explain their responses and to share their ideas about the words.

▶ True or Not True

Children will listen to sentences about the Oral Vocabulary words and tell which ones are true and which ones are not true.

- Review the meanings of the Oral Vocabulary words with children.

- Tell children that you will be saying sentences about the Oral Vocabulary words. Tell them to listen carefully so they can decide whether each sentence is true or not true.

- Then say each sentence and have children decide whether it is true or not true. Model how to tell whether the first sentence is true or not true.

  1. The temperature tells you when it is night or day. *(not true)*

  2. Rabbits use their ears to find a scent. *(not true)*

  3. Dogs communicate when they wag their tails. *(true)*

  4. A sly animal does not hide from people. *(not true)*

  5. A baby cries when she is in a good mood. *(not true)*

  6. Squirrels gather nuts to help them survive in winter. *(true)*

- Revisit the items that are not true. Encourage children to reword the sentences to make them true.

▶ Word Sort

Children will sort the Oral Vocabulary words to learn more about how the words are used.

- Use the word strips from Discuss Oral Vocabulary. On the board or on chart paper, draw a chart like the one below, and tell children they will help you sort the Oral Vocabulary words. Review the meanings of the Oral Vocabulary words, displaying each word as you share its meaning.

- Then explain the chart headings. Tell children they will sort the Oral Vocabulary words into three groups: words that name a thing, words that describe, or words that are verbs, or action words.

- Choose one of the word strips, and read the word aloud. For example, say: *Survive*. **Is *survive* a word for a thing, a word that describes, or an action word? Who can tell me what *survive* is? Where should I put *survive*?** Place the strip in the *Words for Actions* column of the chart.

- Continue with the other words, and encourage children to tell why they think a word belongs in the category they have named.

Words for Things	Words That Describe	Words for Actions
mood	sly	survive
scent		communicate
temperature		

. . . .

▶ Dictate, Draw, and Write

Children will dictate sentences and draw pictures to illustrate some of this week's Oral Vocabulary words.

- Review the meanings of the Oral Vocabulary words with children. Hold up the word strip from Discuss Oral Vocabulary as you review each word. Display the word strips along the chalk ledge.

- Have children think of a sentence using one of the Oral Vocabulary words. As a child says a sentence, record it on the board or on chart paper. Call on another child to say a different sentence using the word, and record that child's sentence as well.

- Continue until there is at least one sentence for each Oral Vocabulary word.

- Then have children choose three words to draw and write about in their Word Study Notebooks to show what they have learned about the words *communicate, mood, scent, sly, survive,* or *temperature.*

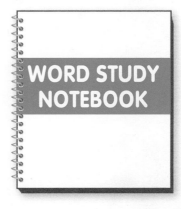

WORD STUDY
NOTEBOOK

Oral Vocabulary Development

ORAL VOCABULARY

1. **crop** A *crop* is a plant or animal that people raise for food or to make things.

2. **golden** If something is *golden*, it is a deep yellow color, like the color of gold.

3. **grind** If you *grind* something, you crush it into very small pieces.

4. **patch** A *patch* of land is a small piece of land.

5. **sprout** When plants *sprout*, they begin to grow.

6. **sturdy** If something is *sturdy*, it is hard to break or bend.

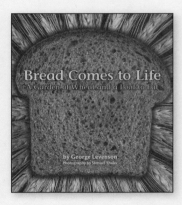

The Oral Vocabulary words appear in the Read Aloud Book "Bread Comes to Life."

▶ Discuss Oral Vocabulary

Children will answer questions about the Oral Vocabulary words from the Read Aloud Book "Bread Comes to Life" to deepen their understanding of the words.

- Write each Oral Vocabulary word on a strip of paper.

- Review with children the meaning of each Oral Vocabulary word, displaying each word as you share its meaning, shown to the left.

- Ask questions about the words, such as the ones below. Encourage children to use the Oral Vocabulary words in their responses.

  1. **Which of these plants would you call a crop, corn or an oak tree? Why?**
  2. **Would you say that the sun is golden? Why or why not?**
  3. **If you wanted to break something into very small pieces, would you grind it or fold it? Explain.**
  4. **What could a farmer do with a patch of land? Explain.**
  5. **When do you think most plants sprout, in the spring or in the winter? Why?**
  6. **Which of these is more sturdy, a plastic fork or a metal fork? Why?**

- As children answer the questions, encourage them to explain their responses and to share their ideas about the words.

▶ Word Sort

Children will sort Oral Vocabulary words to learn about how the words are used.

- Use the word strips from Discuss Oral Vocabulary. On the board or on chart paper, draw a chart like the one below, and tell children they will help you sort the Oral Vocabulary words.

- Review the meanings of the Oral Vocabulary words, displaying each word as you share its meaning.

- Then explain the chart headings. Tell children they will sort the Oral Vocabulary words into three groups: words that name a thing, words that describe, or words that are verbs, or action words.

- Choose one of the word strips, and read the word aloud. For example, say: *Patch*. **Is** *patch* **a word for a thing, a word that describes, or an action word? Who can tell me what** *patch* **is? Where should I put** *patch*? Place the strip in the *Words for Things* column of the chart.

- Continue with the other words, and encourage children to tell why they think a word belongs in the category they have named.

Words for Things	Words That Describe	Words for Actions
patch	golden	sprout
crop	sturdy	grind

▶ Riddles

Children will listen to riddles and identify the matching Oral Vocabulary words.

- Review the meanings of the Oral Vocabulary words with children.

- Tell children that you will be telling them riddles about the Oral Vocabulary words. Tell them to listen carefully so they can guess the Oral Vocabulary word for each riddle.

- Then say each riddle and have children guess which Oral Vocabulary word matches the riddle. Model the process by showing how to solve the first riddle.

- If children have difficulty answering the riddles, ask them yes/no questions, such as the following: *Could a flower that is like sunshine be golden?*

  1. I am a flower that reminds you of sunshine. How could you describe me? *(golden)*

  2. You grow me to eat. What am I? *(crop)*

  3. When you make flour out of wheat, you do this. *(grind)*

  4. I am a piece of wood that is hard to bend or break. How would you describe me? *(sturdy)*

  5. I am something that happens when a seed starts to grow. *(sprout)*

  6. I am a place where you could plant a little garden. What am I? *(patch)*

- Encourage children to think of their own riddles for the Oral Vocabulary words and have their classmates solve them.

▶ Dictate, Draw, and Write

Children will dictate sentences and draw pictures to illustrate some of this week's Oral Vocabulary words.

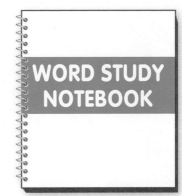

- Review the meanings of the Oral Vocabulary words with children. Hold up the word strip from Discuss Oral Vocabulary as you review each word. Display the word strips along the chalk ledge.

- Have children think of a sentence using one of the Oral Vocabulary words. As a child says a sentence, record it on the board or on chart paper. Call on another child to say a different sentence using the word, and record that child's sentence as well.

- Continue until there is at least one sentence for each Oral Vocabulary word.

- Then have children draw and write in their Word Study Notebooks to tell about a patch of land where a garden is planted. Have them try to use the words *crop, golden, grind, patch, sprout,* or *sturdy* to tell about their drawings.

Oral Vocabulary Development

ORAL VOCABULARY

1. **assistant** An *assistant* is a person who helps someone else do a job.

2. **enormous** Something that is *enormous* is very big.

3. **generous** If you are *generous*, you are willing to share with or to help others.

4. **mayor** A *mayor* is the leader of a city or town.

5. **shocked** If you are *shocked*, you are very surprised.

6. **volunteers** *Volunteers* are people who work for free.

The Oral Vocabulary words appear in the Read Aloud Book "Curious George Makes Pancakes."

▶ Discuss Oral Vocabulary

Children will answer questions about the Oral Vocabulary words from the Read Aloud Book "Curious George Makes Pancakes" to deepen their understanding of the words.

- Write each Oral Vocabulary word on a strip of paper.

- Review with children the meaning of each Oral Vocabulary word, displaying each word as you share its meaning, shown to the left.

- Ask questions about the words, such as the ones below. Encourage children to use the Oral Vocabulary words in their responses.

  1. Who would need an assistant more, someone moving a heavy piano or someone eating her lunch? Explain.
  2. Which of these is enormous, an elephant or a mouse? Why?
  3. Would a generous person give books to a library? Why or why not?
  4. How do you think a mayor could help people? Explain.
  5. Would you be shocked if you saw a horse at school? Why or why not?
  6. Do volunteers get paid money when they do a job? Explain.

- As children answer the questions, encourage them to explain their responses and to share their ideas about the words.

▶ Synonyms

Children will name synonyms for Oral Vocabulary words.

- Tell children that synonyms are words that mean the same or almost the same thing. Provide a few examples of synonym pairs, such as *happy* and *glad*, *hat* and *cap*, and *sleep* and *nap*.

- On the board or on chart paper, draw a chart like the one below. Tell children they will help you name synonyms for the Oral Vocabulary words.

- Review the meanings of the Oral Vocabulary words, displaying each word as you share its meaning.

- Write the word *assistant* in the first column. Guide children to describe or name words that mean the same or almost the same thing. Write their ideas in the second column. If children need help with word meanings, help them use a picture dictionary.

- Continue with the remaining Oral Vocabulary words. Then read the words and synonyms with children.

Word	Synonyms
assistant	helper
enormous	big, huge, large
generous	kind, helpful, giving
shocked	surprised, amazed

▶ Word Sort

Children will sort the Oral Vocabulary words to learn more about how the words are used.

- Use the word strips from Discuss Oral Vocabulary. On the board or on chart paper, draw a chart like the one below, and tell children they will help you sort the Oral Vocabulary words.

- Review the meanings of the Oral Vocabulary words, displaying each word as you share its meaning.

- Then explain the chart headings. Tell children they will sort the Oral Vocabulary words into two groups: words for work or words that describe.

- Choose one of the word strips, and read the word aloud. For example, say: **Enormous. Is *enormous* a word for work or a word that describes? Who can tell me what *enormous* is? Where should I put *enormous*?** Place the strip in the *Words That Describe* column of the chart.

- Continue for the other words, and encourage children to tell why they think a word belongs in the category they have named.

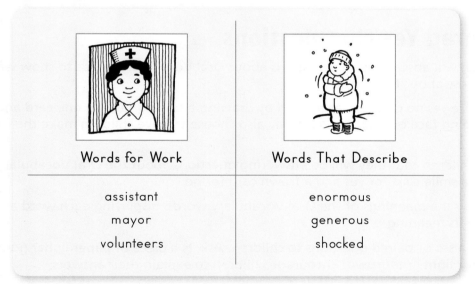

Words for Work	Words That Describe
assistant	enormous
mayor	generous
volunteers	shocked

▶ Dictate, Draw, and Write

Children will dictate sentences and draw pictures to illustrate some of this week's Oral Vocabulary words.

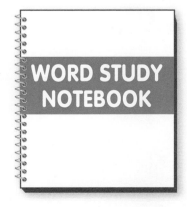

WORD STUDY NOTEBOOK

- Review the meanings of the Oral Vocabulary words with children. Hold up the word strip from Discuss Oral Vocabulary as you review each word. Display the word strips along the chalk ledge.

- Have children think of a sentence using one of the Oral Vocabulary words. As a child says a sentence, record it on the board or on chart paper. Call on another child to say a different sentence using the word, and record that child's sentence as well.

- Continue until there is at least one sentence for each Oral Vocabulary word.

- Then have children draw and write in their Word Study Notebooks to tell about a job that volunteers do in a city. Have them try to use the words *assistant, enormous, generous, mayor, shocked,* or *volunteers* to tell about their drawings.

ORAL VOCABULARY

1. **creatures** *Creatures* are animals.

2. **firmly** If you do something *firmly*, you do it in a strong and steady way.

3. **kite** A *kite* is something that you can fly on a string. It is made from a light frame covered with paper, cloth, or plastic.

4. **launched** If something, such as a rocket, was *launched*, it was sent off into the sky.

5. **light** Something that is *light* doesn't weigh very much.

6. **replied** If you *replied,* you answered someone.

The Oral Vocabulary words appear in the Read Aloud Book "Someone Bigger."

▶ Discuss Oral Vocabulary

Children will answer questions about the Oral Vocabulary words from the Read Aloud Book "Someone Bigger" to deepen their understanding of the words.

- Write each Oral Vocabulary word on a strip of paper.

- Review with children the meaning of each Oral Vocabulary word, displaying each word as you share its meaning, shown to the left.

- Ask questions about the words, such as the ones below. Encourage children to use the Oral Vocabulary words in their responses.

  1. **Which ones are creatures—frogs and lizards or trees and flowers? Why?**

  2. **If you firmly hammered a nail, would it fall out of the wood? Explain.**

  3. **Would you fly a kite or ride on a kite? Why?**

  4. **If a rocket was launched, did the rocket come down or go up? Explain.**

  5. **Would you say that a feather is light or that a brick is light? Why do you think so?**

  6. **If you replied, did you ask a question or answer a question? Why?**

- As children answer the questions, encourage them to explain their responses and to share their ideas about the words.

▶ Paired Yes/No Questions

Children will answer paired questions about Oral Vocabulary words to show what they know about the words.

- Prepare yes/no cards for each child by drawing a smiling face on one card and a frowning face on another. You may also choose to have children make their own cards.

- Tell children that they will be answering questions about the Oral Vocabulary words with a smile card for *yes* and a frown card for *no*.

- Review the meanings of the Oral Vocabulary words, displaying each word as you share its meaning.

- Read a set of paired questions to children. Ask: **Is a piece of paper light?** *(yes/smile)* **Is a car light?** *(no/frown)* Encourage children to explain their answers.

- Continue with the other questions, and encourage children to explain their answers.

  1. **Would you use a kite inside your house?** *(no/frown)* **Would you use a kite outside your house?** *(yes/smile)*

  2. **Are rocks creatures?** *(no/frown)* **Are dogs creatures?** *(yes/smile)*

  3. **Would you have replied if you were asked a question?** *(yes/smile)* **Would you have replied if no one spoke to you first?** *(no/frown)*

  4. **If your papers were glued firmly, would they come apart easily?** *(no/frown)* **If your shoes were firmly tied, could you run without them falling off?** *(yes/smile)*

  5. **Would you have launched a toy plane to see it go up into the air?** *(yes/smile)* **Would you have launched a toy plane to see if it could bounce?** *(no/frown)*

▶ Describe It

Children will respond to prompts about Oral Vocabulary words to show understanding of the words.

- Review the meanings of the Oral Vocabulary words with children.

- Tell children you are going to ask them to say or do something to show that they understand the Oral Vocabulary words.

- Read the following prompts. Ask several children to provide descriptions for each prompt.

  1. **Describe how something light feels when you pick it up.** *(Possible response: It is easy to pick up.)*
  2. **Tell about a time you replied to someone.** *(Possible response: I answered my friend's question.)*
  3. **Describe some creatures you have seen.** *(Possible response: I have seen some colorful birds.)*
  4. **Tell how a rocket looks when it is launched.** *(Possible response: It goes straight up into the sky.)*
  5. **Describe how you would hold something firmly on a windy day.** *(Possible response: I would hold it very tightly in my hands.)*
  6. **Describe a kite you have seen.** *(Possible response: It was long and looked like a dragon.)*

▶ Dictate, Draw, and Write

Children will dictate sentences and draw pictures to illustrate some of this week's Oral Vocabulary words.

- Review the meanings of the Oral Vocabulary words with children. Hold up the word strip from Discuss Oral Vocabulary as you review each word. Display the word strips along the chalk ledge.

- Have children think of a sentence using one of the Oral Vocabulary words. As a child says a sentence, record it on the board or on chart paper. Call on another child to say a different sentence using the word, and record that child's sentence as well.

- Continue until there is at least one sentence for each Oral Vocabulary word.

- Then have children choose three words to draw and write about in their Word Study Notebooks to show what they have learned about the words *creatures, firmly, kite, launched, light,* or *replied.*

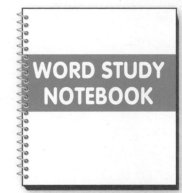

ORAL VOCABULARY

1. **bellowed** If you *bellowed*, you said something in a loud, deep voice.

2. **dingy** Something that is *dingy* looks dull and not shiny.

3. **rumbled** If something *rumbled*, it made a deep, rolling sound.

4. **valley** A *valley* is the low land between two mountains or hills.

5. **waiters** *Waiters* are people who serve food in a restaurant.

6. **weary** When you are *weary*, you feel very tired.

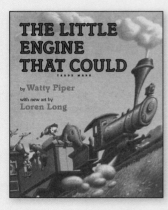

The Oral Vocabulary words appear in the Read Aloud Book "The Little Engine That Could."

▶ Discuss Oral Vocabulary

Children will answer questions about the Oral Vocabulary words from the Read Aloud Book "The Little Engine That Could" to deepen their understanding of the words.

- Write each Oral Vocabulary word on a strip of paper.

- Review with children the meaning of each Oral Vocabulary word, displaying each word as you share its meaning, shown to the left.

- Ask questions about the words, such as the ones below. Encourage children to use the Oral Vocabulary words in their responses.

    1. **If you bellowed, would it be easy or hard to hear you? Why?**
    2. **How would a dingy bike look? Explain.**
    3. **Which of these would more likely have rumbled—thunder or a bird? Why?**
    4. **If you were on top of a mountain, would you look down at a valley or look up at a valley? Why?**
    5. **What would you want waiters to bring you? Explain.**
    6. **When you feel weary, do you want to play or rest? Why?**

- As children answer the questions, encourage them to explain their responses and to share their ideas about the words.

▶ Word Sort

Children will sort the Oral Vocabulary words to learn more about how they are used.

- Use the word strips from Discuss Oral Vocabulary, excluding the word *waiters*. On the board or on chart paper, draw a chart like the one below, and tell children they will help you sort Oral Vocabulary words.

- Review the meanings of the Oral Vocabulary words, displaying each word as you share its meaning.

- Then explain the chart headings. Tell children they will sort the Oral Vocabulary words into three groups: words that name things, words that describe, and words that are verbs, or action words.

- Choose one of the word strips, and read the word aloud. For example, say: ***Dingy. Is dingy a word for a thing, a word that describes, or an action word? Who can tell me what dingy is? Where should I put dingy?*** Place the strip in the *Words That Describe* column of the chart.

- Continue for the other words, and encourage children to tell why they think a word belongs in the category they have named.

Words for Things	Words That Describe	Words for Actions
valley	dingy	bellowed
	weary	rumbled

▶ Riddles

Children will listen to riddles and identify the matching Oral Vocabulary words.

- Review the meanings of the Oral Vocabulary words with children.

- Tell children that you will be telling them riddles about the Oral Vocabulary words. Tell them to listen carefully so they can guess the Oral Vocabulary word for each riddle.

- Then say each riddle and have children guess which Oral Vocabulary word matches the riddle. Model the process by showing how to solve the first riddle.

- If children have difficulty answering the riddles, ask them yes/no questions, such as the following: *Is a valley a low place between mountains or hills?*

  1. I am a low place between high places. What am I? *(valley)*

  2. A big, noisy truck did this when it drove down the street. What did the truck do? *(rumbled)*

  3. We might bring you ice cream in a restaurant. Who are we? *(waiters)*

  4. I am not shiny and new any more. How could you describe me? *(dingy)*

  5. Someone who just fell down hard might have done this. What do you think the person did? *(bellowed)*

  6. You might feel like this after riding your bike all day. How might you feel? *(weary)*

- Encourage children to think of their own riddles for the Oral Vocabulary words and have their classmates solve them.

- -

▶ Dictate, Draw, and Write

Children will dictate sentences and draw pictures to illustrate some of this week's Oral Vocabulary words.

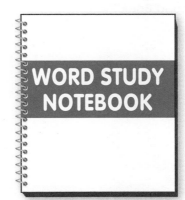

- Review the meanings of the Oral Vocabulary words with children. Hold up the word strip from Discuss Oral Vocabulary as you review each word. Display the word strips along the chalk ledge.

- Have children think of a sentence using one of the Oral Vocabulary words. As a child says a sentence, record it on the board or on chart paper. Call on another child to say a different sentence using the word, and record that child's sentence as well.

- Continue until there is at least one sentence for each Oral Vocabulary word.

- Then have children choose three words to draw and write about in their Word Study Notebooks to show what they have learned about the words *bellowed, dingy, rumbled, valley, waiters,* or *weary.*

Oral Vocabulary Development

ORAL VOCABULARY

1. **certainly** *Certainly* means there is no doubt, or question, about something.

2. **embarrassed** If you feel *embarrassed*, you feel silly or foolish.

3. **languages** *Languages* are the words spoken and understood by large groups of people.

4. **mumbled** If you *mumbled*, you spoke in an unclear way that was hard to understand.

5. **popular** If someone is *popular*, a lot of people like that person.

6. **study** When you *study*, you try to learn something.

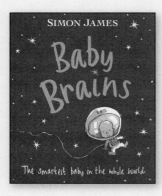

The Oral Vocabulary words appear in the Read Aloud Book "Baby Brains."

▶ Discuss Oral Vocabulary

Children will answer questions about the Oral Vocabulary words from the Read Aloud Book "Baby Brains" to deepen their understanding of the words.

- Write each Oral Vocabulary word on a strip of paper.

- Review with children the meaning of each Oral Vocabulary word, displaying each word as you share its meaning, shown to the left.

- Ask questions about the words, such as the ones below. Encourage children to use the Oral Vocabulary words in their responses.

  1. **If you are certainly going to go to the park, will you go? Explain.**
  2. **Would you feel embarrassed if you dropped your lunch tray at school? Why or why not?**
  3. **What are some languages you have heard people speak?**
  4. **If you mumbled, would people know what you said? Explain.**
  5. **Who might be more popular, someone who likes to share or someone who doesn't like to share? Why?**
  6. **What are some things that you study at school?**

- As children answer the questions, encourage them to explain their responses and to share their ideas about the words.

▶ Antonyms

Children will name antonyms for Oral Vocabulary words.

- Remind children that antonyms are words that mean the opposite. Provide a few examples of antonym pairs, such as *long* and *short, happy* and *sad,* and *day* and *night*.

- On the board or on chart paper, draw a chart like the one below. Tell children they will help you list antonyms for some of the Oral Vocabulary words.

- Review the meanings of the Oral Vocabulary words, displaying each word as you share its meaning.

- Write the word *certainly* in the first column. Guide children to describe or name words that have the opposite meaning. List their ideas in the second column.

- Repeat for the Oral Vocabulary words *embarrassed, popular,* and *mumbled*. Then read the words and antonyms with children.

Word	Antonyms
certainly	doubtful, unsure
embarrassed	proud, happy, pleased
popular	unpopular, disliked
mumbled	shouted, yelled

▸ Complete Sentences

Children will use Oral Vocabulary words to complete sentences.

- Review the meanings of the Oral Vocabulary words with children.

- Tell children you will be saying sentences with a word missing. Ask them to listen carefully so they can choose the Oral Vocabulary word that best completes each sentence.

- Then say each of the following sentences, indicating the missing word by saying *blank*. Repeat the sentence, and have children supply the missing Oral Vocabulary word. Model the process by completing the first sentence.

- If children have difficulty, provide two words as choices for each sentence, and ask children which one is correct.

  1. Pete was _____ when he forgot his cousin's name. *(embarrassed)*

  2. Beth _____, so I didn't understand what she said. *(mumbled)*

  3. Ada was very_____ and well liked by all the children at camp. *(popular)*

  4. I _____ butterflies by reading about them and watching them outdoors. *(study)*

  5. Our teacher can speak three _____. *(languages)*

  6. We will _____ try to come to your birthday party. *(certainly)*

- Call on volunteers to say sentences using the Oral Vocabulary words.

▸ Dictate, Draw, and Write

Children will dictate sentences and draw pictures to illustrate some of this week's Oral Vocabulary words.

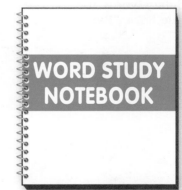

- Review the meanings of the Oral Vocabulary words with children. Hold up the word strip from Discuss Oral Vocabulary as you review each word. Display the word strips along the chalk ledge.

- Have children think of a sentence using one of the Oral Vocabulary words. As a child says a sentence, record it on the board or on chart paper. Call on another child to say a different sentence using the word, and record that child's sentence as well.

- Continue until there is at least one sentence for each Oral Vocabulary word.

- Then have children choose three words to draw and write about in their Word Study Notebooks to show what they have learned about the words *certainly, embarrassed, languages, mumbled, popular,* or *study*.

ORAL VOCABULARY

1. **announced** If you *announced* something, you told it to a group of people.

2. **entrance** The *entrance* is the place where you enter, or go into, a building.

3. **expect** When you *expect* something, you wait for it to happen.

4. **favorite** If something is your *favorite*, you like it more than all the others.

5. **independent** When you are *independent*, you decide or make choices by yourself.

6. **judge** A *judge* is a person who decides who wins a contest.

The Oral Vocabulary words appear in the Read Aloud Book "Pet Show!"

▶ Discuss Oral Vocabulary

Children will answer questions about the Oral Vocabulary words from the Read Aloud Book "Pet Show!" to deepen their understanding of the words.

- Write each Oral Vocabulary word on a strip of paper.

- Review with children the meaning of each Oral Vocabulary word, displaying each word as you share its meaning, shown to the left.

- Ask questions about the words, such as the ones below. Encourage children to use the Oral Vocabulary words in their responses.

  1. **If you announced that you were going to have a party, did you tell one friend or many friends? Why?**
  2. **What does the entrance of our school look like?**
  3. **What is something you expect to happen each day at school? Why?**
  4. **What is your favorite color? Why do you like it?**
  5. **If you were being independent, would you ask for help before painting a picture? Why or why not?**
  6. **Would you need a judge for a contest or for taking a test? Explain.**

- As children answer the questions, encourage them to explain their responses and to share their ideas about the words.

▶ Sentence Clue Game

Children will use sentence clues to explain the meanings of Oral Vocabulary words.

- After reviewing the Oral Vocabulary words with children, tell them that they will play the Sentence Clue Game.

- Remind children that you will ask what a word means. Then you will give sentence clues, and they will use the clues to tell the word's meaning.

- Provide general information in the first sentence clue. Add details in subsequent sentences until children can explain the word's meaning.

- Begin with *judge*. Ask: **What is a *judge*?** Pause after each sentence clue to allow children to define the word: **A *judge* is a person. A *judge* looks at all the entries in a contest. Then the *judge* chooses the winners.** *(Possible response: A judge is the person who decides the winners of a contest.)*

- Continue in the same way with other Oral Vocabulary words as time allows.

▶ Word Associations

Children will answer questions about the Oral Vocabulary words.

- Review the meanings of the Oral Vocabulary words with children.

- Tell children you will be asking questions about the Oral Vocabulary words. Have them listen carefully to decide which Oral Vocabulary word answers each question.

- Read aloud the first question and model how to figure out which Oral Vocabulary word answers it.

- Then read aloud each of the remaining questions for children, and have them name the Oral Vocabulary word that answers it. If children have difficulty answering, provide two answer choices for each question.

  1. **Which word is something I use each time I go into my home?** *(entrance)*
  2. **Which word names a person who decides who will win?** *(judge)*
  3. **Which word tells what I would have done when I wanted to share my big news?** *(announced)*
  4. **Which word tells what I am doing when I just know something will happen?** *(expect)*
  5. **Which word tells what I am being when I clean my desk all by myself?** *(independent)*
  6. **Which word tells about the toy I like most of all?** *(favorite)*

- Have children think of other ways they can use the Oral Vocabulary words in sentences.

▶ Dictate, Draw, and Write

Children will dictate sentences and draw pictures to illustrate some of this week's Oral Vocabulary words.

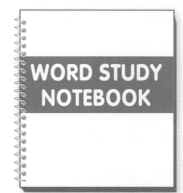

- Review the meanings of the Oral Vocabulary words with children. Hold up the word strip from Discuss Oral Vocabulary as you review each word. Display the word strips along the chalk ledge.

- Have children think of a sentence using one of the Oral Vocabulary words. As a child says a sentence, record it on the board or on chart paper. Call on another child to say a different sentence using the word, and record that child's sentence as well.

- Continue until there is at least one sentence for each Oral Vocabulary word.

- Then have children draw and write in their Word Study Notebooks to tell about a contest of some kind. Have children try to use the words *announced, entrance, expect, favorite, independent,* or *judge* to tell about their drawings.

Teacher's Notes

Meet Irene Fountas

Journeys Leveled Readers offer a variety of engaging, interesting fiction and nonfiction text— very carefully leveled, so you can count on the supports and challenges in each text to be appropriate for children in their development.

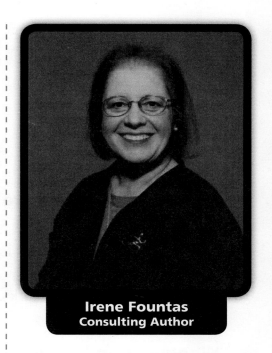

Irene Fountas
Consulting Author

The ***Journeys*** Reader's Workshop approach supports the Common Core's emphasis on children reading and writing complex literature and informational text.

Weekly Plans for Whole Group and Small Group instruction enable teachers to:

- increase children's ability to read, think, and write critically about text.

- meet children at their instructional level and move them forward.

- allow for lesson flexibility to fit the strengths and needs of children.

Irene Fountas is a Professor in the School of Education of Lesley University in Cambridge, Massachusetts. Irene's research has focused on leveled texts, reader's and writer's workshop, assessment, classroom management, and professional development.

Reading Minilessons

Table of Contents

Introduction

What Are Effective Instructional Practices in Literacy?

Your goal in literacy teaching is to bring each child from where he is to as far as you can take him in a school year, with the clear goal of helping each child develop the competencies of proficiency at the level. Proficient readers and writers not only think deeply and critically about texts but also develop a love of reading. The roots of lifelong literacy begin with a rich foundation in the elementary school.

The lessons in this section provide a structure for organizing your literacy teaching, linking understandings across the language and literacy framework, and building a strong foundation of reading strategies and skills. On the pages that follow, you will find an overview of how to use this section along with your *Journeys* materials in three different instructional contexts: Whole-Group Teaching, Small-Group Teaching, and Independent Literacy Work.

WHOLE GROUP
Interactive Read-Aloud/Shared Reading
(heterogeneous)

WHOLE GROUP
Reading Minilesson
(heterogeneous)

SMALL GROUP
Guided Reading
(temporary homogeneous)

SMALL GROUP
Literature Discussion
(heterogeneous)

INDEPENDENT
Independent Reading,
Literacy Work

Whole-Group Teaching

Whole-Group Lessons are related lesson sequences you may want to use across a week. At the core of each lesson is a Journeys literature selection, chosen to highlight a certain aspect of reading that is important for children to learn and apply in various contexts.

> **JOURNEYS RESOURCES FOR WHOLE-GROUP TEACHING**
> - Big Books
> - Read Aloud Books

Interactive Read-Aloud/Shared Reading sets the stage for the day's focus and provides a common foundation of experience for children at various levels of reading proficiency (Fountas and Pinnell, 2006).

As you read aloud to children, use the questions and prompts at planned stopping points in the text to encourage discussion of the reading through classroom collaboration.

Reading aloud to children in this context

- helps children appreciate literature.
- gives children a model of how to think about ideas in the text and from the thinking of their peers.
- models fluent, expressive, phrased reading.
- has children think actively about what they read.
- allows children to hear and share a variety of perspectives and interpretations through classroom collaboration.
- is the common text used in the Reading Minilesson.

The **Reading Minilesson** is focused instruction about a specific topic or skill, called the Minilesson Principle (Fountas and Pinnell, 2001). Using this principle, you help your children think like effective, independent readers. The literature selection from the Interactive Read-Aloud/Shared Reading context is used as the example to demonstrate the principle.

Whole-Group Lessons

▶ What Makes a Family?

What Makes a Family?
Big Book, Lesson 1

Poems About Family
Big Book pp. 26–30, Lesson 1

Building with Dad
Read-Aloud Book, Lesson 1

INTERACTIVE READ-ALOUD/SHARED READING

Read aloud the book to children. Stop periodically for a brief interaction. Use the following suggested stopping points and prompts for quick group response, or give a specific prompt and have partners or threes turn and talk.

- At the end of page 6, say: "We learned from the book that families can have many people. Who are the people in your family?"
- At the end of page 8, ask: "How can friends and neighbors be a part of a family?"
- After reading page 18, display the photos on pages 18 and 19 and say: "Look at these pictures. How are these families helping each other?" Follow-up: "What things do you do to help your family?"
- After reading page 22, ask: "What memories does your family have? Turn and talk about your family memories with a partner."

MINILESSON Main Ideas

TEACH Display the minilesson principle on chart paper, and read it aloud. Tell children they are going to learn how to think about what the author tells mostly about.

1. Discuss the principle with children, using *What Makes a Family?* as an example. Display the title as you read it aloud. Suggested language: "Often, the title of a book is a clue to what the author wants to tell about. What word in the title is a clue that tells you what the book is mostly about?" *(family)*

   > **MINILESSON PRINCIPLE**
   > Think about what the author tells mostly about.

2. Focus on one part of the book, such as what families do together. Suggested language: "This book told about some things families can do together. What are two things families can do together?" *(Families can celebrate things like birthdays, and they can help each other.)*

3. Use children's responses to explain that authors tell mostly about one thing in books. Suggested language: "The author of this book told mostly about families. In telling mostly about families, the author told things about them, such as who is in a family, what families do, and how they help each other."

4. Elicit from children additional details that support the idea that the author tells mostly about families in this book. Record children's ideas in a Web like the one shown here.

Families

SUMMARIZE AND APPLY Restate the minilesson principle. Then tell children to apply it to a book they will listen to or read. Suggested language: "When you read, think about what the author tells mostly about."

GROUP SHARE Ask children to share what they learned from a book they listened to or read. Have children explain what the author told mostly about and how they know.

The **Group Share** has children apply the minilesson principle to the text. As children think deeply about the text, they are able to make the connection to the minilesson principle, deepening their comprehension.

TEACHER'S ROLE

- Engage children in thinking deeply about texts.
- Provide a learning environment in which children feel comfortable sharing their thinking with each other.
- Prepare explicit lessons that are tailored to children's needs.
- Provide a model of phrased, fluent reading in interactive read-aloud.

- Prompt children with comments and questions at planned stopping points to promote active thinking in interactive read-aloud/shared reading.
- Provide explicit teaching of critical literacy concepts in reading minilessons.
- Expose children to a wide variety of genres, authors, and topics.
- Monitor children's understanding to plan for future lessons.

CHILD'S ROLE

- Listen actively.
- Share ideas and opinions with others.
- Make connections to other readings and to own experiences.
- Ask genuine questions and build on the ideas of others.
- Demonstrate understanding of critical literacy concepts.

Informational Text

Genre instruction is a powerful tool for helping children develop the competencies of effective readers and writers. The questions and teaching points in this section can be used over and over across the year as children encounter different genres and increasingly difficult texts within a particular genre.

SUPPORT THINKING

DISCUSSION STARTERS During whole-group and small-group discussion, use questions to spark conversation about genre characteristics.

- What is this book about?
- Are all of the words written in the same size and color?
- What kinds of pictures does the author use?
- What can you learn from the pictures?
- What does the author do to make the book interesting?
- How do you know that the information in the book is true?

COMPARING TEXTS After children have read and listened to several informational books, prompt them to compare books and to recognize common characteristics. Use questions such as these:

- How are the animals/objects/people in [title] and [title] the same?
- Think about [title] and [title]. How are they the same? How are they different?
- How do the pictures in [title] and [title] help you understand the information the author tells?

Genre Characteristics

Informational text gives facts about a topic.

Through repeated exposure to informational text, children should learn to notice common genre characteristics, though they will not be expected to use the technical labels. Use friendly language to help them understand the following concepts:

- **Author's Purpose:** to give information
- **Graphic Features:** pictures that help the reader understand information or show more about the topic
  - **Diagrams:** pictures with labels
  - **Maps:** pictures that show where something is or how to get from one place to another place
  - **Graphs/Charts:** pictures that help readers compare information
- **Text Features:** ways the author makes words stand out
  - **Headings:** type—usually larger, darker, or both—at the beginning of a new section
  - **Labels:** words that name a picture or parts of a picture
  - **Sizes/Colors:** authors use different sizes and colors to help readers see what is most important
- **Main Idea:** what the book is mostly about
- **Details:** information that tells more about the main idea or topic
- **Text Structure:** how the book is organized
- **Facts:** information that is true and can be proved
- **Opinions:** what the author thinks or believes

Discussion Starters are provided to spark discussion about genre characteristics.

Prompts for **Comparing Texts** guide children to compare the various texts they have read in a particular genre.

JOURNEYS Literature

My Five Senses,
Big Book,
Lesson 6

Zinnia's Flower Garden,
Big Book,
Lesson 23

BIG BOOKS
Atlantic
Chameleon, Chameleon
Everybody Works
From Caterpillar to Butterfly
The Handiest Things in the World
Jump into January
Look at Us
Move!
My Five Senses
Turtle Splash!
What a Beautiful Sky!
What Do Wheels Do All Day?
What Do You Do With a Tail Like This?
What Makes a Family?
Zinnia's Flower Garden

BIG BOOKS
Paired Selections
"Amazing Animal Bodies," from Chameleon, Chameleon
"Cross-Country Trip," from One of Three
"Different Kinds of Dogs," from Please, Puppy, Please
"Exploring Land and Water," from Curious George's Dinosaur Discovery
"The Fort Worth Zoo," from Mice Squeak, We Speak
"From Apple Tree to Store," from Pie in the Sky
"Growing Sunflowers," from Zinnia's Flower Garden
"Holidays All Year Long," from Jump into January
"How Water Changes," from Snow

"Jobs People Do," from Something Special
"My School Bus," from How Do Dinosaurs Go to School?
"Schools Then and Now," from Miss Bindergarten Celebrates the Last Day of Kindergarten
"Signs and Shapes," from Mouse Shapes
"What Can a Baby Animal Do?" from Leo the Late Bloomer
"What Will the Weather Be Like?" from What a Beautiful Sky!
"Wheels Long Ago and Today," from What Do Wheels Do All Day?
"Where Animals Live," from Turtle Splash!

254 • Teaching Genre: Informational Text

Small-Group Teaching

Small-group lessons are the individualized sessions in which you help children develop as readers based on their needs, challenges, and sometimes their preferences.

RESOURCES FOR SMALL-GROUP TEACHING
- Leveled Readers
- Leveled Readers Teacher's Guides

In **GUIDED READING** lessons, you use *Journeys* Leveled Readers to work with small groups of children who will benefit from teaching at a particular instructional level. You select the text and guide the readers by supporting their ability to use a variety of reading strategies (Fountas and Pinnell, 1996, 2001). Guided reading groups are flexible and should change as a result of your observations of your children's growth.

In this section, whole-group lessons provide the foundation for small-group instruction. Skills introduced in whole group can be developed and expanded according to children's needs in a smaller group with the appropriate level text. On the planning pages, Leveled Readers that connect to the whole-group experience are suggested, though you may need to select from the complete Leveled Readers Database (pp. 344–353) to match your children's instructional levels.

▲ JOURNEYS Leveled Readers

Select Leveled Readers according to the instructional levels of your children.

Guided Reading Level

Every Reader has been carefully analyzed and leveled by Irene Fountas, and the titles are presented in ascending order.

Reading Recovery Level

Each Reader has been assessed with a quantitative readability score, indicating its Lexile level.

Genre

The Leveled Readers have been written in a wide variety of genres, directly corresponding to those of the Anchor Texts with which they appear. Instruction for and additional information about each genre can be found in the Teaching Genre section of this Guide.

Leveled Readers Database

	Title	Grade	DRA	Lexile		Genre	Word Count
	Animals in the Woods	K	A	BR	A, B	Informational Text	15
	Apples	K ▲	A	BR	A, B	Realistic Fiction	25
	Aquarium, The	K ◆	1	BR	1	Informational Text	29
	At School	K-VR	A	BR	A, B	Informational Text	20
	At the Aquarium	K ▲	1	BR	1	Informational Text	24
	At the Playground	K ▲	1	BR	1	Informational Text	20
	At the Pond	K ●	A	BR	A, B	Realistic Fiction	25
	At the Zoo	K ▲	A	BR	A, B	Fiction	20
	Baker, The	K ●	A	30	A, B	Realistic Fiction	25
	Bears Through the Year	K ▲	A	BR	A, B	Fiction	20
	Bug Parts	K ●	1	BR	1	Informational Text	22
	Bugs for Dinner	K ●	A	180	A, B	Informational Text	35
	Bugs!	K-VR	1	70	1	Informational Text	21
	Choosing a Pet	K ◆	A	BR	A, B	Informational Text	31
	Curious George and the Animals	K ◆	1	90	1	Fiction	29
	Curious George and the Hungry Animals	K ▲	1	90	1	Fiction	23
	Curious George Visits Animal Friends	K ●	1	BR	1	Fiction	26
	Day at School, A	K ▲	1	BR	1	Fiction	15
	Feeding Our Pets	K ▲	1	10	1	Informational Text	25
A	Find the Bug	K ▲	1	70	1	Informational Text	30
A	Fire Fighter, The	K ●	1	BR	1	Informational Text	25
A	Four Frogs	K ◆	A	BR	A, B	Realistic Fiction	25
A	Fun All Year	K ▲	1	BR	1	Informational Text	25
A	Fun at Camp	K ◆	1	BR	1	Fiction	35
A	Garden, The	K ◆	1	BR	1	Informational Text	27
A	Going for a Hay Ride	K ◆	A	BR	A, B	Informational Text	26
A	Hay Ride, The	K ▲	A	BR	A, B	Informational Text	16
A	I Can Do It!	K ●	A	BR	A, B	Informational Text	25
A	In My Yard	K ●	A	BR	A, B	Informational Text	28
A	In the City	K ●	A	BR	A, B	Informational Text	20

344 • Leveled Readers Database

TEACHER'S ROLE

GUIDED READING

- Form groups based on children's instructional levels.
- Establish routines and meeting times.
- Select and introduce the book.
- Monitor children's reading through the use of running records and specific questioning.
- Record observations.

LITERATURE DISCUSSION

- Form groups based on children's reading preferences.
- Demonstrate routines for effective discussion.
- Facilitate discussions, and redirect student talk as needed.
- Summarize children's ideas and engage them in self-evaluation of their contributions.

CHILD'S ROLE

GUIDED READING

- Apply skills learned during whole-group instruction.
- Share ideas.
- Make connections to other readings and to own experiences.
- Ask questions.
- Support thinking with evidence from the text.

LITERATURE DISCUSSION

- Choose a book.
- Prepare by reading and thinking about the text.
- Listen politely and respectfully to others.
- Share opinions and raise questions.

▼ JOURNEYS Leveled Readers Teacher's Guides

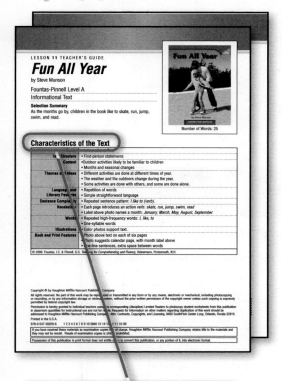

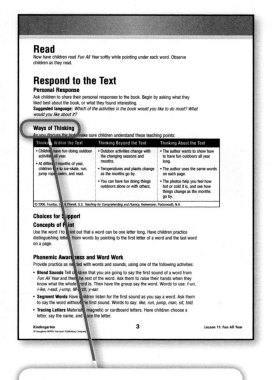

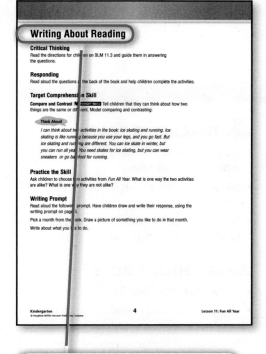

Characteristics of the Text
The qualitative features of each Reader include genre, text structure, content, book and print features, themes and ideas, language and literary features, and sentence complexity.

Ways of Thinking
The Leveled Readers Teacher's Guides outline how to lead children to read closely as they are prompted to think within, beyond, and about the text.

Writing About Reading
Children have multiple opportunities to demonstrate through writing their thinking within, beyond, and about the text they have just read.

In **LITERATURE DISCUSSION,** a small group of children of varying abilities and a common interest—a topic, a genre, or an author—selects one book to read. Each child comes prepared to discuss it.

In this collaborative group, you facilitate discussion of the book and encourage children to share their thinking and to build upon each other's ideas as they gain a deeper understanding of the text (Fountas and Pinnell, 2001).

Literature discussion groups will change as children select different books to read. Guide children to select books by encouraging them to page through a book or read a short segment in order to determine whether it is too easy or too difficult before they make a final selection.

The suggested trade book titles on pp. 354–357 are appropriate for Kindergarten children to engage in literature discussions and represent a wide variety of genres, authors, and topics.

Independent Literacy Work

Independent literacy work includes meaningful and productive activities for your children to do while you work with small groups.

INDEPENDENT READING The best way to develop reading skills is to read more. Independent reading is a time for children to explore their interests, select books that are "just right" for them, and read continuous text for an established period of time.

Support your children as they make book choices because too-hard books will only frustrate them. Teach them how to choose books that they can read with understanding and that don't present too many challenges. Having a large, accessible collection of books—whether in your classroom or in the library—is the best way to support readers.

> **Suggested Trade Book Titles**
> Select books from a variety of genres, topics, and themes for children to read independently or in Literature Discussion Groups.

TEACHER'S ROLE

- Establish classroom routines for independent work time.
- Set expectations for what children should accomplish.
- Confer with individual children to discuss books or sample oral reading.

CHILD'S ROLE

- Follow established classroom routines.
- Engage thoughtfully in reading and writing tasks.
- Take responsibility for assignments, and demonstrate progress.

Literature Discussion

For small-group literature discussion, use the suggested trade book titles on the pages that follow, or select age-appropriate texts from your library or classroom collection.

Engage children in discussions to build understanding of the text, deepen comprehension, and foster their confidence in talking about what they read. Encourage children to share their ideas about the text and also to build upon one another's ideas.

 Classic

 Science

 Social Studies

 Music

 Math

 Art

Suggested Trade Book Titles

BIOGRAPHY

Rau, Dana Meachen. *Dr. Seuss.* A brief introduction to the life of the well-loved author and illustrator Dr. Seuss. Children's Press, 2003 (32p).

Rau, Dana Meachen. *Neil Armstrong.* Intended for beginning readers, this is an introduction to the life of astronaut Neil Armstrong, the first person on the moon. Children's Press, 2003 (32p).

FANTASY

Alexander, Martha. *I'll Protect You from the Jungle Beasts.* A boy and his teddy bear reassure one another during a trip through the forest. Charlesbridge, 2006 (32p).

Brown, Lisa. *How to Be.* Siblings pretend to be various animals, then return to being themselves. HarperCollins, 2006 (32p).

Brown, Marcia. *Dick Whittington and His Cat.* A boy trades his cat for riches. Atheneum, 1988 (32p).

Bunting, Eve and Jeff Mack (il). *Hurry, Hurry!* Barnyard animals hurry to witness the hatching of a chick. Harcourt, 2007 (32p).

Carle, Eric. *The Very Hungry Caterpillar.* An insatiable young caterpillar eats his way through the book. Philomel, 1981 (32p).

Ehlert, Lois. *Leaf Man.* The elusive Leaf Man leads readers on a merry chase. Harcourt, 2005 (40p).

Ehlert, Lois. *Wag a Tail.* Find out what's on the minds of these friendly dogs as they play on their way to the park. Harcourt, 2007 (40p).

Fleming, Denise. *The Cow Who Clucked.* A cow goes in search of her missing moo, visiting other farm animals along the way. Holt, 2006 (40p).

Freeman, Don. *Corduroy.* A teddy bear, locked inside the store, comes to life to search for his missing button and eventually finds a new home. **Available in Spanish as** *Corduroy (Edición española).* Viking, 2008 (28p).

Gág, Wanda. *Millions of Cats.* A man in search of a cat has a hard time choosing among all the cats he finds. Puffin, 2006 (32p).

Geisert, Arthur. *Hogwash.* Little pigs happily get dirty and their mothers don't mind because they have a marvelous scrubbing machine to get them all clean in no time! Houghton, 2008 (32p).

Geisert, Arthur. *Lights Out.* Intricate drawings tell how a young pig concocts a device that helps him get to sleep comfortably before the lights go out at night. Houghton, 2005 (32p).

Gerstein, Mordicai. *Leaving the Nest.* A baby bird falls out of the nest and learns to fly. Foster/Farrar, 2007 (40p).

Henkes, Kevin. *A Good Day.* A bad day turns to good for four animals. Greenwillow, 2007 (24p).

Johnson, Crockett. *Harold and the Purple Crayon.* Harold demonstrates the power of imagination with a single crayon. **Available in Spanish as** *Harold y el lápiz color morado.* HarperCollins, 1958/1998 (64p).

Khing, T. T. *Where Is the Cake?* The mystery of a missing cake's whereabouts is waiting to be solved as young readers search the wordless images for clues. Abrams, 2007 (32p).

Lehman, Barbara. *Rainstorm.* This wordless picture book conveys a rainy-day adventure for a boy who finds a mysterious key. Houghton, 2007 (32p).

Lehman, Barbara. *The Red Book.* A girl in the snow and a boy on a beach connect through a mysterious red book. Houghton, 2004 (32p).

Teacher's Notes

Whole-Group Lessons

What Makes a Family?
Big Book, Lesson 1

Poems About Family
Big Book pp. 26–30, Lesson 1

Building with Dad
Read-Aloud Book, Lesson 1

▶ What Makes a Family?

INTERACTIVE READ-ALOUD/SHARED READING

Read aloud the book to children. Stop periodically for a brief interaction. Use the following suggested stopping points and prompts for quick group response, or give a specific prompt and have partners or threes turn and talk.

- At the end of page 6, say: "We learned from the book that families can have many people. Who are the people in your family?"
- At the end of page 8, ask: "How can friends and neighbors be a part of a family?"
- After reading page 18, display the photos on pages 18 and 19 and say: "Look at these pictures. How are these families helping each other?" Follow-up: "What things do you do to help your family?"
- After reading page 22, ask: "What memories does your family have? Turn and talk about your family memories with a partner."

MINILESSON Main Ideas

TEACH Display the minilesson principle on chart paper, and read it aloud. Tell children they are going to learn how to think about what the author tells mostly about.

1. Discuss the principle with children, using *What Makes a Family?* as an example. Display the title as you read it aloud. Suggested language: "Often, the title of a book is a clue to what the author wants to tell about. What word in the title is a clue that tells you what the book is mostly about?" *(family)*

> **MINILESSON PRINCIPLE**
>
> Think about what the author tells mostly about.

2. Focus on one part of the book, such as what families do together. Suggested language: "This book told about some things families can do together. What are two things families can do together?" *(Families can celebrate things like birthdays, and they can help each other.)*

3. Use children's responses to explain that authors tell mostly about one thing in books. Suggested language: "The author of this book told mostly about families. In telling mostly about families, the author told things about them, such as who is in a family, what families do, and how they help each other."

4. Elicit from children additional details that support the idea that the author tells mostly about families in this book. Record children's ideas in a Web like the one shown here.

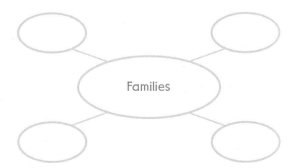

SUMMARIZE AND APPLY Restate the minilesson principle. Then tell children to apply it to a book they will listen to or read. Suggested language: "When you read, think about what the author tells mostly about."

GROUP SHARE Ask children to share what they learned from a book they listened to or read. Have children explain what the author told mostly about and how they know.

▶ Building with Dad

INTERACTIVE READ-ALOUD/SHARED READING

Read aloud the book to children. Stop periodically for a brief interaction. Use the following suggested stopping points and prompts:

- At the end of page 3, ask: "What job do you think the dad has?"
- After reading that the boy climbs in the earthmover's seat on page 10, ask: "Why does the boy get to go into the earthmover's seat? What happened right before so he could do that?"
- At the end of page 30, ask: "How does the boy feel at the end of the story? Turn and talk about your ideas with a partner. Think of words that tell about the boy."

MINILESSON Main Ideas

TEACH Display the minilesson principle on chart paper, and read it aloud to children. Explain that the author of *Building with Dad* tells mostly about one thing. Tell children they are going to think about this one thing that the author tells about.

1. Remind children that the title of a book often has a clue about the main idea of the book. Display and reread the title. Suggested language: "The title of this book gives you a clue about what the author tells mostly about. What word in the title *Building with Dad* is a clue that tells you what the book is mostly about?" *(building)*

> **MINILESSON PRINCIPLE**
>
> Think about what the author tells mostly about.

2. Reread page 6 to children. Suggested language: "There are many steps to building a school. What step did the author just tell about?" *(the first one)*

3. Talk with children about the other steps the author wrote about. Explain to children that building is what the author mostly tells about in this book and that these steps tell about building. Fill in a Web with children's responses about the steps. Write *Building* in the middle circle and the steps to building the school in the outside circles.

SUMMARIZE AND APPLY Restate the minilesson principle. Tell children to apply it to a book they will listen to or read. Suggested language: "When you read, think about what the author tells mostly about. Look for a clue in the title and other parts of the story."

GROUP SHARE Have children share what the author told mostly about in a story they listened to or read.

▶ Poems About Family

INTERACTIVE READ-ALOUD/SHARED READING

Read aloud the poems to children. Stop periodically for a brief interaction. Use the following suggested stopping points and prompts:

- After you read "Frère Jacques," ask: "What is this poem about?" Follow-up: "What do the words *ding, ding, dong* tell about?"
- After you read "My Little Sister," ask: "What is this poem about?" Follow-up: "Why do you think the sister is not very neat? Turn and talk about your ideas with a partner."

MINILESSON Genre: Poetry

TEACH Remind children that they have read four poems: "Frère Jacques," "Everybody Says," "Tortillas for Mommy," and "My Little Sister." Display the minilesson principle on chart paper, and read it aloud to children. Tell children they are going to think about what they notice in a poem.

1. Introduce repetition in poetry by having children sing Frère Jacques. Suggested language: "Some poems have words that are said more than once. How many times did you sing *Are you sleeping?*" *(two times)* Follow-up: "How many times did you sing Brother John?" *(two times)* Repeat with the phrases *Morning bells are ringing* and *ding, ding, dong.* Tell children that they can look for words in a poem that are said more than once. Continue the discussion of repeated words with the Spanish nursery rhyme "Tortillas para mamá."

> **MINILESSON PRINCIPLE**
>
> Think about what you notice in this poem.

2. Model how to notice rhyming words in poems. Read aloud the English adaptation "Tortillas for Mommy," emphasizing the rhyming words *yummy* and *tummy* and *round* and *browned.* Then say the rhyming words in isolation: *yummy, tummy; round, browned.* Say: "These words have the same ending sound. They rhyme."

3. Read aloud the poems "Everybody Says" and "My Little Sister." Ask children to share what they notice in these poems, prompting them to recognize repeating words and rhyming words.

SUMMARIZE AND APPLY Restate the minilesson principle. Tell children to apply it to a poem they will listen to or read. Suggested language: "When you listen to or read a poem, listen and look for words that are said more than once. Listen for words that have the same ending sounds."

GROUP SHARE Ask children to tell about a poem that they listened to or read. Have them share what they noticed.

Whole-Group Lessons

How Do Dinosaurs Go to School?
Big Book, Lesson 2

My School Bus
Big Book pp. 31–38, Lesson 2

Friends at School
Read-Aloud Book, Lesson 2

▶ How Do Dinosaurs Go to School?

INTERACTIVE READ-ALOUD/SHARED READING

Read aloud the book to children. Stop periodically for a brief interaction. Use the following suggested stopping points and prompts for quick group response, or give a specific prompt and have partners or threes turn and talk.

- At the end of page 3, say: "People can get from one place to another in different ways. What are some ways children can get to school?" Follow-up: "Could a large animal like a dinosaur get to school in the same ways that children do?"
- At the end of page 15, ask: "Do you think the dinosaur on these pages is a good classmate? Why or why not?"
- After reading page 30, say: "In this story, some things could not happen in real life. What is one thing in the story that could not happen in real life?"

MINILESSON Understanding Characters

TEACH Display the minilesson principle on chart paper, and read it aloud to children. Tell children they are going to learn to think about who the story is about.

> **MINILESSON PRINCIPLE**
>
> Think about who the story is about.

1. Discuss the principle with children, using examples from *How Do Dinosaurs Go to School?* Display the title page of the book and reread the title. Suggested language: "When authors write a story, they decide who the story will be about. A story can be about a person or an animal. The pictures and the title of a story often give clues. What do you see in the picture?" *(a dinosaur and a girl)* Follow-up: "What word in the title *How Do Dinosaurs Go to School?* tells you who the story might be about?" *(Dinosaurs)*

2. Explain to children that understanding the characters in a story will make the story more enjoyable. Suggested language: "If you understand who the story is about, you will enjoy the story more. This story is about dinosaurs who go to school and the things they might do."

3. Reread pages 10–19 aloud. Then say: "What are some of the silly ways a dinosaur might behave at school?" *(interrupting other children, yelling, fidgeting, talking out of turn)* Follow-up: "How do you think the children and teachers would feel about the dinosaurs if they behaved in these ways?"

4. Reread pages 22–25. Point out that in this part of the story, the author shows better ways for a dinosaur to behave at school. Have children tell what other things the dinosaurs do. Fill in a Web like the one below, using children's responses.

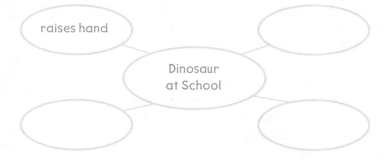

SUMMARIZE AND APPLY Restate the minilesson principle. Then tell children to apply it to a book they will listen to or read. Suggested language: "When you read, think about who the story is about."

GROUP SHARE Ask children to tell about a story they listened to or read. Have them tell who the story was about.

▶ Friends at School

INTERACTIVE READ-ALOUD/SHARED READING

Read aloud the book to children. Stop periodically for a brief interaction. Use the following suggested stopping points and prompts:

• After you read page 4, say: "In this book, we learn about the children who go to school. Who else is at the school?" Follow-up: "What do you think the children learn from Mocha, Sam, and Sara?"

• After you read page 12, ask: "What things do you like to do at school? Turn and talk with your partner about your favorite things to do."

• At the end of the book, say: "Think about what the children do in the book. Do you think they learn a lot each day? Tell why."

MINILESSON Main Ideas

TEACH Display the minilesson principle on chart paper, and read it aloud to children. Tell children they are going to learn how to think about what the author tells mostly about.

1. Discuss the principle with children, using *Friends at School* as an example. Display the title as you read it aloud. Suggested language: "Remember that the title and pictures in a book can give clues to what the author wants to tell about. What do you see in the picture?" *(children)* Follow-up: "What word in the title *Friends at School* is a clue that tells you what the book is mostly about?" *(Friends)*

> **MINILESSON PRINCIPLE**
> Think about what the author tells mostly about.

2. Focus on the activities the children in the book do. Suggested language: "The author told some things that the children did at school. Can you tell two things that the children did?" *(Possible responses: played counting games and sang songs)*

3. Explain to children that authors tell mostly about one thing. Guide them in understanding that the author of this book tells mostly about friends and what they do at school. Create a Web with *Friends at School* in the middle circle. For the outer circles, elicit from children what friends do at school.

SUMMARIZE AND APPLY Restate the minilesson principle. Tell children to apply it to a book they will listen to or read. Suggested language: "When you read, think about what the author tells mostly about. Think about how you know what that one thing is."

GROUP SHARE Ask children to share what they learned from a book they listened to or read. Have children explain what the author told mostly about.

▶ My School Bus

INTERACTIVE READ-ALOUD/SHARED READING

Read aloud the book to children. Stop periodically for a brief interaction. Use the following suggested stopping points and prompts:

• At the end of page 33, ask: "Do you think this book tells about things that could really happen, or is it a made-up story? How do you know?"

• At the end of the book, say: "What things do you see on your way to school? Turn and talk with a partner about the things you see."

MINILESSON Genre: Informational Text

TEACH Display the minilesson principle on chart paper, and read it aloud. Tell children they are going to think about what the pictures show in *My School Bus*.

1. Introduce children to the idea that pictures give important information. Display page 31 and reread the title and text. Suggested language: "How many pictures do you see on the page? What do they show?" *(two; They both show school buses.)* Follow-up: "How are these pictures different?" *(The large one is a photo and the small one is a drawing.)*

> **MINILESSON PRINCIPLE**
> Think about what the pictures in the book show you.

2. As you review pages 32–35 of the book, point out to children that each page shows two pictures. Ask: "What does the large picture show? How is the small picture like the large one?" *(The small picture shows the same thing as the large one.)* Follow-up: "Can you guess why the author has the small pictures on each page?" *(The small pictures go with the map.)*

3. Display the map on pages 36 and 37. Ask: "What can you find out by looking at this map?" *(all the things the girl sees on her way to school)* Explain to children that the small pictures on the previous pages are places on the map. Point to each picture on the map and have children tell what the girl sees on her way to school. For each picture on the map, point out the matching small illustration.

SUMMARIZE AND APPLY Restate the minilesson principle. Tell children to apply it to a book they will listen to or read. Suggested language: "When you read, think about what the pictures show you. They help you understand what you are reading."

GROUP SHARE Ask children to show examples of pictures in a book they listened to or read. Have them explain what the pictures show.

Whole-Group Lessons

Please, Puppy, Please
Big Book, Lesson 3

Different Kinds of Dogs
Big Book pp. 32–38, Lesson 3

I Have a Pet!
Read-Aloud Book, Lesson 3

▶ Please, Puppy, Please

INTERACTIVE READ-ALOUD/SHARED READING

Read aloud the book to children. Stop periodically for a brief interaction. Use the following suggested stopping points and prompts for quick group response, or give a specific prompt and have partners or threes turn and talk.

- At the end of page 4, ask: "What did the puppy do when it stayed inside?" Follow-up: "Why do you think the puppy did this?"
- At the end of page 7, ask: "Where is the puppy going? What do you think will happen next?"
- At the end of page 8, point to the text and say: "The author wrote the word *please* four times. What do you notice about the letters in this word each time it is written?" Follow-up: "Why do you think that the author wrote the letters bigger each time?"
- At the end of the book, ask: "Do you think the puppy is a good puppy? Tell why or why not."

MINILESSON Story Structure

TEACH Display the minilesson principle on chart paper, and read it aloud to children. Tell children they are going to learn to think about where the story happens.

1. Discuss the principle with children, using examples from *Please, Puppy, Please*. Suggested language: "Stories tell about places. The places in a story help you picture in your mind what happens in the story. At the beginning of the story, where were the children and their puppy?" *(inside their home)* Follow-up: "What did the inside of their home look like?" *(messy after the puppy chewed up the newspaper)*

> **MINILESSON PRINCIPLE**
>
> Think about where the story happens.

2. Point out to children that sometimes the places in a story change. Display and reread page 5. Suggested language: "Where are the children and puppy now?" *(still inside their home)* "The children said, 'Let's go play.' Where did they go?" *(in their backyard)* Follow-up: "Think about what the backyard is like. What words can you think of that tell about this place?" *(Possible responses: big place to play in; it has soft grass; it has a broken gate)*

3. Continue discussing the places in the story with children. Have them tell in their own words what the place is like and what happens in each place. Use children's responses to fill in a Column Chart like the one shown below.

Place	What It Is like	What Happens There

SUMMARIZE AND APPLY Restate the minilesson principle. Then tell children to apply it to a book they will listen to or read. Suggested language: "When you read, think about where the story happens."

GROUP SHARE Ask children to tell about the place in a book they listened to or read. Have them tell what the place was like and what happened.

▶ I Have a Pet!

INTERACTIVE READ-ALOUD/SHARED READING

Read aloud the book to children. Stop periodically for a brief interaction. Use the following suggested stopping points and prompts:

- After you read about Bucky on page 7, ask: "What things can Bucky do?" Follow-up: "What things does the boy do to take care of Bucky?"
- After you read page 15, ask: "What does the girl love about George?" Follow-up: "What can George do that Bucky and Fern cannot do?"
- At the end of the book, ask: "Do you have a pet? Turn and talk with a partner about your pet or a pet you would like to have."

MINILESSON Story Structure

TEACH Display the minilesson principle on chart paper, and read it aloud to children. Tell children they are going to think about what happens in a story.

1. Use *I Have a Pet!* to discuss the idea that readers learn what happens in a story by reading the words and looking at the pictures. Suggested language: "The story *I Have a Pet!* is about children who brought their pets to a show. The judge was supposed to give a prize to the best pet. What happened at the beginning of the story?" *(A boy told the judge about his dog Bucky.)* Follow-up: "What happened next?" *(A girl told about her cat Fern.)*

> **MINILESSON PRINCIPLE**
>
> Think about what happens in the story.

2. Display pages 16 and 17 and say, "Pictures can tell you what happens in a story. What does this picture tell you about what happened?" *(The pets got away from the children. The pets were misbehaving.)*

3. Work with children to retell the remaining events in the story. You may wish to record their responses in a Flow Chart.

SUMMARIZE AND APPLY Restate the minilesson principle. Tell children to apply it to a book they will listen to or read. Suggested language: "When you read, think about what happens in the story. Use both the pictures and the words to help you."

GROUP SHARE Have children tell what happened in a story they listened to or read. Have them tell how they learned what happened in the story.

▶ Different Kinds of Dogs

INTERACTIVE READ-ALOUD/SHARED READING

Read aloud the book to children. Stop periodically for a brief interaction. Use the following suggested stopping points and prompts:

- After you read the first page, say: "Some books tell stories that are made-up. Some books tell about real things. What kind of book is *Different Kinds of Dogs*?" Follow-up: "How do you know?"
- At the end of page 35, ask: "Which kind of dog do you think could run faster—a tall dog or a short dog?"
- At the end of the book, point out the labels in the diagram of the dog and ask: "What do these words tell about the picture of the dog?" Follow-up: "Can you think of another animal that you can write these words for?"

MINILESSON Main Ideas

TEACH Explain to children that *Different Kinds of Dogs* is different from the other two books they read this week because it tells about real animals. Display the minilesson principle on chart paper, and read it aloud. Tell children they are going to learn how to think about what the author tells mostly about.

1. Display the title as you read it aloud. Suggested language: "Remember that the title of a book is a clue to what the author wants to tell about. Pictures can also give clues. What do the pictures show?" *(real dogs)* Follow-up: "What word in the title is a clue that tells you what the book is mostly about?" *(Dogs)*

> **MINILESSON PRINCIPLE**
>
> Think about what the author tells mostly about.

2. As you page through the book, point out to children that each page tells about different sizes and shapes of dogs. Ask: "What is the same about each page in this book?" *(They all tell about dogs.)*

3. Fill in a Web with the word *Dogs* in the middle circle. Review with children the descriptions of dogs in the book and use their responses to fill in the outside circles. Use the Web to explain that the author of this book tells mostly about dogs.

SUMMARIZE AND APPLY Restate the minilesson principle. Tell children to apply it to a book they will listen to or read. Suggested language: "When you read, think about what the author tells mostly about. Use the title and pictures to help you."

GROUP SHARE Ask children to share what they learned from a book they listened to or read. Have children explain what the author told mostly about and how they know.

Whole-Group Lessons

Everybody Works
Big Book, Lesson 4

The Elves and the Shoemaker;
The Lion and the Mouse
Big Book pp. 31–38, Lesson 4

Pizza at Sally's
Read-Aloud Book, Lesson 4

▶ **Everybody Works**

INTERACTIVE READ-ALOUD/SHARED READING

Read aloud the book to children. Stop periodically for a brief interaction. Use the following suggested stopping points and prompts for quick group response, or give a specific prompt and have partners or threes turn and talk.

- At the end of page 6, ask: "Do you think this book tells about real people, or is it a made-up story? How do you know?"
- At the end of page 8, ask: "What do these pictures show?" Follow-up: "Why do you think the authors chose those pictures?"
- At the end of page 23, say: "Volunteers are people who offer their help even though they do not earn money for their work. Volunteers work because they want to help others. Have you ever volunteered to help your parents or someone else?"
- At the end of the book, ask: "What jobs do you do now? What job would you like to have when you grow up? Turn and talk with your partner about the jobs you do and what job you would like to have."

MINILESSON Genre: Informational Text

TEACH Display the minilesson principle on chart paper, and read it aloud to children. Tell children they are going to learn to notice what the people in the story do.

1. Discuss the principle with children, using examples from *Everybody Works*. Display the photos on page 3. Suggested language: "In this book, you learned that everybody works in different ways. Who are the people in these pictures?" *(sailors, a doctor and a patient, sanitation workers, caregiver and children)* Follow-up: "What work are they doing?" *(sailors work in the Navy to protect our country; doctors keep people healthy; sanitation workers help keep cities clean; caregivers take care of people who need help)*

> **MINILESSON PRINCIPLE**
>
> Notice what the people in the story do.

2. Focus on one part of the book, such as the places where people work. Reread pages 18–21. Suggested language: "You learned about some places where people work. Can you name places where people work?" *(Possible responses: in an office; at home; outside; or travel from place to place.)* Follow-up: "The authors wrote that some people travel from place to place. Look at the pictures. What are the jobs that take people from place to place?" *(train conductor; school bus driver)*

3. Continue to page through the book and have children identify the jobs people and animals do. Record children's responses in a T-Map like the one shown here.

What the Picture Shows	What Job the Person or Animal Has

SUMMARIZE AND APPLY Restate the minilesson principle. Then tell children to apply it to a book they will listen to or read. Suggested language: "When you read, notice what the people or animals in the book do. Use pictures to help you."

GROUP SHARE Ask children to tell about the people or animals in a book they listened to or read. Have them tell what the people or animals do.

▶ Pizza at Sally's

INTERACTIVE READ-ALOUD/SHARED READING

Read aloud the book to children. Stop periodically for a brief interaction. Use the following suggested stopping points and prompts:

- After you read page 6, say: "The author told you that wheat is a plant that is grown by farmers. The wheat is made into flour. The flour is used to make bread and pizzas. You also read that milk is made into cheese. Where does the milk come from?" *(cows)*
- After you read page 20, say: "There are several steps in making a pizza. What did Sally do first?" *(She made the sauce.)* Follow-up: "What did Sally do next?" *(She made the pizza dough.)*
- At the end of the book, say: "You can put different toppings on a pizza, such as mushrooms or pepperoni. What toppings would you put on a pizza? Turn and talk about your favorite toppings with a partner."

MINILESSON Text and Graphic Features

TEACH Display the minilesson principle on chart paper, and read it aloud. Tell children they are going to think about what the pictures show in *Pizza at Sally's*.

1. Remind children that pictures give important information. Display page 2 and reread the text. Then ask: "What pictures do you see on the page?" *(tomatoes, garden tools, newsletter, a seed packet, a snail, a worm, and a ladybug)* Follow-up: "These pictures are all the same in one way. How are they the same?" *(They all show something to do with growing tomatoes.)*

> **MINILESSON PRINCIPLE**
>
> Think about what the pictures show you.

2. Display page 6 and reread the text. Then ask: "What pictures do you see on this page?" *(different kinds of cheese, butter, yogurt, milk, cream, and ice cream)* Follow-up: "How are these pictures all the same?" *(They all show something about milk and things that can be made from milk.)*

3. Continue to page through the book and have children identify what is common among the grouped pictures. Record children's responses in a T-Map labeled *What the Pictures Show* and *How They Are the Same.*

SUMMARIZE AND APPLY Restate the minilesson principle. Tell children to apply it to a book they will listen to or read. Suggested language: "When you read, think about what the pictures show you."

GROUP SHARE Ask children to show examples of pictures in a book they listened to or read. Have them explain what the pictures show.

▶ The Elves and the Shoemaker; The Lion and the Mouse

INTERACTIVE READ-ALOUD/SHARED READING

Read aloud the book to children. Stop periodically for a brief interaction. Use the following suggested stopping points and prompts:

- After you read *The Elves and the Shoemaker,* ask: "Why do you think the elves helped the shoemaker?"
- After you read *The Lion and the Mouse,* ask: "Do you think you could help someone who is bigger than you are? Tell how you might help."
- After reading both stories, say: "Tell about some of the things in both stories that could not happen in real life."

MINILESSON Genre: Traditional Tales

TEACH Display the minilesson principle on chart paper, and read it aloud to children. Explain to children that *The Elves and the Shoemaker* and *The Lion and the Mouse* are fables. Tell them that a fable is a story that has a lesson. Tell children they are going to think about how the characters in the stories learn lessons.

1. Use *The Elves and the Shoemaker* to discuss the principle. Suggested language: "Tell what you know about the elves." *(They worked hard; they were kind.)* Follow-up: "Why do you think the shoemaker and his wife made clothes and shoes for the elves?" *(The elves had torn clothes and no shoes; the elves were kind to the shoemaker and his wife, so they wanted to be kind to the elves.)* "What lesson did the shoemaker and his wife learn?" *(Helping others is important.)*

> **MINILESSON PRINCIPLE**
>
> Think about the lesson the characters learn in the story.

2. Use *The Lion and the Mouse* to discuss the principle in a similar way. Suggested language: "How did the lion treat the mouse at the beginning of the story?" *(The lion was mean. He wanted to eat the mouse because the mouse woke him up.)* Follow-up: "What did the mouse do to help the lion?" *(She chewed the net and freed the lion.)* "What lesson did the lion learn?" *(He learned that little friends can help just as much as big friends.)*

SUMMARIZE AND APPLY Restate the minilesson principle. Tell children to apply it to a book they will listen to or read. Suggested language: "When you read, think about the lesson a story character learns."

GROUP SHARE Ask children to tell about a character from a book they listened to or read who learned a lesson.

Whole-Group Lessons

The Handiest Things in the World
Big Book, Lesson 5

Stone Soup
Big Book pp. 40–44, Lesson 5

The Little Red Hen
Read-Aloud Book, Lesson 5

▶ The Handiest Things in the World

INTERACTIVE READ-ALOUD/SHARED READING

Read aloud the book to children. Stop periodically for very brief discussion of the text. Use the suggested stopping points and prompts below for quick group response, or give a specific prompt and have partners or threes turn and talk.

- After reading the first three pages, ask: "What do you think this book will be about? Why do you think so?"
- After reading about pouring, ask: "What are some things that your hands help you do? *(eat, hold a dog, count, pour water)* Follow-up: "How do the tools that are shown in the photos help you do those things easier?"
- After reading about pushing air, ask: "How do the photos help you understand what the author is saying?" *(The photos show what hands can do and then they show a tool that can help you do the same thing.)*
- At the end, ask: "Can you think of other things your hands do? What new tools might help your hands do those things better? Turn and talk about your ideas with a partner."

MINILESSON Details

TEACH Display the minilesson principle on chart paper, and read it aloud to children. Tell children that they are going to think about how the pictures in a book can help them understand it better.

1. Discuss the principle with children using examples from *The Handiest Things in the World*. Reread pages 4–5 aloud. Suggested language: "We read that we can use our hands to eat. What tools can we use to help us eat without getting our fingers dirty?" *(chopsticks)* Follow-up: "How did you learn this?" *(The photo shows a boy using chopsticks to eat.)*

> **MINILESSON PRINCIPLE**
>
> Notice things in the pictures to help you understand a book.

2. Reread pages 6–7. Ask: "What can you use to hold a dog more easily? *(a leash)* Follow-up: "How do you know?" *(The photo shows a boy using his hands to hold a dog, and then shows him using a leash. It looks easier to use a leash.)*

3. Continue paging through the book, having children tell how details in the photos helped them understand what the author was saying. Record children's responses in a T-Map like the one shown here.

What Hands Do	What Tool Can Do It

SUMMARIZE AND APPLY Restate the minilesson principle. Tell children to apply it to a book they will listen to or read. Suggested language: "When you read a book, notice things in the pictures to help you understand it."

GROUP SHARE Ask children to tell about something they learned from a picture in a book they listened to or read.

▶ The Little Red Hen

INTERACTIVE READ-ALOUD/SHARED READING

Read aloud the book to children. Stop periodically for a brief interaction. Use the following suggested stopping points and prompts:

- After you read page 10, ask: "What words can you use to tell about the dog, the cat, and the mouse?" Follow-up: "What is the hen like?"
- After you read page 16, say: "In this story, there are words that have the same ending sound." Reread the text, emphasizing the rhyming words. "What words have the same ending sound?"
- At the end of the book, ask: "Do you think the Little Red Hen's friends will be more willing to help next time? Turn and talk about your ideas with a partner."

MINILESSON Details

TEACH Display the minilesson principle on chart paper, and read it aloud to children. Tell children that they are going to think about how details give more information about what is happening in a story.

1. Discuss the principle with children using examples from *The Little Red Hen*. Suggested language: "We read that the Little Red Hen made a cake. Why did she decide to bake a cake?" *(She found wheat seeds.)*

> **MINILESSON PRINCIPLE**
>
> Think about how the details in a story help you better understand why things happen.

2. Guide children to notice details that helped them understand the story. Suggested language: "We read that the Little Red Hen asked her friends for help making the cake. Why do you think she asked for help?" *(It was a lot of work.)* Follow-up: "What details helped you know this?" *(To make the cake, the Little Red Hen had to plant seeds, cut wheat, and grind flour.)*

3. Continue in the same way, asking about details that helped them understand the story. Suggested Language: "How do you think the Little Red Hen felt when the other animals did not help her?" *(upset)* Follow-up: "What details helped you know this?" *(She did not share the cake with them.)*

SUMMARIZE AND APPLY Restate the minilesson principle. Tell children to apply it to a story they will listen to or read. Suggested language: "When you read a story, notice how the details help you understand what is happening."

GROUP SHARE Ask children to share details in a story they listened to or read. Have them tell what the details helped them to understand.

▶ Stone Soup

INTERACTIVE READ-ALOUD/SHARED READING

Read aloud the story to children. Stop periodically for brief discussion of the text. Use the following suggested stopping points and prompts:

- After reading that the villagers don't share their food, ask: "Why do you think the villagers don't share with their neighbors or the traveler?" *(They are afraid they will run out of food.)*
- After reading that the villagers add food to the soup, ask: "What makes the villagers share their food?" *(They want to make the soup taste better.)*
- At the end, ask: "Why do you think the traveler's idea about making stone soup worked? Turn and talk about your ideas with a partner."

MINILESSON Genre: Folktale

TEACH Display the minilesson principle on chart paper, and read it aloud to children. Explain that folktales are stories that have been told over and over for many years. Tell them that they are going to think about how folktales often teach a lesson.

1. Discuss the principle with children, focusing on the characters in *Stone Soup*. Suggested language: "In *Stone Soup*, the villagers did not have enough food to share with the traveler. What did the traveler do to trick the villagers into sharing food?" *(He told them how good the stone soup was and how it would be better with just a little something added to it.)*

> **MINILESSON PRINCIPLE**
>
> Think about how folktales often teach a lesson.

2. Tell children that a lesson in a story is often shown by how the characters change in the story. Ask: "What did the villagers do to change?" *(They started sharing their food.)* Follow-up: "What did they learn from the traveler?" *(that sharing made it better for everyone)*

3. Explain that a lesson that characters learn in a story is also a lesson for everyone who reads the story. Discuss how this lesson might help them in their own lives.

SUMMARIZE AND APPLY Restate the minilesson principle. Tell children to apply it to a story they will listen to or read. Suggested language: "When you read, think about the lesson the author is trying to teach."

GROUP SHARE Ask children to explain the lesson that the author teaches in a story they listened to or read.

Whole-Group Lessons

My Five Senses
Big Book, Lesson 6

Poems About Senses
Big Book pp. 32–38, Lesson 6

Listen, Listen
Read-Aloud Book, Lesson 6

▶ My Five Senses

INTERACTIVE READ-ALOUD/SHARED READING

Read aloud the book to children. Stop periodically for a brief interaction. Use the following suggested stopping points and prompts for quick group response, or give a specific prompt and have partners or threes turn and talk.

- After reading the title page, ask: "What do these pictures show?" Follow-up: "Why do you think the author chose those pictures?"
- At the end of page 8, say: "There are things that taste good and things that taste bad. What are things you like to taste? Turn and talk with a partner about your ideas."
- Display page 11 and say: "The boy is touching a rabbit. How do you think the rabbit's fur feels?" Follow-up: "Can you think of something else that feels soft?"
- At the end of the book, ask: "What senses do you use when you eat a cookie?"

MINILESSON Text and Graphic Features

TEACH Display the minilesson principle on chart paper, and read it aloud to children. Tell children they are going to think about what the pictures show in *My Five Senses*.

1. Remind children that pictures give important information. Display page 2 and have children describe what they see. Suggested language: "What can you tell about this boy's face?" *(He has big eyes.)*

   > **MINILESSON PRINCIPLE**
   >
   > Think about what the pictures show you.

2. Reread the text on page 3 to children and guide them in understanding that the picture helps them understand the words. Suggested language: "We can see that the boy's big eyes are open. Then we read that the boy can see with his eyes. The picture helps you understand the words."

3. Continue to page through the book, matching the illustrations with the text. Record children's responses in a T-Map like the one shown here. Remind children that the pictures help them understand what the five senses are.

What the Picture Shows	What the Sense Is

SUMMARIZE AND APPLY Restate the minilesson principle. Then tell children to apply it to a book they will listen to or read. Suggested language: "When you read, think about what the pictures show you. They help you understand what you are reading."

GROUP SHARE Ask children to show examples of pictures in a book they listened to or read. Have them explain what the pictures show.

▶ Listen, Listen

INTERACTIVE READ-ALOUD/SHARED READING

Read aloud the book to children. Stop periodically for a brief interaction. Use the following suggested stopping points and prompts:

- Show children the illustrations on pages 2–5 and ask: "What do you see in these pictures?" *(bugs, people at the beach)* Follow-up: "What time of the year do you think these pictures show?" *(summer)*

- After you read page 11, say: "Some words have the same ending sound." Reread the text, emphasizing the rhyming words *fly* and *cry* and ask: "What words have the same ending sound?" Follow-up: "What do the words *whoosh* and *whoo* mean?"

- At the end of the book, ask: "What is your favorite time of the year? Why? Turn and talk with a partner about your favorite time of the year."

MINILESSON Compare and Contrast

TEACH Display the minilesson principle on chart paper, and read it aloud to children. Tell children they are going to learn how to think about the ways in which things in a book are different.

> **MINILESSON PRINCIPLE**
>
> Think about how things in the book are different.

1. Discuss the principle with children, using *Listen, Listen* as an example. Suggested language: "In *Listen, Listen,* you learned about summer, autumn, winter, and spring. These are all seasons. In which season can you go swimming outside?" *(summer)*

2. Focus on the differences between summer and winter. Suggested language: "Think about the weather in summer and in winter. How is the weather in summer different from the weather in winter?" *(Summer is hot; winter is cold.)* Follow-up: "What things can you do in the summer? What things can you do in the winter?"

3. Elicit from children more examples of how summer and winter are different. Record children's ideas in a Venn Diagram. Label the left circle *Summer* and the right circle *Winter*. Label the intersection of the circles *Both*.

SUMMARIZE AND APPLY Restate the minilesson principle. Tell children to apply it to a book they will listen to or read. Suggested language: "When you read a book, think about how things in it are different."

GROUP SHARE Have children tell about two things, animals, or people from a book they listened to or read. Have them tell how the two things, animals, or people are different.

▶ Poems About Senses

INTERACTIVE READ-ALOUD/SHARED READING

Read aloud the poems to children. Stop periodically for a brief interaction. Use the following suggested stopping points and prompts:

- After you read "Picnic Day," say: "Some words have the same ending sound." Reread the text, emphasizing the rhyming words *trees/breeze, grass/glass, lemonade/shade.* Ask: "What words have the same ending sound?"

- After you read "Five Wonderful Senses," ask: "What is the nicest sound you have ever heard? Turn and talk with a partner about why it was a nice sound."

MINILESSON Genre: Poetry

TEACH Display the minilesson principle on chart paper, and read it aloud to children. Remind children that they have read four poems. Explain that these poems use words that tell how things look, feel, smell, taste, and sound.

1. Reread "Picnic Day" to children. Then say: "This poem tells about all five senses that we learned about in *My Five Senses.* What words did the poet use to help you understand what the five senses are?" *(see, smell, feel, hear, taste)*

> **MINILESSON PRINCIPLE**
>
> Notice words that tell you how things look, feel, smell, taste, and sound.

2. Repeat the first step with the poem "Five Wonderful Senses." Then guide children to notice that the poet also wrote the body parts that go with the senses. Suggested language: "The poet tells how she can taste. What word did the poet use to tell how she can taste?" *(mouth)* Repeat this step with the other senses mentioned in the poem.

3. Reread "Here Are My Eyes" and "The Storm," and have children tell what senses these poems tell about. Have them identify the words the poets use to tell about the senses.

SUMMARIZE AND APPLY Restate the minilesson principle. Tell children to apply it to a poem they will listen to or read. Suggested language: "When you read a poem, notice the words that tell how things look, feel, smell, taste, and sound."

GROUP SHARE Ask children to share words from a poem they listened to or read. Have them explain how the words the poet used told how things look, feel, smell, taste, and sound.

Whole-Group Lessons

Mice Squeak, We Speak
Big Book, Lesson 7

The Fort Worth Zoo
Big Book pp. 32–38, Lesson 7

Amelia's Show-and-Tell Fiesta
Read-Aloud Book, Lesson 7

▶ Mice Squeak, We Speak

INTERACTIVE READ-ALOUD/SHARED READING

Read aloud the book to children. Stop periodically for a brief interaction. Use the following suggested stopping points and prompts for quick group response, or give a specific prompt and have partners or threes turn and talk.

- At the end of page 11, say: "On pages 7 and 8, we read: *Crickets creak. Mice squeak.* What words have the same ending sound?" *(creak and squeak)* Follow-up: "We read: *Sheep baa. But I speak!* What word sounds like *creak* and *squeak*?" *(speak)*
- At the end of page 16, ask: "How does the author show the dove making its sound?" *(The dove's mouth is opened and word* coo *is written four times.)* Follow-up: "What do you notice about the letters of the words the dove says?" *(The letters get bigger and bigger.)*
- After you read the book, ask: "What is your favorite animal? What sound does it make? Turn and talk with a partner about how your favorite animal sounds."

MINILESSON Compare and Contrast

TEACH Display the minilesson principle on chart paper, and read it aloud to children. Tell children they are going to learn how to think about the ways in which things in a book are different.

1. Discuss the principle with children, using *Mice Squeak, We Speak* as an example. Suggested language: "In *Mice Squeak, We Speak,* you learned that the animals and the children make different sounds. How are their sounds different?" *(Animals make sounds, but children can speak words.)* Follow-up: "Animals and people also look different. What is one way a cat is different from a person?" *(Possible response: Cats have four legs and a person has two.)*

> **MINILESSON PRINCIPLE**
>
> Think about how things in the book are different.

2. Continue in the same way by contrasting two animals from the story. Suggested language: "Now think of the cat and the lion. How are their sounds different?" *(A cat purrs and a lion roars.)* Follow-up: "Cats and lions also look different. What is one way in which cats and lions look different?" *(Cats are small and lions are big.)*

3. Use children's responses to the questions above to create a Venn Diagram like the one shown below. Explain to children that the words in the outer parts of the circles tell how cats and lions are different.

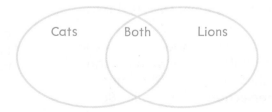

SUMMARIZE AND APPLY Restate the minilesson principle. Then tell children to apply it to a book they will listen to or read. Suggested language: "When you read a book, think about how things are different."

GROUP SHARE Have children tell about two animals, people, places, or things from a book they listened to or read. Have them tell how the two animals, people, places, or things are different.

▶ Amelia's Show-and-Tell Fiesta

INTERACTIVE READ-ALOUD/SHARED READING

Read aloud the book to children. Stop periodically for a brief interaction. Use the following suggested stopping points and prompts:

- After you read that Amelia's plans are *muy grandes* on page 4, say: "The words *muy grandes* mean 'very big.' So, Amelia has big plans that *pull her in like the tide.* Have you ever gone to the beach and felt the tide? What do you think it means that her big plans *pull her in like the tide*?"

- After you display and read page 10, say: "Amelia's dress has three fancy skirts. The author used the Spanish word *rojo* to tell about the first skirt. What clues in the words and pictures tell you what *rojo* means?"

- At the end, ask: "Would you like to have a classmate like Amelia? Turn and talk about your ideas with a partner."

MINILESSON Understanding Characters

TEACH Display the minilesson principle on chart paper, and read it aloud to children. Tell children they are going to learn to think about what the people in the story are like.

1. Using the character Amelia from *Amelia's Show-and-Tell Fiesta,* discuss how children can find clues to learn what Amelia is like. Suggested language: "In the beginning, you read that Amelia went to her new *American* school. What did the clue word *American* tell you about Amelia?" *(She was from another country.)*

> **MINILESSON PRINCIPLE**
> Think about what the people in the story are like.

2. Talk with children about how Amelia felt when she realized the other children brought things for the show-and-tell basket. Suggested language: "When Amelia's teacher called her name, why did Amelia say she made a big mistake?" *(She didn't bring anything to put in the basket.)* Follow-up: "How did Amelia feel?" *(silly, embarrassed)*

3. Discuss with children that the clues in the story, such as things Amelia did and what she said, can help them learn what Amelia was like. Page through the story to find more story clues that tell what Amelia was like. Record children's responses in a T-Map labeled *Story Clues* and *What Amelia Was Like.*

SUMMARIZE AND APPLY Restate the minilesson principle. Tell children to apply it to a book they will listen to or read. Suggested language: "When you read, think about what the people in the story are like."

GROUP SHARE Have children tell about a person from a story they listened to or read. Have them tell what that person was like.

▶ The Fort Worth Zoo

INTERACTIVE READ-ALOUD/SHARED READING

Read aloud the book to children. Stop periodically for a brief interaction. Use the following suggested stopping points and prompts:

- After you read the first page, ask: "Do you think this book tells about real people and animals, or is it a made-up story? How do you know?"

- At the end of the book, ask: "Have you ever been to a zoo?" Follow-up: "What is your favorite zoo animal? Turn and talk with a partner about your favorite animal at the zoo."

MINILESSON Genre: Informational Text

TEACH Explain to children that *The Fort Worth Zoo* is different from the other two books they read this week because it gives information about a real place and shows pictures of real animals. Display the minilesson principle on chart paper, and read it aloud. Tell children they are going to learn to notice the words that tell about the pictures.

1. Display page 33 of *The Fort Worth Zoo* to introduce the idea that the pictures and words on the pictures tell important information. Suggested language: "What animal do you see?" *(parrot)* "Point to the words at the top of the picture. They say 'Parrot Paradise.' Why do you think the author wrote these words?" *(They tell where the parrot lives in the zoo.)* "Now point to the word next to the bird. It says 'Parrot.' Why do you think the author put that word on the picture?" *(It tells what kind of animal is in the picture.)* Continue in this way with the text at the bottom of the page. Explain that these words tell even more about the parrot.

> **MINILESSON PRINCIPLE**
> Notice the words that tell about the pictures.

2. As you page through the book, point out to children the label at the top of each picture, the caption, and the text. Explain that these tell more about the picture of the animal. Suggested language: "The words at the top of the picture tell where the animal lives in the zoo. The word or words next to the animal in the picture tell what kind of animal it is. The words at the bottom of the page tell more about the animal."

SUMMARIZE AND APPLY Restate the minilesson principle. Tell children to apply it to a book they will listen to or read. Suggested language: "When you read, look for words that tell about the pictures."

GROUP SHARE Ask children to tell about words and pictures from a book they listened to or read. Have them explain how the words tell about the pictures.

Whole-Group Lessons

Move!
Big Book, Lesson 8

The Hare and the Tortoise
Big Book pp. 32–38, Lesson 8

Jonathan and His Mommy
Read-Aloud Book, Lesson 8

▶ Move!

INTERACTIVE READ-ALOUD/SHARED READING

Read aloud the book to children. Stop periodically for a brief interaction. Use the following suggested stopping points and prompts for quick group response, or give a specific prompt and have partners or threes turn and talk.

- At the end of page 3, say: "Look at the words underneath the pictures of the gibbon. Why do you think the author wrote the words this way?" *(The gibbon swings. The words are swinging like the gibbon.)*
- At the end of page 17, say: "On page 15, what animal do you see with the praying mantis?" *(the snake)* Follow-up: "Did the snake get the praying mantis? How do you know?" *(No. The praying mantis flew away.)*
- After you read the book, ask: "If you could be one of these animals, which animal would you like to be? Turn and talk with a partner about which animal you would like to be and why."

MINILESSON Details

TEACH Display the minilesson principle on chart paper, and read it aloud to children. Tell children they are going to look for words that tell what things are like.

1. Discuss the principle with children, using examples from *Move!* Suggested language: "In the book *Move!*, you learned that animals move in different ways. You can look for clues to find out more things about the animals. Look at the gibbon. Do you think a gibbon moves fast or slow? What clue helps you?" *(I think it moves fast. The words say that the gibbon swings, so it probably moves fast.)* Follow-up: "Where do you think a gibbon lives? What clue tells you?" *(It lives in the jungle. The words say that the gibbon swings through trees in the jungle.)*

> **MINILESSON PRINCIPLE**
> Notice the words in the book that tell what things are like.

2. Continue, using the jacana as an example. Suggested language: "Where do you think a jacana lives? What clues tell you?" *(It lives near water. The words say that the jacana floats on lily pads. Lily pads grow in water. The words also say that the jacana dives to catch a fish. Fish live in water.)*

3. Use children's responses to the question above to fill in an Inference Map like the one shown here. Record the clues they used in the boxes on top. Record where they think the jacana lives in the big box at the bottom.

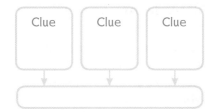

SUMMARIZE AND APPLY Restate the minilesson principle. Then tell children to apply it to a book they will listen to or read. Suggested language: "When you read a book, notice the words that tell what things are like."

GROUP SHARE Have children tell about animals, people, or things from a book they listened to or read. Have them tell what they are like and what word clues they used.

▶ Jonathan and His Mommy

INTERACTIVE READ-ALOUD/SHARED READING

Read aloud the book to children. Stop periodically for a brief interaction. Use the following suggested stopping points and prompts:

- After you read page 5, display pages 4 and 5 and say: "Pictures can help you understand what a word means. Which picture shows what the word *zigzag* means?"
- After you read page 10, ask: "Why do Jonathan and his mother wriggle their noses and ears?" *(They are pretending to be bunnies.)*
- At the end, ask: "Which walk do you like best? Turn and talk with a partner about why you like that walk."

MINILESSON Details

TEACH Display the minilesson principle on chart paper, and read it aloud to children. Tell children they are going to use pictures to learn about where people in the story live.

1. Display the cover of the book to children, and have them tell what they see in the illustration. Suggested language: "People live in different places. Some live in big cities. Some live in small towns. Others live in the country. What do you see in this picture?" *(car, building, a person sitting on steps, a plant in a windowsill)* Follow-up: "Do you think this picture shows things in a city or in the country?" *(city)*

> **MINILESSON PRINCIPLE**
>
> Notice things in the pictures that tell about where the people live.

2. Display pages 2 and 3, and have children tell what they see in the illustrations. Suggested language: "What do you notice about Jonathan and his mommy?" *(They are walking down steps of a building.)* Follow-up: "Do you think Jonathan and his mommy live in a city or do they live in the country? Why do you think so?" *(I think they live in a city. I see lots of buildings, a motorcycle, and cars on the street. If they lived in the country, there might not be so many buildings and cars on the street.)*

3. As you page through the book, point to the different urban scenes and have children tell what they see that belongs in a city. Record children's responses in a Web.

SUMMARIZE AND APPLY Restate the minilesson principle. Tell children to apply it to a book they will listen to or read. Suggested language: "When you read, notice things in the pictures that tell about where the people live."

GROUP SHARE Have children tell about people in a story they listened to or read. Have them tell what clues in the pictures help them understand where the people live.

▶ The Hare and the Tortoise

INTERACTIVE READ-ALOUD/SHARED READING

Read aloud the story to children. Stop periodically for a brief interaction. Use the following suggested stopping points and prompts:

- After you read the first page, ask: "Do you think this book tells about real animals, or is it a made-up story? How do you know?"
- At the end of the story, ask: "What lesson did the hare learn? Turn and talk with a partner about your ideas."

MINILESSON Understanding Characters

TEACH Display the minilesson principle on chart paper, and read it aloud. Tell children they are going to learn to notice what the animals in a story do to help them understand the animals.

1. Explain to children that the things the animals do can help them understand what the animals are like. Suggested language: "In the story *The Hare and the Tortoise,* the tortoise tells the hare that he could beat him in a race. What did the hare do when the tortoise said that?" *(The hare laughed at him.)* Follow-up: "Why did the hare do this?" *(He thinks the tortoise is slow. The hare thinks he is the fastest animal in the forest.)*

> **MINILESSON PRINCIPLE**
>
> Notice what the animals in the story do to help you understand them.

2. Continue the discussion of what the hare did. Suggested language: "What did the hare do when he woke up from his nap and couldn't find the tortoise?" *(He laughed again.)* Follow-up: "Why did he laugh?" *(He thought the tortoise was still far behind him in the race.)*

3. Focus on the tortoise. Suggested language: "What did the tortoise do in the beginning of the story?" *(He made a bet with the hare that he could win a race.)* Follow-up: "What did the tortoise do in the middle?" *(He walked and never stopped.)* "What happened at the end of the race?" *(The tortoise was already at the finish line. The tortoise won.)*

4. Work with children to fill in an Inference Map for each character. Record what the character does in the top three boxes. Then record what the character is like in the large box at the bottom.

SUMMARIZE AND APPLY Restate the minilesson principle. Tell children to apply it to a book they will listen to or read. Suggested language: "When you read, think about what the animals or people do to help you understand them."

GROUP SHARE Ask children to tell about a character from a book they listened to or read. Have them explain what the character was like.

Whole-Group Lessons

What Do Wheels Do All Day?
Big Book, Lesson 9

Wheels Long Ago and Today
Big Book pp. 32–38, Lesson 9

Good Morning, Digger
Read-Aloud Book, Lesson 9

▶ What Do Wheels Do All Day?

INTERACTIVE READ-ALOUD/SHARED READING

Read aloud the book to children. Stop periodically for a brief interaction. Use the following suggested stopping points and prompts for quick group response, or give a specific prompt and have partners or threes turn and talk.

- At the end of page 7, ask: "Can you think of other wheels that make us go?"
- At the end of page 21, ask: "Why did the author write that wheels sometimes *spit and sputter*? What helps you understand what she means?" *(the pictures of the cars)*
- After you read the book, ask: "What wheels do you use? Turn and talk with a partner about the wheels you use."

MINILESSON Text and Graphic Features

TEACH Display the minilesson principle on chart paper, and read it aloud to children.

1. Guide children in using pictures to understand the information in *What Do Wheels Do All Day?* Display page 5, and point to the illustration of the man pushing the banana cart. Suggested language: "What do you see in this picture?" *(a man pushing a cart)*

> **MINILESSON PRINCIPLE**
>
> Think about what you learn from the pictures.

2. Turn back to page 4, and point to the word *Push.* Ask: "How could you use what you see in the picture to figure out what this word means?" *(The cart has one wheel, and I see a man pushing the cart. So, I know that the word is push.)*

3. Continue in the same way with the picture of the dog in the wagon on page 5 and the word *pull* on page 4. Suggested language: "What do you see in the picture?" *(a dog in a wagon)* Follow-up: "How does the wagon move?" *(Someone pulls it.)* Show the word *Pull* on page 4, and point out to children that the picture tells about the word *pull.*

4. Work with other pictures and words throughout the book. Have children tell what the picture shows and what they learned from the picture. Record children's responses in a T-Map like the one shown here.

What the Picture Shows	What I Learned

SUMMARIZE AND APPLY Restate the minilesson principle. Then tell children to apply it to a book they will listen to or read. Suggested language: "When you read a book, think about what you learn from the pictures."

GROUP SHARE Have children tell about pictures in a book they listened to or read. Have them tell what they learned from the pictures.

▶ Good Morning, Digger

INTERACTIVE READ-ALOUD/SHARED READING

Read aloud the book to children. Stop periodically for a brief interaction. Use the following suggested stopping points and prompts:

- Display the book's cover to children and say: "The title and pictures can give you clues as to what the book is about. The title is *Good Morning, Digger*. What do you think this book is about?"
- After you display and read page 18, ask: "What do you think the workers are building? Turn and talk about your ideas with a partner."
- At the end, ask: "Have you ever seen big trucks like the ones in the story? What sounds did they make?"

MINILESSON Text and Graphic Features

TEACH Display the minilesson principle on chart paper, and read it aloud to children. Tell children they are going to learn to think about how the author writes letters and words in different ways.

1. Display page 3 of *Good Morning, Digger* and point to the text. Suggested language: "What do you notice about the letters and words on this page?" *(Some letters and words are darker than others.)* Reread the text on page 3, pointing to each word as you read. Follow-up: "Why do you think the letters and words *Grrr-clank!* are darker than other words?" *(This is what the digger sounds like.)*

> **MINILESSON PRINCIPLE**
>
> Think about how the author made some of the letters and words darker.

2. Reread page 8, pointing to each word as you read. Suggested language: "Why do you think the words *Rolly-roll! Rumble and rattle* are darker than the other words?" *(This is what the dump truck does and sounds like.)* Explain to children that the author of *Good Morning, Digger* wanted them to notice the sounds of the trucks. So, the author wrote these letters and words darker than the others.

3. Continue in the same way with the text on page 14. Record the name of each truck and the sound it makes in a T-Map labeled *Truck* and *What It Sounds Like*.

SUMMARIZE AND APPLY Restate the minilesson principle. Tell children to apply it to a book they will listen to or read. Suggested language: "When you read, think about why the author wrote some letters and words differently."

GROUP SHARE Have children tell about a book they listened to or read. Have them tell how the author made some of the letters and words differently than others.

▶ Wheels Long Ago and Today

INTERACTIVE READ-ALOUD/SHARED READING

Read aloud the book to children. Stop periodically for a brief interaction. Use the following suggested stopping points and prompts:

- After you read the first page, ask: "Do you think this book tells about real things or is it a made-up story? How do you know?"
- After you read page 38, say: "Each thing in these photos has a certain number of wheels. How many wheels can you count on each thing?"

MINILESSON Compare and Contrast

TEACH Display the minilesson principle on chart paper, and read it aloud. Tell children that it is important to think about how things are the same and different as they read.

1. Discuss the principle with children, using *Wheels Long Ago and Today* as an example. Review the photos with children. Suggested language: "What is this book mostly about?" *(wheels)* Follow-up: "What is the same about all the pictures in the book?" *(Every picture shows something that has wheels.)*

> **MINILESSON PRINCIPLE**
>
> Think about how things in the book are the same and how they are different.

2. Focus on the photo of the wagon on page 34 and the car on page 37 to explain how to contrast. Suggested language: "How is the wagon different from the car?" *(An animal pulled the wagon. A car doesn't need an animal to pull it.)* Follow-up: "What is the same about the wagon and the car?" *(They both have four wheels. They both helped people travel to different places.)*

3. Work with children to compare and contrast the bicycle on page 35 with bicycles children have today. Record children's responses in a Venn Diagram labeled *Bicycles Then, Both,* and *Bicycles Today*.

SUMMARIZE AND APPLY Restate the minilesson principle. Tell children to apply it to a book they will listen to or read. Suggested language: "When you read, think about how things in the book are the same and how they are different."

GROUP SHARE Ask children to tell about how things in a book they listened to or read were the same and how they were different.

Whole-Group Lessons

Mouse Shapes
Big Book, Lesson 10

Signs and Shapes
Big Book pp. 31–38, Lesson 10

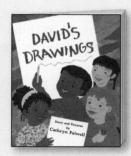

David's Drawings
Read-Aloud Book, Lesson 10

▶ Mouse Shapes

INTERACTIVE READ-ALOUD/SHARED READING

Read aloud the book to children. Stop periodically for a brief interaction. Use the following suggested stopping points and prompts for quick group response, or give a specific prompt and have partners or threes turn and talk.

- After you read page 9, ask: "Whom is the story about? What are their names?"
- At the end of page 13, ask: "What is the same about all triangles?" Follow-up: "Why do you think Violet said triangles are tricky?" *(They can be different sizes.)*
- At the end of page 23, ask: "Why did Violet wish that she and her friends were bigger?"
- After you read page 30, ask: "What shapes did the mice use to make the Swiss cheese?"

MINILESSON Story Structure

TEACH Display the minilesson principle on chart paper, and read it aloud to children. Tell children they are going to think about what happens in a story.

1. Use *Mouse Shapes* to discuss the idea that readers learn what happens in a story by reading the words and looking at the pictures. Suggested language: "The story *Mouse Shapes* is about three mice and a cat. What happens at the beginning of the story?" *(Violet, Martin, and Fred are running from the cat.)* Follow-up: "How did they get away from the cat? How do you know?" *(They hid in some shapes. The pictures showed them hiding in the shapes.)*

> **MINILESSON PRINCIPLE**
>
> Think about what happens in the story.

2. Display page 12 and say, "Pictures can tell you what happens in a story. What does this picture tell you about what happened in the middle of the story?" *(The mice made a house, a tree, and a sun with the shapes.)*

3. Work with children to retell the remaining events in the story. You may wish to record their responses in a Flow Chart labeled *Beginning, Middle,* and *End*. Guide children to identify the most important events from the story.

SUMMARIZE AND APPLY Restate the minilesson principle. Then tell children to apply it to a book they will listen to or read. Suggested language: "When you read, think about what happens in the story. Use both the pictures and the words to help you."

GROUP SHARE Have children tell what happened in a story they listened to or read. Have them tell how they learned what happened in the story.

▶ David's Drawings

INTERACTIVE READ-ALOUD/SHARED READING

Read aloud the book to children. Stop periodically for a brief interaction. Use the following suggested stopping points and prompts:

- After you read page 9, ask: "What do you think might happen next?"
- After you read page 27, ask: "How do you think David felt when his sister said his drawing needed something?"
- At the end of the book, ask: "What things do you like to draw? Where do you get ideas for drawing? Turn and talk with a partner about what you like to draw."

MINILESSON Story Structure

TEACH Display the minilesson principle on chart paper, and read it aloud to children.

> **MINILESSON PRINCIPLE**
>
> Notice how characters help each other in the story.

1. Tell children they are going to think about how the characters in *David's Drawing* help each other. Suggested language: "In the story *David's Drawing*, David saw a tree that he thought was beautiful. What happened after he drew the tree?" *(Amanda helped by coloring the tree brown and drawing some grass.)* Follow-up: "What happened next?" *(Ryan added leaves.)*

2. Have children retell what each child added to the drawing. Then display page 19, and discuss the completed drawing. Suggested language: "This started out as David's drawing. Why did David write *Our Class Picture* on the bottom of his drawing?" Follow-up: "How do you think David felt when he hung the picture on the bulletin board?"

3. Explain to children that, in this story, children helped each other to make a beautiful drawing. Have children retell the steps in creating the drawing, and record their responses in a T-Map labeled *Character* and *What He or She Added*.

SUMMARIZE AND APPLY Restate the minilesson principle. Tell children to apply it to a book they will listen to or read. Suggested language: "When you read, notice how characters help each other in the story."

GROUP SHARE Have children tell what happened in a story they listened to or read. Have them tell how characters helped each other.

▶ Signs and Shapes

INTERACTIVE READ-ALOUD/SHARED READING

Read aloud the book to children. Stop periodically for a brief interaction. Use the following suggested stopping points and prompts:

- At the end of page 31, ask: "What signs have you seen, and what shapes were they?"
- At the end of the book, ask: "Why do you think these signs are important?" Follow-up: "What do you think might happen if we didn't have signs?"

MINILESSON Text and Graphic Features

TEACH Display the minilesson principle on chart paper, and read it aloud. Tell children they are going to think about what they can learn from the pictures.

> **MINILESSON PRINCIPLE**
>
> Think about what you learn from the pictures.

1. Display the title page, and discuss the title and photo. Suggested language: "Look at this picture. How does the picture help you understand the title, *Signs and Shapes*?" *(It shows signs. Each sign has a different shape.)*

2. Display page 34, and ask children to tell what they see in the photo. Suggested language: "What do you see on this sign? What do you think this sign means?" *(The sign shows a person. It probably means to watch out for people.)*

3. As you page through the book, remind children that pictures can help them understand what they are reading. Review each sign, its shape, and its purpose with children and create a Column Chart labeled *Sign, Shape,* and *What the Sign Means*.

SUMMARIZE AND APPLY Restate the minilesson principle. Tell children to apply it to a book they will listen to or read. Suggested language: "When you read, think about what you learn from the pictures. Pictures help you understand what you are reading."

GROUP SHARE Ask children to show pictures in a book they listened to or read. Have them explain what they learned from the pictures.

Whole-Group Lessons

Jump into January
Big Book, Lesson 11

Holidays All Year Long
Big Book pp. 26–30, Lesson 11

Every Season
Read-Aloud Book, Lesson 11

▶ Jump into January

INTERACTIVE READ-ALOUD/SHARED READING

Read aloud the book to children. Stop periodically for a brief interaction. Use the following suggested stopping points and prompts for quick group response, or give a specific prompt and have partners or threes turn and talk.

- At the end of page 9, say: "One thing this book has told about is the weather. What is weather?" Follow-up: "What is the weather today?"
- At the end of page 11, ask: "What was the weather on these two pages?" Follow-up: "How did the pictures help you understand what the weather was like?"
- At the end of page 13, ask: "How did the weather help these gardens grow? Turn and talk with a partner about your ideas."
- After reading pages 24–25, ask: "Where could we turn in the book to see what kind of weather comes next?" *(We could turn to the beginning of the book.)*

MINILESSON Compare and Contrast

TEACH Display the minilesson principle on chart paper, and read it aloud to children. Tell children they are going to learn to notice what is the same and what is different in parts of the year.

1. Discuss the principle with children, using examples from *Jump into January*. Reread pages 2–11 aloud. Suggested language: "We have read about two parts of the year. What was the same about these parts of the year in this book?" *(people playing outside; people wearing coats and hats)* Follow-up: "What was different about these parts of the year?" *(different kinds of weather—snow in one part and wind and rain in another part)*

> **MINILESSON PRINCIPLE**
>
> Notice what is the same and what is different in parts of the year.

2. Continue in the same way, talking about what was the same and what was different in different parts of the year. Reread pages 14–19 aloud. Suggested language: "First, we read about a part of the year with snow. Just now, we read about another part of the year. How was it the same as the part of the year with snow?" *(People were playing outside.)* Follow-up: "What was different about these parts of the year?" *(There was snow in one part, and the weather was cold. People were wearing coats, hats, and gloves. There was no snow in the other part. The weather was hot. People wore swimsuits.)*

3. Use children's responses to the above questions to fill in a Venn Diagram like the one below. Where possible, sketch the item next to the word. As time allows, create additional Venn Diagrams to compare and contrast other seasons.

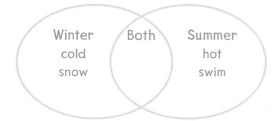

SUMMARIZE AND APPLY Restate the minilesson principle. Then tell children to apply it to a book they will listen to or read. Suggested language: "When you read, tell what is the same and what is different about the things in the book."

GROUP SHARE Ask children to tell about people, places, animals, or things in a book they have listened to or read. Have them tell how two of them were the same and how they were different.

▶ Every Season

INTERACTIVE READ-ALOUD/SHARED READING

Read aloud the book to children. Stop periodically for a brief interaction. Use the following suggested stopping points and prompts:

- At the end of page 6, say: "There are four parts of the year. These parts are called seasons. What season have we been reading about?" Follow-up: "How did the pictures help you understand what happens during spring?"
- At the end of page 12, ask: "Did you like the way the author told about summer?" Follow-up: "Explain why you did or did not like the way the author told about summer."
- At the end of the book, ask: "Which season comes next?" Follow-up: "How do you know? Turn and tell a partner about your ideas."

MINILESSON Compare and Contrast

TEACH Write the minilesson principle on chart paper, and read it aloud to children. Remind children that *Every Season* told about the four seasons of the year. Guide children in recalling that some things are the same about the seasons, and some things are different.

1. Use *Every Season* to discuss how autumn and winter in the book were the same and how they were different. Suggested language: "How was autumn the same as winter?" *(People bundled up to keep warm. Children had fun outside. Animals were outside.)* Follow-up: "What was different about autumn and winter?" *(Leaves turned colors in fall. Snow fell during winter.)*

> **MINILESSON PRINCIPLE**
>
> Think about how things in the book are the same and different.

2. Next, draw a Venn Diagram with sections labeled *Autumn, Both, Winter*. Ask children to tell more ways autumn and winter were the same. Then have them tell more ways autumn and winter were different.

3. Create additional Venn Diagrams to compare and contrast other seasons as described in the book. Remind children to think about the words as well as the pictures.

SUMMARIZE AND APPLY Restate the minilesson principle. Tell children to apply it to a book they will listen to or read. Suggested language: "When you read, think about how things in the book are the same and how they are different."

GROUP SHARE Have children think of a book they listened to or read. Ask them to tell about how things in the book were the same and how things were different.

▶ Holidays All Year Long

INTERACTIVE READ-ALOUD/SHARED READING

Read aloud the book to children. Stop periodically for a brief interaction. Use the following suggested stopping points and prompts:

- After you read page 26, ask: "What is a holiday?"
- After you read page 29, ask: "How are Presidents' Day and Independence Day the same?" Follow-up: "How are they different?"
- At the end of the book, say: "There was a picture with a word above it at the top of each page. What was the same about each of these?" Follow-up: "What was different about each of these? Turn and talk with a partner about your ideas."

MINILESSON Genre: Informational Text

TEACH Explain to children that *Holidays All Year Long* is like the other two books they read this week because it explained things that happened at different times of the year. Tell them it is different from the other two books they read this week because it tells only about holidays. Display the minilesson principle on chart paper, and read it aloud. Tell children they are going to think about what the author wanted them to learn from the book.

1. Use *Holidays All Year Long* to discuss the principle. Suggested language: "*Holidays All Year Long* told about Martin Luther King, Jr. Day. When do we celebrate this day?" *(in January)* "Who was Dr. Martin Luther King, Jr.?" *(a man who wanted all people to be treated fairly)*

> **MINILESSON PRINCIPLE**
>
> Think about what the author wants you to learn from the book.

2. As you page through the book, point out that each page told about a holiday. For each page, name the holiday, and ask: "When do we celebrate this holiday? Why do we celebrate this holiday?" Fill in a Column Chart labeled *Holiday, When,* and *Why* with children's responses.

3. Read aloud the chart entries as you clarify and reinforce understanding that holidays happen throughout the year and are celebrated for a variety of reasons.

SUMMARIZE AND APPLY Restate the minilesson principle. Tell children to apply it to a book they will listen to or read. Suggested language: "When you read about things that really happened, think about what an author wants you to learn from the book."

GROUP SHARE Ask children to tell about things they learned from a book they listened to or read.

Whole-Group Lessons

Snow
Big Book, Lesson 12

How Water Changes
Big Book pp. 31–38, Lesson 12

Storm Is Coming!
Read-Aloud Book, Lesson 12

▶ Snow

INTERACTIVE READ-ALOUD/SHARED READING

Read aloud the book to children. Stop periodically for a brief interaction. Use the following suggested stopping points and prompts for quick group response, or give a specific prompt and have partners or threes turn and talk.

* At the end of page 9, say: "Different animals do different things during winter. The bear says it is time to be sleeping. What will many animals need to find during winter that bears will not need to find?" *(Bears will sleep, so they will not need to look for food, but many other animals will need to find food.)*
* At the end of page 16, ask: "The author said the forest was covered with a sparkling blanket. Was there a real blanket covering the forest?" Follow-up: "Why do you think the author chose these words?"
* At the end of page 27, ask: "What will the geese do during winter?" Follow-up: "Why will the geese fly south? Turn and talk with a partner about your ideas."
* After reading the last page, ask: "What happens to temperatures in the spring?" *(Temperatures get warmer.)* Follow-up: "How do you know what happens to temperatures in spring?" *(I know from what the owl says and from my own life.)*

MINILESSON Conclusions

TEACH Display the minilesson principle on chart paper, and read it aloud to children. Tell children they are going to learn to notice clues that help them know how the animals in the story felt.

1. Discuss the principle with children, using examples from *Snow*. Tell children they can get clues from the pictures, from the words, and from the way animals say the words. Reread pages 1–5 aloud. Suggested language: "We read that snow was coming. Did the geese feel happy or worried?" *(worried)* Follow-up: "What clues helped you understand how the geese felt?" *(In the pictures, the geese looked scared; their eyes were open very wide. The geese said, 'S-s-s-SNOW?' The geese said words with a shiver. They said their lake would freeze.)*

> **MINILESSON PRINCIPLE**
>
> Notice clues that help you know how the animals in the story feel.

2. Continue in the same way, talking about clues that showed how the animals felt. Reread pages 20–21 aloud as you display the pages. Suggested language: "Listen to the words, and look at the pictures. How did the bunnies feel about the snow?" *(They felt happy.)* Follow-up: "What clues showed how they felt?" *(They giggled. They were smiling, and one bunny put its arms up high.)*

3. Use children's responses to the above questions to fill in a Column Chart like the one below. Where possible, add sketches to illustrate the words.

Animals	How They Felt	Clues
geese	scared	"S-s-s-SNOW!"
bunnies	happy	smiles

SUMMARIZE AND APPLY Restate the minilesson principle. Then tell children to apply it to a book they will listen to or read. Suggested language: "When you read, notice clues that tell you how animals or people in a story feel."

GROUP SHARE Ask children to tell about animals or people in a book they have listened to or read. Have them explain how they used clues to tell how the animals or people felt.

▶ Storm Is Coming!

INTERACTIVE READ-ALOUD/SHARED READING

Read aloud the book to children. Stop periodically for a brief interaction. Use the following suggested stopping points and prompts:

- At the end of page 1, ask: "Why should the animals go to the barn if a storm is coming?"
- At the end of page 5, ask: "What did Duck see?" Follow-up: "What did the dark clouds mean?"
- At the end of page 15, say: "The sheep says the Sun is hiding from the storm. Why does the sheep think this?"
- At the end of the book, ask: "Why was this book funny? Turn and tell a partner about your ideas."

MINILESSON Conclusions

TEACH Tell children that characters are the people or animals in a story. Then tell children they will think about the characters in *Storm Is Coming!*

1. Tell children they can use clues to understand what characters are like. Reread page 1. Then direct children's attention to the illustration on page 30. Suggested language: "Was the farmer nice or mean?" *(nice)* Follow-up: "What were the clues that helped you figure this out?" *(At the beginning of the story, the farmer wanted the animals to get to the barn so they would be safe. At the end of the story, the farmer was smiling and hugging the animals.)*

   > **MINILESSON PRINCIPLE**
   >
   > Notice clues in the story that tell what characters are like.

2. Write the minilesson principle on chart paper, and read it aloud to children. Next, draw a Column Chart with sections labeled *Character, What the Character Was Like,* and *Clues.* Use the chart to continue to discuss what the characters in the book were like.

3. As you work with children to complete the chart, remind them to think about the pictures and the words.

SUMMARIZE AND APPLY Restate the minilesson principle. Tell children to apply it to a story they will listen to or read. Suggested language: "When you read, notice clues in the story that tell what characters are like."

GROUP SHARE Have children tell what a character was like in a story they listened to or read. Ask them to tell the clues that helped them figure out what the character was like.

▶ How Water Changes

INTERACTIVE READ-ALOUD/SHARED READING

Read aloud the book to children. Stop periodically for a brief interaction. Use the following suggested stopping points and prompts:

- After you read page 34, say: "We have read that water can turn to ice when it gets very cold. What makes ice turn to water?" Follow-up: "Where would you put a piece of ice if you wanted it to turn to water?"
- At the end of the book, ask: "What are the three things water can be?" Follow-up: "How can you change water? Turn and talk with a partner about your ideas."

MINILESSON Genre: Informational Text

TEACH Explain to children that *How Water Changes* was like the other two books they read this week because it told what a kind of weather was like. Tell children it was different from the other two books they read this week because it did not tell a story that was make-believe. Instead, it gave information. Display the minilesson principle on chart paper, and read it aloud. Tell children they are going to notice the words that tell about pictures.

1. Use *How Water Changes* to discuss the principle. Reread page 32. First, read the text at the bottom of the page. Then point to the oval at the top of the page as you read the caption. Ask: "What do these words tell you about the picture?" *(The words tell that the lake is frozen.)* Follow-up: "How do these words help you better understand this page?" *(The words tell that the ice is frozen, so the ice is hard enough to skate on.)*

   > **MINILESSON PRINCIPLE**
   >
   > Notice the words that tell about the pictures.

2. Reread page 34. First, read the text at the bottom of the page. Then point to the caption in the oval at the top of the page as you read it. Ask: "How do these words help you understand?" Fill in a T-Map labeled *Words* and *How They Tell About the Picture* with children's responses for pages 32, 34, and 36.

3. Read aloud the chart entries as you guide children in noticing words that tell about pictures.

SUMMARIZE AND APPLY Restate the minilesson principle. Tell children to apply it to a book they will listen to or read. Suggested language: "When you read a book, look for words that tell about the pictures. Think about how the words can help you better understand the pictures."

GROUP SHARE Ask children to tell about a book or story they have read that has words to tell about the pictures.

Whole-Group Lessons

What Do You Do With a Tail Like This?
Big Book, Lesson 13

Poems
Big Book pp. 32–37, Lesson 13

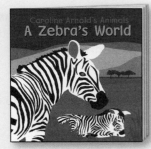

A Zebra's World
Read-Aloud Book, Lesson 13

▶ What Do You Do With a Tail Like This?

INTERACTIVE READ-ALOUD/SHARED READING

Read aloud the book to children. Stop periodically for very brief discussion of the text. Use the suggested stopping points and prompts below for quick group response, or give a specific prompt and have partners or threes turn and talk.

- After reading about ears, say: "Think about two of the animals. What is the same about their ears?" *(A cricket and a humpback whale hear with their ears.)* Follow-up: "What is different?" *(The cricket's ears are on its knees, and the humpback's ears are on its head.)*
- After reading about eyes, ask: "How do these animals use their eyes?" *(to see things underwater, to see at night, to look two ways at once)* Follow-up: "Do people use their eyes in the same way? Why or why not?"
- After reading about feet, ask: "How does the author present the information in this book?" *(The author shows pictures of a body part from different animals, and then tells how each animal uses that body part.)*
- At the end, ask: "How does the author make this book fun to read? Turn and talk about your ideas with a partner."

MINILESSON Author's Purpose

TEACH Display the minilesson principle on chart paper, and read it aloud to children. Tell children that they are going to learn how to think about what the author wants you to learn from a book.

1. Discuss the principle with children using examples from *What Do You Do With a Tail Like This?* Reread pages 4–7 aloud. Suggested language: "What did the author tell about on these pages?" *(how some animals use their noses)* Follow-up: "Which animals use their noses in similar ways?" *(A platypus uses its nose to dig in the mud, and a mole uses its nose to find its way underground.)*

> **MINILESSON PRINCIPLE**
>
> Think about what the author wants you to learn from a book.

2. Page through the book, talking about the different ways animals use parts of their bodies. Suggested language after each spread: "What animals did the author tell us about? How does each of the animals use their (ears, tails, eyes, nose, feet)?" Record children's ideas in an Inference Map like the one shown here.

3. Use children's responses to help children understand what the author wanted them to learn from this book. Suggested language: "You can see that the book gives information about how different animals use different parts of their bodies. What does the author want you to learn?" *(that animals use parts of their bodies in many different ways)*

SUMMARIZE AND APPLY Restate the minilesson principle. Tell children to apply it to a book they will listen to or read. Suggested language: "When you read a book, think about what the author wants you to learn."

GROUP SHARE Ask children to tell about things they learned from a book they listened to or read.

▶ A Zebra's World

INTERACTIVE READ-ALOUD/SHARED READING

INTERACTIVE READ-ALOUD/SHARED READING

Read aloud the book to children. Stop periodically for a brief interaction. Use the following suggested stopping points and prompts:

- At the end of page 1, ask: "Is this book make-believe or is it about things that can really happen?" Follow-up: "How can you tell?"

- At the end of page 12, ask: "What kind of zebra has the author told you about?" *(baby/young zebra)* Follow-up: "How was the young zebra the same as the older zebras? How was it different from the older zebras? Turn and tell a partner about your ideas."

- At the end of the book, ask: "What other parts of the book helped you tell it was about real things—and not make-believe? *(fun facts, map, glossary)* Follow-up: "What is a glossary?"

MINILESSON Author's Purpose

TEACH Display the minilesson principle on chart paper, and read it aloud to children. Remind children that *A Zebra's World* told about a kind of animal. Guide children to think about what the author wanted them to learn.

1. Use *A Zebra's World* to discuss what the author wanted children to learn. Display page 1, and ask: "What did the author want you to learn about on page 1?" *(plains zebras)* Follow-up: "How could you tell?" *(The author told many things about plains zebras. The author told where they live, what they eat, and how big they are.)*

> **MINILESSON PRINCIPLE**
>
> Think about what the author wants you to learn from the book.

2. Next, draw a Web. Label the center oval *Zebras*. Ask children to tell what the author wanted them to learn about zebras. Record what children describe in the outer ovals.

3. When the Web is complete, read aloud all the ideas in the outer ovals. Use the Web to guide children in understanding that the author wanted them to learn many things about zebras.

SUMMARIZE AND APPLY Restate the minilesson principle. Tell children to apply it to a book they will listen to or read. Suggested language: "When you read, think about what the author wants you to learn from the book."

GROUP SHARE Have children tell how they could tell what the author wanted them to learn in a book they listened to or read.

▶ Poems About Animals

INTERACTIVE READ-ALOUD/SHARED READING

Read aloud the poems to children. Stop periodically for brief discussion of the text. Use the following suggested stopping points and prompts:

- After you read "Wings," ask: "What does the author mean by saying that not having any is 'too few'?" *(The author wishes she had wings to fly.)*

- After you read "Dragon," ask: "What does the poet compare a dragonfly's body to?" *(a pin)* "What else is straight and shining like a pin? Turn and talk about your ideas with a partner."

- After you read "On Our Way," say: "This is a poem about people moving like animals. Which animal would you like to move like? Why?"

- After you read "Tails," ask: "Do you agree with the poet that the monkey has the nicest tail? Why or why not?"

MINILESSON Genre: Poetry

TEACH Display the minilesson principle on chart paper, and read it aloud to children. Explain that many poems have words with the same ending sound. Tell children that they are going to notice words in the poems they read that have the same ending sound.

1. Ask children to listen for words that have the same ending sound as you reread "Wings." Have children echo each line after you. Ask: "Which words had the same ending sound?" *(two/few)*

> **MINILESSON PRINCIPLE**
>
> Notice the words that have the same ending sound.

2. Continue with the remaining poems, rereading each one aloud. Have children name the words in each poem that have the same ending sound.

3. Write the rhyming words side by side in a list. Have children chant the pairs of rhyming words. Then reread the poems again, inviting children to chime in on the rhyming words.

SUMMARIZE AND APPLY Restate the minilesson principle. Tell children to apply it to a poem they will listen to or read. Suggested language: "When you read a poem, notice the words that have the same ending sound."

GROUP SHARE Ask children to recite a poem they have listened to or read that has words with the same ending sound. After children recite the poem, have them identify the words with the same ending sound.

Turtle Splash!
Big Book, Lesson 14

Where Animals Live
Big Book pp. 30–38, Lesson 14

Home for a Tiger, Home for a Bear
Read-Aloud Book, Lesson 14

▶ Turtle Splash!

INTERACTIVE READ-ALOUD/SHARED READING

Read aloud the book to children. Stop periodically for a brief interaction. Use the following suggested stopping points and prompts for quick group response, or give a specific prompt and have partners or threes turn and talk.

- Reread pages 1–7. At the end of page 7, ask: "How many turtles were on the log at the beginning of the book?" Follow-up: "How could you tell?"
- At the end of page 8, say: "The author used action words to tell how animals were moving, for example: *rabbit rustles; squirrel scampers.* How did these words help you better understand how the animals moved?"
- After you read page 12, say: "This page told about ducklings and a mallard. What is a mallard?" *(a kind of duck)* Follow-up: "What are ducklings?" *(baby ducks)*
- After reading the last page, ask: "Where do the turtles go for the night?" Follow-up: "What will the turtles do in the morning? Turn and talk to a partner about your ideas."

MINILESSON Cause and Effect

TEACH Display the minilesson principle on chart paper, and read it aloud to children. Tell children they are going to think about how some things make other things happen. Explain to children that understanding what makes things happen will help them understand books and stories.

1. Discuss the principle with children, using an example of cause and effect from *Turtle Splash!* Reread page 4, and draw children's attention to the illustrations on pages 5–7. Suggested language: "In this part of the book, one turtle left the log and went into the water. What happened that made the turtle go into the water?" *(A bullfrog jumped.)*

> **MINILESSON PRINCIPLE**
>
> Think about how some things in the story make other things happen.

2. Use children's responses to explain how to figure out what makes things happen. Suggested language: "The jumping bullfrog made the turtles go into the water. This is one thing that made another thing happen. As you read, it is important to think about why things happen."

3. Work with children to find things in the book that made other things happen. Record children's ideas in a T-Map like the one shown here.

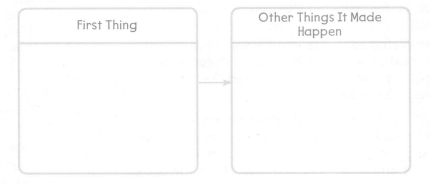

First Thing	Other Things It Made Happen

SUMMARIZE AND APPLY Restate the minilesson principle. Explain that children can apply it to a book they will listen to or read. Suggested language: "When you read or listen to a book, think about how some things in the book make other things happen."

GROUP SHARE Ask children to share an example of one thing that made another thing happen in a book or story they listened to or read.

▶ Home for a Tiger, Home for a Bear

INTERACTIVE READ-ALOUD/SHARED READING

Read aloud the book to children. Stop periodically for a brief interaction. Use the following suggested stopping points and prompts:

- After you read aloud pages 1–3, ask: "What do you think this book will be about? Why do you think so?"
- At the end of the book, ask: "Were you right about what the book would be about?" Point out pages 30–31. Follow-up: "How was this part of the book different from the other parts of the book?"
- Take a picture walk through the book. Point out the illustration on page 13. Say: "Different parts of the world can look very different and have very different kinds of weather. What is this part of the world like?"

MINILESSON Details

TEACH Remind children that *Home for a Tiger, Home for a Bear* told where some animals lived—and this helped children learn more about the animals.

1. Reread pages 4–5 as you guide children in thinking about where the animals in the book lived and in learning more about them. Suggested language: "Where does the deer live?" *(in the forest)* "What kind of place does the deer like to live in?" *(a place with trees; a place that is cool)*

> **MINILESSON PRINCIPLE**
>
> Think about where the animals in the book live to learn more about them.

2. Write the minilesson principle on chart paper, and read it aloud to children. Next, draw a Column Chart with sections labeled *Animal, Where It Lives,* and *Other Things I Learned.* Use the chart to continue to discuss where the other animals in the book lived and more about what they were like. Suggested language: "Where does this animal live? What kind of place is it? What does the place tell you about the animal?"

SUMMARIZE AND APPLY Restate the minilesson principle. Tell children to apply it to a story or book about animals that they will listen to or read. Suggested language: "When you read or listen to a story about animals, think about where they live and what they do there."

GROUP SHARE Have children tell where an animal lived in a story they listened to or read. Ask them to share other things they learned about the animal.

▶ Where Animals Live

INTERACTIVE READ-ALOUD/SHARED READING

Read aloud the book to children. Stop periodically for a brief interaction. Use the following suggested stopping points and prompts:

- After you read page 32, ask: "Does this book give real information, or is it make-believe?" Follow-up: "How can you tell?"
- After you read page 36, say: "Animals live in parts of the world that have the kinds of places and things they need. In what kind of place do sea lions live?" Follow-up: "How do the words and the picture help you understand what a rocky coast is?"
- At the end of the book, say: "The author asks, *What are good places for people to live?* Turn and talk with a partner about your ideas."

MINILESSON Main Ideas

TEACH Explain to children that *Where Animals Live* was like the other two books they read this week because it told about animals and showed where they lived. Tell children that each book told about one thing at a time. Display the minilesson principle on chart paper, and read it aloud. Tell children they are going to notice how the author told about one thing at a time.

1. Use *Where Animals Live* to discuss the principle. Reread page 31. Suggested language: "We are going to look for the one thing that the author tells about on each page. What one thing did the author tell about on this page?" *(places where beavers live)*

> **MINILESSON PRINCIPLE**
>
> Notice how the author tells you about one thing at a time.

2. Continue similarly with the remaining pages. With children, complete a T-Map labeled *Page Number* and *One Thing* with children's responses. In the *One-Thing* column, write the main idea for the page. If possible, provide a sketch for each response.
3. After the chart is complete, read the entries, pointing out that the author told about one thing at a time.

SUMMARIZE AND APPLY Restate the minilesson principle. Tell children to apply it to a book they will listen to or read. Suggested language: "When you read or listen to a book, notice how the author tells you about one thing at a time."

GROUP SHARE Ask children to tell about a book or story they have read. Tell them to point out the one thing the author told them about in the book or one part of the book.

Whole-Group Lessons

What a Beautiful Sky!
Big Book, Lesson 15
What Will the Weather Be Like?
Big Book pp. 26–30, Lesson 15

How Many Stars in the Sky?
Read-Aloud Book, Lesson 15

▶ What a Beautiful Sky!

INTERACTIVE READ-ALOUD/SHARED READING

Read aloud the book to children. Stop periodically for a brief interaction. Use the following suggested stopping points and prompts for quick group response, or give a specific prompt and have partners or threes turn and talk.

- At the end of page 10, say: "We have read about different kinds of clouds. How are they the same?" Follow-up: "How are they different?"
- After you read page 18, say: "Earth spins around once each day. Part of this time, Earth is facing toward the Sun. Part of this time, Earth is facing away from the Sun. This page said, *We can see stars when the Sun says goodbye.* When we see many stars in the sky, is Earth facing toward the Sun, or away from the Sun?" Follow-up: "How do you know? Turn and talk to a partner about your ideas."
- After you read pages 22–23, direct children's attention to each caption as you reread it. Ask: "How do the words and pictures work together to help you understand shapes of the Moon you see?"
- At the end of the book, ask: "What other things have you seen in the sky?"

MINILESSON Details

TEACH Display the minilesson principle on chart paper, and read it aloud to children. Tell children they are going to learn to notice the words in a book that tell what something is like. Explain that this will make books more interesting and easier to understand.

1. Discuss the principle with children, using examples from *What a Beautiful Sky!* Reread page 4 aloud. Then say: "We read about the Sun. Which words told what the Sun was like?" *(big, bright)* Follow-up: "How did these words help you understand what the Sun was like?" *(The words told its size and what it looked like.)*

2. Continue in the same way, talking about words that told what something was like. Reread page 8 aloud. Then say: "Which words told what some of the clouds were like?" *(fluffy, light)* Follow-up: "How did these words help you understand what these clouds were like?" *(The words told what they looked and seemed like.)*

> **MINILESSON PRINCIPLE**
>
> Notice the words in the book that tell you what something is like.

3. Use children's responses to fill small Webs like those below. After the Webs are complete, discuss how noticing the words that told what something was like made the book more interesting and easier to understand.

SUMMARIZE AND APPLY Restate the minilesson principle. Then tell children to apply it to a book they will listen to or read. Suggested language: "When you read or listen to a book, notice the words that tell what something is like."

GROUP SHARE Ask children to think about people, places, animals, or things in a book they listened to or read. Have them tell words in the book that told what one of these was like.

▶ How Many Stars in the Sky?

INTERACTIVE READ-ALOUD/SHARED READING

Read aloud the book to children. Stop periodically for a brief interaction. Use the following suggested stopping points and prompts:

- At the end of page 11, say: "The boy and his father went to town. Why were there no people in town?"
- At the end of page 12, say: "The boy's father talks about Jupiter. Jupiter and Earth are both planets. What are names of other planets?"
- After you read page 14, say: "On this page, we read that the time is 2:45. Is the time 2:45 in the morning or in the afternoon?" Follow-up: "How can you tell?"
- At the end of the book, say: "What was the star that the boy and his father saw at the end of the book?" Follow-up: "Why can't we see stars during the day? Turn and talk to a partner about your ideas."

MINILESSON Sequence of Events

TEACH Write the minilesson principle on chart paper, and read it aloud to children. Tell children that noticing what happens first in a story and what happens next will help them understand the story. To prepare children, ask: "What did you do first when you came to class today?" Follow-up: "What did you do next?"

1. Tell children they can also tell what happens first and what happens next in a story. Use *How Many Stars in the Sky?* to discuss sequence of events, as you focus on the beginning and end of the story. Suggested language: "What happened first in the story?" *(The boy and his dad went out to try to count stars.)* Follow-up: "What happened next?" *(The boy and his dad couldn't count all the stars, but they saw the Sun in the morning.)*

> **MINILESSON PRINCIPLE**
>
> Notice what happens first in the story and what happens next.

2. Next, draw a Flow Chart. Create two large boxes in a row. Draw an arrow from the first box to the second. Use children's responses regarding what happened first and next in the story to complete the Flow Chart.

SUMMARIZE AND APPLY Restate the minilesson principle. Tell children to apply it to a story they will listen to or read. Suggested language: "When you read or listen to a story, notice what happens first and what happens next."

GROUP SHARE Have children tell what happened first and what happened next in a story they have listened to or read.

▶ What Will the Weather Be Like?

INTERACTIVE READ-ALOUD/SHARED READING

Read aloud the book to children. Stop periodically for a brief interaction. Use the following suggested stopping points and prompts:

- After you read page 26, ask: "Did the children on this page like this kind of weather?" Follow-up: "How could you tell?"
- After you read page 27, say: "It was cloudy. What kind of weather do you think we will probably read about next?" Follow-up: "Why do you think so?"
- After reading page 28, ask: "Were you right about the weather that would come next?" Follow-up: "Tell how the picture helps you figure out how the child feels about the rain."
- At the end of the book, ask: "What is the weather like today?" Follow-up: "How do you feel about this kind of weather? Turn and talk with a partner about your ideas."

MINILESSON Genre: Informational Text

TEACH Explain that *What Will the Weather Be Like?* is like the other two books children read this week because it told about things in the sky, such as the Sun. Display the minilesson principle on chart paper, and read it aloud. Tell children they are going to notice what the author tells mostly about.

1. Use *What Will the Weather Be Like?* to discuss the principle. Reread page 26. Suggested language: "What was the weather like on this page?" *(hot, sunny)*

> **MINILESSON PRINCIPLE**
>
> Notice what the author tells mostly about.

2. Continue through the book, asking the same question for each page. Create an Idea-Support Map, a graphic organizer with a large box at the top and smaller boxes below it. Draw an arrow from each small box to the large box. Fill each small box with the response to the question: "What was the weather like on this page?" Add a sketch to illustrate each phrase.

3. After the small boxes have been filled, read aloud the phrases inside all of them. *(hot and sunny; cloudy; cloudy with rain; windy; hot and sunny)* Then say: "Notice all these things the author told us. What did the author tell mostly about?" *(kinds of weather)*

SUMMARIZE AND APPLY Restate the minilesson principle. Tell children to apply it to a book they will listen to or read. Suggested language: "When you read, notice what the author tells mostly about."

GROUP SHARE Ask children to explain what an author told mostly about in a book they have listened to or read.

Whole-Group Lessons

What Is Science?
Big Book, Lesson 16

Benjamin Franklin, Inventor
Big Book pp. 32–38, Lesson 16

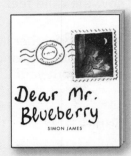

Dear Mr. Blueberry
Read-Aloud Book, Lesson 16

▶ What Is Science?

INTERACTIVE READ-ALOUD/SHARED READING

Read aloud the book to children. Stop periodically for a very brief interaction. Use the following suggested stopping points and prompts for quick group response, or give a specific prompt and have partners or threes turn and talk.

- At the end of page 7, say: "Science is about studying many different kinds of things. Studying means learning about something. What are some things you can learn about in space?"
- At the end of page 10, say: "All the things on the last few pages are the same in some way. Are they all things found in space or all things found on Earth?"
- At the end of page 27, ask: "Why do you think hunting and exploring are part of science? Turn and talk with a partner about your ideas."
- After reading pages 30–31, ask: "Where have you heard these sentences before?" *(These sentences were at the beginning of the book.)*

MINILESSON Details

TEACH Display the minilesson principle on chart paper, and read it aloud to children. Tell children they are going to learn how to use the details in a book to learn about something.

1. Discuss the principle with children, using examples from *What Is Science?* Reread pages 13–15 aloud. Suggested language: "The author wrote a poem about the different things science can be. One thing she wrote about was weather. What words did she use to tell about weather?" *(wind, hurricanes, tornadoes, snow)* Follow-up: "What did these words about weather help you understand?" *(There are different kinds of weather.)*

2. Continue in the same way, using parts of Earth as an example. Reread pages 20–23 aloud. Suggested language: "This part of the poem told about how you can learn about parts of Earth. What were some words the author used to tell about things you find on Earth?" *(glaciers, geysers, clay, sand, mountains, rolling land)*

3. Use children's responses to the above question to fill in a Web like the one shown below. Record the detail words in the outer circles. Reinforce to children that authors use words that tell about things to help them understand and picture in their minds what they are reading about.

> **MINILESSON PRINCIPLE**
>
> Think about how details help you learn about something.

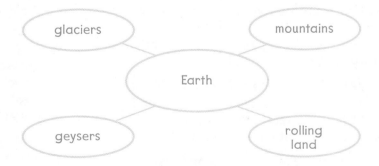

SUMMARIZE AND APPLY Restate the minilesson principle. Then tell children to apply it to a book they will listen to or read. Suggested language: "When you read a book, think about what you learn from the details."

GROUP SHARE Ask children to tell about something they learned from a book they listened to or read. Ask them to tell what details helped them learn about it.

▶ Dear Mr. Blueberry

INTERACTIVE READ-ALOUD/SHARED READING

Read aloud the book to children. Stop periodically for a brief discussion of the story. Use the following suggested stopping points and prompts:

- After you read Emily's first letter on page 2, say: "This kind of writing is a letter. The first line tells the person the letter is for—Mr. Blueberry. The last line says who wrote the letter—Emily. Why do you think Emily wrote to Mr. Blueberry?"
- After Mr. Blueberry writes on page 16 that whales are migratory, ask: "What do you think Mr. Blueberry is like as a teacher?" Follow-up: "What different things has Emily learned from Mr. Blueberry through his letters?"
- At the end of the story, ask: "What do you think Emily is like? Turn and talk about your ideas with a partner. Think of words that tell about Emily."

MINILESSON Genre: Fantasy

TEACH Explain to children that *Dear Mr. Blueberry* is a made-up story. Tell children that it includes some things that could happen in real life and other things that could not really happen.

1. Use *Dear Mr. Blueberry* to discuss the idea that some stories include parts that could not happen in real life. Suggested language: "The story *Dear Mr. Blueberry* told about a girl who wrote letters to her teacher about a whale living in a pond. Which part of this story could really happen?" *(A girl could really write letters to her teacher.)* Follow-up: "Which part of this story could not really happen?" *(A whale could not live in a pond.)*

> **MINILESSON PRINCIPLE**
>
> Notice the parts in the story that could not really happen.

2. Write the minilesson principle on chart paper, and read it aloud to children. Next, draw a T-Map labeled *Could Really Happen* and *Could Not Happen*. Ask children to name other things that happened in *Dear Mr. Blueberry* that fit in each category.

3. Guide children to explain how they know which parts of the story could not really happen. Explain to children that they will better understand what they read if they notice the parts that could not happen in real life.

SUMMARIZE AND APPLY Restate the minilesson principle. Tell children to apply it to a book they will listen to or read. Suggested language: "When you read, notice the parts in the story that could not really happen. Think about how you know they could not really happen."

GROUP SHARE Have children tell about the parts of a book they listened to or read that could not happen in real life.

▶ Benjamin Franklin, Inventor

INTERACTIVE READ-ALOUD/SHARED READING

Read aloud the book to children. Stop periodically for brief discussion. Use the following suggested stopping points and prompts:

- After you read the first page, ask: "Do you think this book tells about things that really happened, or is it a made-up story? How do you know?"
- At the end of the book, say: "In the middle of this book, there are small pictures shown beside bigger pictures. What do the bigger pictures show?" Follow-up: "What do the smaller pictures show? Turn and talk with a partner about why the book shows pairs of pictures."
- Continue discussion of the book with children. Say: "At the end of the book, the author says what she thinks about Benjamin Franklin. She says he was a great man. Do you think she is right?" Follow-up: "Why or why not?"

MINILESSON Details

TEACH Explain to children that *Benjamin Franklin, Inventor* is different from the other two books they read this week because it gives information about a real person. Display the minilesson principle on chart paper, and read it aloud. Tell children they are going to think about what a person did in his life to understand why the person is important.

1. Use *Benjamin Franklin, Inventor* to discuss the principle. Suggested language: "*Benjamin Franklin, Inventor* told about some of the things Benjamin Franklin did in his life. This book told you that an inventor is someone who makes new things. Then it told about some of the new things that Benjamin Franklin invented. What was one of the first things he invented?" *(swim fins)*

> **MINILESSON PRINCIPLE**
>
> Think about what the person did in his life.

2. As you page through the book, point out to children that each page shows another thing Benjamin Franklin did in his life. Ask: "What things did Benjamin Franklin do in his life?" Fill in a Web with children's responses. Write *Benjamin Franklin* in the middle circle and the things he invented in the outside circles.

3. Read aloud all the items in the Web as you guide children to explain why Benjamin Franklin was important.

SUMMARIZE AND APPLY Restate the minilesson principle. Tell children to apply it to a book they will listen to or read. Suggested language: "When you read about a real person, think about what that person did in his or her life."

GROUP SHARE Ask children to tell about a real person from a book they listened to or read.

Whole-Group Lessons

From Caterpillar to Butterfly
Big Book, Lesson 17

Anansi and Grasshopper
Big Book pp. 30–35, Lesson 17

It Is the Wind
Read-Aloud Book, Lesson 17

▶ From Caterpillar to Butterfly

INTERACTIVE READ-ALOUD/SHARED READING

Read aloud the book to children. Stop periodically for very brief discussion of the text. Use the suggested stopping points and prompts below for quick group response, or give a specific prompt and have partners or threes turn and talk.

- After reading the captions on pages 6 and 7, ask: "Why do you think the author includes these captions?" *(to tell more about caterpillars)*
- After the children let the butterfly go, ask: "Why are the children both happy and sad to let the butterfly go?" *(They feel happy that the butterfly is free, but sad because they will miss it.)*
- After reading about different kinds of butterflies, ask: "How are these butterflies the same? How are they different? Turn and talk about your ideas with a partner."

MINILESSON Sequence of Events

TEACH Display the minilesson principle on chart paper, and read it aloud to children. Tell children that they are going to learn about what happens first, next, and last in a book. Explain that this will help them understand the information in the book better.

1. Discuss the principle with children using examples from *From Caterpillar to Butterfly*. Suggested language: "In the book *From Caterpillar to Butterfly*, the children watched a caterpillar change into a butterfly. What was the first thing that happened?" *(A caterpillar hatched out of an egg.)* Follow-up: "What happened next?" *(The caterpillar ate and ate and ate.)*

> **MINILESSON PRINCIPLE**
>
> Notice what happens first, next, and last in the book.

2. Continue in the same way, having children tell the order of events in the life of a caterpillar. Suggested language: "What happened after the caterpillar grew out of its skin?" *(It made a special house, called a chrysalis.)*

3. Finally, ask children about the last thing that happened to the caterpillar. Suggested language: "What happened when the chrysalis cracked?" *(A butterfly hatched.)*

4. Ask children to retell what happened to the caterpillar, using the words *first*, *next*, and *last*. Record their responses in a Flow Chart like the one shown here.

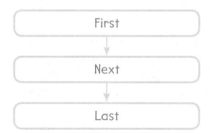

SUMMARIZE AND APPLY Restate the minilesson principle. Tell children to apply it to a book they will listen to or read. Suggested language: "When you read a book, think about what happens first, next, and last."

GROUP SHARE Ask children to share what happened first, next, and last in a book they listened to or read.

▶ It Is the Wind

INTERACTIVE READ-ALOUD/SHARED READING

Read aloud the book to children. Stop periodically for a brief discussion of the story. Use the following suggested stopping points and prompts:

- At the end of page 3, ask: "Which words on this page have the same ending sound?"
- At the end of page 18, ask: "Which words on this page have the same ending sound?" Follow-up: "How do these words make the book more fun to listen to?"
- At the end of the book, ask: "How did the pictures help you better understand the story? Turn and tell a partner about your ideas."

MINILESSON Conclusions

TEACH Tell children they can use what they already know to understand a story. Before beginning the discussion about the book, tap prior knowledge by asking: "Suppose you put an ice cube in a cup outside on a hot day. When you come back, the ice cube is gone, but there is water in the cup. What happened?" *(The ice cube melted.)* Follow-up: "How do you know?" *(from what I already know in my own life)*

1. Use *It Is the Wind* to discuss how children can think about what they already know to understand a story. Reread pages 1–7 aloud. Suggested language: "You already know that there are noises you hear at night that can wake you up. What noises did the author tell you about and show you on these pages?" *(owl hooting, dog howling, swings moving, gate moving)*

> **MINILESSON PRINCIPLE**
>
> Think about what you already know to understand the story.

2. Write the minilesson principle on chart paper, and read it aloud. Then create an Inference Map to record children's ideas about where the boy in the story lives. Ask children to tell the noises named and shown.

3. After you reread page 23, read aloud all the words and phrases you have written in the boxes. Then ask: "Using what you know from your life, do you think you could hear all of these noises in a busy city or in the country?" *(country)* Write *country* in the rectangle at the bottom of the graphic organizer, explaining to children how they used what they knew from their own lives to understand the story.

SUMMARIZE AND APPLY Restate the minilesson principle. Tell children to apply it to a story they will listen to or read. Suggested language: "When you read, think about what you already know to understand a story."

GROUP SHARE Have children tell how they have used what they already knew to understand a story they have read or listened to.

▶ Anansi and Grasshopper

INTERACTIVE READ-ALOUD/SHARED READING

Read aloud the book to children. Stop periodically for brief discussion. Use the following suggested stopping points and prompts:

- After you read page 26, ask: "How are these creatures the same?" Follow-up: "How are they different?"
- After you read page 29, ask: "How is this like something that has already happened in the book?"
- At the end of the book, ask: "What words would you use to tell about what Anansi is like?" Follow-up: "Would you like to have Anansi as a friend? Turn and talk with a partner about your ideas."

MINILESSON Genre: Traditional Tale

TEACH Display the minilesson principle on chart paper, and read it aloud to children. Explain that *Anansi and Grasshopper* was different from the other two books children read this week because it was a kind of story that is told aloud by one person to another for many years. Point out that this kind of story, or tale, often includes a lesson or a trick. Explain to children that they are going to think about the trick that someone plays on someone else.

1. Use *Anansi and Grasshopper* to discuss the principle. Reread page 26, and ask: "What did Anansi want Grasshopper to help with?" *(finding fruit)* "What did Anansi promise for Grasshopper's help?" *(sharing the fruit)*

> **MINILESSON PRINCIPLE**
>
> Think about the trick that someone plays on someone else.

2. Reread page 27, and ask: "Why did Grasshopper tell Anansi to keep the melon?" *(Anansi told Grasshopper there would be something bigger the next day. Grasshopper wanted the bigger fruit.)*

3. Reread pages 28–29, and ask: "Why did Grasshopper tell Anansi to keep the mango?" *(Anansi told Grasshopper they would find a giant goo-goo the next day, and Grasshopper wanted the giant goo-goo.)*

4. Reread page 30, and ask: "What was the trick?" *(There is no such thing as a giant goo-goo. Grasshopper helped Anansi find the other fruit, and Anansi kept all the fruit the two of them found.)*

SUMMARIZE AND APPLY Restate the minilesson principle. Tell children to apply it to a book they will listen to or read. Suggested language: "When you read or listen to a book with a trick, think about the trick that someone plays on someone else."

GROUP SHARE Ask children to tell about a trick someone played on someone else in a book or story they read or listened to.

Whole-Group Lessons

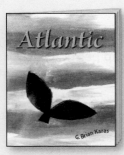

Atlantic
Big Book, Lesson 18

Poems About the Sea
Big Book pp. 32–38, Lesson 18

One-Dog Canoe
Read-Aloud Book, Lesson 18

▶ Atlantic

INTERACTIVE READ-ALOUD/SHARED READING

Read aloud the book to children. Stop periodically for very brief discussion of the text. Use the suggested stopping points and prompts below for quick group response, or give a specific prompt and have partners or threes turn and talk.

- After reading about the beach, ask: "What is this story about?" *(the Atlantic Ocean)* Follow-up: "Who is telling the story?" *(the Atlantic Ocean)"*
- After reading page 11, ask: "Why does the author say that an iceberg could be lapping at your toes?" *(to show how far the ocean water can travel)*
- After reading page 27, ask: "What are some things that people do to show their interest in the ocean?" *(Fishermen fish in it, artists paint it, and poets write about it.)*
- At the end, ask: "How would you describe the Atlantic Ocean? Turn and talk about your ideas with a partner."

MINILESSON Author's Purpose

TEACH Display the minilesson principle on chart paper, and read it aloud to children. Tell children that they are going to think about what the author wants them to learn from the book. Explain that the things the author tells about in the book will help them figure this out.

1. Discuss the principle with children using examples from *Atlantic*. Reread pages 3–11. Suggested language: "This book told about an ocean. What did the author tell about on these pages?" *(how big the ocean is and where it is)*
2. Page through the book, discussing what the ocean is like, what it does, and how it is part of nature. Record children's responses on a Web like the one shown here.
3. Use children's responses to guide children in understanding what the author wants them to understand. Ask: "What do you think the author wants you to learn from this book?" *(what the Atlantic Ocean is like)*

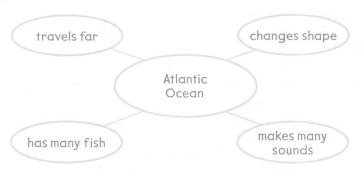

SUMMARIZE AND APPLY Restate the minilesson principle. Tell children to apply it to a book they will listen to or read. Suggested language: "When you read a book, think about what the author wants you to learn."

GROUP SHARE Ask children to tell about a book they have listened to or read. Have them tell what the author wanted them to learn.

▶ One-Dog Canoe

INTERACTIVE READ-ALOUD/SHARED READING

Read aloud the book to children. Stop periodically for a brief discussion of the story. Use the following suggested stopping points and prompts:

- After you read aloud through page 8, ask: "Is this story real or make-believe?" Follow-up: "How can you tell?"
- At the end of page 9, say: "Why does the author compare the wolf to an arrow on the wind?"
- After you read page 26, ask: "What happened to the canoe?" Follow-up: "Why did it happen?"
- At the end of the book, ask: "How is the end of the book like the beginning of the book?"

MINILESSON Author's Purpose

TEACH Write the minilesson principle on chart paper, and read it aloud to children. Explain that authors write for different reasons. Tell children that one reason is to write a story for readers to enjoy. Point out that this is the reason the author wrote *One-Dog Canoe*.

> **MINILESSON PRINCIPLE**
>
> Notice how authors write some stories for you to enjoy.

1. Reread through page 7. Suggested language: "What was this story about?" *(a girl and animals in a canoe)* Continue to read to page 12. Ask: "What word would you use to tell about the story— serious, sad, or funny?" *(funny)*

2. Next, create a Web. Continue to ask children to say words that tell about the book. Fill the outer ovals with words children use to describe the book.

3. After the outer ovals are complete, help children recognize how they could tell the author wrote the story for them to enjoy. Suggested language as you point to the Web: "We can read the words that tell what we thought about the book. The book was funny. We enjoyed the book." In the center oval, write *to enjoy*.

SUMMARIZE AND APPLY Restate the minilesson principle. Tell children to apply it to a story they will listen to or read. Suggested language: "When you read or listen to a story, notice how authors write some stories for you to enjoy."

GROUP SHARE Have children tell about a story that was fun to listen to or read.

▶ Poems About the Sea

INTERACTIVE READ-ALOUD/SHARED READING

Read aloud the poems to children. Stop periodically for brief discussion. Use the following suggested stopping points and prompts:

- After you read "If You Ever," ask: "Why is it silly to say that if you ever touch a whale's tail, you'll never meet another whale?"
- After reading "A Sailor Went to Sea, Sea, Sea," say: "In this poem, two different words that sound alike mean two different things. What are they?" Follow up: "What does each word mean?"
- After you read "Ten Little Fishes," ask: "What are two different things the word *school* can mean? Turn and talk to a partner about your ideas."
- After reading "Undersea," say: "How is this poem like the poem 'Ten Little Fishes'?" Follow-up: "How is it different?"

MINILESSON Genre: Poetry

TEACH Display the minilesson principle on chart paper, and read it aloud to children. Tell children they are going to think about words they hear over and over in poems.

> **MINILESSON PRINCIPLE**
>
> Think about the words that you hear over and over.

1. Use *Poems About the Sea* to discuss the principle. Reread pages 22–23. Ask: "Which words did you hear over and over?" *(ever, never)* Recite the poem again, guiding children to clap for each word part (syllable) of the repeated words. Follow-up: "How did hearing these words over and over make the poem more fun and interesting?" *(Answers will vary, but should reflect that the repeated words provided rhythm, or a beat.)*

2. Continue similarly with "A Sailor Went to Sea" and "Ten Little Fishes." After you complete each poem, write its title on the board, and have children name the repeated words from the poem. Write each repeated word or phrase once in a column below the poem title.

3. After all three lists are complete, ask volunteers to choose a repeated word and say a silly short poem that includes the word over and over.

SUMMARIZE AND APPLY Restate the minilesson principle. Tell children to apply it to a poem they will listen to or read. Suggested language: "When you read or listen to a poem, think about words you hear over and over."

GROUP SHARE Ask children to tell about a poem they read or heard that has the same word over and over.

Whole-Group Lessons

Sheep Take a Hike
Big Book, Lesson 19

Fairy Tales: The Three Billy Goats Gruff;
The Builder and the Oni
Big Book pp. 29–38, Lesson 19

Nicky and the Rainy Day
Read-Aloud Book, Lesson 19

▶ Sheep Take a Hike

INTERACTIVE READ-ALOUD/SHARED READING

Read aloud the book to children. Stop periodically for a brief interaction. Use the following suggested stopping points and prompts for quick group response, or give a specific prompt and have partners or threes turn and talk.

- After you read page 10, ask: "Why can't the sheep find the trail?" Follow-up: "What does it mean to *bicker*?"
- After you read page 18, say: "A compass is something to help you find your way. It has a pointer that always points to the north. Why do you think the sheep had a compass?"
- At the end of page 21, ask: "How did the pictures help you figure out what a swamp was? Turn and talk to a partner about your ideas."
- After you finish the book, ask: "What do you think the author meant by the words on the last page?"

MINILESSON Cause and Effect

TEACH Display the minilesson principle on chart paper, and read it aloud to children. Tell children they are going to notice when one thing in a story makes another thing happen. Remind children that understanding what makes things happen will help them understand books and stories.

1. Discuss the principle with children, using an example of cause and effect from *Sheep Take a Hike*. Reread page 18. Suggested language: "The sheep are lost. What happened to make them feel lost?" *(The compass sank.)*

> **MINILESSON PRINCIPLE**
>
> Notice when one thing in a story makes another thing happen.

2. Use children's responses to explain how to identify cause and effect. Suggested language: "The sheep were in a swamp. The compass sank, so they could not use it to find their way. This was one thing that made another thing happen. As you read, it is important to think about why things happen."

3. Work with children to find things that made other things happen in the book. Record their ideas in a T-Map like the one shown here.

SUMMARIZE AND APPLY Restate the minilesson principle. Explain that children can apply it to a story they will listen to or read. Suggested language: "When you read or listen to a story, notice when one thing makes another thing happen."

GROUP SHARE Ask children to share an example of one thing that made another thing happen in a book or story they listened to or read.

▶ Nicky and the Rainy Day

INTERACTIVE READ-ALOUD/SHARED READING

Read aloud the book to children. Stop periodically for a brief discussion of the story. Use the following suggested stopping points and prompts:

- After you read the title page, ask: "What do you think this book will be about? Why do you think so?" Follow-up after reading page 3: "Were you right about what the book would be about?"
- After you read page 15, say: "Deserts, mountains, and jungles are different kinds of land that are on different parts of Earth. What is the same about these kinds of land?" Follow-up: "What is different about them? Turn and talk to a partner about your ideas."
- After you read page 28, ask: "What do you think the bunnies saw that was green and yellow and orange and red?" Follow-up: "Why do you think so?" After you read page 31, ask children if they were right.
- At the end, ask: "Did the bunnies go to all the places in the book, or did they make-believe they were going to many of these places?" Follow-up: "Where is one place you have pretended to go? Why did you want to go there?"

MINILESSON Cause and Effect

TEACH Remind children that in *Nicky and the Rainy Day,* they read about one thing making another thing happen.

1. Reread page 3 as you guide children in understanding how one thing can make another thing happen. Suggested language: "Why couldn't Nicky and the others go out to play at the beginning of the story?" (*It was raining.*)

> **MINILESSON PRINCIPLE**
> Notice when one thing in a story makes another thing happen.

2. Write the minilesson principle on chart paper, and read it aloud. Next, create a T-Map with sections labeled *First Thing* and *What It Made Happen.* Use the chart to continue to discuss cause and effect. Make certain to include a chart entry to emphasize that, near the end of the book, Nicky and the others could go out for a walk in the meadow (what it made happen) because the rain stopped (first thing).

SUMMARIZE AND APPLY Restate the minilesson principle. Tell children to apply it to a story they will listen to or read. Suggested language: "When you read or listen to a story, notice when one thing makes another thing happen."

GROUP SHARE Have children tell about part of a story they read or heard when they noticed one thing that made another thing happen.

▶ Fairy Tales

INTERACTIVE READ-ALOUD/SHARED READING

Read aloud the book to children. Stop periodically for brief discussion. Use the following suggested stopping points and prompts:

- After you read page 31, ask: "Why did the troll let Little Billy Goat pass?" Follow-up: "Were you surprised that the troll let Little Billy Goat pass?"
- After you read page 33, ask: "Did the troll let Middle Billy Goat pass for the same reason as Little Billy Goat, or for a different reason?"
- At the end of page 35, ask: "Why did the troll swim away? Turn and talk to a partner about your ideas."
- After you finish the book, ask: "How was *The Builder and the Oni* the same as *The Three Billy Goats Gruff*?" Follow-up: "How was it different?"

MINILESSON Understanding Characters

TEACH Explain to children that *The Three Billy Goats Gruff* and *The Builder and the Oni* are fairy tales. Tell children that they can read to see what people and animals do and say. This can help them notice whether the animals and people are good or bad. Display the minilesson principle on chart paper, and read it aloud. Tell children they are going to notice how some of the people and animals in these fairy tales were good and how some of them were bad.

1. Use *The Three Billy Goats Gruff* to discuss the principle. Suggested language: "As I read, I noticed whether the people and animals were good or bad. I could tell what the animals were like by what they were doing. The billy goats only wanted to cross the bridge to get something to eat. There was no reason for the troll to stop them. The troll was bad for trying to stop them."

> **MINILESSON PRINCIPLE**
> Notice that the people and animals can be good or bad.

2. Have children apply the principle to *The Builder and the Oni.* Ask: "Which people and animals were good? Which were bad? How could you tell?" With children's responses, complete a Column Chart labeled *Name, Did and Said,* and *Good or Bad?*

SUMMARIZE AND APPLY Restate the minilesson principle. Tell children to apply it to a book they will listen to or read. Suggested language: "When you read or listen to a story, notice that the people and animals can be good or bad."

GROUP SHARE Ask children to tell about good and bad animals or people in a fairy tale they have read or heard.

Whole-Group Lessons

Curious George's Dinosaur Discovery
Big Book, Lesson 20

Exploring Land and Water
Big Book pp. 25–30, Lesson 20

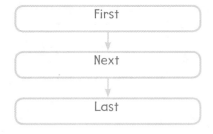

Duck & Goose
Read-Aloud Book, Lesson 20

► Curious George's Dinosaur Discovery

INTERACTIVE READ-ALOUD/SHARED READING

Read aloud the book to children. Stop periodically for a brief interaction. Use the following suggested stopping points and prompts for quick group response, or give a specific prompt and have partners or threes turn and talk.

- At the end of page 8, ask: "Who is the most important person or animal in the story?" Follow-up: "How can you tell?"
- After you read page 10, say: "Scientists who search for dinosaur bones must often sift through dirt. They put the dirt in pans that have very small holes. The dirt goes out through the holes, but any bones stay in the pan. Why do you think scientists must often sift through many pans without finding any bones?"
- After you finish the book, say: "At the end of the book, the author wrote that George got to see HIS dinosaur on display. What did the author mean by *HIS dinosaur*? Turn and talk to a partner about your ideas."

MINILESSON Sequence of Events

TEACH Display the minilesson principle on chart paper, and read it aloud. Tell children they are going to think about what happens first, next, and last in a story. Explain that thinking about the things that happen in order will help them better understand the story.

1. Use *Curious George's Dinosaur Discovery* to discuss the principle. Reread page 4 aloud. Suggested language: "What happened in the beginning of the story?" *(George and his friend went to a rock quarry to watch scientists and help dig for dinosaur bones.)* Follow-up: "What sort of trouble did George get into first?" *(He made a big mess and then knocked over a wheelbarrow.)*

> **MINILESSON PRINCIPLE**
> Think about what happens first, next, and last in the story.

2. Tell children to think about what George did next. Suggested language: "First, George knocked over a wheelbarrow. What did he do next?" *(He ran up a hill and accidentally knocked a rock down the hill.)*
3. Ask children to think about what happened at the end. Suggested language: "First, George knocked over a wheelbarrow. Next, he ran up a hill and knocked down rocks. What happened last in the story?" *(The rocks knocked dirt off of dinosaur bones, and George got to help with the new discovery.)*
4. Use children's answers to tell what happened first, next, and last in the story. Explain that using the words *first, next,* and *last* will help them remember the order of things in the story. Record children's ideas in a Flow Chart like the one shown here.

```
┌─────────────┐
│    First    │
└─────────────┘
       │
       ▼
┌─────────────┐
│    Next     │
└─────────────┘
       │
       ▼
┌─────────────┐
│    Last     │
└─────────────┘
```

SUMMARIZE AND APPLY Restate the minilesson principle. Then tell children to apply it to a book they will listen to or read. Suggested language: "When you read or listen to a story, think about what happens first, next, and last."

GROUP SHARE Have children share stories they read or heard by telling what happened first, next, and last. Remind them to use the words *first, next,* and *last.*

▶ Duck & Goose

INTERACTIVE READ-ALOUD/SHARED READING

Read aloud the book to children. Stop periodically for a brief discussion of the story. Use the following suggested stopping points and prompts:

- At the end of page 4, ask: "What reason does Duck give for owning the egg?" Follow-up: "What reason does Goose give for owning the egg?"
- After you read pages 10–11, ask: "Why are there circles leading from Duck's and Goose's heads to pictures?"
- At the end of the book, ask: "Did the author write this book for you to learn about ducks and geese, or did the author write this book for you to enjoy? Turn and talk to a partner about your ideas."

MINILESSON Sequence of Events

TEACH Display the minilesson principle on chart paper, and read it aloud. Remind children that thinking about what happens first, next, and last will help them understand stories they listen to and read.

1. Reread through page 9 of *Duck & Goose* to discuss sequence of events. Suggested language: "What happened in the beginning of the story?" *(Duck and Goose find an egg.)* Follow-up: "What problem did Duck and Goose have?" *(They both said they owned the egg.)*

> **MINILESSON PRINCIPLE**
>
> Think about what happens first, next, and last in the story.

2. Tell children to think about what Duck and Goose did to try to solve the problem. Suggested language: "First, Duck and Goose both said they owned the egg. What happened next?" *(They took care of the egg by keeping it warm, and they became friends.)*

3. Ask children to think about what happened last, at the end of the story. Suggested language: "First, Duck and Goose both said they owned the egg. Next, they tried to take care of the egg, and they became friends. What happened last in the story?" *(They found out that the egg was really a ball. They played with the ball.)*

4. Create a Flow Chart labeled *First, Next,* and *Last.* Write children's responses to the questions above.

SUMMARIZE AND APPLY Restate the minilesson principle. Tell children to apply it to a story they will listen to or read. Suggested language: "When you read or listen to a story, think about what happens first, next, and last."

GROUP SHARE Have children tell what happened first, next, and last in a story they listened to or read. Tell them to use the words *first, next,* and *last.*

▶ Exploring Land and Water

INTERACTIVE READ-ALOUD/SHARED READING

Read aloud the book to children. Stop periodically for brief discussion. Use the following suggested stopping points and prompts:

- After you read page 25, ask: "How are the places on this page the same?" Follow-up: "How are they different?"
- After you read page 26, ask: "How does the picture help you understand what an ocean is?" Follow-up: "How can you tell the name of the ocean in the picture?"
- After reading page 27, point to the arch in the photo and say: "There are special places around the world. They are called landmarks. One of these special places is the big arch you see here. It is the Gateway Arch. How can you tell what river the Gateway Arch is near?"
- After you read page 30, ask: "How does this key help you understand the map?" Follow-up: "Why do you think this is called a key? Turn and talk with a partner about your ideas."

MINILESSON Genre: Informational Text

TEACH Explain that *Exploring Land and Water* was different from the other two books children read this week because it was not make-believe. It told about things in real life. Display the minilesson principle on chart paper, and read it aloud. Tell children they are going to think about the places in the book so they can learn more about them.

1. Use *Exploring Land and Water* to discuss the principle. Reread page 26. Suggested language: "What did you learn on this page about an ocean?" *(It is a big body of water. It is very big. People swim and fish there.)*

> **MINILESSON PRINCIPLE**
>
> Think about the places in the book so you can learn about them.

2. Continue through the book, asking a similar question for each page. Create a T-Map with the headings *Place* and *What I Learned.* Complete the chart with children's responses.

SUMMARIZE AND APPLY Restate the minilesson principle. Tell children to apply it to a book they will listen to or read. Suggested language: "When you read or listen to a book about places, think about the places so you can learn about them."

GROUP SHARE Ask children to share a book they listened to or read. Have them tell about the places in the book.

Whole-Group Lessons

Zin! Zin! Zin! a Violin
Big Book, Lesson 21

Poems
Big Book pp. 30–35, Lesson 21

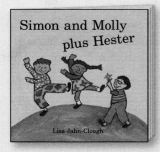

Simon and Molly plus Hester
Read-Aloud Book, Lesson 21

▶ Zin! Zin! Zin! a Violin

INTERACTIVE READ-ALOUD/SHARED READING

Read aloud the book to children. Stop periodically for very brief discussion of the text. Use the suggested stopping points and prompts below for quick group response, or give a specific prompt and have partners or threes turn and talk.

- After reading about the violin, ask: "What is happening in this book?" *(Musical instruments are coming together.)* Follow-up: "Which instruments come together to make a duo?" *(trombone and trumpet)*
- After reading about the harp, ask: What instruments do you think play louder music?" *(trumpet, trombone, French horn)* Follow-up: "What instruments do you think play softer music?" *(cello, violin, harp)*
- After all the instruments are on stage, ask: "What are all the instruments going to do?" *(play for an audience)* Follow-up: "Have you ever heard any of these instruments? What did they sound like?"
- At the end, say: "Think about two instruments. How are the instruments alike? How are they different? Turn and talk about your ideas with a partner."

MINILESSON Details

TEACH Display the minilesson principle on chart paper, and read it aloud to children. Tell children that they are going to look for words that tell what things are like.

1. Discuss the principle with children using examples from *Zin! Zin! a Violin.* Suggested language: "In the book *Zin! Zin! a Violin* you learned about musical instruments that play in an orchestra. You can look for words that help you learn more about these instruments."

2. Reread the description of the trombone. Ask: "Which words tell about how the trombone sounded?" *(mournful moan, silken tone)* Follow-up: "What do the words *gliding, sliding, high notes go low* tell you?" *(how the trombone makes sound)*

3. Continue in the same way, using other musical instruments as examples. Suggested language for each spread: "Which words tell about what a (trumpet) is like?" Use children's responses to complete a T-Map like the one shown here.

> **MINILESSON PRINCIPLE**
>
> Notice words in a book that tell what things are like.

Instrument	Words That Tell About It

SUMMARIZE AND APPLY Restate the minilesson principle. Tell children to apply it to a book they will listen to or read. Suggested language: "When you read a book, notice the words that tell what things are like."

GROUP SHARE Ask children to tell about something they learned from a book they listened to or read. Have them name words that helped them understand what it was like.

▶ Simon and Molly plus Hester

INTERACTIVE READ-ALOUD/SHARED READING

Read aloud the book to children. Stop periodically for a brief interaction. Use the following suggested stopping points and prompts:

- After reading page 4, ask: "What do you think it would be like to have a new kid move into your neighborhood? Turn and talk about your ideas with a partner."
- After reading page 16, ask: "Why do you think Simon spent all afternoon trying to make paper airplanes?"
- At the end of the story, ask: "What other things do you think the three friends will enjoy doing together?"

MINILESSON Understanding Characters

TEACH Display the minilesson principle on chart paper, and read it aloud to children. Tell children they are going to think about how the people in a story feel and why.

1. Discuss the principle with children, using examples from *Simon and Molly plus Hester*. Suggested language: "In the story, we got to know three people. Who were they?" *(Simon, Molly, and Hester)*

> **MINILESSON PRINCIPLE**
> Notice how the people in the story feel.

2. Focus on how Simon felt at the beginning of the story. Suggested language: "At the beginning of the story, Simon felt very upset and jealous that Hester had moved in. We knew Simon was upset by the things he said and did. On page 7, Simon said that he did not like paper airplanes. On page 8, Simon ate his toast plain instead of putting cinnamon-sugar on it as Hester suggested. What did Simon say to Hester on page 10 that showed he was upset?" *(Simon told Hester to leave him alone.)*

3. Have children tell how Simon's feelings changed. Ask: "How did Simon feel at the end of the story?" *(happy)* Follow-up: "What did Simon say and do that helped you figure out how he felt?" *(Simon had fun playing with Molly and Hester. He said that he was glad to be friends with Molly and Hester.)*

4. Have children tell how Molly and Hester felt at different points in the story. Record children's ideas in a T-Map labeled *What the Person Said or Did* and *How the Person Felt*.

SUMMARIZE AND APPLY Restate the minilesson principle. Tell children to apply it to a book they will listen to or read. Suggested language: "When you read, think about how the people in the story feel."

GROUP SHARE Ask children to tell about a person in a book they listened to or read. Have children tell how the person felt and what the person said or did that showed his or her feelings.

▶ Poems About Music

INTERACTIVE READ-ALOUD/SHARED READING

Read aloud the poems to children. Stop periodically for brief discussion of the text. Use the following suggested stopping points and prompts:

- After reading "Celebration," ask: "What will be happening in the night?" *(a party or celebration)* Follow-up: "What do you picture in your mind when you hear the words *when the dusk comes crawling*?"
- After reading "The More We Get Together," ask: "What does the poet mean by *The more we get together, the happier we'll be*?" *(Friends are happiest when they spend time together.)*
- After reading "The Lobsters and the Fiddler Crab," ask: "What is this poem about?" *(lobsters dancing all night)* Follow-up: "How is it like 'Celebration'? Turn and talk about your ideas with a partner."

MINILESSON Genre: Poetry

TEACH Display the minilesson principle on chart paper, and read it aloud to children. Explain that reading a poem can make them feel a certain way. Tell them that thinking about how a poem makes them feel will help them enjoy it more.

1. Reread "Celebration" aloud. Ask: "How does this poem make you feel?" *(lucky, excited)* Follow-up: "What words did the poet use to make you feel that way?"

> **MINILESSON PRINCIPLE**
> Think about how a poem makes you feel.

2. Then reread "The More We Get Together" aloud. Ask: "Did the words in this poem make you feel sad or glad?" *(glad)*

3. Help children notice other words that convey feelings. Reread the second verse of "The Lobsters and the Fiddler Crab" aloud, emphasizing a feeling of excitement. Point out the exclamation mark at the end. Ask: "How do you feel when you hear these words?" *(happy, excited)*

SUMMARIZE AND APPLY Restate the minilesson principle. Tell children to apply it to poems they will listen to or read. Suggested language: "When you read poems, think about how they make you feel."

GROUP SHARE Ask children to tell how certain poems they listened to or read made them feel.

Whole-Group Lessons

Leo the Late Bloomer
Big Book, Lesson 22

What Can a Baby Animal Do?
Big Book pp. 31–38, Lesson 22

A Tiger Grows Up
Read-Aloud Book, Lesson 22

▶ Leo the Late Bloomer

INTERACTIVE READ-ALOUD/SHARED READING

Read aloud the book to children. Stop periodically for a brief interaction. Use the following suggested stopping points and prompts for quick group response, or give a specific prompt and have partners or threes turn and talk.

- At the end of page 7, ask: "How do you think Leo feels about not being able to read, write, or draw?" *(sad)*
- At the end of page 16, say: "*Patience* means that you are able to wait for something without getting upset. When are some times when you need patience?"
- At the end of the book, ask: "How do you think Leo feels when he finally blooms?" *(great)*

MINILESSON Story Structure

TEACH Display the minilesson principle on chart paper, and read it aloud to children. Tell children they are going to learn how to think about the problems in a story.

1. Discuss the principle with children, using *Leo the Late Bloomer* as an example. Suggested language: "In the story *Leo the Late Bloomer,* you learned that Leo had some problems. What was Leo's first problem?" *(He couldn't read.)*

2. Continue to focus on Leo's other problems. Suggested language: "Leo had some other problems, too. What were those problems?"

3. Help children identify the problems Leo had and record their ideas in a Story Map like the one shown here. Reinforce to children that it is important to understand what problems the person or animal in a story has. Guide children to recognize how Leo's problems were solved, and record the solution on the Story Map.

> **MINILESSON PRINCIPLE**
>
> Think about the problem in the story.

Setting	Character
Problem	
Solution	

SUMMARIZE AND APPLY Restate the minilesson principle. Then tell children to apply it to a book they will listen to or read. Suggested language: "When you read, think about the problem in the story."

GROUP SHARE Have children describe the problem in a story they listened to or read.

▶ A Tiger Grows Up

INTERACTIVE READ-ALOUD/SHARED READING

Read aloud the book to children. Stop periodically for a brief interaction. Use the following suggested stopping points and prompts:

- After reading page 3, say: "A *den* is the name for the home of a wild animal. What other animals besides a tiger live in a den?" *(a bear, lion, wolf)*
- After reading page 17, ask: "Why do you think young cubs live together after they leave their mother?" *(to stay safe)*
- At the end of the book, ask: "What was the most interesting thing you learned about a tiger? Turn and talk about your ideas with a partner."

MINILESSON Sequence of Events

TEACH Display the minilesson principle on chart paper, and read it aloud to children. Tell children they are going to find out how things grow and change.

1. Discuss the principle with children, using examples from *A Tiger Grows Up*. Suggested language: "*A Tiger Grows Up* is about the life of a Bengal tiger from the cub's birth to when she is grown-up and becomes a mother herself. What was the cub like at the beginning of the story?" *(The cub was very small and could not even stand up. All the cub could do was drink milk and sleep.)*

> **MINILESSON PRINCIPLE**
> Think about how things grow and change.

2. Have the children tell how the cub grew and changed throughout the story. Suggested language: "As the cub grew, she looked different and was able to do many things besides drink milk and sleep. At the end of the book, what was the cub like?" *(The cub had grown into a tigress. She was big and strong. She could hunt and have cubs of her own.)*

3. Use children's responses to the previous questions to fill in a T-Map labeled *Beginning* and *End* to show how the cub changed from the beginning of the story to the end. You may wish to add sketches to reinforce children's understanding.

SUMMARIZE AND APPLY Restate the minilesson principle. Tell children to apply it to a book they will listen to or read. Suggested language: "When you read, think about how things grow and change over time."

GROUP SHARE Ask children to share how something grew and changed in a book they listened to or read.

▶ What Can a Baby Animal Do?

INTERACTIVE READ-ALOUD/SHARED READING

Read aloud the book to children. Stop periodically for a brief interaction. Use the following suggested stopping points and prompts:

- After reading page 32, say: "A *calf* is the name for a young whale. What other animals call their babies calves?" *(cows, elephants, giraffes, buffalo)*
- After reading about the rabbits, ask: "What else might a rabbit and her bunny be good at?"
- At the end of the book, ask: "What are some things you and your mother or grandmother can both do?"

MINILESSON Conclusions

TEACH Display the minilesson principle on chart paper, and read it aloud. Tell children they are going to learn how to spot clues in a book to help them figure out what comes next.

1. Discuss the principle with children using the patterned language in *What Can a Baby Animal Do?* Reread the first three pages of the book. Suggested language: "In the book *What Can a Baby Animal Do?*, the author repeats some of the words from page to page to make a pattern. How are the sentences about the Humpback whale and its calf the same as the sentences about the cat and its kitten?" *(Both name the mother and tell what she does well and then name the baby and tell what it can do.)*

> **MINILESSON PRINCIPLE**
> Notice clues in the book to help you make guesses about what comes next.

2. Continue by helping children use this repetitive text pattern to guess what comes next in the book. Suggested language: "Once we notice that the author uses some of the same words on every page, we have a big clue about what comes next in the book. If the next page in this book was about a mother dog and her puppy, what do you think the page would say?" *(Possible answer: This mother dog is a good digger. Its puppy said, "I can dig, too.")*

3. Starting with the horse, continue reading about the rest of the animals in the book and have children guess what comes next. Suggested language: "I am going to show you only the pictures and you use the pattern to guess what words come next."

SUMMARIZE AND APPLY Restate the minilesson principle. Tell children to apply it to a book they will listen to or read. Suggested language: "When you read, think about clues to help you guess what comes next."

GROUP SHARE Have children tell what clues they used to make guesses about what came next in a book they listened to or read.

Whole-Group Lessons

Zinnia's Flower Garden
Big Book, Lesson 23

Growing Sunflowers
Big Book pp. 32-37, Lesson 23

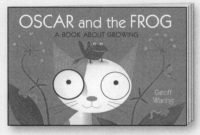

Oscar and the Frog
Read-Aloud Book, Lesson 23

▶ Zinnia's Flower Garden

INTERACTIVE READ-ALOUD/SHARED READING

Read aloud the story to children. Stop periodically for a brief interaction. Use the following suggested stopping points and prompts for quick group response, or give a specific prompt and have partners or threes turn and talk.

- After reading page 6, say: "You can see a small notebook on this page. This is a journal. Zinnia writes about her garden in this journal. What are some things you would write about in a journal?"
- At the end of page 8, ask: "Why is it hard for Zinnia to wait for her seeds to grow?"
- After reading page 14, ask: "What would happen if Zinnia did not water her plants?"
- After reading on page 20 that the first flower bloomed, ask: "How do you think Zinnia felt when she saw the first flower in her garden?"
- After reading page 26, ask: "Do you think selling flowers at Zinnia's lemonade stand was a good idea? Why or why not?"

MINILESSON Sequence of Events

TEACH Display the minilesson principle on chart paper, and read it aloud to children. Tell children they are going to think about what happens first, next, and last in a story. Explain that thinking about what happens in order will help them understand the story.

1. Help children identify the sequence of events in *Zinnia's Flower Garden*. Suggested language: "In *Zinnia's Flower Garden*, what did Zinnia do first to start her garden?" *(She got the soil ready and planted all different kinds of flower seeds.)*

> **MINILESSON PRINCIPLE**
>
> Think about what happens in the story first, next, and last.

2. Tell children to think about what Zinnia did next. Suggested language: "Think about Zinnia's garden. What did she do next after planting the flower seeds?" *(She watered the seeds and watched them grow into flowers.)*

3. Ask children to think about what happened at the end of the story. Suggested language: "Zinnia took care of her garden until the end of the story. What were the last things she did to her garden?" *(She picked all of the flowers and collected the ripe seeds to plant next year.)*

4. Work with children to use their answers to the previous questions to tell what happened first, next, and last in the story. Point out that using the words *first, next,* and *last* will help them remember the order of what happened in the story. Record children's ideas in a Flow Chart like the one shown here.

```
┌──────────────┐
│    First     │
└──────────────┘
        ↓
┌──────────────┐
│     Next     │
└──────────────┘
        ↓
┌──────────────┐
│     Last     │
└──────────────┘
```

SUMMARIZE AND APPLY Restate the minilesson principle. Then tell children to apply it to a book they will listen to or read. Suggested language: "When you listen to or read a book, think about what happens first, next, and last."

GROUP SHARE Have children share stories they read by telling what happened first, next, and last. Remind them to use the words *first, next,* and *last* to help tell the correct order.

▶ Oscar and the Frog

INTERACTIVE READ-ALOUD/SHARED READING

Read aloud the book to children. Stop periodically for a brief interaction. Use the following suggested stopping points and prompts:

- After reading pages 4–5, say: "The word *hatch* means to come out of an egg. What animals do you know that hatch from an egg? Let's read on to see if you're right."
- After reading page 16, ask: "Are you full-grown like Frog, or still growing like Oscar?" *(still growing)* Follow-up: "How do you think you will change as you grow?"
- After reading page 24, ask: "What other animals do you know that are born? Turn and talk about your ideas with a partner."

MINILESSON Text and Graphic Features

TEACH Display the minilesson principle on chart paper, and read it aloud to children. Tell children they are going to use pictures to get information about the topic they are reading about.

1. Use *Oscar and the Frog* to introduce the idea that pictures contain important information. Suggested language: "There are many pictures in the book *Oscar and the Frog*. The pictures are colorful and fun to look at, but they also give us information about the plants and animals in the story. Let's look at the pictures on pages 4–5. What information do these pictures show?" *(the steps of a tadpole growing from an egg into a frog)*

> **MINILESSON PRINCIPLE**
>
> Notice how the pictures give you information.

2. Continue having children find examples of pictures in the story that provide information. Suggested language: "There are other pictures in the story that provided information. Tell about some of these pictures that helped you better understand what you were reading about by giving you information." *(Possible response: The pictures on pages 10–11 gave me information about what different seeds look like and how seeds can be different sizes.)*

SUMMARIZE AND APPLY Restate the minilesson principle. Tell children to apply it to a book they will listen to or read. Suggested language: "When you read, look at the pictures to get information."

GROUP SHARE Ask children to tell what information they learned by looking at the pictures in a book they listened to or read.

▶ Growing Sunflowers

INTERACTIVE READ-ALOUD/SHARED READING

Read aloud the book to children. Stop periodically for a brief interaction. Use the following suggested stopping points and prompts:

- After reading the list of the things you need to grow sunflowers on page 33, say: "The word *moist* means 'just a little wet.' What other words do you know that tell about being wet?" *(damp, soggy, sopping, soaked)* Follow-up: "Why do you think the author lists the things you need to grow sunflowers?"
- At the end of the book, ask: "What are the most important things to remember about growing sunflowers?" *(keep the pot in a sunny place and keep the soil moist)*

MINILESSON Sequence of Events

TEACH Explain to children that some books include information about how to do something. Then display the minilesson principle on chart paper, and read it aloud.

1. Have children look back through *Growing Sunflowers* to find information about how to do something. Suggested language: "The person who wrote *Growing Sunflowers* gave steps telling how to do something. What do the steps tell you how to do?" *(They tell you how to plant and grow sunflowers.)*

> **MINILESSON PRINCIPLE**
>
> Notice when the author tells you how to do something.

2. Draw a Flow Chart labeled Step 1 through Step 6. Have children name the steps for growing sunflowers that appeared in *Growing Sunflowers*. Use this information to fill in the chart. You may wish to add sketches to reinforce children's understanding.

SUMMARIZE AND APPLY Restate the minilesson principle. Tell children to apply it to a book they will listen to or read. Suggested language: "When you read, look for places where the author tells you how to do something."

GROUP SHARE Ask children to name other books they have read that included information about how to do something.

Whole-Group Lessons

Chameleon, Chameleon
Big Book, Lesson 24

Amazing Animal Bodies
Big Book pp. 32–38, Lesson 24

Red Eyes or Blue Feathers
Read-Aloud Book, Lesson 24

▶ Chameleon, Chameleon

INTERACTIVE READ-ALOUD/SHARED READING

Read aloud the book to children. Stop periodically for a brief interaction. Use the following suggested stopping points and prompts for quick group response, or give a specific prompt and have partners or threes turn and talk.

- After reading page 5, ask: "How does the chameleon solve the problem that he is hungry and there isn't any food in his tree?"
- After reading page 12, say: "The words on this page tell us that the tiny chameleon is not dangerous. This means that it cannot hurt the bigger chameleon. What animals might be dangerous or harmful to chameleons?"
- After reading page 16, ask: "How is the scorpion different from the tiny chameleon, the geckos, and the frog?"
- After reading pages 22–23, ask: "How does a chameleon catch its food?"
- At the end of the book, ask: "Why do chameleons change colors?"

MINILESSON Conclusions

TEACH Display the minilesson principle on chart paper, and read it aloud to children. Tell children they are going to look at the pictures in a book to help understand what they are reading.

1. Discuss the principle with children, using pictures from *Chameleon, Chameleon.* Suggested language: "In the book *Chameleon, Chameleon,* there are many pictures of real animals. Looking closely at these pictures will help you understand the words in the book. Look at the picture of the chameleon on the first two pages of the book. How does the picture help you understand the words *His skin has peaceful colors?*" *(The picture shows that peaceful colors are green, blue, and yellow.)*

> **MINILESSON PRINCIPLE**
> Think about the pictures to help you understand the book.

2. Continue showing how pictures can help children understand the information in a book. Suggested language for page 25: "Look at the picture of the girl chameleon up in the tree. How does the picture help you understand the words *Her skin is dark with angry colors?*" *(The picture shows that a dark, angry color is black.)*

3. Work with children to explain how to use pictures on other pages to better understand the book. Record children's ideas in a Column Chart like the one shown here.

What the Pictures Show	What the Words Say	Conclusions

SUMMARIZE AND APPLY Restate the minilesson principle. Then tell children to apply it to a book they will listen to or read. Suggested language: "When you listen to or read a book, look at the pictures to understand what the words mean."

GROUP SHARE Have children share books they read and explain how they used pictures to understand the meaning of the book.

▶ Red Eyes or Blue Feathers

INTERACTIVE READ-ALOUD/SHARED READING

Read aloud the book to children. Stop periodically for a brief interaction. Use the following suggested stopping points and prompts:

- After reading page 1, say: "The word *adapt* means 'to change for a reason or purpose.' What is one animal that you have already read about that has adapted or changed to be able to catch its food from far away?" *(a chameleon)*
- After reading pages 16–17, ask: "Why do you think this bug is called a jewel beetle?"
- At the end of the book, say: "Throughout the book there are words and sentences that appear in smaller letters. What do these sentences tell?" Follow-up: "Why do they appear in small letters?"

MINILESSON Compare and Contrast

TEACH Display the minilesson principle on chart paper, and read it aloud to children. Tell children they are going to learn to think about ways in which things can be the same and different.

> **MINILESSON PRINCIPLE**
>
> Notice how two things in a book are the same and how they are different.

1. Discuss the principle with children, using *Red Eyes or Blue Feathers* as an example. Suggested language: "In *Red Eyes or Blue Feathers,* we read about many animals. In some ways the animals are the same. Let's think about two animals: a polar bear and a red fox. Can you remember what is the same about these two animals?" *(The color of their coat blends into their surroundings.)*

2. Then help children contrast a polar bear and a red fox. Suggested language: "Think again about a polar bear and a red fox. How are these two animals different?" *(Possible response: A polar bear is much bigger than a red fox. A polar bear lives where it is very cold and a red fox doesn't.)*

3. Work with children to choose two different animals from the book and tell how they are the same and how they are different. Record children's ideas in a Venn Diagram with the animal names in the outer parts of the circles and *Both* in the overlapping section.

SUMMARIZE AND APPLY Restate the minilesson principle. Tell children to apply it to a book they will listen to or read. Suggested language: "When you read, think about how things are the same and how they are different."

GROUP SHARE Have children tell how two things in a book they listened to or read were the same and how they were different.

▶ Amazing Animal Bodies

INTERACTIVE READ-ALOUD/SHARED READING

Read aloud the book to children. Stop periodically for a brief interaction. Use the following suggested stopping points and prompts:

- At the end of page 34, ask: "How are snowshoe hares and chameleons the same?"
- At the end of the book, ask: "How do you think the shell helps the clam? Turn and talk about your ideas with a partner."

MINILESSON Conclusions

TEACH Display the minilesson principle on chart paper, and read it aloud to children. Tell children they are going to learn how the pictures in a book can help them understand what they are reading.

> **MINILESSON PRINCIPLE**
>
> Think about the pictures to help you understand the book.

1. Use pictures from *Amazing Animal Bodies* to demonstrate the principle. Suggested language: "The words in the book *Amazing Animal Bodies* tell how the bodies of some animals help them stay alive. If you are reading about an animal and come to a word you don't understand, look at the pictures for help. If you read the page that says *Chameleons change colors to blend into their surroundings* and you do not know the meaning of *surroundings,* how could the picture help you figure out this word?" *(The picture shows that the chameleon's surroundings are the green leaves around it.)*

2. Provide another example of how pictures can help children understand the information in a book. Suggested language: "Look at the picture of the anteater. How does the picture help you understand the word *snout*?" *(The picture shows that the snout is like a nose.)*

3. Work with children to find other pictures in the book that help children understand the words in the story. Record children's ideas in a T-Map with the heading *What the Pictures Show* at the top of the left column and the heading *What the Words Mean* at the top of the right column.

SUMMARIZE AND APPLY Restate the minilesson principle. Tell children to apply it to a book they will listen to or read. Suggested language: "When you read, look at the pictures to help you understand what you are reading about."

GROUP SHARE Have children share books they have read and tell how they used pictures to understand what they read.

Pie in the Sky
Big Book, Lesson 25

From Apple Tree to Store
Big Book pp. 37–45, Lesson 25

Bread Comes to Life
Read-Aloud Book, Lesson 25

▶ Pie in the Sky

INTERACTIVE READ-ALOUD/SHARED READING

Read aloud the story to children. Stop periodically for a brief interaction. Use the following suggested stopping points and prompts for quick group response, or give a specific prompt and have partners or threes turn and talk.

- After reading page 6, say: "When Dad calls the tree a pie tree, he doesn't mean that pies will actually grow on the tree. Instead, Dad means that something will grow on the tree that can be used to make pies. What fruits grow on trees that could be used to make pies?" *(apples and cherries)*
- After reading on page 10 that spring has arrived, ask: "How is the tree different in fall and spring?" *(In fall the tree has buds on it and in spring the buds bloom.)*
- After reading page 16, ask: "What do you think the orange and green balls are?"
- At the end of page 32, ask: "Do you think it is important to follow the steps in order to make the pie? Why or why not? Turn and talk about your ideas with a partner."
- At the end of the story, ask: "Do you think birds would like cherry pie? Why or why not?"

MINILESSON Text and Graphic Features

TEACH Display the minilesson principle on chart paper, and read it aloud to children. Tell children they are going to learn to think about why different sized letters are used in a story.

1. Discuss the principle with children, using examples from *Pie in the Sky.* Suggested language: "In the book *Pie in the Sky,* you will notice some words that are in big letters and other words that are in small letters. Look at the first page where you see both big and small letters. Can you point to the big letters?" Follow-up: "Now can you point to the small letters?"

> **MINILESSON PRINCIPLE**
>
> Think about why the letters are different sizes.

2. Read all of the text on page 4 aloud. Explain that the words in the big letters are used to tell the story about the pie tree. Ask: "What do the words in small letters tell?" *(They tell what can be seen in the picture on the page.)* Help children understand that the big letters are used to tell the main story.

3. Continue looking at and rereading words that are in big letters and words that are in small letters. Work with children to fill in a T-Map to show text that appears in big letters and text that appears in small letters. Remind children that two different sized letters are used to separate the main part of the story from the part that describes what can be seen in the pictures.

Words in Big Letters	Words in Small Letters

SUMMARIZE AND APPLY Restate the minilesson principle. Then tell children to apply it to a book they will listen to or read. Suggested language: "When you read, think about why letters with different sizes are used."

GROUP SHARE Ask children to share examples of words shown in different sizes in a book they listened to or read.

▶ Bread Comes to Life

INTERACTIVE READ-ALOUD/SHARED READING

Read aloud the book to children. Stop periodically for a brief interaction. Use the following suggested stopping points and prompts:

- At the end of page 5, ask: "What kinds of bread have you eaten?" Follow-up: "Which kind is your favorite?"
- At the end of page 12, say: "A *crop* is a group of plants grown for food or other uses. We're reading about a crop of wheat in this story. What other kinds of crops might be grown for food?"
- At the end of the book, ask: "Why do you think this book is called *Bread Comes to Life?* Turn and talk about your ideas with a partner."

MINILESSON Text and Graphic Features

TEACH Display the minilesson principle on chart paper, and read it aloud to children. Tell children they are going to look at the pictures in a book to get information from them.

1. Discuss the principle with children, using examples of pictures on pages 22–23 in *Bread Comes to Life.* Suggested language: "The story *Bread Comes to Life* has pictures that give information about growing wheat and making bread that will help you understand the story. Look at these pictures. What information does this group of pictures give you?" *(steps for preparing bread dough)* Follow-up: "How do the pictures help you see each step in your mind?" *(They show exactly what is done to the dough during each step.)*

> **MINILESSON PRINCIPLE**
>
> Think about how the pictures give you information.

2. Continue having children discuss other pictures in the story that provide important information about making bread. Suggested language: "Flip through the book and pay attention to the pictures. What pictures provide information that help you understand how bread is made?" *(Possible response: The picture of the threshing box on page 15 shows how the wheat is separated from the rest of the plant.)*

SUMMARIZE AND APPLY Restate the minilesson principle. Tell children to apply it to a book they will listen to or read. Suggested language: "When you read, notice the pictures in the book and what information they tell you."

GROUP SHARE Have children tell about the pictures in a book they listened to or read and explain what they learned from the pictures.

▶ From Apple Tree to Store

INTERACTIVE READ-ALOUD/SHARED READING

Read aloud the book to children. Stop periodically for a brief interaction. Use the following suggested stopping points and prompts:

- After reading page 37, say: "*Ripe* means that the apples are full-grown and ready to be picked. How do you think apples would taste if they were picked before they were ripe?"
- After reading page 38, ask: "Why does the apple picker need a ladder?"
- At the end of the book, ask: "What is your favorite thing to eat that is made from apples? Turn and talk about your ideas with a partner."

MINILESSON Sequence of Events

TEACH Display the minilesson principle on chart paper, and read it aloud to children. Tell children they are going to learn how to think about order as they read. Explain that most books happen in a certain order. They tell what happens first, next, and last.

1. Discuss the principle with children, using events from *From Apple Tree to Store.* Suggested language: "In *From Apple Tree to Store,* things happen in order. Let's look at the beginning. What happened first?" *(The apples were picked and put into large bins.)*

> **MINILESSON PRINCIPLE**
>
> Think about what happens in the book first, next, and last.

2. Focus on what happened to the apples next after they were put into the bins. Suggested language: "What happened next after the apples were put into the large bins?" *(A tractor picked up the bins and a big truck took the apples to the store.)*

3. Focus on what happened last. Suggested language: "What was the last thing that happened to the apples?" *(People bought apples in a store and took them home and ate them.)*

4. Work with children to use their answers to the previous questions to put the most important events in order. Record children's ideas in a Flow Chart labeled *First, Next,* and *Last.* Remind children that when they think about the order in which things happen it helps them understand a story.

SUMMARIZE AND APPLY Restate the minilesson principle. Tell children to apply it to a book they will listen to or read. Suggested language: "When you listen to or read a book, think about what happens first, next, and last."

GROUP SHARE Have children tell the sequence of events in a book. Ask them to tell what happened first, next, and last.

Whole-Group Lessons

Kitten's First Full Moon
Big Book, Lesson 26

Poems
Big Book pp. 32–38, Lesson 26

Curious George Makes Pancakes
Read-Aloud Book, Lesson 26

▶ Kitten's First Full Moon

INTERACTIVE READ-ALOUD/SHARED READING

Read aloud the story to children. Stop periodically for very brief discussion of the text. Use the suggested stopping points and prompts below for quick group response, or give a specific prompt and have partners or threes turn and talk.

- After reading the first page, ask: "Why does Kitten think the full moon is a bowl of milk?" *(She's never seen a full moon before, and it is round and white like a bowl of milk.)*
- After Kitten chases the moon, ask: "Why do you think Kitten keeps trying to get the moon?" *(She is hungry; cats love milk.)*
- After Kitten jumps in the lake, ask: "Why does Kitten jump in the lake?" *(She thinks the reflection of the moon is a bigger bowl of milk.)*
- At the end, ask: "Have you ever seen a full moon? What did it look like to you? Turn and talk about your ideas with a partner."

MINILESSON Conclusions

TEACH Display the minilesson principle on chart paper, and read it aloud to children. Explain that the characters in a story are the people or animals that the story is about. Tell them they are going to learn how to notice clues in a story to help them figure out what a character is like.

1. Discuss the principle with children, using *Kitten's First Full Moon*. Suggested language: "In *Kitten's First Full Moon*, there is one character. Who is the character?" *(Kitten)* Follow-up: "What did Kitten try to do?" *(get the moon)*

> **MINILESSON PRINCIPLE**
>
> Notice clues in a story that tell what characters are like.

2. Focus on the things Kitten did to try to get the moon. Suggested language: "Kitten first tried to lick the moon, but ended up with a bug on her tongue. Did that stop her from trying?" *(no)* Follow-up: "What did she do next?" *(She tried to jump up and get it.)*

3. Page through the book, asking children to tell about the things Kitten did. Use children's responses to complete an Inference Map like the one shown below. Point out that what Kitten did can help them figure out what she is like. Suggested language: "Kitten kept trying, even when she got hurt and scared. That tells me that Kitten doesn't give up easily. The author didn't tell you this, but you can figure it out from the things she did."

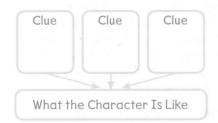

SUMMARIZE AND APPLY Restate the minilesson principle. Tell children to apply it to a story they will listen to or read. Suggested language: "When you read, notice clues in the story that tell what characters are like."

GROUP SHARE Ask children to tell about a character in a story they listened to or read. Have them tell about the clues that helped them figure out what the character was like.

▶ Curious George Makes Pancakes

INTERACTIVE READ-ALOUD/SHARED READING

Read aloud the story to children. Stop periodically for a brief interaction. Use the following suggested stopping points and prompts:

- After reading page 2, say: "*Fundraisers* are different ways to make money for people who need it. The pancake breakfast George was going to was a fundraiser. People paid money to go to the breakfast and that money would be given to the hospital. How could you try to help raise money for children in a hospital? Turn and talk about your ideas with a partner."
- After reading page 11, ask: "How were George's pancakes different from the pancakes being made at the beginning of the story?"
- After reading page 16, say: "George is sticky. Do you think napkins will solve this problem? Why or why not?"

MINILESSON Cause and Effect

TEACH Display the minilesson principle on chart paper, and read it aloud to children. Tell children they are going to notice how one thing can make another thing happen. Explain that understanding why things happen will help them better understand a whole story.

1. Discuss the principle with children, using an example from *Curious George Makes Pancakes*. Suggested language: "In *Curious George Makes Pancakes*, you learned that the line of people waiting to get pancakes grew very, very long. What happened to make the line for pancakes so long?" *(George's pancakes were so delicious that everyone got in line to get some.)*

> **MINILESSON PRINCIPLE**
> Notice that one thing in the story can make another thing happen.

2. Use children's responses to explain how one thing can make another thing happen. Suggested language: "George's delicious blueberry pancakes made many people line up to get them. It is one thing that made another thing happen. As you read, it is important to look for the reasons why things happen."

3. Work with children to find other causes and effects in the story. Record children's ideas in a T-Map labeled *First Thing* and *Other Thing It Made Happen*.

SUMMARIZE AND APPLY Restate the minilesson principle. Tell children to apply it to a story they will listen to or read. Suggested language: "When you read, notice how one thing can make another thing happen."

GROUP SHARE Have children share an example of one thing that made another thing happen from a story they listened to or read.

▶ Poems About Trying and the Moon

INTERACTIVE READ-ALOUD/SHARED READING

Read aloud the poems to children. Stop periodically for a brief interaction. Use the following suggested stopping points and prompts:

- After reading "Drinking Fountain," ask: "What is the boy's problem?" *(He can't get a drink of water.)* "How do you think the fountain is supposed to work?"
- After reading "The Puppy Chased the Sunbeam," say: "How does this poem make you feel? Why does it make you feel that way?"
- After reading "Silvery" and "Moon Boat," ask: "How are these two poems alike? How are they different? Turn and talk about your ideas with a partner."

MINILESSON Genre: Poetry

TEACH Display the minilesson principle on chart paper, and read it aloud to children. Tell children that they are going to think about how words in the poems help them make pictures in their minds. Explain that this will help them understand and enjoy the poems.

1. Ask children to close their eyes and listen as you reread the first verse of "Silvery." Then have them describe what they pictured in their minds. Suggested language: "What did you see in your mind when I read these lines?" Follow-up: "What words helped you make that picture?"

> **MINILESSON PRINCIPLE**
> Think about how words in poems make pictures in your mind.

2. Repeat, rereading the last verse of "Silvery." Have children think about the pictures they made in their minds when they heard these words. Ask: "What helped you make a picture in your mind?"

3. Continue in the same way, rereading each poem. Discuss with children words in the poems that helped them make pictures in their minds. Write their ideas in a T-Map labeled *Words in the Poem* and *Pictures in My Mind*.

SUMMARIZE AND APPLY Restate the minilesson principle. Tell children to apply it to a poem they will listen to or read. Suggested language: "When you read a poem, think about how the words help you make pictures in your mind."

GROUP SHARE After listening to or reading a poem, have children describe the pictures the words in the poem made in their minds.

Whole-Group Lessons

One of Three
Big Book, Lesson 27

Cross-Country Trip
Big Book pp. 31–38, Lesson 27

Someone Bigger
Read-Aloud Book, Lesson 27

▶ One of Three

INTERACTIVE READ-ALOUD/SHARED READING

Read aloud the story to children. Stop periodically for a brief interaction. Use the following suggested stopping points and prompts for quick group response, or give a specific prompt and have partners or threes turn and talk.

- At the end of page 9, ask: "Do you think the three sisters are friends with each other? How do you know?"
- After reading page 15, explain to children that a *subway* is a train that runs under the ground. Tell them that people in big cities use subways to get from one place to another instead of driving a car or taking a bus. Ask: "What do you think would be fun about riding on a subway with your family?"
- After reading page 21, ask: "Why do you think Eva and Nikki go out without their little sister sometimes?" *(because she is too young to do some of the things they like to do)*
- At the end of page 29, ask: "What do you think the youngest sister enjoys most about staying home with her mom and dad?"
- At the end of the story, ask: "Do you think Eva and Nikki miss their little sister when they've been out for a while without her? Why or why not?"

MINILESSON Compare and Contrast

TEACH Display the minilesson principle on chart paper, and read it aloud to children. Tell children they are going to learn to think about how people they read about are the same and how they are different.

1. Discuss the principle with children, using examples of characters from *One of Three*. Suggested language: "The story *One of Three* is about three sisters. Sisters can be the same in many ways, but they can also be different. Think about how the three sisters in the story look. How do they look the same?" *(All three sisters have long hair and brown eyes.)* Follow-up: "How do the three sisters look different?" *(Eva and Nikki look older and taller than their little sister.)*

> **MINILESSON PRINCIPLE**
>
> Think about how people in the story are the same and how they are different.

2. Work with children to notice other similarities and differences between the two older sisters and the youngest sister. Record children's ideas in a Venn Diagram like the one shown here.

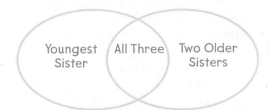

SUMMARIZE AND APPLY Restate the minilesson principle. Then tell children to apply it to a story they will listen to or read. Suggested language: "When you read, think about how people are the same and how they are different."

GROUP SHARE Ask children to share how people in a story they read were the same and how they were different.

▶ Someone Bigger

INTERACTIVE READ-ALOUD/SHARED READING

Read aloud the story to children. Stop periodically for a brief interaction. Use the following suggested stopping points and prompts:

- At the end of page 11, ask: "Why do the townspeople tell Sam that the kite needs someone bigger to hold it?"

- At the end of page 17, say: "Everyone keeps saying that the kite needs someone bigger to hold it. The word *bigger* compares the size of two people or things. What animal can you think of that is even bigger than a rhino that might be able to hold the kite?"

- At the end of the book, ask: "The next time Sam asks his father if he can do something, what do you think he will say? Turn and talk about your ideas with a partner."

MINILESSON Story Structure

TEACH Display the minilesson principle on chart paper, and read it aloud to children. Tell children they are going to think about the beginning of a story and the end of a story.

1. Discuss the principle with children, using *Someone Bigger* as an example. Suggested language: "What happened at the beginning of the story *Someone Bigger*?" (*Sam and his dad made a kite. Sam asked his dad if he could fly the kite and his dad said that the kite needed someone bigger to hold it.*) Follow-up: "How do you think that made Sam feel?" (*sad, mad*)

> **MINILESSON PRINCIPLE**
>
> Think about how the story begins and how it ends.

2. Tell children to think about what happened when the kite flew away and how the story ended. Suggested language: "What happened at the end of the story?" (*Sam finally got a hold of the kite and the kite did not pull him up. Sam rescued all of the people and animals holding on to the kite and brought them back down on the ground. Sam got to fly the kite by himself.*) Follow-up: "How did Sam feel then?" (*happy and proud that everyone knew he was big enough to fly the kite on his own*)

3. Work with children to use their answers to the previous questions to tell what happened in the beginning, middle, and end of the story. Record children's ideas in a Flow Chart labeled *Beginning, Middle,* and *End*.

SUMMARIZE AND APPLY Restate the minilesson principle. Tell children to apply it to a story they will listen to or read. Suggested language: "When you read a story, think about how it begins and how it ends."

GROUP SHARE Have children tell the beginning and ending of a story they listened to or read.

▶ Cross-Country Trip

INTERACTIVE READ-ALOUD/SHARED READING

Read aloud the book to children. Stop periodically for a brief interaction. Use the following suggested stopping points and prompts:

- After reading page 32, say: "This is what a postcard looks like. There is usually a picture on the front of the postcard. On the back of the postcard is a place for you to write a short letter and the person's address you are writing to. Why do you think the author chose to write this story on postcards?" (*to make information about the trip interesting*)

- After reading page 33, ask: "Would you rather visit New York City or Washington, D.C.? Why?"

- At the end of the book, ask: "Which postcard do you think was Granny's favorite? Why? Turn and talk about your ideas with a partner."

MINILESSON Genre: Informational Text

TEACH Display the minilesson principle on chart paper, and read it aloud to children. Tell children they are going to learn to think about how they get information about different things in a book.

1. Discuss the principle with children, using examples from *Cross-Country Trip*. Suggested language: "In the information book *Cross-Country Trip,* the author writes about a family's trip across the country. The author shares information about many different things the family members see on their trip. What are some of the things the author gives you information about?" (*Possible response: The author gives information about New York City and things to see there like the Empire State Building and the Statue of Liberty.*)

> **MINILESSON PRINCIPLE**
>
> Think about how the author gives you information about different things.

2. Work with children to record their responses in a Web. Write *Things We Learned* in the center circle and record children's suggestions in the outer circles. You may wish to draw sketches to reinforce children's understanding. Ask: "How did learning about all of these different things make the book fun to read?" (*It was interesting to learn about things in different cities and parts of the country.*)

SUMMARIZE AND APPLY Restate the minilesson principle. Tell children to apply it to a book they will listen to or read. Suggested language: "When you read, notice when the author gives you information about different things."

GROUP SHARE Ask children to share the different things they learned about in an information book they listened to or read.

Whole-Group Lessons

You Can Do It, Curious George!
Big Book, Lesson 28

Poems About Doing Things
Big Book pp. 26–30, Lesson 28

The Little Engine That Could
Read-Aloud Book, Lesson 28

▶ You Can Do It, Curious George!

INTERACTIVE READ-ALOUD/SHARED READING

Read aloud the story to children. Stop periodically for a brief interaction. Use the following suggested stopping points and prompts for quick group response, or give a specific prompt and have partners or threes turn and talk.

- After reading page 2, say: "George was always curious. If you are *curious,* it means that you want to know about something. What are some things you are curious about?"
- After reading page 3, ask: "What do you think is special about this museum?"
- After reading about George's sledding experience on pages 13–15, ask: "Why wasn't sledding George's best sport?" *(because he didn't know how to stop the sled and he ran into a skier)*
- At the end of page 20, ask: "What do you think George is going to try to be the best at next?"
- At the end of the story, ask: "If you wanted to be the very best swimmer or musician, what things would you need to do? Turn and talk about your ideas with a partner."

MINILESSON Story Structure

TEACH Display the minilesson principle on chart paper, and read it aloud to children. Tell children they are going to think about how a story begins and how it ends.

1. Discuss the principle with children, using *You Can Do It, Curious George!* Suggested language: "What happened in the beginning of the story?" *(George and his friend went to a museum and found out that it won a prize for being the best museum.)*

2. Tell children to think about what George did next and how the story ended. Suggested language: "George decided to find out what he was the best at doing. How did he do this?" *(He tried doing many different things such as sledding and kite flying.)* Follow-up: "What happened to George at the end of the story?" *(George warned everyone about a fire and got a prize for being the Best Helper.)*

3. Work with children to use their answers to the previous questions to tell what happened in the beginning, in the middle, and at the end of the story. Record children's ideas in a Flow Chart like the one shown here.

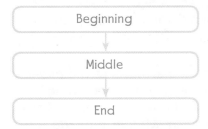

SUMMARIZE AND APPLY Restate the minilesson principle. Then tell children to apply it to a story they will listen to or read. Suggested language: "When you read a story, think about how it begins and how it ends."

GROUP SHARE Have children share a story they read by telling how the story begins and how it ends. Suggest that they use the words *in the beginning* and *at the end of the story.*

▶ The Little Engine That Could

INTERACTIVE READ-ALOUD/SHARED READING

Read aloud the story to children. Stop periodically for a brief discussion of the story. Use the following suggested stopping points and prompts:

- At the end of page 11, say: "The engine is usually on the front of a train. The engine is what pulls the train and makes it go. What other things do you know of that have an engine?"
- At the end of page 17, ask: "How were the Passenger Engine and the Freight Engine different?" *(The Passenger Engine carried people and the Freight Engine carried big machines.)*
- At the end of the story, ask: "What was the problem in this story?" *(The train engine broke down.)* Follow-up: "How did the problem get solved?" *(The Little Blue Engine pulled the train over the mountain and into the city.)*

MINILESSON Genre: Fantasy

TEACH Explain that *The Little Engine That Could* is a made-up story. Tell children that it includes some things that could happen in real life and other things that could not really happen.

1. Focus on *The Little Engine That Could* to introduce the idea that some stories include parts that could not happen in real life. Suggested language: "The story *The Little Engine That Could* tells about a train with a broken engine that needs to get over a mountain to deliver toys and food to boys and girls. What is one part of this story that could really happen?" *(Possible answer: A train engine could break down.)* Follow-up: "What is one part of this story that could not really happen?" *(Possible answer: Toys cannot really talk.)*

> **MINILESSON PRINCIPLE**
> Think about the parts in the story that could not really happen.

2. Ask children to name other things that happened in *The Little Engine That Could* that could not happen in real life. Write the minilesson principle on chart paper. Explain to children that they will better understand what they read if they notice the parts that could not happen in real life.

SUMMARIZE AND APPLY Restate the minilesson principle. Tell children to apply it to a book they will listen to or read. Suggested language: "When you read, look for parts of the story that could not really happen."

GROUP SHARE Have children tell about something that could not really happen in a story they read or listened to.

▶ Poems About Things You Can Do

INTERACTIVE READ-ALOUD/SHARED READING

Read aloud the poems to children. Stop periodically for a brief interaction. Use the following suggested stopping points and prompts:

- After reading "Whistling" on pages 26–27, ask: "How do you think the boy feels about not being able to whistle?"
- After reading "Time to Play" on pages 28–29, ask: "What things do you enjoy playing outside?"
- After reading "By Myself" on page 30, ask: "What are some other things you could imagine yourself to be when you close your eyes?"

MINILESSON Genre: Poetry

TEACH Remind children of ways that poems are different from other things they might read. Explain that many poems have words that sound alike, or rhyme, for example. Tell children that poems also include words that help readers make pictures in their minds. Write the minilesson principle on chart paper, and read it aloud to children. Explain to children that they will look at the poems they read to find words that help them make pictures in their minds.

1. Turn the book so it is facing you and not the children. Then reread "Whistling" for children, having them listen for words that help them picture a person who is whistling. Suggested language: "Which words help you picture someone whistling?" *(lips, small and round)*

> **MINILESSON PRINCIPLE**
> Think about how the words make pictures in your mind.

2. Repeat the first step using the poem "Time to Play." Have children name words that help them picture playing. *(bike, pretend, hopscotch)*
3. You may wish to have volunteers act out or draw parts of the poem to show what they pictured as they read.

SUMMARIZE AND APPLY Restate the minilesson principle. Tell children to apply it to a book they will listen to or read. Suggested language: "When you read, think about how the author's words help you make pictures in your mind."

GROUP SHARE Ask children to tell how they used words from a poem or book they read to make pictures in their minds.

Whole-Group Lessons

Look at Us
Big Book, Lesson 29

The Three Little Pigs
Big Book pp. 26–30, Lesson 29

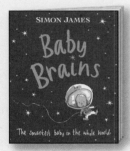

Baby Brains
Read-Aloud Book, Lesson 29

▶ Look at Us

INTERACTIVE READ-ALOUD/SHARED READING

Read aloud the book to children. Stop periodically for a brief interaction. Use the following suggested stopping points and prompts for quick group response, or give a specific prompt and have partners or threes turn and talk.

- At the end of page 5, ask: "On your first day of school, did you feel the same as the kindergartners in this book or different? Explain your answer."
- After reading on page 10 that the children learned about bugs, ask: "What are some things you think the children learned about bugs?"
- At the end of page 18, say: "A *community* is the area or neighborhood you live in. Who are some people who help you in your community?"
- At the end of page 22, ask: "How did the children get ready for their play?"
- At the end of the book, ask: "What do you think was the hardest thing about being in this kindergarten class?" Follow-up: "What thing was the most fun? Turn and talk about your ideas with a partner."

MINILESSON Main Ideas

TEACH Display the minilesson principle on chart paper, and read it aloud to children. Tell children they are going to learn to think about what a book is mostly about.

1. Using *Look at Us,* discuss with children that a book is about one main idea. Suggested language: "*Look at Us* is a book made by teachers and students. What is the book mostly about?" *(all of the things a class of kindergarten students did throughout the school year)*

> **MINILESSON PRINCIPLE**
>
> Think about what the author tells mostly about.

2. Talk with children about the specific things the kindergartners did. Suggested language: "What were some of the things the children did in kindergarten?" *(Possible answer: They learned how to write their names and other words.)*

3. Use children's answers to the previous questions to complete an Idea-Support Map like the one shown here. You may wish to add symbols or simple sketches to help children understand the content of the final map.

SUMMARIZE AND APPLY Restate the minilesson principle. Then tell children to apply it to a book they will listen to or read. Suggested language: "When you read, think about what the book is mostly about to understand it."

GROUP SHARE Ask children to tell what a book they read or listened to was mostly about.

▶ Baby Brains

INTERACTIVE READ-ALOUD/SHARED READING

Read aloud the story to children. Stop periodically for a brief interaction. Use the following suggested stopping points and prompts:

- At the end of page 7, say: "Mr. Brains said that his baby was bright. *Bright* is another way of saying 'smart.' What made Mr. Brains say this?"
- At the end of page 16, ask: "How is Baby Brains like other babies you know?" *(He is small and he cries and sleeps in a crib.)* Follow-up: "How is he different from other babies you know?" *(He can walk, talk, read, go to school, fix cars, work as a doctor, and travel in space.)*
- At the end of the story, ask: "Why do you think the author wrote this book?" *(to make people laugh)*

MINILESSON Story Structure

TEACH Display the minilesson principle on chart paper, and read it aloud to children. Tell children they are going to learn how to think about the most important parts of a story.

1. Discuss the principle with children, using examples from *Baby Brains*. Suggested language: "In the story *Baby Brains,* some parts of the story are important and other parts are not as important. Which part of the story do you think is more important: Baby Brains reading the morning newspaper or Baby Brains flying on a space mission? Why?" *(Baby Brains flying on a space mission because he realized that he was just a baby and wasn't big enough to be away from home.)*

> **MINILESSON PRINCIPLE**
>
> Think about the most important parts of the story.

2. Elicit from children other important parts of the story. Suggested language: "What other parts of the story are important?" *(Possible answer: Baby Brains becoming a doctor; Baby Brains coming home after the space mission and doing the things babies do)*

SUMMARIZE AND APPLY Restate the minilesson principle. Tell children to apply it to a story they will listen to or read. Suggested language: "When you read, think about the most important parts of the story."

GROUP SHARE Ask children to share the most important parts of a story they listened to or read.

▶ The Three Little Pigs

INTERACTIVE READ-ALOUD/SHARED READING

Read aloud the story to children. Stop periodically for a brief interaction. Use the following suggested stopping points and prompts:

- At the end of the first page of the story, say: "This story begins with the words *Once upon a time*. This is how fairy tales begin. *The Three Little Pigs* is a fairy tale. What else do you know about fairy tales?"
- At the end of page 28, ask: "Why was the wolf able to blow down the houses made of straw and sticks?"
- At the end of the story, ask: "Why do you think the three little pigs decided to live together?"

MINILESSON Story Structure

TEACH Display the minilesson principle on chart paper, and read it aloud. Tell children they are going to learn to look for the most important parts of the story and use their own words to tell about them. Explain to children that this means thinking about what the author wrote and then saying it in a different way.

1. Discuss the principle with children, using examples from *The Three Little Pigs*. Suggested language: "In the story *The Three Little Pigs,* we read about a big, bad wolf visiting the houses of three little pigs. What is the most important part at the beginning of the story?" *(The wolf blows down the little pig's house made of straw.)*

> **MINILESSON PRINCIPLE**
>
> Think about the most important parts of the story and tell them in your own words.

2. Continue having children identify the most important parts of the story and telling them in their own words. Suggested language: "What is the most important thing that happened in the middle of the story? Tell about it using your own words." *(The wolf blew down the pig's house that was made out of sticks.)* Follow-up: "The end of the story was important, too. Tell about the most important thing that happened at the end in your own words." *(The wolf tried to blow down the pig's house made of bricks but could not. The three little pigs lived together in this strong house.)*

SUMMARIZE AND APPLY Restate the minilesson principle. Tell children to apply it to a book they will listen to or read. Suggested language: "When you read, think about the most important parts of the story and use your own words to tell about them."

GROUP SHARE Ask children to use their own words to share the most important parts of a book they listened to or read.

Whole-Group Lessons

Miss Bindergarten Celebrates the Last Day of Kindergarten
Big Book, Lesson 30

Schools Then and Now
Big Book pp. 41–46, Lesson 30

Pet Show!
Read-Aloud Book, Lesson 30

▶ ## Miss Bindergarten Celebrates the Last Day of Kindergarten

INTERACTIVE READ-ALOUD/SHARED READING

Read aloud the story to children. Stop periodically for a very brief interaction. Use the following suggested stopping points and prompts for quick group response, or give a specific prompt and have partners or threes turn and talk.

- After reading pages 6–7, say: "*Celebrates* means to show that you are happy that something special is happening by doing things such as playing music or eating together. What are some things you have celebrated?"
- At the end of page 15, ask: "How do you know that the children in Miss Bindergarten's class have learned how to work together?"
- At the end of page 25, ask: "Why do you think the children are decorating bags and putting their names on them?"
- At the end of the story, ask: "Would you like to have Miss Bindergarten as a teacher? Why or why not? Turn and talk about your ideas with a partner."

MINILESSON Understanding Characters

TEACH Display the minilesson principle on chart paper, and read it aloud to children. Tell children they are going to learn how to notice clues about characters as they read. Explain that these clues will help them figure out what the characters are like.

> **MINILESSON PRINCIPLE**
>
> Notice clues that help you know what characters in the story are like.

1. Discuss the principle with children, using examples of characters from *Miss Bindergarten Celebrates the Last Day of Kindergarten*. Suggested language: "In the story, you learned about Miss Bindergarten and many of her students. What did Miss Bindergarten's students bring her on the last day of school?" Follow-up: "What did this tell you about Miss Bindergarten?"

2. Continue to focus on Miss Bindergarten. Suggested language: "Miss Bindergarten celebrated the last day of kindergarten with her students. She held her students' hands and ran through the sprinkler with them. What did this tell you about her?" *(She enjoys having fun with her students.)*

3. Explain how the author also gives clues about what Miss Bindergarten is like by what she says. Suggested language: "At the end of the story Miss Bindergarten gave each student a gift and said something special. The author did not tell you that Miss Bindergarten is caring and kind, but you can figure this out because of what she said and did."

4. Work with children to determine what other characters in the story are like by using clues such as what they say and do. Record children's ideas in a Column Chart.

Character	Clues	What Character Is Like

SUMMARIZE AND APPLY Restate the minilesson principle. Then tell children to apply it to a story they will listen to or read. Suggested language: "When you read, look for clues to help you figure out what the characters are like."

GROUP SHARE Have children share a description of one character in a story. Ask them what clues they used to figure out what the character was like.

▶ Pet Show!

INTERACTIVE READ-ALOUD/SHARED READING

Read aloud the book to children. Stop periodically for a brief interaction. Use the following suggested stopping points and prompts:

- At the end of page 9, say: "Archie's mother describes Archie's cat as being independent. *Independent* means you are able to do things on your own. What are some things you can do on your own?"
- At the end of page 29, ask: "Why were there judges at the pet show?" *(to decide which pet got which prize)* Follow-up: "What other types of shows or contests are judged?"
- At the end of the story, ask: "If you could own any pet, what would it be? Why? Turn and talk about your ideas with a partner."

MINILESSON Understanding Characters

TEACH Display the minilesson principle on chart paper, and read it aloud to children. Tell children they are going to learn to think about how people in the story feel.

1. Discuss the principle with children, using examples from *Pet Show!* Suggested language: "In the story *Pet Show!*, we got to know some people as we read. Who was the child who could not find his pet cat?" *(Archie)*

> **MINILESSON PRINCIPLE**
>
> Think about how people in the story feel.

2. Focus on Archie in the story. Suggested language: "What did Archie tell his friends when he couldn't find his cat anywhere?" *(He told them to start the show without him.)*

3. Use children's responses to explain that what people say and do in a story are clues that help readers understand how the people feel. Suggested language: "The author used what Archie said to show readers that he was sad and frustrated that he could not find his cat."

4. Elicit from children additional examples from the story. Record children's ideas in a T-Map labeled *What the Person Said or Did* and *How the Person Felt*.

SUMMARIZE AND APPLY Restate the minilesson principle. Tell children to apply it to a story they will listen to or read. Suggested language: "When you read, think about how the people in the story feel."

GROUP SHARE Ask children to describe how a person felt in a story they listened to or read.

▶ Schools Then and Now

INTERACTIVE READ-ALOUD/SHARED READING

Read aloud the book to children. Stop periodically for a brief interaction. Use the following suggested stopping points and prompts:

- At the end of page 42, ask: "What might be good about having children who are older than you in your class?"
- After reading pages 44–45, ask: "What problems do you think children had long ago writing with feathers and ink?" *(The feathers broke and the ink was messy.)*
- At the end of the book, ask: "Do you think you would have liked going to school long ago? Why or why not? Turn and talk about your answers with a partner."

MINILESSON Compare and Contrast

TEACH Display the minilesson principle on chart paper, and read it aloud. Tell children they are going to learn how to think about how things are the same and how they are different to help them better understand a book.

1. Discuss the principle with children, using examples from *Schools Then and Now*. Suggested language: "In *Schools Then and Now*, we learned that schools long ago and today are the same in some ways and different in some ways. How are schools long ago and today the same?" *(Children learn how to read, write, and do math. Children play with friends.)*

> **MINILESSON PRINCIPLE**
>
> Think about how things in the book are the same and how they are different.

2. Page through the book with children to find examples of how schools long ago were different from schools today. Suggested language: "Let's look in the book. In what ways are schools from long ago different from schools today?" *(Possible answer: Schools long ago only had one small classroom. Schools today are much bigger and have many classrooms.)*

3. Work with children to compare schools long ago and today using a Venn Diagram. In the first circle, write *Schools Long Ago*. In the overlapping section, write *Both*. In the second circle, write *Schools Today*. Record children's ideas.

SUMMARIZE AND APPLY Restate the minilesson principle. Tell children to apply it to a book they will listen to or read. Suggested language: "When you read, think about how things in the book are the same and how they are different."

GROUP SHARE Ask children to share an example of things in a book that are the same. Then have them share an example of things that are different.

Teacher's Notes

Teaching Genre

Table of Contents

Genre instruction and repeated exposure to a variety of genres are essential components of any high-quality literacy program. Access to the tools children need to understand information in different genres will make them better readers. When children understand the characteristics of a variety of genres, they will be able to:

- gain an appreciation for a wide range of texts
- develop a common vocabulary for talking about texts
- begin reading texts with a set of expectations related to genre
- make evidence-based predictions
- develop preferences as readers
- understand purposes for reading and writing
- recognize the choices an author makes when writing
- compare and contrast texts
- think deeply about what they read

The pages in this section provide a framework for discussing genre with your children in an age-appropriate way. You can use the lists on the following pages to organize for genre discussion.

- **Genre Characteristics:** teach and review the salient features
- **Discussion Starters:** begin and maintain productive discussions
- **Comparing Texts:** encourage children to make connections across texts
- **Literature:** select *Journeys* literature for discussion

Fantasy

Genre Characteristics

SUPPORT THINKING

DISCUSSION STARTERS During whole-group and small-group discussion, use questions to spark conversation about genre characteristics.

- Who is this story about?
- What is [character name] like?
- What is happening in this story? What happens at the end?
- What does [character name] do in this story?
- Where is this story happening?
- Which parts of this story could not happen in real life?
- Which people could not live in the real world? How do you know?
- Would you like to read more stories that are like [title]? Why or why not?

COMPARING TEXTS After children have read and listened to several fantasy stories, prompt them to compare stories and to recognize common characteristics. Use questions such as these:

- How are the people/animals in [title] and [title] alike? How are they different?
- How is [title] the same as other stories you have read? How is it different?
- How is the ending of [title] different from the ending of [title]?

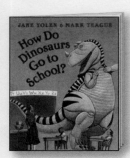 

How Do Dinosaurs Go to School?, Big Book, Lesson 2

Curious George's Dinosaur Discovery, Big Book, Lesson 20

A fantasy story is a made-up story that could not happen in real life.

Through repeated exposure to fantasy stories, children should learn to notice common genre characteristics, though in Kindergarten they will not be expected to use the technical labels. Use friendly language to help them understand the following concepts:

- **Author's Purpose:** to entertain
- **Characters:** the people or animals in a story; characters in fantasy stories often have special abilities or are able to do things that would not be possible in real life
- **Characters' Actions/Qualities:**
  - may have both real and make-believe qualities
  - animals and objects may talk or act like people do in real life
  - people may have feelings like those of real people but can do amazing things
- **Setting:** where and when the story takes place
  - the story may be set in a different time
  - may be a real place or a make-believe place
- **Plot:** what happens in the story
  - stories have a beginning, a middle, and an ending
  - people/animals may have realistic or make-believe solutions to problems
- **Dialogue:** the words that characters say to each other
- **Theme/Message:** what the author is trying to say to readers

JOURNEYS Literature

BIG BOOKS
Curious George's Dinosaur Discovery
How Do Dinosaurs Go to School?
Leo the Late Bloomer
Miss Bindergarten Celebrates the Last
    Day of Kindergarten
Mouse Shapes
Sheep Take a Hike
Snow
You Can Do It, Curious George!

READ-ALOUD BOOKS
Baby Brains
Curious George Makes Pancakes
Dear Mr. Blueberry
Duck & Goose
The Little Engine That Could
Nicky and the Rainy Day
One-Dog Canoe
Someone Bigger
Storm Is Coming!

LEVELED READERS
Bears Through the Year A
Come for a Swim! D
The Costume Box B
Curious George and the Animals A
Curious George and the Hungry
    Animals A
Curious George and the Newspapers F
Curious George Goes for a Ride B
Curious George Likes to Ride B
Curious George Visits Animal Friends A
Curious George Visits the Woods E
A Day at School A
Dressing Up B
Fun at Camp A
Good Job, Sam! D
A Hat for Cat C
Helping Mr. Horse D
It's a Party! A
Look at the Bears A
Making a Tree House A

Mouse and Bear A
Mouse and Bear Are Friends A
My Backpack A
No Snow! D
Our Class Band A
Our Family Vacation A
Our School A
Show and Tell A
Summer Camp A
Taking Pictures A
Teamwork C
Tell All About It A
Things I Can Do B
Things I Like to Do B
Time for Breakfast! A
The Tree House A
Up and Away, Curious George A
A Very Nice Lunch D
Winter Sleep C

Traditional Tale

Genre Characteristics

Traditional tales have been told over and over for many years. Some of the most common traditional tales are fairy tales, folktales, and fables. These are all made-up stories in which characters can do unusual things.

Through repeated exposure to traditional tales, children should learn to notice common genre characteristics, though they will not be expected to use the technical labels. Use friendly language to help them understand the following concepts:

- **Author's Purpose:** the reason why the author wrote the story
  - to entertain
  - fables and folktales may also teach a lesson
- **Characters:** the people or animals in a story
  - may be able to do special or magical things
  - can be good or bad
  - animals may talk and act like people
- **Setting:** where and when the story takes place
  - fairy tales are usually set long ago in a faraway place
  - folktales usually happen long ago in the place where the story started
  - fables may not have a specific time or place
- **Plot:** what happens in the story
  - includes a beginning, a middle, and an ending
  - there is usually a problem that is solved in the end
- **Dialogue:** the words that characters say to each other
- **Storybook Language:**
  - fairy tales have memorable beginning and ending language such as *Once upon a time* and *happily ever after*
  - folktales may have words or sentences that repeat throughout the story
- **Transformations:** magical changes happen mostly in fairy tales
  - people or objects that change form
- **Theme/Message:** what the author is trying to say to readers
  - folktales often tell what a group of people believes
  - may tell a group's explanation for why things are the way they are
  - in fables, readers usually learn a lesson from what happens in the story

SUPPORT THINKING

DISCUSSION STARTERS During whole-group and small-group discussion, use questions to spark conversation about genre characteristics of traditional tales.

- Who is this story about?
- What is happening in this story?
- What problem does [character name] have?
- How do things turn out for people who are good? For people who are bad?
- Where is this story happening?
- What parts of this story could not happen in real life?
- Which people/animals are not like those in the real world? How do you know?
- Which person/animal in the story makes you think about someone you know?
- Do you like the way the story ended? Why or why not?
- What lesson can you learn by reading this story?

COMPARING TEXTS After children have read and listened to several traditional tales, prompt them to compare selections and to recognize common characteristics. Use questions such as these:

- How is [title] the same as other stories you have read?
- How is [character name] like people/animals in other stories you have read?
- Have you read about any other people/animals that can do the same kinds of things as [character name]?
- Which story do you like better — [title] or [title]? Why?

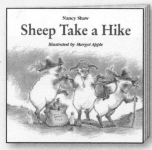

The Builder and the Oni and ***The Three Billy Goats Gruff,*** in Big Book, Lesson 19

JOURNEYS Literature

FAIRY TALE

BIG BOOKS

Paired Selections

"The Builder and the Oni," from Sheep Take a Hike

"The Elves and the Shoemaker," from Everybody Works

"The Three Billy Goats Gruff," from Sheep Take a Hike

"The Three Little Pigs," from Look at Us

FOLKTALE

BIG BOOKS

Paired Selections

"Anansi and Grasshopper," from From Caterpillar to Butterfly

"Stone Soup," from The Handiest Things in the World

READ-ALOUD BOOK

The Little Red Hen

FABLE

BIG BOOKS

Paired Selections

"The Hare and the Tortoise," from Move!

"The Lion and the Mouse," from Everybody Works

Realistic Fiction

SUPPORT THINKING

DISCUSSION STARTERS During whole-group and small-group discussion, use questions to spark conversation about genre characteristics.

- Who is this story about?
- What is [character name] like?
- What is happening in this story?
- What problem does [character name] have?
- How do things turn out for [character name]?
- Where is this story happening?
- When is this story happening?
- What parts of the story could really happen?
- Which person in [title] makes you think about someone you know?

COMPARING TEXTS After children have read and listened to several realistic fiction stories, prompt them to compare stories and to recognize common characteristics. Use questions such as these:

- How are the people in [title] and [title] alike?
- How is [title] the same as other stories you have read? How is it different?
- Which story seems more real—[title] or [title]? Explain.

Please, Puppy, Please, Big Book, Lesson 3

Pie in the Sky, Big Book, Lesson 25

Genre Characteristics

Realistic fiction is a made-up story that could happen in real life.

Through repeated exposure to realistic fiction, children should learn to notice common genre characteristics, though they will not be expected to use the technical labels. Use friendly language to help them understand the following concepts:

- **Author's Purpose:** the reason why the author wrote the story
  - to entertain
- **Characters:** the people or animals in a story
  - characters in realistic fiction might remind children of people they know
- **Setting:** where and when the story happens
  - could be a real place
- **Plot:** what happens in the story
  - includes a beginning, a middle, and an ending
  - a problem is usually solved in the end
- **Dialogue:** the words that characters say to each other
  - characters talk like real people

JOURNEYS Literature

BIG BOOKS
Kitten's First Full Moon
Mice Squeak, We Speak
One of Three
Pie in the Sky
Please, Puppy, Please

READ-ALOUD BOOKS
Amelia's Show-and-Tell Fiesta
Building with Dad
David's Drawings
Good Morning, Digger
How Many Stars in the Sky?
I Have a Pet!
It Is the Wind

Jonathan and His Mommy
Pet Show!
Pizza at Sally's
Simon and Molly plus Hester

LEVELED READERS
Apples **A**
At the Pond **A**
At the Zoo **A**
The Baker **A**
Dan and His Brothers **C**
Four Frogs **A**
Kevin and Lucy **E**
Lola, the Muddy Dog **D**
Look in the Woods **C**

Making a Mud Pie **C**
My Big Brother Ned **B**
My Brother **B**
My Cat **A**
My Dog **A**
My Pet Cat **A**
Our Room **A**
The Show **A**
Splash! **A**
Visiting the Zoo **A**
A Walk in the Woods **A**
We Like Apples **A**
Winter Vacation **A**

Biography

Genre Characteristics

A biography is the true story of a real person's life.

Through repeated exposure to biographies, children should learn to notice common genre characteristics, though they will not be expected to use the technical labels. Use friendly language to help them understand the following concepts:

- **Author's Purpose:** the reason why the author wrote the biography
  - to give information
  - to show why this person's life is important
- **Narrative Structure:**
  - events are told in order as a story
  - may tell about all of the person's life or just part of the person's life
  - important events told in the order they happened
  - setting is where and when the person lived or worked
- **Facts and Opinions:**
  - facts give information about events that really happened
  - opinions show how the author feels about the person
  - both facts and opinions can tell why the person's life was important
- **Graphic Features:** visual aids
  - may include photographs or illustrations of the person
  - may include a timeline of important events in the person's life

JOURNEYS Literature

BIG BOOK

Paired Selection

"Benjamin Franklin, Inventor," from What Is Science?

SUPPORT THINKING

DISCUSSION STARTERS During whole-group and small-group discussion, use questions to spark conversation about genre characteristics.

- Who is this book about?
- What is this person like?
- What important things happened to [subject name]?
- Where did [subject name] live?
- What did other people think about [subject name]?
- What is the author trying to tell readers about [subject name]?
- Why is it important to know about [subject name]'s life?

COMPARING TEXTS After children have read and listened to several biographies, prompt them to compare selections and to recognize common characteristics. Use questions such as these:

- How are [subject name] and [subject name] the same?
- How is [title] the same as other stories about real people that you have read? How is it different?
- Which person would you like to read more about? Explain.

Benjamin Franklin, Inventor, in Big Book, Lesson 16

Informational Text

Genre Characteristics

Informational text gives facts about a topic.

Through repeated exposure to informational text, children should learn to notice common genre characteristics, though they will not be expected to use the technical labels. Use friendly language to help them understand the following concepts:

- **Author's Purpose:** to give information
- **Graphic Features:** pictures that help the reader understand information or show more about the topic
  - **Diagrams:** pictures with labels
  - **Maps:** pictures that show where something is or how to get from one place to another place
  - **Graphs/Charts:** pictures that help readers compare information
- **Text Features:** ways the author makes words stand out
  - **Headings:** type—usually larger, darker, or both—at the beginning of a new section
  - **Labels:** words that name a picture or parts of a picture
  - **Sizes/Colors:** authors use different sizes and colors to help readers see what is most important
- **Main Idea:** what the book is mostly about
- **Details:** information that tells more about the main idea or topic
- **Text Structure:** how the book is organized
- **Facts:** information that is true and can be proved
- **Opinions:** what the author thinks or believes

JOURNEYS Literature

My Five Senses, Big Book, Lesson 6

Zinnia's Flower Garden, Big Book, Lesson 23

READ-ALOUD BOOKS

Bread Comes to Life
Every Season
Friends at School
Listen, Listen
Oscar and the Frog
Red Eyes or Blue Feathers
A Tiger Grows Up

LEVELED READERS

Animals in the Snow **B**
Animals in the Woods **A**
The Aquarium **A**
At School **A**
At the Aquarium **A**
At the Beach **B**
At the Playground **A**
Bug Parts **A**
Bugs! **A**
Bugs for Dinner **A**
By the Sea **B**
Camping Under the Stars **B**
Choosing a Pet **A**
A City Garden **C**
Curious About Playing Ball **B**
Curious About the Animal Park **C**
Family Fun **B**
Feeding Our Pets **A**
Find the Bug **A**
The Fire Fighter **A**
The Flower **B**
Friends **B**
Fun All Year **A**
Fun in July **B**

Fun With Friends **B**
The Garden **A**
Going Fast **D**
Going for a Hay Ride **A**
Going for a Hike **B**
Going to School **B**
The Hay Ride **A**
How Many Ducks? **B**
I Can! **B**
I Can Do It! **A**
In My Yard **A**
In the City **A**
In the Desert **D**
In the Garden **A**
In the Rain Forest **B**
In the Sky **C**
In the Tree **C**
Jobs on the Farm **D**
June Vacation **C**
Let's Climb! **A**
Let's Have Fun! **B**
Let's Sell Things! **A**
Let's Swim **A**
The Lion **B**
Look at Me! **A**
Look for Bugs **A**
Look Up! **A**
Lots of Birds **B**
Lots of Flowers **A**
Lots of Helpers **C**
Make a Kite **A**
The Market **A**
My Bike **A**
My Family **A**

My Family Pictures **A**
My Flower Garden **A**
My House **B**
My Pet **A**
My School **C**
My Yard **A**
October Days **A**
On the Farm **A**
Our Classroom **B**
Our Jobs **A**
Pets at School **A**
The Pet Show **A**
The Playground **A**
The Puppy **A**
Rain Today **A**
Rainy Day **A**
Riding to School **B**
Rosie and the Bug Jar **D**
The Sea **A**
Selling Things **A**
Sisters and Brothers **A**
Snack Time **C**
The Storm **D**
Swimming **A**
Trip to the Fire Station **C**
The Vegetable Garden **A**
Visiting a Park **B**
Visiting Grandma and Grandpa **A**
What Animals Eat **D**
When I Was Little **B**
A Year of Fun **A**
Zoom! **A**

Poetry

SUPPORT THINKING

DISCUSSION STARTERS During whole-group and small-group discussion, use questions to spark conversation about genre characteristics.

- What does this poem tell about?
- Which words in the poem rhyme?
- What words in the poem help you picture something?
- Which words in the poem tell about sounds? Which words tell about smells? Which words tell about tastes?
- Is the poem silly or serious? How do you know?

COMPARING TEXTS After children have read and listened to several poems, prompt them to compare poems and to recognize common characteristics. Use questions such as these:

- How are [title] and [title] the same?
- How are the poems in [title] the same as other poems you have read?
- Which poem did you like more—[title] or [title]? What did you like about it?

What Is Science?, Big Book, Lesson 16

Zin! Zin! Zin! a Violin, Big Book, Lesson 21

Genre Characteristics

Poetry is a piece of writing in which words are used to show feelings and ideas.

Through repeated exposure to poetry, children should learn to notice common genre characteristics, though they will not be expected to use the technical labels. Use friendly language to help them understand the following concepts:

- **Author's Purpose:** the reason the author wrote the poem
  - to entertain; to express
- **Form:** the style of poem; includes traditional rhymes, songs and chants, free verse (which does not rhyme), and list poems
- **Rhyme:** the use of words with the same ending sound; makes poems fun to read and easy to remember
- **Rhythm:** the beat of how the words are read
  - children may tap their fingers or clap their hands to the beat
  - rhythm can make a poem sound like a song
- **Sensory Words:** words that describe how things look, feel, taste, smell, and sound
- **Repeated Readings:** poems are often enjoyed and understood more when read many times

JOURNEYS Literature

BIG BOOKS

What Is Science?
Zin! Zin! Zin! a Violin

BIG BOOKS
Paired Selections

"By Myself," from You Can Do It, Curious George!

"Celebration," from Zin! Zin! Zin! a Violin

"Dragonfly," from What Do You Do With a Tail Like This?

"Drinking Fountain," from Kitten's First Full Moon

"Everybody Says," from What Makes a Family?

"Five Wonderful Senses," from My Five Senses

"Frère Jacques," from What Makes a Family?

"Here Are My Eyes," from My Five Senses

"If You Ever," from Atlantic

"The Lobsters and the Fiddler Crab," from Zin! Zin! Zin! a Violin

"Moon Boat," from Kitten's First Full Moon

"The More We Get Together," from Zin! Zin! Zin! a Violin

"My Little Sister," from What Makes a Family?

"On Our Way," from What Do You Do With a Tail Like This?

"Picnic Day," from My Five Senses

"The Puppy Chased the Sunbeam," from Kitten's First Full Moon

"A Sailor Went to Sea, Sea, Sea," from Atlantic

"Silverly," from Kitten's First Full Moon

"The Storm," from My Five Senses

"Tails," from What Do You Do With a Tail Like This?

"Ten Little Fishes," from Atlantic

"Time to Play," from You Can Do It, Curious George!

"Tortillas for Mommy," from What Makes a Family?

"Undersea," from Atlantic

"Wings," from What Do You Do With a Tail Like This?

"Whistling," from You Can Do It, Curious George!

Writing Handbook Minilessons

Writing Handbook Minilessons

COMMON CORE WRITING HANDBOOK ▪ GRADE K

Contents

How to Use This Book

The Common Core Writing Handbook is a unique instructional tool that was designed to complement the writing instruction in your reading program as well as meet all of the Common Core State Standards for writing. At Kindergarten, this manual supports instruction by providing two minilessons for every key writing lesson in your reading program. This book consists of a 64-page Teacher's Guide with 60 minilessons and an abundance of copying masters to motivate children's writing. A student handbook is also available that may be used instead of the copying masters.

Minilessons

The minilessons are short, focused lessons on specific topics that address the Common Core State Standards. Two Teacher's Guide minilessons are provided for every writing topic and include an objective and guiding question; easy-to-follow instructions; modeled, collaborative, and independent writing; conference and evaluation information; and writing copying masters.

Writing Copying Masters

Thirty writing copying masters are provided that directly correlate to thirty minilessons in the Teacher's Guide. The copying masters are motivational and provide children with opportunities for expressing themselves while having them learn how to write opinion, informative/ explanatory, and narrative pieces that are developmentally appropriate at their level.

Purposes for Writing

Before children write, or share information with others, they need to think about why they are writing. This is the purpose for writing. It is important for children to understand that knowing their purpose for writing will help them improve the focus of their writing. Children might use the following prompts to help them better understand their purpose, or main reason for writing:

- Do I want to show information about something I know or learned?
- Do I want to tell how something is done or how something works?
- Do I want to tell a story, either real or made up?
- Do I want to express thoughts or feelings?

The Writing Process

The Common Core Writing Handbook presents the writing process as a strategy that children can use to help them write for any task, audience, or purpose. Children can use the writing process independently or as part of writing workshops in which they respond to each other's writing. The writing process can help children understand how to plan, write, and revise for various purposes and genres. It is thus useful in helping children meet the Common Core State Standards for opinion, informative/explanatory, and narrative writing.

What Process Writing Is

The writing process, or process writing, is an instructional approach to writing that consists of five basic stages. The stages are recursive in nature, meaning that children are encouraged to go back and forth between the stages as needed.

Prewriting: children begin to plan writing.

Drafting: children put their ideas into writing and drawing.

Revising: children reread the draft and decide how to rework and improve it.

Editing: children polish the draft.

Publishing: children share their writing and drawing with others.

The Writing Traits

Along with understanding the writing process, children will benefit from having a beginning understanding of the traits of good writing covered in the *Common Core Writing Handbook.* The "Traits of Writing" is an approach in which children analyze their writing for the characteristics, or qualities, of what good writing looks like. These qualities include ideas, organization, voice, word choice, sentence fluency, and conventions.

A Common Language

One of the advantages of instructing children in the traits of writing is that you give them a working vocabulary and thus build a common language for writing that they can all use and understand as they progress up the grades. Children can use the traits as a framework for improving any kind of writing they are doing. To this end, a systematic, explicitly taught focus on the traits of writing has proved to be an effective tool for discussing writing, enabling children to analyze and improve their own writing, and providing teachers with a way to assess children's compositions and developing skills in a fair, even-handed manner.

The Writing Workshop

Since writing is an involved process that children accomplish at varying speeds, it is usually a good idea to set aside a block of time for them to work on their writing. One time-tested model that has worked well in classrooms is the Writing Workshop. In this model during a set period of time, children work individually and collaboratively (with classmates and/or with the teacher) on different writing activities. Two of these activities are for children to comment on interactive writing produced during class time or to collaborate in reviewing each other's manuscripts. One effective technique used in many workshops as a way for children to comment on aspects of each other's writing is to use the language of the traits when they comment.

Writing Workshops are often most effective when they adhere to a dependable schedule and follow a set of clearly posted guidelines (for example, keep voices down, point out the good things about someone's writing as well as comment on parts that might be revised, listen politely, and put away materials when the workshop is over). In addition, children should know what areas of the classroom they can use and should have free access to writing materials, including their handbooks.

Introducing the Traits

Share an overview of the Writing Traits with children. Discuss each trait briefly and explain to children that they will learn about the traits, which they can use to help them as they plan, draft, revise, edit, and publish their writing.

When you use the minilessons to instruct children on different topics in writing, use the language of the traits with them. Encourage them to use it, too, any time they interact with text. Over time, they will develop an important common writing vocabulary that will help them as they progress up the grades.

Evaluating Writing

While children are learning about the writing process and writing traits they will also benefit from knowing how to evaluate their own writing as well as the writing of others. Children will learn that creating a checklist will help them become better writers. They can ask themselves the following questions to check their writing:

- Did I leave spaces between words?
- Did I start my sentences with capital letters?
- Did I end my sentences with a period or other end mark?

To signal that their writing is complete, children may draw a happy or smiling face next to each part of the writing that completes their checklist. Children may then want to complete any section that did not get a happy face. With practice, children will learn the importance of evaluating their writing and how it improves their overall writing skills.

Writing Handbook Minilessons

Names

Minilesson 1

Using Capital Letters for Names

Common Core State Standard: L.K.1b

Objective: Use initial capital letters to write names.
Guiding Question: How do I write people's names?

Teach/Model—I Do

Tell children that most people have two names—a first name and a last name. Say the first and last names of a friend or relative. Explain that this is the name of a person you know. Write both names on the board in all lower case letters. Read the names aloud, running your hand beneath each name. Then say, *Oops! I forgot something important!* Replace the first letter of the first name with a capital letter. Repeat with the first letter of the last name. Explain that when people write first or last names, they need to start with a capital letter.

Guided Practice—We Do

Ask a volunteer to say his or her first and last names. Have the rest of the class repeat both names. Then ask children to help you write the name on the board. Help children identify the first letter of the child's first name. Guide them to remind you that the first letter must be a capital. Have a volunteer write the capital letter. Write the remaining letters yourself or have a child write them as you dictate. Do the same with the last name. Underline the capitalized letters to draw attention to them. Have children read the names with you.

Practice/Apply—You Do

Ask children to draw a self-portrait. Then help them write their first and last names beneath the picture. Suggest that they spell and write as much of their names as they can. Encourage them to write the first letter of each of their names on their own and tell you that each of these initial letters is a capital.

Conference/Evaluate

Offer help writing and spelling names as needed, especially for last names.

Minilesson 2

Drafting a List of Names

Common Core State Standard: L.K.1b

Objective: Write a list of names.
Guiding Question: How can I make a list of the names of some people I know?

Teach/Model—I Do

Tell children that you had some good friends when you were in school. Say the first names of 3 people you remember from your own childhood. Explain that you want to make a list to help you remember their names. Write one of the names on the board, read it with children, and point out the initial capital letter. Below it, repeat with the other names in list form, lining up the names' initial letters vertically. Read the names with children and reemphasize that this list names some of your friends when you were younger.

Guided Practice—We Do

Ask 3 children to come stand near you. Tell the class that you want to make a list of these children's names. Have seated children say the first names of the 3 children who are standing. Then have children help you write the names in a list. Stress that the names need to begin with capital letters and that they should be written in list format—that is, in a vertical column. When you are done, read the list with children, running your hand under each name in turn. Repeat with another group of 3 children as time permits.

Practice/Apply—You Do

Distribute copies of the **blackline master** on **page 7**. Read aloud the directions. Have children draw a picture of themselves and two other children they know; these can be friends, classmates, or relatives. Then help children write the first names of the people in the picture, using list form. Ask children to share their work with a partner.

Conference/Evaluate

Remind children to begin each name with a capital letter. Encourage them to spell and write the names on their own as much as possible.

6 • Writing for Common Core

Name _____

WRITING FORMS

Names

Teacher: On the top, have children draw a picture showing themselves and two other children, who can be friends, relatives, or classmates. Below that, have children list the first names of the three people in the picture, one on each set of lines.

Grade K • 7

Writing Handbook Minilessons

Labels

Minilesson 3	Minilesson 4

Describing a Picture

Common Core State Standard: W.K.2

Objective: Write about a picture.

Guiding Question: What words can I use to tell about a picture?

Teach/Model—I Do

On the board, sketch a picture of a house. Include windows, a chimney, and a door. Explain that you want to write some words that describe, or tell about, the picture. Write the word *house* and read it aloud. Tell children that this word describes the whole picture but that you could use other words to tell about parts of the picture, too. Write *windows*, *door*, and *chimney* in list form and read them aloud. Point out that all of these words tell about the picture you drew in different ways.

Guided Practice—We Do

Draw a picture of a tree with leaves and branches. Add several birds and a nest. Ask children what words they could use to describe the picture. Remind them to think of the whole picture as well as the parts that make it. Guide children to give words to describe the picture, such as *tree*, *leaf*, and *nest*. Have the class help you write or spell the words. Read the completed list aloud with children.

Practice/Apply—You Do

Provide magazines or catalogs and scissors. Help children cut out one or more pictures. Then have children describe their pictures in writing, as they did in the *I Do* and *We Do* sections.

Conference/Evaluate

Move through the room, checking that children are on task. Engage them in conversation about the words they choose. Look for children to come up with at least three words. Take dictation or help with spelling as necessary, but encourage children to write on their own as much as possible.

Drafting Labels

Common Core State Standard: W.K.2

Objective: Write labels.

Guiding Question: What is a label?

Teach/Model—I Do

Hold up a long wooden block and identify it. Write *block* on an index card and read it with children. Then tape the card to the block. Explain that you have just made a label; you have written the name of an object and put the word with the object. Tell children that labels are very useful. Explain or elicit that labels can help children learn to read words or learn the names of objects. Repeat the activity with a chair and a puppet or stuffed animal.

Guided Practice—We Do

Display or point out several more ordinary classroom objects, such as a book, a shelf, and a box. Have children name the objects. Then display index cards and ask children to help you write a label for each object. Say the words slowly and carefully, encouraging children to help you name the letters. When each label is complete, ask children to tape it to the correct object. Explain that children can use the labels to help them learn to read the names of the objects.

Practice/Apply—You Do

Distribute the **blackline master** on **page 9**. Read the directions aloud. Point out that children are writing labels to go with pictures this time instead of writing labels that will be attached to objects but that the process is still the same. Remind children to leave spaces between letters and to form letters carefully and correctly.

Conference/Evaluate

Be sure that children's labels match the pictures. Encourage them to write any letters they know and to think about letter-sound combinations.

8 • Writing for Common Core

Name _____

WRITING FORMS

Labels

Directions Have children think about four kinds of animals they like. Ask them to draw one animal in each box. Have children write a label below each drawing that names the kind of animal they drew (deer, puppy, giraffe, etc.).

Writing Handbook Minilessons

Captions

Minilesson 5

Telling About a Picture

Common Core State Standards: W.K.2, L.K.6, SL.K.4

Objective: Talk about the action in a picture.

Guiding Question: How can I tell someone else what is happening in a picture?

Teach/Model—I Do

Sketch a simple picture on the board that shows a person running (stick figures are fine). Tell children that this picture shows a person named Bernie. Add that Bernie is doing something in the picture and that you can use words to tell what he is doing. Say *Bernie is running*. Emphasize that you told what was happening in the picture. Repeat with a picture showing a bird in the air and the sentence *The bird is flying*.

Guided Practice—We Do

Sketch a simple picture of two people throwing a ball back and forth. Tell children that the people in the picture are named Beth and Fred. Ask children to describe what is happening in the picture. Guide them to focus especially on the action. Help them put together short sentences such as *Beth and Fred are playing ball*. If time permits, repeat with another picture of your choice. Again, ask children to focus on describing the action in the picture.

Practice/Apply—You Do

Give each child a photograph or drawing clipped from a newspaper or a magazine. All pictures should show some type of action (no portraits or pictures of objects). Then divide the class into pairs or small groups. Instruct children to describe what is happening in their picture and tell their ideas to their partner or group members. If time permits, have children exchange pictures with classmates and repeat the activity.

Conference/Evaluate

Make sure children are describing the action in the picture rather than saying *This is a girl* or something similar. Ask guiding questions as necessary to make sure children focus on the action in the picture.

10 • Writing for Common Core

Minilesson 6

Drafting Captions

Common Core State Standards: W.K.2, L.K.6

Objective: Write about the action in a picture.

Guiding Question: How can I write about a picture?

Teach/Model—I Do

Draw a simple sketch of a fish. Include small lines to suggest motion. Tell children that they can probably tell what is going on just by looking at your picture, but that you want to write some words to make sure people who see the picture understand it. On the board, write *The fish is swimming*. Begin the sentence with a capital letter and end it with a period. Read the sentence aloud, running your hand under the words and pointing out the initial capital and the final period. Explain that when words tell what is happening in a picture, we call the words a caption.

Guided Practice—We Do

Display a picture that you have cut from a magazine or newspaper. Be sure the picture focuses on action, such as an athlete catching a ball or an animal digging in the dirt. Have children talk about what is happening in the picture. Then guide them to write a short sentence to serve as a caption for the picture. Help children write the caption on the board. Read it aloud with them, pointing to each word as you say it.

Practice/Apply—You Do

Distribute copies of the **blackline master** on **page 11**. Ask children to think of something they like to do. Then have them draw a picture of themselves engaged in that activity. Next, ask children to write a short caption telling what they are doing in their picture, with an emphasis on the activity (dancing, building, reading). Have children share their work with a partner or the whole class as time permits.

Conference/Evaluate

Encourage children to do as much writing on their own as they can. Help them write sentences with an initial capital letter and a final period.

Name _____

Captions

Teacher: Have children draw a picture showing themselves taking part in a favorite activity. Then have them write a caption to explain what is happening in the picture.

Story Sentences

WRITING FORMS

Minilesson 7

Choosing Events to Describe

Common Core State Standard: W.K.3

Objective: Describe which ideas or events to include in a story.

Guiding Question: What events do we want to tell about?

Teach/Model—I Do

Say that you have an idea for a story that could go with the setting *at the beach*. Tell children that you can think of two interesting events for a story with that setting. Explain that an event is something that happens. Say *One idea I have is that a character would go in a boat. That would be one event that would go with the setting of a beach.* Sketch a stick figure in a simple boat. Write *go in a boat* below the drawing. Repeat with the event *find seashells*.

Guided Practice—We Do

Tell children that they will soon be starting a class story. Work together to choose a setting for the story. Then guide children to suggest events that could happen in that setting. Write children's ideas on the board in bullet form and encourage them to sketch quick pictures. Remind children that the events they describe must be connected to the setting. After 5–6 suggestions, read the list aloud.

Practice/Apply—You Do

Have children draw pictures of an event they would like to include in a story. Then have children share their work and vote to choose which events they'll include in their story.

Conference/Evaluate

Move through the room, engaging children in conversation about their pictures. Offer assistance with writing as needed. Children may simply write labels, but encourage them to write longer phrases or complete sentences, if possible.

Minilesson 8

Drafting Story Sentences

Common Core State Standards: W.K.3, L.K.1f

Objective: Write a sentence for a story.

Guiding Question: How can I write a sentence that can be part of a story?

Teach/Model—I Do

Review that in the previous minilesson you were thinking about a person who went to the beach. Say *I had an idea for a story about this person. I thought the person might go on a boat.* Explain that today you will write a whole sentence about that idea. On the board, write *Eddy sailed away from the beach in a little blue boat.* Read the sentence aloud with children, touching the words in turn. Explain that this is a sentence because it begins with a capital letter and ends with a period, and that it could be part of a story about Eddy and his trip to the beach.

Guided Practice—We Do

Explain that you would like to write more sentences, this time about a girl named Nola who finds seashells on a beach. Ask children to think about what the shells might look like (color, size, shape), and how Nola feels about finding them. Guide children to tell you 3–4 sentences that could be part of a story about Nola, such as *Nola found 3 big purple shells* or *Nola was happy that she found so many seashells.* Write the sentences on the board as children say them.

Practice/Apply—You Do

Distribute copies of the **blackline master** on **page 13**. Read the directions aloud. Have children use the prompt to draw a picture and write a story sentence about it. Emphasize that the character must be make-believe and come from their own imagination. Have children share their work with a partner.

Conference/Evaluate

Make sure children compose a complete sentence rather than just a phrase. If you take dictation, ask them to tell you where the period should go.

Name _____

Story Sentences

Teacher: Ask children to think of ideas for a made-up character they might like to write a story about. Ask them to draw a picture that shows their character. Then have children write a story sentence to tell more about the picture.

Grade K • **13**

Class Story

Minilesson 9

Telling a Story in Words and Pictures

Common Core State Standard: W.K.3

Objective: Use words and pictures to tell a class story.

Guiding Question: How can we combine words and pictures to help us tell a class story?

Teach/Model—I Do

Show children a familiar book that has both words and pictures. Explain that the words and the pictures both help tell the story. Then point out that children can also tell stories through words and pictures. Model by sketching three pictures on the board: a tall building; a bird flying to the building; the bird landing on top of the building. Then write the words *There was an apartment building. A bird flew to the building to look around. She liked it so much that she decided to move in!* Read the words aloud and point to the pictures as you read.

Guided Practice—We Do

Tell children that you will write a story together about a fox that lives in a cave. Draw three boxes on the board and explain that these boxes are for the pictures. Draw lines below the pictures for the words. Ask children to think of events that could happen in the story. Have volunteers draw the pictures and have them help you write words beneath the boxes. Remind children that they need to be respectful of one another's ideas. Read the completed story aloud.

Practice/Apply—You Do

Have children work in pairs. Ask them to make up a story about a cat that went in a car. Have them tell the story in words and pictures. Have children check that their ideas make sense.

Conference/Evaluate

Move through the room, checking that partners are working productively together. Remind them to use words as well as pictures; it's a good idea to limit the number of pictures children draw to three.

14 • Writing for Common Core

Minilesson 10

Drafting a Class Story

Common Core State Standard: W.K.3

Objective: Write a story as a group.

Guiding Question: How can we write a story together?

Teach/Model—I Do

Display two sock or finger puppets and explain that they will tell a story together. Have the puppets take turns telling a story about a rainy day. Early on, compliment the puppets for listening to each other so they are sure that the story makes sense. Near the end of the story, however, have one puppet angrily interrupt to say that it doesn't like the other puppet's idea. Gently remind the puppet that it's important to take turns and to say kind things. Have the puppet apologize; then proceed with the story.

Guided Practice—We Do

Remind children that they planned to write a group story. Review the setting they chose; then ask for the story's first line. Model checking to be sure that the opening sentence matches the setting. Then write it on chart paper and read it with children. Continue as above with the next 2–3 sentences, checking also that the sentences include details and relate to one another.

Practice/Apply—You Do

Continue the process described above, but ask children to take over the task of checking that each new sentence fits the story. When the story is done, read it aloud with children. Then explain that the story needs pictures. Distribute copies of the **blackline master** on **page 15.** Have children follow the directions.

Conference/Evaluate

Check children's ability to work as part of a group. Note whether children are willing to try to write words on their own. If necessary, help children identify the initial sound and the letter that goes with it, and then show them how to write that letter.

Name _____

WRITING FORMS

Class Story

_____
- -
_____
- -
_____
- -
_____

Directions Ask children to choose their favorite part of the class story they just wrote. Have them write about it at the top of the paper. Encourage them to use their own words to tell what happened in that part of the story. Then have them draw a picture to go with the words.

Descriptive Sentences

WRITING FORMS

Minilesson 11

Using Sensory Details

Common Core State Standard: SL.K.4

Objective: Describe using sensory words.

Guiding Question: How can I tell my readers what things look like and feel like?

Teach/Model—I Do

Display a small rock or a similar object. Explain that you want to describe this rock as carefully as you can. On the board, write *How It Looks*. Read the words aloud. Explain that you get information through your eyes, by seeing, and that you know some words to describe what the rock looks like. Say *round*, *black*, *shiny*, or other words that apply, and write them on the board. Repeat with *What It Feels Like*, using words such as *bumpy*, *smooth*, and *warm*. Point out that these words can help readers feel that they are part of a story.

Guided Practice—We Do

Write two columns on the board: *How It Looks* and *What It Feels Like*. Hold up several red checkers. Explain that the checkers are red, and write *red* in the *How It Looks* column. Then guide children to add other words to that list. Repeat with what the checkers feel like, passing them around the group so everyone has a chance to touch them. Supply *smooth* or *rough* to start the list, if needed.

Practice/Apply—You Do

Have children work in pairs. Ask them to choose an object in the room. Have them write its name and then write words that describe how it looks and feels.

Conference/Evaluate

Circulate, checking children's work. Encourage children to separate their words into two lists—the way the object looks and the way it feels. Try to have children list at least three words for each category.

Minilesson 12

Drafting Descriptive Sentences

Common Core State Standard: SL.K.4

Objective: Write descriptive sentences about an object.

Guiding Question: How can I describe an object?

Teach/Model—I Do

Place a pencil, an oblong eraser, and a rubber ball where children can see them. Tell children that you're thinking of one of these objects and that you'll write a description of it. Explain that a description uses words that help you see and feel the object, as in the previous lesson, and that it puts those words into sentences. Write *My object is round and [white]. It feels smooth, and it feels good in my hand.* Read the description aloud and have children identify the sensory words. Then have children identify the object (the ball) and tell how they know.

Guided Practice—We Do

Ask children to help you write a description of the pencil. Start them off by writing *This pencil is long and. . . .* Go around the room, helping children add a word or a sentence to the description. Call children's attention to certain aspects of the pencil (the tip, the eraser), if needed. When children are done, read their work aloud.

Practice/Apply—You Do

Give each child a copy of the **blackline master** on **page 17**. Have children follow the directions. Explain that they should include at least one description of how the object feels and at least one that tells how it looks.

Conference/Evaluate

Move around the room, offering help as needed. Check that children are writing in sentences and that they write the name of the object they chose.

16 • Writing for Common Core

Name _____

Descriptive Sentences

I chose a _____.

_____

_____

_____

_____

Directions Ask children to choose an object from the classroom, draw it, and write its name. Then have them write a description of the object, using words that describe the way it looks and feels. If appropriate, children can add how the object sounds or how it smells. Remind them to write in sentences.

Grade K • 17

Writing Handbook Minilessons

Descriptive Sentences

Minilesson 13	Minilesson 14
Showing Information in a Drawing	**Drafting Descriptive Sentences**

Common Core State Standard: W.K.2

Common Core State Standards: W.K.2, L.K.5c

Minilesson 13 — Showing Information in a Drawing

Objective: Draw a picture to communicate information.

Guiding Question: How can I use a picture to share my ideas with others?

Teach/Model—I Do

Explain that you are going to draw a picture of something you saw this morning. On the board, draw a sketch of a person. Then draw a sketch of a dog and draw a leash from the dog to the person's hand. Ask children to describe what you drew. Elicit or explain that you saw a person walking a dog. Repeat with another example, such as a school bus with a person standing nearby to represent seeing a school bus picking up a child. Emphasize that you can use a picture to tell other people what you know or what you saw, heard, smelled, or touched.

Guided Practice—We Do

Guide children to think about things they saw earlier in the day. Invite a few volunteers to come to the board one by one and draw a simple picture to show something they saw, heard, smelled, or touched. Encourage other children to guess what each drawing represents. Then guide the artist to explain in words what he or she had in mind. Point out that the drawing shows information about what each person saw.

Practice/Apply—You Do

Have children draw a picture on their own that shows them doing an activity they enjoy. Ask them to share and discuss their completed picture with a partner.

Conference/Evaluate

Circulate and engage children in conversation about their work. Find something positive to say about each child's work. Point out how their pictures show other people what they like to do.

Minilesson 14 — Drafting Descriptive Sentences

Objective: Write a descriptive sentence.

Guiding Question: How do I write a descriptive sentence?

Teach/Model—I Do

Remind children that they have been learning about words that describe objects, people, or events. Review a few of these kinds of words with children, such as *purple*, *loud*, *bumpy*, and *small*. Then draw a quick picture of a tall tree on the board, showing several thick branches. Tell children that you are going to use words that describe the tree to write a sentence about it. Say *Here are some words that tell about the tree: tall, strong, thick. I'll put some of those words into a sentence.* Write on the board *The tree is tall and has strong branches.* Read the sentence aloud to children, pointing out the initial capital letter and the final period. Point to the describing words *tall* and *strong*.

Guided Practice—We Do

On a sheet of paper or on the board, sketch a quick picture of a large leaf. Display the picture. Invite children to name words or phrases that describe the leaf, such as *big*, *green*, and *pointy*. Guide them to create sentences about the leaf that use these words, such as *The leaf is big and green* or *This leaf has sharp points*. Write the sentences on the board and read them aloud. Help children find the descriptive words, the initial capitals, and the final periods.

Practice/Apply—You Do

Distribute copies of the **blackline master** on **page 19**. Write *butterfly*, *flower*, and *fish* on the board and ask children to choose one. Have them draw a picture and write a sentence to describe it.

Conference/Evaluate

Circulate, guiding children to use complete sentences rather than simply writing down words and phrases. Ask them to point out descriptive words they used.

18 • Writing for Common Core

Name _____

Descriptive Sentences

Teacher: Have children draw a picture of a butterfly, a flower, or a fish. Then have children write a descriptive sentence to tell about what they drew.

Grade K • **19**

Captions

Minilesson 15

Using Words for Colors and Shapes

Common Core State Standard: SL.K.4

Objective: Use color and shape words to describe objects.

Guiding Question: How can I describe objects carefully?

Teach/Model—I Do

Hold up a penny. Tell children that this is a coin called a penny but that you want to use more exact words to describe it. Say *This coin is the color brown. So, I can call it a* brown coin. Write the words *brown coin* on the board. Repeat with the coin's shape (round). Write *round coin* and read it aloud. Explain that you have used two words to help describe the coin: the word *brown*, which tells the coin's color, and the word *round*, which tells its shape. Repeat with a square blue tile or other object.

Guided Practice—We Do

Display a red checker. Guide children to use a shape word (*round or circle*) to describe the checker. Repeat with a color word (*red*). Help children call the checker a *round red checker*. Next, display a square object such as a tile, a pattern block, or a number cube. Help children use words to describe the object; elicit that they can use shape and color words such as *square* and *white*. Continue with several other simple objects.

Practice/Apply—You Do

Ask children to choose an object in the classroom that has a simple shape. Have children draw the object they chose and label it. Then ask them to write color and shape words to describe the object as clearly as they can.

Conference/Evaluate

Circulate, checking that children are using color and shape words. If children are unsure of an object's shape, steer them toward more specific items, such as blocks, marbles, and the like. Have children read their descriptions to a partner, and encourage partners to guess the object based on the color and shape words.

Minilesson 16

Drafting Caption Sentences

Common Core State Standards: W.K.2, SL.K.4, SL.K.6

Objective: Write a sentence that tells about a picture.

Guiding Question: How can I write a sentence to tell what I know about a picture?

Teach/Model—I Do

Use yellow marker or chalk to draw a full moon on the board or on a sheet of paper. Surround it with dark colors to represent the night sky. Explain that you have drawn a full moon and that you will write a sentence to tell about your picture. Remind children that this kind of writing is called a *caption*. Add that you will use color or shape words in your caption. Say *The moon is yellow. That's a color word. It's round. That's a shape word.* Then write the sentence *The round moon is in the sky* on the board and read it with children. Repeat with *The picture shows a yellow moon*. Point out the initial capital letter and the final period in each sentence. Stress that both sentences work as captions for the picture.

Guided Practice—We Do

Draw a quick picture showing a child holding a large red box in the shape of a cube. Invite children to use color and shape words to describe what they see. Then guide children to compose simple sentences that use these words and can serve as captions for the picture, such as *The girl has a red box* or *Her box is shaped like a square*. Help children write the sentences on the board. Read them aloud.

Practice/Apply—You Do

Distribute copies of the **blackline master** on **page 21**. Have children draw a color picture that shows themselves with a favorite toy, book, or other object. Then have them write a caption sentence that includes color or shape words.

Conference/Evaluate

Circulate, checking that children are using complete sentences rather than words and phrases.

20 • Writing for Common Core

Name _____

Captions

Teacher: Have children use color to draw a picture of themselves together with a favorite object, such as a toy, a stuffed animal, a ball, or a book. Then guide them to write a simple caption sentence that uses color or shape words to describe the picture.

Grade K • **21**

Description

Minilesson 17

Choosing Descriptive Words

Common Core State Standards: W.K.2, SL.K.4, L.K.6

Objective: Use words that are specific, not vague.

Guiding Question: What words should I use to describe?

Teach/Model—I Do

Display a picture of an elephant. Explain that you can write about the elephant by using words that describe it. On the board, write *An elephant is an animal.* Read the sentence aloud. Then frown. Tell children that you can use words that are more specific; that is, words that tell more about the elephant. Erase *an animal* and replace it with *gray and has a long trunk.* Read the new sentence aloud. Help children understand that *gray* and *long trunk* help them visualize the elephant more than just *an animal.* Repeat with *has thick legs and a short tail.*

Guided Practice—We Do

Display an apple, which can be plastic or real. On the board, write *An apple is nice.* Read it with children. Then shake your head and explain that lots of things can be nice, so *nice* might not be the best word to use to describe the apple. Guide children to replace *nice* with more specific words or phrases, such as *red, round, smooth, tasty,* or *my favorite fruit.* Read the resulting sentences with children.

Practice/Apply—You Do

Display a pencil. On the board, write *This pencil is good* and read it aloud. Tell children that you believe they can think of better words to describe pencils. Give children a pencil and a sheet of paper, and ask them to write a sentence that tells about their pencil. Possible specific words might include *sharp, yellow, long,* or *made of wood.*

Conference/Evaluate

Walk through the room, checking that children are on task. Help with spelling or take dictation as needed.

22 • Writing for Common Core

Minilesson 18

Revising a Description with Number Words

Common Core State Standards: W.K.2, SL.K.4, L.K.6

Objective: Write a description that uses number words.

Guiding Question: How can I include number words in a description?

Teach/Model—I Do

Display a toy car. Explain that you can write a description of the car. On the board, write *Our toy car has wheels.* Read the description aloud with children. Then say: *This is a good description, but I can make it better. I can tell how many wheels it has.* Revise the sentence so it reads *Our toy car has four wheels.* Explain that the sentence is clearer because you revised it so it includes a number word.

Guided Practice—We Do

Draw a quick sketch of a ladybug on the board. Draw two spots on each wing. On the board, write *This cute ladybug has wings and some spots.* Read the sentence with children. Tell children that the sentence could be better if it included number words. Invite children to count the wings and the spots. Then have them revise the sentence so it reads *This cute ladybug has two wings and four spots.*

Practice/Apply—You Do

Distribute copies of the **blackline master** on **page 23**. Remind children that they have been learning about using specific words to describe objects and animals. Read the sentence at the top of the page with children. Tell them to draw an animal they like and then revise the initial sentence by writing a new sentence at the bottom that uses descriptive words and at least one number word. Encourage children to share their work with a partner.

Conference/Evaluate

Move around the room, offering assistance as needed. Help children write the name of their animal correctly.

Name _____

Description

My animal has legs.

_____

- -

_____

_____

- -

_____

Teacher: Read the sentence at the top of the page as children follow along. Ask children to draw a picture of an animal they like. Then have them revise the sentence at the top and rewrite the new sentence at the bottom. The new sentence should use describing words and at least one number word to tell about their animal.

Grade K • 23

Writing Handbook Minilessons

Description

Minilesson 19

Using Peer Feedback to Revise

Common Core State Standards: W.K.2, L.K.2a, L.K.2b

Objective: Revise a piece of writing based on others' ideas.

Guiding Question: How can I use my classmates' suggestions to make my writing better?

Teach/Model—I Do

On the board, write *I saw a rabbit. It was moving.* Display a puppet. Read the sentences aloud as if you are reading them to the puppet. Ask the puppet if it has any suggestions for improving your writing. Have the puppet say *You could tell the color of the rabbit or when you saw it.* Tell children you think this is a good suggestion. Revise the first sentence to read *I saw a brown rabbit today.* Read the sentences again. Have the puppet suggest that you can add the way the rabbit moved. Revise the last sentence to read *It was hopping on the lawn.* Thank the puppet. Explain that writers can get good ideas from others to help them revise.

Guided Practice—We Do

On the board, write *I saw a dog. It had paws.* Explain that this is your puppet's work. Tell children that you like the puppet's work, but you think it could be better. Ask children what suggestions they could make that would improve the writing such as *spotted dog* or *big paws.* Include all suggestions, highlighting those that add details or describing words. Have the puppet thank the children who shared their ideas.

Practice/Apply—You Do

Have children write about something they saw this morning. Then have them alternate reading their work to a partner. Each partner should make suggestions about revision. Encourage children to use the suggestions, but do not insist that they do so.

Conference/Evaluate

Remind children that they need to be respectful of their classmates and their suggestions.

Minilesson 20

Revising a Description with Size and Shape Words

Common Core State Standards: W.K.2, L.K.2a, L.K.2b

Objective: Revise a description so that it uses size and shape words.

Guiding Question: How can I include size and shape words in a description?

Teach/Model—I Do

Display a small square tile. Write on the board *This is a tile.* Read the sentence aloud. Then frown. Explain that your sentence is not very interesting. Tell children that your writing would be better if you told about the tile's size and shape. Say *The tile is small; that tells about the size.* Revise the sentence to read *This tile is small.* Then say *The tile is square; that tells about the shape.* Revise the sentence again to read *This tile is small and square.* Tell children that adding size and shape made the description clearer.

Guided Practice—We Do

Show children a playground ball. On the board, write *A ball is in our room* and read it with children. Then explain to children that you would like to add to your sentence to tell about the ball's size and shape. Invite children to suggest words that describe these features. Then help the class revise the sentence so it reads *A big round ball is in our room.* Read the sentence aloud with children and talk about why it is an improvement over the original.

Practice/Apply—You Do

Distribute copies of the **blackline master** on **page 25**. Read the sentence at the top with children. Have them rewrite the sentence to include size and shape words at the bottom of the page. Children should share their work with a partner.

Conference/Evaluate

Help children spell words as needed. Take dictation if necessary. Ask children if they think their new sentence is an improvement over the original, and why.

Name _____

WRITING FORMS

Description

Here are some grapes.

_____

- -

_____

- -

_____

Teacher: Read the sentence at the top of the page with children. Have them revise the sentence to include information about the size and shape of the grapes. Then have them write the revised sentence at the bottom of the page. Children can color the picture when they are done.

Story Sentences

| Minilesson 21 | Minilesson 22 |

Writing a Great Beginning

Common Core State Standard: W.K.3

Objective: Write an interesting beginning for a story.

Guiding Question: How can I start writing a story so the reader will want to read more?

Teach/Model—I Do

Tell children that you are going to write the beginning of a story. On the board, write *I saw a bird. It was flying. It was big*. Read it aloud; then frown. Explain that these sentences aren't very interesting. Tell children that you want your writing to "grab" the reader, or make the reader want to keep reading to see what happens next. Write *An enormous bird was flying right at me!* Read it aloud. Say that the new version is more interesting and uses more descriptive words. Repeat with *There was a shark* and *"Help!" I yelled as I swam away from the angry shark.*

Guided Practice—We Do

On the board, write *I saw a cat. It was walking on the sidewalk*. Tell children that this is the beginning of a story but that you aren't satisfied with it. Ask children to help you change it so that it will grab the reader. Guide children by suggesting that they use more descriptive words (*running* instead of *walking*), use more exciting subjects (*lion* instead of *cat*), or include words that show feelings (*the cat looked frightened*). Read the new beginning aloud. Make further changes if you want, explaining why you made them. Then repeat with the story starter *There were some bugs. They were little.*

Practice/Apply—You Do

Ask children to work with a partner. Have them write the first sentence or two of a story. Remind them that the story beginning should grab the reader. Ask them to share their writing with another pair.

Conference/Evaluate

Move through the room, asking children to read their work aloud to you.

26 • Writing for Common Core

Drafting Story Sentences

Common Core State Standards: W.K.3, L.K.2a, L.K.2b

Objective: Write a story sentence that uses exact nouns.

Guiding Question: How do I use exact nouns?

Teach/Model—I Do

Sketch a picture of a horse on the board, or display one from a magazine. Tell children that you would like to make up a story about the picture. On the board, write *This animal is running home to see someone*. Read the sentence aloud. Then tell children that you could make some of the words more exact. Explain that the animal in the picture has a more exact name: a horse. Add that you could also tell exactly who the horse wants to see. Rewrite the sentence so it reads *This horse is running home to see its brother*. Explain that using exact names for animals and objects can improve writing.

Guided Practice—We Do

On the board, write the sentence *The boy played with his toy in the room*. Read the sentence aloud and tell children that it is from a story you want to write. Underline the words *toy* and *room* and tell children that you think they can help you write more exact words. Guide children to provide more specific words, such as *basketball* and *bedroom*. Write their sentences on the board. Talk with children about how words that are more specific improve the sentence.

Practice/Apply—You Do

Distribute copies of the **blackline master** on **page 27**. Read the sentence at the top aloud. Then have children draw a picture showing a meal they would like to eat and rewrite the new story sentence, using more exact words, at the bottom of the page. Invite children to share their work with a partner.

Conference/Evaluate

Circulate, offering help as needed. Encourage children to name at least two different foods in their writing and, if possible, to tell who *they* refers to.

Name _____

Story Sentences

They ate some food.

_____

- -

_____

_____

- -

_____

Teacher: Tell children that the sentence at the top of the page comes from a story. Ask them to draw a picture that shows some foods that they especially like to eat. Then have children rewrite the sentence about the picture, using the exact names of the foods they drew.

Grade K • **27**

Story Sentences

Minilesson 23

Reacting to Events

Common Core State Standards: W.K.3, L.K.1b

Objective: Write a sentence about a reaction to an event.

Guiding Question: How do I write about my feelings after something that happened to me?

Teach/Model—I Do

Tell children that something very surprising happened to you yesterday: you were washing dishes when a bowl fell on the floor and broke. On the board, write *I felt surprised when the bowl broke*. Read the sentence aloud. Explain that this tells how you felt when something happened. Repeat with another event, such as laughing when you accidentally put your keys in the refrigerator, and write a sentence about it: *I laughed when I found what I did with my keys*.

Guided Practice—We Do

Guide children to imagine how they would feel if a lion at the zoo roared at them. Write their ideas in sentence form, such as *I would feel scared/excited/angry if the lion roared at me*. Repeat, having children imagine how they would react if they saw two sea lions tossing a ball.

Practice/Apply—You Do

Ask children to think about something interesting that happened to them in the last few days and to draw a picture of that event. Then have children write words or phrases to tell how the event made them feel. Encourage them to write or dictate full sentences if they are able to, but accept single words such as *surprised*, *happy*, or *funny* as well. Ask children to share their work with a partner.

Conference/Evaluate

Walk around the room, checking that children are on task. Ask children to tell you what is happening in their pictures and to discuss how they felt about what happened.

Minilesson 24

Drafting Story Sentences

Common Core State Standards: W.K.3, L.K.1b

Objective: Write story sentences that use exact verbs.

Guiding Question: How do I use verbs in my writing?

Teach/Model—I Do

Write the following sentence on the board: *The children are standing on the playground.* Read the sentence aloud. Tell children that the sentence helps you picture what is happening. Then replace *standing* with *jumping* and read the sentence again. Explain that the verb *jumping* gives you a very different picture about what is happening. Repeat with *running*, *hopping*, and *climbing*. Point out that writing can be improved by choosing exact verbs that help readers get pictures in their heads.

Guided Practice—We Do

On the board, write *Tanya _____ the ball.* Read it aloud. Guide children to suggest verbs that could go in the blank, such as *threw*, *kicked*, and *hit*. Write each sentence and read it with children. Encourage children to picture what is happening in each. You can also have children sketch simple pictures on the board to illustrate the sentences. If children have difficulty thinking of an appropriate word, use the verb *rolled* to get them started. Discuss how the writing is made clearer by adding exact verbs.

Practice/Apply—You Do

Give each child a copy of the **blackline master** on **page 29.** Ask children to think of an activity they would enjoy doing. Have them draw a picture of themselves engaged in that activity. Then have them write a sentence that uses an exact verb to describe what they are doing in the picture.

Conference/Evaluate

Move through the room, offering assistance as needed. Help children identify the exact verbs they used. Tell children how the verbs help you understand exactly what is happening in the picture.

Name _____

WRITING FORMS

Story Sentences

Teacher: Ask children to think of something fun they would like to do. Have them draw a picture of themselves engaged in this activity. Then have them write a sentence about the picture, using an exact verb.

Grade K • **29**

Story Sentences

Minilesson 25

Writing a Strong Ending

Common Core State Standard: W.K.3

Objective: Write a strong ending to a story.
Guiding Question: What makes a good story ending?

Teach/Model—I Do

Remind children that they wrote story beginnings in a previous lesson. Explain that stories also need good endings. Tell children that most stories have a problem and that the ending often tells how the characters solve the problem. Write the following on the board and read it aloud: *Jane the eagle thought she was the best flyer in the world!* Next, write the middle of the story: *One day she saw an airplane. It made her sad. The plane could fly higher than she could.* Finally, write *So Jane bought a ticket to ride the plane. Now she could fly as high as the plane!* Read the story aloud, emphasizing that the ending is funny but tells how Jane solves the problem.

Guided Practice—We Do

Write the following on the board and read it aloud: *It was cold in the woods. The wind felt like ice. Big Bear was freezing. Even her fur couldn't help her stay warm.* Review the story's problem and explain that the ending should tell how the bear solves the problem. Guide children to suggest endings. Point out that the endings can be funny (she bought a coat) or serious (she found a warmer cave).

Practice/Apply—You Do

Write the following on the board and read it aloud: *Fred the Alligator swam through the swamp. He was hungry, and he was looking for things to eat. But he couldn't find any food.* Review the problem in the story. Have children write and share a strong ending that solves the problem.

Conference/Evaluate

Circulate, offering help as needed. Be sure that children's endings provide a solution to the problem.

30 • Writing for Common Core

Minilesson 26

Drafting Story Sentences

Common Core State Standards: W.K.3, L.K.1f

Objective: Write story sentences in sequence.
Guiding Question: How can I use sentences to tell a story?

Teach/Model—I Do

Remind children that they wrote endings for stories in the previous minilesson. Emphasize that stories have beginnings, middles, and ends and that the ideas in the story should go in order. On the board, write the following: *A mouse was walking along. It saw a cat. The mouse ran away.* Read the sentences aloud, indicating the initial capitals and the periods. Ask children to get a picture in their heads of what happened in the story. Then read the sentences in a different order: *It saw a cat. The mouse ran away. A mouse was walking along.* Point out that if children try to picture the story now, they will see that the story does not make sense when the sentences are in this order.

Guided Practice—We Do

On the board, write the sentences *I went swimming. I swam all day.* Read the sentences aloud. Ask children to provide an appropriate ending sentence, such as *After that, I was tired.* Repeat, asking children to supply a beginning sentence to precede *We went on the slide. Then we played on the swings.* Finally, ask children to provide a sentence that could go between *I visited my friend* and *We had a great time.* Review the importance of sequence with children.

Practice/Apply—You Do

Distribute copies of the **blackline master** on **page 31**. Read the two sentences aloud. Explain that the sentences are part of a story but that the middle part of the story is missing. Have children write a second sentence for the story and then illustrate their work.

Conference/Evaluate

Read completed stories aloud with children to help them determine whether the sentences fit together.

Name _____

Story Sentences

A bird was in the tree.

_____

- -

_____

- -

_____

Then the bird flew away.

Teacher: Read the two sentences aloud. Tell children that these sentences are part of a story. Point out that the middle sentence is missing. Ask children to write an appropriate middle sentence that fits with the two existing sentences. Then ask children to draw a picture to illustrate their story.

Grade K • **31**

Story

Minilesson 27

Organizing a Story

Common Core State Standards: W.K.3, SL.K.3, L.K.1f

Objective: Use time-order words to organize a story.

Guiding Question: How can I tell a story in order?

Teach/Model—I Do

Tell children that when they write stories, it is important to tell the events in order. One way of doing this is to use the words *first*, *next*, and *last*. On the board, write the following: *First, Ms. Lin went to the park. Next, she went to the store. Last, she went home.* Read the story aloud with children, emphasizing the time-order words. Stress that words like *first* and *last* help readers better understand what is happening.

Guided Practice—We Do

On the board, write *First, _____.* Below that, write *Next, _____.* Finally, write *Last, _____.* Read the words with children. Then have them carry out the following actions as a group: in order, they should clap their hands, then touch their noses, and finally fold their arms. Repeat, making sure children understand the order. Guide them to complete the sentence frames to tell what they did first, next, and last; for example, the first might read *First, we clapped our hands.* Read the completed frame aloud.

Practice/Apply—You Do

Have children think of three things they did after they woke up this morning, such as eating breakfast, getting dressed, and getting on the school bus. Have children order the events. At the top of a sheet of paper, have them draw what happened first and label it *first*. Repeat with the other two events, labeling them *next* in the middle of the page and *last* on the bottom of the paper. Have children keep their work for the next minilesson.

Conference/Evaluate

Circulate, making sure that children are on task. Ask them to use the pictures and the words *first*, *next*, and *last* to tell you their stories.

Minilesson 28

Drafting a Story

Common Core State Standards: W.K.3, SL.K.3, L.K.1f

Objective: Write a story based on pictures.

Guiding Question: How can I use pictures to write a story?

Teach/Model—I Do

Remind children that in the previous minilesson they used the words *first*, *next*, and *last* to help them tell a story. Tell children that they will turn their pictures into stories today. On the board, draw three sketches as follows: from left to right, a stick figure lying in bed; a stick figure standing up; a stick figure running. Touch the pictures in turn and say *first*, *next*, *last*. Explain that these pictures tell a story about your friend Jed. On the board, write the following and read it aloud: *First, Jed was asleep. Next, he got up. Last, he went jogging.* Emphasize that you took your story pictures and turned them into a story with words.

Guided Practice—We Do

Draw the following pictures, from left to right: a sun; a cloud partly covering the sun; a cloud with rain falling from it. Explain that this story tells about something that happened one day. Touch the pictures one by one and say *first*, *next*, *last*. Then guide children to tell a simple story about the pictures, using *first*, *next*, and *last*. Possible stories might include *First, the sun was out. Next, a cloud came. Last, it rained.* Write the story on the board and read it aloud.

Practice/Apply—You Do

Make sure children have the work they began during the previous minilesson. Then distribute copies of the **blackline master** on **page 33**. Ask children to complete the sentence frames to tell what is happening in each picture. Ask children to share their work with a partner.

Conference/Evaluate

Check that children's sentences refer to the pictures they drew earlier. Encourage them to write or copy as many words on their own as they can.

WRITING FORMS

Story

First, _____.

Next, _____.

Last, _____.

Teacher: Have children look at the picture story they created in the previous minilesson. Read the time-order words on the page. Ask children to complete the sentence frames by writing what is happening in each picture of the story, making sure to retell the events in the correct order. Offer dictation and spelling help as needed, and encourage children to keep their writing simple and short. Children can draw a picture when their writing is complete.

Grade K • **33**

Writing Handbook Minilessons

Minilesson 29	Minilesson 30
Revising a Story	**Editing a Story**

Common Core State Standards: W.K.3, L.K.2a, L.K.2b

Common Core State Standards: W.K.3, L.K.2a, L.K.2b

Objective: Revise a story.

Guiding Question: How can I make my story better?

Teach/Model—I Do

Tell children that you have a story idea. On the board, write the sentence *A bear was walking.* Read the sentence; then shake your head. Explain that you like the idea of the story, but that it isn't very clear. Say *I'll revise this story to add some more details. That will help my readers get a better picture of what is happening.* Add the words *big black* before *bear* and *in the forest* after *walking.* Read the changes aloud; then write the new sentence on the board. Read it with children. Point out that revising your sentence made it clearer and better.

Guided Practice—We Do

Tell children that you have another story idea. On the board, write the sentence *A girl had a pet.* Read the sentence aloud. Elicit from children that the sentence is not very interesting. Ask the class for suggestions about how they could revise the sentence to make it better, such as by naming the girl or describing the pet. Insert or change words as needed; then write the new sentence on the board. Repeat with other suggestions.

Practice/Apply—You Do

Distribute copies of the **blackline master** on **page 35**. Explain that the sentence at the top of the page is a good story idea, but that you think children can revise it to make the sentence better. Guide children to add or change words, then write the full sentence at the bottom of the page. Close by having children draw a picture in the frame.

Conference/Evaluate

Circulate through the room, offering spelling and dictation help as needed. Talk with children about how their revisions improve the original sentence.

34 • Writing for Common Core

Objective: Use editing symbols to edit a story.

Guiding Question: How can I make changes to my story?

Teach/Model—I Do

On the board, write the sentence *my pet is blac and white* as below. Read the sentence aloud and explain that there are some things wrong with this sentence. Add that you can use special signs called editing symbols to help you fix the problems. Place a caret under the word *my* and explain that this symbol means that you are adding or changing a word. Above *my*, rewrite the word with an upper-case *M*. Then repeat, placing a caret under *blac* and writing *black* above it. Finally, insert a caret at the end and add a final period. Read the sentence with children. Explain that all the problems have been fixed.

My   black   .
my pet is blac and white
^   ^   ^

Guided Practice—We Do

Write *the caat has big teeth* on the board, as below. Read the sentence with children and ask them what is wrong with it. Review the use of the caret. Then guide them to fix the sentence as shown.

The cat   .
the caat has big teeth
^ ^   ^

Practice/Apply—You Do

Ask children to use a piece of writing they did that has not been edited. Have them use editing symbols to make necessary changes.

Conference/Evaluate

Circulate through the room, making suggestions about what parts of the sentences need fixing. Guide children to use appropriate spelling and punctuation.

Name _____

Story

I saw a dog.

_____

- -

_____

_____

- -

_____

Teacher: Read the first sentence aloud. Tell children that this sentence is a story idea, but explain that children can revise the sentence to make it better. Ask children to add or change words at the top of the page, then write the complete sentence at the bottom of the page. Finally, ask children to draw a picture to illustrate their story sentence.

Grade K • 35

Writing Handbook Minilessons

Message

WRITING FORMS

Minilesson 31

Writing Facts and Opinions

Common Core State Standards: W.K.2, L.K.6, SL.K.4

Objective: Write facts and opinions.

Guiding Question: What is the difference between facts and opinions?

Teach/Model—I Do

Sketch a picture of a horse on the board. Explain that you are going to write a fact about horses: that is, you will write something that is true. Write the sentence *Horses eat hay* and read it aloud. Point out that horses really do eat hay, so this sentence is true; the sentence tells a fact about horses. Then say that you will write an opinion about horses. Explain that an opinion is something that some people think, while other people disagree. Write *Horses are my favorite animals.* Read it aloud. Point out that some would agree that horses are their favorites, but others could have different favorite animals.

Guided Practice—We Do

Sketch a picture of a bird on the board. Guide children to think of facts about birds, such as *Some birds fly*, *Birds lay eggs*, and *Birds have two feet*. Write these facts on the board under the heading *Facts*. Then repeat with children's opinions about birds, which might include *I like birds*, *Birds would make good pets*, or *Birds are funny-looking*. Write these under the heading *Opinions*. Review the difference between fact and opinion with children.

Practice/Apply—You Do

Have children choose an animal. Ask them to write one fact about the animal and one opinion about it. Encourage them to share their work with a partner.

Conference/Evaluate

Circulate, asking guiding questions such as the following: *Would everybody agree that a tiger has sharp teeth/that rabbits are the friendliest animals?* Check whether children grasp the difference between opinion and fact.

36 • Writing for Common Core

Minilesson 32

Drafting a Message

Common Core State Standards: W.K.1, L.K.1f

Objective: Write the body of a short message.

Guiding Question: How can I write a message to a person in my family?

Teach/Model—I Do

Explain to children that a message is a short letter that gives somebody information. Tell them that you need to write a message for the principal. Write on the board: *Ms./Mr. _____, You should know that my class is doing a great job in writing.* Then sign the message. Read it aloud. Step back and smile. Say *There! When the principal gets this message, he/she will learn some very important information about our class!* If possible, deliver a copy of the message.

Guided Practice—We Do

Tell children that they will now write a message to another adult in the school. Guide children to choose an appropriate person, such as a custodian, an office worker, or another teacher. Write the recipient's name on the board, followed by a comma. Ask children what they would like this person to know. Guide the class to compose a polite and respectful message about what they are doing in school or another topic. Write the body of the message on the board and read it with children. Then sign it *Mr./Ms. ___'s Class.* Deliver a copy of the message if appropriate.

Practice/Apply—You Do

Distribute copies of the **blackline master** on **page 37**. Tell children to think of a family member they want to write a message to. Then ask children to write a message to that person. They should put the recipient's name at the top, write the body of the message below that, and sign it. Have them draw a picture to match the message.

Conference/Evaluate

Walk through the room, offering spelling and dictation help as needed.

Name _____

WRITING FORMS

Message

_____

- - - - - - - - - - - - - - - - - - -

_____

_____

- -

_____

_____

- -

_____

                                        _____

                                        - - - - - - - - - - - - - - - - - - -

                                        _____

Teacher: Tell children that they will use this page to write a message to a family member. Help them write the recipient's name at the top and the body of the message below that. Have children end by signing their names and drawing a picture to illustrate the message.

Thank-You Note

Minilesson 33

Expressing Thanks

Common Core State Standards: W.K.1, L.K.1f, L.K.2a

Objective: Thank a person and explain why he or she is being thanked.

Guiding Question: How do I tell someone thank you?

Teach/Model—I Do

Explain that when people do nice things for you, it is a good idea to thank them. Display a puppet. Tell children that the puppet did something for you, and you would like to thank it. Say *Thank you* to the puppet. Have the puppet say *But what did I do?* Tell children that you forgot something important: when you thank people, you should always explain your reasons for thanking them. Speak to the puppet and say *Thank you for helping to sort my markers!* Have the puppet reply *You're welcome! I was glad to help.*

Guided Practice—We Do

Ask a child to bring you a pencil. Tell the class that you would like to thank the child. Say: *I can begin by saying* Thank you, *but I want to give a reason.* Guide children to suggest sentences such as *Thank you for bringing me the pencil.* Repeat, asking other children to carry out tasks such as putting away a toy.

Practice/Apply—You Do

Give each child a sheet of paper and three markers of different colors; if possible, children sitting next to each other should not have the same colors. Tell children that they should use their markers to draw a picture. Add that if they want a different color, they can borrow one from a neighbor. Explain that when they borrow a marker, they must thank the child who is lending them the marker and explain why.

Conference/Evaluate

Move through the room, checking that children say *Thank you for letting me use your marker* or a similar sentence. If children are reluctant to borrow a marker on their own for any reason, guide them to borrow one from a classmate or from you.

38 • Writing for Common Core

Minilesson 34

Drafting a Thank-You Note

Common Core State Standards: W.K.1, L.K.1f, L.K.2a

Objective: Write a thank-you note.
Guiding Question: How can I write a thank-you letter?

Teach/Model—I Do

Tell children that people can thank each other in person but that they can also write a special letter called a thank-you note. Explain that your brother took you to a play recently, and you want to send him a thank-you note. On the board, write *Dear Bobby, Thank you for taking me to the play! I loved the play because it was funny.* Sign your name; then read the note aloud. Point out that the note names the person you are thanking, tells what that person did for you, and gives an opinion.

Guided Practice—We Do

Have the class name an adult in the school who did something nice for them, such as a specialist teacher or a custodian. Explain that the class will write a note to thank this person. On the board, write *Dear* and then fill in the name of the person followed by a comma. Then have children express their thanks, being sure they give a reason and an opinion. Sign the note and read the completed letter aloud. If possible, copy the note and deliver it to the recipient.

Practice/Apply—You Do

Distribute copies of the **blackline master** on **page 39**. Ask children to think of a person they know who did something nice for them. Guide them to draft a thank-you note to this person. Remind them that a thank-you note gives a reason and an opinion. Ask children to draw a picture after they are done.

Conference/Evaluate

Circulate, taking dictation or helping with spelling as needed. Help children identify the reason and the opinion in the note. Ask guiding questions, such as *Where did you go with Uncle James?* or *What did you like about it when Shane let you ride his bike?*

Name _____

WRITING FORMS

Thank-You Note

_____

- - - - - - - - - - - - - - - - - -

_____

_____

- -

_____

_____

- -

_____

_____

- -

_____

_____

- - - - - - - - - - - - - - - - - -

_____

Teacher: Tell children to think of someone who did something nice for them and whom they would like to thank. Ask them to write a thank-you note to that person. Assist them in writing the recipient's name at the top and the body of the thank-you note, including their reason and opinion, below that. Children should also sign their names and draw a picture.

Writing Handbook Minilessons

Letter

Minilesson 35	Minilesson 36

Using Parts of a Letter

Common Core State Standard: RF. K.1

Objective: Identify and use a date, greeting, body, and signature in a letter.

Guiding Question: What are the parts of a letter?

Teach/Model—I Do

Ask children if they have ever written or gotten a letter in the mail or via computer. Explain that letters always have certain parts. Write the date at the top of a sheet of chart paper. Say *Letters always start with the date*. Then write and read aloud *Dear [principal's name]*. Explain that this part is called the greeting; it tells who the letter is for. Next, write a message such as *I went to the zoo. I liked it a lot.* and follow it with *Sincerely, [your name]'s class*. Explain that these are called the body of the letter, the closing, and the signature. Review the terms *date*, *greeting*, *body*, *closing*, and *signature*.

Guided Practice—We Do

Tell children you want to write a letter to a friend. Ask what goes at the top. Elicit that this place is for the date, and write the date on chart paper. Continue with the greeting, body, closing, and signature, guiding children to name these parts in order. Refer children to the letter you wrote in the *I Do* section, if needed. Close the letter with *Love, [your name]* and point out that different letters use different closings.

Practice/Apply—You Do

Write a short letter on the board with the date, greeting, body, closing, and signature. Read it aloud. Challenge children to point to the signature, date, and greeting. Continue until children have pointed to all the parts. Then reverse the task by pointing to the parts in turn and having children name them.

Conference/Evaluate

Check children's ability to identify the parts of the letter. Encourage them to participate even if they think they might give a wrong answer.

Drafting a Letter

Common Core State Standard: W.K.2

Objective: Draft a letter.

Guiding Question: What should I say in a letter?

Teach/Model—I Do

Explain that you want to write a letter to another kindergarten class in the school. Write the date at the top of a sheet of chart paper. Then write the greeting. Read these parts aloud. Then explain that letters are often about telling people your news. Write something newsworthy from your classroom as the body of your letter; keep it to 1–2 sentences at most. For example, you might write *We thought our fish was sick, but it was really okay*. Read your writing aloud. Then add a closing and a signature. Read the whole letter, naming the parts (date, body, etc.) as you touch each section.

Guided Practice—We Do

Guide children to write a letter to a friend about a place and how they liked it. Then help children name and identify the parts of the letter as you write each on the board. Pay particular attention to the body of the letter; ask children what they would like to tell their friend about the visit. Read the entire letter aloud, having children help you review the names of the parts.

Practice/Apply—You Do

Give each child a copy of the **blackline master** on **page 41**. Have children follow the directions to complete a short letter to a family member.

Conference/Evaluate

Move through the room, asking children who they are writing to and helping with spelling, as needed. Check children's willingness to write on their own. Review the parts of a letter to help children make sure they have included them all.

40 • Writing for Common Core

Name _____

Letter

Dear _____,

Love,
_____

Directions Have children choose a family member and write a letter to that person. Encourage them to share some interesting news they have.

Grade K • **41**

Writing Handbook Minilessons

Opinion Sentences

Minilesson 37

Sharing Writing in Groups

Common Core State Standards: W.K.3, SL.K.4, L.K.1f

Objective: Ask and answer questions about writing.
Guiding Question: How can I talk about my writing?

Teach/Model—I Do

Explain that when you share your writing in a group, you answer questions, and that when someone else is sharing, you listen carefully and ask questions. On the board, write the following: *I went to the park. I walked for a while. Then I sat and read my book.* Display a puppet. Explain that the puppet is in your sharing group. Read your work aloud. Then have the puppet ask questions like *Did you have fun?*, *What book did you read?*, *What else did you do?*, and *What sounds did you hear?* Answer the questions thoughtfully.

Guided Practice—We Do

Write the following on the board: *I went bowling. Bowling is my favorite sport.* Read it aloud. Guide children to ask you questions about the writing. Offer prompts as needed by having the puppet ask a question or two. Repeat with *I saw some flowers near the sidewalk. They smelled wonderful.*

Practice/Apply—You Do

Ask children to write a sentence about something they saw or heard. Then divide the class into groups of 4 or 5 children. Have children take turns sharing their writing with the group. Invite listeners to ask questions and have the writer respond. Remind children to be polite when speaking. If time is an issue, you can distribute children's completed writing and have them share this work instead.

Conference/Evaluate

Walk around the room, checking that groups are working smoothly and that children are being respectful to one another. Suggest questions to ask if children are having difficulty formulating their own. Compliment children on their ability to share ideas.

Minilesson 38

Drafting Opinion Sentences

Common Core State Standards: W.K.3, SL.K.4, L.K.1f

Objective: Write an opinion.
Guiding Question: How is an opinion different from a fact?

Teach/Model—I Do

Explain that sometimes people write opinions, and sometimes people write facts. On the board, write *Giraffes are very tall.* Read it aloud and explain that this is a fact because it is true; everyone knows that giraffes are tall. Then write *I think giraffes are the funniest-looking animals in the world.* Read it aloud and explain that this is an opinion because it tells what you think; some people might agree with you, but others probably do not. Repeat with *Giraffes have long necks* (fact) and *Giraffes are my favorite animals* (opinion).

Guided Practice—We Do

Write the word *cats* on the board. Guide children to tell their opinions about cats. Possible opinions might include *Cats are not very friendly*, *I love cats*, or *I think cats have the softest fur of any animal.* Help children distinguish these opinions from facts about cats, such as *Cats are animals* or *Cats have four legs.* Write children's opinions on the board, using full sentences, and read them aloud. Repeat with another animal, such as dogs or lions.

Practice/Apply—You Do

Pass out copies of the **blackline master** on **page 43.** Ask children to think of an animal they have an opinion about. Have them draw a picture of the animal and then write one or two sentences that tell their opinion about it. Ask children to share their writing in small groups, taking turns asking and answering questions.

Conference/Evaluate

Offer assistance as needed and make sure that children are on task. Check whether children are able to distinguish facts and opinions.

Name _____

Opinion Sentences

Teacher: Have children choose an animal and draw a picture of it. Then have them write one or two opinion sentences about the animal.

Grade K • **43**

Opinion Sentences

WRITING FORMS

Minilesson 39

Changing Words

Common Core State Standard: W.K.5

Objective: Use clear and descriptive words to improve writing.

Guiding Question: Can I change the words I wrote to make my writing clearer?

Teach/Model—I Do

On the board, write the sentence *I saw some animals yesterday*. Read it aloud. Then tell children that the word *animals* isn't very clear; you could have seen any kind of animal. Cross out the word *animals* and write *chickens* above it. Use a caret to indicate where *chickens* belongs in the sentence; tell children what the caret is for. Read the new sentence aloud. Point out that by changing *animals* to *chickens*, you made the sentence clearer and more interesting.

Guided Practice—We Do

Repeat the above process with children. Write *I ate something for dinner*. Guide children to help you change *something* so that the sentence is clearer. Encourage children to direct you how to make the change by crossing out *something* and suggesting more specific words, such as *pizza* or *salad*; remind them to remember the carets. Read each new sentence aloud and point out how each change makes the sentence more interesting.

Practice/Apply—You Do

On the board, write *The girl played with toys*. Point out that the word *toys* isn't very clear. Have children change the word *toys* to a more specific word or words, such as *stuffed animals*. Ask children to share their work with a partner and make other suggestions for revising the sentence.

Conference/Evaluate

Circulate and offer assistance as necessary. Have children tell you how they made the sentence clearer and more interesting.

44 • Writing for Common Core

Minilesson 40

Revising Opinion Sentences

Common Core State Standards: L.K.2a, L.K.2b

Objective: Revise a sentence that gives an opinion.

Guiding Question: How can I use exact words to make my opinion sentences better?

Teach/Model—I Do

On the board, write the sentence *I think that some animals are very graceful*. Read the sentence with children, and explain the meaning of *graceful* if necessary. Point out that this is an opinion sentence, but that it is not very clear or detailed: you can make your sentence better by telling exactly what animals you think are graceful. Use editing symbols to delete *some animals* and insert *swans and dolphins*. Read the changes aloud; then write a clean copy of the new sentence below the original. Point out that revising made your sentence better.

Guided Practice—We Do

On the board, write this sentence: *My favorite thing is playing with toys*. Read the sentence with children. Underline the word *toys* and explain that this word is not very exact; it doesn't tell what kinds of toys the speaker likes best. Guide children to suggest more exact words that would improve the sentence; possibilities include substituting *dolls*, *toy cars*, or *blocks*. Write the new sentences and discuss why they are improvements over the original.

Practice/Apply—You Do

Distribute copies of the **blackline master** on **page 45**. Read the opinion sentence with children. Tell children that they can revise the sentence to make the opinion clearer. Remind children to use editing symbols to add, change, or delete words. Then have children write the full sentence at the bottom of the page and draw a picture to illustrate their work.

Conference/Evaluate

Help with writing and spelling as needed. Talk with children about how they improved the original.

Name _____

Opinion Sentences

I love to eat fruit.

_____

- -

_____

_____

- -

_____

Teacher: Read the first sentence aloud. Remind children that this is an opinion sentence but that they can revise the sentence to make their opinion clearer. Ask children to use editing symbols to add, delete, or change words at the top of the page, then make a clean copy of the complete sentence at the bottom of the page. Have children draw pictures to illustrate their opinion.

Grade K • 45

List

Minilesson 41

Making Lists for Different Purposes

Common Core State Standard: W.K.8

Objective: Work with lists.

Guiding Question: What is a list and how do I use it?

Teach/Model—I Do

On the board, write *Things I Need to Buy* and read the words aloud. Tell children that you need to go to the grocery store and that you want to remind yourself of the things you want to buy. Say *I need to buy apples and grapes*, and write the words *apples* and *grapes* on the board in list form. Read the words aloud. Add *milk* to the list and read it aloud. Then add two other items. Point out that the list is made up of words, not whole sentences, and that the things are listed in a column that goes from top to bottom.

Guided Practice—We Do

On the board, write *Children in Our Class*. Read the words aloud. Ask children why someone might want to make a list of all the children in the class. Elicit or explain that a teacher might need it to be sure he or she doesn't leave anyone out. Ask children what a list of children in the class would look like; guide children to explain that it would include all their names in a column.

Practice/Apply—You Do

Help children generate possible topics for lists, such as *Dangerous Animals* or *My Favorite Books*. Then ask children to think of a list they might need to make. Have them write the title of the list on a sheet of paper and tell a partner why this list would be a good one to have.

Conference/Evaluate

Move around the room, listening to children's conversations. Ask whether they think their list would be long or short and why they think so.

46 • Writing for Common Core

Minilesson 42

Drafting a List

Common Core State Standard: W.K.8

Objective: Draft a list.

Guiding Question: What do I need to put on my list?

Teach/Model—I Do

On the board, write the title *My Favorite Sports*. Read it aloud. Tell children that you would like to remember every one of your favorite sports so that it is included on the list. Name 4–5 sports one by one, writing their names in list form below the title. Name 1–2 others that you don't especially like; then shake your head and say that you don't like it enough for it to be one of your favorites. Add 1–2 more sports to the list and read them aloud. Explain that your list is complete.

Guided Practice—We Do

On the board, write *Things to Do on the Playground*. Read the words aloud. Guide children to help you draft a list of the things they can do on the playground. Start by saying *You can use the swings on the playground* and writing *swings* under the list title. Then guide children to add to the list. Have them help you determine where the next item should go. When children are finished, read the list aloud one item at a time. Explain that if a visitor ever wants to know about the school playground, children just need to show the visitor the list.

Practice/Apply—You Do

Distribute copies of the **blackline master** on **page 47**. Give children the directions. Remind them to use their best spelling and handwriting.

Conference/Evaluate

Circulate through the room, offering assistance with spelling and sounding out words. Help children read their lists back to you. Note which sounds children can easily associate with letters and which sounds are much more difficult.

Name _____

List

My Favorite Foods

Directions Ask children to draft a list of their favorite foods. Remind them to put one food on each line. Encourage them to continue their lists on the back of the paper, if needed.

Grade K • **47**

Lists

Minilesson 43

Writing Lists with Numbers

Common Core State Standard: W.K.2

Objective: Use numbers to indicate items on a list.
Guiding Question: How can I use numbers to make a list?

Teach/Model—I Do

Remind children they have recently learned about lists. Explain that sometimes people use numbers when they make lists. Using numbers in a list helps writers know the order of the things. On a large sheet of paper, write *1*, *2*, and *3*, each on its own line. Say *Here's what I did to make breakfast today*. Next to *1*, sketch two eggs and say *Number 1, I cracked the eggs*. Next to *2*, sketch a frying pan and say *Number 2, I cooked the eggs*. Next to *3*, sketch a person at a table and say *Number 3, I ate the eggs!* Have children use the numbers and pictures to retell the story. Keep the sheet of paper for the next lesson.

Guided Practice—We Do

Ask children to think about what they do when they get ready to go home from school. Tell them they will make a numbered list to show these steps. Write item numbers 1–3 on another large sheet of paper. Then guide children to draw pictures to show activities like getting their backpacks or pushing the chairs in. Help children read the lists. Save the paper.

Practice/Apply—You Do

Have children think about things they do to get ready for school in the morning. Possible activities might include brushing teeth, eating breakfast, or feeding the cat. Ask each child to come up with three activities. Hand out sheets of paper. Have children write the number 1 at the top and draw the first thing they do. Have them continue with 2 and 3. Ask children to share their drawings and sequence with partners. Save completed papers for the next lesson.

Conference/Evaluate

Help children order their ideas. Remind them to include a number with a period after it for each item.

48 • Writing for Common Core

Minilesson 44

Drafting a Numbered List

Common Core State Standard: W.K.2

Objective: Write a list with item numbers.
Guiding Question: How can I write a list that uses numbers?

Teach/Model—I Do

Review the previous minilesson, in which children created numbered lists with pictures. Explain that children can use the pictures they made to draft a written list with numbers. Display the paper with the breakfast story you created in the previous lesson. Use the pictures and numbers to retell what happened with children. Then explain that you will use words and numbers to make a new list. Write *1*, *2*, and *3* on the board, each on its own line. Model writing the information in the pictures into a list, so that the first item, for example, reads *1. I cracked the eggs*. Read the list with children, saying the number names and the words.

Guided Practice—We Do

Display the picture list children made earlier, which shows what they do to get ready to go home from school. Review the list with children and use the numbers and pictures to list the items one by one. Then have children help you write the item numbers 1–3 on the board and write each activity in words next to it. Read the list with children.

Practice/Apply—You Do

Distribute copies of the **blackline master** on **page 49**. Also distribute the individual picture lists children made during the previous minilesson; these lists show what children do to get ready for school. Guide children to convert the pictures to words and make a written list with numbers. Have children share their work in small groups or with a partner.

Conference/Evaluate

Take dictation as needed. Check that children use numbers to order the activities.

Name _____

WRITING FORM

Lists

Getting Ready for School

_____

- -

_____

_____

- -

_____

_____

- -

_____

_____

- -

_____

_____

- -

_____

Teacher: Give children the picture lists they created during the previous minilesson. Have them describe the pictures in words and write the list on this page, using numbers for each activity.

Invitation

Minilesson 45

Choosing Important Information

Common Core State Standard: W.K.2

Objective: Choose what to put in an invitation.
Guiding Question: What should I say in an invitation?

Teach/Model—I Do

Tell children that you want to write an invitation to a friend. Explain that when you write an invitation, you are asking someone to do something with you. Explain that you will make a list of important information you need so the friend knows what is going on. Say *I need to tell my friend what we will do.* Add that you need to tell your friend the day, the time, and the place. On the board, write in list form *What: Play games; When: 3:00 Friday; Where: My House.*

Guided Practice—We Do

Tell children that you want to write an invitation to the class next door to come and share a snack. Ask them what information needs to go in the invitation. Help them use the list on the board as a guide. Guide them to determine what the invitation will be for (snack), where the other class should go (your classroom), and when they are invited (choose a time and day that's reasonable). Write this information on the board and read it aloud. Copy it on a sheet of paper for the next minilesson.

Practice/Apply—You Do

Ask children to plan an invitation to send to a friend or family member. Have them list important information to include: *whom* they are inviting, *what* they are inviting them to do, and *where* and *when* the invitation is for. Collect children's lists for the next minilesson.

Conference/Evaluate

If children leave something out, prompt them by asking *Where should your friend go? What will you and your friend do?*

Minilesson 46

Drafting an Invitation

Common Core State Standard: W.K.2

Objective: Draft an invitation.
Guiding Question: How do I write an invitation?

Teach/Model—I Do

Remind children that in the previous lesson you were planning to invite a friend to play games with you. Tell children that you will now use your information to write an actual invitation. Start by writing *Dear Jenny.* Follow it with a comma and point out that this part of the invitation tells who it is for. Then write *You're invited to play games at my house!* Read it aloud. Point out that some information is in the invitation, but some is left out. Add *We'll play at 3:00 on Friday.* Compare the invitation with the list you made during the previous lesson. Then explain that all you have to do now is sign the invitation so Jenny knows who wrote it.

Guided Practice—We Do

Remind children that they were planning an invitation for the class next door to come and eat a snack. Write *Dear Ms. Snowe's Class* on the board and read the words aloud. Then guide children to express ideas from the invitation in sentence form, using your invitation to Jenny as a model. Write down their ideas as complete sentences and read them aloud. Help children check that all the important information is included. Then have them sign their name.

Practice/Apply—You Do

Distribute copies of the **blackline master** on **page 51.** Have children follow directions to complete the activity.

Conference/Evaluate

Move through the room, offering assistance as needed. Take dictation when necessary, especially when children have a lot to say.

Name _____

WRITING FORMS

Invitation

_____

- -

_____

_____

- -

_____

Teacher: Ask children to use the invitation plan they made in Minilesson 45. Have them draft an invitation to a friend or family member based on this plan. They should write *Dear ___* at the top and their own name at the bottom.

Report

Minilesson 47

Researching Facts

Common Core State Standards: W.K.2, W.K.8

Objective: Use books to find information.

Guiding Question: How do I learn about a topic?

Teach/Model—I Do

Tell children that you are going to write a report. Explain that a report is a piece of writing that tells facts, or things that are true. Tell the class that when people write a report they first do research, or find facts about their topic in books or elsewhere. Display a picture book that tells about animals. Choose an animal described in the book. Show how you can look through the book to find information about that animal. Identify the facts you find and show children where in the book they appear. Then write each fact in words and phrases on a sheet of paper. For example, for a mouse you might write *small*, *4 legs*, and *squeaks*. Save the paper for the next lesson.

Guided Practice—We Do

Choose another animal that is described in a picture book. Tell children that they will do research together to learn about this animal. Read a section aloud about the animal and display the pictures. Then help children to share facts that they learned about the animal. Write these on a sheet of paper as in the previous section of the lesson. Repeat as needed with a second animal. Save the sheet of paper.

Practice/Apply—You Do

Ask children to work with a partner. Give each pair a book that contains factual information about animals and ask them to choose an animal in the book to learn about. Have children use the pictures and words in the text to find facts about the animal. Ask them to record these facts on a paper. Save the papers.

Conference/Evaluate

Circulate, making sure that both members of each pair are involved. Encourage groups to list at least 3 facts.

52 • Writing for Common Core

Minilesson 48

Drafting a Report

Common Core State Standards: W.K.2, W.K.8

Objective: Write a report with facts about a topic.

Guiding Question: How do I write a report that gives facts?

Teach/Model—I Do

Review the previous minilesson, in which children looked through books to find facts about animals. Tell children that they can use these facts to write a report with sentences about their animals. Display the sheet with the facts you wrote in the previous lesson's *I Do* section. Read the facts aloud. Model how you can turn them into full sentences, such as *A mouse is a small animal. Mice have 4 legs. They squeak.* Write the sentences on the board and read them with children. Give the work a title. Point out that now you have finished your report.

Guided Practice—We Do

Display the paper with the information children found in the *We Do* section of the previous minilesson. Read the information aloud. Then guide children to turn the words and phrases into full sentences, such as *Ducks can swim.* Write the sentences on the board and read them with children. Ask the class to help you think of a title. Congratulate the class on completing a report.

Practice/Apply—You Do

Give each child a copy of the **blackline master** on **page 53**. Also distribute the papers with the facts children found during the *You Do* part of the previous minilesson. Guide children to write 2–3 facts in sentence form on the master. Though this task does not involve partners, children should sit by their partner from the previous minilesson so each child has access to the facts he or she found.

Conference/Evaluate

Move around the room, offering help as needed. Provide the beginning of a sentence if children are having difficulty, such as *A mouse has _____.*

Name _____

Report

Teacher: Give children the papers they completed earlier, in which they noted facts they learned about animals. Guide children to choose 2–3 of these facts and write them in sentence form, then draw a picture.

Grade K • **53**

Writing Handbook Minilessons

Report

| Minilesson 49 | Minilesson 50 |

Making Ideas Complete

Common Core State Standard: W.K.5

Objective: Add new ideas to complete a piece of writing.

Guiding Question: What else do I want to say about my topic?

Teach/Model—I Do

On the board, write the sentences *The sun is big. The sun is very hot.* Read them aloud. Then explain that you just realized that you have one more thing to say about the sun. Insert a caret directly after *big* and remind children that this symbol shows that words are being added. Above the caret, write *and bright*. Read the sentences again, running your hand below the words; pay special attention to the new words. Sum up by explaining that adding the words told more information and made your writing complete.

Guided Practice—We Do

On the board, write *Horses live on farms. They neigh.* Read the sentences aloud. Tell children that you want to add another fact about horses. Ask for a suggestion and show children how to include the new idea, such as by adding the new sentence *They eat grass.* Continue with other ideas, writing the original sentences again each time.

Practice/Apply—You Do

On the board, write *Cars go fast. They have wheels.* Read the sentences aloud. Distribute paper. Have children draw a car and write a sentence that tells one more idea about cars, such as *Cars go on roads.* Have children discuss ideas with peers.

Conference/Evaluate

Circulate, making sure that children are coming up with a new idea and not recycling one of the two you wrote on the board. Emphasize that their writing can help complete what you wrote.

Revising a Report

Common Core State Standards: W.K.2, L.K.2a, L.K.2b

Objective: Revise a written report.

Guiding Question: How can I improve a report?

Teach/Model—I Do

Remind children that revision is an important part of writing. Review that children have recently been working on writing reports, and tell them that they can make changes to make their reports better. On the board, write the title *Apples* and then write *Apples grow. Apples are sold in stores.* Read the sentences aloud. Explain that your report makes sense but that you think you can improve it. Rewrite the report so it reads *Apples grow on trees. You can buy apples in grocery stores.* Read the report aloud. Point out that you did not change much, but you did add details and change around some of the words.

Guided Practice—We Do

On the board, write the title *Cars* and read it aloud. Explain that this is a report on cars. Then write these sentences: *Cars have wheels. A car has glass.* Read the sentences with children. Guide children to suggest ways of improving the report. A possible change might be *Cars have four wheels. They also have glass windows.* Write the new sentences and discuss why they are improvements over the original.

Practice/Apply—You Do

Distribute copies of the **blackline master** on **page 55**. Read the sentences at the top of the page with children. Tell children that they can revise the report to make it clearer. Have children revise the report and write a clean copy at the bottom of the page. They can also draw a picture to illustrate their work.

Conference/Evaluate

Move through the room, asking guiding questions such as *Does the report tell us what cows eat?* and *What sounds do cows make?* Offer to take dictation as needed.

54 • Writing for Common Core

Name _____

Report

Cows

Cows eat.

Cows make sounds.

_____

- - - - - - - - - - - - - - - -

_____

- - - - - - - - - - - - - - - -

_____

- - - - - - - - - - - - - - - -

_____

Teacher: Read the report on cows aloud. Ask children to revise the report so it is clearer and gives better information. Ask children to write a clean copy of their revision at the bottom of the page and draw a picture.

Grade K • 55

Response to Literature

Minilesson 51

Writing an Opinion

Common Core State Standard: W.K.1

Objective: Describe characters and events in a story.

Guiding Question: What ideas do I have about books I've read?

Teach/Model—I Do

Explain that when people tell what they think about a book they've read, they are giving their *opinion*. Remind children that two important parts of a story are the characters and events. Hold up a book you've recently read aloud. Briefly review the story. Then give an opinion about your favorite part (e.g., *The chase was very exciting*) and an opinion about a character (e.g., *I think the girl needs to be nicer*). Repeat with another book. Explain that when you give opinions about a book, you are *responding* to the book.

Guided Practice—We Do

Display another book that children know well. Do a brief picture walk and help children respond to the characters and events in the book. Remind them that this means telling their opinions and that they can use words like *silly* or *scary* to tell what they think of parts of the story. Kick off the process with a response of your own if children seem uncertain what to do. Write their ideas on the board in note form (e.g., *scary* or *fox was mean*).

Practice/Apply—You Do

Ask children to work with a partner. Each child chooses a book he or she knows well. Then have children tell their partners their opinions about the characters and events of the book. Encourage children to list some of their opinions in note form, as you did in the *We Do* section above.

Conference/Evaluate

Circulate, listening to children talk. Make sure their comments relate to the book they chose. Ask for clarification if necessary. Remind them to take turns.

56 • Writing for Common Core

Minilesson 52

Drafting a Response to Fiction

Common Core State Standard: W.K.1

Objective: Draft a literature response.

Guiding Question: How do I write a response to literature?

Teach/Model—I Do

Display another book you've recently read with children. Do a brief picture walk to refresh children's recollections of the story. Then explain that you'll use sentences to draft a response to the book. Write the title of the book at the top of the board or on a sheet of chart paper. Then write 3–4 simple sentences about the book. For *The Cat in the Hat*, for instance, you might write *This is a very silly book! I liked Sally a lot. I think the children should tell their mom what happened.* Read your response aloud. Point out that all your sentences tell your opinions about the book.

Guided Practice—We Do

Have children continue the activity above, dictating new sentences for responses to the same book. Point out that opinions should be expressed in full sentences. Help children expand phrases and fragments into sentences, if needed. Write their sentences on the board and read them aloud. Compliment children on their thoughtful responses.

Practice/Apply—You Do

Choose another book of fiction that is familiar to children. Reproduce the **blackline master** on **page 57** and give each child a copy. Have them follow the directions. Encourage children to write one or two opinion sentences and then share their work with a classmate.

Conference/Evaluate

Note children's willingness to spell and write words on their own. Ask guiding questions to help them clarify their ideas. Check that they give responses to the pictures and plot as well as characters.

Name _____

Response To Literature

Teacher: Display the book you chose. Do a brief picture walk so you're sure the book is familiar to children. Then have children write sentences to respond to the book and draw a picture to go with their response.

Grade K • **57**

Response to Literature

Minilesson 53

Understanding Characters

Common Core State Standard: W.K.1

Objective: Describe and analyze characters in fiction.

Guiding Question: What are my opinions about a character?

Teach/Model—I Do

Display a fiction book you have read to children recently. Do a brief picture walk to remind them of the story. Then write the name of one of the main characters on the board. Tell children that you have some opinions about that character. On the board, write some words or phrases that describe the character, as suggested by the information in the text. For example, you might write *greedy* and point out that the character tries to take her sister's candy, or you might write *good friend* and explain that she comforts a child who is crying. Read the list aloud and explain how the story supports your opinion.

Guided Practice—We Do

Have children choose another character from the story you just reviewed, or invite them to choose a character from a different story. Ask children their opinions of the character. Write words and phrases on the board. Help children explain what parts of the text their opinions are based on. If children have difficulty thinking of words and phrases, prompt them with questions like *Is he happy or sad? What kinds of games does she like to play?*

Practice/Apply—You Do

Ask children to choose a familiar fiction book. Give them a few minutes to reacquaint themselves with the story. Then have them choose a character and write words and phrases that tell their opinion of that character. Have them share with a partner.

Conference/Evaluate

Circulate and help make sure children's reasons make sense.

Minilesson 54

Drafting a Response to Realistic Fiction

Common Core State Standard: W.K.1

Objective: Write a response to a piece of realistic fiction.

Guiding Question: How do I write down my feelings and thoughts about a realistic story?

Teach/Model—I Do

Tell children that *realistic fiction* tells about people who do things that real people might do. Display 3–4 books that are examples of realistic fiction. Then explain that you will write a response to one of the books. Do a picture walk with children. Next, write 2–3 sentences on the board to respond to the story, focusing if possible on the realism in the book. For example, you might write *The kitchen in the story looks a lot like my kitchen* or *The main character has the same color hair as me.*

Guided Practice—We Do

Guide children to offer other responses to the story you chose, or have them begin again with a different piece of realistic fiction. Encourage responses that deal in some way with the realism in the book, but accept all responses. Help children express their ideas in full sentences. Write their responses on the board. Read the list aloud when children are finished.

Practice/Apply—You Do

Choose a story that qualifies as realistic fiction and that you have recently shared with children. Do a picture walk and a brief retelling with children to remind them of the characters, setting, and plot. Then distribute the **blackline master** on **page 59**. Ask children to write 2 or more sentences in response to the book, focusing on what makes the story realistic.

Conference/Evaluate

Circulate through the room, offering help as needed. Help children write complete sentences. Ask guiding questions if needed, such as *Does the main character remind you of anyone?*

58 • Writing for Common Core

Name _____

Response to Literature

Realistic Fiction Response

_____
- - - - - - - - - - - - - - - - - - -
_____

_____
- - - - - - - - - - - - - - - - - - -
_____
- - - - - - - - - - - - - - - - - - -
_____
- - - - - - - - - - - - - - - - - - -
_____
- - - - - - - - - - - - - - - - - - -
_____

Teacher: Display a book of realistic fiction and review it with children. Help children copy the title of the book onto the top of the page. Then have children write 2 or more sentences to respond to the story, focusing especially on the realistic parts. Have them close by drawing a picture that goes with their response.

Grade K • **59**

Response to Literature

Minilesson 55

Understanding Different Kinds of Writing

Common Core State Standard: W.K.1

Objective: Compare different genres.

Guiding Question: How are books alike and different?

Teach/Model—I Do

Display 3 books that children are familiar with. One should be realistic fiction, one fantasy fiction, and one nonfiction. Tell children that these books fit in 3 different categories. Hold up the two fiction books. Explain that these books are both fiction but that one is realistic (it could really happen) and the other is fantasy (it cannot happen). Put one book beside a label reading *realistic fiction* and the other by a label *fantasy fiction*. Explain that the third book is in a new category, nonfiction (about real things). Put this book next to the label *nonfiction*. Review the categories and labels with children.

Guided Practice—We Do

Display several other books children have read or heard. Briefly review the text and pictures for each. Then ask questions such as *Is this book about real things? Is it about things that could be real? Is it about things that cannot happen?* Guide children to identify the genre of each book and place it in the correct pile. Try to show 5–6 books total.

Practice/Apply—You Do

Give pairs of children some sticky notes and a picture book that clearly fits into one of the categories above. Have children look through the book and say whether it is realistic fiction (RF), fantasy fiction (FF), or nonfiction (NF). When they have decided, they can write RF, FF, or NF on a sticky note and attach it to the book cover. Repeat with 4–5 books.

Conference/Evaluate

Move through the room, asking partners how they know which book belongs in which category.

Minilesson 56

Drafting a Response to Literature

Common Core State Standard: W.K.1

Objective: Write a response to a piece of nonfiction.

Guiding Question: How do I respond to nonfiction?

Teach/Model—I Do

Remind children that some books are nonfiction; that is, they are about real people, places, and things. Review a few examples from the previous minilesson. Explain that children can write responses to nonfiction just as they can to fiction. Model this process by displaying a nonfiction book children know well and reviewing it. Then close the book and write 2–3 sentences about it on the board. Try to emphasize things that you learned from the text and the pictures. Examples might include *I had no idea trees could be so old* or *I think Martin Luther King was very brave*. Read the sentences aloud with children.

Guided Practice—We Do

Guide children to suggest other responses to the nonfiction book you used in the *I Do* part of the lesson, or have them begin again with a different nonfiction title. Suggest that children mention things they learned from the book, but accept other responses as well. Write children's responses on the board as complete sentences. Read the list with children after collecting 6–7 responses.

Practice/Apply—You Do

Display a nonfiction book that children have read or heard. Do a brief review with children to remind the class of the subject of the book; you may want to read some of the facts aloud. Distribute the **blackline master** on **page 61**. Ask children to write at least 2 sentences in response to the book, focusing on what they learned from it.

Conference/Evaluate

Move through the room, offering help as needed. Ask questions such as *What did you learn about sharks?*

Name _____

Response to Literature

Nonfiction Response

_____

- -

_____

_____

- -

_____

_____

- -

_____

_____

- -

_____

Teacher: Display a nonfiction book. Review it with children. Have children write the title at the top of the page. Then have them write at least two sentences in response to the book, focusing on things they learned. They should then draw a picture that goes with their response.

Grade K • **61**

Writing Handbook Minilessons

Journal

Minilesson 57

Responding in a Journal

Common Core State Standards: W.K.1, W.K.5

Objective: Draw and talk about the year's work.
Guiding Question: What made me proud this year?

Teach/Model—I Do

Tell children that people often do a special kind of writing called *keeping a journal*. Explain that when you keep a journal, you record your ideas and feelings about things you did. Add that keeping a journal means recording new ideas or feelings every few days and dating each entry. Explain that people keep all their journal writing in one place, such as a notebook or a computer file, so they can easily find it again. On the board, write the date and then sketch a quick picture of several children holding hands and smiling. Say *This picture tells about one of my thoughts: I am proud that this class has worked so well together this year!* Explain that you will write this thought in your journal later on.

Guided Practice—We Do

On the board, write the sentence frame *I liked learning about _____* and read it aloud. Ask children to reflect on what they learned during the year. Then guide children to complete the sentence orally. Record their responses. Point out that these could be journal entries because they tell children's thoughts and feelings about things they did.

Practice/Apply—You Do

Have children create a journal by stapling three sheets of paper together. Ask children to think back over the school year and think of 3 things they did that made them proud. Then ask children to record these accomplishments in pictures, one accomplishment on each page. Have them date the pages and share their work with a partner or in a small group.

Conference/Evaluate

Circulate. Point out that thinking about what makes you proud makes a great topic for a journal entry.

62 • Writing for Common Core

Minilesson 58

Drafting a Journal Entry

Common Core State Standards: W.K.1, W.K.5

Objective: Write a journal entry.
Guiding Question: How can I write a journal entry?

Teach/Model—I Do

Remind children that they learned about creating journals. Review that journal entries need to be dated and that they should be about feelings or thoughts regarding things that the journal keeper did. Explain that journal entries can include pictures but that they usually have words and complete sentences as well. Tell children that you are going to write a journal entry that describes your feelings about something you did recently. Write the date on the board; below that, write *It felt great to get outside for a walk! The sun was shining and it made me very happy.* Read the sentences aloud. Point out that you can also draw a picture to help you remember how it felt to go for the walk, and add that you will write this in a more permanent journal later on.

Guided Practice—We Do

On the board, write the date; then write the sentence frame *I liked _____.* Read it aloud. Guide children to think about something they did recently, in school or out, that they enjoyed. Have volunteers complete the sentence frame orally. Write their responses on the board. Point out that these are wonderful journal entries because they tell about thoughts and feelings.

Practice/Apply—You Do

Distribute copies of the **blackline master** on **page 63**. Explain that children will write and draw a journal entry on this sheet. Have children write the date at the top of the page and write one or more sentences about their favorite part of school this year. Ask children to draw a picture.

Conference/Evaluate

Remind children to use capital letters and periods when writing their sentences.

Name _____

Journal

Teacher: Tell children that they will use this page to write and draw a journal entry. Have them write the date at the top of the page. Ask them to think of their favorite part of the school year. Then have them write one or more sentences about that topic and draw a picture.

Grade K • **63**

Writing Handbook Minilessons

Journal

Minilesson 59	Minilesson 60

Using Your Own Voice

Common Core State Standards: W.K.1, W.K.5

Objective: Use your own voice in a journal entry.
Guiding Question: What is my own writing voice?

Teach/Model—I Do

Have three children come to the front of the room. Ask other children to close their eyes. Then have the three children say in turn *Can you guess who I am?* Have the class identify each speaker. Stress that you can often identify people by their voice. Then say that people also have their own "voices" when they write: the words and tone they write with sound like the things they would say. Write *I love giraffes because they are so cool!* Explain that your niece wrote this; add that your niece is bubbly, so the sentence sounds like something she would write. Repeat with *Giraffes are very interesting* and explain that your nephew wrote this sentence; add that he rarely gets excited, so this sentence sounds like him. Explain that people use their own voices in many kinds of writing, such as when keeping a journal.

Guided Practice—We Do

Guide children to tell what they are going to do after school. Write their ideas on the board. Point out the way that children's voices come through in their words and phrasing: *Kishi writes that she is going to her grandma's house and that her grandma is awesome—Kishi's voice is enthusiastic!* Wrap up by pointing out that all writers have their own voice.

Practice/Apply—You Do

Ask children to write a journal entry that tells about their favorite food. Have them pay close attention to the voice they use. Ask them to read their completed entries to a partner. Have pairs describe their writing voices using words such as *funny* or *excited*.

Conference/Evaluate

Point out words and phrases that especially reveal the writer's voice.

64 • Writing for Common Core

Sharing Your Work Online

Common Core State Standards: W.K.1, W.K.5

Objective: Write a journal entry for sharing online.
Guiding Question: What do I do to share my writing online?

Teach/Model—I Do

Ask children what they know about computers. Draw out or explain that people can use a computer to go online and share their writing with others. Add that many people keep online journals called blogs, which are available for anyone to read. If possible, show children how you can access a blog or other piece of online writing on a computer. Next, on the board, write the date and the sentence *I like blue because blue is the color of the sky*. Read it with children. Then explain that you can type this sentence onto the computer and post it online so other people can read it, even if they live far away. If possible, post it to a blog or school-related website; if not, using a word processing program is fine. If a computer is not available, tell children you can post it another time.

Guided Practice—We Do

On the board, write the date. Ask children what they might like to say about the day so far. Write their sentences on the board. Then demonstrate, if possible, how these sentences could be written on the computer. Stress that children should do this only with an adult's permission and with an adult present.

Practice/Apply—You Do

Distribute copies of the **blackline master** on **page 65**. Have children write a journal entry on this sheet on a topic of their choice and add a picture. Remind them that this piece of writing can be shared by typing it onto the computer and posting it online. Help children post this work online if possible.

Conference/Evaluate

Circulate, checking that children are on task. Ask children who they would especially like to see their work once it is posted online.

Name _____

Journal

Teacher: Ask children to write a journal entry on a topic of their choice. They should include the date and a picture. If possible, help them to type their writing on a computer and post it online.

Grade K • **65**

Teacher's Notes

Resources

Table of Contents

Linguistic Transfer Support

In the charts that follow, the mark • identifies areas in which primary language speakers may have some difficulty pronouncing and perceiving spoken English. The sound may not exist in the primary language, may exist but be pronounced somewhat differently, or may be confused with another sound. Sound production and perception issues affect phonics instruction.

CONSONANTS

Sound	Spanish	Vietnamese	Hmong	Cantonese	Haitian Creole	Korean	Khmer
/b/ as in bat			•	•		•	
/k/ as in cat and kite			•				
/d/ as in dog				•		•	
/f/ as in fan						•	
/g/ as in goat			•	•		•	•
/h/ as in hen					•		
/j/ as in jacket	•	•	•	•		•	
/l/ as in lemon						•	
/m/ as in money							
/n/ as in nail							
/p/ as in pig			•				
/r/ as in rabbit	•		•	•	•	•	
/s/ as in sun			•				
/t/ as in teen		•	•				
/v/ as in video	•			•		•	•
/w/ as in wagon	•		•				•
/y/ as in yo-yo							
/z/ as in zebra	•		•	•		•	•
/kw/ as in queen			•				
/ks/ as in X-ray			•	•			

SHORT VOWELS

Sound	Spanish	Vietnamese	Hmong	Cantonese	Haitian Creole	Korean	Khmer
short a as in hat	•	•		•		•	
short e as in set	•		•	•	•	•	
short i as in sit	•	•	•	•	•	•	
short o as in hot	•		•			•	
short u as in cup	•		•	•	•	•	

LONG VOWELS

Sound	Spanish	Vietnamese	Hmong	Cantonese	Haitian Creole	Korean	Khmer
long *a* as in d<u>a</u>te			•	•			
long *e* as in b<u>e</u>				•		•	
long *i* as in <u>i</u>ce				•			
long *o* as in r<u>oa</u>d			•	•			
long *u* as in tr<u>u</u>e				•		•	

VOWEL PATTERNS

Sound	Spanish	Vietnamese	Hmong	Cantonese	Haitian Creole	Korean	Khmer
oo as in b<u>oo</u>k	•	•	•		•	•	•
aw as in s<u>aw</u>	•					•	

DIPHTHONGS

Sound	Spanish	Vietnamese	Hmong	Cantonese	Haitian Creole	Korean	Khmer
oy as in b<u>oy</u>			•				
ow as in h<u>ow</u>	•						

R-CONTROLLED VOWELS

Sound	Spanish	Vietnamese	Hmong	Cantonese	Haitian Creole	Korean	Khmer
ir as in b<u>ir</u>d	•	•	•	•	•	•	•
ar as in h<u>ar</u>d	•	•	•	•	•	•	•
or as in f<u>or</u>m	•	•	•	•	•	•	•
air as in h<u>air</u>	•	•	•	•	•	•	•
ear as in h<u>ear</u>	•	•	•	•	•	•	•

CONSONANT DIGRAPHS

Sound	Spanish	Vietnamese	Hmong	Cantonese	Haitian Creole	Korean	Khmer
sh as in <u>sh</u>oe	•*	•		•			•
ch as in <u>ch</u>ain		•	•				
th as in <u>th</u>ink	•	•	•	•	•	•	•
ng as in si<u>ng</u>	•		•		•		

CONSONANT BLENDS

Sound	Spanish	Vietnamese	Hmong	Cantonese	Haitian Creole	Korean	Khmer
bl, *tr*, *dr*, etc. (start of words) as in <u>bl</u>ack, <u>tr</u>ee, <u>dr</u>ess		•	•	•		•	
ld, *nt*, *rt*, etc. (end of words) as in co<u>ld</u>, te<u>nt</u>, sta<u>rt</u>		•	•	•	•	•	•

* Spanish speakers from Mexico or Central America who also speak Nahuatl or a Mayan language will be familiar with this sound, written as an *x* in words like *mixteca* (pronounced *mishteca*).

Sound–Symbol Transfer Support

The following charts identify sound–symbol transfer issues for four languages that use the Roman alphabet. (The remaining three do not.) The mark • identifies symbols which do not represent the corresponding sound in the writing system of the primary language.

CONSONANTS

Sound	Spanish	Vietnamese	Hmong	Haitian Creole
b as in <u>b</u>at			•	
c as in <u>c</u>at		•	•	•
as in <u>c</u>ent		•	•	
d as in <u>d</u>og				
f as in <u>f</u>ish				
g as in <u>g</u>oat			•	
as in <u>g</u>iant	•		•	
h as in <u>h</u>en	•			
j as in <u>j</u>acket	•	•	•	
k as in <u>k</u>ite			•	
l as in <u>l</u>emon				
m as in <u>m</u>oon				
n as in <u>n</u>ice				
p as in <u>p</u>ig				
qu as in <u>qu</u>een	•		•	•
r as in <u>r</u>abbit	•		•	
s as in <u>s</u>un			•	
t as in <u>t</u>een			•	
v as in <u>v</u>ideo	•			
w as in <u>w</u>agon		•	•	
x as in <u>X</u>-ray		•	•	•
y as in <u>y</u>o-<u>y</u>o	•			
z as in <u>z</u>ebra	•	•	•	

CONSONANT DIGRAPHS

Sound	Spanish	Vietnamese	Hmong	Haitian Creole
sh as in <u>sh</u>oe	•			
ch as in <u>ch</u>air				•
th as in <u>th</u>ink as in <u>th</u>at	•			•

VOWELS AND VOWEL PATTERNS

Sound	Spanish	Vietnamese	Hmong	Haitian Creole
a as in b<u>a</u>t	•		•	
aCe as in d<u>a</u>te	•	•		
ai as in r<u>ai</u>n	•	•	•	•
ay as in d<u>ay</u>	•		•	•
au as in <u>au</u>thor	•	•	•	•
aw as in s<u>aw</u>	•	•	•	•
e as in b<u>e</u>t	•		•	•
ee as in s<u>ee</u>d	•	•	•	•
ea as in t<u>ea</u>	•	•	•	•
ew as in f<u>ew</u>	•	•	•	•
i as in s<u>i</u>t	•		•	•
iCe as in p<u>i</u>pe	•	•	•	•
o as in h<u>o</u>t	•		•	•
o as in r<u>o</u>de	•	•	•	•
oo as in m<u>oo</u>n	•	•	•	•
oo as in b<u>oo</u>k	•		•	•
oa as in b<u>oa</u>t	•	•	•	•
ow as in r<u>ow</u>	•	•	•	•
ow as in h<u>ow</u>	•	•	•	•
ou as in s<u>ou</u>nd	•	•	•	•
oi as in b<u>oi</u>l			•	•
oy as in b<u>oy</u>		•	•	•
u as in c<u>u</u>p	•	•	•	•
uCe as in J<u>u</u>ne	•	•		
ui as in s<u>ui</u>t	•	•	•	•
ue as in bl<u>ue</u>	•	•	•	•
y as in tr<u>y</u>	•	•	•	•
ar as in st<u>ar</u>			•	•
er as in f<u>er</u>n	•		•	•
ir as in b<u>ir</u>d	•		•	•
or as in t<u>or</u>n	•		•	
ur as in b<u>ur</u>n	•		•	

English–Spanish Vocabulary Transfer Support

English and Spanish share some basic linguistic characteristics. Both languages use word parts like prefixes and suffixes, and both have verbs that change in form. The example words below are not intended to be cognates, but words that illustrate the similar meanings of the word parts. Note that Haitian Creole, Cantonese, Hmong, and Vietnamese do not use word parts to construct new words in the same way that English does.

PREFIXES

English Word Part or Parts	English Example Words	Spanish Word Part or Parts	Spanish Example Words	Word Part Purpose
un-, non-, in-, dis-	<u>un</u>happy <u>non</u>stop <u>in</u>correct <u>dis</u>like	*in-, des-/dis-* *no* plus the verb *sin* plus the noun or verb	<u>in</u>feliz, <u>in</u>correcto <u>des</u>conocido <u>dis</u>parejo <u>no</u> gustar <u>sin</u> parar	Means "not"
re-	<u>re</u>do	*re-*	<u>re</u>hacer	Means "again"
pre-	<u>pre</u>teen	*pre-*	<u>pre</u>escolar	Means "before"

SUFFIXES

English Word Part or Parts	English Example Words	Spanish Word Part or Parts	Spanish Example Words	Word Part Purpose
-ful	power<u>ful</u>	*-oso/a*	poder<u>oso/a</u>	Means "with"; turns a noun into an adjective
-able	read<u>able</u> like<u>able</u>	*-ible* *-able*	leg<u>ible</u> agrad<u>able</u>	Turns a verb into an adjective
-less	fear<u>less</u> care<u>less</u>	*sin* plus the noun prefix *des-*	<u>sin</u> miedo <u>des</u>cuidado	Means "without"; turns a noun into an adjective
-ness	happi<u>ness</u>	*-idad*	feli<u>cidad</u>	Turns an adjective into a noun
-ion/-tion, -ment	react<u>ion</u> pay<u>ment</u> amaze<u>ment</u>	*-ción/-sión* verb stem + *-o*	rea<u>cción</u> conclu<u>sión</u> pag<u>o</u> asombr<u>o</u>	Turns a verb into a noun
-ly	quick<u>ly</u>	*-mente*	rápida<u>mente</u>	Turns an adjective into an adverb

▶ Qualitative Spelling Inventory (QSI)

You may use this inventory and the **Qualitative Spelling Inventory Checklist** (pages 330–331) to gather information about where students fall within a specific developmental level. In this QSI, the words are presented in increasing difficulty. As the spelling assessment proceeds, you will see what features students are learning by the quality of their spelling and the number of words and features they spell correctly. With the words in ascending difficulty, consider stopping the assessment when students make enough errors to determine a phase of spelling. To avoid frustration level testing, small groups can continue this or another list the next day.

The inventory and the checklist will help you identify what students have learned, what they are still "using but confusing" and thus need to learn, and what is beyond their present level. The inventory can be given at the beginning and end of the year and one or two times in between to monitor progress.

Students who score between 40% and 90% on the **Qualitative Spelling Inventory** can begin instruction on grade level. Consider alternate lists for students who score below 40% and above 90%.

Grade 1	Grade 2	Grade 3	Grade 4	Grade 5	Grade 6
1. net	1. class	1. paint	1. shown	1. scowl	1. pledge
2. pig	2. went	2. find	2. thirst	2. beneath	2. advantage
3. job	3. chop	3. comb	3. lodge	3. pounce	3. changeable
4. bell	4. when	4. knife	4. curve	4. brighten	4. inspire
5. trap	5. milk	5. scratch	5. suit	5. disgrace	5. conference
6. chin	6. shell	6. crawl	6. bounce	6. poison	6. relying
7. with	7. sock	7. throat	7. middle	7. destroy	7. amusement
8. drum	8. such	8. voice	8. clue	8. weary	8. conclusion
9. track	9. sleep	9. nurse	9. traced	9. sailors	9. carriage
10. bump	10. boat	10. weigh	10. hurry	10. whistle	10. advertisement
11. smoke	11. size	11. waving	11. noisier	11. chatting	11. description
12. pool	12. plain	12. letter	12. striped	12. legal	12. appearance
13. slide	13. tight	13. useful	13. collar	13. human	13. cooperation
14. shade	14. knife	14. tripping	14. medal	14. abilities	14. democratic
15. brave	15. start	15. early	15. skipping	15. decided	15. responsible
16. white	16. fought	16. dollar	16. palace	16. settlement	16. invisible
17. pink	17. story	17. mouthful	17. civil	17. surround	17. official
18. father	18. clapped	18. starry	18. wrinkle	18. treasure	18. commission
19. batted	19. saving	19. slammed	19. fossil	19. service	19. civilize
20. hugging	20. funny	20. thousand	20. disappear	20. confession	20. inherited
	21. patches	21. circle	21. damage	21. frequency	21. accidental
	22. pinned	22. laughter	22. capture	22. commotion	22. spacious
	23. village	23. carried	23. parading	23. evidence	23. sensibility
	24. pleasure	24. happiest	24. trouble	24. predict	24. composition
	25. question		25. imagine	25. community	25. accomplish
			26. favorite	26. president	26. opposition
				27. responsible	
				28. sensibility	
				29. symphonies	
				30. permission	

Qualitative Spelling Inventory Checklist

This checklist can assist you in identifying a phase of spelling development for each student and whether the student is in the early, middle, or late part of that phase.

When a feature is regularly spelled correctly, check "Yes." If the feature is spelled incorrectly or is omitted, check "No." The last feature that you check as "Often" corresponds to the student's phase of development.

Student's Name_____

Letter Name–Alphabetic Phase

EARLY

- Are beginning and ending consonants included?   Yes _____ No _____ Often _____
- Is there a vowel in each word?   Yes _____ No _____ Often _____

MIDDLE

- Are consonant digraphs and blends correct? (**sh**ade/**tr**ack)   Yes _____ No _____ Often _____

LATE

- Are short vowels spelled correctly? (h**i**d, ch**o**p, s**u**ch)   Yes _____ No _____ Often _____
- Are *m* and *n* included in front of other consonants? (bu**m**p, pi**n**k)   Yes _____ No _____ Often _____

Within Word Pattern Phase

EARLY

- Are long vowel spellings in single-syllable words "used but confused"? (SLIED for *slide*, MAIK for *make*)   Yes _____ No _____ Often _____
- Is there a vowel in each word?   Yes _____ No _____ Often _____

MIDDLE

- Are most long vowels in single-syllable words spelled correctly but some long vowel spellings still "used but confused"? (MANE for *main*)   Yes _____ No _____ Often _____

LATE

- Are *r*- and *l*-controlled vowels in single-syllable words spelled correctly? (sta**r**t/mi**l**k)   Yes _____ No _____ Often _____

Syllables and Affixes Phase

EARLY

- Are inflectional endings added correctly to base words with short vowel patterns? (hug**ging**, pin**ned**)

Yes _____ No _____ Often _____

MIDDLE

- Are inflectional endings added correctly to base words with long vowel patterns? (wa**ving**, stri**ped**)

Yes _____ No _____ Often _____

LATE

- Are unaccented final syllables spelled correctly? (cat**tle**, accur**ate**)

Yes _____ No _____ Often _____

- Are less frequent prefixes and suffixes spelled correctly? (**con**fession, **pro**duction, cap**ture**, coll**ar**)

Yes _____ No _____ Often _____

Derivational Relations Phase

EARLY

- Are multisyllabic words spelled correctly? (expansion, community)

Yes _____ No _____ Often _____

MIDDLE

- Are unaccented vowels in derived words spelled correctly? (proh**i**bition, opp**o**sition)

Yes _____ No _____ Often _____

LATE

- Are words from derived forms spelled correctly? (comp**e**tition, conf**i**dent)

Yes _____ No _____ Often _____

- Are absorbed prefixes spelled correctly? (**ir**relevant, **ac**complish)

Yes _____ No _____ Often _____

Adapted from Words Their Way *by Donald Bear, Marcia Invernizzi, Shane Templeton, & Francine Johnston (Englewood Cliff, NJ: Prentice-Hall 2004).*

▶ Comprehensive List of Spelling/Phonics Lessons and Words, Grades K–6

The effectiveness of word study instruction begins with its word list. The lessons and words on pages 332–342 are organized by the phases of spelling development to guide your selection of lessons for students, based on assessment results. Lessons that are not in your grade-level version of this Guide can be accessed online at **www.thinkcentral.com**.

Emergent Phase

LATE

Letters *Aa–Jj*
Grade K, Lesson 1

The Letters in Your Name
Grade K, Lesson 2

Letters *Aa–Tt*
Grade K, Lesson 3

The Alphabet
Grade K, Lesson 4

Beginning Sounds in Words
Grade K, Lesson 5

Beginning Sounds in Words
Grade K, Lesson 6

Beginning Sounds /m/m, /s/s
Grade K, Lesson 7

Beginning Sounds /m/m, /s/s, /t/t
Grade K, Lesson 8

Beginning Sounds /t/t, /k/c, /p/p
Grade K, Lesson 9

Beginning Sounds /n/n, /m/m
Grade K, Lesson 14

Beginning Sounds /p/p, /f/f
Grade K, Lesson 16

Beginning Sounds /d/d, /r/r, /g/g
Grade K, Lesson 21

Letter Name–Alphabetic Phase

EARLY

Ending Sounds in Words
Grade K, Lesson 10

Ending Sounds /s/s, /p/p, /t/t
Grade K, Lesson 11

Ending Sounds /g/g, /b/b
Grade K, Lesson 18

Short *a* /ă/
Grade K, Lesson 12

Words with -*an*, -*ap*, -*at*
Grade K, Lesson 13

Short *a* Words and High-Frequency Words
Grade K, Lesson 15

Short *i* /ĭ/
Grade K, Lesson 17

Words with Short *a* and Short *i*
Grade K, Lesson 19

Words with -*ig*, -*in*, -*it*
Grade K, Lesson 20

Short *o* /ŏ/
Grade K, Lesson 22

MIDDLE

Words for One and More than One (-*s*)
Grade K, Lesson 23

Words with -*at*, -*it*, -*ot*
Grade K, Lesson 24

Words with Short *o* and Short *e*
Grade K, Lesson 25

Words with -*et* and -*en*
Grade K, Lesson 26

Short *u* /ŭ/
Grade K, Lesson 27

Words with Short *e* and Short *u*
Grade K, Lesson 28

Words with -*ap*, -*up*, -*op*
Grade K, Lesson 29

Words with Short Vowels
Grade K, Lesson 30

Words with Short *a*
Grade 1, Lesson 1
1. am
2. at
3. sat
4. man
5. dad
6. mat

Words with Short *i*
Grade 1, Lesson 2
1. if
2. is
3. him
4. rip
5. fit
6. pin

Words with Short *o*
Grade 1, Lesson 3
1. log
2. dot
3. top
4. hot
5. lot
6. ox

Words with Short *e*
Grade 1, Lesson 4
1. yet
2. web
3. pen
4. wet
5. leg
6. hen

Words with Short *u*
Grade 1, Lesson 5
1. up
2. bug
3. mud
4. nut
5. hug
6. tub

Words with Short *a*
Grade 1, Lesson 6
1. an
2. bad
3. can
4. had
5. cat
6. ran

Words with Short *i*
Grade 1, Lesson 7
1. in
2. will
3. did
4. sit
5. six
6. big

Words with Short *o*
Grade 1, Lesson 8
1. on
2. got
3. fox
4. pop
5. not
6. hop

Words with Short *e*
Grade 1, Lesson 9
1. yes
2. let
3. red
4. ten
5. bed
6. get

Words with Short *u*
Grade 1, Lesson 10
1. us
2. sun
3. but
4. fun
5. bus
6. run

Words with *th*
Grade 1, Lesson 11
1. that
2. then
3. this
4. them
5. with
6. bath

Words with *ch*
Grade 1, Lesson 12
1. chin
2. chop
3. much
4. chip
5. rich
6. chick

Words with *sh*, *wh*
Grade 1, Lesson 13
1. ship
2. shop
3. which
4. when
5. whip
6. fish

Short Vowels *a*, *i*
Grade 2, Lesson 1
1. sad
2. dig
3. jam
4. glad
5. list
6. win
7. flat
8. if
9. fix
10. rip
11. kit
12. mask

Short Vowels *o*, *u*, *e*
Grade 2, Lesson 2
1. wet
2. job
3. hug
4. rest
5. spot
6. mud
7. left
8. help
9. plum

10. nut
11. net
12. hot

Consonant Blends with *r, l, s*
Grade 2, Lesson 5
1. spin
2. clap
3. grade
4. swim
5. place
6. last
7. test
8. skin
9. drag
10. glide
11. just
12. stage

Common Final Blends *nd, ng, nk, nt, xt, mp*
Grade 2, Lesson 6
1. next
2. end
3. camp
4. sank
5. sing
6. drink
7. hunt
8. stand
9. long
10. stamp
11. pond
12. bring

Words with *ar*
Grade 1, Lesson 21
1. far
2. arm
3. yard
4. art
5. jar
6. bar
7. barn
8. bark
9. card
10. yarn

Double Consonants and *ck*
Grade 2, Lesson 7
1. rock
2. black
3. trick
4. kick
5. full
6. dress
7. neck
8. add
9. spell
10. stuck
11. class
12. doll

Words with *th, sh, wh, ch*
Grade 2, Lesson 8
1. dish
2. than
3. chest
4. such
5. thin
6. push
7. shine
8. chase
9. white
10. while
11. these
12. flash

Short Vowels
Grade 3, Lesson 1
1. crop
2. plan
3. thing
4. smell
5. shut
6. sticky
7. spent
8. lunch
9. pumpkin
10. clock
11. gift
12. class
13. skip
14. swing

Within Word Pattern Phase

Words with Long *a*
Grade 1, Lesson 14
1. came
2. make
3. brave
4. late
5. gave
6. shape

Words with Long *i*
Grade 1, Lesson 15
1. time
2. like
3. kite
4. bike
5. white
6. drive

Long Vowels *a, i*
Grade 2, Lesson 3
1. cake
2. mine
3. plate
4. size
5. ate
6. grape
7. prize
8. wipe
9. race

10. line
11. pile
12. rake

Words with Long *o*
Grade 1, Lesson 16
1. so
2. go
3. home
4. hole
5. no
6. rope
7. joke
8. bone
9. stove
10. poke

Words with Long *e*
Grade 1, Lesson 17
1. me
2. be
3. read
4. feet
5. tree
6. keep
7. eat
8. mean
9. sea
10. these

Words with Long *a*
Grade 1, Lesson 18
1. play
2. grain
3. sail
4. mail
5. may
6. rain
7. way
8. day
9. stay
10. pain

Words with Long *o*
Grade 1, Lesson 19
1. show
2. row
3. grow
4. low
5. blow
6. snow
7. boat
8. coat
9. road
10. toad

Words with *er, ir, ur*
Grade 1, Lesson 22
1. her
2. fern
3. girl
4. sir
5. stir
6. bird
7. fur
8. hurt
9. turn
10. third

Words with *oo* (/o͞o/)
Grade 1, Lesson 23
1. look
2. book
3. good
4. hook
5. brook
6. took
7. foot
8. shook
9. wood
10. hood

Words with *oo, ou, ew*
Grade 1, Lesson 24
1. soon
2. new
3. noon
4. zoo
5. boot
6. too
7. moon
8. blew
9. soup
10. you

Words with Long *i*
Grade 1, Lesson 28
1. my
2. try
3. sky
4. fly
5. by
6. dry
7. pie
8. cried
9. night
10. light

Long Vowels *o, u*
Grade 2, Lesson 4
1. doze
2. nose
3. use
4. rose
5. pole
6. close
7. cute
8. woke
9. mule
10. rode
11. role
12. tune

Contractions
Grade 2, Lesson 10
1. I'm
2. don't
3. isn't
4. can't
5. we'll
6. it's
7. I've
8. didn't
9. you're
10. that's
11. wasn't
12. you've

Words with *ai, ay*
Grade 2, Lesson 12
1. pay
2. wait
3. paint
4. train
5. pail
6. clay
7. tray
8. plain
9. stain
10. hay
11. gray
12. away

Words with *ee, ea*
Grade 2, Lesson 13
1. free
2. teach
3. teeth
4. please
5. beach
6. wheel
7. team
8. speak
9. sneeze
10. sheep
11. meaning
12. weave

Long *o (o, oa, ow)*
Grade 2, Lesson 14
1. own
2. most
3. soap
4. float
5. both
6. know
7. loan
8. goat
9. flow
10. loaf
11. throw
12. coach

Long *i (i, igh, y)*
Grade 2, Lesson 17
1. night
2. kind
3. spy
4. child
5. light
6. find
7. right
8. high
9. wild
10. July
11. fry
12. sigh

Words with ar
Grade 2, Lesson 19
1. car
2. dark
3. arm
4. star
5. park
6. yard

7. party
8. hard
9. farm
10. start
11. part
12. spark

Words with *or, ore*
Grade 2, Lesson 20
1. horn
2. story
3. fork
4. score
5. store
6. corn
7. morning
8. shore
9. short
10. born
11. tore
12. forget

Words with *er*
Grade 2, Lesson 21
1. father
2. over
3. under
4. herd
5. water
6. verb
7. paper
8. cracker
9. offer
10. cover
11. germ
12. master

Homophones
Grade 2, Lesson 22
1. meet
2. meat
3. week
4. weak
5. mane
6. main
7. tail
8. tale
9. be
10. bee
11. too
12. two

Words with *oo (ew, oo, ou)*
Grade 2, Lesson 26
1. root
2. crew
3. spoon
4. few
5. bloom
6. grew
7. room
8. you
9. stew
10. boost
11. scoop
12. flew

Words with *oo (book)*
Grade 2, Lesson 27
1. took
2. books
3. foot
4. hoof
5. cook
6. nook
7. hood
8. wood
9. stood
10. shook
11. crook
12. cookbook

Words with *ai, ay, igh, y*
Grade 2, Lesson 29
1. aim
2. snail
3. bay
4. braid
5. ray
6. always
7. gain
8. sly
9. chain
10. shy
11. bright
12. fright

Words with *oa, ow, ee, ea*
Grade 2, Lesson 30
1. seated
2. keeps
3. speed
4. seen
5. means
6. clean
7. groan
8. roast
9. bowls
10. crow
11. owe
12. grown

V-C-e Spellings
Grade 3, Lesson 2
1. spoke
2. mile
3. save
4. excuse
5. cone
6. invite
7. cube
8. price
9. erase
10. ripe
11. broke
12. flame
13. life
14. rule

More Long *a* and Long *e* Spellings
Grade 3, Lesson 3
1. lay
2. real

3. trail
4. sweet
5. today
6. dream
7. seem
8. tea
9. treat
10. afraid
11. leave
12. bait
13. screen
14. speed

More Long *o* Spellings
Grade 3, Lesson 4
1. load
2. open
3. told
4. yellow
5. soak
6. shadow
7. foam
8. follow
9. glow
10. sold
11. window
12. coach
13. almost
14. throat

Spelling Long *i*
Grade 3, Lesson 5
1. slight
2. mild
3. sight
4. pie
5. mind
6. tie
7. pilot
8. might
9. lie
10. tight
11. blind
12. fight
13. die
14. midnight

Vowel + /r/ Sounds in *air* and *fear*
Grade 3, Lesson 16
1. air
2. wear
3. chair
4. stairs
5. bare
6. bear
7. hair
8. care
9. pear
10. pair
11. share
12. near
13. ear
14. beard

Words with *aw, al, o*
Grade 2, Lesson 25
1. tall
2. saw
3. dog
4. draw
5. call
6. fall
7. soft
8. paw
9. ball
10. yawn
11. log
12. small

More Short and Long Vowels
Grade 3, Lesson 6
1. math
2. toast
3. easy
4. socks
5. Friday
6. stuff
7. paid
8. cheese
9. June
10. elbow
11. program
12. shiny
13. piles
14. sticky

Words with *ou, ow*
Grade 1, Lesson 25
1. how
2. now
3. cow
4. owl
5. ouch
6. house
7. found
8. out
9. gown
10. town

Words with *ow, ou*
Grade 2, Lesson 28
1. cow
2. house
3. town
4. shout
5. down
6. mouse
7. found
8. loud
9. brown
10. ground
11. pound
12. flower

LATE

Three-Letter Clusters
Grade 3, Lesson 7
1. three
2. scrap
3. street

4. spring
5. thrill
6. scream
7. strange
8. throw
9. string
10. scrape
11. spray
12. threw
13. strong
14. scratch

Unexpected Consonant Spellings
Grade 3, Lesson 8
1. itch
2. wreck
3. knee
4. patch
5. wrap
6. knot
7. watch
8. knife
9. stretch
10. write
11. knew
12. knock
13. match
14. wrong

Vowel Sound in *town*
Grade 3, Lesson 9
1. clown
2. round
3. bow
4. cloud
5. power
6. crown
7. thousand
8. crowd
9. sound
10. count
11. powder
12. blouse
13. frown
14. pound

Vowel Sound in *talk*
Grade 3, Lesson 10
1. talk
2. cross
3. awful
4. law
5. cloth
6. cost
7. crawl
8. chalk
9. also
10. raw
11. salt
12. wall
13. lawn
14. always

Vowel Sound in *joy*
Grade 3, Lesson 11
1. joy
2. point

3. voice
4. join
5. oil
6. coin
7. noise
8. spoil
9. toy
10. joint
11. boy
12. soil
13. choice
14. boil

Homophones
Grade 3, Lesson 12
1. hole
2. whole
3. its
4. it's
5. hear
6. here
7. won
8. one
9. our
10. hour
11. their
12. there
13. fur
14. fir

Contractions
Grade 3, Lesson 13
1. I'd
2. he's
3. haven't
4. doesn't
5. let's
6. there's
7. wouldn't
8. what's
9. she's
10. aren't
11. hasn't
12. couldn't
13. he'd
14. they're

Vowel + /r/ Sounds
Grade 3, Lesson 14
1. horse
2. mark
3. storm
4. market
5. acorn
6. artist
7. March
8. north
9. barking
10. stork
11. thorn
12. forest
13. chore
14. restore

Vowel + /r/ Sound in nurse
Grade 3, Lesson 15
1. nurse
2. work
3. shirt
4. hurt
5. first
6. word
7. serve
8. curly
9. dirt
10. third
11. worry
12. turn
13. stir
14. firm

Words with /j/ and /s/
Grade 3, Lesson 17
1. age
2. space
3. change
4. jawbone
5. jacket
6. giant
7. pencil
8. circle
9. once
10. large
11. dance
12. jeans
13. bounce
14. huge

Spelling the /k/ and /kw/ Sounds
Grade 3, Lesson 18
1. shark
2. check
3. queen
4. circus
5. flake
6. crack
7. second
8. squeeze
9. quart
10. squeak
11. quick
12. coldest
13. Africa
14. Mexico

Vowel Sounds in *spoon* and *wood*
Grade 3, Lesson 19
1. mood
2. wooden
3. drew
4. smooth
5. blue
6. balloon
7. true
8. crooked
9. chew
10. tooth
11. hooves
12. cool
13. food
14. pooch

ough and *augh*
Grade 3, Lesson 28
1. taught
2. thought
3. rough
4. laugh
5. bought
6. cough
7. ought
8. caught
9. fought
10. daughter
11. tough
12. through
13. enough
14. brought

Short *o* and Long *o*
Grade 4, Lesson 4
1. block
2. shown
3. oatmeal
4. wrote
5. fellow
6. scold
7. coast
8. odd
9. locate
10. slope
11. throat
12. host
13. online
14. shock
15. solve
16. known
17. remote
18. stock
19. boast
20. globe

Homophones
Grade 4, Lesson 5
1. wait
2. weight
3. heard
4. herd
5. days
6. daze
7. heel
8. heal
9. peak
10. peek
11. sent
12. cent
13. scent
14. feet
15. feat
16. vain
17. vane
18. vein
19. miner
20. minor

Short *a* and Long *a*
Grade 4, Lesson 1
1. blade
2. gray
3. past
4. afraid
5. magic
6. delay
7. amaze
8. drain
9. maybe

10. break
11. sale
12. hang
13. stain
14. glass
15. raft
16. jail
17. crayon
18. fact
19. stale
20. steak

Short *e* and Long *e*
Grade 4, Lesson 2
1. west
2. steep
3. member
4. gleam
5. fresh
6. freedom
7. speed
8. steam
9. beast
10. believe
11. speck
12. kept
13. cheap
14. pretend
15. greed
16. shelf
17. least
18. eager
19. reason
20. chief

Short *i* and Long *i*
Grade 4, Lesson 3
1. skill
2. crime
3. grind
4. tonight
5. brick
6. flight
7. live
8. chill
9. delight
10. build
11. ditch
12. decide
13. witness
14. wind
15. district
16. inch
17. sigh
18. fright
19. remind
20. split

Vowel Sounds /ŭ/, /yo͞o/, and /o͞o/
Grade 4, Lesson 6
1. bunch
2. fruit
3. argue
4. crumb
5. crew
6. tune
7. juice
8. refuse
9. truth

10. young
11. clue
12. trunk
13. amuse
14. suit
15. rude
16. trust
17. dew
18. stuck
19. rescue
20. brush

Vowel Sounds /o͞o/ and /o͝o/
Grade 4, Lesson 7
1. bloom
2. cookbook
3. tool
4. shampoo
5. put
6. wool
7. stool
8. proof
9. prove
10. group
11. brook
12. foolish
13. bush
14. crooked
15. booth
16. raccoon
17. hook
18. groom
19. roof
20. soup

Vowel Sounds /ou/ and /ô/
Grade 4, Lesson 8
1. aloud
2. bald
3. hawk
4. south
5. faucet
6. proud
7. claw
8. tower
9. stalk
10. couple
11. howl
12. false
13. dawn
14. allow
15. drown
16. pause
17. fault
18. cause
19. amount
20. cloudier

Vowel + /r/ Sounds
Grade 4, Lesson 9
1. spark
2. prepare
3. cheer
4. tear
5. scarf
6. scare
7. repair
8. earring

9. scarce
10. weird
11. sharp
12. rear
13. spare
14. gear
15. hairy
16. compare
17. alarm
18. harsh
19. upstairs
20. square

More Vowel + /r/ Sounds
Grade 4, Lesson 10
1. learn
2. dirty
3. worn
4. sore
5. thirst
6. burn
7. record
8. cure
9. board
10. course
11. worth
12. early
13. return
14. pure
15. world
16. search
17. worse
18. thirteen
19. sport
20. current

Syllables and Affixes Phase

EARLY

Compound Words
Grade 1, Lesson 20
1. bedtime
2. sunset
3. bathtub
4. sailboat
5. flagpole
6. backpack
7. playpen
8. raincoat
9. inside
10. himself

Base Words with -ed, -ing
Grade 1, Lesson 26
1. mix
2. mixed
3. hop
4. hopped
5. hope
6. hoping
7. run
8. running
9. use
10. used

Base Words with -er, -est
Grade 1, Lesson 27
1. hard
2. harder
3. hardest
4. fast
5. faster
6. fastest
7. slow
8. slower
9. slowest
10. sooner

Words with Suffixes -ly, -y, -ful
Grade 1, Lesson 29
1. sad
2. sadly
3. slow
4. slowly
5. dust
6. dusty
7. trick
8. tricky
9. help
10. helpful

Compound Words
Grade 2, Lesson 15
1. cannot
2. pancake
3. maybe
4. baseball
5. playground
6. someone
7. myself
8. classroom
9. sunshine
10. outside
11. upon
12. nothing

Base Words with Endings -ed, -ing
Grade 2, Lesson 9
1. liked
2. using
3. riding
4. chased
5. spilled
6. making
7. closed
8. hoping
9. baked
10. hiding
11. standing
12. asked

Base Words with Endings -ed, -ing
Grade 2, Lesson 16
1. running
2. clapped
3. stopped
4. hopping
5. batted
6. selling
7. pinned
8. cutting
9. sitting
10. rubbed
11. missed
12. grabbed

Base Words with Endings -s, -es
Grade 2, Lesson 11
1. hens
2. eggs
3. ducks
4. bikes
5. boxes
6. wishes
7. dresses
8. names
9. bells
10. stamps
11. dishes
12. grapes

Suffixes -ly, -ful
Grade 2, Lesson 23
1. helpful
2. sadly
3. hopeful
4. thankful
5. slowly
6. wishful
7. kindly
8. useful
9. safely
10. painful
11. mouthful
12. weakly

Long e Spelled y
Grade 2, Lesson 18
1. happy
2. pretty
3. baby
4. very
5. puppy
6. funny
7. carry
8. lucky
9. only
10. sunny
11. penny
12. city

Prefixes re-, un-
Grade 2, Lesson 24
1. unhappy
2. retell
3. untangle
4. unkind
5. repaint
6. refill
7. unlike
8. remake
9. unpack
10. reread
11. unlock
12. replay

Compound Words
Grade 3, Lesson 20
1. birthday
2. anyone
3. sometimes
4. everything
5. homework
6. afternoon
7. airplane
8. grandmother
9. something
10. without
11. himself
12. faraway
13. sunburned
14. daylight

Words with -ed and -ing
Grade 3, Lesson 21
1. coming
2. swimming
3. dropping
4. tapping
5. taping
6. invited
7. saving
8. stared
9. planned
10. changing
11. joking
12. loved
13. gripped
14. tasted

Changing Final y to i
Grade 3, Lesson 22
1. cities
2. cried
3. puppies
4. hurried
5. stories
6. flies
7. parties
8. tried
9. pennies
10. fried
11. carried
12. babies
13. spied
14. ponies

The Suffixes -ful, -ly, and -er
Grade 3, Lesson 23
1. singer
2. loudly
3. joyful
4. teacher
5. fighter
6. closely
7. powerful
8. farmer
9. quickly
10. careful
11. friendly
12. speaker
13. wonderful
14. truly

The Prefixes re- and un-
Grade 3, Lesson 24
1. unfold
2. rejoin
3. untie
4. reheat
5. unfair
6. unclear
7. repaid
8. rewrite
9. unhurt
10. recheck
11. unlucky
12. unwrap
13. reuse
14. unsure

The Suffixes -less and -ness
Grade 3, Lesson 25
1. painless
2. sickness
3. sadness
4. helpless
5. thankless
6. kindness
7. hopeless
8. darkness
9. fearless
10. thickness
11. careless
12. goodness
13. spotless
14. softness

Compound Words
Grade 4, Lesson 11
1. somebody
2. fireplace
3. nearby
4. toothbrush
5. homesick
6. make-believe
7. anything
8. all right
9. goodbye
10. forehead
11. classmate
12. flashlight
13. haircut
14. twenty-two
15. driveway
16. alarm clock
17. baby-sit
18. airport
19. forever
20. mailbox

Words with -ed or -ing
Grade 4, Lesson 12
1. rising
2. traced
3. stripped
4. slammed
5. dancing
6. striped
7. winning

Comprehensive Word List

8. snapping
9. bragging
10. handled
11. dripped
12. begged
13. dared
14. skipped
15. hitting
16. spotted
17. raced
18. dimmed
19. spinning
20. escaped

More Words with -ed or -ing
Grade 4, Lesson 13
1. wiped
2. covered
3. mapped
4. pleasing
5. slipped
6. putting
7. traveled
8. seeking
9. visiting
10. mixed
11. shipped
12. phoning
13. offered
14. smelling
15. hiking
16. checking
17. fainted
18. landed
19. becoming
20. wandering

Final Long e
Grade 4, Lesson 14
1. turkey
2. lonely
3. colony
4. steady
5. hungry
6. valley
7. hockey
8. starry
9. melody
10. movie
11. duty
12. drowsy
13. chimney
14. plenty
15. daily
16. alley
17. fifty
18. empty
19. injury
20. prairie

Changing Final y to i
Grade 4, Lesson 15
1. tiniest
2. hobbies
3. copied
4. countries
5. pitied
6. easier

7. laziest
8. families
9. spied
10. happiest
11. ladies
12. friendlier
13. studied
14. busier
15. breezier
16. prettiest
17. noisier
18. healthier
19. butterflies
20. funniest

Words with /k/, /ng/, and /kw/
Grade 4, Lesson 16
1. risky
2. track
3. topic
4. blank
5. question
6. pocket
7. monkey
8. junk
9. equal
10. ache
11. public
12. attack
13. struck
14. earthquake
15. picnic
16. banker
17. electric
18. blanket
19. mistake
20. stomach

Prefixes re-, un-, dis-
Grade 4, Lesson 18
1. unused
2. refresh
3. dislike
4. replace
5. unpaid
6. redo
7. disorder
8. unplanned
9. distrust
10. rewind
11. untrue
12. unload
13. recall
14. displease
15. uneven
16. rebuild
17. restart
18. uncover
19. untidy
20. discolor

Suffixes -ful, -less, -ness, -ment
Grade 4, Lesson 19
1. colorful
2. weakness
3. movement
4. endless

5. truthful
6. illness
7. cheerful
8. useless
9. beautiful
10. restless
11. clumsiness
12. pavement
13. peaceful
14. fondness
15. neatness
16. speechless
17. statement
18. wasteful
19. penniless
20. treatment

Words with -ed or -ing
Grade 5, Lesson 16
1. scrubbed
2. listening
3. stunned
4. knitting
5. carpeting
6. wandered
7. gathering
8. beginning
9. skimmed
10. chatting
11. shrugged
12. bothering
13. whipped
14. quizzed
15. suffering
16. scanned
17. ordered
18. totaled
19. answered
20. upsetting

More Words with -ed or -ing
Grade 5, Lesson 17
1. tiring
2. borrowed
3. freezing
4. delivered
5. whispered
6. losing
7. decided
8. amazing
9. performing
10. resulting
11. related
12. attending
13. damaged
14. remarked
15. practicing
16. supported
17. united
18. expected
19. amusing
20. repeated

Changing Final y to i
Grade 5, Lesson 18
1. duties
2. earlier

3. loveliest
4. denied
5. ferries
6. sunnier
7. terrified
8. abilities
9. dirtier
10. scariest
11. trophies
12. cozier
13. enemies
14. iciest
15. greediest
16. drowsier
17. victories
18. horrified
19. memories
20. strategies

Suffixes: -ful, -ly, -ness, -less, -ment
Grade 5, Lesson 19
1. lately
2. settlement
3. watchful
4. countless
5. steadily
6. closeness
7. calmly
8. government
9. agreement
10. cloudiness
11. delightful
12. noisily
13. tardiness
14. forgetful
15. forgiveness
16. harmless
17. enjoyment
18. appointment
19. effortless
20. plentiful

Prefixes: in-, un-, dis-, mis-
Grade 5, Lesson 24
1. mislead
2. dismiss
3. insincere
4. unable
5. indirect
6. mistreat
7. disaster
8. dishonest
9. insecure
10. unknown
11. incomplete
12. unequal
13. unstable
14. misspell
15. disagree
16. informal
17. discover
18. unwise
19. mislaid
20. disgrace

Words with Syllable Pattern CV
Grade 1, Lesson 30
1. even
2. open
3. begin
4. baby
5. tiger
6. music
7. paper
8. zero
9. table
10. below

VCCV Syllabication
Grade 3, Lesson 26
1. person
2. helmet
3. until
4. carpet
5. Monday
6. enjoy
7. forget
8. problem
9. Sunday
10. garden
11. order
12. mistake
13. umpire
14. herself

Words with Double Consonants
Grade 3, Lesson 27
1. jelly
2. bottom
3. pillow
4. happen
5. butter
6. lesson
7. cherry
8. sudden
9. arrow
10. dollar
11. hello
12. rabbit
13. letter
14. button

Words Ending with -er or -le
Grade 3, Lesson 29
1. apple
2. river
3. little
4. October
5. ladder
6. summer
7. purple
8. later
9. November
10. giggle
11. uncle
12. winter
13. center
14. double

Words that Begin with a- or be-
Grade 3, Lesson 30
1. below
2. about
3. belong
4. around
5. again
6. alone
7. because
8. above
9. between
10. alive
11. behind
12. begin
13. along
14. before

Words with VCV Pattern
Grade 4, Lesson 21
1. event
2. humor
3. rapid
4. music
5. relief
6. planet
7. detail
8. unite
9. frozen
10. figure
11. siren
12. polite
13. hotel
14. protest
15. punish
16. defend
17. relay
18. habit
19. student
20. moment

VCCV and VCV Patterns
Grade 4, Lesson 22
1. dentist
2. final
3. finish
4. narrow
5. shelter
6. ahead
7. corner
8. hollow
9. divide
10. famous
11. recent
12. silver
13. capture
14. cabin
15. dinner
16. minus
17. minute
18. value
19. reward
20. broken

Words with VCCV Pattern
Grade 4, Lesson 23
1. poster
2. secret
3. whether
4. author
5. rocket
6. bushel
7. agree
8. bucket
9. ticket
10. declare
11. chicken
12. clothing
13. apron
14. whiskers
15. degree
16. gather
17. achieve
18. rather
19. bracket
20. machine

Words with VCCCV Pattern
Grade 4, Lesson 24
1. hundred
2. supply
3. single
4. middle
5. explain
6. surprise
7. pilgrim
8. sandwich
9. instead
10. complete
11. monster
12. settle
13. address
14. farther
15. sample
16. although
17. turtle
18. athlete
19. orchard
20. kingdom

Words with VV Pattern
Grade 4, Lesson 25
1. idea
2. lion
3. usual
4. radio
5. liar
6. poem
7. India
8. piano
9. January
10. quiet
11. poet
12. science
13. diary
14. violin
15. period
16. February
17. cereal
18. video
19. meteor
20. rodeo

Final Schwa + /r/ Sound
Grade 4, Lesson 26
1. enter
2. banner
3. sugar
4. shower
5. motor
6. collar
7. labor
8. finger
9. mirror
10. beggar
11. favor
12. bother
13. fever
14. doctor
15. temper
16. actor
17. polar
18. sweater
19. traitor
20. whenever

Final Schwa + /l/ Sound
Grade 4, Lesson 27
1. title
2. towel
3. battle
4. pedal
5. metal
6. simple
7. eagle
8. special
9. total
10. trouble
11. nickel
12. gentle
13. barrel
14. model
15. tangle
16. ankle
17. marvel
18. juggle
19. squirrel
20. riddle

More Vowel + /r/ Sounds
Grade 5, Lesson 7
1. earth
2. peer
3. twirl
4. burnt
5. smear
6. further
7. appear
8. worthwhile
9. nerve
10. pier
11. squirm
12. weary
13. alert
14. murmur
15. thirsty
16. reverse
17. worship
18. career
19. research
20. volunteer

Short Vowels
Grade 6, Lesson 1
1. batch
2. reject
3. vanish
4. sloppy
5. rhythm
6. blunder
7. strict
8. meadow
9. recover
10. cleanse
11. text
12. mystery
13. expand
14. bluff
15. promptly
16. initials
17. statue
18. polish
19. somehow
20. dreadful

Short Vowels
Grade 5, Lesson 1
1. breath
2. wobble
3. blister
4. crush
5. direct
6. promise
7. grasp
8. numb
9. hymn
10. shovel
11. gravity
12. frantic
13. swift
14. feather
15. comic
16. bundle
17. solid
18. weather
19. energy
20. stingy

Long a and Long e
Grade 5, Lesson 2
1. awake
2. feast
3. stray
4. greet
5. praise
6. disease
7. repeat
8. display
9. braces
10. thief
11. ashamed
12. sleeve
13. waist
14. beneath
15. sheepish

Long i and Long o
Grade 5, Lesson 3
1. sign
2. groan
3. reply
4. thrown
5. strike
6. mighty
7. stroll
8. compose
9. dough
10. height
11. excite
12. apply
13. slight
14. define
15. odor
16. spider
17. control
18. silent
19. brighten
20. approach

Vowel Sounds: /o͞o/, /yo͞o/
Grade 5, Lesson 4
1. glue
2. flute
3. youth
4. accuse
5. bruise
6. stew
7. choose
8. loose
9. lose
10. view
11. confuse
12. cruise
13. jewel
14. execute
15. route
16. cartoon
17. avenue
18. include
19. assume
20. souvenir

VCCV Pattern
Grade 5, Lesson 11
1. bargain
2. journey
3. pattern
4. arrive
5. object
6. suppose
7. shoulder
8. permit
9. sorrow
10. tunnel
11. subject
12. custom
13. suggest
14. perhaps

Long i and Long o (continued)
16. release
17. remain
18. sway
19. training
20. niece

15. lawyer
16. timber
17. common
18. publish
19. burden
20. scissors

VCV Pattern
Grade 5, Lesson 12
1. human
2. exact
3. award
4. behave
5. credit
6. basic
7. vivid
8. evil
9. modern
10. nation
11. robot
12. panic
13. select
14. cousin
15. item
16. police
17. prefer
18. menu
19. novel
20. deserve

VCCCV Pattern
Grade 5, Lesson 13
1. conflict
2. orphan
3. instant
4. complex
5. simply
6. burglar
7. laundry
8. laughter
9. employ
10. anchor
11. merchant
12. improve
13. arctic
14. mischief
15. childhood
16. purchase
17. dolphin
18. partner
19. complain
20. tremble

VV Pattern
Grade 5, Lesson 14
1. actual
2. cruel
3. patriot
4. diet
5. museum
6. casual
7. ruin
8. pioneer
9. trial
10. visual
11. realize
12. create
13. riot
14. genuine

15. area
16. annual
17. audio
18. dial
19. theater
20. influence

Vowel Sounds: /ou/, /ô/, /oi/
Grade 5, Lesson 5
1. ounce
2. sprawl
3. launch
4. loyal
5. avoid
6. basketball
7. moist
8. haunt
9. scowl
10. naughty
11. destroy
12. saucer
13. pounce
14. poison
15. August
16. auction
17. royal
18. coward
19. awkward
20. encounter

Vowel + /r/ Sounds
Grade 5, Lesson 6
1. glory
2. aware
3. carton
4. adore
5. aboard
6. dairy
7. ordeal
8. pardon
9. warn
10. vary
11. barely
12. torch
13. barge
14. soar
15. beware
16. absorb
17. armor
18. stairway
19. perform
20. former

Words with VCCV Pattern
Grade 4, Lesson 20
1. million
2. collect
3. lumber
4. pepper
5. plastic
6. borrow
7. support
8. thirty
9. perfect
10. attend
11. canyon
12. traffic

13. fortune
14. danger
15. soccer
16. engine
17. picture
18. survive
19. seldom
20. effort

LATE

Words with Final /j/ and /s/
Grade 4, Lesson 17
1. glance
2. judge
3. damage
4. package
5. twice
6. stage
7. carriage
8. since
9. practice
10. marriage
11. baggage
12. office
13. message
14. bridge
15. chance
16. notice
17. ridge
18. manage
19. palace
20. bandage

Words with Silent Consonants
Grade 4, Lesson 29
1. half
2. comb
3. mortgage
4. honor
5. fasten
6. kneel
7. wreath
8. calm
9. answer
10. handsome
11. wrinkle
12. listen
13. fetch
14. yolk
15. climb
16. honest
17. knuckle
18. plumber
19. limb
20. folktale

Unusual Spellings
Grade 4, Lesson 30
1. meant
2. routine
3. style
4. flood
5. month
6. pleasant
7. guess
8. women

9. either
10. against
11. disguise
12. sweat
13. magazine
14. guard
15. receive
16. wonder
17. league
18. type
19. ceiling
20. money

Three-Syllable Words
Grade 4, Lesson 28
1. library
2. another
3. hospital
4. example
5. deliver
6. history
7. however
8. several
9. vacation
10. important
11. victory
12. imagine
13. camera
14. potato
15. remember
16. together
17. memory
18. favorite
19. continue
20. president

Homophones
Grade 5, Lesson 8
1. steel
2. steal
3. aloud
4. allowed
5. ring
6. wring
7. lesson
8. lessen
9. who's
10. whose
11. manor
12. manner
13. pedal
14. peddle
15. berry
16. bury
17. hanger
18. hangar
19. overdo
20. overdue

Compound Words
Grade 5, Lesson 9
1. wildlife
2. uproar
3. home run
4. headache
5. top-secret
6. teammate
7. wheelchair

8. light bulb
9. well-known
10. throughout
11. life preserver
12. barefoot
13. part-time
14. warehouse
15. overboard
16. post office
17. outspoken
18. up-to-date
19. awestruck
20. newscast

Final Schwa + /r/ Sound
Grade 5, Lesson 10
1. cellar
2. flavor
3. cougar
4. chapter
5. mayor
6. anger
7. senator
8. passenger
9. major
10. popular
11. tractor
12. thunder
13. pillar
14. border
15. calendar
16. quarter
17. lunar
18. proper
19. elevator
20. bitter

Final Schwa + /l/ Sound
Grade 5, Lesson 15
1. formal
2. whistle
3. label
4. puzzle
5. legal
6. angle
7. normal
8. needle
9. angel
10. pupil
11. struggle
12. level
13. local
14. bicycle
15. channel
16. global
17. stumble
18. quarrel
19. article
20. fossil

Final /n/ or /ən/, /chər/, /zhər/
Grade 5, Lesson 21
1. nature
2. certain
3. future
4. villain

5. mountain
6. mixture
7. pleasure
8. captain
9. departure
10. surgeon
11. texture
12. curtain
13. creature
14. treasure
15. gesture
16. fountain
17. furniture
18. measure
19. feature
20. adventure

Unstressed Syllables
Grade 5, Lesson 23
1. entry
2. limit
3. talent
4. disturb
5. entire
6. wisdom
7. dozen
8. impress
9. respond
10. fortress
11. neglect
12. patrol
13. kitchen
14. forbid
15. pirate
16. spinach
17. adopt
18. frighten
19. surround
20. challenge

Words from Other Languages
Grade 5, Lesson 20
1. salsa
2. mattress
3. tycoon
4. burrito
5. bandana
6. tomato
7. poncho
8. dungarees
9. lasso
10. patio
11. siesta
12. cargo
13. vanilla
14. tsunami
15. iguana
16. plaza
17. caravan
18. hammock
19. pajamas
20. gallant

Plurals
Grade 6, Lesson 19
1. echoes
2. halves
3. solos

4. leaves
5. heroes
6. cliffs
7. scarves
8. potatoes
9. pianos
10. volcanoes
11. sheriffs
12. calves
13. tomatoes
14. cellos
15. wolves
16. ratios
17. stereos
18. yourselves
19. studios
20. bookshelves

Long Vowels
Grade 6, Lesson 2
1. scene
2. bracelet
3. mute
4. strive
5. faithful
6. devote
7. rhyme
8. succeed
9. coax
10. rely
11. conceal
12. forgave
13. lonesome
14. delete
15. confine
16. exceed
17. terrain
18. reproach
19. abuse
20. defeat

Vowel Sounds: /ou/, /o͞o/, /ô/, /oi/
Grade 6, Lesson 3
1. mound
2. gloomy
3. caution
4. annoy
5. dawdle
6. counter
7. haughty
8. rejoice
9. devour
10. thoughtful
11. flawless
12. maroon
13. droop
14. doubt
15. bamboo
16. hoist
17. oyster
18. exhausted
19. scoundrel
20. boundary

Vowel + /r/ Sounds
Grade 6, Lesson 4
1. source
2. flirt
3. hurdle

4. parka
5. frontier
6. forward
7. radar
8. earnest
9. afford
10. urban
11. discard
12. smirk
13. rehearse
14. mourn
15. surface
16. parcel
17. yearn
18. fierce
19. starch
20. formula

Words with *ie* or *ei*
Grade 6, Lesson 6
1. brief
2. field
3. reign
4. review
5. fiery
6. receipt
7. relieve
8. conceited
9. neither
10. foreign
11. grief
12. veil
13. freight
14. belief
15. deceive
16. yield
17. beige
18. perceive
19. seize
20. leisure

Derivational Relations Phase

EARLY

Final /ĭj/, /ĭv/, /ĭs/
Grade 5, Lesson 22
1. storage
2. olive
3. service
4. relative
5. cabbage
6. courage
7. native
8. passage
9. voyage
10. knowledge
11. image
12. creative
13. average
14. justice
15. detective
16. postage
17. cowardice
18. adjective

19. village
20. language

Suffix: *-ion*
Grade 5, Lesson 25
1. elect
2. election
3. tense
4. tension
5. react
6. reaction
7. confess
8. confession
9. decorate
10. decoration
11. contribute
12. contribution
13. express
14. expression
15. imitate
16. imitation
17. connect
18. connection
19. admire
20. admiration

Word Parts: *com-, con-, pre-, pro-*
Grade 5, Lesson 26
1. produce
2. company
3. protect
4. preview
5. contain
6. combat
7. prejudge
8. commotion
9. contest
10. prefix
11. progress
12. computer
13. confide
14. convince
15. prospect
16. confirm
17. preflight
18. provide
19. propose
20. promotion

Homophones
Grade 6, Lesson 5
1. waist
2. waste
3. patience
4. patients
5. rite
6. right
7. write
8. muscle
9. mussel
10. principal
11. principle
12. summary
13. summery
14. sight
15. cite
16. site
17. stationary
18. stationery

19. coward
20. cowered

Final /ər/
Grade 6, Lesson 7
1. fiber
2. similar
3. regular
4. barrier
5. superior
6. grammar
7. rumor
8. character
9. director
10. acre
11. consider
12. junior
13. senior
14. solar
15. scholar
16. razor
17. surrender
18. particular
19. familiar
20. laser

Final /ən/, /əl/, and /ər/
Grade 6, Lesson 8
1. triangle
2. mental
3. error
4. panel
5. litter
6. pollen
7. gallon
8. cancel
9. abandon
10. rival
11. soldier
12. recycle
13. salmon
14. counsel
15. rural
16. vehicle
17. citizen
18. monitor
19. physical
20. oxygen

Words with *-ed* or *-ing*
Grade 6, Lesson 9
1. happening
2. limited
3. forgetting
4. equaled
5. fitting
6. reasoning
7. labored
8. permitting
9. scrapped
10. tutoring
11. admitted
12. honored
13. skidding
14. pardoned
15. modeling
16. preferred
17. scarred

18. favored
19. glistening
20. shuddered

Endings and Suffixes
Grade 6, Lesson 10

1. reserved
2. unlikely
3. purposeful
4. adorable
5. amazement
6. gentleness
7. sparkling
8. homeless
9. excitement
10. mileage
11. graceful
12. sincerely
13. advanced
14. usable
15. amusement
16. entirely
17. wireless
18. excluding
19. scarcely
20. changeable

Final /īz/, /īv/, and /ĭj/
Grade 6, Lesson 15

1. revise
2. advantage
3. memorize
4. active
5. organize
6. criticize
7. shortage
8. advertise
9. attractive
10. college
11. explosive
12. exercise
13. encourage
14. summarize
15. wreckage
16. recognize
17. positive
18. percentage
19. sensitive
20. heritage

Suffixes: -ion or -ation
Grade 6, Lesson 11

1. correct
2. correction
3. explore
4. exploration
5. admire
6. admiration
7. subtract
8. subtraction
9. examine
10. examination
11. separate
12. separation
13. alter
14. alteration
15. preserve

16. preservation
17. reflect
18. reflection
19. substitute
20. substitution

Spelling /sh/
Grade 6, Lesson 18

1. section
2. shallow
3. direction
4. musician
5. rash
6. position
7. astonish
8. pressure
9. attention
10. crucial
11. impression
12. official
13. emotion
14. bashful
15. delicious
16. establish
17. ancient
18. situation
19. suspicion
20. permission

Prefixes: dis-, ex-, inter-
Grade 6, Lesson 20

1. disobey
2. explosion
3. dislike
4. interview
5. disapprove
6. interoffice
7. Internet
8. disallow
9. disappear
10. international
11. disrespect
12. exchange
13. exclaim
14. dissolve
15. disconnect
16. interact
17. distaste
18. export
19. disappoint
20. interstate

Prefixes: pre-, pro-
Grade 6, Lesson 21

1. prediction
2. project
3. prevent
4. prepaid
5. prevail
6. proclaim
7. prehistoric
8. prejudge
9. preapprove
10. pregame
11. precaution
12. preorder
13. prescreen
14. preshow
15. pretreat

16. prolong
17. process
18. protrude
19. provision
20. production

More Words with -ion
Grade 6, Lesson 13

1. circulate
2. circulation
3. conclude
4. conclusion
5. instruct
6. instruction
7. possess
8. possession
9. introduce
10. introduction
11. except
12. exception
13. discuss
14. discussion
15. collide
16. collision
17. oppose
18. opposition
19. estimate
20. estimation

Suffixes: -ent, -ant, -able, -ible, -ism, -ist
Grade 5, Lesson 27

1. vacant
2. insistent
3. reversible
4. patriotism
5. finalist
6. honorable
7. contestant
8. observant
9. urgent
10. pessimist
11. comfortable
12. absorbent
13. optimism
14. journalism
15. novelist
16. terrible
17. frequent
18. laughable
19. radiant
20. collectible

Greek Word Parts
Grade 5, Lesson 28

1. telephone
2. autograph
3. microscope
4. photograph
5. televise
6. biology
7. microphone
8. paragraph
9. symphony
10. telegraph
11. megaphone
12. microwave
13. photocopy
14. biography

15. saxophone
16. telescope
17. calligraphy
18. xylophone
19. homophone
20. homograph

Latin Word Roots
Grade 5, Lesson 29

1. inspect
2. export
3. erupt
4. predict
5. respect
6. bankrupt
7. dictate
8. porter
9. report
10. spectacle
11. deport
12. interrupt
13. dictator
14. import
15. disrupt
16. portable
17. transport
18. spectator
19. verdict
20. dictionary

More Words from Other Languages
Grade 5, Lesson 30

1. ballet
2. echo
3. bouquet
4. cassette
5. coupon
6. safari
7. portrait
8. barrette
9. depot
10. courtesy
11. petite
12. denim
13. brunette
14. buffet
15. garage
16. khaki
17. crochet
18. chorus
19. essay
20. alphabet

MIDDLE

Prefixes: in-, im-, ir-, il-
Grade 6, Lesson 12

1. illegal
2. indent
3. imperfect
4. irregular
5. insecure
6. illogical
7. inappropriate
8. impatient
9. individual
10. inability
11. impolite

12. illegible
13. irresistible
14. immobile
15. impartial
16. inaudible
17. improper
18. ineffective
19. immovable
20. irrational

Word Parts: com-, con-
Grade 6, Lesson 14

1. contrast
2. contact
3. compound
4. concentrate
5. combine
6. comment
7. conference
8. compete
9. community
10. convert
11. conversation
12. commute
13. constitution
14. conduct
15. consumer
16. continent
17. composition
18. communicate
19. compliment
20. condition

Suffixes: -ent, -ant
Grade 6, Lesson 16

1. confident
2. confidence
3. fragrant
4. fragrance
5. excellent
6. excellence
7. decent
8. decency
9. truant
10. truancy
11. brilliant
12. brilliance
13. resident
14. residence
15. evident
16. evidence
17. occupant
18. occupancy
19. reluctant
20. reluctance

Suffixes: -able/-ible, -ate
Grade 6, Lesson 17

1. visible
2. enjoyable
3. celebrate
4. incredible
5. horrible
6. desperate
7. cooperate
8. valuable
9. appreciate
10. considerate

11. audible
12. delicate
13. washable
14. graduate
15. capable
16. miserable
17. sensible
18. fortunate
19. noticeable
20. responsible

Words with Silent Letters
Grade 6, Lesson 22
1. aisle
2. align
3. island
4. crumbs
5. gnaw
6. design
7. knotty
8. bustle
9. shepherd
10. soften
11. sword
12. thistle
13. knock
14. wrestle
15. column
16. autumn
17. knowledge
18. debt
19. numb
20. raspberry

Suffixes: -ic, -ure, -ous
Grade 6, Lesson 23
1. fantastic
2. culture
3. curious
4. nervous
5. posture
6. jealous
7. scientific

8. generous
9. signature
10. dangerous
11. tragic
12. gigantic
13. sculpture
14. precious
15. lecture
16. serious
17. specific
18. fracture
19. romantic
20. ambitious

Prefixes: de-, trans-
Grade 6, Lesson 24
1. transform
2. deject
3. destruct
4. detour
5. transmit
6. default
7. describe
8. defend
9. transplant
10. descend
11. derail
12. defrost
13. transcript
14. deploy
15. dethrone
16. deodorize
17. transatlantic
18. decompose
19. decrease
20. transaction

Word Parts
Grade 6, Lesson 25
1. existence
2. refreshment
3. convention
4. intermission
5. uneventful
6. perfectly

7. completion
8. improvement
9. information
10. attendance
11. reversible
12. invention
13. development
14. respectful
15. unhappiness
16. preparation
17. irrigate
18. disagreement
19. unbelievable
20. concentration

Words from Other Languages
Grade 6, Lesson 26
1. opera
2. vague
3. antique
4. drama
5. tornado
6. debut
7. stampede
8. gourmet
9. unique
10. academy
11. sonnet
12. brochure
13. cocoon
14. fatigue
15. mosquito
16. diploma
17. fiesta
18. debris
19. cafeteria
20. quartet

Greek Word Parts
Grade 6, Lesson 27
1. geography
2. democracy
3. microbiology
4. technology

5. thermos
6. automatic
7. mythology
8. democratic
9. thermometer
10. chronology
11. automobile
12. aristocrat
13. thermal
14. geology
15. aristocracy
16. geometry
17. anthology
18. apology
19. thermostat
20. psychology

Latin Word Roots
Grade 6, Lesson 28
1. prescribe
2. contract
3. manufacture
4. progression
5. vocal
6. manual
7. audience
8. eject
9. impose
10. management
11. Congress
12. expose
13. inject
14. audition
15. manuscript
16. vocabulary
17. objection
18. manicure
19. proposal
20. extract

Greek and Latin Word Parts
Grade 6, Lesson 29
1. pedal
2. peddler

3. pedestrian
4. pedestal
5. centipede
6. dental
7. dentist
8. dentures
9. vocalize
10. vocalist
11. vocation
12. memoir
13. memorial
14. tripod
15. podium
16. memorable
17. manager
18. manifest
19. mortal
20. mortified

Words Often Confused
Grade 6, Lesson 30
1. desert
2. dessert
3. hardy
4. hearty
5. moral
6. morale
7. laying
8. lying
9. personal
10. personnel
11. formally
12. formerly
13. healthy
14. healthful
15. precede
16. proceed
17. conscious
18. conscience
19. immigrate
20. emigrate

Teacher's Notes

Leveled Readers Database

Guided Reading Level	Title	Grade Pack	DRA Level	Lexile Level	Reading Recovery Level	Genre	Word Count
A	Animals in the Woods	K ●	A	BR	A, B	Informational Text	15
A	Apples	K ▲	A	BR	A, B	Realistic Fiction	25
A	Aquarium, The	K ◆	1	BR	1	Informational Text	29
A	At School	K-VR	A	BR	A, B	Informational Text	20
A	At the Aquarium	K ▲	1	BR	1	Informational Text	24
A	At the Playground	K ▲	1	BR	1	Informational Text	20
A	At the Pond	K ●	A	BR	A, B	Realistic Fiction	25
A	At the Zoo	K ▲	A	BR	A, B	Fiction	20
A	Baker, The	K ●	A	30	A, B	Realistic Fiction	25
A	Bears Through the Year	K ▲	A	BR	A, B	Fiction	20
A	Bug Parts	K ●	1	BR	1	Informational Text	22
A	Bugs for Dinner	K ●	A	180	A, B	Informational Text	35
A	Bugs!	K-VR	1	70	1	Informational Text	21
A	Choosing a Pet	K ◆	A	BR	A, B	Informational Text	31
A	Curious George and the Animals	K ◆	1	90	1	Fiction	29
A	Curious George and the Hungry Animals	K ▲	1	90	1	Fiction	23
A	Curious George Visits Animal Friends	K ●	1	BR	1	Fiction	26
A	Day at School, A	K ▲	1	BR	1	Fiction	15
A	Feeding Our Pets	K ▲	1	10	1	Informational Text	25
A	Find the Bug	K ▲	1	70	1	Informational Text	30
A	Fire Fighter, The	K ●	1	BR	1	Informational Text	25
A	Four Frogs	K ◆	A	BR	A, B	Realistic Fiction	25
A	Fun All Year	K ▲	1	BR	1	Informational Text	25
A	Fun at Camp	K ◆	1	BR	1	Fiction	35
A	Garden, The	K ◆	1	BR	1	Informational Text	27
A	Going for a Hay Ride	K ◆	A	BR	A, B	Informational Text	26
A	Hay Ride, The	K ▲	A	BR	A, B	Informational Text	16
A	I Can Do It!	K ●	A	BR	A, B	Informational Text	25
A	In My Yard	K ◆	A	BR	A, B	Informational Text	28
A	In the City	K ●	A	BR	A, B	Informational Text	20

- Go to www.thinkcentral.com for the complete *Journeys* Online Leveled Readers Database.
- Search by grade, genre, title, or level.

Author's Purpose	Cause and Effect	Compare and Contrast	Conclusions	Fact and Opinion	Main Ideas and Details	Sequence of Events	Story Structure	Text and Graphic Features	Theme	Understanding Characters
●		●	●	●				●		
●		●	●		●	●		●		
●				●	●			●		
●			●	●	●					
●	●	●			●	●	●	●		●
		●			●			●		
	●	●				●	●			
●			●	●	●			●		●
			●	●	●			●		●
		●	●		●		●		●	●
●		●	●		●			●	●	
●	●		●	●		●		●		
●		●		●	●			●		
●			●	●	●			●		
	●	●					●	●		●
	●	●	●				●	●	●	
						●	●			●
●	●	●			●				●	
●	●		●		●			●		
●		●	●		●	●				
●			●		●					
	●	●	●	●		●	●			●
●	●	●	●		●		●	●	●	●
	●	●	●				●		●	
●			●			●		●		
●			●		●			●		
●			●	●	●		●	●	●	●
		●			●			●		
●		●	●		●			●		
●					●			●		

Leveled Readers Database

Guided Reading Level	Title	Grade Pack	DRA Level	Lexile Level	Reading Recovery Level	Genre	Word Count
A	In the Garden	K ▲	1	BR	1	Informational Text	20
A	It's a Party!	K ●	A	BR	A, B	Fiction	15
A	Let's Climb!	K ●	A	BR	A, B	Informational Text	19
A	Let's Sell Things!	K ◆	1	BR	1	Informational Text	28
A	Let's Swim	K ▲	A	BR	A, B	Informational Text	19
A	Look at Me!	K-VR	A	BR	A, B	Informational Text	25
A	Look at the Bears	K ◆	1	BR	1	Fiction	28
A	Look for Bugs	K ◆	1	70	1	Informational Text	30
A	Look Up!	K ●	A	BR	A, B	Informational Text	25
A	Lots of Flowers	K ◆	A	BR	A, B	Informational Text	28
A	Make a Kite	K-VR	1	BR	1	Informational Text	24
A	Making a Tree House	K ◆	1	BR	1	Fiction	27
A	Market, The	K ●	A	BR	A, B	Informational Text	15
A	Mouse and Bear	K ▲	1	100	1	Fiction	26
A	Mouse and Bear Are Friends	K ◆	1	100	1	Fiction	35
A	My Backpack	K ●	A	BR	A, B	Fiction	21
A	My Bike	K-VR	1	BR	1	Informational Text	22
A	My Cat	K ▲	A	60	A, B	Realistic Fiction	25
A	My Dog	K ●	1	BR	1	Realistic Fiction	22
A	My Family	K ◆	A	BR	A, B	Informational Text	25
A	My Family Pictures	K ▲	A	BR	A, B	Informational Text	20
A	My Flower Garden	K ▲	A	BR	A, B	Informational Text	19
A	My Pet	K ▲	A	BR	A, B	Informational Text	25
A	My Pet Cat	K ◆	A	60	A, B	Realistic Fiction	32
A	My Yard	K ▲	A	BR	A, B	Informational Text	19
A	October Days	K ●	A	BR	A, B	Informational Text	24
A	On the Farm	K-VR	A	BR	A, B	Informational Text	21
A	Our Class Band	K ●	1	BR	1	Fiction	30
A	Our Family Vacation	K ●	A	BR	A, B	Fiction	29
A	Our Jobs	K-VR	A	BR	A, B	Informational Text	19

ONLINE LEVELED READERS DATABASE

• Go to www.thinkcentral.com for the complete *Journeys* Online Leveled Readers Database.

• Search by grade, genre, title, or level.

Author's Purpose	Cause and Effect	Compare and Contrast	Conclusions	Fact and Opinion	Main Ideas and Details	Sequence of Events	Story Structure	Text and Graphic Features	Theme	Understanding Characters
●		●	●	●		●	●	●	●	●
			●				●			●
●		●	●	●	●			●		
●	●		●	●	●			●		
●	●		●					●		
●			●		●			●		
			●						●	●
●		●			●	●		●		
●	●		●			●		●		
●	●		●		●			●		
●	●		●	●	●	●		●		
	●		●		●	●	●		●	●
●		●						●		
	●		●		●	●	●		●	●
		●	●		●		●			●
		●	●	●	●			●		●
●			●	●				●		
	●		●		●	●	●		●	●
			●				●	●		●
●		●	●		●			●		
●		●			●			●		
●	●	●			●	●	●	●		●
●	●	●	●			●	●	●	●	●
	●		●			●	●			●
●			●	●	●			●		
		●						●		
●	●	●	●		●					
		●	●		●		●			●
	●	●	●			●	●			●
●			●		●			●		

Leveled Readers Database

Guided Reading Level	Title	Grade Pack	DRA Level	Lexile Level	Reading Recovery Level	Genre	Word Count
A	Our Room	K ●	A	BR	A, B	Realistic Fiction	22
A	Our School	K ◆	1	BR	1	Fiction	22
A	Pet Show, The	K ●	1	BR	1	Informational Text	25
A	Pets at School	K ◆	1	10	1	Informational Text	33
A	Playground, The	K ◆	A	BR	A, B	Informational Text	20
A	Puppy, The	K-VR	A	BR	A, B	Informational Text	15
A	Rain Today	K ◆	A	BR	A, B	Informational Text	25
A	Rainy Day	K ▲	A	BR	A, B	Informational Text	20
A	Sea, The	K ●	A	BR	A, B	Informational Text	20
A	Selling Things	K ▲	1	BR	1	Informational Text	20
A	Show, The	K ●	1	BR	1	Fiction	25
A	Show and Tell	K ▲	A	BR	A, B	Fiction	20
A	Sisters and Brothers	K-VR	1	BR	1	Informational Text	24
A	Splash!	K ▲	A	BR	A, B	Realistic Fiction	21
A	Summer Camp	K ▲	1	BR	1	Fiction	25
A	Swimming	K ◆	A	BR	A, B	Informational Text	24
A	Taking Pictures	K ●	A	BR	A, B	Fiction	20
A	Tell All About It	K ◆	A	BR	A, B	Fiction	27
A	Time for Breakfast!	K ●	1	BR	1	Fiction	20
A	Tree House, The	K ▲	A	BR	A, B	Fiction	20
A	Up and Away, Curious George	K ●	1	BR	1	Fiction	22
A	Vegetable Garden, The	K ●	A	BR	A, B	Informational Text	21
A	Visiting Grandma and Grandpa	K ●	A	BR	A, B	Informational Text	24
A	Visiting the Zoo	K ◆	A	BR	A, B	Fiction	26
A	Walk in the Woods, A	K ●	1	BR	1	Fiction	20
A	We Like Apples	K ◆	A	BR	A, B	Realistic Fiction	35
A	Winter Vacation	K ●	A	BR	A, B	Fiction	24
A	Year of Fun, A	K ◆	1	BR	1	Informational Text	32
A	Zoom!	K ●	A	BR	A, B	Informational Text	24
B	Animals in the Snow	K-VR	2	BR	2	Informational Text	41

ONLINE LEVELED READERS DATABASE

• Go to www.thinkcentral.com for the complete *Journeys* Online Leveled Readers Database.
• Search by grade, genre, title, or level.

Author's Purpose	Cause and Effect	Compare and Contrast	Conclusions	Fact and Opinion	Main Ideas and Details	Sequence of Events	Story Structure	Text and Graphic Features	Theme	Understanding Characters
		•			•		•		•	•
	•					•	•		•	•
•					•			•		
•			•	•	•			•		
•		•			•			•		
•			•	•				•		
•	•			•	•	•		•		
•	•			•	•	•		•		
•		•		•				•		
			•		•		•	•	•	
	•		•		•	•	•			•
•				•	•					
		•	•					•		
	•		•			•	•			•
•		•			•	•				
•		•	•	•	•			•		
	•	•				•	•		•	•
			•		•		•		•	
	•		•				•		•	•
	•		•	•	•					•
	•		•			•			•	•
•				•	•	•		•		
•			•		•			•		
			•	•			•		•	•
	•		•			•				•
	•		•	•	•					•
	•		•				•			•
•		•			•	•		•		
•			•	•	•			•		
•	•	•	•		•			•		

Leveled Readers Database

Guided Reading Level	Title	Grade Pack	DRA Level	Lexile Level	Reading Recovery Level	Genre	Word Count
B	At the Beach	K-VR	2	60	2	Informational Text	31
B	By the Sea	K ■	2	180	2	Informational Text	65
B	Camping Under the Stars	K-VR	2	BR	2	Informational Text	31
B	Costume Box, The	K ▲	2	BR	2	Fiction	55
B	Curious About Playing Ball	K-VR	2	BR	2	Informational Text	45
B	Curious George Goes for a Ride	K ▲	2	190	2	Fiction	35
B	Curious George Likes to Ride	K ◆	2	190	2	Fiction	44
B	Dressing Up	K ◆	2	BR	2	Fiction	66
B	Family Fun	K-VR	2	BR	2	Informational Text	30
B	Flower, The	K-VR	2	BR	2	Informational Text	28
B	Friends	K-VR	2	BR	2	Informational Text	24
B	Fun in July	K-VR	2	BR	2	Informational Text	25
B	Fun with Friends	K ■	2	40	2	Informational Text	113
B	Going for a Hike	K-VR	2	210	2	Informational Text	41
B	Going to School	K ◆	2	100	2	Informational Text	40
B	How Many Ducks?	K-VR	2	40	2	Informational Text	24
B	I Can!	K-VR	2	BR	2	Informational Text	23
B	In the Rain Forest	K ■	2	BR	2	Informational Text	65
B	Let's Have Fun!	K-VR	2	BR	2	Informational Text	43
B	Lion, The	K-VR	2	BR	2	Informational Text	22
B	Lots of Birds	K-VR	2	BR	2	Informational Text	45
B	My Big Brother Ned	K ▲	2	210	2	Realistic Fiction	38
B	My Brother	K ◆	2	210	2	Realistic Fiction	48
B	My House	K ■	2	BR	2	Informational Text	74
B	Our Classroom	K-VR	2	BR	2	Informational Text	24
B	Riding to School	K ▲	2	90	2	Informational Text	35
B	Things I Can Do	K ▲	2	BR	2	Fiction	47
B	Things I Like to Do	K ◆	2	40	2	Fiction	56
B	Visiting a Park	K-VR	2	60	2	Informational Text	30
B	When I Was Little	K ■	2	BR	2	Informational Text	79

- Go to www.thinkcentral.com for the complete *Journeys* Online Leveled Readers Database.
- Search by grade, genre, title, or level.

Author's Purpose	Cause and Effect	Compare and Contrast	Conclusions	Fact and Opinion	Main Ideas and Details	Sequence of Events	Story Structure	Text and Graphic Features	Theme	Understanding Characters
●	●		●		●			●		
●				●	●			●		
●	●		●		●	●		●		
	●	●	●	●	●	●	●			●
●		●	●		●			●		
●			●		●					
			●		●		●			●
		●			●		●		●	●
●	●		●	●	●			●		
●	●		●			●		●		
●		●	●	●	●			●	●	
●	●	●	●	●	●			●		
●	●		●	●	●	●		●		
●	●		●		●	●		●		
●	●	●	●		●			●		
●	●	●	●		●	●		●		
●		●	●	●	●			●		
●		●	●		●			●		
●		●	●	●	●			●		
●		●	●	●	●			●		
●		●	●	●	●	●		●		
		●	●	●			●			●
			●		●		●		●	●
●		●	●					●		
●			●		●			●		
●		●	●	●	●			●		
●	●		●		●	●				
	●		●				●		●	●
●		●		●	●			●		
●			●		●	●		●		

Leveled Readers Database

Guided Reading Level	Title	Grade Pack	DRA Level	Lexile Level	Reading Recovery Level	Genre	Word Count
C	City Garden, A	K ■	4	BR	4	Informational Text	111
C	Curious About the Animal Park	K-VR	4	BR	4	Informational Text	52
C	Dan and His Brothers	K ■	4	80	4	Realistic Fiction	105
C	Hat for Cat, A	K ■	4	70	4	Fiction	85
C	In the Sky	K-VR	3	BR	3	Informational Text	38
C	In the Tree	K ■	4	BR	4	Informational Text	110
C	June Vacation	K ■	4	BR	4	Informational Text	86
C	Look in the Woods	K ■	4	50	4	Realistic Fiction	71
C	Lots of Helpers	K ■	3	130	3	Informational Text	92
C	Making a Mud Pie	K ■	4	230	4	Realistic Fiction	105
C	My School	K-VR	4	BR	4	Informational Text	46
C	Snack Time	K-VR	3	170	3	Informational Text	50
C	Teamwork	K ■	4	80	4	Fiction	112
C	Trip to the Fire Station	K-VR	4	BR	4	Informational Text	50
C	Winter Sleep	K ■	4	160	4	Fiction	92
D	Come for a Swim!	K ■	6	140	6	Fiction	107
D	Going Fast	K ■	6	BR	6	Informational Text	116
D	Good Job, Sam!	K ■	6	70	5	Fiction	108
D	Helping Mr. Horse	K ■	6	80	6	Fiction	82
D	In the Desert	K ■	6	130	6	Informational Text	109
D	Jobs on the Farm	K ■	6	30	6	Informational Text	107
D	Lola, the Muddy Dog	K ■	6	50	5	Realistic Fiction	107
D	No Snow!	K ■	6	40	6	Fiction	94
D	Rosie and the Bug Jar	K-VR	6	360	6	Informational Text	93
D	Storm, The	K ■	6	BR	6	Informational Text	71
D	Very Nice Lunch, A	K ■	6	120	6	Fiction	115
D	What Animals Eat	K ■	6	70	6	Informational Text	112
E	Curious George Visits the Woods	K ■	8	BR	8	Fiction	91
E	Kevin and Lucy	K ■	8	120	7	Fiction	130
F	Curious George and the Newspapers	K ■	10	110	10	Fiction	137

ONLINE LEVELED READERS DATABASE

• Go to www.thinkcentral.com for the complete *Journeys* Online Leveled Readers Database.
• Search by grade, genre, title, or level.

Author's Purpose	Cause and Effect	Compare and Contrast	Conclusions	Fact and Opinion	Main Ideas and Details	Sequence of Events	Story Structure	Text and Graphic Features	Theme	Understanding Characters
●	●	●	●			●		●		
●	●		●	●				●		
		●	●				●		●	●
●		●				●	●			●
●	●	●	●		●	●		●		
●		●	●		●			●		
●		●			●			●		
	●					●		●		●
●			●	●	●					
			●				●	●		●
●			●	●				●		
●	●	●	●	●	●			●		
	●	●	●			●	●		●	●
●	●		●	●	●			●		
	●					●	●			●
	●		●			●	●		●	●
●			●		●			●		
	●					●	●			●
							●			●
●			●		●			●		
●			●	●	●			●		
		●				●	●			●
	●		●				●			●
			●		●	●				
●	●	●			●	●		●		
	●		●				●		●	●
●		●		●			●	●		●
	●		●			●	●			●
	●		●		●	●	●			●
	●		●				●		●	●

Literature Discussion

For small-group literature discussion, use the suggested trade book titles on the pages that follow, or select age-appropriate texts from your library or classroom collection.

Engage children in discussions to build understanding of the text, deepen comprehension, and foster their confidence in talking about what they read. Encourage children to share their ideas about the text and also to build upon one another's ideas.

 Classic

 Science

 Social Studies

 Music

 Math

 Art

Suggested Trade Book Titles

BIOGRAPHY

Rau, Dana Meachen. *Dr. Seuss.* A brief introduction to the life of the well-loved author and illustrator Dr. Seuss. Children's Press, 2003 (32p).

Rau, Dana Meachen. *Neil Armstrong.* Intended for beginning readers, this is an introduction to the life of astronaut Neil Armstrong, the first person on the moon. Children's Press, 2003 (32p).

FANTASY

Alexander, Martha. *I'll Protect You from the Jungle Beasts.* A boy and his teddy bear reassure one another during a trip through the forest. Charlesbridge, 2006 (32p).

Brown, Lisa. *How to Be.* Siblings pretend to be various animals, then return to being themselves. HarperCollins, 2006 (32p).

Brown, Marcia. *Dick Whittington and His Cat.* A boy trades his cat for riches. Atheneum, 1988 (32p).

Bunting, Eve and Jeff Mack (il). *Hurry, Hurry!* Barnyard animals hurry to witness the hatching of a chick. Harcourt, 2007 (32p).

Carle, Eric. *The Very Hungry Caterpillar.* An insatiable young caterpillar eats his way through the book. Philomel, 1981 (32p).

Ehlert, Lois. *Leaf Man.* The elusive Leaf Man leads readers on a merry chase. Harcourt, 2005 (40p).

Ehlert, Lois. *Wag a Tail.* Find out what's on the minds of these friendly dogs as they play on their way to the park. Harcourt, 2007 (40p).

Fleming, Denise. *The Cow Who Clucked.* A cow goes in search of her missing moo, visiting other farm animals along the way. Holt, 2006 (40p).

Freeman, Don. *Corduroy.* A teddy bear, locked inside the store, comes to life to search for his missing button and eventually finds a new home. **Available in Spanish as** *Corduroy (Edición española).* Viking, 2008 (28p).

Gág, Wanda. *Millions of Cats.* A man in search of a cat has a hard time choosing among all the cats he finds. Puffin, 2006 (32p).

Geisert, Arthur. *Hogwash.* Little pigs happily get dirty and their mothers don't mind because they have a marvelous scrubbing machine to get them all clean in no time! Houghton, 2008 (32p).

Geisert, Arthur. *Lights Out.* Intricate drawings tell how a young pig concocts a device that helps him get to sleep comfortably before the lights go out at night. Houghton, 2005 (32p).

Gerstein, Mordicai. *Leaving the Nest.* A baby bird falls out of the nest and learns to fly. Foster/Farrar, 2007 (40p).

Henkes, Kevin. *A Good Day.* A bad day turns to good for four animals. Greenwillow, 2007 (24p).

Johnson, Crocket. *Harold and the Purple Crayon.* Harold demonstrates the power of imagination with a single crayon. **Available in Spanish as** *Harold y el lápiz color morado.* HarperCollins, 1958/1998 (64p).

Khing, T. T. *Where Is the Cake?* The mystery of a missing cake's whereabouts is waiting to be solved as young readers search the wordless images for clues. Abrams, 2007 (32p).

Lehman, Barbara. *Rainstorm.* This wordless picture book conveys a rainy-day adventure for a boy who finds a mysterious key. Houghton, 2007 (32p).

Lehman, Barbara. *The Red Book.* A girl in the snow and a boy on a beach connect through a mysterious red book. Houghton, 2004 (32p).

Lehman, Barbara. *Trainstop.* In a wordless daydream, a girl meets miniature people when her train makes a strange stop. Houghton, 2008 (32p).

Lionni, Leo. *Alexander and the Wind-up Mouse.* A story about friendship between a toy mouse and the real mouse that wants to be liked by people. Knopf, 2006 (32p).

Lobel, Arnold. *Frog and Toad Are Friends.* Best friends Frog and Toad experience the small moments of life together. HarperCollins, 1970 (64p).

Lobel, Arnold and Anita Lobel. *On Market Street.* In a twist on an alphabet book, a boy buys presents for a friend on busy Market Street. Greenwillow, 1981 (40p).

Marshall, James. *George and Martha.* Five short stories about the classic hippo friends in their first book. Sandpiper, 1974 (48p).

McCloskey, Robert. *Make Way for Ducklings.* A family of ducks settles in Boston Common. **Available in Spanish as *Abran paso a los patitos*.** Viking, 1941 (68p).

McPhail, David. *Big Brown Bear's Birthday Surprise.* Big Brown Bear and Rat float down a stream to adventure and to a welcome surprise. Harcourt, 2007 (32p).

Newman, Jeff. *Hippo! No, Rhino!* A rhino grows increasingly upset at the mislabeling of his zoo habitat. Little, 2006 (32p).

Onishi, Satoru. *Who's Hiding?* This is a hide-and-seek of animals that will engage readers as they look for the hidden animals on each page. Kane/Miller, 2007 (32p).

Rohmann, Eric. *My Friend Rabbit.* Rabbit means well, but trouble follows him no matter what he tries to do. **Available in Spanish as *Mi amigo conejo*.** Square Fish, 2007 (32p)

Seeger, Laura Vaccaro. *Dog and Bear: Two Friends, Three Stories.* Three stories about a tender friendship between a dachshund and a teddy bear. Roaring Brook, 2007 (32p).

Seeger, Laura Vaccaro. *Dog and Bear: Two's Company.* Three more tales of friends helping each other through hurt feelings, birthdays, and feeling sick. Roaring Brook, 2008 (32p).

Silverstein Shel. *The Giving Tree.* A selfless tree supports a boy as he grows up. HarperCollins, 1964 (64p).

Tankard, Jeremy. *Grumpy Bird.* Bird wakes up in a bad mood, but before long his friends help make the day better. Scholastic, 2007 (32p).

Varon, Sara. *Chicken and Cat.* In this wordless picture book, two friends plant a garden to brighten Chicken's city home. Scholastic, 2006 (40p).

Willems, Mo. *Elephant and Piggie: I Am Invited to a Party!* When Piggie is invited to a party, Elephant helps him select proper attire. Hyperion, 2007 (64p).

Willems, Mo. *Elephant & Piggie: There Is a Bird on Your Head!* Elephant panics when his head becomes an unexpected home for birds. Hyperion, 2007 (64p).

INFORMATIONAL TEXT

Banks, Kate. *Fox.* In poetic style, a baby fox learns survival skills through the seasons of the year. Foster/Farrar, 2007 (40p).

Barton, Byron. *Planes.* A simple text introduces different kinds of planes. Harper, 2006 (32p).

Bullard, Lisa. *Fast and Slow: An Animal Opposites Book.* Brief text, along with inviting photographs, introduces the concepts of fast and slow. **Available in Spanish as *Veloces y lentos: Un libro de animals opuestos*.** Capstone, 2005 (32p).

Cipriano, Jeri. *At the Park.* Simple text and photographs present the many different things people can do in parks. **Available in Spanish as *En el parque*.** Yellow Umbrella, 2004 (16p).

Crews, Donald. *Truck.* A big red truck goes about its travels in this wordless picture book. Greenwillow, 1980 (32p).

Eckart, Edana. *Watching the Weather.* A simple introduction to how weather changes and how meteorologists do their work. Children's Press, 2004 (24p).

Frazee, Marla. *Walk On!* Frazee's clever instructions on how to walk are easily applied to all new experiences. Harcourt, 2006 (32p).

Gravett, Emily. *Orange Pear Apple Bear.* With only five words, this book deals with shapes, colors, and order. Simon, 2007 (32p).

Hoban, Tana. *Count and See.* This classic counting book provides numerals, words, and models along with helpful photographs. Simon, 1972 (40p).

Johnson, Stephen T. *Alphabet City.* Readers will be drawn into the realistic illustrations to search for the letters of the alphabet hidden in plain sight throughout a city. Viking, 1995 (32p).

Ljungkvist, Laura. *Follow the Line Around the World.* A simple but interactive tour of the globe. Viking, 2008 (32p).

Lobel, Anita. *Hello, Day!* Animals greet the day in their customary ways. Greenwillow, 2008 (32p).

McCarthy, Mary. *A Closer Look.* Children will delight in discovering a new way of seeing a ladybug, a bird, and a flower. Greenwillow, 2007 (40p).

Neubecker, Robert. *Wow! School!* Young Izzy is very excited about all there is to see on her first day at school. Hyperion, 2007 (32p).

Reiser, Lynn. *Hardworking Puppies.* Ten puppies find their callings in life and young readers see real-life jobs for dogs. Harcourt, 2006 (32p).

Literature Discussion

Robbins, Ken. *Seeds.* Photos and simple text pair seeds with the plants they will become. Atheneum, 2005 (32p).

Seeger, Laura Vaccaro. *First the Egg.* In what could be the answer to the classic question, "Which comes first?," this book uses spare text to illustrate the concept of sequence of events. Porter/Roaring Brook, 2007 (32p).

Trumbauer, Lisa. *Living in a Suburb.* Simple text and photographs describe life in the suburbs. Pebble, 2005 (24p).

Winter, Jeanette. *Mama.* Two words (mama and baby) tell the true story of an orphaned young hippo adopted by a tortoise. Harcourt, 2006 (32p).

POETRY

Cauley, Lorinda Bryan. *Clap Your Hands.* Rhyming text instructs children in a variety of playful activities. Penguin, 2001 (32p).

Elliott, David. *On the Farm.* Short poems paint a picture of each farm animal's personality. Candlewick, 2008 (32p).

Hamilton, Kersten. *Red Truck.* Simple rhyming text tells how a little red tow truck saves the day. Viking, 2008 (32p).

Harter, Debbie. *Walking Through the Jungle.* Told in lively verse, a young explorer discovers many different animals on a romp outdoors. **Available in Spanish as** *De paseo por la selva.* Barefoot, 2004 (32p).

Johnson, David A. *Snow Sounds: An Onomatopoeic Story.* Simple poems convey the sounds of a snowy day. Houghton, 2006 (32p).

Lyon, George Ella. *Trucks Roll!* Simple rhyming verse tells of the many features, traits, and uses of trucks. Jackson/Atheneum, 2007 (40p).

Martin Jr., Bill. *Chicka Chicka Boom Boom.* Letters play by a coconut tree in this timeless beginner alphabet book. **Available in Spanish as** *Chica Chica Bum Bum.* Simon, 1989 (40p).

Mitton, Tony. *Down by the Cool of the Pool.* Animals have fun at the pond, flapping and stamping, wiggling and dancing, until they all flop and plop into the pool. Scholastic, 2002 (32p).

Sturges, Philemon. *I Love Trains!* A boy expresses his love of trains and all that he knows about them in rhyming text. Harper, 2006 (32p).

Updike, John. *A Child's Calendar.* Twelve poems celebrate the cycles of seasons. Holiday, 1999 (32p).

Wheeler, Lisa. *Jazz Baby.* Rhythm, rhyme, and a little dancing helps the whole family put the baby to sleep. Harcourt, 2007 (40p).

REALISTIC FICTION

Blackaby, Susan. *Riley Flies a Kite.* Riley keeps trying until he finds the perfect place to fly his kite. **Available in Spanish as** *El papalote de Pablo.* Picture Window, 2006 (24p).

Cooney, Barbara. *Miss Rumphius.* An adventurous young lady grows up to fulfill all her dreams and leaves behind a lasting gift for her community. **Available in Spanish as** *La señorita Emilia.* Viking, 1982 (32p).

Crews, Nina. *Snowball.* A child eagerly awaits snowfall, then has a great time celebrating its arrival. Simple text from the narrator's viewpoint. Harper, 1997 (32p).

Guy, Ginger Foglesong. *Siesta.* This bilingual book reinforces color names as siblings gather items for an afternoon rest. Greenwillow, 2005 (32p).

Henderson, Kathy. *Look at You!* A celebration of all the activities toddlers can do introduces new verbs. Candlewick, 2007 (40p).

Keats, Ezra Jack. *The Snowy Day.* A small boy delights in the aftermath of a snowstorm. **Available in Spanish as** *Un día de nieve.* Viking, 1962 (32p).

Krauss, Ruth. *The Carrot Seed.* A little boy cares for the carrot seed that he just knows will eventually grow. **Available in Spanish as** *La semilla de zanahoria.* HarperCollins, 2004 (32p).

Krauss, Ruth, reillustrated by Helen Oxenbury. *The Growing Story.* As the seasons change, a boy sees the animals around him growing. The age-old childhood question, "Am I getting bigger?," is answered in this classic story. HarperCollins, 2007 (32p).

McPhail, David. *My Little Brother.* A boy describes all the things he does not like about having a little brother—and the things that he does like. Harcourt, 2004 (32p).

McPhail, David. *Sisters.* Two sisters find that although they are different in many ways, they are also alike in others, especially in their love for each other. **Available in Spanish as** *Hermanas.* Harcourt, 2003 (32p).

Milgrim, David. *Time to Get Up, Time to Go.* In the company of his doll, a boy goes about his very busy day. Clarion, 2006 (32p).

Reiser, Lynn. *My Way/A mi manera.* In this bilingual format, friends Margaret and Margarita tell how they are alike and different and show their individuality. Greenwillow, 2007 (32p).

Schwartz, Amy. *Bea and Mr. Jones.* When kindergartner Bea and her father trade places at school and work, life gets interesting for both of them. Harcourt, 2006 (32p).

Shulevitz, Uri. *Snow.* A hopeful boy doesn't let grumpy grown-ups ruin his hopefulness as he waits for snow. Farrar, 1998 (32p).

Wiesner, David. *Flotsam.* A wordless and intricate picture book in which beach treasures are more than they at first seem. Clarion, 2006 (40p).

Williams, Sue. *I Went Walking/Salí de paseo.* A child goes for a walk, encountering animals along the way. Harcourt, 2006 (32p).

Yashima, Taro. *Umbrella.* Momo can't wait to use her birthday present, an umbrella. Viking, 1958 (40p).

TRADITIONAL TALE

Aardema, Verna. *Why Mosquitoes Buzz in People's Ears.* Repetitive and cumulative text, paired with vibrant illustrations, make this retelling of a tale from West Africa a favorite. Dial, 1975 (32p).

Barton, Byron. *The Little Red Hen.* The little red hen finds none of her friends are willing to help with the hard work, but they do want to share in the harvest. Harper, 1994 (32p).

Barton, Byron. *The Three Bears.* In a slight variation on the Goldilocks tale, the three bears complain about their uninvited visitor. Harper, 1991 (32p).

Brett, Jan. *The Mitten.* In this retelling of a Ukrainian folktale, animals take shelter in a boy's lost mitten. Putnam, 1989 (32p).

Professional Bibliography

Abbott, M. (2001). Effects of traditional versus extended word-study spelling instruction on students' orthographic knowledge. *Reading Online, 5*(3).

Barrentine, Shelley. "Engaging with reading through interactive read-alouds." *The Reading Teacher, 50(1):* 36–43.

Baumann, J. F., Edwards, E. C., Font, G., Tereshinski, C. A., Kame'enui, E. J., & Olejnik, S. (2003). Teaching morphemic and contextual analysis to fifth-grade students. *Reading Research Quarterly, 37*(2), 150–176.

Bear, D. R., Invernizzi, M., Templeton, S., & Johnston, F. (2012). *Words their way: Word study for phonics, vocabulary, and spelling instruction* (5th Ed.). Upper Saddle River, NJ: Pearson/Prentice-Hall.

Beck, I., McKeown, M. G., & Kucan, L. (2008). *Creating robust vocabulary.* New York: Guilford.

Berninger, V. W., Abbott, R. D., Nagy, W., & Carlisle, J. (2009). Growth in phonological, orthographic, and morphological awareness in grades 1 to 6. *Journal of Psycholinguistic Research. 39*(2), 141–163.

Berninger, V. W., Vaughan, K., & Abbott, R. D. (2000). Language-based spelling instruction: Teaching children to make multiple connections between spoken and written words. *Learning Disability Quarterly,* 23, 117–135.

Biemiller, A. (2005). Size and sequence in vocabulary development: Implications for choosing words for primary grade vocabulary instruction. In E. H. Hiebert & M. L. Kamil (Eds.), *Teaching and learning vocabulary: Bringing research to practice* (pp. 223–242). Mahwah, NJ: Lawrence Erlbaum Associates.

Bowers, P. N., & Kirby, J. R. (2010). Effects of morphological instruction on vocabulary acquisition. *Reading and Writing: An Interdisciplinary Journal.* 23(5), 515–537.

Brooks, A., Begay, K., Curtin, G., Byrd, K., & Graham, S. (2000). Language-based spelling instruction: Teaching children to make multiple connections between spoken and written words. *Learning Disability Quarterly,* 2, 117–135.

Carlisle, J. F. (2010). Effects of instruction in morphological awareness on literacy achievement: An integrative review. *Reading Research Quarterly, 45*(4), 464–487.

Clay, Marie M. *Becoming Literate: The Construction of Inner Control.* Heinemann, 1991.

Clay, Marie M. *Change Over Time in Children's Literacy Development.* Heinemann, 2001.

Conrad, N. J. (2008). From reading to spelling and spelling to reading: Transfer goes both ways. *Journal of Educational Psychology, 100*(4), 869–878.

Dale, E., & O'Rourke, J. (1981). *Living word vocabulary.* Chicago: World Book/ Childcraft International.

Ehri, L. C. (2005). Learning to read words: Theory, findings, and issues. *Scientific Studies of Reading, 9*(2), 167–188.

Fountas, Irene. C. and G. S. Pinnell. *Guided Reading: Good First Teaching for All Children.* Heinemann, 1996.

Fountas, Irene C. and G. S. Pinnell. *Guiding Readers and Writers: Teaching Comprehension, Genre, and Content Literacy.* Heinemann, 2001.

Fountas, Irene C. and G. S. Pinnell. *Leveled Books, K–8: Matching Texts to Readers for Effective Teaching.* Heinemann, 2005.

Fountas, Irene C. and G. S. Pinnell. *Teaching for Comprehending and Fluency: Thinking, Talking, and Writing About Reading, K–8.* Heinemann, 2006.

Henderson, E. H., & Templeton, S. (1986). The development of spelling abilities through alphabet, pattern, and meaning. *Elementary School Journal, 86,* 305–316.

Hiebert, E. H. (2005). In pursuit of an effective, efficient vocabulary curriculum for elementary students. In E. H. Hiebert & M. L. Kamil (Eds.), *Teaching and learning vocabulary: Bringing research to practice* (pp. 243–263). Mahwah, NJ: Lawrence Erlbaum Associates.

Holdaway, Don. *The Foundations of Literacy.* Ashton Scholastic, 1979 (also Heinemann).

Invernizzi, M., & Hayes, L. (2004). Developmental-spelling research: A systematic imperative. *Reading Research Quarterly, 39,* 2–15.

Juel, C, & Minden-Cupp, C. (2000). Learning to read words: Linguistic units and instructional strategies. *Reading Research Quarterly, 35,* 458–492.

Kieffer, M. J., & Lesaux, N. K. (2007). Breaking down words to build meaning: Morphology, vocabulary, and reading comprehension in the urban classroom. *Reading Teacher, 61*(2), 134–144.

Morris, D., Bloodgood, J. W., Lomax, R. G., & Perney, J. (2003). Developmental steps in learning to read: A longitudinal study in kindergarten and first grade. *Reading Research Quarterly, 38,* 302–328.

Morris, D., Nelson, L., & Perney, J. (1986). Exploring the concept of "spelling instructional level" through the analysis of error-types. *Elementary School Journal, 87,* 181–200.

Nunes, T., & Bryant, P. (2006). *Improving literacy by teaching morphemes.* London: Routledge.

Ouellette, G. P., & Sénéchal, M. (2008). A window into early literacy: Exploring the cognitive and linguistic underpinnings of invented spelling. *Scientific studies of reading, 12*(2), 195–219.

Pikulski, J., & Templeton, S. (2010). *Comprehensive vocabulary instruction for reading and school success* (Professional Paper). Boston: Houghton Mifflin Harcourt.

Pinnell, Gay Su and Irene C. Fountas. *The Continuum of Literacy Learning, Grades K–8: Behaviors and Understandings to Notice, Teach, and Support.* Heinemann, 2007.

Santoro, L. E., Chard, D. J., Howard, L., & Baker, S. K. (2008). Making the most of classroom read-alouds to promote comprehension and vocabulary. *The Reading Teacher, 61,* 396–408.

Templeton, S. (2003). Teaching of spelling. In J. Guthrie (Senior Ed.), *Encyclopedia of Education* (2nd Ed.) (pp. 2302–2305). New York: Macmillan.

Templeton, S. (2011). Teaching spelling in the English/language arts classroom. In D. Lapp & D. Fisher (Eds.), *The handbook of research on teaching the English language arts* (3rd ed.) (pp. 247–251). IRA/NCTE: Erlbaum/Taylor Francis.

Templeton, S. (2012). The vocabulary-spelling connection and generative instruction: Orthographic development and morphological knowledge at the intermediate grades and beyond. In J. F. Baumann & E. J. Kame'enui (Eds.), *Vocabulary instruction: Research to Practice* (2nd ed.) New York: Guilford Press.

Templeton, S., & Bear, D. R. (Eds.). (1992). *Development of orthographic knowledge and the foundations of literacy: A memorial festschrift for Edmund H. Henderson.* Hillsdale, NJ: Lawrence Erlbaum Associates.

Templeton, S., & Bear, D. R. (2006). *Spelling and Vocabulary.* Boston: Houghton Mifflin.

Templeton, S., & Bear, D. R. (2011). Phonemic awareness, word recognition, and spelling. In T. Rasinski (Ed.), *Developing reading instruction that works.* Bloomington, IN: Solution Tree Press.

Templeton, S., Bear, D. R., Invernizzi, M., & Johnston, F. (2010). *Vocabulary their way: Word study with middle and secondary students.* Boston: Allyn & Bacon.

Templeton, S., Bear, D. R., & Madura, S. (2007). Assessing students' spelling knowledge: Relationships to reading and writing. In J. R. Paratore & R. L. McCormack (Eds.), *Classroom literacy assessment: Making sense of what students know and do.* New York: Guilford Press.

Templeton, S., & Gehsmann, K. (in press). *Teaching reading and writing, K-8: The developmental approach.* Boston: Pearson/Allyn & Bacon.

Templeton, S., & Morris, D. (1999). Questions teachers ask about spelling. *Reading Research Quarterly, 34,* 102–112.

Templeton, S., & Morris, D. (2000). Spelling. In M. Kamil, P. Mosenthal, P. D. Pearson, & R. Barr (Eds.), *Handbook of reading research: Vol. 3* (pp. 525–543). Mahwah, NJ: Lawrence Erlbaum Associates.

White, T. G. (2005). Effects of systematic and strategic analogy-based phonics on Grade 2 students' word reading and reading comprehension. *Reading Research Quarterly, 40*(2), 234–255.

Zeno, S. M., Ivens, S. H., Millard, R. T., & Duvvuri, R. (1996). *The educator's word frequency guide.* New York: Touchstone Applied Science Associates.